Dear NFT User:

We released our first book, the NFT Guide t
of research and development in which we
hurt. Looking back on those heady first da
be working on our fifteenth edition of the g
when they see it written out.

But even after 15 editions it always warms each of our cold, crusty, curmudgeonly hearts when we come across someone on the street consulting their little black book. Whether you're navigating your way through this "concrete jungle where dreams are made of" (as Alicia once sang) using our specially formulated maps that at least one optometrist has ensured us is at least 30 percent less strain-inducing than it once was, or just quietly taking in the full force of our collective genius as we distill the best bar on the block down to a haiku-like three- to ten-word blurb, trust us, we always feel a flush of pride when we see people out in public reading a NFT guide.

That's because like the best house-cured meat along Arthur Avenue, the finest crust on a Staten Island pizza pie or the most transcendent Brooklyn mayonnaise, this little black guide is, at its core, an artisanal product. With NFT, the blurbs you get are all house made, never processed, especially via some faceless algorithm—because, let's face it, our servers could never handle it anyway. Like that roomy boutique on that sketchy block down by the waterfront, NFT is carefully curated to offer you the best of what a neighborhood has to offer. And if a trendy, stinky or otherwise unfun place isn't worth your or anyone else's time, we feel free to exclude it, because at NFT we pride ourselves on not only being "well edited" but actually "best edited."

A word about some of this year's listings: Not only has Superstorm Sandy permanently turned us off to the glory days of Dodger baseball (as in Sandy Koufax), Wheat Thins (as in Sandy Duncan) and certain canine companions featured in vintage cartoons (as in Little Orphan Annie's dog Sandy) but it also shut down many of our favorite spots in low-lying areas of the city, especially around the South Street Seaport. At press time, some of these spots had not yet reopened. We are keeping them in the book as active listings because we hope these closures are only temporary and not permanent. In the meantime, you can help do your part by making an effort to patronize the establishments that are still open or have reopened—even months later, they can use the business.

Anyway, as we like to say, wrap your furry paws around this superior guide of all things New York City and get ready to scout the holes in the wall so holey the Department of Buildings should have long since shut them down, bars so divey you'll need a scuba tank to get there and shops so indispensable they're still working for Lehman Brothers years after the collapse. Of course if and when you come across something we missed, please send us a note at www.notfortourists.com, because at its core, NFT is a family, and we wouldn't be who we are without you. So if you're new to us, welcome! And if you're coming back, thanks for continuing to trust us enough to show us around in public…

ane, Scott, et al.

Downtown

Midtown

Uptown

Way Uptown

Outer Boroughs

Table of Contents

Map 1 • Financial District

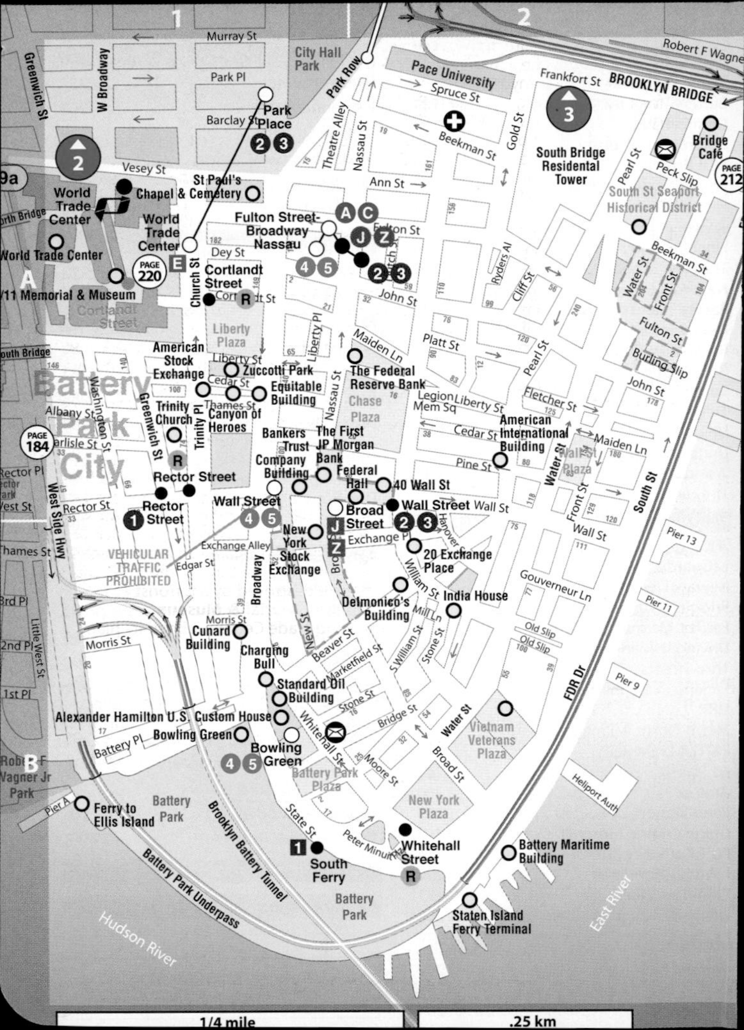

1
2
A
B
Murray St
Park Pl
Barclay St
Vesey St
Greenwich St
W Broadway
City Hall Park
Park Row
Park Place
St Paul's Chapel & Cemetery
World Trade Center
World Trade Center
World Trade Center
North Bridge
9/11 Memorial & Museum
Cortlandt Street
PAGE 220
Church St
Dey St
Cortlandt Street
Cortlandt St
Liberty Plaza
Fulton Street-Broadway Nassau
Pace University
Spruce St
Frankfort St
BROOKLYN BRIDGE
Robert F Wagner
Beekman St
Gold St
Theatre Alley
Nassau St
Ann St
Fulton St
Dutch St
John St
Liberty Pl
South Bridge Residential Tower
Pearl St
Peck Slip
Bridge Café
PAGE 212
South St Seaport Historical District
Beekman St
Water St
Front St
Fulton St
Burling Slip
John St
Ryders Al
Cliff St
Platt St
Maiden Ln
The Federal Reserve Bank
Chase Plaza
Legion Mem Sq
Liberty St
Fletcher St
American International Building
Cedar St
Pine St
Maiden Ln
Wall St Plaza
Front St
Wall St
South St
Pier 13
Pier 11
Pier 9
Gouverneur Ln
Old Slip
Old Slip
South Bridge
American Stock Exchange
Liberty St
Zuccotti Park
Cedar St
Equitable Building
Battery Park City
Washington St
Greenwich St
Trinity Pl
Trinity Church
Thames St
Canyon of Heroes
Albany St
PAGE 184
Carlisle St
Rector Pl
West St
West Side Hwy
Rector St
Rector Street
Rector Street
Bankers Trust Company Building
The First JP Morgan Bank
Federal Hall
40 Wall St
Wall Street
Wall Street
Wall St
Broad Street
Hanover Sq
New York Stock Exchange
Exchange Pl
20 Exchange Place
Exchange Alley
Thames St
VEHICULAR TRAFFIC PROHIBITED
Edgar St
Broadway
Broad St
William St
India House
Delmonico's Building
Mill Ln
3rd Pl
2nd Pl
1st Pl
Little West St
Morris St
Morris St
Cunard Building
Charging Bull
New St
Beaver St
Marketfield St
S William St
Stone St
Standard Oil Building
Stone St
Bridge St
Water St
Vietnam Veterans Plaza
FDR Dr
Alexander Hamilton U.S. Custom House
Bowling Green
Bowling Green
Whitehall St
Moore St
Broad St
Battery Pl
Robert F Wagner Jr Park
Battery Park Plaza
New York Plaza
Heliport Auth
Pier A
Ferry to Ellis Island
Battery Park
Brooklyn Battery Tunnel
State St
Peter Minuit Plz
Whitehall Street
South Ferry
Battery Maritime Building
Battery Park Underpass
Battery Park
Staten Island Ferry Terminal
East River
Hudson River
1/4 mile
.25 km

Neighborhood Overview

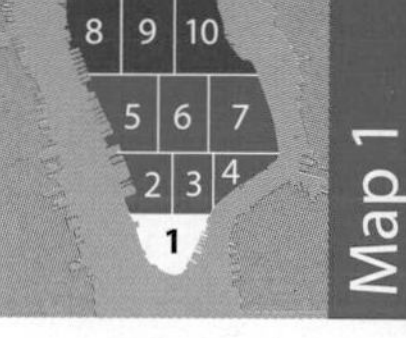

This is where it all began. Site of the original Dutch settlement on Manhattan Island, the Financial District contains more historical markers than any other part of the city. If you're looking for a place to start, check out **St. Paul's Chapel and Cemetery**, which dates back to 1766, **Trinity Church**, whose spire was once the tallest point in Manhattan, and **Federal Hall**, site of the first capitol of the United States. You can also head to Battery Park to take the **ferry** to the Statue of Liberty, and, far more interestingly, to Ellis Island where you can explore the history of immigration in the United States.

That's just the beginning. The importance of New York as a financial and commercial center is evident on practically every street. To take it in, check out, in no particular order, the **New York Stock Exchange**, the NYSE Amex Equities (formerly known as the **American Stock Exchange**), the **Federal Reserve Bank**, the first **JP Morgan Bank** (still visibly scarred from a bombing in 1920), John D. Rockefeller's **Standard Oil Building**, and the **Alexander Hamilton US Custom House** (now the National Museum of the American Indian). The architecture of the chocolate brown federal-style **India House** and stunning maritime-themed interior of the **Cunard Building** both represent distinct eras of New York's commercial past. Rivaling Grand Central and Brooklyn Bridge as Manhattan's most gorgeous gateway, the **Battery Maritime Building** is the departure point for the summer ferry to Governor's Island, where you can stroll around fortifications built during the Revolutionary War. Last but not least, the **Charging Bull** statue at **Bowling Green**, initially installed as a piece of guerrilla art, has become the ultimate symbol for New York's financial strength, and beloved by photo-snapping tourists from all over the world. Financial growth led to the creation of the modern skyscraper, and many famous examples soar above these streets. Notable buildings include **40 Wall Street** (now known as the "Trump Building"), art-deco gems **20 Exchange Place** and the **American International Building**, the massive Equitable Building, and the Bankers Trust Company Building. Of course, the most famous structure is the one that's missing—the World Trade Center Towers, which were destroyed by a terrorist attack on September 11, 2001. **The National September 11 Memorial & Museum** now marks the footprint of the towers and as of 2012, One World Trade Center claimed its place as the city's tallest skyscraper.

When you're ready for a break from all that history and architecture, take in some people watching at **Zuccotti Park** (onetime hub for the Occupy Wall Street protest), reflect in the relative peace and quiet of the **Vietnam Veterans Plaza**, or mix history and pleasure history and pleasure by having a drink at New York's oldest bar, the **The Bridge Cafe**. The best way to chill out might be by simply grabbing a beer on board the free **Staten Island Ferry** and checking out the awesome views of New York Harbor commuters get to enjoy every day. The tourists will all be at **South Street Seaport**, which might be best avoided unless you like crowded cobblestoned shopping malls. If you're a foodie, though, New Amsterdam Market, open Sundays at the site of the much-missed Fulton Fish Market, is worth a visit. As far as kicking back in quaint downtown is concerned, Stone Street and Front Street are perfect spots to grab a bite and a drink after a day of wandering around. We'll see you there!

Landmarks

O Landmarks

- **20 Exchange Place •**
20 Exchange Pl [William St]
Cool facade with bronze depictions of various modes of transport.
- **40 Wall St •** 40 Wall St [William St]
Tallest building in the world for a day in 1930. Oh and Trump owns it.
- **Alexander Hamilton U.S. Custom House •**
1 Bowling Green [State St]
Stately Cass Gilbert building; check out the oval staircases.
- **American International Building •**
70 Pine St [Pearl St]
Great Art Deco skyscraper.
- **American Stock Exchange •**
86 Trinity Pl [Thames St]
212-306-1000
New York's other stock exchange.
- **Bankers Trust Company Building •**
14 Wall St [Nassau St]
More neck-craning excitement from the NYC skyline!
- **Battery Maritime Building •**
10 South St [Broad St]
Ready-to-be-converted riverfront building.
- **Bowling Green •** Broadway & State St
Watch the tourists take pics of the bull. New York's first park.
- **Bridge Cafe •** 279 Water St [Dover St]
212-227-3344
The oldest bar in NYC. Great vibe, good food too.
- **Canyon of Heroes •**
Broadway b/n Bowling Green & City Hall Park
Markers in the sidewalk remember those honored with a ticker tape parade.
- **Charging Bull •** Bowling Green Park
Rub his cojones for luck.
- **Cunard Building •** 25 Broadway [Morris St]
Former Cunard headquarters, former post office, currently a locked building with great ceiling mosaics.
- **Delmonico's •** 56 Beaver St [S William St]
212-509-1144
Once the site of THE restaurant in New York.
- **Equitable Building •** 120 Broadway [Cedar St]
Its massiveness gave momentum to zoning laws for skyscrapers.
- **Federal Hall •** 26 Wall St [Broad St]
212-825-6888
Where George the First was inaugurated.
- **Federal Reserve Bank of New York •**
33 Liberty St [William St]
212-720-6130
Where *Die Hard 3* took place.
- **Ferry to Ellis Island •** Pier A & Battery Park
The main building features beautiful domed ceilings and Guastavino tiled arches.
- **The First JP Morgan Bank •**
23 Wall St [Broad St]
Still visibly scarred from an anarchist bombing in 1920.
- **India House Club •** 1 Hanover Sq [Stone St]
212-269-2323
Members-only club in historic, nautical-themed house.
- **New York Stock Exchange •**
20 Broad St [Exchange Pl]
212-656-5168
Where *Wall Street* took place.
- **One World Trade Center •** Vesey St [West St]
1,776 foot tall tower to be completed in 2013.
- **September 11 Memorial and Museum •**
Greenwich St
212-266-5211
Awe-inspiring tribute to those lost, surrounded by rebirth.
- **South Street Seaport •** 12 Fulton St [South St]
212-732-7678
Mall with historic ships as backdrop.
- **St. Paul's Chapel & Cemetery •**
Broadway & Fulton St
212-233-4164
Old-time NYC church and cemetery.
- **Standard Oil Building •**
26 Broadway [Morris St]
Sweeping wall of a building overlooking Bowling Green.
- **Staten Island Ferry •** 1 Whitehall St [Stone St]
Grab a tall boy on board and enjoy the view.
- **Vietnam Veterans Memorial Plaza •**
55 Water St [Coenties Slip]
212-471-9496
A nice quiet spot to contemplate our faded dreams of empire.
- **World Trade Center Site •**
Church St & Vesey St
We still can't believe what happened.
- **Zuccotti Park •** Trinity Pl & Cedar St
Birthplace of Occupy Wall Street, ca. 2011.

It ain't the village by any stretch, but Front Street has some good options like wine bar **Bin 220** and **Fresh Salt**. Old stalwarts like the **The Paris Cafe** and the **Bridge Cafe** capture the history of the area. The semi-secret Blue Bar at **India House** is a NFT favorite—you can thank us later.

Bars

- **Beekman Beer Garden Beach Club** • 89 South St [Beekman St]
  212-896-4600
  Seaport sandbox with awesome Brooklyn Bridge views.
- **Bin 220** • 220 Front St [Beekman St]
  212-374-9463
  Escape the tourists at this excellent little wine bar.
- **Bridge Cafe** • 279 Water St [Dover St]
  212-227-3344
  Oldest bar in NYC; good whiskey selection.
- **The Dead Rabbit** • 30 Water St [Broad St]
  646-422-7906
  Fancy cocktails in an old-timey, Irish-American atmosphere.
- **Fresh Salt** • 146 Beekman St [Front St]
  212-962-0053
  Where architects go for happy hour.
- **Harry's Cafe & Steak** • 1 Hanover Sq [Pearl St]
  212-785-9200
  The vintage French wine flows like a river. Or at least it used too.
- **Heartland Brewery** • 93 South St [Fulton St]
  646-572-2337
  Heartland HeartLAND HEARTLAND!
- **India House Club** • 1 Hanover Sq [Stone St]
  212-269-2323
  Secret bar to the left up the stairs. You're welcome.
- **Killarney Rose** • 127 Pearl St [Hanover St]
  212-422-1486
  Irish pub where you can pregame for the Staten Island Ferry.
- **Liquid Assets** • 55 Church St [Fulton St]
  212-693-2001
  Plush seating and soft lighting.
- **Paris Café** • 119 South St [Peck Slip]
  212-240-9797
  Good, historic bar but used to be better. Best very late.
- **Ulysses Folk House** • 95 Pearl St [Hanover Sq]
  212-482-0400
  Slightly hipper downtown bar.
- **Vintry** • 57 Stone St [Mill Ln]
  212-480-9800
  Fine wine and whiskey for sophisticated grape and grain lovers.
- **Whitehorse Tavern** • 25 Bridge St [Whitehall St]
  212-668-9046
  Downtown dive. Not to be confused with the one in the West Village.

Restaurants

Our Stone Street favorite is **Adrienne's Pizza Bar**, and on Front Street it's the New Zealand goodness of **Nelson Blue**. You can eat cheaply at **Sophie's**, **Financier Patisserie**, **Zaitzeff**, and greasy spoon **Pearl Street Diner** while you wait for financial success and a table at **Mark Joseph**.

Restaurants

- **Adrienne's Pizzabar** • 54 Stone St [S William St] 212-248-3838 • $$ Modern, thin crust pizza.
- **Battery Gardens** • Battery Park [Across from 17 State St] 212-809-5508 • $$$$$ Panoramic views of NY harbor with a wood-burning fireplace.
- **Bayard's** • 1 Hanover Sq [Pearl St] 212-514-9454 • $$$$ Elegant Continental cuisine in the historic India House.
- **Bridge Cafe** • 279 Water St [Dover St] 212-227-3344 • $$$$$ Expensive but effective Seaport dining. Historic.
- **Financier Patisserie** • 62 Stone St [Mill Ln] 212-344-5600 • $$ Have your cake and a light meal too.
- **Grotto Pizzeria** • 69 New St [Beaver St] 212-809-6990 • $$ More quick, tasty Italian. Less nudity than that other grotto.
- **The Growler** • 55 Stone St [Mill Ln] 917-409-0251 • $$ Pub grub, craft beer and a dog-friendly patio.
- **Harry's Cafe & Steak** • 1 Hanover Sq [Pearl St] 212-785-9200 • $$$$ When the market is flush so is Harry.
- **Les Halles** • 15 John St [Broadway] 212-285-8585 • $$$ Excellent French steakhouse. Thanks Mr. Bourdain.
- **Mark Joseph Steakhouse** • 261 Water St [Peck Slip] 212-277-0020 • $$$$ Luger's wannabe: damn close, actually, and they take plastic.
- **Nelson Blue** • 233 Front St [Peck Slip] 212-346-9090 • $$$ New Zealand lollichop lollichop, whoah Lollichop…
- **Paris Café** • 119 South St [Peck Slip] 212-240-9797 • $$$ Good burgers and seafood, a bit pricey though.
- **Pearl Street Diner** • 212 Pearl St [Platt St] 212-344-6620 • $ Greasy spoon hidden among the skyscrapers.
- **Smorgas Chef** • 53 Stone St [Mill Ln] 212-422-3500 • $$ Best 'balls on Wall Street…
- **Sophie's Cuban** • 73 New St [Beaver St] 212-809-7755 • $ Great cheap Cuban/Caribbean.
- **Suteishi** • 24 Peck Slip [Front St] 212-766-2344 • $$$ Hip seaport sushi. Get the Orange/Red Dragon split.
- **Toloache** • 83 Maiden Ln [Gold St] 212-809-9800 • $$ Upscale Mexican and a gigantic tequila selection.
- **Ulysses Folk House** • 95 Pearl St [Hanover Sq] 212-482-0400 • $$$ Highlight: the buffet spread.
- **Wall Street Bath & Spa** • 88 Fulton St [Gold St] 212-766-8600 • $$ Pre-and Post rub and tub grub.
- **Zaitzeff** • 72 Nassau St [John St] 212-571-7272 • $$ Quick and organic burgers for lunch.
- **Zeytuna** • 59 Maiden Ln [William St] 212-742-2436 • $$ Gourmet take-out. NFT fave.

Bagels, Coffee, & Shopping

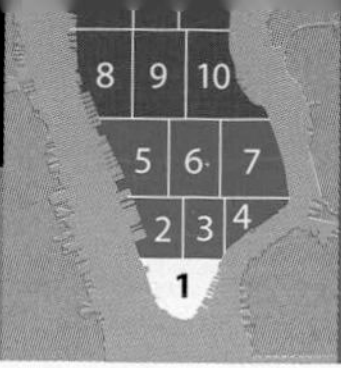

8 9 10
5 6 7
2 3 4
1

Map 1

Gourmet markets **Jubilee** and **Zeytuna** keep Financial District dwellers fed. Pick up some wine from **Downtown Cellars** or **Pasanella**, grab a coffee at **Fika**, then blow your own money at—where else? **J & R**.

Coffee

- **Dean & DeLuca** • 100 Broadway [Pine St]
  212-577 2153
  Expensive espresso for executives.
- **Fika** • 66 Pearl St [Broad St]
  212-832-0022
  Great coffeehouse run by friendly Swedes.
- **Financier Patisserie** • 35 Cedar St [Liberty St]
  212-952-3838
  Tres bien croissants.
- **Jack's Stir Brew Coffee** •
  222 Front St [Peck Slip]
  212-227-7631
  Excellent little coffehouse, especially for these parts.

Shopping

- **Barclay Rex** • 75 Broad St [S William St]
  212-962-3355
  For all your smoking needs.
- **Bowne & Co Stationers** •
  211 Water St [Beekman St]
  212-748-8651
  Old fashioned presses make prints, maps & cards.
- **Century 21** • 22 Cortlandt St [Broadway]
  212-227-9092
  Where most New Yorkers buy their underwear.
- **Dick's Cut Rate Hardware** • 9 Gold St [Platt St]
  212-425-1070
  Not a sex shop.
- **Downtown Cellars** • 55 Liberty St [Nassau St]
  212-406-9463
  Fantastic everything—small label wines, champagnes, and spirits.
- **Drago Shoe Repair** • 123 Fulton St [Dutch St]
  212-947-8496
  When your sole needs fixin'.
- **Flowers of the World** •
  110 Maiden Ln [Pearl St]
  800-582-0428
  Fulfill any feeling, mood, budget, or setting.
- **J&R Music & Computer World** •
  23 Park Row [Beekman St]
  212-238-9000
  Computers, electronics, and a good record store, to boot!
- **Jubilee Marketplace** • 99 John St [Cliff St]
  212-233-0808
  Godsend for Financial District dwellers.
- **La Petite Cave** • 83 Maiden Ln [Liberty St]
  212-514-9817
  Friendly owner with well curated wine selection.
- **Little Airplane Productions** •
  207 Front St [Beekman St]
  212-965-8999
  Cute little toy store run by "Wonder Pets" creators.
- **New Amsterdam Market** • South St b/w Beekman St & Peck Slip
  Awesome outdoor market, open every Sunday.
- **Pasanella and Son Vintners** •
  115 South St [Peck Slip]
  212 233 8383
  Great wine shop. Movies screenings in the back tasting room!
- **Zeytuna** • 59 Maiden Ln [William St]
  212-742-2436
  Excellent gourmet store—fish, meat, cheese counters. Yum.

Map 2 • TriBeCa

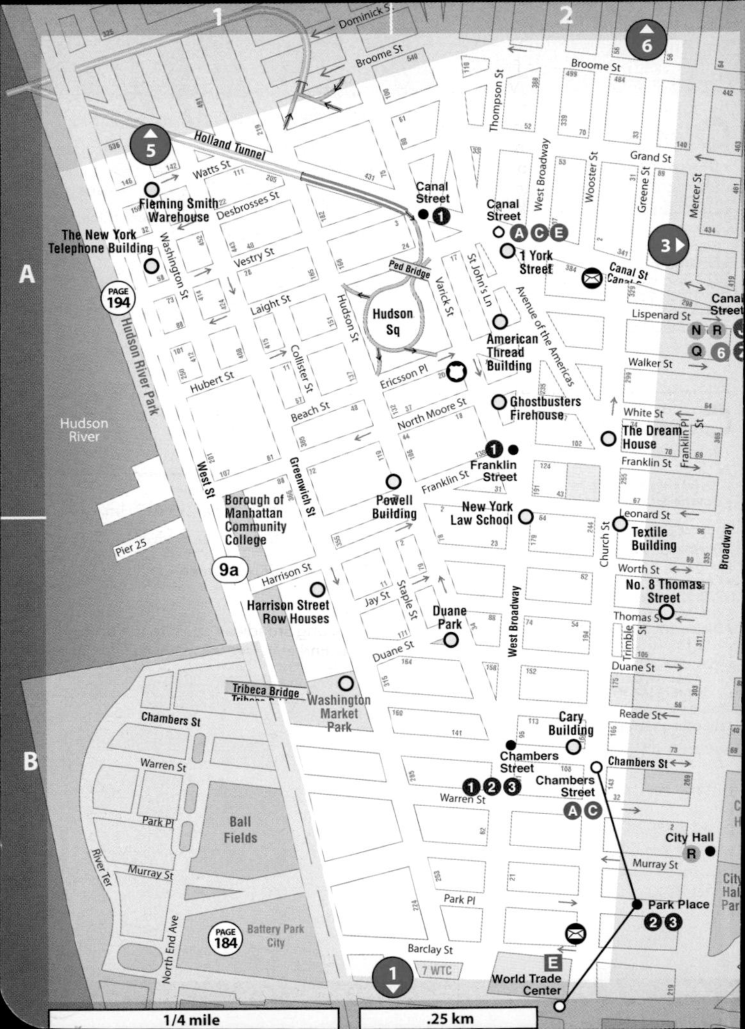

Canal Street
Canal Street
1 York Street
Canal St
Canal Street
Fleming Smith Warehouse
The New York Telephone Building
Hudson Sq
American Thread Building
Ghostbusters Firehouse
The Dream House
Franklin Street
Powell Building
New York Law School
Textile Building
Borough of Manhattan Community College
No. 8 Thomas Street
Harrison Street Row Houses
Duane Park
Washington Market Park
Cary Building
Chambers Street
Chambers Street
City Hall
Ball Fields
Park Place
Battery Park City
World Trade Center
7 WTC
Hudson River
Hudson River Park
Pier 25
Tribeca Bridge
Ped Bridge
Holland Tunnel
Dominick St
Broome St
Grand St
Watts St
Desbrosses St
Vestry St
Laight St
Hubert St
Beach St
North Moore St
Ericsson Pl
Franklin St
Harrison St
Jay St
Duane St
Chambers St
Warren St
Park Pl
Murray St
Barclay St
Lispenard St
Walker St
White St
Leonard St
Worth St
Thomas St
Reade St
Thompson St
West Broadway
Wooster St
Greene St
Mercer St
St John's Ln
Varick St
Avenue of the Americas
Hudson St
Collister St
Greenwich St
Washington St
West St
Staple St
Church St
Franklin Pl
Trimble Pl
Broadway
River Ter
North End Ave

PAGE 194

PAGE 184

1/4 mile
.25 km

Neighborhood Overview

Thinking of moving to TriBeCa? Well, then, congratulations—you've clearly made your first 10 million dollars! And, if you already live there…well, you're not reading a guidebook anyway…but maybe your assistant is. As for the rest of us, we'll just have to be content with walking around the neighborhood and choosing which fabulous converted loft building we'd live in when WE make our first 10 million. Such is life in one of New York's prime neighborhoods—minutes away from downtown, the West Village, SoHo, and Chinatown, decent subway access, a few minutes' walk to either the Battery Park City promenade or Hudson River Park, excellent restaurants, a few killer bars—if you can afford it, of course.

But even if you can't, there's no question that walking around is our favorite pastime in the Triangle Below Canal Street (Canal Street being the north side of the triangle, Broadway being the east side of the triangle, and the West Side Highway being the west side of the triangle). On your walk, you'll pass one of the city's oldest parks (**Washington Market Park**), some ancient row houses (the **Harrison Street Row Houses**) and our favorite TriBeCa landmark, the **Ghostbusters Firehouse** (you'll know it when you see it, trust us). A great starting point for seeing TriBeCa is its nexus, lovely little **Duane Park.** It's a quaint little triangle surrounded on all sides by gorgeous factory buildings converted into lofts you'd give an arm and a leg to live in.

As for the buildings themselves, there are a several worth noting, including Henry J. Hardenbergh's **Textile Building**, Carrère & Hastings' **Powell Building**, which now houses **Nobu**, Ralph Walker's massive **New York Telephone Company Building**, the rounded front of the **American Thread Building**, the Venetian mash-up of **No. 8 Thomas Street**, cast-iron gem the **Cary Building**, and, the "pièce de résistance," Stephen Decatur Smith's **Fleming Smith Warehouse** on Washington Street, which houses TriBeCa classic **Capsouto Freres**.

Although most of the new construction (especially along Broadway) fits into the boring/puerile category, one new building to check out is Enrique Norten's postmodern **One York Street**; his insertion of a glass tower in the middle of two 19th-century buildings is pretty cool. **New York Law School's** new building at 185 West Broadway shines brightly at night as its law students burn the candle at both ends. Meanwhile, Herzog & de Meuron's eagerly awaited 56 Leonard Street project, stalled since the recession days of 2009, is scheduled to open in 2015.

Unfortunately, we just don't get to TriBeCa as much at night any more, as two of its most interesting cultural hotspots—the Knitting Factory and Roulette—have both moved to Brooklyn. However, one of the coolest long-running sound and light installations in the world is here, at 275 Church Street, just steps from the swanky **TriBeCa Grand Hotel**. La Monte Young and Marian Zazeela's **Dream House**, open October thru June on Thursday, Friday, and Saturday nights, is a special place to chill out and get in touch with your inner being in the midst of all this residential poshness.

Landmarks

- **American Thread Building** • 260 W Broadway [Beach St]
  Check out cool rounded front; watch out for tunnel traffic.
- **Cary Building** • 105 Chambers St [Church St]
  Cast-iron goodness on Chambers. We like it.
- **Dream House** • 275 Church St [White St]
  212-925-8270
  Cool sound + light installation by La Monte Young and Marian Zazeela. Closed during summer.
- **Duane Park** • Duane St & Hudson St
  One of the nicest spots in all of New York.
- **Fleming Smith Warehouse** • 451 Washington St [Watts St]
  TriBeCa's most sublimely beautiful structure. Believe it.
- **Ghostbusters Firehouse** • 14 N Moore St [Varick St]
  Are you the gatekeeper?
- **Harrison Street Row Houses** • Harrison St & Greenwich St
  Unique collection of preserved Federalist architecture.
- **New York Law School** • 185 W Broadway [Leonard St]
  212-431-2100
  New York Law's new main building burns brightly on cold TriBeCa nights.
- **New York Telephone Company Building** • 140 West Street [Vestry St]
  Massive Art Deco gem still looms over now-fashionable TriBeCa.
- **No. 8 Thomas Street** • 8 Thomas St [Broadway]
  Bizarre Venetian townhouse in the middle of downtown. Really.
- **One York Street** • 1 York St [Canal St]
  Enrique Norten's postmodern offering is pretty damned good.
- **Powell Building** • 105 Hudson St [Franklin St]
  Carrere & Hastings gem w/ Nobu on the ground floor.
- **Textile Building** • 66 Leonard St [Church St]
  Henry J. Hardenbergh goodness in TriBeCa.
- **Washington Market Park** • 310 Greenwich St [Chambers St]
  One of the city's oldest marketplaces.

Nightlife is quieter here than in other neighborhoods, but upscale drinks can be found at **TriBeCa Grand** and **Bubble Lounge** and **Nancy Whiskey** and **Puffy's** are classic dives. Old school hangout **Walker's** is a New York classic and should not be missed; otherwise, check out the Flea Theatre's calendar or wait for the **TriBeCa Film Festival**.

Bars

- **Anotheroom** • 249 W Broadway [N Moore St]
  212-226-1418
  Cosy, cute, and narrow.
- **B Flat** • 277 Church St [White St]
  212-219-2970
  Stylish Japanese basement cocktail den.
- **Brandy Library** • 25 N Moore St [W Broadway]
  212-226-5545
  Refined but cozy with lots of free tasting events.
- **Broome Street Bar** •
  363 W Broadway [Broome St]
  212-784-6650
  Real low-key for this part of town.
- **Bubble Lounge** • 228 W Broadway [White St]
  212-431-3433
  Champagne bar; the more $$$ you spend, the nicer they'll be.
- **Church Bar** • 2 6th Ave [Church St]
  212-519-6600
  Luxurious space with pricey drinks and occasional live music.
- **Lucky Strike** • 59 Grand St [W Broadway]
  212-941-0772
  Hipsters, locals, ex-smoky. Recommended.
- **Naked Lunch** • 17 Thompson St [Grand St]
  212-343-0828
  Average lounge.
- **Nancy Whiskey Pub** •
  1 Lispenard St [W Broadway]
  212-226-9943
  Good dive. As if there were any other kind.
- **Puffy's Tavern** • 81 Hudson St [Harrison St]
  212-227-3912
  Suits, old timers, and hipsters. Top TriBeCa watering hole.
- **Smith & Mills** • 71 N Moore St [Greenwich St]
  212-226-2515
  Upscale cool cocktails. Limited seating.
- **Soho Grand Hotel** •
  310 W Broadway [Canal St]
  212-965-3000
  Swank sophistication.
- **Terroir** • 24 Harrison St [Greenwich St]
  212-625-9463
  Happening wine bar with funky list and tasty eats.
- **Toad Hall** • 57 Grand St [W Broadway]
  212-431-8145
  Laid back vibe with SoHo locals.
- **Tribeca Grand Hotel** • 2 6th Ave [White St]
  212-519-6600
  Posh drinks in an uber-cool space; service is another matter.
- **Walker's** • 16 N Moore St [W Broadway]
  212-941-0142
  Where old and new Tribeca neighbors mix.
- **Ward III** • 111 Reade St [W Broadway]
  212-240-9194
  Fantastic cocktail den. Awesome drinks, no attitude.
- **Warren 77** • 77 Warren St [Greenwich St]
  212-227-8994
  Do you believe in miracles? A classy sports bar in NYC.

Movie Theaters

- **Tribeca Cinemas** • 54 Varick St [Laight St]
  212-941-2001
  Home base of De Niro's Tribeca Film Festival.

Theaters/Performing Arts

- **TriBeCa Performing Arts Center** •
  199 Chambers St [Greenwich St]
  212-220-1460
  Downtown performing arts center connected to BMCC. Cool.

Restaurants

If you've got cash, Tribeca's got you covered. **Nobu** has top-shelf sushi, **Odeon** has the cool factor, **Landmarc** has killer steaks, **Il Giglio** has white-tablecloth-Italian, and **Capsouto Freres** has upscale French. **Bouley** is a top NYC dining experience. Otherwise, we go for the far-above-average pub grub at **Walker's** or cabbie favorite **Pakistan Tea House**.

Restaurants

- **Acappella** • 1 Hudson St [Chambers St]
  212-240-0163 • $$$$
  Sopranos-worthy Northern Italian cuisine.
- **Bouley** • 163 Duane St [W Broadway]
  212-964-2525 • $$$$$
  Absolute top NYC dining. Love the apples in the foyer.
- **Bread Tribeca** • 301 Church St [Walker St]
  212-334-0200 • $$$
  Country-style Italian.
- **Bubby's** • 120 Hudson St [N Moore St]
  212-219-0666 • $$
  Great atmosphere—good home-style eats and homemade pies.
- **Capsouto Freres** •
  451 Washington St [Watts St]
  212-966-4900 • $$$
  Excellent brunch, great space, oldish (in a good way) vibe.
- **City Hall** • 131 Duane St [Church St]
  212-227-7777 • $$$$$
  Bright, expensive, lots of suits, but still cool.
- **Corton** • 239 W Broadway [N Moore St]
  212-219-2777 • $$$$
  Bruni and Platt love this place. So should you.
- **Duane Park** • 157 Duane St [Hudson St]
  212-732-5555 • $$$$$
  Underrated New American.
- **Dylan Prime** • 62 Laight St [Greenwich St]
  212-334-4783 • $$$$$
  Excellent steakhouse, great location, TriBeCa prices.
- **Edward's** • 136 W Broadway [Duane St]
  212-233-6436 • $$
  Middle-of-the-road, kid's menu, mostly locals, sometimes great.
- **Estancia 460** • 460 Greenwich St [Watts St]
  212-431-5093 • $$
  Louche Argentines and brilliant french toast. Formerly Sosa Borella.
- **The Harrison** • 355 Greenwich St [Harrison St]
  212-274-9310 • $$$$$
  Great New American—understandably popular.
- **Il Giglio** • 81 Warren St [Greenwich St]
  212-571-5555 • $$$$$
  Stellar Italian. Trust us.
- **Ivy's Bistro** • 385 Greenwich St [N Moore St]
  212-343-1139 • $$
  Down-to-earth neighborhood Italian.
- **Kitchenette** • 156 Chambers St [Hudson St]
  212-267-6740 • $$
  Great breakfast. Try the bacon.
- **Kori** • 253 Church St [Leonard St]
  212-334-0908 • $$$
  Korean. Hip space. It's TriBeCa.
- **Landmarc** • 179 W Broadway [Leonard St]
  212-343-3883 • $$$$$
  Modern, posh, great steaks and wines; and, of course, pricey.
- **Lupe's East LA Kitchen** •
  110 6th Ave [Watts St]
  212-966-1326 • $
  Tex-Mex. Quaint. Eat here.
- **Nobu** • 105 Hudson St [Franklin St]
  212-219-0500 • $$$$$
  Designer Japanese. When we have 100 titles, we'll go here.
- **The Odeon** • 145 W Broadway [Thomas St]
  212-233-0507 • $$$$
  We can't agree about this one, so go and make your own decision.
- **Pakistan Tea House** •
  176 Church St [Reade St]
  212-240-9800 • $
  The real deal. Where cabbies eat. The Naan is perfect.
- **Saluggi's** • 325 Church St [Lispenard St]
  212-226-7900 • $$
  Brussels sprout, bacon, caramelized onion pie: get it.
- **Tribeca Grill** • 375 Greenwich St [Franklin St]
  212-941-3900 • $$$$$
  Are you looking at me?
- **Walker's** • 16 N Moore St [W Broadway]
  212-941-0142 • $$
  Surprisingly good food for a pub!
- **Zutto** • 77 Hudson St [Harrison St]
  212-233-3287 • $$$
  Neighborhood Japanese.

Bagels, Coffee, & Shopping

Hit up **Grandaisy Bakery** and **Duane Park Patisserie** for baked goods and **MarieBelle** for chocolate. We like **Selima Optique** for cool specs, **Steven Alan** and **Jack Spade** for trendy threads, **Korin** for cutlery, and **Tent & Trails** for plotting NYC escapes.

Coffee

- **Bikini Bar** • 148 Duane St [W Broadway] 212 571 6737 Surf's always up at this beachy coffee shop.
- **Kaffe 1668** • 275 Greenwich St [Murray St] 212-693-3750 Excellent coffee in a really cool space.
- **La Colombe Torrefaction** • 319 Church St [Lipsenard St] 212-343-1515 New York's first outpost of top-notch Philly roasters.
- **Moomah Cafe** • 161 Hudson St [Laight St] 212-226-0345 Take an art class with your coffee.

Shopping

- **All Good Things** • 102 Franklin St [6th Ave] 212-966-3663 Urban market selling fancy seafood & meat, fresh bread, and veggies.
- **Amish Market** • 53 Park Pl [W Broadway] 212-608-3863 Lots prepared foods. Do they deliver by horse and buggy?
- **Balloon Saloon** • 133 W Broadway [Duane St] 212-227-3838 We love the name.
- **Boffi Soho** • 31 Greene St [Grand St] 212-431-8282 Hi-end kitchen and bath design.
- **Duane Park Patisserie** • 179 Duane St [Staple St] 212-274-8447 Yummy!
- **Grandaisy Bakery** • 250 W Broadway [Beach St] 212-334-9435 Breads and pizzas by the one and only.
- **Issey Miyake** • 119 Hudson St [N Moore St] 212-226-0100 Flagship store of this designer.
- **Jack Spade** • 56 Greene St [Broome St] 212-625-1820 Barbie's got Ken, Kate's got Jack. Men's bags.
- **Korin** • 57 Warren St [W Broadway] 212-587-7021 Supplier to Japanese chefs and restaurants.
- **Let There Be Neon** • 38 White St [Church St] 212-226-4883 Neon gallery and store.
- **MarieBelle's Fine Treats & Chocolates** • 484 Broome St [Wooster St] 212-925-6999 Top NYC chocolatier. Killer hot chocolate.
- **New York Nautical** • 158 Duane St [Thomas St] 212-962-4522 Armchair sailing.
- **Oliver Peoples** • 366 W Broadway [Watts St] 212-925-5400 Look as good as you see, and vice-versa.
- **Selima Optique** • 59 Wooster St [Broome St] 212-343-9490 Funky eyewear for the vintage inclined.
- **Shoofly** • 42 Hudson St [Thomas St] 212-406-3270 Dressing your child for social success.
- **SoHo Art Materials** • 7 Wooster St [Crosby St] 212-431-3938 A painter's candy store.
- **Steven Alan** • 103 Franklin St [Church St] 212-343-0692 Trendy designer clothing and accessories. One-of-a-kind stuff.
- **Tent & Trails** • 21 Park Pl [Church St] 212-227-1761 Top outfitter for gearheads.
- **Tribeca Wine Merchants** • 40 Hudson St [Duane St] 212-393-1400 High quality for a high rollers neighborhood.
- **Urban Archaeology** • 143 Franklin St [W Broadway] 212-431-4646 Retro fixtures.
- **We Are Nuts About Nuts** • 166 Church St [Chambers St] 212-227-4695 They're nuts. We're nuts. We're all nuts.
- **What Goes Around Comes Around** • 351 W Broadway [Broome St] 212-343-1225 LARGE, excellent collection of men's, women's, and children's vintage.
- **Whole Foods** • 270 Greenwich St [Murray St] 212-349-6555 Tribeca natural market outpost means strollers and celebrities.

Map 3 • City Hall / Chinatown

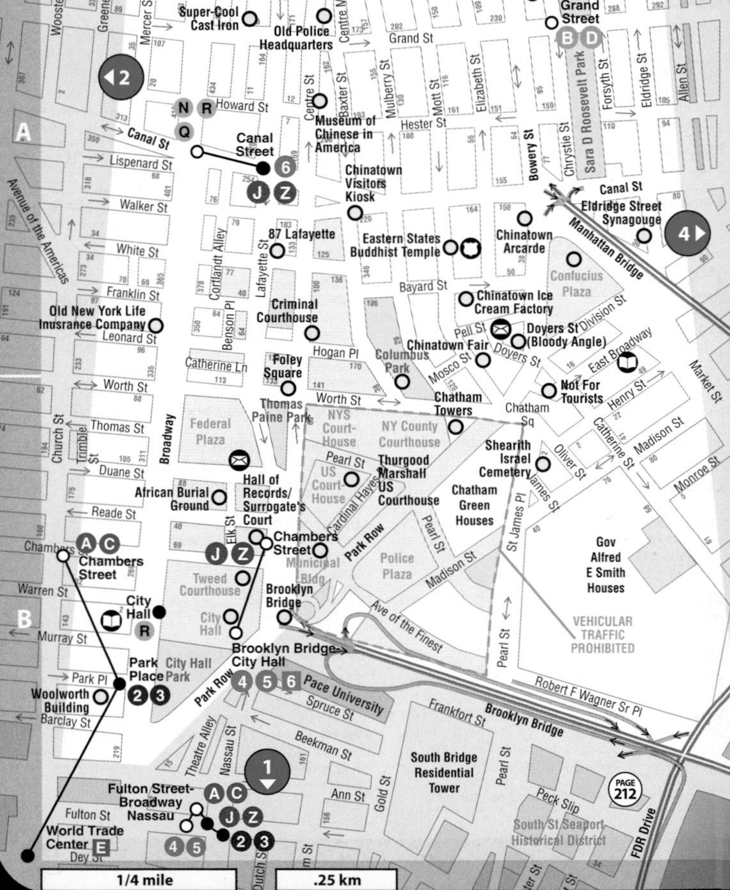

Neighborhood Overview

Chinatown. Home of the NFT offices from 1998 until 2010, we truly have a love-hate relationship to this neighborhood. On one hand you have one of the highest concentrations of great (and cheap!) food in all of New York, one of the city's most interesting and diverse **parks,** lots of history, and a daytime hustle-and-bustle that is probably only matched by midtown Manhattan.

On the other hand ... it's quite possibly New York's grimiest neighborhood, there is almost no nightlife, and peace and quiet is, of course, nonexistent during daylight hours. But hey—if you want peace and quiet, what are you doing in the middle of New York City anyway?

Our advice is to just get in there and mix it up with the locals, many of whom live in the huge **Confucius Towers** complex at the base of the Manhattan Bridge. And mixing it up is something that New Yorkers have been doing in this area for hundreds of years, starting with the incredibly dangerous "Five Points" area north of Collect Pond (the setting for Scorcese's seething Gangs of New York). Both the Five Points and Collect Pond are gone (the area itself is now **Columbus Park**), but little **Doyers Street** (aka "Bloody Angle") was the scene of Chinese gang wars for over 50 years.

Today, though, you can stroll around like the most clueless tourist and have absolutely no problems at all—gang wars have been replaced with street and shop commerce, from the tourist vendors of Mott Street to the **produce market** in the shadow of the Manhattan Bridge, with all of Canal Street's wall of tourists and locals connecting the two. The mass of humanity is sometimes overwhelming.

Fortunately, there are some cool places to try and hide away for a few moments, including the Eastern States Buddhist Temple and Maya Lin's new **Museum of Chinese In America**. The best "living museum," however, is without a doubt Columbus Park, which has an incredible range of activities—from early-morning tai chi to afternoon mah-jongg—happening within its borders throughout the day. In summer, a stop at classic **Chinatown Ice Cream Factory** will also cool your jets momentarily.

Columbus Park also serves as the northeast border of the **City Hall** area. There are several standout examples of civic architecture, including City Hall itself, the **Tweed Courthouse**, the **US Courthouse**, the condo-ized **Woolworth Building**, the sublime **Hall of Records/Surrogate Court** building, and, one of our favorite buildings in all of New York, McKim, Mead, & White's masterful **Municipal Building**, complete with a wedding-cake top and the Brooklyn Bridge stop of the 4-5-6 trains underneath.

From the Municipal Building, a walk over the **Brooklyn Bridge** is almost a de rigueur activity; if you'd rather stay in Manhattan, though, check out the recently-discovered **African Burial Ground** or watch Law & Order episodes being filmed from Foley Square. Or head back east a bit to discover another bit of New York City history, an ancient **Jewish Burial Ground** on St. James Place.

No matter what you do here don't forget to EAT. It's worth the traffic, the smells, the lines, and the general rudeness of people. Believe it

Landmarks

Landmarks

- **87 Lafayette St** • 87 Lafayette St [White St]
  Ex-firehouse designed in Chateau style by Napoleon LeBrun.
- **African Burial Ground** •
  290 Broadway [Duane St]
  212-637-2019
  Colonial burial ground for 20,000+ African-American slaves.
- **Brooklyn Bridge** • Chambers St & Centre St
  The granddaddy of them all. Walking towards Manhattan at sunset is as good as it gets.
- **Centre Marketplace** • Centre St & Broome St
  Another great street we can't afford to live on.
- **Chatham Towers** • 170 Park Row [Worth St]
  1960s poured-concrete apartment buildings overlooking Chatham Square. Nice windows.
- **Chinatown Arcade** • 48 Bowery [Canal St]
  Hidden dirty hallway connecting Elizabeth to the Bowery.
- **Chinatown Fair** • 8 Mott St [Bowery]
  551-697-5549
  Sneak out of the office to play Ms. Pac Man here.
- **Chinatown Ice Cream Factory** •
  65 Bayard St [Mott St]
  212-608-4170
  The best ice cream (ginger, black sesame, mango, red bean…), ever.
- **Chinatown Visitors Kiosk** •
  Walker St & Baxter St
  Good meeting point. Just lookout for the dragon.
- **City Hall** • 260 Broadway [Park Pl]
  212-788-3000
  Beautiful and slightly less barricaded than last year.
- **Columbus Park Playground** •
  67 Mulberry St [Bayard St]
  212-408-0100
  Former Five Points hub now operates as prime Chinatown hangout.
- **Confucius Plaza** • Bowery & Division St
  Confucius say: live here!
- **Criminal Courthouse** •
  100 Centre St [Leonard St]
  212-374-4423
  Imposing.
- **Doyers Street (Bloody Angle)** •
  Doyers St [Chatham Sq]
  One of few curvy streets in New York. Has a decidedly otherworldly feel.
- **Eldridge Street Synagogue** •
  12 Eldridge St [Division St]
  212-219-0888
  The first large-scale building by Eastern Euro immigrants in NY.
- **Foley Square** • Worth St & Centre St
  Now with bizarre black obelisk. Guiliani hated it.
- **Lighting District** • Bowery [Broome]
  Light up your life with products from these fine purveyors…
- **Municipal Building** • Chambers St & Park Row
  Wonderful McKim, Mead & White masterpiece.
- **Museum of Chinese in America** •
  215 Centre St [Howard St]
  212-619-4785
  Beautiful new home designed by Maya Lin.
- **Not For Tourists** • 2 E Broadway [Chatham Sq]
  212-965-8650
  NFT headquarters from 1998 to 2010.
- **Old New York Life Insurance Company** •
  346 Broadway [Leonard St]
  Great narrow McKim, Mead & White with hand-wound clock and cool internal stairwells.
- **Old Police Headquarters** •
  240 Centre St [Grand St]
  A beautiful building in the center of the not so beautiful Little Italy/Chinatown area.
- **Shearith Israel Cemetery** •
  55 St James Pl [Oliver St]
  Oldest Jewish cemetery in New York.
- **Super-Cool Cast Iron** • Crosby St & Grand St
  We want to live on the top floor of this building.
- **Surrogate's Courthouse** •
  31 Chambers St [Elk St]
  Great lobby and zodiac-themed mosaics.
- **Thurgood Marshall US Courthouse** •
  40 Centre St [Pearl St]
  Cass Gilbert masterpiece from 1935.
- **Tweed Courthouse** •
  52 Chambers St [Broadway]
  Great interior dome, but will we ever see it?
- **Woolworth Building** • 233 Broadway [Park Pl]
  A Cass Gilbert classic. Stunning lobby.

Think Kansas is boring at night? You haven't been to Chinatown at 10 pm on a Monday. Fortunately, one of the best dive/Chinese gangster Karaoke bars, the inimitable **Winnie's**, is here for your pleasure. Otherwise, hit sprawling **Fontana's** (the site of several NFT parties), or dance with hipsters at **Santos Party House**.

Bars

- **Apotheke** • 9 Doyers St [Bowery]
  212-406-0400
  Flaming expensive Euro-cocktails in a (supposedly) former opium den.
- **Capitale** • 130 Bowery [Grand St]
  212-334-5500
  Formerly the Bowery Savings Bank. Cool space.
- **Experimental Intermedia** • 224 Centre St [Grand St]
  212-431-5127
  Experimental art/performance art shows involving a variety of artistic media.
- **Fontana's** • 105 Eldridge St [Grand St]
  212-334-6740
  A big, band-playing, art-hanging LES slice in borderline Chinatown.
- **Happy Ending** • 302 Broome St [Forsyth St]
  212-334-9676
  Still taking the edge off.
- **Randolph Beer** • 343 Broome St [Elizabeth St]
  212-334-3706
  Lots of wood and even more beer.
- **Santos Party House** • 96 Lafayette St [Walker St]
  212-584-5492
  Eclectic music is the rule at this terrific venue.
- **Southside** • 1 Cleveland Pl [Broome St]
  212-680-5601
  Models, bankers, wealthy hipsters...you know the drill.
- **Tropical 128** • 128 Elizabeth St [Broome St]
  212-925-8219
  Challenge the Chinatown champions.
- **Winnie's** • 104 Bayard St [Mulberry St]
  212-732-2384
  Chinese gangster karaoke. We kid you not.

Restaurants

First stop: the crab soup dumplings at **Joe's Shanghai**. Second stop: the salt-and-pepper squid at **Pho Viet Huong**. On from there, classic Thai at **Pongsri Thai,** dim sum at **Mandarin Court**, **88 Palace**, or **Dim Sum Go Go**. In a hurry? Get a kebab at street cart **Xinjiang**. Too much Asian? Head to SoHo gem **Despaña** for Spanish sandwiches.

Restaurants

- **88 Palace** • 88 E Broadway [Forsyth St]
  212-941-8886 • $$
  Dim sum madness under the Manhattan Bridge.
- **Aux Epices** • 121 Baxter St [Canal St]
  212-274-8585 • $$
  Sweet little Malaysian spot doling out gourmet plates.
- **Banh Mi Saigon** • 198 Grand St [Mulberry St]
  212-941-1541 • $
  The best Vietnamese sandwiches. Ever.
- **Bo Ky** • 80 Bayard St [Mott St]
  212-406-2292 • $
  Chinese/Vietnamese hybrid. Killer soups.
- **Buddha Bodai** • 5 Mott St [Worth St]
  212-566-8388 • $$
  Veg heads dig this place.
- **Cong Ly** • 124 Hester St [Chrystie St]
  212-343-1111 • $
  Most interesting Pho in the city. Plus grilled pork!
- **Cup & Saucer** • 89 Canal St [Eldridge St]
  212-925-3298 • $
  Where NFT eats when sick of Chinese food. Well, just Rob.
- **Despana** • 408 Broome St [Centre St]
  212-219-5050 • $
  Excellent Spanish take-out/gourmet grocery, complete w/ bull.
- **Dim Sum Go Go** • 5 E Broadway [Catherine St]
  212-732-0797 • $$
  New, hip, inventive dim sum; essentially, post-modern Chinese.
- **East Corner Wonton** •
  70 E Broadway [Market St]
  212-343-9896 • $
  Consistently good wonton noodle soups.
- **Excellent Pork Chop House** •
  3 Doyers St [Bowery]
  212-791-7007 • $
  Fried chicken leg and spicy wontons are excellent.
- **Food Sing 88** • 2 E Broadway [Chatham Sq]
  212-219-8223 • $
  Outstanding beef soup with hand-pulled noodles.
- **Fuleen Seafood** • 11 Division St [Catherine St]
  212-941-6888 • $$$
  Chinatown gem; amazing lunch specials.
- **Great NY Noodletown** • 28 Bowery [Bayard St]
  212-349-0923 • $
  Cheap Chinese soups and BBQ and deep-fried squid. At 2 am.
- **Joe's Shanghai** • 9 Pell St [Bowery]
  212-233-8888 • $$
  Crab Soup Dumpling Mecca. Worth the wait.
- **Mandarin Court** • 61 Mott St [Bayard St]
  212-608-3838 • $$
  Consistently good and frenetic dim sum.
- **New Malaysia** • 46 Bowery [Canal St]
  212-964-0284 • $$
  A hidden gem that's literally hidden. Try the specials.
- **Nha Trang** • 87 Baxter St [White St]
  212-233-5948 • $$
  Excellent Vietnamese. Pho Beef Satee is good.
- **Nice Green Bo** • 66 Bayard St [Mott St]
  212-625-2359 • $
  Amazing Shanghainese. Nice alternative to Joe's.
- **Old Sichuan** • 65 Bayard St [Mott St]
  212-227-9888 • $
  Spicy and delicious, get the fish stew.
- **Pho Viet Huong** • 73 Mulberry St [Bayard St]
  212-233-8988 • $$
  Very good Vietnamese—get the salt and pepper squid.
- **Ping's** • 22 Mott St [Mosco St]
  212-602-9988 • $$
  Eclectic Asian seafood. And we mean "eclectic."
- **Pongsri Thai** • 106 Bayard St [Baxter St]
  212-349-3132 • $$
  Ever wonder where district attorneys go for cheap, tasty Thai?
- **Sanur Restaurant** • 18 Doyers St [Bowery]
  212-267-0088 • $
  Amazing, super cheap Malaysian.
- **Shanghai Cafe** • 100 Mott St [Canal St]
  212-966-3988 • $
  Killer soup dumplings and spicy garlic broccoli.
- **Tasty Hand-Pulled Noodles Inc.** •
  1 Doyers St [Bowery]
  212-791-1817 • $
  Stop by for a bowl on your post office run.
- **Wah Mei Fast Food** • 190 Hester St [Baxter St]
  212-925-6428 • $
  Linoleum floors, fluorescent lights, and an amazing pork chop over rice.
- **Xi'an Famous Foods** • 67 Bayard St [Mott St]
  $
  Hand pulled noodles and tasty lamb burgers.
- **Xinjiang Kebab Cart** • Division St & Market St
  $
  Charcoal grilled chicken hearts anyone? Get them spicy.

Bagels, Coffee, & Shopping

Rule Number One: Stay away from tourist trap Canal Street, unless you're headed to **Pearl Paint** for art supplies. Hit **New Beef King** for homemade jerky, **DiPalo Fine Foods** for Italian imports, **K & M Camera** for shutterbug stuff, **Pearl River Mart** for a massive selection of Chinese housewares, and **Papabubble** to watch candy-making magic happen.

Coffee

- **Saturdays Surf** • 31 Crosby St [Grand St]
  212-966-7875
  Small espresso bar with laid-back surfer vibe.

Shopping

- **Aji Ichiban** • 37 Mott St [Pell St]
  212-233-7650
  Load up on free samples from the huge selection of Asian candies and snacks.
- **Alleva** • 188 Grand St [Mulberry St]
  212-226-7990
  Killer Italian import shop.
- **Bangkok Center Grocery** •
  104 Mosco St [Mulberry St]
  212-349-1979
  Curries, fish sauce, and other Thai products.
- **Catherine Meat Market** •
  21 Catherine St [Henry St]
  212-693-0494
  Fresh pig deliveries every Tuesday!
- **Chinatown Arcade** • 48 Bowery [Canal St]
  Bizarre indoor mall/passageway. Check it out.
- **Chinatown Ice Cream Factory** •
  65 Bayard St [Mott St]
  212-608-4170
  Take home a quart of mango. Oddest flavors in NYC.
- **Clic** • 255 Centre St [Broome St]
  Art books and an art gallery.
- **Di Palo Fine Foods** • 200 Grand St [Mott St]
  212-226-1033
  Delicacies from across Italy. Excellent cheese.
- **Downtown Music Gallery** •
  13 Monroe St [Catherine St]
  212-473-0043
  Independent labels and artists.
- **Fay Da Bakery** • 83 Mott St [Canal St]
  212-791-3884
  Chinese pastry and boba like nobody's business.
- **Forsyth Outdoor Produce Market** •
  Forsyth St & Division St
  Cheapest veggies and fruit in Manhattan. Long lines.
- **Fountain Pen Hospital** •
  10 Warren St [Broadway]
  212-964-0580
  They don't take Medicaid.
- **Harney & Sons** • 433 Broome St [Crosby St]
  212-933-4853
  Awe-inspiring tea selection. Sampling encouraged.
- **K & M Camera** • 385 Broadway [White St]
  212-523-0954
  Good all-around camera store; open Saturdays!
- **Lendy Electric** • 176 Grand St [Baxter St]
  212-431-3698
  Great bastion of the electrical supply world.
- **Lung Moon Bakery** • 83 Mulberry St [Canal St]
  212-349-4945
  Chinese bakery.
- **New Beef King** • 89 Bayard St [Mulberry St]
  212-233-6612
  Serious jerky for serious jerks.
- **New York City Store** •
  1 Centre St [Chambers St]
  212-669-7452
  NYC books and municipal publications.
- **No 6** • 6 Centre Market Pl [Grand St]
  212-226-5759
  Notable selection of carefully selected original American and European vintage.
- **Opening Ceremony** •
  35 Howard St [Crosby St]
  212-219-2688
  Expensive hipster threads for tiny bodies.
- **Oro Bakery and Bar** • 375 Broome St [Mott St]
  212-941-6368
  Euro baked goods when you need a break from egg tarts.
- **Papabubble** • 380 Broome St [Mulberry St]
  212-966-2599
  Candy labratory. Willy Wonka would be proud.
- **Pearl Paint** • 308 Canal St [Mercer St]
  212-431-7932
  Mecca for artists, designers, and people who just like art supplies.
- **Pearl River Mart** • 477 Broadway [Broome St]
  212-431-4770
  Chinese housewares and more. Almost mind-numbing.
- **Piemonte Ravioli** • 190 Grand St [Mulberry St]
  212-226-0475
  Old-school and homemade.
- **Yunhong Chopsticks Shop** • 50 Mott St [Bayard St]
  212-566-8828
  Super-cute chopstick shop in C-town.

Map 4 • Lower East Side

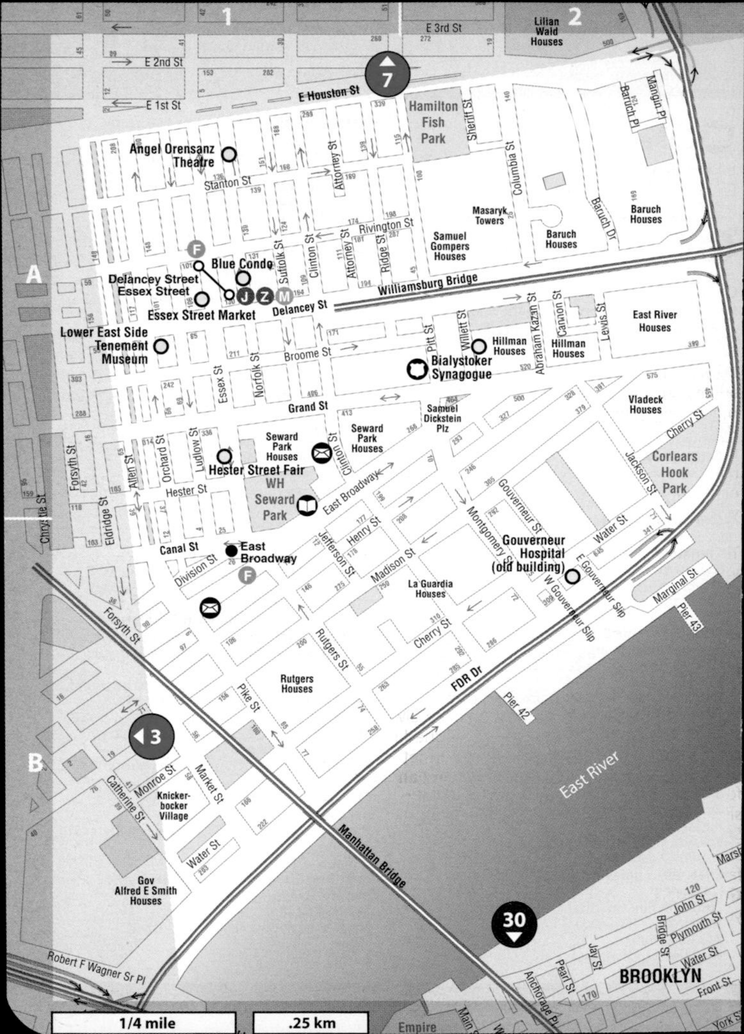

Neighborhood Overview

Now characterized by bars and nightclubs and the high-heeled, cologne-drenched crowds that flock to them, the Lower East Side has traditionally been known as the epicenter of immigrant cultures. At one time the term "Lower East Side" applied to what's now called the East Village as well, but starting in the latter part of the 20th century, the two neighborhoods have commonly been referred to separately, with Houston Street as the dividing line. While the Lower East Side has the grittier reputation, with its sprawl of housing projects along the East River, and shared border with Chinatown on the southern and western edges, gentrification is quickly sweeping across the landscape; one of the more obvious signs is the incongruous **Blue Condo** rising above Norfolk Street.

Of all the groups who settled here, the area is perhaps most known for its Jewish roots, and traces can still be found if you look hard enough. A number of historic synagogues still stand, including **Bialystoker Synagogue** on Willett St, and the **Angel Orensanz Foundation**, which has been converted into an art gallery. The venerable **Katz's Delicatessen** on Houston St. **(Map 7)** is an obvious starting point for any culinary tour, and if you still have room after all that pastrami, head to **Russ & Daughters (Map 7)** for bagels, smoked fish, and old world appetizing. If a light snack is what you're after, **Kossar's Bialys** is still one of the best deals in town. Once your belly is full, walk along the tenement buildings and discount clothing stores along Orchard Street until you reach the **Lower East Side Tenement Museum**. There you can tour restored apartments of actual people who lived in the area long ago, and thank your lucky stars that at least you don't share your tiny studio with a half dozen relatives.

The overlapping of Jewish, Puerto Rican and Chinese cultures, as well as the changes wrought by the neighborhood's rising attractiveness to developers make any walking tour fascinating. Along Clinton Street, old school Latino businesses stand side-by-side with cutting-edge eateries. On Broome Street, pungent Chinese vegetable markets encounter pricey boutiques. Art center **ABC No Rio**, which grew out of downtown's squatter movement and punk rock scene is located a couple blocks from the swanky **Hotel on Rivington**. You get the picture.

When you're done with history, you can always do some more eating. Check out the stalls at **Essex Street Market**—established in the 1930s to replace the pushcarts that once clogged these streets—for gourmet groceries, meats, and produce. If you're passing by on a Saturday, **Hester Street Fair** will give you a taste of the city's booming foodie scene with its many artisanal delights. And then there's the infamous nightlife, a slice of party heaven (or hell) clustered around Orchard, Clinton, Ludlow, Rivington, and Stanton Streets. If you're not up for impressing bouncers at **Libation** or downing vodka shots at **Mehanata**, do what we do and catch a show. **Mercury Lounge** is one of our favorite venues, and there's always something going on at **Cake Shop** or **Arlene's Grocery**. This is best attempted on a week night, of course. Don't say we didn't warn you.

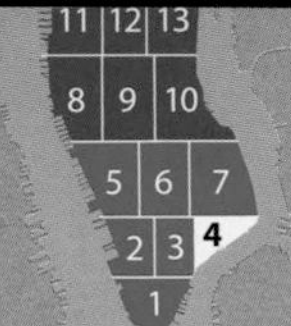

Landmarks

Landmarks

- **Angel Orensanz Foundation for the Arts •**
  172 Norfolk St [Stanton St]
  212-529-7194
  Performance space in ex-synagogue. Amazing.
- **Bialystoker Synagogue •**
  7 Bialystoker Pl [Grand St]
  212-475-0165
  The oldest building in NY to currently house a synagogue. Once a stop on the Underground Railroad.
- **Blue Condo •** 105 Norfolk St [Delancey St]
  Bernard Tschumi's odd masterpiece.
- **Gouverneur Hospital •**
  621 Water St [Gouverneur St]
  One of the oldest hospital buildings in the world.
- **Lower East Side Tenement Museum •**
  108 Orchard St [Broome St]
  212-982-8420
  Great illustration of turn-of-the-century (20th, that is) life.

Ready for a night out on the Lower East Side? Chug some $2 PBRs at **Welcome to the Johnsons** then head to **Arlene's Grocery** for rock n' roll karaoke. Or check out burlesque at Nurse Bettie, then get cozy on a couch at **The Back Room**. Or sample beers at **Spitzer's Corner** then catch a show at **Cake Shop** or **Fat Baby.** Go!

Bars

- **169 Bar** • 169 E Broadway [Rutgers St]
  646-833-7199
  Sometimes good, sometimes not.
- **Arlene's Grocery** • 95 Stanton St [Ludlow St]
  212-358-1633
  Cheap live tunes.
- **The Back Room** • 102 Norfolk St [Delancey St]
  212-228-5098
  The secret room is behind a bookcase.
- **Barramundi** • 67 Clinton St [Rivington St]
  212-529-6900
  Great garden in summer.
- **Cake Shop** • 152 Ludlow St [Stanton St]
  212-253-0036
  Coffee, records, beer, rock shows, and a "Most Radical Jukebox."
- **Chloe 81** • 81 Ludlow St [Broome St]
  212-677-0067
  Another secret bar you won't get into.
- **Clandestino** • 35 Canal St [Ludlow St]
  212-475-5505
  Inviting bar off the beaten track.
- **Dark Room** • 165 Ludlow St [Stanton St]
  212-353-0536
  For dark deeds. Ask Lindsay Lohan.
- **The Delancey** • 168 Delancey St [Clinton St]
  212-254-9920
  Overrated, but the roof is cool if you can get up there.
- **Donnybrook** • 35 Clinton St [Stanton St]
  212-228-7733
  Upscale yet rustic pub for the professional crowd.
- **Fat Baby** • 112 Rivington St [Essex St]
  212-533-1888
  Excellent venue to see "Friend Rock."
- **Libation** • 137 Ludlow St [Rivington St]
  212-529-2153
  If you like this place, please leave New York.
- **Local 138** • 138 Ludlow St [Rivington St]
  212-477-0280
  Great happy hour. No douchebags most of the time.
- **Lolita Bar** • 266 Broome St [Allen St]
  212-966-7223
  Hipster-haven.
- **Los Feliz** • 109 Ludlow St [Delancey St]
  212-228-8383
  Taqueria/tequileria full of revolutionary splendor and a hidden subterranean labyrinth.
- **The Magician** • 118 Rivington St [Essex St]
  212-673-7851
  Hipster haven. The NFT cartographer loves it.
- **Max Fish** • 178 Ludlow St [Stanton St]
  212-529-3959
  Where the musicians go. Still.
- **Mehanata** • 113 Ludlow St [Delancey St]
  212-625-0981
  Keep an eye out for DJ Eugene Hutz.
- **Motor City Bar** • 127 Ludlow St [Rivington St]
  212-358-1595
  Faux biker bar. Still good, though.
- **Nurse Bettie** • 106 Norfolk St [Rivington St]
  212-477-7515
  Cozy cocktails and burlesque. Recommended on weeknights.
- **Rivington 151** • 151 Rivington St [Suffolk St]
  212-228-4139
  Dependable, with cheap specials.
- **The Skinny** • 174 Orchard St [Stanton St]
  212-228-3668
  Shimmy through sweating crowds in this appropriately named dive bar.
- **The Slipper Room** •
  167 Orchard St [Stanton St]
  212-253-7246
  Striptease for the arty crowd.
- **Spitzer's Corner** •
  101 Rivington St [Ludlow St]
  212-228-0027
  40 beers on tap best enjoyed Sunday through Wednesday.
- **The Ten Bells** • 247 Broome St [Ludlow St]
  212-228-4450
  Organic wine bar with candlelit Euro-vibe. Nice!
- **Verlaine** • 110 Rivington St [Essex St]
  212-614-2494
  Mellow, French-Vietnamese motif with deceptively sweet cocktails.
- **Welcome to the Johnsons** •
  123 Rivington St [Essex St]
  212-420-9911
  Great décor, but too crowded mostly.

Restaurants

Sliders at the **Meatball Shop** and brunch at **Clinton St Baking Company** keep 'em lined up, but if you're with a group, just get a big table at **Congee Village**. We love **Tiny's Giant Sandwich** shop and **Nonna's L.E.S. Pizza** for a quick bite, **'intoteca** for sidewalk sitting, **wd~50** for inventive cuisine, and **Shopsin's** when we just need some good old fashioned mac n' cheese pancakes.

Restaurants

- **'inoteca** • 98 Rivington St [Ludlow St]
  212-614-0473 • $$
  Late-night tapas, mafia-style.
- **Barrio Chino** • 253 Broome St [Orchard St]
  212-228-6710 • $$
  Started as a tequila bar, but now more of a restaurant.
- **Cafe Katja** • 79 Orchard St [Broome St]
  212-219-9545 • $$$
  The LES Euro zone welcomes Austria into the fold.
- **Cheeky Sandwiches** •
  35 Orchard St [Hester St]
  646-504-8132 • $
  New Orleans Po'boys dressed. The real deal.
- **Clinton Street Baking Co.** •
  4 Clinton St [E Houston St]
  646-602-6263 • $$
  Homemade buttermilk everything. LES laid back. Top 5 bacon.
- **Congee Village** • 100 Allen St [Delancey St]
  212-941-1818 • $$
  Porridge never tasted so good.
- **Creperie** • 135 Ludlow St [Rivington St]
  212-979-5543 • $
  A hole-in-the-wall that serves sweet and savory crepes.
- **El Castillo de Jagua** •
  113 Rivington St [Essex St]
  212-982-6412 • $
  Great cheap Dominican.
- **El Sombrero** • 108 Stanton St [Ludlow St]
  212-254-4188 • $$
  Cheap margaritas. Dates back to earlier days of the LES.
- **The Fat Radish** • 17 Orchard St [Canal St]
  212-300-4053 • $$$
  Modern British eats with a hip, industrial backdrop.
- **Hi Thai** • 123 Ludlow St [Rivington St]
  212-677-7624 • $
  Tasty Thai eatery near bustling nightlife and shops.
- **Kuma Inn** • 113 Ludlow St [Delancey St]
  212-353-8866 • $$
  Spicy southeast Asian tapas.
- **Kupersmith** • 49 Clinton St [Rivington St]
  212-614-3234 • $$
  British pub food with great brunch menu.
- **Les Enfants Terribles** • 37 Canal St [Ludlow St]
  212-777-7518 • $$$
  Cozy French-African. Recommended.
- **The Meatball Shop** • 84 Stanton St [Allen St]
  212-982-8895 • $$
  Amazing balls in many different varieties.
- **Mission Chinese** • 154 Orchard St [Stanton St]
  212-529-8800 • $$
  Always packed Chinese hipster spot is worth the hype.
- **Noah's Ark Original Deli** •
  399 Grand St [Suffolk St]
  212-674-2200 • $$
  Great Jewish deli.
- **Nonna's L.E.S. Pizzeria** •
  105 Clinton St [Delancey St]
  212-477-2708 • $
  Get a grandma slice.
- **Pok Pok Phat Thai** •
  137 Rivington St [Norfolk St]
  212-477-1299 • $$
  Tiny Thai with big flavors.
- **San Marzano** • 71 Clinton St [Rivington St]
  212-228-5060 • $$
  Personal pies with gourmet toppings.
- **Schiller's Liquor Bar** •
  131 Rivington St [Norfolk St]
  212-260-4555 • $$$$
  Loud, good, loud, good.
- **Shopsin's** • 120 Essex St [Rivington St]
  $
  Kenny's back! Get your Blisters on My Sisters in the Essex St Market.
- **Sorella** • 95 Allen St [Delancey St]
  212-274-9595 • $$$$
  Top end Northern Italian.
- **Sticky Rice** • 85 Orchard St [Broome St]
  212-274-8208 • $$
  Thai treats, Asian BBQ, BYOB, and Wi-Fi?!
- **Teanyssimo** • 90 Rivington St [Orchard St]
  212-475-9190 • $$
  Vegan tea room and Moby hang-out.
- **Tiny's Giant Sandwich Shop** •
  129 Rivington St [Norfolk St]
  212-228-4919 • $
  Great art work on the walls, complements delicious sandwiches in your belly.
- **wd~50** • 50 Clinton St [Stanton St]
  212-477-2900 • $$$$
  Michelin-starred gastronomical wonderworld on Clinton Street.
- **Zucco Le French Diner** •
  188 Orchard St [Stanton St]
  212-677-5200 • $
  Cozy, inexpensive French brasserie where the owner serves your quiche.

Bagels, Coffee, & Shopping

We buy our gear at **Ludlow Guitars**, retro glasses at Moscot, jewelry at Windy Mink, groceries at **Essex Street Market**, and uhhh...just browse at Babeland. **Bluestockings** is worth a look for activist lit, Economy Candy has everything, and if you're hungry, hit **Kossar's Bialys**, and **Doughnut Plant**.

Bagels

- **Kossar's Bialys** • 367 Grand St [Essex St]
  212-473-4810
  Where NFT gets their morning treats.

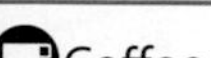

Coffee

- **Lost Weekend** • 45 Orchard St [Hester St]
  917-261-2401
  Great coffee with a side of hipster.
- **Roasting Plant** • 81 Orchard St [Broome St]
  212-775-7755
  Custom-ground coffee. Theatrical.

Shopping

- **Babeland** • 94 Rivington St [Ludlow St]
  212-375-1701
  Sex toys without the creepy vibe.
- **BabyCakes** • 248 Broome St [Ludlow St]
  855-462-2292
  A bakery dedicated solely to vegan, gluten-free goodies.
- **Bluestockings** • 172 Allen St [Stanton St]
  212-777-6028
  Specialty - Political/Left Wing.
- **Chari & Co.** • 175 Stanton St [Clinton St]
  212-475-0102
  Cozy Japanese bike shop with down-to-earth staff.
- **Doughnut Plant** • 379 Grand St [Norfolk St]
  212-505-3700
  Great, weird, recommended.
- **Economy Candy** • 108 Rivington St [Essex St]
  212-254-1531
  Floor-to ceiling candy madness.
- **Edith Machinist** •
  104 Rivington St [Ludlow St]
  212-979-9992
  Where to buy your vintage boots and bags.
- **Essex Street Market** •
  120 Essex St [Rivington St]
  212-388-0449
  Classic public market with a great combo of old-school and fresh-faced vendors.
- **Il Laboratorio del Gelato** •
  188 Ludlow St [E Houston St]
  212-343-9922
  Mind-bogglingly incredible artisanal gelato.
- **Labor Skate Shop** • 46 Canal St [Orchard St]
  646-351-6792
  Hip skate kids roll on in to hang and pick up a cool board.
- **Ludlow Guitars** • 172 Ludlow St [Stanton St]
  212-353-1775
  New and used vintage guitars, accessories, and amps.
- **Moishe's Bakery** • 504 Grand St [E Broadway]
  212-673-5832
  Best babka, challah, hamantaschen, and rugalach.
- **Moscot** • 118 Orchard St [Delancey St]
  212-477-3796
  Glasses like your grandfather used to wear.
- **Narnia** • 161 Rivington St [Clinton St]
  212-979-0661
  So many awesome articles. So few dollars to buy them with. Expensive, beautiful vintage.
- **Project No. 8** • 38 Orchard St [Hester St]
  212-925-5599
  Fashionable Euro-boutique.
- **Roni-Sue's Chocolates** •
  120 Essex St [Rivington St]
  212-260-0421
  Chocolate-covered bacon and other sweets sold from inside Essex Market.
- **Saxelby Cheesemongers** •
  120 Essex St [Rivington St]
  212-228-8204
  All-American and artisinal.
- **September Wines & Spirits** •
  100 Stanton St [Ludlow St]
  212-388-0770
  Wines from a variety of family-operated vineyards. Free tastings!
- **Streit's Matzos** • 148 Rivington St [Suffolk St]
  212-475-7000
  Making the real deal since 1925.
- **Top Hops** • 94 Orchard St [Delancey St]
  212-254-4677
  Sip a beer while you shop for more beer.
- **Wendy Mink** • 72 Orchard St [Broome St]
  212-260-5298
  Unique, affordable jewelry that's handmade in NYC.
- **Zarin Fabrics** • 314 Grand St [Allen St]
  212-925-6112
  Major destination in the fabric district.

Map 5 • West Village

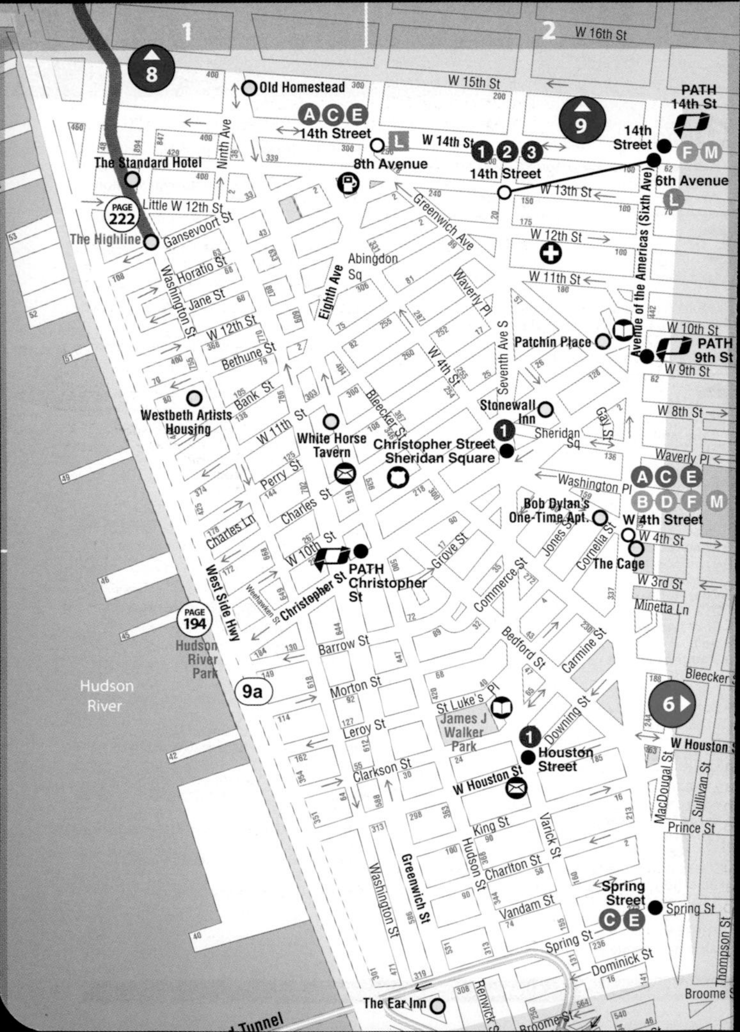

Old Homestead
14th Street
8th Avenue
14th Street
PATH 14th St
14th Street
6th Avenue
The Standard Hotel
The Highline
Abingdon Sq
Patchin Place
PATH 9th St
Westbeth Artists Housing
White Horse Tavern
Christopher Street Sheridan Square
Stonewall Inn
Sheridan Sq
Bob Dylan's One-Time Apt.
W 4th Street
The Cage
PATH Christopher St
Hudson River Park
Hudson River
St Luke's Pl
James J Walker Park
Houston Street
Spring Street
The Ear Inn

W 16th St
W 15th St
W 14th St
W 13th St
W 12th St
W 11th St
W 10th St
W 9th St
W 8th St
Little W 12th St
Gansevoort St
Horatio St
Jane St
W 12th St
Bethune St
Bank St
W 11th St
Perry St
Charles St
Charles Ln
W 10th St
Christopher St
Weehawken St
Barrow St
Morton St
Leroy St
Clarkson St
W Houston St
King St
Charlton St
Vandam St
Spring St
Dominick St
Broome St
Ninth Ave
Eighth Ave
Greenwich Ave
Waverly Pl
W 4th St
Bleecker St
Seventh Ave S
Avenue of the Americas (Sixth Ave)
Gay St
Washington Pl
Jones St
Cornelia St
W 3rd St
Minetta Ln
Grove St
Commerce St
Bedford St
Carmine St
Downing St
Bleecker St
W Houston St
MacDougal St
Sullivan St
Prince St
Thompson St
Washington St
West Side Hwy
Greenwich St
Hudson St
Varick St
Renwick St
Holland Tunnel

Neighborhood Overview

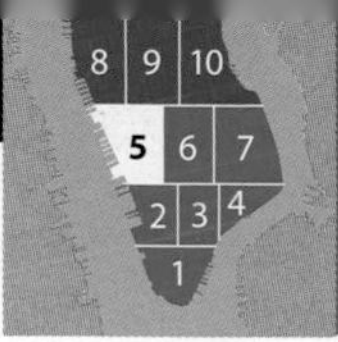

Ah, the West Village. This is the idyllic neighborhood of Jane Jacobs, the district of odd-angled streets designed to disorient grid-seasoned New Yorkers. Bordered by collegiate Greenwich Village to the east, millionaire stronghold Tribeca to the South, and factory-turned-gallery heaven Chelsea to the North, this neighborhood has quaint beauty, a thriving restaurant scene, and top-notch shopping, making it the ultimate address for the very, very rich. But its draw goes deeper than finding the boots or the cheeseburger that will change your life, because of all the famous artists, musicians, and writers who once lived, worked, drank, strolled, and starved here.

To catch a glimpse of more Bohemian times, head to the **White Horse Tavern** (1880), which has the dubious honor of being the place where Dylan Thomas drank himself to death. You can see where Edgar Allen Poe was treated at **Northern Dispensary** (1831), and visit Bob Dylan's old apartment at **161 West 4th Street**. Charming, gated **Patchin Place** (1849) was once home to writers Theodore Dreiser, e.e. Cummings, and Djuna Barnes. Thelonious Monk, Miles Davis, and every other jazz great under the sun played at **Village Vanguard** (1935). Poet Edna St. Vincent Millay helped found **Cherry Lane Theater** (1924), which remains the oldest continuously operating off-Broadway theater. Absent is Gertrude Vanderbilt Whitney's Studio Club on West 8th Street, which became the Whitney Museum of Art (1931). The museum moved uptown in the 1950s, but a new building at Washington and Gansevoort Street will bring it back to the neighborhood sometime in 2015.

The atmosphere of artistic creativity and non-conformity that permeated this neighborhood in the early 20th century (and still does, to some extent) gave rise to the gay rights movement, sparked by the 1969 riots at the **Stonewall Inn**. The West Village has also been the scene of vehement preservation efforts. **The Ear Inn** (1817), one of the oldest bars in Manhattan, was an early example of the New York City Landmarks Preservation Commission acting to protect a historic building. The **Jefferson Market Courthouse** (1877), now part of the New York Public Library, was also saved by the outcry of the community when faced with demolition. Since 1969 much of the area has been preserved as a historic district that runs from 14th Street to West 4th or St. Luke's Place, and from Washington St. to University Place.

Despite all that architectural preservation, perhaps no area has seen as dramatic change in recent years as the blocks between 14th, Gansevoort, and Hudson Streets, also known as the Meatpacking District. The slaughterhouses, meat markets, hookers, and johns have been displaced by highest of high-end shops, nightclubs, and glittering hotels, paving the way for a different kind of meat market entirely. The Standard Hotel, one of the most visible signs of the area's resurgence, straddles the newly renovated **High Line Park**, converted from a railway to a green public space that runs all the way up to 30th Street. It's worth a stroll, if only to remind yourself that you're (literally) above all the luxury below. Continue your walk along ever-popular Hudson River Park, before hitting one of the West Village's fine bars and restaurants and having more fun than you can afford.

Landmarks

Landmarks

- **Bob Dylan's One-Time Apartment** •
161 W 4th St [Cornelia St]
Bob Dylan lived here in the '60s.
- **The Cage (Basketball Court)** •
6th Ave & W 4th St
Where everybody's got game…
- **The Ear Inn** • 326 Spring St [Greenwich St]
212-431-9750
Second-oldest bar in New York; great space.
- **The High Line** •
Gansevoort to 30th St b/n 10th & 11th Ave
212-500-6035
Stunning elevated park; a testament to human creativity.
- **Jefferson Market** • 425 6th Ave [W 10th St]
212-243-4334
Now a library.
- **Old Homestead Steakhouse** •
56 9th Ave [W 14th St]
212-242-9040
Said to be NY's oldest steakhouse, circa 1868.
- **Patchin Place** •
W 10th St b/n 6th Ave & Greenwich Ave
Tiny gated enclave, once home to E.E. Cummings.
- **The Standard** • 848 Washington St [W 12th St]
212-645-4646
Hip Meatpacking District hotel straddling the High Line.
- **The Stonewall Inn** •
53 Christopher St [7th Ave S]
212-488-2705
Uprising here in 1969 launched the gay rights movement.
- **Westbeth Artists Housing** •
55 Bethune St [Washington St]
Cool multifunctional arts center.
- **White Horse Tavern** •
567 Hudson St [W 11th St]
212-989-3956
Another old, cool bar. Dylan Thomas drank here (too much).

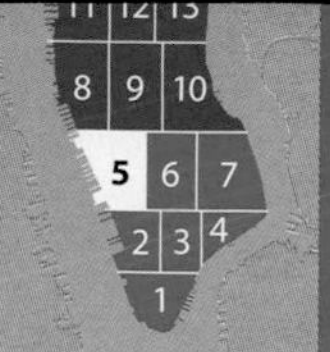

So many bars, so little time. The **Ear Inn** and **White Horse Tavern** are classics while **Employees Only** and **Little Branch** have speakeasy cocktails covered. Check out live jazz at **Jazz Gallery** and **Village Vanguard**, world music at **SOB's**, cabaret at **Marie's Crisis** and the **Duplex** and movies at **IFC** or revival house **Film Forum**.

Bars

- **Art Bar** • 52 8th Ave [W 4th St]
  212-727-0244
  Great spaces, cool crowd.
- **Arthur's Tavern** • 57 Grove St [Bleecker St]
  212-675-6879
  Featuring great jazz and blues since 1937.
- **Barrow's Pub** • 463 Hudson St [Barrow St]
  212-741-9349
  Low-key, old man bar.
- **Blind Tiger Ale House** •
  281 Bleecker St [Jones St]
  212-462-4682
  Beer heaven. Good food. Good vibe.
- **The Duplex** • 61 Christopher St [7th Ave S]
  212-255-5438
  Everything's still fun.
- **The Ear Inn** • 326 Spring St [Greenwich St]
  212-431-9750
  2nd oldest bar in NYC. A great place.
- **Employees Only** • 510 Hudson St [W 10th St]
  212-242-3021
  Classy cocktails for big bucks.
- **Fat Cat** • 75 Christopher St [7th Ave S]
  212-675-6056
  Laid back vibe. Plus ping pong and jazz!
- **Henrietta Hudson** •
  438 Hudson St [Morton St]
  212-924-3347
  Good lesbian vibe.
- **Kettle of Fish** • 59 Christopher St [7th Ave S]
  212-414-2278
  Cozy couches and darts.
- **Little Branch** • 22 7th Ave S [W 12th St]
  212-929-4360
  Clever cocktails in an intimate, cavernous setting.
- **Marie's Crisis** • 59 Grove St [7th Ave S]
  212-243-9323
  Showtunes only! And no, Billy Joel doesn't count.
- **The Other Room** •
  143 Perry St [Washington St]
  212-645-9758
  Surprisingly decent beer selection with great, low-key vibe.
- **SOB's** • 204 Varick St [W Houston St]
  212-243-4940
  World music venue with salsa lessons on Mondays.
- **Standard Biergarten** •
  848 Washington St [W 13th St]
  212-645-4100
  Gallons of beer, pretzels and partying young ones.
- **The Stonewall Inn** •
  53 Christopher St [7th Ave S]
  212-488-2705
  From the L to the GB and T, this is where it all began.
- **Village Vanguard** • 178 7th Ave S [Perry St]
  212-255-4037
  Classic NYC jazz venue. Not to be missed.
- **Vin Sur Vingt** • 201 W 11th St [Greenwich St]
  212-924-4442
  Bold wine choices and French small plates in a cozy space.
- **Vol de Nuit** • 148 W 4th St [6th Ave]
  212-982-3388
  Belgian beers, cool vibe.
- **White Horse Tavern** •
  567 Hudson St [W 11th St]
  212-989-3956
  Another NYC classic.

Movie Theaters

- **Film Forum** • 209 W Houston St [Varick St]
  212-727-8110
  Best place to pick up a film geek.
- **IFC Center** • 323 6th Ave [W 3rd St]
  212-924-7771
  Great midnights, special events, and Manhattan exclusives

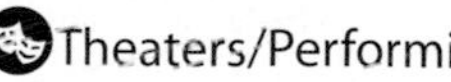

Theaters/Performing Arts

- **Cherry Lane Theater** •
  38 Commerce St [Bedford St]
  212-989-2020
  Founded by Edna St. Vincent Millay & her boho buddies.
- **HERE** • 145 6th Ave [Dominick St]
  212-647-0202
  Cool avant-garde multiplex with a nice cafe.
- **Lucille Lortel Theatre** •
  121 Christopher St [Bedford St]
  212-279-4200
  Play Twister on the Off-Off Broadway Playwright's Walk of Fame.

Restaurants

No burger crawl would be complete without a trip to **Corner Bistro** and **BLT Burger**. Save up for dinner at the **Spotted Pig** or **Spice Market** by grabbing a slice at **Joe's Pizza**—one of NYC's finest. Head to and **Pearl Oyster Bar** for seafood, **Pó** for Italian, and for diner grub, try **Waverly Restaurant** (not to be confused with **Waverly Inn**).

Restaurants

- **Aquagrill** • 210 Spring St [Sullivan St]
212-274-0505 • $$$$$
NFT's favorite straight-up seafood restaurant. Great feel.
- **Bar Six** • 502 6th Ave [W 13th St]
212-691-1363 • $$$
Pretty much a perfect French bistro.
- **BLT Burger** • 470 6th Ave [W 11th St]
212-243-8226 • $$
Really, really freakin' good burgers.
- **Café Asean** • 117 W 10th St [Patchin Pl]
212-633-0348 • $$
Pan-Asian, via Mr. Wong.
- **Café Condesa** • 183 W 10th St [7th Ave]
212-352-0050 • $$
Cozy Latin bistro with a seriously tasty Mexican brunch.
- **Corner Bistro** • 331 W 4th St [Jane St]
212-242-9502 • $
Top NYC burgers. Perfect at 3 am.
- **Ditch Plains** • 29 Bedford St [Downing St]
212-633-0202 • $$$
Great for seafood or breakfast.
- **EN Japanese Brasserie** •
435 Hudson St [Leroy St]
212-647-9196 • $$$$
Amazing izakaya not to be missed.
- **Fatty Crab** • 643 Hudson St [Gansevoort St]
212-352-3592 • $$$
West Village favorite for Malaysian street food.
- **French Roast** • 78 W 11th St [6th Ave]
212-533-2233 • $$
Open 24 hours. French comfort food.
- **Home** • 20 Cornelia St [W 4th St]
212-243-9579 • $$$$
There's no place like it.
- **Joe's Pizza** • 7 Carmine St [Bleecker St]
212-366-1182 • $
Excellent slices.
- **John's Pizzeria** • 278 Bleecker St [Jones St]
212-243-1680 • $$
Quintessential NY pizza.
- **Keste Pizzeria** • 271 Bleecker St [Jones St]
212-243-1500 • $$$
So authentic, it's the headquarters for the APN (look it up).
- **La Bonbonniere** • 28 8th Ave [Jane St]
212-741-9266 • $
Best cheap breakfast in the city.
- **Landbrot** • 137 7th Ave S [Charles St]
212-255-7300 • $$
German baked goods along with beer and pretzels.
- **The Marrow** • 99 Bank St [Greenwich Ave]
212-428-6000 • $$$$
Excellent German and Italian tastes with a high price.
- **Mary's Fish Camp** • 64 Charles St [W 4th St]
646-486-2185 • $$$
Amy Sedaris used to wait tables here for fun. Killer food!
- **Mercadito** • 100 7th Ave S [Grove St]
212-647-0830 • $$$$
Inventive Mexican with great fish taco choices.
- **Pearl Oyster Bar** • 18 Cornelia St [W 4th St]
212-691-8211 • $$$
For all your lobster roll cravings. NFT fave.
- **Po** • 31 Cornelia St [W 4th St]
212-645-2189 • $$$$
Creative Italian. Intimate feel.
- **Spice Market** • 403 W 13th St [9th Ave]
212-675-2322 • $$$$$
Another Jean-George joint. Thai-Malaysian street food and beautiful people.
- **The Spotted Pig** •
314 W 11th St [Greenwich St]
212-620-0393 • $$$$
We finally got in. All great except for pig ears.
- **Taim** • 222 Waverly Pl [Perry St]
212-691-1287 • $$
Gourmet falafel with mind-blowing housemade sauces.
- **Tartine** • 253 W 11th St [W 4th St]
212-229-2611 • $$$
BYOB + Solid French = NFT pick.
- **Tea & Sympathy** •
108 Greenwich Ave [W 13th St]
212-989-9735 • $$$
Eccentric English. Cult favorite.
- **Tertulia** • 359 6th Ave [Washington Pl]
646-559-9909 • $$$
Trendy tapas.
- **Wallse** • 344 W 11th St [Washington St]
212-352-2300 • $$$$
Top-notch Austrian cuisine keeps the West Villagers coming back.
- **The Waverly Inn** • 16 Bank St [Waverly Pl]
917-828-1154 • $$$$
Hip, revamped café-cum-speakeasy. Good luck getting in.
- **Waverly Restaurant** •
385 6th Ave [Waverly Pl]
212-675-3181 • $$
Great old-school diner with classy waiters.
- **Westville** • 210 W 10th St [Bleecker St]
212-741-7971 • $$
Trendy organic belly timber served with a fresh market flair.

oodies, hit **Murray's Cheese**, **Myers of Keswick**, **Ottomanelli & Sons**, **Citarella**, **Faiccos**, and **Murray's Bagels**. Sip java at **Joe The Art of Coffee**, browse for books at **Three Lives & Company**, or go ahead and blow your bonus at **Jeffrey**, **Alexander McQueen**, and **Stella McCartney**.

Bagels

- **Murray's Bagels** • 500 6th Ave [W 13th St]
  212-462-2830
  Classic. But they don't toast, so don't ask.

Coffee

- **Joe the Art of Coffee** • 141 Waverly Pl [Gay St]
  212-924-6750
  Excellent espresso.
- **Mojo Coffee** • 128 Charles St [Greenwich St]
  212-691-6656
  Tiny, perfect cafe.
- **Roasting Plant** • 75 Greenwich Ave [7th Ave]
  212-775-7755
  Techno-coffee beans flying through the air!

Shopping

- **Alexander McQueen** • 417 W 14th St [9th Ave]
  212-645-1797
  Brit bad boy designs.
- **Bien Cuit** • 35 Christopher St [Waverly Pl]
  646-590-3341
  Stand out breads and pastries.
- **C.O. Bigelow Chemists** • 414 6th Ave [W 9th St]
  212-533-2700
  Classic village pharmacy. Do try and patronize it.
- **Citarella** • 424 6th Ave [W 9th St]
  212-874 0383
  Wealthy foodies love this place.
- **The End of History** • 548 Hudson St [Perry St]
  212-647-7598
  Very cool shop specializing in antique glass.
- **Faicco's Italian Specialties** •
  260 Bleecker St [Cornelia St]
  212-243-1974
  Proscuitto bread, homemade sausage, huge heros, pork heaven.
- **Flight 001** • 96 Greenwich Ave [Jane St]
  212-989-0001
  Cute hipster travel shop. And they sell NFT!
- **Grom** • 233 Bleecker St [6th Ave]
  212-206-1738
  This gelato is so good and so expensive.
- **Health & Harmony** • 470 Hudson St [Barrow St]
  212-691-3036
  Small health food store with good selection and decent prices.
- **House of Oldies** • 35 Carmine St [Bleecker St]
  212-243-0500
  Everything on vinyl.
- **Jacques Torres** • 350 Hudson St [Charlton St]
  212-414-2462
  Tastebud bliss brought to you by the Master of Chocolate.
- **Jeffrey** • 449 W 14th St [Washington St]
  212-206-1272
  Avant garde (and wildly expensive) mini-department store.
- **The Leather Man** •
  111 Christopher St [Bedford St]
  212-243-5339
  No, you won't look like James Dean. But it'll help.
- **Murray's Cheese** • 254 Bleecker St [Leroy St]
  212-243-3289
  We love cheese, and so does Murray's.
- **Myers of Keswick** • 634 Hudson St [Horatio St]
  212-691-4194
  Killer English sausages, pasties, etc. And "Bounty!"
- **O. Ottomanelli & Sons** •
  285 Bleecker St [Jones St]
  212 675-4217
  High quality meats and the friendliest butchers in town.
- **Rebel Rebel Records** •
  319 Bleecker St [Christopher St]
  212-989-0770
  Small CD and LP shop with knowledgeable staff.
- **Scott Jordan Furniture** •
  137 Varick St [Spring St]
  212-620-4682
  Solid hardwood furniture. Super-cool and mostly unaffordable.
- **Stella McCartney** • 112 Greene St [Prince St]
  212-255-1556
  Hip, animal-friendly fashion.
- **Steven Alan** • 69 8th Ave [W 13th St]
  212-242-2677
  The West Village outpost for the preppy-cool NYC-based label.
- **Three Lives & Company** • 154 W 10th St [Waverly Pl]
  212-741-2069
  General Interest books.
- **Vitra** • 29 9th Ave [W 13th St]
  212-463-5700
  Sleek and modern home furnishings. Super-cool.

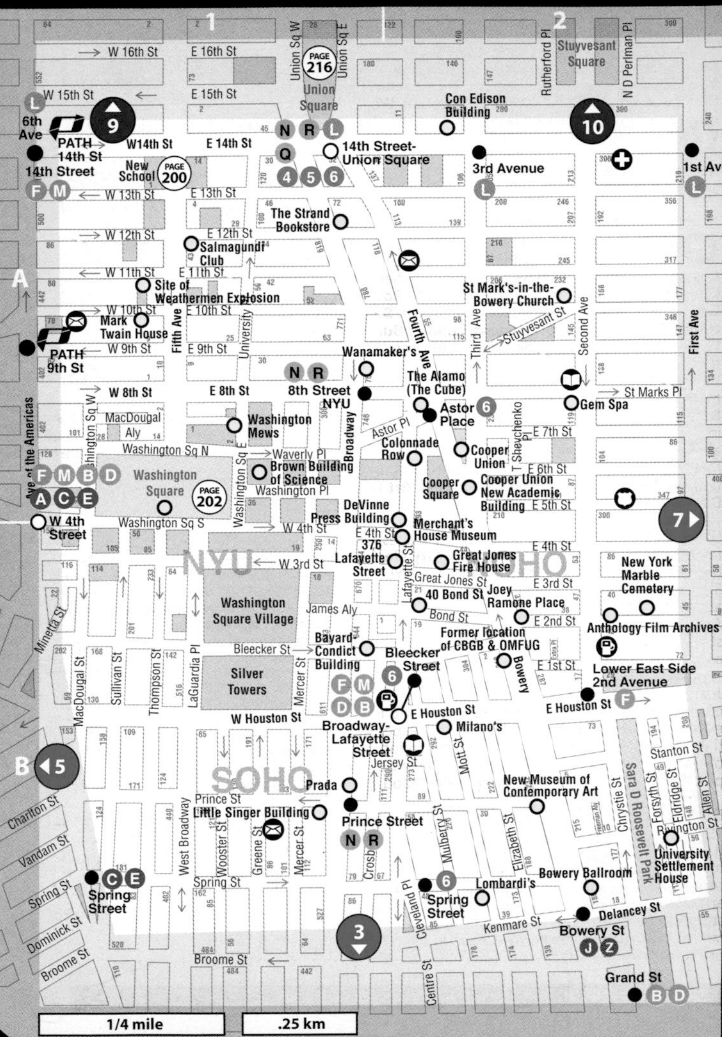
W 16th St
E 16th St
W 15th St
E 15th St
Union Square
14th Street-Union Square
Con Edison Building
6th Ave
PATH 14th St
W14th St
E 14th St
14th Street
New School
3rd Avenue
1st Ave
W 13th St
E 13th St
The Strand Bookstore
W 12th St
E 12th St
Salmagundi Club
W 11th St
E 11th St
Site of Weathermen Explosion
St Mark's-in-the-Bowery Church
W 10th St
E 10th St
Mark Twain House
PATH 9th St
W 9th St
E 9th St
Fifth Ave
University Pl
Fourth Ave
Third Ave
Second Ave
First Ave
Stuyvesant St
Stuyvesant Square
Rutherford Pl
N D Perlman Pl
Wanamaker's
8th Street NYU
The Alamo (The Cube)
W 8th St
E 8th St
St Marks Pl
Gem Spa
Astor Place
Astor Pl
MacDougal Aly
Washington Mews
Colonnade Row
Cooper Union
E 7th St
T Shevchenko Pl
Washington Sq N
Waverly Pl
Brown Building of Science
E 6th St
Washington Square
Washington Pl
Cooper Square
Cooper Union New Academic Building
E 5th St
Ave of the Americas
Washington Sq W
Washington Sq E
W 4th Street
Washington Sq S
DeVinne Press Building
W 4th St
E 4th St
Merchant's House Museum
376 Lafayette Street
Great Jones Fire House
NYU
NOHO
W 3rd St
Washington Square Village
Great Jones St
E 3rd St
New York Marble Cemetery
40 Bond St
Joey Ramone Place
James Aly
Bond St
E 2nd St
Anthology Film Archives
Bayard-Condict Building
Former location of CBGB & OMFUG
Bleecker St
Bleecker Street
Minetta St
Silver Towers
E 1st St
Lower East Side 2nd Avenue
MacDougal St
Sullivan St
Thompson St
LaGuardia Pl
Mercer St
Broadway
Lafayette St
Bowery
E Houston St
W Houston St
Broadway-Lafayette Street
Milano's
Jersey St
Mott St
Stanton St
SOHO
Prada
New Museum of Contemporary Art
Chrystie St
Sara D Roosevelt Park
Forsyth St
Eldridge St
Allen St
Charlton St
Prince St
Little Singer Building
Prince Street
Rivington St
Vandam St
West Broadway
Wooster St
Greene St
Crosby St
Mulberry St
Elizabeth St
University Settlement House
Bowery Ballroom
Spring St
Spring Street
Lombardi's
Cleveland Pl
Delancey St
Kenmare St
Bowery St
Dominick St
Broome St
Centre St
Grand St
1/4 mile
.25 km

Neighborhood Overview

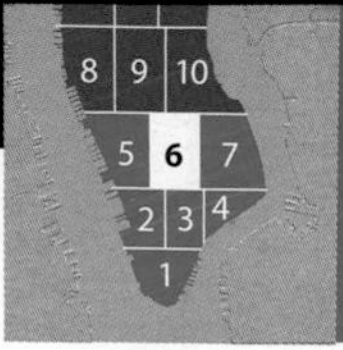

8 9 10
5 6 7
2 3 4
1

Map 6

Simply put, this is still the center of the universe. It all radiates from the corner of Broadway and Houston, which serves as the intersection for four of New York City's most exciting neighborhoods: Greenwich Village, Soho, NoHo, and NoLiTa. While the area is far from bucolic—green space is limited to a few patches of grass in **Washington Square Park**—it has everything one could possibly want in terms of culture. Architecture, art galleries, movie theaters, live music, shopping, restaurants, old New York, new New York, and every other kind of New York are all here for the taking. If you're new to the city and ready to dive in and explore, start here.

One of this area's highlights is the sheer number of buildings from every period of New York City's development. Just walk the streets and you'll traverse over two hundred years of architectural history. Start with the somewhat-hidden former stables at **Washington Mews** for a taste of 18th-century New York. Other ancient (for New York) buildings include **St. Marks Church in-the-Bowery** (1799), **Colonnade Row** (1830s), the **Old Merchant's House** (1832), **Grace Church** (1846) and the **Cooper Union Building** (1859). The stunning white terra cotta exterior of Louis Sullivan's **Bayard-Condict Building** (1899), and Ernest Flagg's **Great Jones Fire House** (1899) and **Little Singer Building** (1904) hearken back to New York at the turn of the 20th century. In the early 20th century Daniel Burnham (**Wanamaker's**, 1904/1907) and Henry J Hardenbergh (**376 Lafayette St**, 1888, and the **Con Edison Building**, 1914) added their contributions to the area. Our ultimate favorite is the little-known **DeVinne Press Building** (1885) by Babb, Cook & Willard (and not just because we buy our **wine** there). Starting in the 21st century, modern (or should we say postmodern?) architecture has run rampant along the Bowery, transforming the once derelict district. Notable examples include Thom Mayne's **Cooper Union New Academic Building** (2009), Kazuyo Sejima and Ryue Nishizawa's brilliant **New Museum of Contemporary Art** (2007), and Herzog & de Mauron's bizarre **40 Bond** (2007).

Unlike these buildings, some historical places of interest seem hidden in plain sight. Our favorite of these is the lovely **New York City Marble Cemetery**, tucked away on Second Street between The Bowery and Second Avenue. NYU's **Brown Building** was the site of the Triangle Shirtwaist Fire, while **18 West 11th Street** was the site of the Weathermen explosion. A plaque at the **Mark Twain House** on West 4th Street commemorates his time as a Greenwich Villager. And, while you can't rock out at **CBGB** anymore, you can still visit the site (now a John Varvatos store), right around the corner from where Joey Ramone lived on East 2nd Street, also known as **Joey Ramone Place**.

Just as there's no shortage of history, the cultural options here can make your head spin. A few of our favorites include the **Salmagundi Club** for art, the Astor Center for food and cooking events, and **Anthology Film Archives** for experimental film. The **Bowery Ballroom** is one of the best venues in NYC to catch up-and-coming musical acts. Browsing **The Strand**'s 18 miles of books is a must, as is checking out the critics' picks at **Other Music**, which has outlasted practically every other record store in this 'hood.

For all the history and culture here, signs of the area's down-and-out heyday in the 1970s and 1980s are few and far between. **Milano's** still serves up divey goodness, as it's been doing since the 1800s. Skate punks still hang out at **The Alamo** (give it a spin), even while fancy glass towers rise around it. You can still get your punk rock and goth gear at **Trash & Vaudeville**, and browse the magazine racks at **Gem Spa**. Much of the rest of St. Mark's Place between Second and Third Avenues now resembles a cross between a strip mall and Little Tokyo, which stretches along 9th Street as well. If you're ready for a break from all this excitement, grab some ramen, then get a cocktail at **Angel's Share** (one flight up and behind a Japanese restaurant) or explore the sake list at **Decibel** while feeling like you've left the Village far behind.

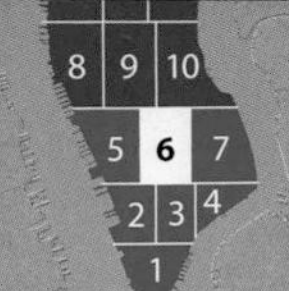

Landmarks

- **376 Lafayette St** • 376 Lafayette St [Great Jones St] Henry Hardenbergh's NoHo masterpiece, circa 1888.
- **40 Bond** • 40 Bond St [Bowery] Uber-futuristic condo projects by Herzog & de Meuron et al.
- **The Alamo (The Cube)** • 4th Ave & Astor Pl Give it a spin sometime.
- **Bayard-Condict Building** • 65 Bleecker St [Crosby St] Louis Sullivan's only New York building.
- **Brown Building of Science** • 23-29 Washington Pl [Greene St] Site of the Triangle Shirtwaist Fire.
- **Colonnade Row** • 428 Lafayette St [Astor Pl] Remains of a very different era.
- **Con Edison Building** • 145 E 14th St [Irving Pl] Cool top.
- **Cooper Union** • 30 Cooper Sq [Bowery] 212-353-4100 Great brownstone-covered building.
- **Cooper Union New Academic Building** • 41 Cooper Square [E 6th St] Supercool, futuristic, and eco-friendly architecture.
- **DeVinne Press Building** • 399 Lafayette St [E 4th St] Killer 1885 brick-and-glass masterpiece by Babb, Cook & Willard.
- **Former location of CBGB & OMFUG** • 315 Bowery [Bleecker St] Now houses high-end retail. Ew.
- **Great Jones Firehouse** • Bowery & Great Jones St The coolest firehouse in NYC.
- **Joey Ramone Place** • Bowery & E 2nd St It's Joey Ramone's place. Period.
- **Little Singer Building** • 561 Broadway [Prince St] A fine building by Ernest Flagg.
- **Mark Twain House** • 14 W 10th St [5th Ave] Mark Twain lived here. It's also NYC's most haunted portal.
- **Merchant's House Museum** • 29 E 4th St [Lafayette St] 212-777-1089 The merchant is now dead.
- **New Museum** • 235 Bowery [Prince St] 212-219-1222 Brilliant white stacked cubes houses contemporary art and killer bookstore. Yah.
- **New York City Marble Cemetery** • 74 E 2nd St [1st Ave] 212-228-6401 Cool, but generally closed. But you can still see in.
- **Salmagundi Club** • 47 5th Ave [E 12th St] 212-255-7740 Cool building.
- **Site of the Weathermen Explosion** • 18 W 11th St [5th Ave] Townhouse where the Weathermen's plans to destroy Columbia's library went awry.
- **St. Mark's Church In The Bowery** • 131 E 10th St [3rd Ave] 212-674-6377 Old church with lots of community ties.
- **University Settlement** • 184 Eldridge St [Rivington St] 212-453-0242 Providing a haven for lower east siders of all ages since 1886.
- **Wanamaker's** • E 8th St & Broadway Former classiest department store in the city is now a Kmart. Ugh.
- **Washington Mews** • University Pl (entrance) [5th Ave] Where horses and servants used to live. Now coveted NYU space.
- **Washington Square Park** • W 4th St & Washington Square W Dime bag, anyone?

Nightlife

For better or worse, this area is why New York is called the city that never sleeps. For dives, we like Scratcher, **Milano's**, and **Blue & Gold**. For cocktails, check out **Mayahuel** or **Angel's Share**. Catch a reading at **KGB**, an indie film at **Angelika Film Center** or **Sunshine Cinema**, or live music at **Joe's Pub** or **Le Poisson Rouge** or **Bowery Ballroom**. We guarantee you won't be bored.

Bars

- **Angel's Share** • 8 Stuyvesant St [E 9th St]
  212-777-5415?
  Semi-hidden cocktail spot. Bring someone special.
- **Blue & Gold Tavern** • 79 E 7th St [1st Ave]
  212-473-8918
  Another fine East Village dive.
- **Booker & Dax** • 207 2nd Ave [13th St]
  212-254-3500
  Near perfect cocktails from the Momofuku team.
- **Botanica Bar** • 47 E Houston St [Mulberry St]
  212-343-7251
  Good bar, but we still miss the Knitting Factory.
- **Bowery Ballroom** • 6 Delancey St [Bowery]
  212-533-2111
  Great space that attracts great bands.
- **Fanelli's Cafe** • 94 Prince St [Mercer St]
  212-226-9412
  Old-time SoHo haunt. Nice tiles.
- **Grassroots Tavern** • 20 St Marks Pl [2nd Ave]
  212-475-9443
  That mass of fur in the corner is a cat.
- **The Immigrant** • 341 E 9th St [1st Ave]
  212-677-2545
  Wine and snacks in a sexy tenement.
- **Jimmy's No. 43** • 43 E 7th St [2nd Ave]
  212-982-3006
  Basement bar that knows its beer.
- **Joe's Pub** • 425 Lafayette St [Astor Pl]
  212-967-7555
  Excellent range of acts in intimate space.
- **KGB Bar** • 85 E 4th St [2nd Ave]
  212-505-3360
  Former CP HQ. Meet your comrades. Readings, too.
- **Le Poisson Rouge** •
  158 Bleecker St [Sullivan St]
  212-505-3474
  Seductive and strangely fun eclectic live music.
- **Marshall Stack** • 66 Rivington St [Allen St]
  212-228-4667
  Winner for best bar that seemed like it would be awful.
- **Mayahuel** • 304 E 6th St [2nd Ave]
  212-253-5888
  Tequila and mezcal den with awesome old Mexico décor.
- **McSorley's Old Ale House** •
  15 E 7th St [3rd Ave]
  212-474-9148
  Lights or darks?
- **Milady's** • 160 Prince St [Thompson St]
  212-226-9340
  Friendly spot keeping in real in this unreal 'hood.
- **Milano's** • 51 E Houston St [Mott St]
  212-226-8844
  Grungy, narrow, awesome, narrow, grungy.
- **Mother's Ruin** • 18 Spring St [Elizabeth St]
  212-219-0942
  Handcrafted cocktails and small plates.
- **Sake Bar Decibel** • 240 E 9th St [2nd Ave]
  212-979-2733
  Hip, underground sake bar.
- **Webster Hall** • 125 E 11th St [Fourth Ave]
  212-353-1600
  Feel the music through the floor.

Bowling

- **Bowlmor Lanes** • 110 University Pl [E 12th St]
  212-255-8188
  Bright, loud, expensive, and sometimes really fun.

Movie Theaters

- **Angelika** • 18 W Houston St [Mercer St]
  212-995-2570
  Higher profile indies play here first.
- **Anthology Film Archives** •
  32 2nd Ave [E 2nd St]
  212-505-5181
  Quirky retrospectives, revivals, and other rarities.
- **Cinema Village** • 22 E 12th St [University Pl]
  212-924-3363
  Charming and tiny with exclusive documentaries and foreign films.
- **Landmark Theatres Sunshine Cinema** •
  143 E Houston St [Eldridge St]
  212-260-7289
  High luxury indie film multiplex.
- **Quad Cinema** • 34 W 13th St [Fifth Ave]
  212-255-2243
  Gay-themed world premieres and second run Hollywood releases.

Restaurants

It's probably unfair for one neighborhood to claim all the glory, but this one's tops for restaurants too, from wallet-busting upscale (**Babbo** and **Strip House**), to awesome street carts (NY Dosas in Washington Square Park). We like **Frank** for Italian, **Zabb Elee** for Thai, **Num Pang** for sandwiches, and **Ssam Bar** for everything. Stayed out late? **Veselka** and **Blue Ribbon** have your back.

Restaurants

- **ACME** • 9 Great Jones St [Lafayette St]
212-203-2121 • $$$$
Nordic hotspot for the chic and loaded.
- **Artichoke Basille's Pizza** •
328 E 14th St [2nd Ave]
212-228-2004 • $$
Stand in line for amazing Sicilian slices.
- **Arturo's** • 106 W Houston St [Thompson St]
212-677-3820 • $$
Classic NYC pizza joint with live jazz. NFT favorite.
- **B&H Dairy** • 127 2nd Ave [St Mark's Pl]
212-505-8065 • $
Eat mushroom barley soup and homemade challah at the counter.
- **Babbo** • 110 Waverly Pl [MacDougal St]
212-777-0303 • $$$$
Super Mario: Go for the pasta tasting menu.
- **Balthazar** • 80 Spring St [Crosby St]
212-965-1414 • $$$$$
Simultaneously pretentious and amazing.
- **Blue Hill** • 75 Washington Pl [MacDougal St]
212-539-1776 • $$$$$
Wonderful food in an unexpected location.
- **Blue Ribbon** • 97 Sullivan St [Spring St]
212-274-0404 • $$$$$
Open 'til 4am. Everything's great.
- **Boukies** • 29 East 2nd St [2nd Ave]
212-777-2502 • $$
Contemporary Greek small plates look and taste good.
- **Forcella** • 334 Bowery [Great Jones St]
212-466-3300 • $$
Can you argue with deep fried Neapolitan pizza? No, you can not.
- **Frank** • 88 2nd Ave [E 5th St]
212-420-0106 • $$
Good food, great breakfast.
- **Freemans** • Freeman Alley [Rivington]
212-420-0012 • $$$
Taxidermy-filled hideaway with fab cocktails and delicious, rustic fare.
- **Il Buco** • 47 Bond St [Bowery]
212-533-1932 • $$$$$
Lovely Italian food. Great wines by the glass. Uber-hip scene.
- **Ippudo** • 65 4th Ave [E 10th St]
212-388-0088 • $$$
People waiting hours for a bowl of ramen? Yes, it's that good.
- **John's of 12th Street** • 302 E 12th St [2nd Ave]
212-475-9531 • $$
Classic Italian. Get the rollatini.
- **Jules Bistro** • 65 St Marks Pl [1st Ave]
212-477-5560 • $$$
Small French bistro with live unimposing jazz.
- **La Esquina** • 114 Kenmare St [Cleveland Pl]
646-613-7100 • $
Taqueria trifecta: taco stand, corner cantina, and secret subterranean abode.
- **Lahore Deli** • 132 Crosby St [E Houston St]
212-965-1777 • $
Indo-Pak deli popular with cabbies.
- **Lombardi's** • 32 Spring St [Mott St]
212-941-7994 • $$$
Said to be the first pizzeria in the US, circa 1905.
- **Mighty Quinn's** • 103 2nd Ave [E 7th St]
212-677-3733 • $$
Wood smoked meats with a Texas and Carolina twang.
- **Miss Lily's** • 132 W Houston St [Sullivan St]
646-588-5375 • $$$
Jamaican plates with a dub beat from a resident DJ.
- **Momofuku Noodle Bar** •
171 1st Ave [E 10th St]
$$$$
Because who can get into M. Ko?
- **Momofuku Ssam Bar** •
207 2nd Ave [E 13th St]
212-254-2296 • $$
Pork. Pork. Other stuff. Pork. Yum.
- **Num Pang** • 21 E 12th St [University Pl]
212-255-3271 • $
Tasty Cambodian sandwiches.
- **Parm** • 248 Mulberry St [Prince St]
212-993-7189 • $$
Chicken, eggplant, and meatball hero heaven is only an hour wait away.
- **Sammy's Roumanian** •
157 Chrystie St [Delancey St]
212-673-0330 • $$$$
An experience not to be missed. Chopped liver which will instantly kill you.
- **Strip House** • 13 E 12th St [5th Ave]
212-328-0000 • $$$$$
Super downtown steakhouse. NFT favorite.
- **Veselka** • 144 2nd Ave [E 9th St]
212-228-9682 • $
Pierogies absorb beer. At 4 am that's all you need to know.
- **Zabb Elee** • 75 2nd Ave [E 4th St]
212-505-9533 • $$
Authentic Thai by way of Queens. Keep the water coming.

Bagels, Coffee, & Shopping

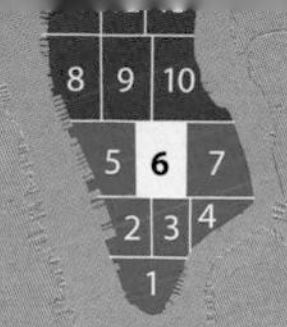

Outside Soho's glorified mall, the city's most eclectic shopping waits. Sample lotions at Kiehl's, and browse for housewares at **John Derian**, trendy threads at **Odin**, books at **The Strand**, music at **Other Music**, old prints at **Pageant Print Shop**, and cool gifts at **MoMA Design Store**. The selections at **Astor Wines & Spirits** and **New Beer Distributors** remind us why we live here.

Coffee

- **Caffe Reggio** • 119 MacDougal St [W 3rd St]
  212-475-9557
  A New York classic. Check out the custom coffee cups.
- **Gimme! Coffee** • 228 Mott St [Prince St]
  212-226-4011
  Amazing cappuccinos from the Ithaca experts.
- **Joe The Art of Coffee** • 9 E 13th St [5th Ave]
  212-924-3300
  Joe really knows his joe.
- **La Colombe Torrefaction** •
  400 Lafayette St [E 4th St]
  212-677-5834
  Philly's Stumptown.
- **Mudspot** • 307 E 9th St [Second Ave]
  212-529-8766
  The Mudtruck's stationary shop.

Shopping

- **Astor Wines & Spirits** •
  399 Lafayette St [E 4th St]
  212-674-7500
  NFT fav. The king of all NYC liquor stores.
- **Black Hound New York** •
  170 2nd Ave [E 11th St]
  212-979-9505
  Killer desserts. NFT Favorite.
- **Blick Art Materials** •
  1 Bond Street [Lafayette St]
  212-533-2444
  Huge, super organized, recommended.
- **Bond Street Chocolate** • 63 E 4th St [Bowery]
  212-677-5103
  The hippest chocolate this side of Belgium. Get the skulls.
- **Dual Specialty Store** • 91 1st Ave [E 6th St]
  212-979-6045
  Indian grocery store stocked with every spice imaginable.
- **East Village Cheese** • 40 3rd Ave [E 10th St]
  212-477-2601
  Super cheap cheeses, olives, and meats. No samples!
- **Forbidden Planet** • 832 Broadway [E 13th St]
  212-473-1576
  Let your inner sci-fi/fantasy nerd run wild.
- **Gem Spa** • 131 2nd Ave [St Marks Pl]
  212-995-1866
  Magazine stand that serves fantastic egg creams.
- **Happy Bones Publications** •
  7 Bond St [Broadway]
  Tiny book shop with an under-the-radar espresso shop.
- **John Derian** • 6 E 2nd St [Bowery]
  212-677-3917
  Whimsical découpage plates and curios for the home.
- **MoMA Design Store** • 81 Spring St [Crosby St]
  646-613-1367
  Cutting-edge, minimalist, ergonomic, offbeat, and funky everything.
- **New Beer Distributors** •
  167 Chrystie St [Rivington St]
  212-473-8757
  Enormous beer selection.
- **Odin New York** • 199 Lafayette St [Broome St]
  212-966-0026
  Boutique with stylish street clothes.
- **Other Music** • 15 E 4th St [Lafayette St]
  212-477-8150
  Underground, experimental CD's, LP's, imports, and out-of-print obscurities.
- **Pageant Print Shop** • 69 E 4th St [2nd Ave]
  212-674-5296
  Just prints, really. But really great prints.
- **Pino's Prime Meats** •
  149 Sullivan St [Prince St]
  212-475-8134
  Old-world Italian butcher. Pino's tips are priceless.
- **Porto Rico Importing Co.** •
  201 Bleecker St [MacDougal St]
  212-477-5421
  Beans by the barrel full.
- **Raffetto's** • 144 W Houston St [MacDougal St]
  212-777-1261
  Take-home Italian foods. Ravioli like mamma used to make.
- **Strand Book Store** • 828 Broadway [E 12th St]
  212-473-1452
  Used mecca; world's messiest and best bookstore.
- **Taschen** • 107 Greene St [Prince St]
  212-226-2212
  God (and the Devil's) gift to publishing.
- **Trash & Vaudeville** • 4 St Marks Pl [Third Ave]
  212-982-3590
  Decades-old NYC HQ for punk and goth gear.

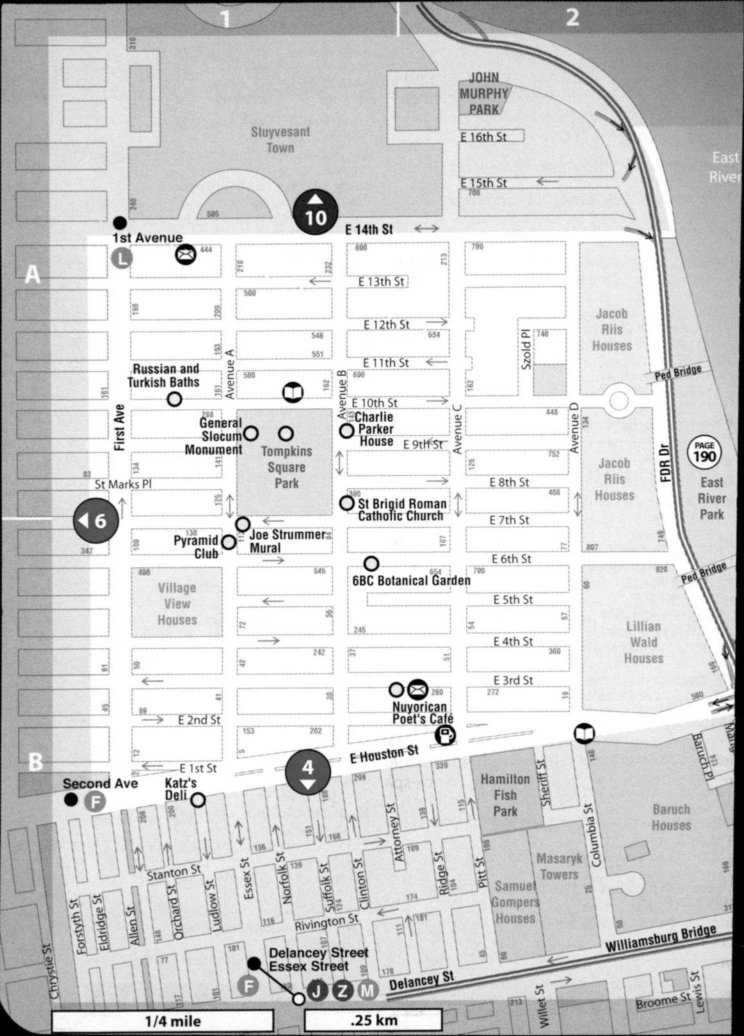

Map 7 • East Village

1 2
A B

Stuyvesant Town
JOHN MURPHY PARK
E 16th St
E 15th St
East River
1st Avenue
E 14th St
E 13th St
E 12th St
E 11th St
E 10th St
E 9th St
E 8th St
E 7th St
E 6th St
E 5th St
E 4th St
E 3rd St
E 2nd St
E 1st St
E Houston St
St Marks Pl
First Ave
Avenue A
Avenue B
Avenue C
Avenue D
Szold Pl
FDR Dr
Ped Bridge
Jacob Riis Houses
Russian and Turkish Baths
General Slocum Monument
Tompkins Square Park
Charlie Parker House
St Brigid Roman Catholic Church
Joe Strummer Mural
Pyramid Club
6BC Botanical Garden
Village View Houses
Lillian Wald Houses
East River Park
Nuyorican Poet's Café
Second Ave
Katz's Deli
Hamilton Fish Park
Sheriff St
Columbia St
Baruch Pl
Baruch Houses
Masaryk Towers
Samuel Gompers Houses
Stanton St
Rivington St
Delancey St
Williamsburg Bridge
Broome St
Lewis St
Willet St
Pitt St
Ridge St
Attorney St
Clinton St
Suffolk St
Norfolk St
Essex St
Ludlow St
Orchard St
Allen St
Eldridge St
Forsyth St
Chrystie St
Delancey Street Essex Street

10
6
4
PAGE 190

1/4 mile
.25 km

Neighborhood Overview

It's no longer the city's Bohemia—we hear it's somewhere in Brooklyn. But if you're dead-set on staying in Manhattan, the East Village is downtown's most livable neighborhood. Blame that on all the well-worn tenements and their (relatively) affordable small studios and "junior" one-bedrooms, some of them rent stabilized. In these apartments dwell old timers, NYU kids, and everyone in between, making for awesome people watching, day or night. A stroll through **Tompkins Square Park** on any warm weekend pretty much sums it up. Cute pooches and their oh-so-hip owners convene at the dog run while bongo drums echo over near Avenue B. Little kids shriek at the playground while crusty punks and gritty old men occupy the benches on the Southwestern side. Just a typical slice of life in the East Village, and a sweet life it is if you can swing the rent.

Before the crowds young professionals lived here, and before the artists, musicians, and squatters that preceded them, this area was home to waves of German, Irish, Italian, Jewish, Ukrainian, and Polish immigrants. A few historical sites remain from those times. One of our favorites is **Saint Brigid's Church** (1848), which was built by Irish immigrants. It's currently undergoing restoration after nearly being demolished. Another holdout, **Russian and Turkish Baths** (1892) still offers old-world platza treatments. One more significant marker from the neighborhood's past is the **General Slocum Monument**, which commemorates one of the worst disasters in the city's history—the sinking of the General Slocum steamship in 1904. Over 1,000 lives were lost, mainly German women and children from the neighborhood.

In the 1960s, Puerto Rican immigrants flooded into Alphabet City, another name for the blocks between Avenue A and Avenue D. Avenue C, also known as Loisaida Avenue, retains some of this character today, even while bars and restaurants catering to more recent arrivals open shop. The loveliest aspects of this area are the many community gardens, planted on once blighted lots and maintained by volunteers. We particularly like the always-tranquil **6BC Botanical Garden** on 6th Street between Avenue B and Avenue C. The best times to visit are Saturday and Sunday afternoons from May through October.

The term "East Village" came into use in the 1960s, when artists, musicians, writers, performers, intellectuals, and political radicals flocked to the neighborhood. A hugely influential art scene sprang up from the 1960s through the 1980s, but unfortunately, many of those galleries and performance spaces fell victim to skyrocketing rents in the 1990s and early 2000s. A few institutions have survived, though—you can still catch a poetry slam at the **Nuyorican Poet's Café**, or dance the night away like it's still 1984 at **The Pyramid Club**. One of our favorite summer events, the Charlie Parker Jazz Festival, takes place in **Tompkins Square Park**, right across the street from the **Charlie Parker House**. When you visit the park be sure to pass by the **Joe Strummer Mural**, a neighborhood landmark honoring one of the icons of punk rock. For live rock n' roll (or any kind of music scene), you're better off heading to the Lower East Side. But if you've come for the awesome bars, restaurants, and shopping that make this the neighborhood you'll never want to leave, read on.

Landmarks

Landmarks

- **6BC Botanical Garden** • 624 E 6th St [Ave C]
  Early Alphabet City community garden, now permanent park.
- **Charlie Parker Residence** •
  151 Ave B [E 10th St]
  The Bird lived here. Great festival every summer in Tompkins Square.
- **General Slocum Monument** •
  Tompkins Sq Park [Ave A]
  Memorial to one of the worst disasters in NYC history.
- **Joe Strummer Mural** •
  112 Avenue A [E 7th St]
  Ha, you think it's funny…turning rebellion into money?
- **Katz's Delicatessen** •
  205 E Houston St [Ludlow St]
  212-254-2246
  Classic NY deli, interior hasn't changed in decades.
- **Nuyorican Poets Café** •
  236 E 3rd St [Avenue C]
  212-780-9386
  Where mediocre poets die of humiliation.
- **The Pyramid Club** • 101 Avenue A [E 7th St]
  212-228-4888
  Classic '80s and '90s club.
- **Russian and Turkish Baths** •
  268 E 10th St [1st Ave]
  212-674-9250
  Sweat away all your urban stress.
- **St. Brigid Roman Catholic Church** •
  119 Avenue B [E 8th St]
  Historic Irish church spared demolition, still standing on Tompkins Square.
- **Tompkins Square Park** • E 9th St & Ave A
  212-387-7685
  Home to many.

Dive bars are an East Village specialty, and some of the finest specimens in the city are right here: try **Manitoba's**, **Lucy's**, **7B**, **International Bar**, and **Coal Yard.** This hood rules for cocktails too: check out **Summit Bar**, **Elsa**, or **Louis 649** if you can't bear the wait at **Death and Company**. **Drop Off Service** has our favorite happy hour this side of the East River. Cheers!

Bars

- **11th Street Bar** • 510 E 11th St [Avenue A]
  212-982-3929
  Darts, Irish, excellent.
- **2A** • 25 Avenue A [E 2nd St]
  212-505-2466
  Great upstairs space.
- **7B (Horseshoe Bar)** • 108 Avenue B [E 7th St]
  212-677-6742
  Godfather II shot here. What can be bad?
- **Amor y Amargo** • 443 E 6th St [Avenue A]
  212-614-6818
  Closet bitters bar.
- **Blarney Cove** • 510 E 14th St [Avenue A]
  212-473-9284
  The dive to end all East Village dives. Opens at 8 a.m.
- **Burp Castle** • 41 E 7th St [2nd Ave]
  212-982-4576
  Belgian ales and hushed voices.
- **Cherry Tavern** • 441 E 6th St [1st Ave]
  212-777-1448
  Get the Tijuana Special.
- **Coal Yard** • 102 1st Ave [E 6th St]
  212-677-4595
  Awesome dive bar that draws a fascinating cross section of locals.
- **d.b.a.** • 41 First Ave [E 2nd St]
  212-475-5097
  Awesome beer list and outdoor patio. NFT fave.
- **Death and Company** • 433 E 6th St [Avenue A]
  212-388 0882
  Classy cocktails served Prohibition style. No password required.
- **Drop Off Service** • 211 Avenue A [E 13th St]
  212-260-2914
  Awesome half-off everything happy hour 'til 8 p.m.
- **Elsa** • 217 E 3rd St [Ave B]
  917-882-7395
  Former dive bar, now serving elegant cocktails.
- **Good Beer** • 422 E 9th St [1st Ave]
  212-677-4836
  Ridiculous microbrew selection. Is this heaven?
- **Heathers** • 506 E 13th St [Avenue A]
  212-254-0979
  Usually low-key for the East Village.
- **Hi-Fi** • 169 Avenue A [E 11th St]
  212-420-8392
  The BEST jukebox in town.
- **Louis 649** • 649 E 9th St [Avenue C]
  212-673-1190
  Low-key cocktails and an impressive whiskey list. Check out their Tuesday night tastings.
- **Manitoba's** • 99 Avenue B [E 6th St]
  212-982-2511
  Punk scene.
- **Mercury Lounge** • 217 E Houston St [Essex St]
  212-260-4700
  Rock venue with occasional top-notch acts.
- **Nublu** • 62 Avenue C [E 5th St]
  646-546-5206
  Sexy lounge with world music, nice ambience, and outdoor porch.
- **The Phoenix** • 447 E 13th St [First Ave]
  212-477-9979
  Gay dive bar with great jukebox.
- **The Pyramid Club** • 101 Avenue A [E 7th St]
  212-228-4888
  Classic '80s and '90s club.
- **The Stone** • 69 Avenue C [E 2nd St]
  All proceeds go to the avant-garde jazz artists. Go now.
- **The Summit Bar** • 133 Avenue C [E 8th St]
  No Phone
  Clean classic cocktails.
- **Upright Citizens Brigade** •
  153 E 3rd St [Ave A]
  212-366-9231
  See smart, new comics and sometimes famous ones too.
- **WCOU Radio (Tile Bar)** • 115 1st Ave [E 7th St]
  212-254-4317
  East Village survivor. Low key and great.

Theaters/Performing Arts

- **Nuyorican Poets Café** •
  236 E 3rd St [Avenue C]
  212-780-9386
  Where mediocre poets die of humiliation.
- **Performance Space 122** •
  150 1st Ave [First Ave]
  212-477-5288
  Where Penny Arcade turned vomiting into art.
- **Theater for the New City** •
  155 1st Ave [E 10th St]
  212-254-1109
  A hot box of crazy theatre.

Restaurants

Residents here are spoiled rotten when it comes to food. Just head to 7th Street between First and A: sandwiches at **Porchetta,** lobster rolls at **Luke's Lobster**, arepas at **Caracas Arepa Bar**, and delicious Greek fare at **Pylos**. **7A's** always open, **Banjara** holds it down in Little India, and if you still have room, check out **Puddin'** for—take a wild guess.

Restaurants

- **7A Cafe** • 109 Avenue A [E 7th St]
  212-475-9001 • $$
  Open 24 hours. Great burgers.
- **Back Forty** • 190 Avenue B [E 12th St]
  212-388-1992 • $$
  Farm fresh, simple, and good.
- **Banjara** • 97 1st Ave [E 6th St]
  212-477-5956 • $$$
  Best Indian on 6th Street, hands-down. Awesome lamb chops.
- **The Beagle** • 162 Avenue A [E 10th St]
  212-228-6900 • $$$
  Classy cocktails and nibbles. Great date spot.
- **Bereket Turkish Kebab House** •
  187 E Houston St [Orchard St]
  212-475-7700 • $
  Middle Eastern delights. Open late.
- **Big Arc Chicken** • 233 1st Ave [E 14th St]
  212-477-0091 • $
  Cheap Middle Eastern food complete with Arabic TV.
- **Black Iron Burger** • 540 E 5th St [Avenue B]
  646-439-0276 • $
  Burgers with horseradish cheese and awesome onion rings.
- **Buenos Aires** • 513 E 6th St [Ave A]
  212-228-2775 • $
  Superior Argentine food: steaks, wine, friendly atmosphere.
- **Caracas Arepa Bar** • 93 E 7th St [1st Ave]
  212-228-5062 • $$
  Authentic Venezuelan.
- **Crif Dogs** • 113 St Marks Pl [Avenue A]
  212-614-2728 • $
  Kick-ass wieners.
- **Dirt Candy** • 430 E 9th St [Avenue A]
  212-228-7732 • $$$
  Translation: gourmet vegetarian.
- **Dok Suni's** • 119 1st Ave [E 7th St]
  212-477-9506 • $$$
  Excellent Korean fusion. NFT fav.
- **Edi & the Wolf** • 102 Avenue C [E 7th St]
  212-598-1040 • $$$
  Fantastic Austrian food, excellent variety, rustic atmosphere
- **El Maguey y La Tuna** •
  321 E Houston St [Attorney St]
  212-473-3919 • $$
  LES Mexican.
- **Flea Market Bistro** •
  131 Avenue A [St Marks Pl]
  212-358-9282 • $$
  French, good brunch.
- **Hummus Place** • 109 St Marks Pl [1st Ave]
  212-529-9198 • $
  Authentic! Best hummus this side of Tel Aviv.
- **Il Posto Accanto** • 190 E 2nd St [Avenue B]
  212-228-3562 • $$$
  Tiny, rustic Italian enoteca.
- **Jeepney** • 201 1st Ave [E 12th St]
  212-533-4121 • $$
  Shabby chic Filipino gastropub.
- **Korzo Haus** • 178 E 7th St [Ave B]
  212-780-0181 • $$
  Killer, unique burgers wrapped in Hungarian fried bread.
- **Luke's Lobster** • 93 E 7th St [1st Ave]
  212-387-8487 • $$
  Fresh-from-the sea lobster rolls, without sticker shock.
- **Luzzo's** • 211 1st Ave [E 13th St]
  212-473-7447 • $$
  Real coal oven. Top ten worthy.
- **Mercadito** • 179 Avenue B [E 11th St]
  212-529-6490 • $$
  This gourmet taqueria is always packed.
- **Odessa** • 119 Avenue A [St Marks Pl]
  212-253-1470 • $
  Diner. Awesome deep-fried meat pierogies.
- **Porchetta** • 110 E 7th St [1st Ave]
  212-777-2151 • $$
  Best Italian pork sandwiches. Ever.
- **Puddin'** • 102 St. Mark's Pl [1st Ave]
  212-477-3537 • $
  Make-your-own pudding parfaits. Best dessert in the hood.
- **Punjabi Grocery & Deli** • 114 E 1st St [1st Ave]
  212-533-3356 • $
  Deli, grocery, and cabbie-worthy Indian eats.
- **Pylos** • 128 E 7th St [Avenue A]
  212-473-0220 • $$
  Delicious Greek, cool hanging-pot ceiling.
- **Royale** • 157 Avenue C [E 10th St]
  212-254-6600 • $$
  Perfect burgers with stellar fixin's, and a deal to boot.
- **Sigiri** • 91 1st Ave [E 6th St]
  212-614-9333 • $$
  Excellent BYOB Sri Lankan above a great beer shop.
- **Supper** • 156 E 2nd St [Avenue A]
  212-477-7600 • $$$
  Spaghetti con limone is yummy. Great brunch. Otherworldly atmosphere.
- **Takahachi** • 85 Avenue A [E 6th St]
  212-505-6524 • $$$
  Super-good Japanese and sushi. A mainstay.

We can't decide if we like **Abraço** or **Ninth Street Espresso** better—we'll take both! Browse vintage oddities at **Obscura Antiques**, used tomes at **Mast Books,** and jewelry at **The Shape of Lies**. Cute boutiques? 9th Street between First and Second. Late-night bodega taco fix? **Zaragoza**.

Coffee

- **Abraco** • 86 E 7th St [1st Ave]
  212-388-9731
  Sip an amazing espresso by the window.
- **Cafe Pick Me Up** • 145 Ave A [E 9th St]
  212-673-7231
  Late-night caffeine hang out. Open 'til 12:30 a.m.
- **Ciao for Now** • 523 E 12th St [Ave A]
  212-677-2616
  Neighborhood fave for coffee and pastries.
- **Ninth Street Espresso** • 700 E 9th St [Ave C]
  212-358-9225
  Absolutely fantastic coffee drinks. Cool Portland vibe.
- **Ost Cafe** • 441 E 12th St [Ave A]
  212-477-5600
  Great space to hang out for a few hours.

Shopping

- **11th Street Flea Market** • 1st Ave & E 11th St
  Stuff you didn't even know you needed!
- **Alphabets** • 115 Avenue A [E 7th St]
  212-475-7250
  Fun miscellany store.
- **Big Gay Ice Cream Shop** •
  125 E 7th St [Avenue A]
  212-533-9333
  Imaginative swirled soft serve treats. Try a salty pimp.
- **Butter Lane** • 123 E 7th St [Avenue A]
  212-677-2880
  Riding the cupcake trend...
- **East Village Books** • 99 St Marks Pl [1st Ave]
  212-477-8647
  Messy pile of used stuff.
- **East Village Wines** • 138 1st Ave [St Marks Pl]
  212-677-7070
  Classic EV liquor store. With booze!
- **Exit 9** • 51 Avenue A [E 3rd St]
  212-228-0145
  Always fun and changeable hipster gifts. First place to sell NFT!
- **First Flight Music** • 174 1st Ave [E 11th St]
  212-539-1383
  Good guitars and amps, spotty service.
- **Gringer & Sons** • 29 1st Ave [E 2nd St]
  212-475-0600
  Kitchen appliances for every price range
- **Lancelotti Housewares** •
  66 Avenue A [E 5th St]
  212-475-6851
  Fun designer housewares, not too expensive.
- **Mast Books** • 66 Avenue A [E 4th St]
  646-370-1114
  Small but excellent selection.
- **No Relation Vintage** • 204 1st Ave [E 13th St]
  212-228-5201
  Cheap vintage basics for patient sifters.
- **Obscura Antiques & Oddities** •
  207 Avenue A [E 13th St]
  212-505-9251
  Kitschy & Arbitrary Americana. Pricey, but sociologically fascinating.
- **Ray's Candy Store** • 113 Avenue A [E 7th St]
  212-505-7609
  Avenue A's Belgian fries-and-ice cream Institution.
- **Russ & Daughters** •
  179 E Houston St [Orchard St]
  212-475-4880
  Fab Jewish soul food—lox, herring, sable, etc.
- **Saifee Hardware & Garden** •
  114 1st Ave [E 7th St]
  212-979-6396
  Classic East Village hardware store. It has everything.
- **The Shape of Lies** • 127 E 7th St [Avenue A]
  212-533-5920
  Vintage and locally-made jewelry.
- **Tinto Fino** • 85 1st Ave [E 5th St]
  212-254-0850
  Great selection of Spanish wines.
- **Zaragoza Mexican Deli and Grocery** •
  215 Avenue A [E 13th St]
  212-780-9204
  Bodega with burritos.

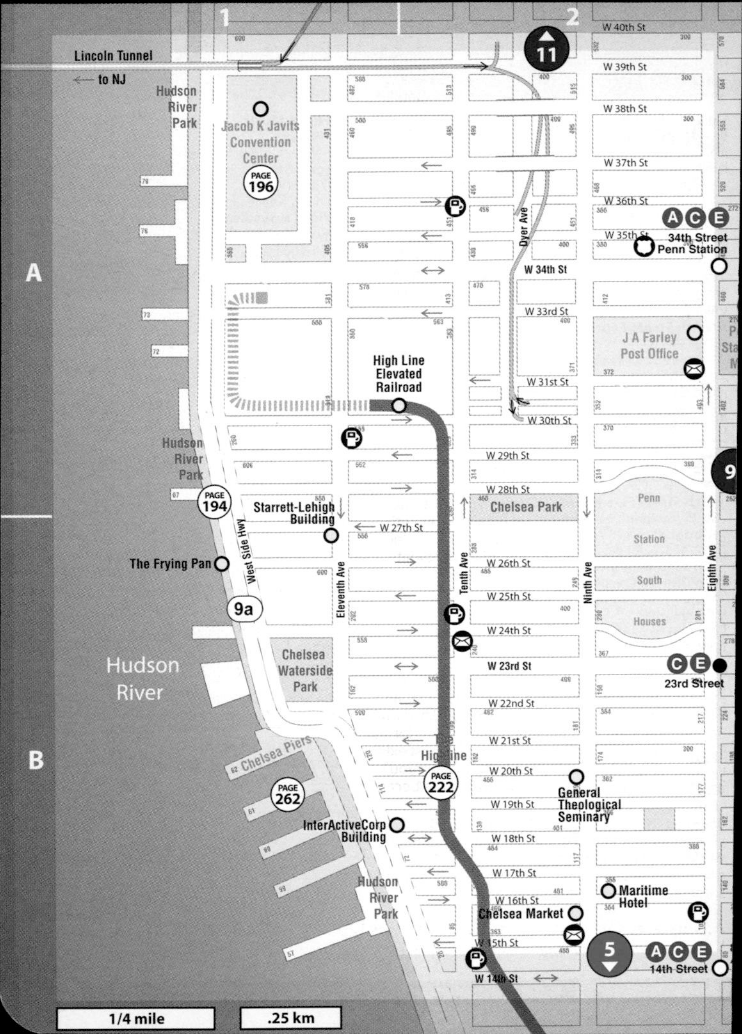

Map 8 • Chelsea

Neighborhood Overview

Located due south of Midtown's gazillion office buildings and due north of the West Village and the Financial District, Chelsea is a magnet for the young, the beautiful, and the wealthy. A polished mix of quaint, restored townhouses and sparkling new condos in the sky combine to create a unique and appealing neighborhood that deftly bridges the transition from downtown to Midtown. With the opening of the long-awaited **High Line Park** in 2009, luxury marched west towards the river, with multiple shiny new buildings clustered around the new ribbon of green that cuts through the heart of the neighborhood.

While the neighborhood is diverse and welcoming to all, it would be dishonest to pretend that it isn't best known as the epicenter of all things gay. A substantial, muscle bound gay population spawned the term "Chelsea boy," used either derisively or admiringly depending on one's taste. Several of the city's best gay bars, book stores, and social service organizations are located within the borders of this neighborhood. And while the gyms aren't exclusively gay, they know who their best and most loyal customers are.

But even if you're not a gay male, the charms of Chelsea are many and unmistakable: a thriving, inclusive nightlife with something for everyone, great dining for almost any budget, and great shopping for middle budgets and upwards (though the odd deal can certainly be found tucked into a side street or a more modest storefront on one of the avenues). On top of that, there are ample opportunities for recreation here—aside from the aforementioned High Line, there's the Hudson River Park (which, unsurprisingly, is alongside the body of water bearing the same name), massive sports complex Chelsea Piers, brilliant **Chelsea Market**, with its wonderfully diverse food vendors, and the safety-first, divided bike lanes on 8th and 9th Avenues.

The architecture of the neighborhood is some of New York's most noteworthy. Frank Gehry's translucent, iceberg/schooner hybrid **InterActiveCorp Building** is regrettably too short to be seen from vantage points that aren't near its location at the intersection of 18th Street and the West Side Highway. But it's a leading candidate for coolest building in Chelsea and one of the loveliest, most unique buildings erected in Manhattan in recent years. A few blocks away lies the gorgeous, Neo-Gothic campus of The General Theological Seminary, the oldest Episcopal theological school. Just north of there, the historic **London Terrace** luxury apartment complex fills an entire city block. Up a few blocks more, the **Starrett-Lehigh Building** is an art deco freight warehouse and factory that now houses several high-profile media and fashion companies.

Farther uptown, on 8th Avenue between 31st and 33rd Streets, the **James A. Farley Post Office** stands in proud, marble magnificence across the street from the grotesquely ugly Madison Square Garden (the unworthy replacement for the demolished Penn Station). A couple blocks west of there is the **Javits Center**, the biggest exhibition hall in the city and another architectural lowlight. As a New Yorker, the best reason you'll ever have for going there is a jobs fair or an industry expo—the latter being preferable because there's likely to be free food or booze.

Instead of heading up into the 30s, take a walk through west Chelsea in the 20s and you'll find yourself in one of the great visual art districts of the world. Over 300 galleries show the newest work of the best artists working today. Despite the occasional dud, you have a better-than-even chance of encountering exhilarating, high-quality work. Now and then, you might even find something you can afford to buy!

Add in some of the best people watching in the city, and you'll know why so many other New Yorkers choose to pay a small fortune every month to live in a shoebox here.

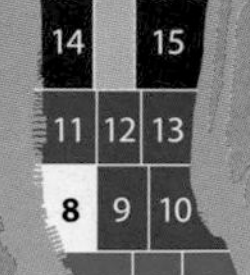

Landmarks

O Landmarks

- **Chelsea Market** • 75 9th Ave [W 16th St]
  Foodies flock here. So should you.
- **Frying Pan** • 12th Ave & W 26th St
  212-989-6363
  Old ship makes for amazing party digs.
- **General Theological Seminary** •
  440 W 21st St [9th Ave]
  212-243-5150
  Oldest seminary of the Episcopal Church; nice campus.
- **Jacob K. Javits Convention Center** •
  655 W 34th St [11th Ave]
  212-216-2000
  IM Pei's attempt to make sense out of New York. Love the location.
- **James A. Farley Post Office** •
  421 Eighth Ave [W 31st St]
  212-330-3296
  Another McKim, Mead & White masterpiece. Slated to become Moynihan Station.
- **Starrett-Lehigh Building** •
  601 W 26th St [11th Ave]
  One of the coolest factories/warehouses ever built.

The **Half King** is perfectly positioned for a drink apres-gallery. **The Kitchen's** list of performances over the years is legendary, and rock shows still happen at the **Hammerstein** and **Highline Ballrooms**. Various gay crowds have their home bars here: **Gym** (hunks!) and **The Eagle** (leather-daddies and cubs) are two of the best.

Bars

- **Billymark's West** • 332 9th Ave [W 29th St]
  212-629-0118
  Down and dirty dive.
- **Chelsea Brewing Company** • [W 18th St]
  212-336-6440
  When you're done playing basketball.
- **The Distinguished Wakamba Cocktail Lounge** •
  543 8th Ave [W 37th St]
  212-244-9045
  Plastic palm trees and provocatively-clad barmaids.
- **The Eagle** • 554 W 28th St [11th Ave]
  646-473-1866
  Get your leather on (or off).
- **Flight 151** • 151 8th Ave [W 17th St]
  212-229-1868
  Prepare for takeoff on Mondays with $4 Margaritas.
- **Gym Sports Bar** • 167 8th Ave [W 19th St]
  212-337-2439
  Where the boys go to watch the game—and each other.
- **The Half King** • 505 W 23rd St [10th Ave]
  212-462-4300
  Always the perfect drinking choice in Chelsea. Amazing brunch.
- **Hammerstein Ballroom** •
  311 W 34th St [8th Ave]
  212-279-7740
  Lofty rock venue.
- **Highline Ballroom** • 431 W 16th St [10th Ave]
  212-414-5994
  New venue for rock, folk, dance, whatever.
- **The Molly Wee Pub** • 402 8th Ave [W 30th St]
  212-967-2627
  You may just need a pint after a trip to Penn Station.
- **The Park** • 118 10th Ave [W 17th St]
  212-352-3313
  Good patio. We're split on this one.
- **Tippler** • 425 W 15th St [10th Ave]
  212-206-0000
  Perfectly mixed cocktails in a dark room under Chelsea Market.
- **Westside Tavern** • 360 W 23rd St [9th Ave]
  212-366-3738
  Local mixture.

Bowling

- **300** • [12th Ave]
  212-835-2695
  VIP bowling on Chelsea Piers.

Movie Theaters

- **AMC Loews 34th Street 14** •
  312 W 34th St [Eighth Ave]
  212-244-4556
  The biggest and most comfortable of the midtown multiplexes.

Theaters/Performing Arts

- **American Place Theatre** •
  266 W 37th St [Eighth Ave]
  212-594-4482
  Theatre for the literary-minded.
- **Atlantic Theater Company** •
  336 W 20th St [Eighth Ave]
  212-691-5919
  David Mamet's theatre company. F*** you!
- **Hudson Guild** • 441 W 26th St [W 27th St]
  212-760-9800
  Nice, intimate space.
- **Joyce Theater** • 175 8th Ave [W 19th St]
  212-691-9740
  Built for dance, with excellent sightlines.
- **The Kitchen** • 512 W 19th St [10th Ave]
  212-255-5793
  The kind of place Jesse Helms would have hated.
- **Sanford Meisner Theatre** •
  164 11th Ave [W 22nd St]
  212-206-1764
  If you're swimming in the Hudson you've gone too far.
- **Upright Citizen's Brigade Theatre** •
  307 W 26th St [8th Ave]
  212-366-9176
  See hilarious improv comics before SNL makes them suck.

14 15
11 12 13
8 9 10
5 6 7

Restaurants

For some tasty Thai, try **Spice** or **Room Service**. For diner food, try **The Highliner** (fancy) or the **Skylight** (cheap). **Grand Sichuan Int'l** is one of our favorite spots for Chinese in all of New York. Across the street, check out **Co.'s** stellar pizzas. Got a bailout bonus? Indulge at **Buddakan**, **Del Posto** or **Morimoto**.

Restaurants

- **Better Burger** • 178 8th Ave [W 19th St] 212-989-6688 • $ Ostrich burger? Check. Soy burger? Check. Antibiotic-free meat? Check.
- **Bottino** • 246 10th Ave [W 24th St] 212-206-6766 • $$$ Good, clean Italian. A good post-gallery spot.
- **Buddakan** • 75 9th Ave [W 16th St] 212-989-6699 • $$$$$ NYC branch of Stephen Starr's insanely popular Philadelphia behemoth.
- **Clyde Frazier's Wine & Dine** • 485 10th Ave [37th St] 212-842-1110 • $$$ Sleek and over the top food and design, just like Clyde.
- **Co.** • 230 9th Ave [W 24th St] 212-243-1105 • $$ Pizza of the gods.
- **Cola's** • 148 8th Ave [W 17th St] 212-633-8020 • $ Intimate and inexpensive.
- **Colicchio & Sons** • 85 Tenth Ave [15th St] 212-400-6699 • $$$$$ Colicchio's latest piece on loan to Manhattan's High Line annex.
- **Cookshop** • 156 10th Ave [W 20th St] 212-924-4440 • $ New, loft-like, local ingredient-focused eatery.
- **Del Posto** • 85 Tenth Ave [15th St] 212-497-8090 • $$$$$ Marble-lined, multi-level temple to the Italian food gods.
- **El Quinto Pino** • 401 W 24th St [9th Ave] 212-206-6900 • $$ Tiny, table-free tapas joint from owners of Tia Pol.
- **Flor de Sol** • 100 Tenth Avenue [W 16th St] 212-366-1640 • $$$$ Tapas with—of course—a scene.
- **Grand Sichuan** • 229 9th Ave [W 24th St] 212-620-5200 • $$ Some of the best Chinese in NYC. Recommended.
- **The Highliner** • 210 Tenth Ave [22nd St] 212-206-6206 • $$$ The classic Empire goes upscale. Open until 5 a.m.
- **La Luncheonette** • 130 10th Ave [W 18th St] 212-675-0342 • $$$$ A truly great French restaurant. Recommended.
- **La Taza de Oro** • 96 8th Ave [W 15th St] 212-243-9946 • $$ Sit at the counter with the locals for great Puerto Rican.
- **Meatball Shop** • 200 9th Ave [22nd St] 212-257-4363 • $ Fancy Italian balls in pork, chicken and beef form.
- **Morimoto** • 88 10th Ave [W 16th St] 212-989-8883 • $$$$$ Stephen Starr's couture Japanese temple. Iron Chef-prepared cuisine.
- **Pepe Giallo** • 253 10th Ave [W 25th St] 212-242-6055 • $$ Takeout Italian.
- **Pomodoro** • 518 Ninth Ave [W 39th St] 212-239-7019 • $$ Takes "fast food" Italian to the next level; superb foccacia.
- **The Red Cat** • 227 10th Ave [W 23rd St] 212-242-0199 • $$$$ Hip and expensive.
- **Room Service** • 166 8th Ave [W 18th St] 212-691-0299 • $$$ This place is truly "Thai"rific—try the iced coffee.
- **Sandwich Planet** • 522 Ninth Ave [W 39th St] 212-273-9768 • $ Unlimited sandwich selection.
- **Sergimmo Salumeria** • 456 9th Ave [W 35th St] 212-967-4212 • $ Serious sandwiches stuffed with mouthwatering Italian meats.
- **Skylight Diner** • 402 W 34th St [9th Ave] 212-244-0395 • $ 24-hour diner. If you must.
- **Spice** • 199 8th Ave [W 20th St] 212-989-1116 • $$ Good, straightforward Thai.
- **Tia Pol** • 205 10th Ave [W 22nd St] 212-675-8805 • $$ Very good, very popular (crowded) tapas joint.
- **Tick Tock Diner** • 481 Eighth Ave [W 34th St] 212-268-8444 • $ 24-hour diner. Time's awastin'.
- **Tipsy Parson** • 156 9th Ave [W 19th St] 212-620-4545 • $$$ Scrumptious Southern and comfy brunch spot.
- **Trestle on Tenth** • 242 10th Ave [W 24th St] 212-645-5659 • $$$ Hip, local, small menu, recommended.
- **Txikito** • 240 9th Ave [W 24th St] 212-242-4730 • $$$ Unique gourmet Basque cooking.

Bagels, Coffee, & Shopping

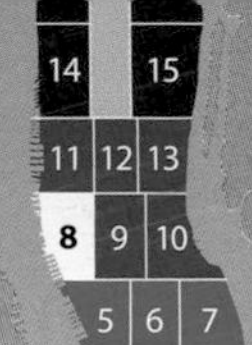

B&H Photo Video remains a go-to electronics store (closed Saturdays) and **Printed Matter's** selection of artists' books is probably the best in the world. For food, simply hit brilliant Chelsea Market to get Italian imports (**Buon Italia**), wine (**Chelsea Wine Vault**), dairy (**Ronnybrook Farm**), fish (**The Lobster Place**), cheese (**Lucy's Whey**) and bread (**Amy's Bread**).

Bagels

- **Murray's Bagels** • 242 8th Ave [W 22nd St]
  646-638-1335
  Classic. But they don't toast, so don't ask.

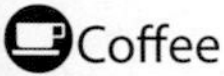

Coffee

- **Billy's Bakery** • 184 9th Ave [W 21st St]
  212-647-9956
  Mindblowingly good cakes to go with your coffee.
- **Blue Bottle Coffee** • 450 W 15th St [10th Ave]
  Cult coffee that's more lab than shop.
- **Joe The Art of Coffee** •
  405 W 23rd St [9th Ave]
  212-206-0669
  Joe really knows his joe.
- **Ninth Street Espresso** •
  75 9th Ave [W 15th St]
  212-228-2930
  Gourmet coffee counter inside Chelsea Market.
- **Paradise Café & Muffins** •
  139 8th Ave [W 17th St]
  212-647-0066
  Friendly spot. We'll let you decide if it's actually paradise.

Shopping

- **192 Books** • 192 10th Ave [W 21st St]
  212-255-4022
  Reads like a library—with a premium on art books and literature.
- **Amy's Bread** • 75 9th Ave [W 15th St]
  212-462-4338
  Perfect breads.
- **Aperture Bookstore** • 547 W 27th St [10th Ave]
  212-505-5555
  We love Aperture. Say hi for us.
- **Apple Store (Chelsea)** • 401 W 14th St [9th Ave]
  212-444-3400
  Less crowded than the other locations.
- **B&H Photo** • 420 9th Ave [W 33rd St]
  212-444-6615
  Where everyone in North America buys their cameras and film. Closed Saturdays.
- **The Blue Store** • 206 8th Ave [W 21st St]
  212-924-8315
  Tobias Funke's dream store. Not kid-friendly.
- **Brooklyn Industries** • 161 8th Ave [W 19th St]
  212-206-0477
  A little bit of Brooklyn in the heart of Chelsea.
- **Buon Italia** • 75 9th Ave [W 16th St]
  212-633-9090
  Italian import mecca—get the 24-month prosciutto.
- **Chelsea Market Baskets** •
  75 9th Ave [W 16th St]
  212-727-1111
  Gift baskets for all occasions.
- **Chelsea Wine Vault** • 75 9th Ave [W 16th St]
  212-462-4244
  Excellent shop inside the Chelsae Market.
- **Eleni's** • 75 9th Ave [W 16th St]
  888-435-3647
  When a card won't do, iced cookies in every shape will.
- **Esposito's Pork Store** •
  354 W 38th St [9th Ave]
  212-868-4142
  Authentic 1890 butcher shop.
- **Fat Witch Bakery** • 75 9th Ave [W 16th St]
  888-419-4824
  Excellent chocolate brownies.
- **Knickerbocker Meat Market** •
  166 9th Ave [W 20th St]
  212-243-3151
  Fantastic butchers that serve only top-notch meat.
- **L'Arte del Gelato** • 75 9th Ave [W 16th St]
  212-366-0570
  Gelato to make you sing an aria. Or just pig out.
- **The Lobster Place** • 75 9th Ave [W 16th St]
  212-255-5672
  Fresh fish and Maine lobster, if you can afford it.
- **Lucy's Whey** • 75 9th Ave [W 16th St]
  212-463-9500
  American artisinal cheeses in Chelsea Market.
- **Printed Matter** • 195 10th Ave [W 22nd St]
  212-925-0325
  Astounding selection of artist's books; highly recommended.
- **Ronnybrook Farm Dairy** •
  75 9th Ave [W 16th St]
  212-741-6455
  All things dairy, fresh from the Hudson Valley. Great shakes.

Map 9 • Flatiron / Lower Midtown

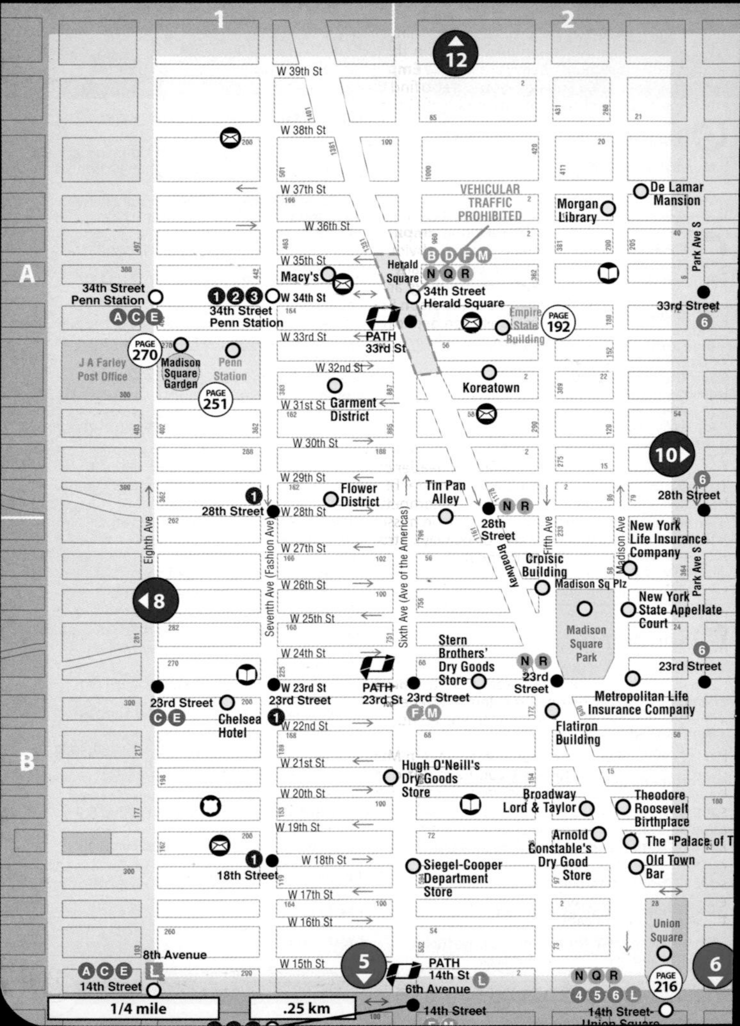

eighborhood Overview

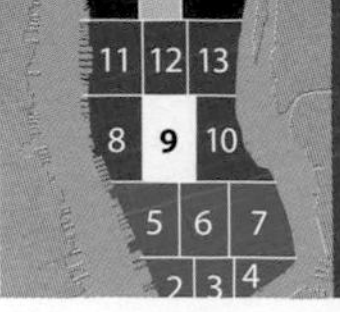

The amazing variety of people, places and things that typifies New York cannot be better experienced than in this area. Containing some of the most tourist-heavy areas—the **Empire State Building** and **Macy's** at Herald Square—you will also find the hip, expensive, and fabulously exclusive communities of Gramercy (to the east) and Chelsea (to the west). Flatiron is also the home to the lesser-known "Silicon Alley," coined as a reflection of the recent influx of start-up Internet companies in the area. In this incredibly diverse and unassuming neighborhood you will see moms pushing strollers, hipsters in low-slung pants, and wealthy elderly women walking their perfectly groomed poodles.

One of the most obvious draws of the area is the impressive architecture. You certainly can't miss the amazing sight of the towering **Empire State Building** or the aptly-named **Flatiron Building**. But also not to miss is the less-obvious **Chelsea Hotel**, a favorite of many musicians and artists from Bob Dylan to Sid Vicious. Early 20th century additions to the area include the **MetLife Tower**, the **New York Life Building**, and the **New York State Appellate Court**, all of which are ranged on the east side of **Madison Square Park**. Equally impressive are the myriad number of current and former cast-iron department store buildings that make up the historic "Ladies' Mile" area, including the **Arnold Constable Dry Goods Store**, the **Broadway Lord & Taylor**, the **Croisic Building**, the **Hugh O'Neill Dry Goods Store**, the **Stern Brothers' Dry Goods Store**, and, our all-time favorite, the **Siegel-Cooper Department Store**. We can't help but mention that this area was also the scene of one of the greatest crimes against architecture—namely, the destruction of McKim, Mead & White's original Penn Station in 1963.

Venture to the **Garment District** and you will be surrounded by the shops and people that helped make New York City the fashion leader of the world in the late 1800's and early 1900's. The nearby **Flower District** was once several blocks filled with lush greenery of every variety. In 2010 however, high rent and massive competition have squeezed most retailers out, it's less than a block in size now and can easily be missed. Luckily **Koreatown** is still going strong on 32nd Street (between Fifth and Broadway). Stroll through here on a Friday night to find the restaurants and bars packed to the brim.

Look down as you walk on 28th Street between Fifth Avenue and Broadway and you will see a plaque in the sidewalk dedicated to **Tin Pan Alley**. If you're a music buff you'll want to take in the historical significance of this area, dated back to 1885 when a group of songwriters and music publishers got together to lobby for copyright laws.

For a piece of Presidential history, visit the **Birthplace of Theodore Roosevelt**. A recreated version of the brownstone President Roosevelt was born in on October 27th 1858 now serves as a museum dedicated to the 26th President.

Finding a small patch of fresh green grass in Manhattan is almost as challenging as finding a parking spot, but in this area you have not one, but two parks. **Madison Square Park** is a beautifully manicured park where you can be sure to catch hundreds of sunbathers on any summer Saturday. It is also home to the long lines of the **Shake Shack**. If you can afford to wait an hour or two, you will be treated to one of the best hamburgers of all-time. Farther south, **Union Square** is one of the more famous parks in Manhattan, having had several historic rallies and riots as well as being a main subway hub; it is busier than most parks. If you can squeeze yourself into a spot on one of the overflowing park benches, you'll be treated to some entertaining people watching. It's also worth noting for the dog lovers out there, that both of these parks have sizable dog parks.

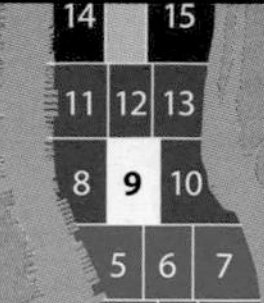

Landmarks

- **The "Palace of Trade" •**
  885 Broadway [E 19th St]
  The mansard roof to end all mansard roofs.
- **Croisic Building •** 220 5th Ave [E 26th St]
  Just another outstanding NYC building. Circa 1912.
- **De Lamar Mansion •**
  233 Madison Ave [E 37th St]
  Dutch sea captain's mansion now inhabited by Polish diplomats.
- **Empire State Building •**
  350 5th Ave [W 33rd St]
  212-736-3100
  The roof deck at night is unmatched by any other view of New York.
- **Flatiron Building •** 175 5th Ave [W 22nd St]
  A lesson for all architects: design for the actual space.
- **Flower District •** W 28th St b/n 6th & 7th Aves
  Lots of flowers by day, lots of nothing by night.
- **Garment District •**
  34th to 40th St b/n 6th to 9th Ave
  Clothing racks by day, nothing by night. Gritty, grimy.
- **Hotel Chelsea •** 222 W 23rd St [7th Ave]
  The scene of many, many crimes.
- **Hugh O'Neill's Dry Goods Store •**
  655 6th Ave [W 20th St]
  Brilliant cast-iron from Mortimer Merritt.
- **Koreatown •**
  W 32nd St b/n Broadway & 5th Ave
  Korean restaurants, bars, and shops. Bustling on the weekends.
- **Lord & Taylor Building •**
  901 Broadway [E 20th St]
  Incredible detail on former Lord & Taylor outlet.
- **Macy's •** 151 W 34th St [7th Ave]
  212-695-4400
  13 floors of wall-to-wall tourists! Sound like fun?
- **Madison Square Garden •**
  4 Penn Plaza [W 31st St]
  212-465-6741
  Crappy, uninspired venue for Knicks, Rangers, Liberty, and over-the-hill rock bands.
- **Madison Square Park •** E 23rd St & Broadway
  212-538-1884
  One of the most underrated parks in the city. Lots of great weird sculpture.
- **Metropolitan Life Insurance Co •**
  1 Madison Ave [E 23rd St]
  Cool top, recently refurbished.
- **The Morgan Library & Museum •**
  225 Madison Ave [E 37th St]
  212-685-0008
  See cool stuff the dead rich dude collected.
- **New York Life Insurance Company •**
  51 Madison Ave [E 26th St]
  The gold roof? Your insurance premiums at work.
- **New York State Appellate Court •**
  Madison Ave & E 25th St
  Insanely ornate 1899 courthouse; where new lawyers get sworn in.
- **Old Town Bar •** 45 E 18th St [Broadway]
  212-529-6713
  Classic NY pub housed in former speak-easy.
- **Penn Station •** 8th Ave & W 32nd St
  Well, the old one was a landmark, anyway.
- **Siegel-Cooper Co. Department Store •**
  616 6th Ave [W 18th St]
  Beaux-Arts retail madness. Now a f***in' Bed, Bath & Beyond.
- **Stern Brothers' Dry Goods Store •**
  32 W 23rd St [6th Ave]
  Awesome ornate cast-iron; now houses Home Depot. Whatever.
- **Theodore Roosevelt Birthplace •**
  28 E 20th St [Broadway]
  212-260-1616
  Teddy was born here, apparently.
- **Tin Pan Alley •**
  W 28th St b/n 6th Ave & Broadway
  Where American popular music climbed out of the crib.
- **Union Square •** E 14th St & University Pl
  Famous park for protests and rallys. Now bordered by chain stores.

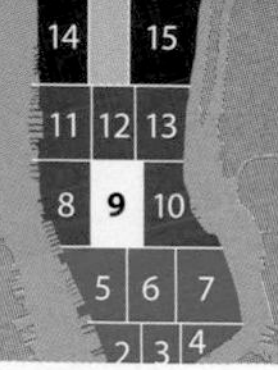

Whether you prefer celebrity sighting at **Raines Law Room**, dress-code mandatory joints like **230 5th**, classic NYC watering holes like **Old Town Bar** and **Peter McManus**, or gulping Guinness at low key Irish pubs like **Dewey's**; you have options. NFT cabaret experts state unequivocally that the **Metropolitan Room** is the best cabaret club in the city.

Bars

- **230 Fifth** • 230 5th Ave [E 26th St] 212-725-4300 Dress code and overpriced drinks. Best view of NYC makes it worthwhile.
- **Ace Hotel Lobby Bar** • 20 W 29th St [Broadway] 212-679-2222 Amazing cocktails in an amazing space.
- **The Archive** • 12 E 36th St [Madison Ave] 212-213-0093 Relaxed, subdued; solid cocktails.
- **Belgian Beer Cafe** • 220 5th Ave [26th St] Belgian fare and brews, plus growlers to go.
- **Birreria** • 200 5th Ave [W 23rd St] 212-937-8910 Retractable-roof beer garden atop Eataly.
- **Dewey's** • 210 5th Ave [W 25th St] 212-696-2337 Generic, inexpensive and comfortable.
- **The Ginger Man** • 11 E 36th St [Madison Ave] 212-532-3740 Where button-down midtown types loosen up over bitter beers.
- **Hotel Metro Rooftop Bar** • 45 W 35th St [6th Ave] 212-279-3535 Fresh air + beer 14 floors above Manhattan.
- **Jazz Gallery** • 1160 Broadway [W 27th St] 212-242-1063 Not-for-profit jazz venue.
- **Lillie's** • 13 E 17th St [5th Ave] 212-337-1970 Perfect for anyone with an Irish-Victorian fetish.
- **Limerick House** • 69 W 23rd St [6th Ave] 212-243-8898 Friendly bar. Plain and simple.
- **Live Bait** • 14 E 23rd St [Madison Ave] 212-353-2400 Still a great feel. A mainstay.
- **Merchants** • 112 7th Ave [W 17th St] 212-366-7267 Good mixed space.
- **Metropolitan Room** • 34 W 22nd St [6th Ave] 212-206-0440 Best cabaret club in the city.
- **No Idea Bar** • 30 E 20th St [Broadway] 212-777-0100 Very laid back for this part of town. Nice happy hour.
- **Old Town Bar** • 45 E 18th St [Broadway] 212-529-6713 Excellent old-NY pub.
- **Peter McManus** • 152 7th Ave [W 19th St] 212-929-9691 Refreshingly basic. Gorgeous old phone booths.
- **The Raines Law Room** • 48 W 17th St [6th Ave] Cocktails worth your time. And money.
- **Rattle N Hum** • 14 E 33rd St [Madison Ave] 212-481-1586 40 beers on tap!
- **Splash** • 50 W 17th St [6th Ave] 212-691-0073 Men dancing in waterfalls.
- **VU Rooftop Bar** • 17 W 32nd St [5th Ave] 212-991-8842 Reliably chill K-town rooftop bar.

Movie Theaters

- **AMC Loews 19th St East 6** • 890 Broadway [E 19th St] 212-260-8173 Standard multiplex.
- **Clearview Cinemas Chelsea** • 260 W 23rd St [Eighth Ave] 212-691-5519 Manhattan's big, comfy, and gay multiplex.

Theaters/Performing Arts

- **29th Street Repertory Theatre** • 212 W 29th St [Seventh Ave] 212-465-0575 "Where Brutal Theater Lives!"
- **Dance Theatre Workshop** • 219 W 19th St [Seventh Ave] 212-691-6500 Great contemporary dance since 1965.
- **People's Improv Theater** • 154 W 29th St [Seventh Ave] 212-563-7488 "The Pit" to all us insiders.
- **TADA! Theater** • 15 W 28th St [Broadway] 212-252-1619 Screw Disney; this is where you go for great affordable theatre for kids.

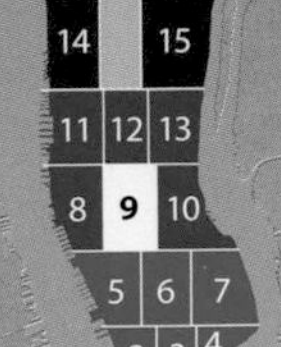

Restaurants

Impress a date with the size of your wallet at **Gramercy Tavern**, **Eleven Madison Park** and NFT-fave **Craft**, or impress them with your wit and conversation over tapas at **Boqueria**. Otherwise, hit **City Bakery** for their pretzel croissants, **Eisenberg's** for egg creams, **Dogmatic** for sausages, or **Kang Suh** for all-night Korean BBQ.

Restaurants

- **ABC Kitchen** • 35 E 18th St [Broadway]
  212-475-5829 • $$$$
  Fancy farm-to-table. In a carpet store.
- **BLT Fish** • 21 W 17th St [5th Ave]
  212-691-8888 • $$$$$
  Downstairs: New England clam shack fare. Upstairs: High-brow seafood.
- **Boqueria** • 53 W 19th St [6th Ave]
  212-255-4160 • $$$
  Cheese stuffed dates wrapped in bacon? We're there.
- **The Breslin** • 16 W 29th St [Broadway]
  212-679-1939 • $$$
  Meet. Wait. Meat. Lamb burgers is a culinary gem.
- **Butterfield 8** • 5 E 38th St [5th Ave]
  212-679-0646 • $$$
  Walnut-paneled Murray Hill American with cool, Hitchcockian cityscape mural.
- **Chat 'n Chew** • 10 E 16th St [5th Ave]
  212-243-1616 • $$
  Home cookin'.
- **City Bakery** • 3 W 18th St [5th Ave]
  212-366-1414 • $$
  Stellar baked goods.
- **Craft** • 43 E 19th St [Broadway]
  212-780-0880 • $$$$$
  Outstanding. A top-end place worth the $$$$$$$$$$$.
- **Dogmatic** • 26 E 17th St [Broadway]
  212-414-0600 • $$
  Sausages magically stuffed into a fresh baked baguette.
- **Eisenberg's Sandwich Shop** •
  174 5th Ave [W 22nd St]
  212-675-5096 • $$
  Old-school corned beef and pastrami.
- **Eleven Madison Park** •
  11 Madison Ave [E 24th St]
  212-889-0905 • $$$$$
  Where the elite meet to greet.
- **Evergreen Shanghai Restaurant** •
  10 E 38th St [5th Ave]
  212-448-1199 • $
  Their scallion pancakes are worth the wait, and they know it.
- **Gramercy Tavern** • 42 E 20th St [Broadway]
  212-477-0777 • $$$$$
  Expensive, but good, New American.
- **Hangawi** • 12 E 32nd St [5th Ave]
  212-213-0077 • $$$$
  Serene, top-end vegetarian Korean.
- **Hill Country** • 30 W 26th St [Broadway]
  212-255-4544 • $$$
  Good ol' Texas 'cue; go for the wet brisket.
- **Kang Suh** • 1250 Broadway [W 32nd St]
  212-564-6845 • $$$
  Late-night Korean. Go for the private rooms.
- **Kunjip** • 9 W 32nd St [Broadway]
  212-216-9487 • $$
  The best Korean food in Manhattan; try the Bo Saam!
- **La Vie en Szechuan** •
  14 E 33rd St [Madison Ave]
  212-683-2779 • $$
  Spiced up Chinese in an unlikely neighborhood.
- **Mesa Grill** • 102 Fifth Ave [E 15th St]
  212-807-7400 • $$$$$
  Southwest heaven.
- **Olympic Pita** • 58 W 38th St [6th Ave]
  212-869-7482 • $
  Scrumptious shawarma.
- **Periyali** • 35 W 20th St [5th Ave]
  212-463-7890 • $$$$
  Upscale Greek. Pretty damned great.
- **Rye House** • 11 W 17th St [5th Ave]
  212-255-7260 • $$$
  Small plates and agreat selection of spirits.
- **Sala One Nine** • 35 W 19th St [6th Ave]
  212-229-2300 • $$
  Garlic on everything, bring breathmints. Must try: Filet Mignon sandwich.
- **Seoul Garden** • 34 W 32nd St [Broadway]
  212-736-9002 • $$
  The soon tofu soup hits the spot.
- **Shake Shack** • 11 Madison Ave [E 23rd St]
  212-889-6600 • $
  Enjoy homemade shakes 'n burgers in the park. On a 2-hour line.
- **Socarrat** • 259 W 19th St [8th Ave]
  212-462-1000 • $$$
  Authentic Paella feast, sit next to the Spaniards at the communal table.
- **Szechuan Gourmet** • 21 W 39th St [6th Ave]
  212-921-0233 • $$$
  Amazing Chinese in this part of the city? Believe it.
- **Tarallucci E Vino** • 15 E 18th St [5th Ave]
  212-228-5400 • $$
  Espresso in the morning, wine after work. Delicious and versatile.
- **Tocqueville** • 1 E 15th St [5th Ave]
  212-647-1515 • $$$$$
  Lovely everything—and you can actually hear each other speak!

Bagels, Coffee, & Shopping

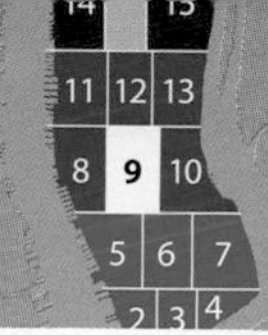

Need sporting goods? **Paragon** is the paragon of sporting goods stores. Food heaven is found at **Eataly**—just bring your credit card. **30th Street Guitars** and **Rogue Music** will rock your world. **Yamak** is a boutique alternative to the the complete mess of humanity that is **Macy's**. **Idlewild** is one of New York's finest bookshops, specializing in travel and literature.

Coffee

- **Café Grumpy** • 224 W 20th St [7th Ave]
  212-255-5511
  Best coffee on the island.
- **Culture Espresso** • 72 W 38th St [6th Ave]
  212-302-0200
  Amazing coffee right near Bryant Park.
- **Stumptown Coffee** • 18 W 29th St [Broadway]
  The real deal straight outta Portland.

Shopping

- **30th Street Guitars** • 236 W 30th St [7th Ave]
  212-868-2660
  Ax heaven. Seriously.
- **A.I. Friedman** • 44 W 18th St [5th Ave]
  212-243-9000
  Art supplies, frames, office furniture, and more.
- **ABC Carpet & Home** •
  888 Broadway [E 19th St]
  212-473-3000
  A NYC institution for chic, even exotic, home décor and design.
- **Abracadabra** • 19 W 21st St [5th Ave]
  212-627-5194
  Magic, masks, costumes—presto!
- **Academy Records** • 12 W 18th St [5th Ave]
  212-242-3000
  Top Jazz/Classical mecca.
- **Adorama** • 42 W 18th St [5th Ave]
  212-741-0052
  Good camera alternative to B&H. Still closed Saturdays, though.
- **Ariston Flowers** • 110 W 17th St [6th Ave]
  212-929-4226
  Excellent florist with orchids as well.
- **Beecher's Cheese** • 900 Broadway [20th St]
  212-466-3340
  Handmade cheese by the block or in gourmet grilled sandwiches.
- **Books of Wonder** • 18 W 18th St [5th Ave]
  212-989-3270
  Top NYC children's bookstore, always has signed copies around too.
- **Bottlerocket Wine & Spirit** •
  5 W 19th St [5th Ave]
  212-929-2323
  Free tastings every Thursday, Friday, and Saturday!
- **Eataly** • 200 5th Ave [23rd St]
  646-398-5100
  Over the top (in a good way) Italian culinary superstore.
- **Fishs Eddy** • 889 Broadway [E 19th St]
  212-420-9020
  Bizarre dishes to complete your cool abode.
- **Idlewild Books** • 12 W 19th St [5th Ave]
  212-414-8888
  One of the best travel + literature bookstores on the planet.
- **Jazz Record Center** • 236 W 26th St [7th Ave]
  212-675-4480
  All that jazz!
- **LA Burdick** • 5 E 20th St [5th Ave]
  212-796-0143
  Mood-altering hot chocolate & astounding pastries.
- **M&J Trimmings** • 1008 6th Ave [W 38th St]
  212-391-6200
  For your DIY sewing projects.
- **Macy's** • 151 W 34th St [7th Ave]
  212-695-4400
  Love the wooden escalators.
- **Muji Chelsea** • 16 W 19th St [5th Ave]
  212-414-9024
  Beautiful Japanese aesthetic applied to daily living.
- **NYC Racquet Sports** • 157 W 35th St [7th Ave]
  212-695-5353
  Serious tennis supplies.
- **Paragon Sporting Goods** •
  867 Broadway [E 18th St]
  212-255-8889
  Top NYC sporting goods store, plus tennis permits!
- **Rogue Music** • 220 W 30th St [7th Ave]
  212-629-5073
  Used equipment you probably still can't afford.
- **Samuel's Hats** • 255 W 36th St [8th Ave]
  212-513-7322
  Decorate your head at this old-school hat shop.
- **Sound by Singer** • 242 W 27th St [8th Ave]
  212-924-8600
  High end audio and video. And we mean "high-end."
- **Tekserve** • 119 W 23rd St [6th Ave]
  212-929-3645
  Apple computer sales and repairs.
- **Yamak** • 6 W 23rd St [5th Ave]
  212-255-7771
  Unique clothing/jewelry from Japan/Europe.

Map 10 • Murray Hill / Gramercy

E 39th St
E 38th St
E 37th St
E 36th St
E 35th St
E 34th St
E 33rd St
E 32nd St
E 31st St
E 30th St
E 29th St
E 28th St
E 27th St
E 26th St
E 25th St
E 24th St
E 23rd St
E 22nd St
E 21st St
E 20th St
E 19th St
E 18th St
E 17th St
E 16th St
E 15th St
E 14th St
Park Ave S
Lexington Ave
Third Ave
Second Ave
First Ave
Tunnel Approach St
Tunnel Exit St
Queens Midtown Tunnel
Sniffen Ct
Broadway Aly
Irving Pl
Union Sq E
Rutherford Pl
Nathan D Perlman Pl
Asser Levy Pl
Avenue C
FDR Dr
Marginal St
The Corinthian
Sniffen Court
St. Vartan Park
33rd Street
Kips Bay Plaza
NYU Medical Center
East River
Curry Hill
28th Street
Bellevue Hospital Center
69th Armory
Baruch College
Waterside Plaza
Vet Adm Medical Center
Marina & Skyport
23rd Street
Protestant Welfare Agencies Building
Mayor James Harper Residence
Baruch Field
Peter Cooper Village
Gramercy Park
National Arts Club
The Players
Augustus St. Gaudens Playground
Pete's Tavern
Tammany Hall/ Union Sq Theater
Stuyvesant Town
Union Square
Friends Meeting House
Stuyvesant Square
PAGE 216
14th Street-Union Square
3rd Avenue
1st Avenue
1/4 mile
.25 km

Neighborhood Overview

The Murray Hill/Gramercy area of New York is one of New York's largest studies in contrast. On one hand, there are massive housing and hospital complexes that take up several city blocks; on the other hand, there are narrow alleys and small, gated parks of unparalleled beauty. Add it all together and we get (ho-hum) just another brilliant slice of New York.

Murray Hill's contrast, for instance, can be found by checking out lovely little **Sniffen Court**, one's of Manhattan's finest residential alleys, and then walking south to teeming **Kips Bay Plaza**, a set of two parallel housing towers designed by I.M. Pei. Or by watching kids play in St. Vartan's Park, then walking south on First Avenue to gaze at the humongous **NYU** and **Bellevue** Medical Centers (by which time, the "hill" portion of Murray Hill has evaporated). For the hill itself, head to Park Avenue and Lexington Avenue in the upper 30s—from there, you can get a sense of why this area is so-named (our unofficial guess is that Park Avenue and 38th Street is about the highest point in these parts). Then walk the side streets in the East Thirties to see some really prime real estate, as well as consulates, hotels, and lots of other stuff you can't afford.

Moving south from Murray Hill, the neighborhood changes rather dramatically in the East 20s. You first encounter "**Curry Hill**" on Lexington Avenue in the upper 20s, a fantastic strip of Indian restaurants and groceries. Two large landmarks, one old and one new, punctuate the southern end of this strip—the looming brickwork of the **69th Armory**, now home to many special events throughout the year, and then **Baruch College's** postmodern new main building just south of there (architects like to call this type of building a "vertical campus;" what that means is a 15-minute wait for an elevator between classes). Baruch is joined in this area by two other schools of note, the **School of Visual Arts** and **NYU's Dental School**, both on East 23rd Street.

The area changes again south of 23rd Street, becoming one of New York's loveliest residential neighborhoods, Gramercy Park. The **park itself** is gated, controlled and accessed by those who actually live around it. For the rest of us, we'll just need to be content with looking in at the park through its wrought-iron gates and staring at incredible period architecture facing the park. Our favorite three examples of this architecture are the **Mayor James Harper Residence** on the west side of the park, and the **Players** and **National Arts** Clubs on the southwestern side of the park. Then stroll down hidden Irving Place, a six-block long stretch of restaurants and nightlife options which dead-ends at 14th Street. Classic watering hole **Pete's Tavern**, where writer O. Henry drank, is a must-stop on this walk.

But the aforementioned contrast is still alive and kicking down here, because a few blocks to the east of warm, intimate Gramercy are the hulking **Stuyvesant Town** and Peter Cooper Village housing complexes, which together comprise over 11,000 residential units. Controversy has marked these two huge complexes for the past several years, as longtime owner Met Life spurned a (lower) offer from a tenant's group to buy the complex, instead selling to Tishman Speyer for $5.4 billion in 2006. It was the largest single sale of American property, which, now thanks to a deflated housing market, is now undoubtedly the largest property fiasco in American history (since Tishman had to turn over the property to its creditors to avoid bankruptcy). For us: no thanks, we'll stick with our Brooklyn walk-ups, and just visit.

Landmarks

- **69th Armory** • 68 Lexington Ave [26th St]
  Event space, historic landmark, hookers at night.
- **Baruch College** • 55 Lexington Ave [E 25th St]
  646-312-1000
  Baruch's "vertical campus;" very cool unless you need an elevator quickly.
- **Curry Hill** • Lexington Ave & E 28th St
  Eat your way down Lexington in the 20s!
- **Gramercy Park** • E 20th St & Irving Pl
  New York's only keyed park. This is where the revolution will doubtlessly start.
- **Kips Bay Plaza** • 1st Ave & E 30th St
  I.M. Pei does the superblock, 1960s-style. A tad brutalist.
- **Mayor James Harper Residence** •
  4 Gramercy Park W [E 21st St]
  Cool wrought-iron madness from 1846.
- **MeetingHouse of the Religious Society of Friends** •
  15 Rutherford Pl [E 16th St]
  212-475-0466
  Quaker meeting house from 1861. No guns, please.
- **The National Arts Club** •
  15 Gramercy Park S [E 20th St]
  212-475-3424
  One of two beautiful buildings on Gramercy Park South.
- **Pete's Tavern** • 129 E 18th St [Irving Pl]
  212-473-7676
  Where O. Henry hung out. And so should you, at least once.
- **The Players** • 16 Gramercy Park S [E 20th St]
  212-475-6116
  The other cool building on Gramercy Park South.
- **Protestant Welfare Agencies Building** •
  281 Park Ave S [E 22nd St]
  Looming Gothic structure circa 1894. Worth a look.
- **Sniffen Court** • 3rd Ave & E 36th St
  Great little space.
- **St. Vartan Park** • 1st Ave & E 35th St
  Murray Hill kid/playground nexus.
- **Stuyvesant Town** • 1st Ave & E 20th St
  Would you really want to live here? Really?
- **Tammany Hall/Union Square Theater** •
  100 E 17th St [Park Ave S]
  212-505-0700
  Once housed NYC's Democratic political machine.

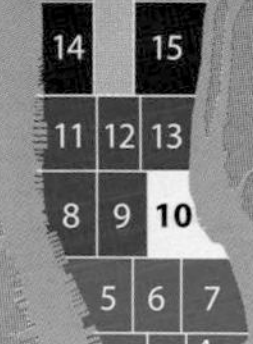

rish pubs abound in this neighborhood, and all of them (**Failte**, **Molly's**, **Paddy Reilly's**, **Rocky Sullivan's**) have their devotees. We prefer dive bars **McSwiggan's** or **Whiskey River**, live music venues **Irving Plaza**, **Rodeo Bar**, or the **Jazz Standard**, and (of course!) classic watering hole **Pete's Tavern**.

Bars

- **Bar Jamon** • 125 E 17th St [Irving Pl]
  212-253-2773
  Pig out at this wine bar.
- **Belmont Lounge** • 117 E 15th St [Irving Pl]
  212-533-0009
  Be seen.
- **Failte Irish Whiskey Bar** •
  531 2nd Ave [E 29th St]
  212-725-9440
  Sip Guiness by the fire. Shoot a round of pool. A favorite of Irish Ex-pats.
- **Irving Plaza** • 17 Irving Pl [E 15th St]
  212-777-6800
  Staple rock venue.
- **Jazz Standard** • 116 E 27th St [Lexington Ave]
  212-576-2232
  Solid shows. BBQ upstairs!
- **McSwiggan's** • 393 2nd Ave [E 23rd St]
  212-683-3180
  One of the best dive bars on the island.
- **Molly's** • 287 3rd Ave [E 22nd St]
  212-889-3361
  Great Irish pub with a fireplace.
- **New York Comedy Club** •
  241 E 24th St [3rd Ave]
  212-696-5233
  And the bartender asks, "where did you get that?"
- **Paddy Reilly's Music Bar** •
  519 2nd Ave [E 29th St]
  212-686-1210
  Sunday night means pints of Guinness and live Irish fiddlin'.
- **Pete's Tavern** • 129 E 18th St [Irving Pl]
  212-473-7676
  Where O. Henry hung out. And so should you, at least once.
- **Plug Uglies** • 257 3rd Ave [E 20th St]
  212-780-1944
  Full length shuffle board table!
- **Rodeo Bar** • 375 3rd Ave [E 27th St]
  212-683-6500
  As close to a honky-tonk as you'll get, partner.
- **Rolf's** • 281 3rd Ave [E 22nd St]
  212-477-4750
  December holiday visit is a must for some German bier.
- **Rose Bar** • 2 Lexington Ave [E 21st St]
  212-920-3300
  Another classy hotel bar NFT can't afford.
- **The Stand** • 239 3rd Ave [20th Street]
  212-677-2600
  Intimate comedy club attracting hip names.
- **Waterfront Ale House** •
  540 2nd Ave [E 30th St]
  212-696-4104
  Decent local vibe.
- **Whiskey River** • 575 2nd Ave [E 32nd St]
  212-679-6799
  Dive bar. Neighborhood joint. Great beer selection.

Movie Theaters

- **AMC Loews Kips Bay 15** •
  570 2nd Ave [E 31st St]
  212-447-0638
  This multiplex is starting to show its age.
- **The Scandinavia House** •
  58 Park Ave [E 38th St]
  212-879-9779
  Scandinavian movies. Bergman and beyond.

Theaters/Performing Arts

- **Baruch Performing Arts Center** •
  55 Lexington Ave [E 25th St]
  646-312-4085
  Leave a trail of bread crumbs to find your way out.
- **Daryl Roth Theatre** • 101 E 15th St [E 15th St]
  212-239-6200
  Used to be a bank; now loses money with theatre.
- **Union Square Theater** •
  100 E 17th St [Park Ave S]
  212-307-4100
  The former site of Tammany Hall.

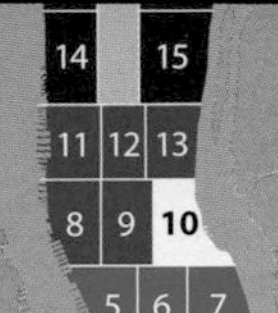

Restaurants

Everyone has their Curry Hill favorite; ours is vegetarian dosa house **Pongal**. If you're into meat, upscale burger joint **Rare** or steakhouse **BLT Prime** both make the cut. Tom Colicchio's **Riverpark** spiffs up an underserved corner of Kips Bay. And good Thai (**Jaiya Thai**) can be found, but the sleeper pick here is **Turkish Kitchen**, our favorite Turkish in all of New York.

Restaurants

- **Baoguette** • 61 Lexington Ave [E 25th St]
  212-532-1133 • $
  Gourmet sandwiches like catfish and sloppy bao.
- **BLT Prime** • 111 E 22nd St [Park Ave S]
  212-995-8500 • $$$$$
  Steakhouse with Craft-like, a-la-carte sides.
- **Blue Smoke** • 116 E 27th St [Park Ave S]
  212-447-7733 • $$$$
  Finger lickin' BBQ, Danny Meyer style (with downstairs jazz club).
- **Brasserie Les Halles** •
  411 Park Ave S [E 29th St]
  212-679-4111 • $$$
  The original. Steak frites and French vibe.
- **The Cannibal** • 113 E 29th St [Park Ave]
  212-686-5480 • $$$
  Hope you like meat. And beer.
- **Carl's Steaks** • 507 3rd Ave [E 34th St]
  212-696-5336 • $
  Cheesesteaks, chickensteaks, and chili fries.
- **Chennai Garden** •
  129 E 27th St [Lexington Ave]
  212-689-1999 • $$
  Indian food that happens to be vegetarian, kosher, and very tasty.
- **Chinese Mirch** • 120 Lexington Ave [E 28th St]
  212-532-3663 • $$$
  Fiery Chinese food by way of Mumbai.
- **Curry Leaf** • 99 Lexington Ave [E 27th St]
  212-725-5558 • $$$
  Best basic Indian.
- **Defonte's of Brooklyn** •
  261 3rd Ave [E 21st St]
  212-614-1500 • $$
  Legendary Brooklyn sandwich takes Manhattan.
- **El Parador Café** • 325 E 34th St [2nd Ave]
  212-679-6812 • $$$
  NY's oldest and friendliest Mexican.
- **Franchia** • 12 Park Ave [E 35th St]
  212-213-1001 •
  Modern Korean tea and treats.
- **Gramercy Cafe** • 184 3rd Ave [E 17th St]
  212-982-2121 • $$
  Open 24 hours. Diner. You know the drill.
- **Haandi** • 113 Lexington Ave [E 28th St]
  212-685-5200 • $$
  Stellar Pakistani grilled meats.
- **I Trulli** • 122 E 27th St [Lexington Ave]
  212-481-7372 • $$$$$
  Italian. Great garden.
- **Jaiya** • 396 3rd Ave [E 28th St]
  212-889-1330 • $$$
  Inventive, spicy Thai.
- **L'Express** • 249 Park Ave S [E 20th St]
  212-254-5858 • $$
  Always-open French diner.
- **La Posada** • 364 3rd Ave [E 26th St]
  212-213-4379 • $
  Authentic Mexican burritos, tacos and enchiladas.
- **Maoz Vegetarian** • 38 Union Sq E [E 16th St]
  212-260-1988 • $
  Cheap and tasty falafel take-out chain from Amsterdam.
- **Mexico Lindo** • 459 2nd Ave [E 26th St]
  212-679-3665 • $$$
  Famous Mexican food.
- **Penelope** • 159 Lexington Ave [E 30th St]
  212-481-3800 • $$
  Gingham décor but oh, what a menu!
- **Pongal** • 110 Lexington Ave [E 28th St]
  212-696-9458 • $$
  Possibly NY's best vegetarian Indian. Sada dosa…mmmm.
- **Posto** • 310 2nd Ave [E 18th St]
  212-716-1200 • $$
  Savory thin-crust pizza, salads.
- **Rare Bar & Grill** •
  303 Lexington Ave [E 37th St]
  212-481-1999 • $$$
  Should be better, given the focus. We're divided on this one.
- **Resto** • 111 E 29th St [Park Ave S]
  212-685-5585 • $$
  Belgian gastropub that's pretty darn great.
- **Riverpark** • 450 E 29th St [First Ave]
  212-729-9790 • $$$$$
  Colicchio brings his vision to underserved corner of Kips Bay.
- **Tiffin Wallah** • 127 E 28th St [Lexington Ave]
  212-685-7301 • $
  Veggie lunch buffet for a few bucks.
- **Turkish Kitchen** • 386 3rd Ave [E 28th St]
  212-679-6633 • $$$
  Excellent Turkish, great décor, brilliant bread. NFT pick!
- **The Water Club** • FDR Drive & 30th St
  212-683-3333 • $$$$
  Romantic, good brunch on the East River.

Bagels, Coffee, & Shopping

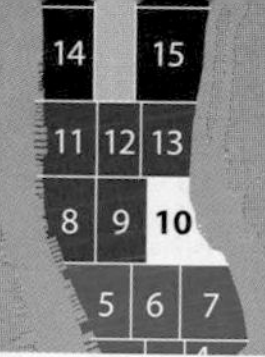

Hit either **Lamarca** or **Lamazou** cheese shops to go along with pastries from **La Delice**. Indian shops **Kalustyan's**, **Foods of India**, and **Om Sari Palace** are always worth a look. **Jam** will have any envelope you could ever need and **Nuthouse Hardware** is New York's only 24-hour hardware store, with power tool rentals. Cool.

Bagels

- **David's Bagels** • 273 First Ave [E 16th St]
212-780-2308
Some argue hands-down best NYC bagel.
- **Ess-A-Bagel** • 359 1st Ave [E 21st St]
212-260-2252
Bagels (and service) with attitude.

Coffee

- **71 Irving Place Coffee & Tea Bar** •
71 Irving Pl [E 19th St]
212-995-5252
Brilliant coffee.
- **Fika** • 407 Park Ave S [E 28th St]
646-649-5133
Swedish coffee is really great. Seriously!
- **Franchia** • 12 Park Ave [E 35th St]
212-213-1001
Modern Korean tea and treats.
- **Lady Mendl's Tea Salon** •
56 Irving Pl [E 17th St]
212-533-4466
It's tea time for the ladies of Manhattan.
- **Maialino** • 2 Lexington Ave [E 21st St]
212-777-2410
Drip bar located in the Gramercy Park Hotel.
- **Oren's Daily Roast** • 434 3rd Ave [E 30th St]
212-779-1241
Hip staff pours superior java at local mini-chain.

Shopping

- **City Opera Thrift Shop** •
222 E 23rd St [3rd Ave]
212-684-5344
They always have something or other.
- **DaVinci Artist Supply** •
137 E 23rd St [Lexington Ave]
212-982-8607
Discounts to student, teachers, and art professionals.
- **Foods of India** • 121 Lexington Ave [E 28th St]
212-683-4419
Huge selection including harder to find spices.
- **Housing Works Thrift Shop** •
157 E 23rd St [Lexington Ave]
212-529-5955
Our favorite thrift store.
- **Jam Paper & Envelope** •
135 3rd Ave [E 15th St]
212-473-6666
And the envelope, please.
- **Kalustyan's** • 123 Lexington Ave [E 28th St]
212-685-3451
Indian specialty foods.
- **La Delice Pastry Shop** •
372 3rd Ave [E 27th St]
212-532-4409
Delectable pastries, buttery croissants, layer cakes.
- **Lamarca Cheese Shop** •
161 E 22nd St [3rd Ave]
212-673-7920
Italian culinary goodies.
- **Lamazou** • 370 3rd Ave [E 27th St]
212-532-2009
Great selection of cheese and gourmet products.
- **Ligne Roset** • 250 Park Ave S [E 20th St]
212-375-1036
Modern, sleek furniture. Only for people with very good jobs.
- **Max Nass** • 118 E 28th St [Lexington Ave]
212-679-8154
Vintage jewelry. repairs, restringing, and restoration.
- **Nemo Tile Company** • 48 E 21st St [Broadway]
212-505-0009
Good tile shop for small projects.
- **Nuthouse Hardware** • 202 E 29th St [3rd Ave]
212-545-1447
Open 24-hours; equipment rentals, too.
- **Om Saree Palace** •
134 E 27th St [Lexington Ave]
212-532-5620
Saris, bangles, earrings, sandals and accessories.
- **Pookie & Sebastian** • 541 3rd Ave [E 36th St]
212-951-7110
Murray Hill outpost for fun, flirty, girly garb.
- **Todaro Bros.** • 555 2nd Ave [E 30th St]
212-532-0633
Home made mozzerella, pastas, high quality groceries.
- **Vintage Thrift Shop** • 286 3rd Ave [E 22nd St]
212-871-0777
Vintage clothes you can actually afford.

Map 11 • Hell's Kitchen

1
2
A
B

W 60th St
W 59th St
W 58th St
W 57th St
W 56th St
W 55th St
W 54th St
W 53rd St
W 52nd St
W 51st St
W 50th St
W 49th St
W 48th St
W 47th St
W 46th St
W 45th St
W 44th St
W 43rd St
W 42nd St
W 41st St
W 40th St
W 39th St
W 38th St
W 37th ST

Henry Hudson Pkwy
West Side Hwy
Hudson River Park
Eleventh Ave
Tenth Ave
Ninth Ave
Eighth Ave
Dyer Ave
Hudson River

PAGE 198
Time Warner Center
Columbus Circle
59th Street Columbus Circle
Dewitt Clinton Park
Daily Show Studio
PAGE 194
50th Street
Associated Musicians of Greater New York
Restaurant Row
Intrepid Sea, Air and Space Museum
Broadway Dance Center
42nd Stre[et]
Port Authori[ty]
Bus Termin[al]
Theatre Row
PAGE 254
Port Authority Bus Terminal
The Annex/ Hell's Kitchen Flea Market
Lincoln Tunnel
Jacob K Javits Convention Center
PAGE 196

14
12
8

1/4 mile
.25 km

Neighboorhood Overview

Named for the squalor its early immigrant tenements epitomized, the scruffy patch of bodega-infused real estate between Broadway and that unlikely landing strip known as the Hudson is home to intimate theaters, niche restaurants and—along with a rising tide of gentrification—an army of toy dogs likely to stage a coup one day. The neighborhood is also characterized by an abundance of things too big and ugly to put anywhere else in Manhattan: car dealerships, cell phone towers, cruise liners, the Port Authority, and stables for those hansom cab horses, the last of which accounts for certain odors and the distinct clip-clop of every rush hour.

It's also further west than the subways venture, harshly industrial-looking and often beset by Lincoln Tunnel traffic or gale force nautical winds. Yes, Hell's Kitchen may seem like the edge of the civilized world, and the panoramic view of New Jersey does little to dampen this grungy impression. Yet most locals come to cherish the mellow vibe and dearth of McDonald's locations that come with living just outside Manhattan's hyperkinetic and tourist-infested core. Here you'll have no trouble hailing a cab, or getting the bartender's attention. And as for the out of-towners—well, they only get as far in as Ninth Avenue before their legs get tired.

Hell's Kitchen may be close to Central Park, but why fight the crowds? Instead explore Hudson River Park, an elegantly sculpted swath of greenery running along the coast of the island. Its linearity makes for ideal bikers and joggers, but the idle will find plenty of lovely spots to spread a picnic blanket and watch lunatics paddle by in kayaks. **Dewitt Clinton Park** always has an entertaining game going on its baseball/soccer/everything field; it also boasts two popular dog runs for the bonding of canines and their owners alike. Community gardens have sprung up there and close by, thanks to green-thumbed volunteers from the area.

Two essential elements to absorb: one you find on stage, and the other you find on the end of a fork—usually in that order. The former is available at one of the countless off and off-off-Broadway theatres lying around—you know, the type that aren't showing something along the lines of "A Musical Loosely Cobbled Together From A String Of #1 Hit Singles"? **Theatre Row** is, as the name suggests, a lineup of such venues featuring, ahem, riskier fare—though perhaps not as scandalous as the peepshows that once littered that stretch of 42nd Street. Satirical mainstays **The Daily Show** and The Colbert Report also tape around here, if you're looking for entertainment that's as free as it is hilarious. Head up to **Restaurant Row** on 46th to sample one of the cozy eateries and candlelit nightlife nooks that cater to audiences after the curtain falls. Almost every sub-genre of food is accounted for, and authenticity is rampant—don't be surprised to find actual French people eating at a French bistro!

Mom-and-pop places have proved resilient—everything from artisanal bread to custom-made paints can be got at tiny stores run by devoted experts. You might even see an old-school coffee shop without so much as a name on a sign out front. But the best spot for browsing is brand new: the **Hell's Kitchen Flea Market**, nestled between bus ramps on 39th Street, offers outdoor bargain-hunting on summer weekends. The usual gridlock is traded for a bazaar of vintage clothing, jewelry and collectibles, most priced a bit cheaper than they were before these particular vendors moved from a Chelsea location known as The Annex.

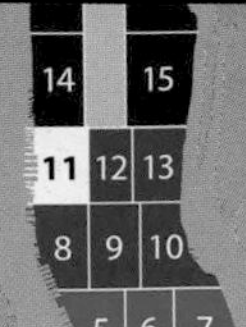

Landmarks

o Landmarks

- **Broadway Dance Center •**
  322 W 45th St [Broadway]
  212-582-9304
  The place for tap lessons.
- **Daily Show Studio •** 733 11th Ave [W 52nd St]
  Home of our favorite TV show. Thank you Jon Stewart.
- **Dewitt Clinton Park •** 11th Ave & W 52nd St
  Where the neighborhood mutts meet to sniff butts.
- **Hell's Kitchen Flea Market •**
  W 39th St & Dyer Ave
  212-243-5343
  Old Chelsea Annex flea market is now located here.
- **Intrepid Sea, Air and Space Museum •**
  12th Ave & W 46th St
  212-245-0072
- **Restaurant Row •** 8th Ave & W 46th St
  Mingle with tourists during pre-theater dinners.
- **Theatre Row •** W 42nd St b/n 9th & Dyer Aves
  Cluster of off-Broadway theatres including Playwrights Horizons.

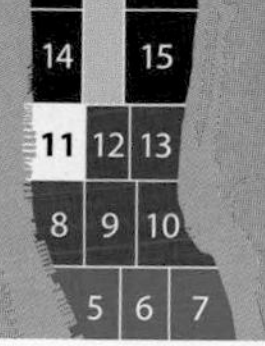

and of contrast: Reservations are essential at **Bar Centrale**, with its peakeasy vibe and classic cocktails—and then there's an utter dive like **udy's Bar & Grill,** which serves each beer with a free hot dog. Elsewhere, ou've got a decadent club-style concert venue and legendary smoker's oof in **Terminal 5.**

Bars

- **Bar Centrale** • 324 W 46th St [8th Ave]
  212-581-3130
  Make reservations to see Broadway stars relaxing after the show.
- **Birdland** • 315 W 44th St [8th Ave]
  212-581-3080
  Top-notch jazz.
- **Blue Ruin** • 538 9th Ave [W 40th St]
  917-945-3497
  Pressed tin ceiling and lots of booze.
- **Don't Tell Mama** • 343 W 46th St [8th Ave]
  212-757-0788
  Good cabaret space.
- **Flaming Saddles** • 793 9th Ave [W 53rd St]
  212-713-0481
  Country-western, gay, bartenders dance on the bar, lots of cuties.
- **Holland Bar** • 532 9th Ave [W 40th St]
  212-502-4609
  One of the last great dives of New York.
- **The House of Brews** • 363 W 46th St [9th Ave]
  212-245-0551
  Pratty but friendly atmosphere, great beer selection.
- **Hudson Hotel Library** •
  356 W 58th St [9th Ave]
  212-554-6000
  Super-super-super pretentious.
- **Industry** • 355 W 52nd St [9th Ave]
  646-476-2747
  Large space with great decor, hot bartenders; come with friends.
- **The Pony Bar** • 637 10th Ave [W 45th St]
  212-586-2707
  Beer beer everywhere. Get a growler to go.
- **Port 41** • 355 W 41st St [9th Ave]
  212-244-4408
  Perfect stop before or after a grueling trip on Greyhound.
- **Rudy's Bar & Grill** • 627 9th Ave [W 44th St]
  646-707-0890
  Classic Hell's Kitchen. Recommended.
- **Smith's** • 701 8th Ave [W 44th St]
  212-246-3268
  Beautiful sign, but beware the testosterone.
- **Swing 46** • 349 W 46th St [9th Ave]
  212-262-9554
  Good place for a drink before a show.
- **The Tank** • 151 W 46th St [7th Ave]
  212-563-6269
  Major destination for experimental music.
- **Terminal 5** • 610 W 56th St [11th Ave]
  212-665-3832
  Ex-club space now used for mid level Indie bands
- **Valhalla** • 815 9th Ave [W 54th St]
  212-757-2747
  Warm, wooden watering hole with staggering beer selection.
- **Vintage** • 753 9th Ave [W 51st St]
  212-581-4655
  Ginormous martini menu. Good beers.
- **XL Nightclub** • 512 W 42nd St [Eleventh Ave]
  212-239-2999
  Gay club featuring Hot Mess drag show Wednesday nights.

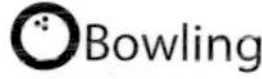

Bowling

- **Lucky Strike Lanes** •
  624 W 42nd St [12th Ave]
  646-829-0170
  America's other, drunker pastime—with a lounge and dress code.

Theaters/Performing Arts

- **Mint Theatre** •
  311 W 43rd St, 3rd Fl [Eighth Ave]
  212-315-0231
  Terrific company that does old plays even Michael Dale has never heard of.
- **Pearl Theatre Co** •
  555 W 42nd St [Eleventh Ave]
  212-598-9802
  The classics done right.

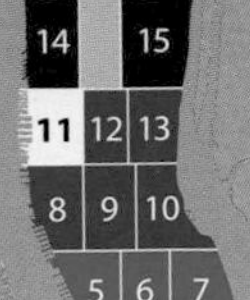

Restaurants

The breadth and depth of deliciousness is staggering here. **Hallo Berlin** boasts German soul food, **Esca** serves top-notch splurge/splash seafood, and **Island Burgers** features about forty variations of their signature dish. Middle Eastern lovers get their fix at BYOB gem **Gazala Place** or **Hummus Kitchen**. Pre-theater pick is French stalwart **Tout Va Bien**.

Restaurants

- **Amma** • 246 E 51st St [3rd Ave]
  212-644-8330 • $$$$
  Posh Indian worth the $$$. In Midtown, no less.
- **Aquavit** • 65 E 55th St [Park Ave]
  212-307-7311 • $$$$$
  Stellar dining experience: top-drawer Scandinavian.
- **BLT Steak** • 106 E 57th St [Park Ave]
  212-752-7470 • $$$$$
  Pricey and good, not great.
- **Chola** • 232 E 58th St [3rd Ave]
  212-688-4619 • $$$$
  Pricey south Indian cuisine.
- **Dawat** • 210 E 58th St [3rd Ave]
  212-355-7555 • $$$$
  Top-end Indian.
- **Docks Oyster Bar** • 633 3rd Ave [E 40th St]
  212-986-8080 • $$$$
  Great seafood, good atmosphere.
- **Felidia** • 243 E 58th St [3rd Ave]
  212-758-1479 • $$$$
  Top Northern Italian.
- **The Four Seasons** • 99 E 52nd St [Park Ave]
  212-754-9494 • $$$$$
  Designer everything. Even the cotton candy.
- **Grand Central Oyster Bar** •
  89 E 42nd St [Park Ave]
  212-490-6650 • $$$
  Classic New York seafood joint. Go for the Saloon.
- **Hide-Chan Ramen** • 248 E 52nd St [2nd Ave]
  212-813-1800 • $$
  This broth is porktastic.
- **La Fonda Del Sol** • E 44th St & Vanderbilt Ave
  212-867-6767 • $$$$
  Excellent tapas in a semi-corporate setting.
- **Le Relais De Venise L'Entrecote** • 590 Lexington Ave [E 52nd St]
  212-758-3989 • $$$
  Good steak frites and salad via Paris.
- **Lexington Brass** • 517 Lexington Ave [48th St]
  212-392-5976 • $$$
  Gastropub grub and a stellar brunch, not bad for Midtown.
- **Menchanko Tei** •
  131 E 45th St [Lexington Ave]
  212-986-6805 • $$
  Japanese noodle shop.
- **Monkey Bar** • 60 E 54th St [Madison Ave]
  212-288-1010 • $$$$
  Graydon Carter does Midtown with old-New York menu.
- **New York Luncheonette** •
  135 E 50th St [Lexington Ave]
  212-838-0165 • $$
  Diner where Obama lunched with Bloomy.
- **Opia** • 130 E 57th St [Lexington Ave]
  212-688-3939 • $$$$
  Midtown spot for moules frites and steak au poivre.
- **P.J. Clarke's** • 915 3rd Ave [E 55th St]
  212-317-1616 • $$$
  Pub grub. A fine burger.
- **Palm One** • 837 2nd Ave [E 45th St]
  212-687-2953 • $$$$$
  Steaks and chops. Go to Luger's.
- **Patroon** • 160 E 46th St [3rd Ave]
  212-883-7373 • $$$$$
  An oasis of civility.
- **Pershing Square** • 90 E 42nd St [Park Ave]
  212-286-9600 • $$$$
  Excellent food and awesome space.
- **Sakagura** • 211 E 43rd St [3rd Ave]
  212-953-7253 • $$$
  Midtowners are very happy to have this excellent izakaya.
- **Shun Lee Palace** •
  155 E 55th St [Lexington Ave]
  212-371-8844 • $$$$$
  Top-end Chinese.
- **Smith & Wollensky** • 797 Third Ave [E 49th St]
  212-753-1530 • $$$$$
  Don't order the fish.
- **Sparks Steak House** • 210 E 46th St [3rd Ave]
  212-687-4855 • $$$$$
  If you can't go to Luger's.
- **Sushi Yasuda** • 204 E 43rd St [3rd Ave]
  212-972-1001 • $$$$
  Best sushi in NYC. Let the debate begin...
- **Taksim** • 1030 2nd Ave [E 54th St]
  212-421-3004 • $$$
  All manner of Turkish delights.
- **Yuva** • 230 E 58th St [3rd Ave]
  212-339-0090 • $$$$
  Inventive new addition to upscale Indian row.

Bagels, Coffee, & Shopping

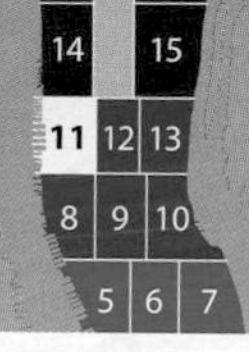

Map 11

Amish Market is the top-end supermarket; **Ninth Avenue International** is amazing for Greek groceries. **Sullivan Street Bakery** makes bundles of heaven disguised as bread. **Delphinium** is the store where you can buy a non-Hallmark card, and **Chelsea Garden Center**, in spite of its geographic indifference, can provide the perfect flowers to go with it.

Coffee

- **Bis.Co. Latte** • 667 10th Ave [W 47th St]
212-581-3900
Mmmm…homemade biscotti.
- **Empire Coffee & Tea** • 568 9th Ave [W 41st St]
212-268-1220
Best coffee in these tourist filled parts.

Shopping

- **10th Avenue Wines & Liquors** •
812 10th Ave [W 54th St]
212-245-6700
Boozehound specials and tastings.
- **Amish Market** • 731 9th Ave [W 50th St]
212-245-2360
Lots prepared foods. Do they deliver by horse and buggy?
- **Amy's Bread** • 672 9th Ave [W 47th St]
212-977-2670
Providing the heavenly smells that wake up Hell's Kitchen.
- **Bouchon Bakery** • 10 Columbus Cir [8th Ave]
212-823-9366
Heavenly pastries in a gigantic mall.
- **Chelsea Garden Center** •
580 11th Ave [W 44th St]
212-727-7100
Urban gardener's delight.
- **Coco and Toto** • 730 11th Ave [W 52nd St]
212-956-5822
Adorable pet boutique grooms, walks and babysits beloved furballs.
- **Coup de Coeur** • 609 9th Ave [W 43rd St]
212-586-8636
Trendy, eclectic shop with great vibes.
- **Delphinium Home** • 353 W 47th St [9th Ave]
212-333-7732
For the "too lazy to make my own card" set.
- **Epstein's Paint Center** •
822 10th Ave [W 55th St]
212-265-3960
Honest advice, top quality from century-old shop.
- **Happy Feet** • 754 10th Ave [W 51st St]
212-757-8400
Reliable deals on all imaginable pet supplies.
- **Hell's Kitchen Flea Market** •
W 39th St & Dyer Ave
212-243-5343
Vintage treasures abound every Sat & Sun.
- **Janovic** • 771 9th Ave [W 52nd St]
212-245-3241
Top NYC paint store. Shades/blinds too.
- **Liberty Bicycles** • 846 9th Ave [W 55th St]
212-757-2418
This bike shop totally rocks.
- **Little Pie Company** • 424 W 43rd St [9th Ave]
212-736-4780
A homemade dessert equals happiness.
- **Luthier Music** • 341 W 44th St [9th Ave]
212-397-6038
One of the best for classical and flamenco guitars.
- **Ninth Avenue International Grocery** •
543 9th Ave [W 40th St]
212-279-1000
Mediterranean/Greek specialty store
- **Ninth Avenue Vintner** •
669 9th Ave [W 46th St]
212-664-9463
Good suggestions from the staff.
- **Pan Aqua Diving** • 460 W 43rd St [10th Ave]
212-736-3483
SCUBA equipment and courses.
- **Poseidon Greek Bakery** •
629 9th Ave [W 44th St]
212-757-6173
Old-school Greek delicacies like spanakopita.
- **Radio Shack** • 333 W 57th St [8th Ave]
212-586-1909
Kenneth, what is the frequency?
- **Sea Breeze Fish Market** •
541 9th Ave [W 40th St]
212-563-7537
Bargains on fresh seafood.
- **Sullivan Street Bakery** •
533 W 47th St [11th Ave]
212-265-5580
Artisan breads, foodie approved. NFT approved. God approved.
- **Tumi** • 10 Columbus Cir [8th Ave]
212-823-9390
When your luggage gets lost and insurance is paying.
- **Whole Foods** • 10 Columbus Cir [8th Ave]
212-823-9600
"Whole Paycheck" everywhere except NYC, where it beats Food Emporium.

Map 12 • Midtown

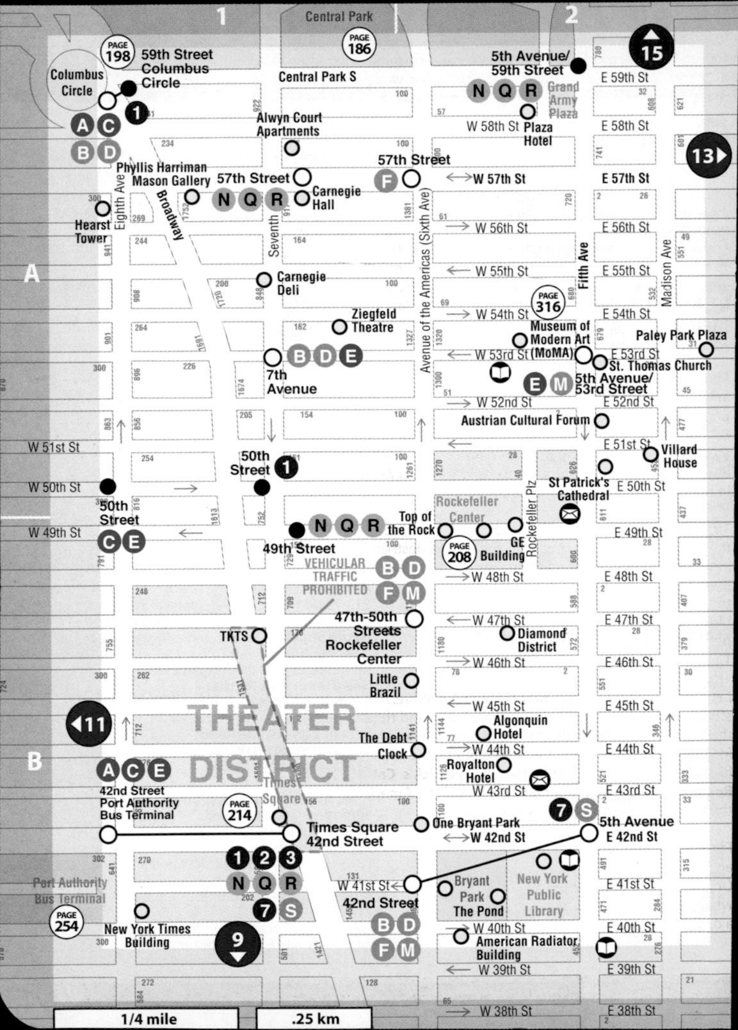

1
2
A
B

Central Park
PAGE 186
Central Park S
PAGE 198
59th Street Columbus Circle
Columbus Circle
1
A C
B D
Alwyn Court Apartments
Phyllis Harriman Mason Gallery
57th Street
N Q R
Carnegie Hall
Hearst Tower
Eighth Ave
Broadway
Seventh Ave
57th Street
F
Avenue of the Americas (Sixth Ave)
5th Avenue/ 59th Street
N Q R
Grand Army Plaza
Plaza Hotel
W 58th St
W 57th St
W 56th St
W 55th St
W 54th St
W 53rd St
W 52nd St
W 51st St
W 50th St
W 49th St
W 48th St
W 47th St
W 46th St
W 45th St
W 44th St
W 43rd St
W 42nd St
W 41st St
W 40th St
W 39th St
W 38th St
E 59th St
E 58th St
E 57th St
E 56th St
E 55th St
E 54th St
E 53rd St
E 52nd St
E 51st St
E 50th St
E 49th St
E 48th St
E 47th St
E 46th St
E 45th St
E 44th St
E 43rd St
E 42nd St
E 41st St
E 40th St
E 39th St
E 38th St
Fifth Ave
Madison Ave
15
13
Carnegie Deli
Ziegfeld Theatre
PAGE 316
Museum of Modern Art (MoMA)
Paley Park Plaza
St. Thomas Church
5th Avenue/ 53rd Street
E M
7th Avenue
B D E
Austrian Cultural Forum
Villard House
50th Street
1
50th Street
C E
St Patrick's Cathedral
Rockefeller Center
Rockefeller Plz
Top of the Rock
GE Building
PAGE 208
49th Street
N Q R
VEHICULAR TRAFFIC PROHIBITED
B D
F M
47th-50th Streets Rockefeller Center
Diamond District
TKTS
Little Brazil
THEATER DISTRICT
Times Square
11
Algonquin Hotel
The Debt Clock
Royalton Hotel
A C E
42nd Street Port Authority Bus Terminal
PAGE 214
Times Square 42nd Street
One Bryant Park
7 S
5th Avenue
1 2 3
N Q R
7 S
Port Authority Bus Terminal
PAGE 254
New York Times Building
9
42nd Street
B D
F M
Bryant Park
The Pond
New York Public Library
American Radiator Building
1/4 mile
.25 km

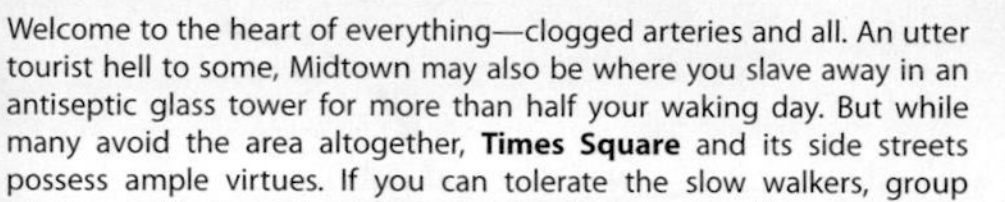

Neighborhood Overview

Welcome to the heart of everything—clogged arteries and all. An utter tourist hell to some, Midtown may also be where you slave away in an antiseptic glass tower for more than half your waking day. But while many avoid the area altogether, **Times Square** and its side streets possess ample virtues. If you can tolerate the slow walkers, group photos, and incessant invitations to comedy shows, you'll be rewarded with some of New York's finest art and most impressive architecture, the brightest lights this side of Tokyo, world-famous hotels and cathedrals, a pair of iconic animal statues, and of course a little animal known as Broadway.

Topping our Midtown list is **The Museum of Modern Art.** Yes, it's pricey and gets packed on the weekend, but the art will blow your mind and the sculpture garden is divine. Bargain tip: it's free on Friday evenings. If you still enjoy the smell and feel of real-live books, the main branch of the **New York Public Library** (guarded by the famous lion statues Patience and Fortitude) is spectacular. Inside, visit The Map Room and The Rose Main Reading Room, one of the most beautiful spaces in the world to get lost in a book. Right outside, you can bask on the lawn of beautiful **Bryant Park**, stare up at the sky, and transcend the chaos of the city. Until a pigeon poops on you or the crazy guy in the smelly trench coat starts yelling at himself.

For a dose of glamour and history, stop in at the **Algonquin Hotel**, where famous writers, entertainers, and socialites used to cavort and carouse in the 1920s. To see how the ultra-rich used to (and still) live, pop into the gorgeous **Plaza Hotel**. If you have a small fortune lying around unused, we hear the Edwardian Suite is quite suitable. Gaze at the exquisite, 1908 façade of the **Alwyn Court Apartments** and decide if you would rather live behind those walls or just look at them like a fine sculpture. When it's movie time, catch it at the plush, gold-trimmed **Ziegfeld Theatre**, which boasts the biggest screen in the city.

Times Square is the dominion of tourists, but it's worth sneaking in late at night when they're back in their hotels, so you can check out the cool pedestrian plaza where the street used to be (though we kind of miss the comfy lawn chairs from the first summer they tried it). One of the area's greatest assets is, of course, the Broadway theatre scene. If you need cheap tickets to a play or musical, weave through the crowds to the **TKTS** booth. After braving the line, grab a seat on the actually-really-awesome bleachers that climb over the booth like a staircase. The real gems, though, can be found on the periphery of the square, including the striking **New York Times Building**, the exhibits at **Discovery Times Square** (brave the tourists – it's worth it!), and the rare tourist-free bar, **Jimmy's Corner**.

Midtown is home to oodles of thrilling architecture. Arguably, the most exciting is the **Hearst Tower,** a stunning masterpiece blending old and new, and the first "green" skyscraper in New York. Sprouting through the roof of the original 1928 building is an angular tower built with recycled steel, completed in 2006. Duck into the lobby to check out the one-of-a-kind water sculpture. Other architectural highlights include **Carnegie Hall**, **St. Patrick's Cathedral**, **St. Thomas Church**, **Villard House**, **Rockefeller Center**, **One Bryant Park**, and the **American Radiator Building**. And finally, don't miss the trippy **Austrian Cultural Forum**, which hosts a number of events open to the public.

For a change of pace, check out **Little Brazil's** small strip of restaurants, bars (some with live music), and shops. Or go north a block to the famous **Diamond District**, which appeared in the 1940s when Orthodox Jews transplanted here from war-torn Europe. Finally, stare up at **The Debt Clock**, wondering what your share is and why Bill Gates needs another tax cut. Whereupon, you will need a drink. Possibly a double.

Landmarks

Landmarks

- **Algonquin Hotel** • 59 W 44th St [6th Ave]
  212-840-6800
  Where snark was invented.
- **Alwyn Court Apartments** •
  180 W 58th St [7th Ave]
  100-year-old apartment building with awesomely detailed exterior.
- **American Radiator Building** •
  40 W 40th St [6th Ave]
  Massive gold-and-black Art Deco gem looms over Bryant Park.
- **Bryant Park** • 6th Ave & 42nd St
  Summer movies, winter ice-skating, hook-ups year round.
- **Carnegie Hall** • 881 7th Ave [W 57th St]
  212-247-7800
  Stock up on free cough drops in the lobby.
- **The Debt Clock** • 6th Ave & W 44th St
  How much the US has borrowed—pennies, really.
- **Diamond District** •
  W 47th St b/n 5th and 6th Ave
  Big rocks abound! Center of the world's diamond industry.
- **GE Building** • 60 Rockefeller Plaza [W 51st St]
  The tallest building at Rock Center.
- **Hearst Tower** • 300 W 57th St [8th Ave]
  It's green! It's mean! It's fit to be seen!
- **Little Brazil** • W 46th St b/n 5th & 6th Ave
  Small stretch of Brazilian businesses. Gisele not included.
- **Museum of Modern Art (MoMA)** •
  11 W 53rd St [5th Ave]
  212-708-9400
  The renovation worked! Admire the beauty of architecture and art.
- **New York Public Library** •
  5th Ave & W 42nd St
  917-275-6975
  A wonderful Beaux Arts building. Great park behind it. The Map Room rules.
- **New York Times Building** •
  8th Ave & W 40th St
  Renzo Piano's impressive new home for The Gray Lady.
- **One Bryant Park** • 1111 Sixth Ave [W 42nd St]
  212-764-0694
  New York's third-tallest building: sleek, elegant, and environmentally friendly.
- **The Plaza Hotel** • 768 5th Ave [W 58th St]
  212-759-3000
  Now anyone can be Eloise with her own Plaza condo.
- **Rockefeller Center** •
  45 Rockefeller Plaza [W 49th St]
  212-332-6868
  Sculpture, ice skating, and a mall!
- **St. Patrick's Cathedral** • 5th Ave & 50th St
  212-753-2261
  NYC's classic cathedral.
- **Times Square** • 7th Ave & W 42nd St
  It looks even cooler than it does on TV!
- **TKTS** • Broadway & W 47th St
  Get cheap Broadway tix underneath the cool looking stairs.
- **Villard House** • 457 Madison Ave [E 51st St]
  Killer brownstone palazzos by holy fathers McKim, Mead & White.
- **Ziegfeld Theatre** • 141 W 54th St [6th Ave]
  212-765-7600
  Glorious 1969 movie palace. 1,100 seats and red carpeting.

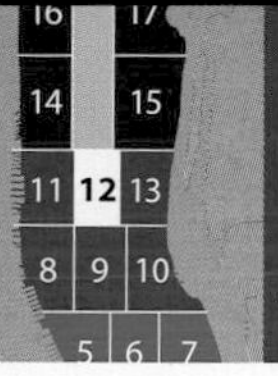

Grab a cocktail at the elegant and laid-back **Faces and Names**, or belly up to the bar at the aforementioned **Jimmy's Corner** for a beer and a shot. Bowl some frames at, uh, **Frames** in **Port Authority** or the nearby **Bowlmor Lanes.** Other options: **Iridium** for jazz, **King Cole** for class, **Caroline's** or **HA!** for comedy, or escape it all on the patio of **Bookmarks**.

Bars

- **Blue Bar** • 59 W 44th St [6th Ave]
  212-840-6800
  If you're in the mood for a Harvey Wallbanger.
- **Bookmarks** • 299 Madison Ave [E 41st St]
  212-983-4500
  Escape the Midtown ruckus at this nifty rooftop bar.
- **The Carnegie Club** • 156 W 56th St [7th Ave]
  212-957-9676
  Drink your 50-year-old cognac with your 22-year-old date.
- **Caroline's on Broadway** •
  1626 Broadway [W 50th St]
  212-757-4100
  Laughs in Times Square. A classic.
- **Emmett O'Lunney's Irish Pub** •
  210 W 50th St [Broadway]
  212-957-5100
  Above-average Irish pub popular with the after-work crowd.
- **HA! Comedy Club** • 232 W 44th St [7th Ave]
  212-789-9061
  Stop in for some great laughs and a minimum of two drinks.
- **The House of Brews** • 302 W 51st St [8th Ave]
  212-541-7080
  Fratty but friendly atmosphere, great beer selection.
- **Iridium Jazz Club** •
  1650 Broadway [W 51st St]
  212-582-2121
  Good mainstream jazz venue. Pricey.
- **Jimmy's Corner** • 140 W 44th St [Broadway]
  212-221-9510
  This cozy joint is the best bar around here, trust us.
- **King Cole Bar** • 2 E 55th St [5th Ave]
  212-339-6857
  Drink a red snapper and admire the gorgeous mural.
- **Paramount Bar** • 235 W 46th St [Broadway]
  212-827-4116
  Tiny, pretentious, unavoidable.
- **R Lounge** • 714 7th Ave [W 48th St]
  212-261-5200
  Sip cocktails with (gulp) tourists and take in the fine view.
- **Roseland Ballroom** • 239 W 52nd St [Broadway]
  212-247-0200
  Big-time rock venue.
- **Royalton Hotel** • 44 W 44th St [5th Ave]
  212-869-4400
  Phillippe Starck is the SH—!
- **Russian Vodka Room** •
  265 W 52nd St [8th Ave]
  212-307-5835
  Russian molls and cranberry vodka. Awesome.
- **Sardi's** • 234 W 44th St [7th Ave]
  212-221-8440
  Absorb the sacred DNA at the upstairs bar.
- **St. Andrews** • 140 W 46th St [6th Ave]
  212-840-8413
  Over 200 Scotches at this bar and restaurant.

Bowling

- **Bowlmor Lanes** • 222 W 44th St [Eighth Ave]
  212-680-0012
  Fifty lanes and seven themed rooms of awesome.
- **Frames** • 550 9th Ave [W 40th St]
  212-268-6909
  Bowl before you get on the bus to Bridgewater.

Movie Theaters

- **AMC Empire 25** •
  234 W 42nd St [Seventh Ave]
  212-398-2597
  Buy tickets ahead. It's Times Square.
- **MoMA** • 11 W 53rd St [Fifth Ave]
  212-708-9400
  Arty programming changes every day.
- **Paris Theatre** • 4 W 58th St [Fifth Ave]
  212-688-3800
  Art house equivalent of the Ziegfeld.
- **Ziegfeld Theatre** • 141 W 54th St [6th Ave]
  212-765-7600
  Beloved NY classic with a gigantic screen. Don't miss.

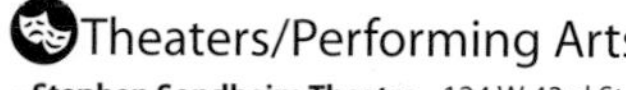

Theaters/Performing Arts

- **Stephen Sondheim Theatre** • 124 W 43rd St
  212-719-1300
  The Landmark facade still calls it Henry Miller's Theatre.

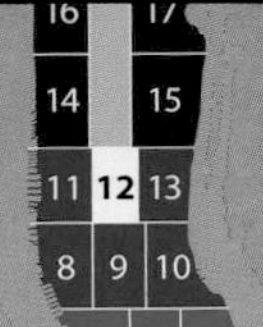

Restaurants

There's something for every taste in this area. Greasy burgers tucked inside a fancy hotel at **Burger Joint**, cheap but ah-mazing chicken parm at **Luigi's**, street food at the halal cart at **53rd & 6th**. For high-end experiences, savor the French-American fare at **The Modern**, the seafood at **Le Bernardin**, David Chang's **Ma Peche**, or the vintage charms of **21 Club**. **Stage** and **Carnegie** are two old standby delis, while **Cafe Edison** is great for lunch or pre-show dinner.

Restaurants

• **53rd & 6th Halal Cart** • 6th Ave & W 53rd St
$
Serving halal food to cabbies and devoted fans (7:30 p.m.–4 a.m.).

• **Afghan Kebab House** •
764 9th Ave [W 51st St]
212-307-1612 • $$
Great kebabs, friendly.

• **Asiate** • 80 Columbus Cir [Broadway]
212-805-8881 • $$$$$
Highest-end Japanese/French. Bring lots of Yen/Euro.

• **Breeze** • 661 9th Ave [W 46th St]
212-262-7777 • $$
Always great Thai/French fusion.

• **Burrito Box** • 885 9th Ave [W 57th St]
212-489-6889 • $
Cheap and tasty Mexican with killer guac.

• **Casellula** • 401 W 52nd St [9th Ave]
212-247-8137 • $$$
Sophisticated wine and cheese pairings.

• **Chili Thai** • 712 9th Ave [W 49th St]
212-265-5054 • $
Tiny, friendly, and delicious.

• **Churrascaria Plataforma** •
316 W 49th St [8th Ave]
212-245-0505 • $$$$
Brazilian Feast! Don't eat all day…then come here.

• **Daisy May's BBQ USA** •
623 11th Ave [W 46th St]
212-977-1500 • $$
Takeout BBQ and sides Mon–Fri. Plus, various Manhattan street carts!

• **Danji** • 346 W 52nd St [9th Ave]
212-586-2880 • $$$
Gourmet Korean small plates with a twist.

• **Don Giovanni** • 358 W 44th St [9th Ave]
212-581-4939 • $$
One of the better cheap pies in the city.

• **Eatery** • 798 9th Ave [W 53rd St]
212-765-7080 • $$
A comfort food favorite. All de-lish.

• **Empanada Mama** • 763 9th Ave [W 51st St]
212-698-9008 • $
No one fries them better.

• **Esca** • 402 W 43rd St [Ninth Ave]
212-564-7272 • $$$$$
Dave Pasternack knows fish, some of which he catches himself.

• **etcetera etcetera** • 352 W 44th St [9th Ave]
212-399-4141 • $$$$
Beautiful bar, delicious Italian food.

• **Gazala Place** • 709 9th Ave [W 48th St]
212-245-0709 • $$
Brilliant Middle Eastern food. Share an appetizer platter.

• **Gossip Bar & Restaurant** • 733 9th Ave [W 50th St]
212-265-2720 • $$
Irish fare, amazing staff, guilty-pleasure menu, awesome bar.

• **Hallo Berlin** • 626 10th Ave [W 44th St]
212-977-1944 • $$
The best wurst in the city! Check out their street cart at 54th & Fifth.

• **Hudson Common** • 356 W 58th St [9th Ave]
212-554-6217 • $$$$$
Lovely and pricey and goody.

• **Hummus Kitchen** • 768 9th Ave [W 51st St]
212-333-3009 •
Hummus so good they named a kitchen after it.

• **Joe Allen** • 326 W 46th St [8th Ave]
212-581-6464 • $$$
De rigueur stargazing, open late.

• **Marseille** • 630 9th Ave [W 44th St]
212-333-2323 • $$$$
True to the name, an expatriate's delight.

• **Meske** • 468 W 47th St [10th Ave]
212-399-1949 • $$
Friendly and consistently good Ethiopian.

• **Nizza** • 630 9th Ave [W 45th St]
212-956-1800 • $$
Share some fantastic antipasti: socca, tapenade, focaccette, and more.

• **Nook** • 746 9th Ave [W 50th St]
212-247-5500 • $$$
Delicious New American (with after-hours parties).

• **Per Se** • 10 Columbus Cir [W 58th St]
212-823-9335 • $$$$$
Divine—but you practically have to sell a kidney to afford it.

• **Pio Pio** • 604 10th Ave [W 44th St]
212-459-2929 • $$
Excellent Peruvian in great setting, especially the cebiche and chicken.

• **Pure Thai Cookhouse** • 766 9th Ave [51st St]
212-581-0999 • $$
Tasty, affordable Thai in a classy little dining room.

• **Totto Ramen** • 366 W 52nd St [9th Ave]
212-582-0052 • $$
Incredible ramen, just be prepared to line up.

• **Tout Va Bien** • 311 W 51st St [8th Ave]
212-265-0190 • $$$$
Warm, homey, pre-theater, French. NFT approved.

Bagels, Coffee, & Shopping

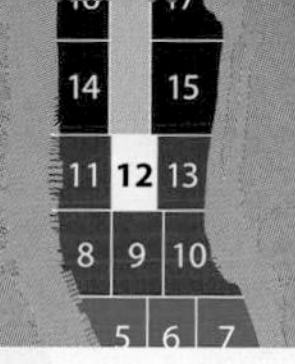

Midtown is home to one of the great world shopping districts. Legendary retailers like **Bergdorf Goodman** and **Saks Fifth Avenue** are majestic retail palaces, while numerous boutiques and flagships for individual brands jostle for position. In **Times Square**, there are several touristy chains, as well as a **Forever 21** that's open until 1 AM and comes in handy for late-night wardrobe emergencies. For unique finds, check out **MoMA Design Store** or **Muji**, and stock up on spirits at **Park Avenue Liquor** or **Oak and Steel**.

Coffee

- **Blue Bottle Coffee** •
  1 Rockefeller Center [5th Ave]
  Cult coffee that's more lab than shop.
- **Fika** • 41 W 58th St [5th Ave]
  212-832-0022
  Swedish oasis in Midtown: strong coffee and homemade pastries.
- **Zibetto** • 1385 6th Ave [W 56th St]
  A real Italian espresso bar. Un caffe, per favore!

Shopping

- **Apple Store** • 767 5th Ave [E 59th St]
  212-336-1440
  Giant glass shrine houses all things Apple.
- **Bergdorf Goodman** • 754 5th Ave [W 57th St]
  212-753-7300
  Hands down—the best windows in the business.
- **Burberry** • 9 E 57th St [5th Ave]
  212-407-7100
  Signature "beige plaid" purveyor.
- **Chanel** • 15 E 57th St [5th Ave]
  212-355-5050
  Official outfitter of "ladies who lunch."
- **Ermenegildo Zegna** • 663 5th Ave [E 57th St]
  212-421-4488
  A truly stylish and classic Italian designer.
- **Forever 21** • 1540 Broadway [W 45th St]
  212-302-0594
  Open til 1 a.m., lifesaver during late-night wardrobe emergencies.
- **Henri Bendel** • 712 5th Ave [W 56th St]
  212-247-1100
  Offbeat department store specializing in the unusual and harder-to-find.
- **Lee's Art Shop** • 220 W 57th St [Broadway]
  212-247-0110
  Excellent art store in surprising location.
- **Mets Clubhouse Shop** •
  11 W 42nd St [5th Ave]
  212-768-9534
  For Amazin' stuff!
- **MoMA Design and Book Store** •
  11 W 53rd St [5th Ave]
  212-708-9700
  Cutting-edge, minimalist, ergonomic, offbeat, and funky everything.
- **Muji Times Square** • 620 8th Ave [W 40th St]
  212-382-2300
  Like a Japanese IKEA, but cooler and without meatballs.
- **Oak and Steel Fine Wines & Spirits** •
  1776 Broadway [W 57th St]
  212-262-7702
  Excellent selection, very knowledgeable staff.
- **Park Avenue Liquor Shop** •
  292 Madison Ave [E 41st St]
  212-685-2442
  Amazing selection of scotch. Makes us wish we had more $$$.
- **Petrossian Boutique** •
  911 7th Ave [W 58th St]
  212-245-2217
  Caviar and other delectables. Bring the Gold Card.
- **Roberto's Winds** • 149 W 46th St [6th Ave]
  212-391-1315
  Saxophones, horns, clarinets, and flutes. If it blows, bring it here.
- **Saks Fifth Avenue** • 611 5th Ave [E 49th St]
  212-753-4000
  Fifth Avenue mainstay with lovely holiday windows and bathrooms.
- **Steinway & Sons** • 109 W 57th St [6th Ave]
  212-246-1100
  Cheap knockoff pianos. Just kidding.
- **The Store at Museum of Arts and Design** •
  2 Columbus Cir [8th Ave]
  212-299-7700
  Not your average museum store.
- **Tiffany & Co.** • 727 5th Ave [E 56th St]
  212-755-8000
  Grande dame of the little blue box.
- **Uniqlo** • 666 5th Ave [48th St]
  877-486-4756
  Japanese t-shirts and more t-shirts—in every color!

Map 13 • East Midtown

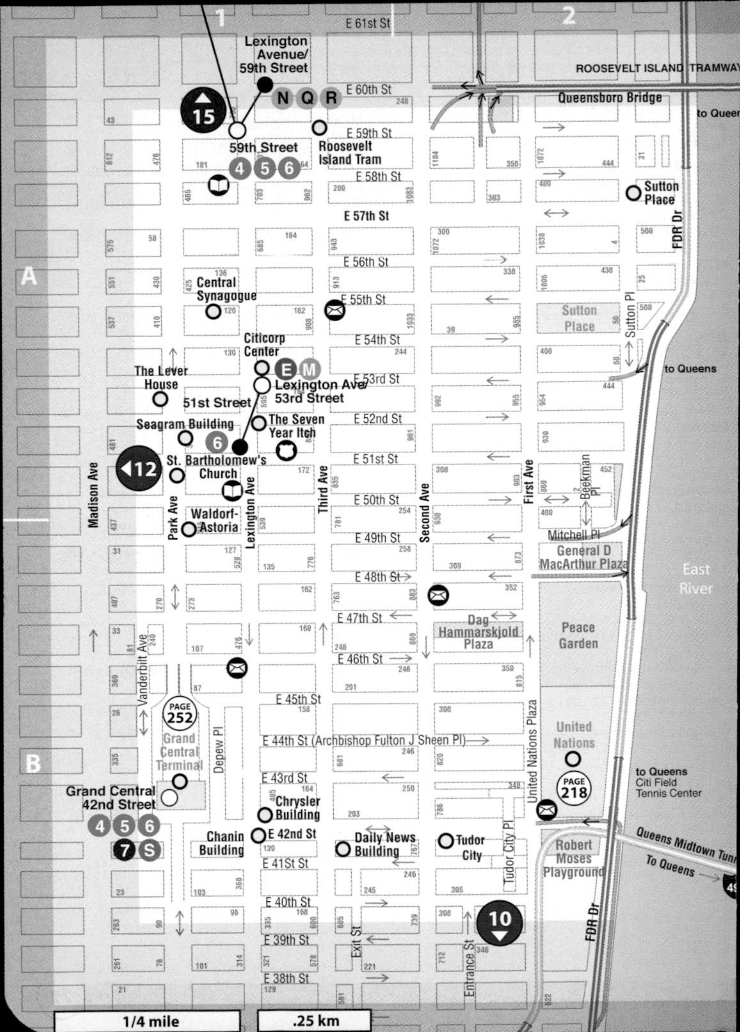

Lexington Avenue/ 59th Street
N Q R
59th Street
4 5 6
Roosevelt Island Tram
Central Synagogue
Citicorp Center
E M
Lexington Ave/ 53rd Street
The Lever House
51st Street
Seagram Building
6
The Seven Year Itch
St. Bartholomew's Church
Waldorf-Astoria
Dag Hammarskjold Plaza
Grand Central Terminal
Grand Central 42nd Street
4 5 6
7 S
Chanin Building
Chrysler Building
Daily News Building
Tudor City
Sutton Place
Mitchell Pl
General D MacArthur Plaza
Peace Garden
United Nations
Robert Moses Playground
East River
Roosevelt Island Tramway
Queensboro Bridge
to Queens
Citi Field
Tennis Center
Queens Midtown Tunnel
To Queens
FDR Dr
Madison Ave
Park Ave
Vanderbilt Ave
Lexington Ave
Third Ave
Second Ave
First Ave
United Nations Plaza
Depew Pl
Tudor City Pl
Beekman Pl
Sutton Pl
Exit St
Entrance St
E 61st St
E 60th St
E 59th St
E 58th St
E 57th St
E 56th St
E 55th St
E 54th St
E 53rd St
E 52nd St
E 51st St
E 50th St
E 49th St
E 48th St
E 47th St
E 46th St
E 45th St
E 44th St (Archbishop Fulton J Sheen Pl)
E 43rd St
E 42nd St
E 41St St
E 40th St
E 39th St
E 38th St

15
12
10
PAGE 252
PAGE 218

1/4 mile
.25 km

Neighborhood Overview

No matter how angry, late, or tired we are from dealing with the overwhelming crowds in this part of town, one glance up at Grand Central Terminal with the Chrysler Building looming in the background never fails to give us a burst of energy and a shot of civic pride. Welcome to East Midtown, which has a major personality disorder—in a good way. It's got the tranquility of elegant Sutton Place and Tudor City, the rowdy nightlife along Second Avenue, the commuter bustle of Grand Central, the international crowd around the UN, and legendary architecture bursting from every corner of this neighborhood.

The hub of this neighborhood—and arguably the city—is **Grand Central Terminal**. One of the busiest train stations in the world, this gorgeous building also houses many hidden surprises under its vaunted ceiling. Start in the main concourse where you'll see a magnificent clock above the Information booth. This spot is what New Yorkers mean when they say, "Meet me at the clock." Some of these meet ups turn into dates at the deluxe and hard-to-find cocktail lounge **Campbell Apartment**. Others wisely opt for a trip into the world of old-school New York dining at the highly recommended **Oyster Bar**. Ask to sit in the Saloon for a real treat. Shopping options abound here with lots of cool shops (books, MTA souvenirs, etc.) and the best food shopping in Midtown at **Grand Central Market**. For a real inside look, even locals enjoy the free tours on Wednesdays at 12:30 pm. Just meet at the clock.

You may have heard of a little organization called the **United Nations**. It's housed in an iconic glass building perched on the edge of the East River. We highly recommend the public tour where you get to see the General Assembly, an amazing art collection, and international diplomats scurrying about. Currently the UN headquarters is undergoing a massive $3 billion renovation. The project is estimated to be completed around the same time the UN finally ends world poverty. We can still dream, right?

Architecture nerds rave and worship at Mies van der Rohe's **Seagram Building**, argue over the value of Phillip Johnson's **Lipstick Building**, and contemplate the public art underneath **The Lever House.** One of the city's most unique places of worship is the **Central Synagogue** with vivid Moorish details. Stroll by at night for an otherworldly experience. **St. Bart's** on Park Avenue is gorgeous in a more traditional way, while the **Chrysler Building**, **Chanin Building**, and **GE Building** are worshipped for their Art Deco brilliance.

If you want a break from all the tall buildings, check out the **Seven Year Itch** subway grate where Marilyn Monroe's dress blows up for all the world to see. Head way east to walk down **Sutton Place** to see where lots of exclusive New Yorkers take up residence. Or stroll around Tudor City and marvel at the handsome Neo-Gothic apartments that diplomats and divas call home. It's a nice way to unwind and enjoy this unique urban enclave without having to drop $2.7 million on a condo.

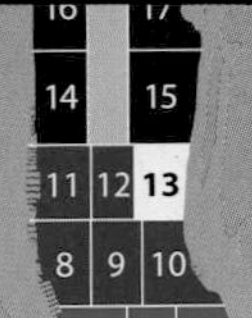

Landmarks

Landmarks

- **Chanin Building** • 122 E 42nd St [Lexington Ave]
  Not the Chrysler, but still a way-cool Art Deco masterpiece.
- **Chrysler Building** • 405 Lexington Ave [E 42nd St]
  212-682-3070
  The stuff of Art Deco dreams. Wish the Cloud Club was still there.
- **Citicorp Center** • 153 E 53rd St [Lexington Ave]
  How does it stand up?
- **Daily News Building** • 220 E 42nd St [2nd Ave]
  Great Caesar's ghost! An Art Deco gem.
- **Grand Central Terminal** • 89 E 42nd St [Park Ave]
  212-340-2583
  Another Beaux Arts masterpiece. Ceiling, staircases, tiles, clock, Oyster Bar, all great.
- **The Lever House** • 390 Park Ave [E 54th St]
  Great example of modernism, but even better, it's so fresh and so clean!
- **Lipstick Building** • 885 3rd Ave [E 53rd St]
  Philip Johnson does New York, deliriously (well).
- **Seagram Building** • 375 Park Ave [E 53rd St]
  Or, "how to be a modernist in 3 easy steps!"
- **The Seven Year Itch** • E 52nd St & Lexington Ave
  Marilyn Monroe's lucky subway grate.
- **St. Bartholomew's Church** • 325 Park Ave [E 51st St]
  212-378-0222
  Brilliant Byzantine-style church with great dome, performances, etc.
- **Sutton Place** • Sutton Pl b/n E 57th & E 59th St
  Quiet, exclusive little lane for the rich and sometimes famous.
- **Tudor City** • Tudor City Place [E 42nd St]
  3000 apartments in "American" Tudor style. Hmmmm.
- **United Nations** • 405 E 42nd St [1st Ave]
  212-963-8687
  NYC is the capital of the planet. Just sayin'.
- **Waldorf Astoria** • 301 Park Ave [E 49th St]
  212-355-3000
  Great hotel, although the public spaces aren't up to the Plaza's.

Not many budget drinking options around here (except **Blarney Stone**), so go high brow at **The Brasserie** inside The Seagram Building, **Campbell Apartment** inside Grand Central, **World Bar** inside the Trump Tower, or **Sir Harry's** inside the Waldorf. If you like to drink with the suits after work, **PJ Clarke's** is your spot.

Bars

- **Blarney Stone** • 710 3rd Ave [E 45th St]
  212-490-0457
  The only bar in purgatory.
- **Brasserie** • 100 E 53rd St [Park Ave]
  212-751-4840
  Posh drinks in hip Diller + Scofidio-designed space.
- **The Campbell Apartment** •
  15 Vanderbilt Ave [E 42nd St]
  212-953-0409
  Awesome space, awesomely snooty!
- **Le Bateau Ivre** • 230 E 51st St [2nd Ave]
  212-583-0579
  Open 'til 4 am. French wine bar.
- **Manchester Pub** • 920 2nd Ave [E 49th St]
  212-935-8901
  You could do a lot worse in this part of town.
- **Midtown 1015 Sutton Place** •
  1015 2nd Ave [E 54th St]
  212-207-3777
  Fabulous roofdeck makes it worth the climb.
- **P.J. Clarke's** • 915 3rd Ave [E 55th St]
  212-317-1616
  Old-timey midtown pub.
- **Sir Harry's** • 301 Park Ave [E 49th St]
  212-872-4890
  Nice little Art-Deco bar inside the Waldorf-Astoria. Bring $$$.
- **Sofia Wine Bar & Cafe** •
  242 E 50th St [2nd Ave]
  212-888-8660
  Italian wine bar, plus food goodies...
- **The World Bar** •
  845 United Nations Plaza [E 46th St]
  212-935-9361
  Expensive, classy hideaway for diplomats and Derek Jeter.

Movie Theaters

- **Instituto Cervantes New York** •
  211 E 49th St [Third Ave]
  212-308-7720
  Spanish gems, but call to make sure there's subtitles.

Theaters/Performing Arts

- **59E59 Theaters** • 59 E 59th St [Madison Ave]
  212-753-5959
  Primary Stages always has something interesting playing here.
- **St Bart's Playhouse** • E 50th St & Park Ave
  212-378-0248
  Manhattan's most beloved community theatre.

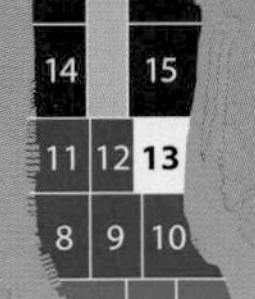

Restaurants

The Oyster Bar should be on any New Yorker's list of must eats. **Aquavit's** Scandanavian Sunday buffet brunch is as amazing as it is expensive. **Sakagura** is a great option for Japanese and sake, while **Sushi Yasada** has the best raw fish in the city. For a classic NYC burger, **PJ Clarke's** is a good bet.

Restaurants

- **21 Club** • 21 W 52nd St [5th Ave]
  212-582-7200 • $$$$
  Old, clubby New York.
- **Akdeniz** • 19 W 46th St [5th Ave]
  212-575-2307 • $$
  Turkish oasis in Midtown.
- **Blue Fin** • 1567 Broadway [W 47th St]
  212-918-1400 • $$$
  Sleek, stylish seafood & sushi spot in the W Hotel.
- **Brasserie 8 1/2** • 9 W 57th St [5th Ave]
  212-829-0812 • $$$$$
  A must for brunch. Lovely for cocktails and dinner too.
- **Burger Joint** • 119 W 56th St [6th Ave]
  212-708-7414 • $
  Fancy hotel lobby leads to unexpected burger dive. Awesome.
- **Café Edison** • 228 W 47th St [Broadway]
  212-840-5000 • $
  Theater district mainstay for Jewish soul food.
- **Cafe Zaiya** • 18 E 41st St [Madison Ave]
  212-779-0600 • $$
  Japanese food court that's cheap and fast.
- **Carnegie Deli** • 854 7th Ave [W 55th St]
  212-757-2245 • $$$
  Still good. Still really, really good.
- **Faces & Names** • 159 W 54th St [7th Ave]
  212-586-9311 • $$
  Fabulous staff, elegant vibe, superb bar and very good food.
- **Gallagher's Steak House** •
  228 W 52nd St [Broadway]
  212-245-5336 • $$$$
  Dine on fancy steak with grizzled old New Yorkers.
- **Haru** • 205 W 43rd St [7th Ave]
  212-398-9810 • $$$$
  Excellent mid-range Japanese. Loud, good.
- **Joe's Shanghai** • 24 W 56th St [5th Ave]
  212-333-3868 • $$
  Uptown version of killer dumpling factory.
- **John's Pizzeria** • 260 W 44th St [8th Ave]
  212-391-7560 • $$
  A tad touristy, but fantastic pizza and a great space.
- **La Bonne Soupe** • 48 W 55th St [5th Ave]
  212-586-7650 • $$
  Ooh la la, the best salad dressing accompanies my soupe a l'oignon.
- **Le Bernardin** • 155 W 51st St [7th Ave]
  212-554-1515 • $$$$$
  Top NYC seafood.
- **Luigi's Gourmet Pizza** •
  936 8th Ave [W 55th St]
  212-265-7159 • $$
  Best chicken parm under $20 in town.
- **Ma Peche** • 15 W 56th St [Fifth Ave]
  212-757-5878 • $$$
  Hip food in Midtown? Sir David Chang has arrived.
- **Margon** • 136 W 46th St [7th Ave]
  212-354-5013 • $
  Great Cuban sandwiches but the coffee is the real hit.
- **The Modern** • 9 W 53rd St [5th Ave]
  212-333-1220 • $$$$
  With gnocchi to die for, spend a lot and then STILL splurge on dessert.
- **Molyvos** • 871 7th Ave [W 56th St]
  212-582-7500 • $$$$
  Top Greek. Someday we'll check it out w/ your credit card.
- **The Palm Restaurant** •
  250 W 50th St [8th Ave]
  212-333-7256 • $$$$
  Upscale but friendly, everything is delicious and staff is superb.
- **Pigalle** • 790 8th Ave [W 48th St]
  212-489-2233 • $$$
  French bistro, friendly atmosphere, great food.
- **Pongsri** • 244 W 48th St [Broadway]
  212-582-3392 • $$
  Great, spicy Thai.
- **Russian Samovar** • 256 W 52nd St [8th Ave]
  212-757-0168 • $$$
  Classic Russian food and flavored vodkas.
- **The Russian Tea Room** •
  150 W 57th St [7th Ave]
  212-581-7100 • $$$$$
  Exquisite Russian dining experience & New York icon.
- **Stage Deli** • 834 7th Ave [W 54th St]
  212-245-7850 • $$
  Deliciously clogs your arteries just as well as Carnegie.
- **Thalia** • 828 8th Ave [W 50th St]
  212-399-4444 • $$$
  Chic atmosphere, excellent food.
- **Toloache** • 251 W 50th St [8th Ave]
  212-581-1818 • $$$
  Designer Mexican in Midtown.
- **Virgil's Real BBQ** • 152 W 44th St [6th Ave]
  212-921-9494 • $$$
  It's real. Hush puppies and CFS to die for.

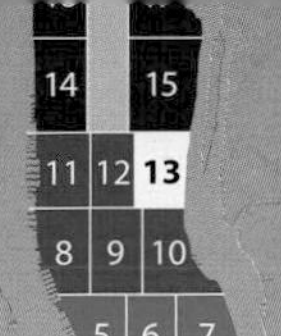

am Flax is where we stock up on art and office supplies. **The Food mporium** under bridge is actually kind of cool. **Sherry Lehmann** has a diculous selection of fancy booze you can't afford. **Jeffrey Wine** has een serving the 'hood for over 30 years. And there's a **Home Depot** in a asement on 59th Street? That's just plain weird.

Bagels

- **Ess-A-Bagel** • 831 3rd Ave [E 51st St]
  212-980-1010
  Bagels with attitude.
- **Tal Bagels** • 977 1st Ave [E 54th St]
  212-753-9080
  Pretty good. Lots of cream cheese options.

Coffee

- **Aroma Espresso Bar** • 205 E 42nd St [3rd Ave]
  212-557-1010
  The Israeli version of Starbucks comes stateside.
- **ING Direct Cafe** • 968 3rd Ave [E 58th St]
  212-752-8432
  Good coffee, inexpensive, clean and uncrowded.
- **Joe The Art of Coffee** •
  Grand Central Terminal [Park Ave]
  212-661-8580
  Located in the Graybar passage off Lexington Ave.

Shopping

- **Amish Market** • 240 E 45th St [3rd Ave]
  212-370-1761
  Lots prepared foods. Do they deliver by horse and buggy?
- **Architects & Designers Building** •
  150 E 58th St [Lexington Ave]
  212-644-2766
  Over 200,000 sq. ft. of commercial and residential furnishings. Wow.
- **Buttercup Bake Shop** •
  973 2nd Ave [E 52nd St]
  212-350-4144
  Move over Magnolia. Buttercup's all grown up.
- **Cohen & Taliaferro** •
  59 E 54th St [Madison Ave]
  212-751-8135
  Antique maps and rare travel books. Cool!
- **Crush Wine & Spirits** •
  153 E 57th St [Lexington Ave]
  212-980-9463
  Stock up on booze to survive the walk through Midtown.
- **Grand Central Market** •
  87 E 42nd St [Park Ave]
  212-878-7034
  Pick up fixings for a gourmet dinner before jumping on the train.
- **Home Depot** • 980 3rd Ave [E 59th St]
  212-888-1512
  Mega home improvement chain comes to the city.
- **Ideal Cheese** • 942 1st Avenue [E 52nd St]
  888-743-1913
  All cheese is ideal.
- **Innovative Audio Video** •
  150 E 58th St [Lexington Ave]
  212-634-4444
  Quality music systems and home theaters.
- **Jeffrey Wine & Liquors** •
  939 1st Ave [E 52nd St]
  212-753-3725
  Jeffrey will treat you right. No Midtown attitude.
- **New York Transit Museum Gallery Annex & Store** •
  Grand Central Terminal, Main Concourse
  212-878-0106
  Specialty - NYC/Transit books.
- **Nicola's Specialty Emporium** •
  997 1st Ave [E 55th St]
  212-753-9275
  Italian brothers with top Italian goods.
- **Radio Shack** • 940 3rd Ave [E 57th St]
  212-750-8409
  Kenneth, what's the frequency?
- **Sam Flax** • 900 3rd Ave [E 55th St]
  212-813-6666
  Portfolios, frames, furniture, and designer gifts.
- **Sherry-Lehmann Wine & Spirits** •
  505 Park Ave [E 59th St]
  212-838-7500
  Wines and spirits for the connaisseur.
- **Sports Authority** • 845 3rd Ave [E 51st St]
  212-355-9725
  Sporting goods for the masses.
- **Whole Foods** • 226 E 57th St [3rd Ave]
  646-497-1222
  "Whole Paycheck" but great, fresh food.
- **Yankees Clubhouse Shop** •
  110 E 59th St [Park Ave]
  212-758-7844
  Any Yankee fan's paradise.

Map 14 • Upper West Side (Lower)

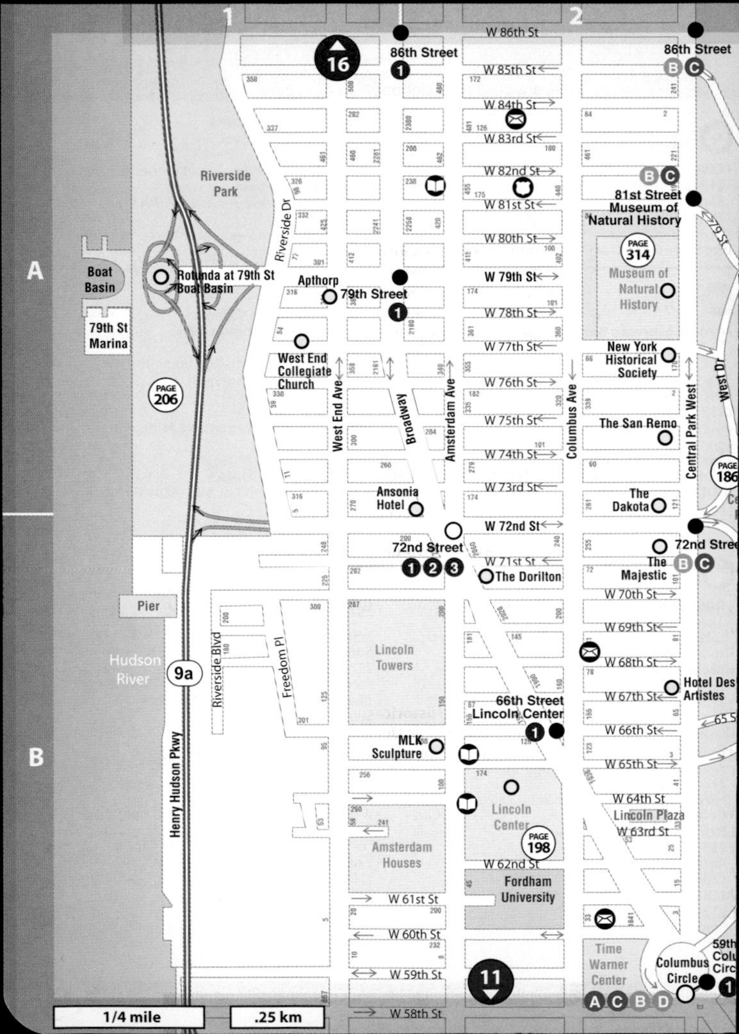

16

W 86th St
86th Street
W 85th St
W 84th St
W 83rd St
W 82nd St
W 81st St
81st Street
Museum of
Natural History
W 80th St
W 79th St
Riverside Park
Riverside Dr
Boat Basin
Rotunda at 79th St
Boat Basin
79th St
Marina
Apthorp
79th Street
PAGE
314
Museum of
Natural
History
W 78th St
W 77th St
West End
Collegiate
Church
New York
Historical
Society
PAGE
206
W 76th St
West End Ave
Broadway
Amsterdam Ave
Columbus Ave
Central Park West
West Dr
W 75th St
The San Remo
W 74th St
PAGE
186
W 73rd St
Ansonia
Hotel
The
Dakota
W 72nd St
72nd Street
72nd Street
The
Majestic
W 71st St
The Dorilton
W 70th St
Pier
W 69th St
Lincoln
Towers
W 68th St
Hudson
River
9a
Riverside Blvd
Freedom Pl
Hotel Des
Artistes
W 67th St
66th Street
Lincoln Center
W 66th St
MLK
Sculpture
W 65th St
Henry Hudson Pkwy
W 64th St
Lincoln
Center
Lincoln Plaza
W 63rd St
Amsterdam
Houses
PAGE
198
W 62nd St
Fordham
University
W 61st St
W 60th St
Time
Warner
Center
Columbus
Circle
59th
W 59th St
11
W 58th St
1/4 mile
.25 km

Neighborhood Overview

Away from the bustle of midtown and downtown Manhattan, the lower part of the Upper West Side offers a decidedly different, slower pace. But by no means does this neighborhood feel sleepy. Sandwiched between two parks, this neighborhood offers great food, museums, dive bars, and beautiful Art Deco architecture, not to mention the cultural meccas of Lincoln Center and the American Museum of Natural History, all of which remind you that New York is a livable city after all.

Many of the buildings that line the streets of the Upper West Side are landmarks. **The Ansonia** (built between 1899 and 1904) was originally a hotel and is now an exclusive apartment building. It has had many famous residents including Babe Ruth and Theodore Dreiser. **The Dakota** (built from 1880-1884) is best known for being the home of John Lennon and Yoko Ono, and the place where Lennon was killed at the entrance to the building. **The Dorilton** (built in 1902), the **Majestic** (built in 1894), and the **San Remo** (completed in 1931) all attest to bygone days of elaborate building construction.

Green space surrounds this neighborhood. To the east lies Central Park, but most locals head west to the gorgeous Riverside Park. It is filled with beautiful flower gardens, wonderful playgrounds, and some great spots to sit down and relax by the water. For those looking for something more active, a path runs along the Hudson River, perfect for jogging and biking. **The Boat Basin at 79th Street** is the only facility in the city that allows year-round residency in boats. It is also used as a launch site for kayaks, canoes, and sailboats, which you can rent in the summer. The rotunda overlooks the marina and is the site of the Boat Basin café (open April to October), a great place to unwind with a beer as the sun sets over the Hudson.

Like a city unto itself, **The American Museum of Natural History** is one of the largest museums in the world. Founded in 1869, the museum contains 25 interconnected buildings with lots of famous permanent exhibits (anthropological collections, rooms on human biology and evolution, a life-sized model blue whale, and the world's largest sapphire in the world, to name a few). Connected to the museum is the always popular **Hayden Planetarium**, part of the Rose Center for Earth and Space. It's a great spot to experience the wonders of the universe narrated by Robert Redford or Whoopi Goldberg.

Just south of AMNH is **The New-York Historical Society** which has a fabulous collection documenting the history of New York and the United States. Some highlights include many of James Audubon's watercolors, paintings from the Hudson River School, and materials from the Civil War and Reconstruction.

When Upper West Siders tire from museums, they join the rest of the city's cultural elite at **Lincoln Center**, probably the most famous arts and culture center in the world. Home of the Film Society of Lincoln Center, Jazz at Lincoln Center, the Lincoln Center Theater, the Metropolitan Opera, the City Opera, the City Ballet, and the New York Philharmonic, as well as Juilliard, the School of American Ballet, and the Library for the Performing Arts, this place is just bursting with artistic brilliance.

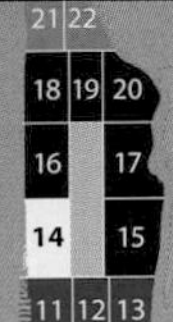

Landmarks

○ Landmarks

- **American Museum of Natural History** • Central Park W & 79th St 212-769-5100 Includes an outstanding planetarium and lots and lots of stuffed animals.
- **The Ansonia** • 2109 Broadway [W 73rd St] 212-877-9800 Truly unique residence on Broadway.
- **The Apthorp** • 2201 Broadway [W 78th St] Huge, city-block-spanning condos complete with inner courtyard.
- **The Dakota** • W 72nd St & Central Park W Classic Central Park West apartment building, designed by Henry J Hardenbergh.
- **The Dorilton** • Broadway & W 71st St Understated it ain't. But damn, it's pretty.
- **Hotel Des Artistes** • 1 W 67th St [Central Park W] $4,000,000 artist studios on CPW. Nice one.
- **Lincoln Center** • 70 Lincoln Center Plaza [W 62nd St] 212-875-5000 A rich and wonderful complex. Highly recommended—movies, theater, music, opera.
- **The Majestic** • 115 Central Park W [W 71st St] Great brick by Chanin.
- **MLK Sculpture** • 122 Amsterdam Ave [W 65th St] Massive brutalist-but-cool square monument to MLK.
- **New-York Historical Society** • 170 Central Park W [W 77th St] 212-873-3400 Oldest museum in New York City.
- **Rotunda at 79th St Boat Basin** • W 79th St [Riverside Dr] 212-496-2105 Rotunda, arcade, arches and boats.
- **The San Remo** • Central Park West & W 74th St Emery Roth's contribution to the Upper West Side skyline.
- **West End Collegiate Church** • 368 West End Ave [W 77th St] 212-787-1566 Dutch/Flemish goodness from Robert Gibson, circa 1892.

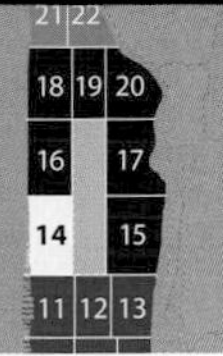

For a night of culture, go to Lincoln Center or see a concert at the **Beacon Theater**. For drunken revelries and beer pong, hit **Jake's Dilemma**. Was that out loud? We meant to say, With a selection of wine for everyone, seek out Barcibo Enoteca. Harry and Sally set up their best friends at **Cafe Luxembourg**. And speaking of which, date night happens at **Cava Wine Bar**.

Bars

- **Bln 71** • 237 Columbus Ave [W 71st St]
  212-362-5446
  Sip wine with 30-something Upper West Siders.
- **Blondies Sports Bar** •
  212 W 79th St [Amsterdam Ave]
  212-362-4360
  Want to catch a game? Any game? Come here.
- **Café Luxembourg** •
  200 W 70th St [Amsterdam Ave]
  212-873-7411
  Hey, is that Tom Hanks over there?
- **Cava Wine Bar** •
  185 W 80th St [Amsterdam Ave]
  212-724-2282
  Cozy. Can you say date night?
- **The Dead Poet** •
  450 Amsterdam Ave [W 82nd St]
  212-595-5670
  Good Irish feel. No secret society that we know of.
- **Dive 75** • 101 W 75th St [Columbus Ave]
  212-362-7518
  The quintessential dive bar with the friendliest staff around.
- **Dublin House** • 225 W 79th St [Broadway]
  212-874-9528
  Great dingy Irish pub. Recommended.
- **Fred's** • 476 Amsterdam Ave [W 83rd St]
  212-579-3076
  Sort of old-school. Sort of fun.
- **George Keeley** •
  485 Amsterdam Ave [W 83rd St]
  212-873-0251
  A rotation of good draft beers and all the sports you need.
- **Hi Life Bar & Grill** •
  477 Amsterdam Ave [W 83rd St]
  212-787-7199
  Not a bad option for this part of town.
- **Jake's Dilemma** •
  430 Amsterdam Ave [W 81st St]
  212-580-0556
  Drink beer and pretend you're still in college.
- **The Tangled Vine Wine Bar and Kitchen** •
  434 Amsterdam Ave [W 81st St]
  646-863-3896
  Have an environmentally friendly wine trio at this UWS hot spot.
- **Wine and Roses** •
  286 Columbus Ave [W 74th St]
  212-579-9463
  A wine-o's paradise. Not as sappy as it sounds.

Movie Theaters

- **AMC Loews Lincoln Square 13** •
  1998 Broadway [W 68th St]
  212-336-5020
  Classy Upper West Side multiplex with IMAX.
- **Jewish Community Center in Manhattan** •
  334 Amsterdam Ave [W 77th St]
  646-505-4444
  Jewish premieres, previews, and festivals.
- **Lincoln Plaza Cinemas** •
  1886 Broadway [W 63rd St]
  212-757-2280
  Uptown version of the Angelika.
- **Walter Reade Theater** •
  144 W 65th St [Broadway]
  212-875-5456
  Amazing festivals and rare screenings.

Theaters/Performing Arts

- **Alice Tully Hall** • Broadway & 65th St
  212-875-5050
  Lincoln Center's house for chamber music and small ensembles.
- **ArcLight Theatre** •
  152 W 71st St [Amsterdam Ave]
  212-595-0355
  A classic church basement theatre.
- **Beacon Theater** • 2124 Broadway [W 74th St]
  212-465-6500
  Former movie palace with beautiful neo-Grecian interior.
- **Mitzi E Newhouse Theater** •
  Amsterdam Ave & W 65th St
  212-239-6200
  Lincoln Center's Off-Broadway space.

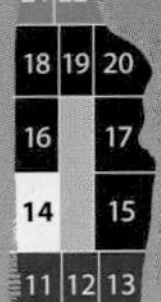

Restaurants

Trendy chefs galore have made their reappearance in the Upper West Side over the last few years. For Daniel Boulud's take on seasonal French cuisine, check out **Bar Boulud** and its charcuterie bar. Or take a walk to **Telepan** where Bill **Telepan** serves up rock-steady seasonal tasting menus and great cocktails. But if breaking the bank isn't in the agenda, check out **Kefi** for the best Greek food around. Meanwhile, sushi snobs don't even have to leave the neighborhood with **Gari** close by.

Restaurants

- **'cesca** • 164 W 75th St [Amsterdam Ave]
  212-787-6300 • $$$$
  Sunday Sauce worthy of a cameo in *Goodfellas*.
- **Ali Baba** • 515 Amsterdam Ave [W 85th St]
  212-787-6008 • $
  Yemenite-Israeli chef brings twist to Kosher takeout.
- **Artie's Delicatessen** •
  2290 Broadway [W 83rd St]
  212-579-5959 • $$
  Hot pastrami on rye never goes out of style.
- **Bar Boulud** • 1900 Broadway [W 63rd St]
  212-595-0303 • $$$
  Before the opera, stop in for the fabulous charcuterie plate.
- **Barcibo Enoteca** • 2020 Broadway [W 69th St]
  212-595-2805 • $$$
  An incredible wine list for the post Lincoln Center crowd.
- **Bello Giardino** • 71 W 71st St [Columbus Ave]
  212-875-1512 • $$
  Check out the back patio and enjoy some Italian fare.
- **Bettola** • 412 Amsterdam Ave [W 80th St]
  212-787-1660 • $$
  Try the wood-fired pizza at this authentic Italian restaurant.
- **Big Nick's Burger & Pizza Joint** •
  2175 Broadway [W 77th St]
  212-362-9238 • $$
  Death by burger. Recommended.
- **Café Luxembourg** •
  200 W 70th St [Amsterdam Ave]
  212-873-7411 • $$$$$
  Top-end bistro. Anyone know what Luxembourgian cuisine is?
- **Celeste** • 502 Amsterdam Ave [W 84th St]
  212-874-4559 • $$
  Cheap and tasty homemade pastas. A true gem.
- **Cocina Economica Mexico** •
  452 Amsterdam Ave [W 82nd]
  212-501-7755 • $$
  Nuevo Mexican in a cute space for only a few pesos.
- **Firehouse Tavern** •
  522 Columbus Ave [W 85th St]
  212-787-3473 • $$
  Where to go for after-softball wings.
- **Freddie & Pepper's Pizza** •
  303 Amsterdam Ave [W 74th St]
  212-799-2378 • $
  Thin crust pizza. Has been around forever.
- **French Roast** • 2340 Broadway [W 85th St]
  212-799-1533 • $$
  Open 24 hours. Good croque-monsieur.
- **Gari** • 370 Columbus Ave [W 78th St]
  212-362-4816 • $$$$$
  Why UWS sushi snobs no longer have to take the cross-town bus.
- **Gray's Papaya** • 2090 Broadway [W 71st St]
  212-799-0243 • $
  Open 24 hours. An institution.
- **Jacob's Pickles** • 509 Amsterdam Ave [84th St]
  212-470-5566 • $$
  Upmarket Southern-style menu and booze, and yes, plenty of pickles.
- **Kefi** • 505 Columbus Ave [W 84th St]
  212-873-0200 • $$
  Greek food gets an upgrade at this amazingly affordable gem.
- **La Caridad 78** • 2199 Broadway [W 78th St]
  212-874-2780 • $$
  Cheap Cuban paradise.
- **Monaco** • 421 Amsterdam Ave [W 80th St]
  212-873-3100 • $$
  Cute bistro. Outdoor tables in the summer.
- **Nanoosh** • 2012 Broadway [W 69th St]
  212-362-7922 • $
  Cheap, fast Middle-Eastern food. Good for before the movies.
- **Nice Matin** • 201 W 79th St [Amsterdam Ave]
  212-873-6423 • $$$
  Traditional French food staple with outdoor seating.
- **Nougatine** • 1 Central Park W [Columbus Cir]
  212-299-3900 • $$$$$
  Brilliant $24.07 prix fixe lunch!
- **Rosa Mexicano** •
  61 Columbus Ave [W 62nd St]
  212-977-7700 • $$$$
  Inventive Mexican. Great guac.
- **Salumeria Rosi Parmacotto** •
  283 Amsterdam Ave [W 73rd St]
  212-877-4801 • $$
  Eatery doubles as excellent salami shop. Beware of '80s glam interior.
- **Shake Shack** • 366 Columbus Ave [W 77th St]
  646-747-8770 • $$
  Now you can get your Shack Burger year round.
- **Telepan** • 72 W 69th St [Columbus Ave]
  212-580-4300 • $$$$$
  Bill Telepan's seasonal menus never disappoint.

Bagels, Coffee, & Shopping

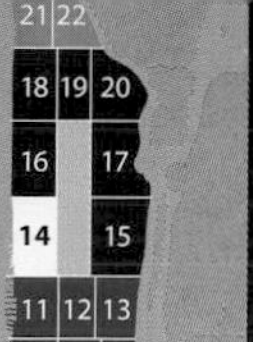

ew York's prime food shopping can be found in this neighborhood. abar's (cheeses, fish, coffee, free samples) and **Fairway** (fresh produce, reads, dry goods, total chaos) are within blocks of each other. To pair some ine with that fine food, we like **67 Wine & Spirits.** And everyone can find omething to wear at the uptown outpost of **Century 21**.

Coffee

- **Aroma Espresso Bar** • 161 W 72nd St [Amsterdam Ave] 212-595-7700 The Israeli version of Starbucks comes stateside.
- **Joe The Art of Coffee** • 514 Columbus Ave [W 85th St] 212-875-0100 Joe really knows his Joe.
- **Le Pain Quotidien** • 60 W 65th St [Lincoln Sq] 212-721-4001 Excellent coffee and pastries. Thanks Belgium.

Shopping

- **67 Wine** • 179 Columbus Ave [W 68th St] 212-724-6767 Top-notch selection and helpful staff. Lots of tastings.
- **Century 21** • 1972 Broadway [66th St] 212-518-2121 Where most New Yorkers buy their underwear.
- **Fairway Market** • 2127 Broadway [W 74th St] 212-595-1888 Top-notch supermarket, but always packed.
- **Gracious Home** • 1992 Broadway [W 68th St] 212-231-7800 A side of hardware with your fancy housewares.
- **Grandaisy Bakery** • 176 W 72nd St [Amsterdam Ave] 212-334-9435 Uptown outpost of famous Sullivan Street location.
- **Jonathan Adler** • 304 Columbus Ave [W 74th St] 212-787-0017 Funky, fun housewares.
- **Laytner's Linen & Home** • 2276 Broadway [W 82nd St] 212-724-0180 Things that'll make you want to stay home more.
- **Nancy's Wines** • 313 Columbus Ave [W 75th St] 212-877-4040 Nancy will help you plan your next tasting party.
- **Patagonia** • 426 Columbus Ave [W 81st St] 917-441-0011 Eco-conscious store selling fleece for your adventurous subway ride.
- **Pookie & Sebastian** • 322 Columbus Ave [W 75th St] 212-580-5844 Flirty tops, girly dresses, and fly jeans—for UWS chicks.
- **Tani** • 2020 Broadway [W 69th St] 212-873-4361 Excellent selection of men's and women's shoes.
- **Town Shop** • 2273 Broadway [W 82nd St] 212-787-2762 Where experts will fit you for the perfect bra.
- **Western Beef** • 75 West End Ave [W 63rd St] 212-459-2800 If you don't have time for Fairway and Zabar's.
- **Westsider Records** • 233 W 72nd St [Broadway] 212-874-1588 Cool record store. You'll find some interesting stuff.
- **The Yarn Company** • 2274 Broadway [W 82nd St] 212-787-7878 The nitty gritty for knitters in the city.
- **Zabar's** • 2245 Broadway [W 80th St] 212-787-2000 Manhattan supermarket legend. NFT's favorite.

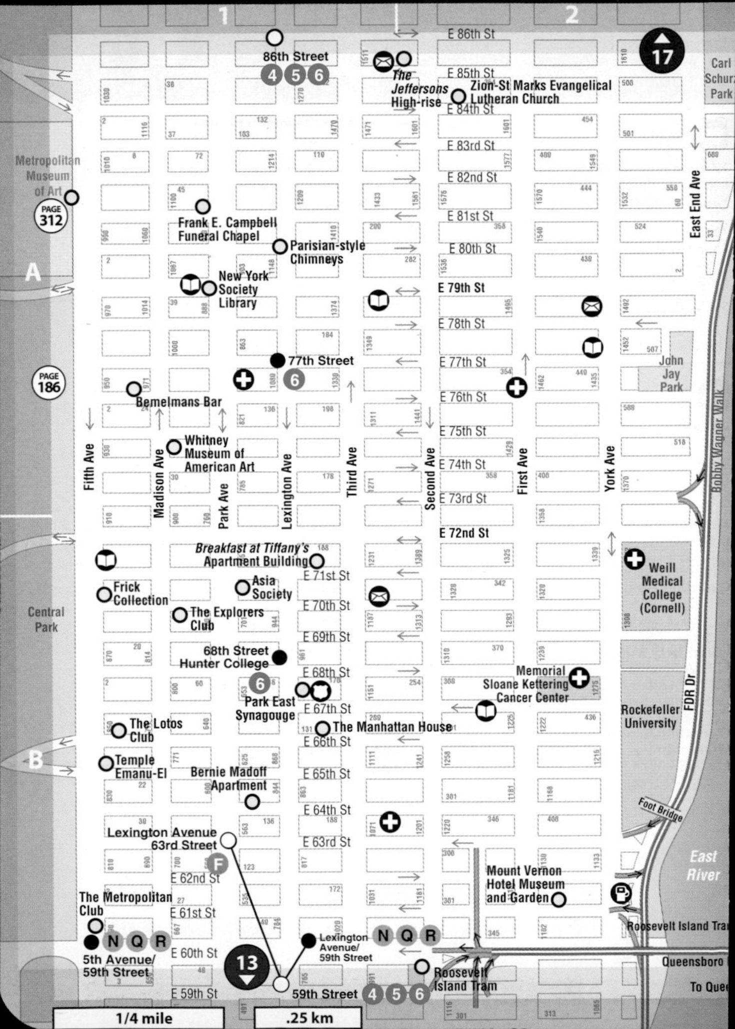

86th Street
4 5 6
The Jeffersons High-rise
Zion-St Marks Evangelical Lutheran Church
Carl Schurz Park
17
Metropolitan Museum of Art
PAGE 312
Frank E. Campbell Funeral Chapel
Parisian-style Chimneys
New York Society Library
77th Street
6
PAGE 186
Bemelmans Bar
Whitney Museum of American Art
John Jay Park
Bobby Wagner Walk
East End Ave
Fifth Ave
Madison Ave
Park Ave
Lexington Ave
Third Ave
Second Ave
First Ave
York Ave
E 86th St
E 85th St
E 84th St
E 83rd St
E 82nd St
E 81st St
E 80th St
E 79th St
E 78th St
E 77th St
E 76th St
E 75th St
E 74th St
E 73rd St
E 72nd St
E 71st St
E 70th St
E 69th St
E 68th St
E 67th St
E 66th St
E 65th St
E 64th St
E 63rd St
E 62nd St
E 61st St
E 60th St
E 59th St
Breakfast at Tiffany's Apartment Building
Weill Medical College (Cornell)
Frick Collection
Asia Society
Central Park
The Explorers Club
68th Street Hunter College
Memorial Sloane Kettering Cancer Center
Park East Synagouge
The Manhattan House
Rockefeller University
FDR Dr
The Lotos Club
Temple Emanu-El
Bernie Madoff Apartment
Foot Bridge
Lexington Avenue 63rd Street
F
East River
Mount Vernon Hotel Museum and Garden
The Metropolitan Club
Roosevelt Island Tram
N Q R
5th Avenue/ 59th Street
13
Lexington Avenue/ 59th Street
Queensboro
To Quee
Roosevelt Island Tram
59th Street
1/4 mile
.25 km

Neighborhood Overview

21 22
18 19 20
16 17
14 15
11 12 13

If you ever saw the TV show Gossip Girl, you know the reputation of the Upper East Side: Snooty, fancy and rich. While this historical neighborhood is home to some of the oldest wealth in New York, it's home to a lot more than you see on the CW: On the weekends, especially in the warm days, check out everyone in their flip flops and sunglasses (designer please) heading to the most green space in Manhattan, Central Park. If you're not sunbathing or throwing a Frisbee, check out some of the most famous museums in the world, lively restaurants, shopping and brunch—oh you must be a lady/gentleman who brunches if you wander up here. Old or young, this neighborhood is changing—and especially in the summer, sans a trip to the Hamptons, there is no better place to be.

Long before **Bernie Madoff** made this neighborhood infamous, the fabulously wealthy started settling into the Upper East Side over a century ago. As a result, there are beautiful high rises up and down Park Avenue. Fifth Avenue is the home of what was dubbed "Millionaires Row" at the turn of the 19th century—the Carnegies, the Vanderbilts, the Astors, and their friends all walked the streets lined with glorious mansions, now known as Museum Mile. For a different sort of landmark head up to 85th for **The Jeffersons High Rise**...you know, that dee-luxe apartment in the sky from the classic TV show. Or walk by where Holly Golightly frolicked at the **Breakfast at Tiffany's Apartment**.

There are many historical sites to check out in one of the most historic districts in New York. Check out the **New York Society Library**, which moved to its current location on 79th Street from University Place in 1937. **Temple Emanu-El** on 65th Street is one of the oldest temples in New York City—it was founded as a result of the second wave of immigration of Jews to America. Established in 1845, the reform congregation moved to its current location in 1927, where it welcomes Jews whose families have been going for generations and those who just moved to the city.

Want to stop and see a couple of exhibits? How about some of the most famous museums in the world. **The Frick Collection**, housed in the 1914 mansion of industrialist Henry Clark Frick, includes works by Rembrant, Degas, Goya, and many more of the art world's best-known names. (Visitor's tip: "Pay what you wish" admission every Sunday between 11 am and 1 pm.) **The Whitney Museum** is a smaller and edgier house of contemporary American art. For a look into the art of worlds past, head over to **The Met** which houses over two million pieces and can take days to see it all. One last stop? **The Asia Society and** Museum**, which houses an impressive art collection and performing arts program.**

If you love classic New York entertainment (and have a giant wad of cash), this your neighborhood. Step inside the Carlye Hotel to find **Bemelmans Bar**, named for the Austrian-born artist who created Madeline children's books. It's a lovely place to stop for a drink and hear some piano during happy hour. Right next door is **Café Carlye** which attracts stars like Judy Collins, Elaine Strich, and Woody Allen on clarinet.

Landmarks

Landmarks

- **Asia Society** • 725 Park Ave [E 70th St]
212-288-6400
Small-scale modernism.
- **Bemelmans Bar** • 35 E 76th St [Madison Ave]
212-744-1600
Features lovely mural by creator of Madeline books, Ludwig Bemelmans.
- **Bernie Madoff Apartment** •
133 E 64th St [Park Ave]
Madoff lived here, before he went to The Big House.
- **Breakfast at Tiffany's Apartment** •
169 E 71st St [Lexington Ave]
Where Holly Golightly and "Fred" lived in *Breakfast at Tiffany's*.
- **The Explorers Club** • 46 E 70th St [Park Ave]
212-628-8383
Indiana Joneses of the world hang out here. Some events open to the public.
- **Frank E. Campbell Funeral Chapel** •
1076 Madison Ave [E 81st St]
212-288-3500
Undertaker to the famously deceased like Lennon and Joan Crawford.
- **The Frick Collection** • 1 E 70th St [5th Ave]
212-288-0700
Lots of furniture.
- **The Jeffersons High-Rise** •
185 E 85th St [3rd Ave]
We're movin' on up to a dee-luxe apartment in the sky-hi.
- **The Lotos Club** • 5 E 66th St [5th Ave]
212-737-7100
Twain loved this private literary club. NFT is still waiting for an invite.
- **The Manhattan House** •
200 E 66th St [3rd Ave]
Seminal UES "white-brick" building.
- **Metropolitan Club of New York** •
1 E 60th St [5th Ave]
212-838-7400
1894 millionaire's clubhouse built by McKim, Mead & White.
- **Metropolitan Museum of Art** •
1000 5th Ave [E 81st St]
212-535-7710
The mother of all art musuems. Check out: temple, roof garden, Clyfford Still room, baseball cards.
- **Mount Vernon Hotel Museum and Garden** •
421 E 61st St [1st Ave]
212-838-6878
Nice old building.
- **New York Society Library** •
53 E 79th St [Madison Ave]
212-288-6900
A subscription library that predates the public library (1754!).
- **Parisian-Style Chimneys** •
E 80th St & Park Ave
A touch of Paris on the UES.
- **Park East Synagogue** •
163 E 67th St [3rd Ave]
212-737-6900
1890 Moorish-Jewish asymmetrical brilliance from Schneider & Herter.
- **Roosevelt Island Tram** • E 59th St & 2nd Ave
As featured in *Spider Man*.
- **Whitney Museum of American Art** •
945 Madison Ave [E 75th St]
212-570-3600
Always has something to talk about, like the controversial Biennial.
- **Zion-St Mark's Evangelical Lutheran Church** •
339 E 84th St [2nd Ave]
212-288-0600
Last "Germantown" church (see the General Slocum memorials inside).

or a down and out dive (translation: our kind of bar) ride the **Subway Inn** r go old country Irish whiskey tasting at **Donohues.** For a little more ass grab the perfect glass of wine at **Uva**. For even more class, no old oney Upper East Side evening is complete without a visit to **emelman's Bar**.

Bars

- **American Trash** • 1471 1st Ave [E 77th St]
212-988-9008
Punk rockin' I-Bankers unite.
- **Bailey's Corner Pub** •
1607 York Ave [E 85th St]
212-650-1341
Friendly Irish local. Watch the game or play darts.
- **Bar Seine** • 37 E 64th St [Madison Ave]
212-734-9100
Check into this classy hotel bar for rest, relaxation and cocktails
- **Bemelmans Bar** • 35 E 76th St [Madison Ave]
212-744-1600
When NFT actually has money, we drink here. Classic UES vibe.
- **Brandy's Piano Bar** • 235 E 84th St [3rd Ave]
212-744-4949
Good ol' rollicking time.
- **Café Carlyle** • 35 E 76th St [Madison Ave]
212-744-1600
Classic cabaret venue where Woody plays. Hellishly expensive.
- **Caledonia Scottish Pub** •
1609 2nd Ave [83rd St]
212-879-0402
Put on your kilt to sip Scotch and nibble on haggis.
- **Donohue's Steak House** •
845 Lexington Ave [E 64th St]
212-744-0938
Old-school Irish. Sit at the bar and drink whiskey.
- **Finnegan's Wake** • 1361 1st Ave [E 73rd St]
212-737-3664
Standard Irish pub. Therefore, pretty good.
- **Iggy's** • 1452 2nd Ave [E 75th St]
212-327-3043
Super-friendly bartenders help cue up the cheesy karaoke action.
- **Jones Wood Foundry** • 401 E 76th St [1st Ave]
212-249-2700
Chill with the European expats and cheer on their favorite 'football' squads
- **Lexington Bar & Books** • 1020 Lexington Ave [E 73rd St]
212-717-3902
Proper attire required but James Bond films available upon request.
- **The Library at Loew's Regency** •
540 Park Ave [E 61st St]
212-339-4050
Signature cocktails and desserts in an upscale hotel lounge.
- **O'Flanagan's** • 1215 1st Ave [E 66th St]
212-439-0660
Unpretentious bar where recent grads and college kids mix peacefully.
- **Phoenix Park** • 206 E 67th St [3rd Ave]
212-717-8181
Chill place to watch the Yankees or eat some burgers.
- **Ryan's Daughter** • 350 E 85th St [2nd Ave]
212-628-2613
Free chips!
- **The Stumble Inn** • 1454 2nd Ave [E 76th St]
212-650-0561
Thanks to the amazing specials, expect to stumble out.
- **Subway Inn** • 143 E 60th St [Lexington Ave]
212-223-8929
Sad, bad, glare, worn-out, ugh. Totally great.
- **Trinity Pub** • 299 E 84th St [2nd Ave]
212-327-4450
Low on the UES meathead scale. Thank goodness!
- **Uva** • 1486 2nd Ave [E 77th St]
212-472-4552 • $
Come for the wine list, food optional.

Movie Theaters

- **Beekman Theatre** • 1271 2nd Ave [E 67th St]
212-585-4141
Another good choice owned by the folks behind the Paris.

Theaters/Performing Arts

- **Sylvia and Danny Kaye Playhouse** • 695 Park Ave [E 69th St]
212-772-5207
Guess which one slept with Laurence Olivier.
- **Theater Ten Ten** • 1010 Park Ave [E 85th St]
212-288-3246
Good resident company puts on musicals and plays.

Restaurants

The burger at **JG Melon** is one of the best reasons to go above 14th Street. Wallet-friendly Mexican from the counter at **Cascabel** is pretty awesome or for an old-time UES Mexican fare favorite, try **Cilantro**. Get your seafood any way you like it at **Atlantic Grill** or grab a lobster roll from the Upper East Side's branch of **Luke's Lobster**. after all that you need a giant sundae and a candy fix, try **Dylan's Candy Bar**, a magical wonderland created by Ralph Lauren's daughter, Dylan, for the sugar-high of a lifetime.

Restaurants

- **Agora Turkish** • 301 East 80th St [2nd Ave]
  212-288-5444 • $$
  BYOY family-run Turkish with big flavors and a small price.
- **Alice's Tea Cup Chapter II** •
  156 E 64th St [Lexington Ave]
  212-486-9200 • $$
  Eat brunch or take tea in a fairy tale setting.
- **Andre's Cafe** • 1631 2nd Ave [E 85th St]
  212-327-1105 • $$
  Low-key Hungarian savories (goulash) and sweets (strudel).
- **Atlantic Grill** • 1341 3rd Ave [E 77th St]
  212-988-9200 • $$$$$
  Seafood galore. Old money loves this place.
- **Beyoglu** • 1431 3rd Ave [E 81st St]
  212-650-0850 • $$$
  Make a meal out of meze.
- **Bistro Chat Noir** • 22 E 66th St [Madison Ave]
  212-794-2428 • $$$$
  Flavorful and quaint. Prices aren't too shabby for Madison Ave.
- **Café Boulud** • 20 E 76th St [Madison Ave]
  212-772-2600 • $$$$$
  Elegant, slightly more relaxed sibling of Daniel.
- **Café Mingala** • 1393 2nd Ave [E 73rd St]
  212-744-8008 • $
  Burmese. $5.50 lunch special!
- **Candle Café** • 1307 3rd Ave [E 75th St]
  212-472-0970 • $$$
  Delicious vegetarian café ironically next door to Le Steak.
- **Cascabel Taqueria** • 1538 2nd Ave [E 80th St]
  212-717-8226 • $
  Great Mexican food at Taco Bell prices.
- **Cilantro** • 1321 1st Ave [E 71st St]
  212-537-4040 • $$$
  Where transplanted Texans satiate cravings for Southwestern fare.
- **Donguri** • 309 E 83rd St [2nd Ave]
  212-737-5656 • $$$$$
  Transcendent, UES Japanese standout.
- **EAT** • 1064 Madison Ave [E 81st St]
  212-772-0022 • $$$
  Great brunch spot—part of the Eli Zabar empire.
- **Elio's** • 1621 2nd Ave [E 84th St]
  212-772-2242 • $$$$$
  UES Italian where schmoozing with the "who's-who" goes down.
- **Farinella** • 1132 Lexington Ave [E 79th St]
  212-327-2702 • $$
  4-ft long pizzas and fresh panini. Napoli-style service.
- **Flex Mussels** • 174 E 82nd St [3rd Ave]
  212-717-7772 • $$$
  23 flavors—try the Abbey or Spaniard.
- **Heidelberg** • 1648 2nd Ave [E 86th St]
  212-628-2332 • $$$$
  Dirndls and lederhosen serving colossal beers and sausage platters.
- **Indian Tandoor Oven** •
  175 E 83rd St [3rd Ave]
  212-628-3000 • $$
  Delectable Indian specialties in cozy, color-draped surroundings.
- **Jacques Brasserie** • 204 E 85th St [3rd Ave]
  212-327-2272 • $$$$
  UES spot for tasty moules frites and Stella on tap.
- **JG Melon** • 1291 3rd Ave [E 73rd St]
  212-650-1310 • $$
  Top NYC burgers. Always crowded. Open 'till 2:30 a.m.
- **Le Veau d'Or** • 129 E 60th St [Lexington Ave]
  212-838-8133 • $$$
  Classic Parisian bistro with a $20 prix fixe.
- **Lexington Candy Shop** •
  1226 Lexington Ave [E 83rd St]
  212-288-0057 • $
  Charming old-timey soda shop with twirly stools.
- **Luke's Lobster** • 242 E 81st St [2nd Ave]
  212-249-4241 • $$
  Fresh-from-the sea lobster rolls, without sticker shock.
- **Malaga** • 406 E 73rd St [1st Ave]
  212-737-7659 • $$$
  Sleeper Spanish joint dishing up terrific tapas and swell sangria.
- **Neil's Coffee Shop** •
  961 Lexington Ave [E 70th St]
  212-628-7474 • $$
  Friendly diner for Hunter students and old timers.
- **Pastrami Queen** •
  1125 Lexington Ave [E 78th St]
  212-734-1500 • $$
  Meats worthy of their royal names.
- **Poke** • 343 E 85th St [2nd Ave]
  212-249-0569 • $$
  Good sushi. BYO Sake.

Bagels, Coffee, & Shopping

an't afford $600 socks on Madison Avenue? Check out **Housing Works Thrift** **hop** or **BIS Designer Resale** for clothes handed down from Park Avenue. lthough pricey, **Eli's** is one of the best places to buy food in the city, and **airway** is another great option for UES victuals. For unique wine breads try **rwasher's** and for all your fastening needs, hit up **Tender Buttons**.

Bagels

- **Bagelworks** • 1229 1st Ave [E 67th St]
  212-744-6444
  Truly excellent.
- **H&H Midtown Bagel East** •
  1551 2nd Ave [E 81st St]
  212-717-7312
  Hot & Heavenly.

Coffee

- **Joe The Art Of Coffee** •
  1045 Lexington Ave [75th St]
  212-988-2500
  Joe really knows his joe.
- **Via Quadronno** • 25 E 73rd St [Madison Ave]
  212-650-9880
  Straight up Italian espresso from Milan.

Shopping

- **Barneys New York** •
  660 Madison Ave [E 61st St]
  212-826-8900
  Museum-quality fashion (with prices to match). Recommended.
- **Bis Designer Resale** •
  1134 Madison Ave [E 84th St]
  212-396-2760
  Where you can actually afford Gucci and Prada.
- **Bloomingdale's** • 1000 3rd Ave [E 60th St]
  212-705-2000
  Where your mother disappears when she's in town.
- **Butterfield Market** •
  1114 Lexington Ave [E 78th St]
  212-288-7800
  UES gourmet grocer circa 1915.
- **Cheese on 62nd** •
  134 E 62nd St [Lexington Ave]
  212-980-5544
  For your next marvelous cocktail party.
- **Crawford Doyle Booksellers** •
  1082 Madison Ave [E 82nd St]
  212-288-6300
  Lovely place to browse and find a classic.
- **Dylan's Candy Bar** • 1011 3rd Ave [E 60th St]
  646-735-0078
  Keeping NYC pediatric dentists in business since 2001.
- **Eli's Manhattan** • 1411 3rd Ave [E 80th St]
  212-717-8100
  Blissful gourmet shopping experience. Just bring $$$.
- **Fairway** • 240 E 86th St [2nd Ave]
  212-327-2008
  So big. So good. So New York.
- **Gagosian Shop** • 988 Madison Ave [E 77th St]
  212-744-9200
  Top quality (and expensive) art & books. Think Damien Hirst and Jeff Koons originals.
- **Housing Works Thrift Shop** •
  202 E 77th St [3rd Ave]
  212-772-8461
  Our favorite thrift store.
- **In Vino Veritas** • 1375 1st Ave [E 73rd St]
  212-288-0100
  These bros know their wine.
- **Maison Kayser** • 1294 3rd Ave [E 74th St]
  212-744-3100
  Spectacular baguettes straight from a Paris legend.
- **Orwashers** • 308 E 78th St [2nd Ave]
  212-288-6569
  Handmade wine breads. Best challah on the east side.
- **Ottomanelli Butcher Shoppe** •
  1549 York Ave [E 82nd St]
  212-772-7900
  Old-school butcher still going strong.
- **Park East Kosher** • 1623 2nd Ave [E 84th St]
  212-737-9800
  Meats and smoked fish. It's all good, and it's all kosher.
- **Tender Buttons** •
  143 E 62nd St [Lexington Ave]
  212-758-7004
  Antique, rare, and unusual buttons.
- **Two Little Red Hens** •
  1652 2nd Ave [E 86th St]
  212-452-0476
  Lovely cases of cakes and pies flanked by kitschy hen memorabilia.
- **Venture Stationers** •
  1156 Madison Ave [E 85th St]
  212-288-7235
  Great neighborhood stationers. Do people still use paper?

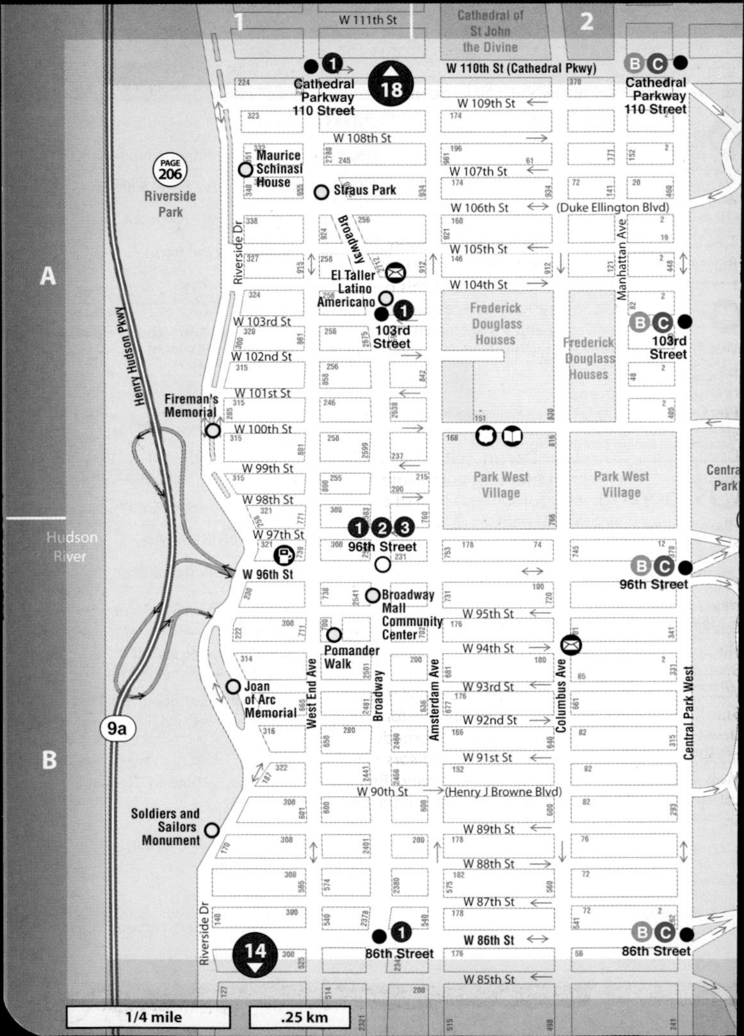

W 111th St
Cathedral of St John the Divine
W 110th St (Cathedral Pkwy)
Cathedral Parkway 110 Street
W 109th St
W 108th St
Maurice Schinasi House
W 107th St
Straus Park
W 106th St (Duke Ellington Blvd)
Broadway
W 105th St
Riverside Dr
El Taller Latino Americano
W 104th St
Frederick Douglass Houses
W 103rd St
103rd Street
W 102nd St
W 101st St
Fireman's Memorial
W 100th St
Park West Village
W 99th St
W 98th St
W 97th St
96th Street
W 96th St
Broadway Mall Community Center
W 95th St
W 94th St
Pomander Walk
W 93rd St
Joan of Arc Memorial
W 92nd St
W 91st St
W 90th St (Henry J Browne Blvd)
W 89th St
Soldiers and Sailors Monument
W 88th St
W 87th St
W 86th St
86th Street
W 85th St
Riverside Park
Henry Hudson Pkwy
Hudson River
Manhattan Ave
West End Ave
Amsterdam Ave
Columbus Ave
Central Park West
Central Park
9a
18
14
A
B
1
2
1/4 mile
.25 km

PAGE 206

Neighborhood Overview

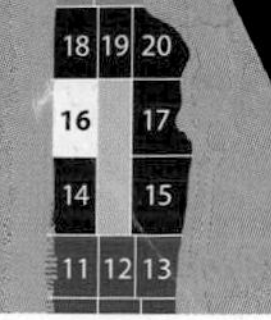

Close to Columbia University, this neighborhood is home to much of New York's liberal intelligentsia. It is not uncommon to overhear discussions about the fate of health care reform or the latest Phillip Roth novel at the dog run, or on line for coffee at a neighborhood bakery. But the neighborhood is far from snobby. Mixed in with the college professors, theater directors, doctors, and lawyers are many families with young children, and twenty-somethings, all of whom enjoy the slower pace of life and physical beauty of Manhattan's Upper West Side.

This neighborhood is one of the greenest spaces in New York. Situated between Riverside and Central Park, there are many places to run, bike, or sit in the shade of a tree. There are few tourist attractions in this part of Central Park, but the natural beauty of the park and its recreational spaces are abundant. You can enter the reservoir from this end of the park, and enjoy a scenic view while running 1.6 miles around a dirt path. Walking west from Central Park to Riverside Park, peek into **Pomander Walk**, a tiny, pedestrian-only street of tiny houses. In Riverside Park, take the time to explore the many famous monuments. After 9/11, neighborhood residents gathered at the **Fireman's Memorial** to commemorate those that were lost. The statue of **Joan of Arc** sits within an island on Riverside Drive that is maintained by neighborhood residents. Dedicated on Memorial Day in 1902 and modeled after a Corinthian temple, the **Soldiers and Sailors Monument** commemorates those who served during the Civil War. If you're just looking for someplace to sit and read, **Straus Park**, a small green island between West End and Broadway, offers a quiet place to rest amid the bustle of the street.

For a neighborhood so far from the bustling theater hub of Times Square and museum mile, the Upper West Side offers its fair share of cultural entertainment. **Symphony Space** is a multidisciplinary arts center. There is always a reading or concert on the main stage, and the **Leonard Nimoy Thalia** next door is always showing a classic movie. Symphony Space also occasionally hosts free marathon concerts, most recently Wall-to-Wall Broadway. Come early to get a seat and stay as long as you want. For jazz, check out **Smoke**; many well-known musicians perform. They also have excellent food. **The Underground Lounge** hosts decent comedy nights and also occasionally has live music. The West Side Arts Coalition sponsors visual arts exhibitions at the **Broadway Mall Community Center** in the renovated Beaux-Arts Community Center. **El Taller Latino Americano** has live music, salsa dancing and an occasional film, as well as Spanish classes, all very affordable.

Landmarks

- **Broadway Mall Community Center** •
W 96th St & Broadway
Beaux-Arts home of The West Side Arts Coalition.
- **El Taller** • 2710 Broadway [W 104th St]
212-665-9460
Vibrant cultural hub for Latino art, music, and dance.
- **Firemen's Memorial** •
W 100th St & Riverside Dr
Memorial to fallen fire fighters.
- **Joan of Arc Memorial** •
Riverside Dr & W 93rd St
Impressive statue erected in 1915.
- **Pomander Walk** • 261 W 94th St [Broadway]
Great little hideaway.
- **Schinasi Mansion** •
351 Riverside Dr [W 107th St]
My name is Elmer J. Fudd, I own a mansion...
- **Soldiers and Sailors Monument** •
W 89th St & Riverside Dr
It's been seen in *Law & Order*, along with everything else in New York.
- **Straus Park** • Broadway & W 106th St
Green respite just off the craziness of Broadway.

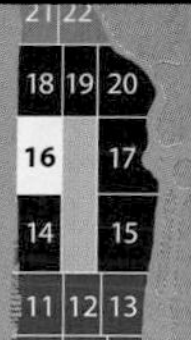

For cheap drinks, check out **Abbey Pub**, **Broadway Dive**, or the **Ding Dong Lounge**. For a good LGBT spot, head to **Suite**. Go Euro with the Beligum brews at **B. Cafe**. **Cleopatra's Needle** is jamming with open mike and jam sessions around the grand piano and **Smoke** is, uh, smokin' with live jazz. The **Village Pourhouse** is where the football fans and softball teams go.

Bars

- **Abbey Pub** • 237 W 105th St [Broadway]
  212-222-8713
  Cozy Columbia hangout.
- **Amsterdam Tavern** •
  938 Amsterdam Ave [W 106th St]
  212-280-8070
  Great beer selection. Annoying TVs.
- **B. Cafe** • 566 Amsterdam Ave [W 87th St]
  212-873-0003
  Belgian beer tastes good. Really good.
- **Broadway Dive** • 2662 Broadway [W 101st St]
  212-865-2662
  Where everyone who reads this book goes.
- **Buceo 95** • 201 W 95th St [Amsterdam Ave]
  212-662-7010
  Surprisingly affordable wine bar with delicious tapas.
- **Cleopatra's Needle** •
  2485 Broadway [W 92nd St]
  212-769-6969
  Solid middle eastern food and solid live jazz performances.
- **Ding Dong Lounge** •
  929 Columbus Ave [W 105th St]
  212-663-2600
  Downtown punk brought Uptown.
- **Dive Bar** • 732 Amsterdam Ave [W 96th St]
  212-749-4358
  Columbia hangout. Not really a dive.
- **Lion's Head Tavern** •
  995 Amsterdam Ave [W 109th St]
  212-866-1030
  Sports bar where locals and Columbia students drink cheaply.
- **The Parlour** • 250 W 86th St [Broadway]
  212-580-8923
  Irish pub, two spaces, good hangout.
- **Smoke** • 2751 Broadway [W 106th St]
  212-864-6662
  Local jazz hangout. Sunday nights are fun.
- **Suite** • 992 Amsterdam Ave [W 109th St]
  212-222-4600
  Karaoke on Thursdays. Only gay bar in the neighborhood.
- **Tap A Keg** • 2731 Broadway [W 104th St]
  212-749-1734
  Cheap beer and pool tables!
- **The Underground Lounge** •
  955 West End Ave [W 107th St]
  212-531-4759
  Stand up comedy and live music. Some really good!
- **Village Pourhouse** •
  982 Amsterdam Ave [W 109th St]
  212-979-2337
  Drink good beer and catch the big game here.

Movie Theaters

- **Leonard Nimoy Thalia at Symphony Space** •
  2537 Broadway [W 95th St]
  212-864-5400
  A different classic movie every week. Good variety.

Theaters/Performing Arts

- **Symphony Space** •
  2537 Broadway [W 95th St]
  212-864-5400
  Neighborhood concert hall with eclectic programs.
- **West End Theatre** • 263 W 86th St [Broadway]
  212-352-3101
  The Prospect Theater Company does some kickass musicals here.

Restaurants

Have the quintessential New York breakfast of bagels and lox at **Barney Greengrass**. Eat old-school at the diner **Broadway Restaurant**. For cheap rice and beans, try **Flor de Mayo** or **El Malecon**. Dine on awesome Mexican at the tiny and cheap **Taqueri Y Fonda** and rich Indian food at **Indus Valley**. For eating on the go, hit **Roti Roll** for inexpensive Indian treats, **Absolute Bagels** for fresh, warm bagels right out of the oven, and pastry as good as any you would find in Paris at **Silver Moon Bakery**.

Restaurants

- **Asia Kan** • 710 Amsterdam Ave [W 94th St]
212-280-8878 • $$$
Super sushi & so hip!
- **Awash** • 947 Amsterdam Ave [W 106th St]
212-961-1416 • $$
Tasty Ethiopian.
- **Barney Greengrass** •
541 Amsterdam Ave [W 86th St]
212-724-4707 • $$$
Sturgeon and eggs make the perfect NYC b-fast.
- **Bella Luna** • 584 Columbus Ave [W 88th St]
212-877-2267 • $$$
Old fashion Italian with live jazz Tuesdays.
- **Broadway Restaurant** •
2664 Broadway [W 101st St]
212-865-7074 • $
Great breakfast and sandwiches, good place to start the day.
- **Café Con Leche** •
424 Amsterdam Ave [W 80th St]
212-595-7000 • $$
Cuban-Dominican haven.
- **Café du Soleil** • 2723 Broadway [W 104th St]
212-316-5000 • $$$$
French bistro that draws locals. Nice bar.
- **Cascabel Taqueria** •
2799 Broadway [W 108th St]
212-665-1500 •
Great Mexican food and drinks; nice outdoor seating.
- **El Malecon** • 764 Amsterdam Ave [W 97th St]
212-864-5648 • $
Roast chicken and a con leche.
- **El Rey de la Caridad** •
973 Amsterdam Ave [W 108th St]
212-222-7383 • $$
Enjoy a Dominican feast. Bring your Spanish dictionary.
- **Flor de Mayo** • 2651 Broadway [W 101st St]
212-663-5520 • $$
Cuban-Chinese-Chicken-Chow.
- **Gennaro** • 665 Amsterdam Ave [W 92nd St]
212-665-5348 • $$$
Crowded Italian.
- **Indian Cafe** • 2791 Broadway [W 108th St]
212-749-9200 • $$
Neighborhood Indian. Nice ambiance.
- **Indus Valley** • 2636 Broadway [W 100th St]
212-222-9222 • $$$
Locals rave about this Indian food but it costs.
- **Jerusalem Restaurant** •
2715 Broadway [W 104th St]
212-865-2295 • $
Good Middle Eastern, friendly service, open late.
- **Kouzan** • 685 Amsterdam Ave [W 93rd St]
212-280-8099 • $$
Upscale Japanese dining with a pseudo nightclub-like atmosphere.
- **Krik Krak** • 844 Amsterdam Ave [W 101st St]
212-222-3100 • $$
Cozy Haitian for great island meal.
- **La Mirabelle** • 102 W 86th St [Columbus Ave]
212-496-0458 • $$$
New York old-timers keep coming back for classic French cuisine.
- **Momofuku Milk Bar** •
561 Columbus Ave [W 87th St]
$$
A dessert-lover's delight (try the cake truffles!).
- **Pio Pio Salon** •
702 Amsterdam Ave [W 94th St]
212-665-3000 • $$
Tasty rotisserie chicken with all the fixins. Thanks Peru!
- **Popover Cafe** •
551 Amsterdam Ave [W 87th St]
212-595-8555 • $$
Neighborhood favorite. Popovers with strawberry butter are a must-try.
- **Roti Roll Bombay Frankie** •
994 Amsterdam Ave [W 109th St]
212-666-1500 • $
Hole-in-the-wall rotis to soak up alcohol.
- **Saigette** • 935 Columbus Ave [W 106th St]
212-866-6888 • $
Damn good Vietnamese including unique banh mi sandwiches.
- **Taqueria Y Fonda** •
968 Amsterdam Ave [W 108th St]
212-531-0383 • $$
Amazing Mexican dive. Columbia kids love this place.
- **Trattoria Pesce Pasta** •
625 Columbus Ave [W 91st St]
212-579-7970 • $$$
Decent neighborhood Italian. Good antipasti.
- **Turkuaz** • 2637 Broadway [W 100th St]
212-665-9541 • $$
Craving gelenseksel yemekler (traditional dish)? It's all here.

Bagels, Coffee, & Shopping

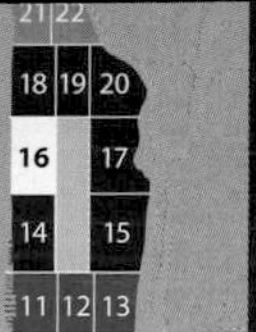

ooking for a nice bottle of wine to bring to dinner? Try **Whole Foods Wine**, hich is the first branch of the upscale grocery store to have one. **Barzini's** as nice fresh produce as does Garden of Eden. For smoked fish and repared foods try **The Kosher Marketplace**. **Schatzie's** is the best butcher round and **Joon Fine Seafood** has fresh fish at fair prices.

Bagels

- **Absolute Bagels •** 2788 Broadway [W 108th St] 212-932-2052 Amazing. Home of the hard to-find pumpernickel raisin.
- **Barney Greengrass •** 541 Amsterdam Ave [W 86th St] 212-724-4707 Classic New York shop. Good bagels.

Coffee

- **Le Pain Quotidien •** 2463 Broadway [W 91st St] 212-769 8879 Excellent coffee and pastries. Thanks Belgium.
- **Silver Moon Bakery •** 2740 Broadway [W 105th St] 212-866-4717 Delicious morning coffee and croissant.
- **Three Star Coffee Shop •** 541 Columbus Ave [W 86th St] 212-874-6780 Old-school diner.

Shopping

- **Ace Hardware •** 610 Columbus Ave [W 90th St] 212-580-8080 The place.
- **Barzini's •** 2455 Broadway [W 91st St] 212-874-4992 Huge selection of cheeses. Fresh bread and produce.
- **Gotham Wines And Liquors •** 2517 Broadway [W 94th St] 212-932 0990 Friendly neighborhood favorite.
- **Gothic Cabinet Craft •** 2652 Broadway [W 101st St] 212-678-4368 Real wood furniture. Made in Queens!
- **Janovic •** 2680 Broadway [W 102nd St] 212-531-2300 Top NYC paint store.
- **Joon Fine Seafood •** 774 Amsterdam Ave [W 98th St] 212-531-1344 Fresh fish market that will fry 'em up right there.
- **The Kosher Marketplace •** 2442 Broadway [W 90th St] 212-580-6378 For all of your Kosher needs.
- **Mani Marketplace •** 697 Columbus Ave [W 94th St] 212-662-4392 Fantastic little grocery with jazz on the sound system.
- **Mitchell's Wine & Liquor Store •** 200 W 86th St [Amsterdam Ave] 212-874-2255 Worth a trip just for the gorgeous neon sign.
- **Mugi Pottery •** 993 Amsterdam Ave [W 109th St] 212-866-6202 Handcrafted pottery. Like in the movie Ghost.
- **Murray's Sturgeon Shop •** 2429 Broadway [W 90th St] 212-724-2650 UWS comfort food: rugelah, knishes, and, lots of sturgeon.
- **New York Flowers & Plant Shed •** 209 W 96th St [Amsterdam Ave] 212-662-4400 Makes you wish you had more (or any) garden space.
- **Schatzie The Butcher •** 555 Amsterdam Ave [W 87th St] 212-410-1555 Butcher with good prime meat and poultry.
- **Sport Trax & Shoes •** 2621 Broadway [W 99th St] 212-866-0217 Affordable sporting equipment and clothing.
- **Upper 90 Soccer & Sport •** 697 Amsterdam Ave [W 94th St] 646-863-7076 Great selection of soccer apparel and accessories.
- **Variazioni •** 2389 Broadway [W 88th St] 212-595-1760 Funky tops, designer jeans, high prices.
- **Whole Foods •** 808 Columbus Ave [W 97th St] 212-222-6160 Finally. Good fresh food north of 96th Street.

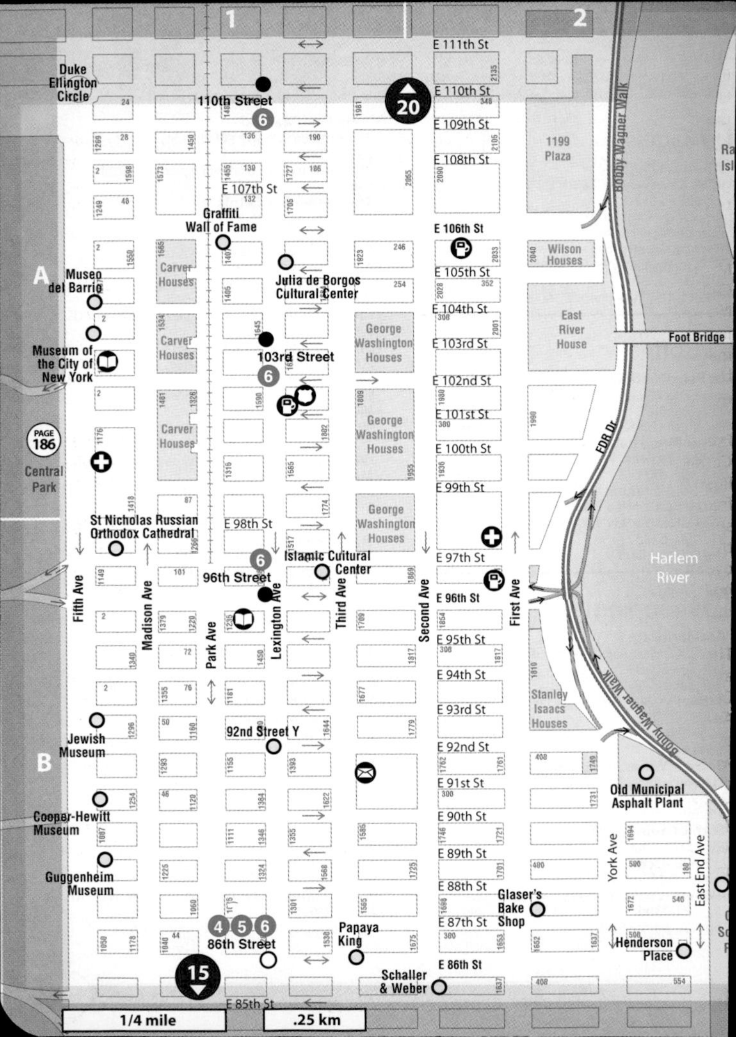

1
2
A
B
Duke Ellington Circle
110th Street
6
20
E 111th St
E 110th St
E 109th St
E 108th St
E 107th St
1199 Plaza
Bobby Wagner Walk
Graffiti Wall of Fame
E 106th St
Wilson Houses
Museo del Barrio
Carver Houses
Julia de Borgos Cultural Center
E 105th St
E 104th St
East River House
Foot Bridge
E 103rd St
Museum of the City of New York
103rd Street
George Washington Houses
E 102nd St
E 101st St
PAGE 186
Central Park
E 100th St
FDR Dr
E 99th St
St Nicholas Russian Orthodox Cathedral
E 98th St
Islamic Cultural Center
96th Street
E 97th St
E 96th St
Harlem River
Fifth Ave
Madison Ave
Park Ave
Lexington Ave
Third Ave
Second Ave
First Ave
E 95th St
E 94th St
E 93rd St
Stanley Isaacs Houses
Jewish Museum
92nd Street Y
E 92nd St
E 91st St
Old Municipal Asphalt Plant
Cooper-Hewitt Museum
E 90th St
E 89th St
York Ave
East End Ave
Guggenheim Museum
E 88th St
Glaser's Bake Shop
E 87th St
4 5 6
86th Street
Papaya King
Henderson Place
15
E 86th St
Schaller & Weber
E 85th St
1/4 mile
.25 km

Neighborhood Overview

Whew, finally a break from the chaos. This part of the Upper East Side is a place for families, young, old, black, white, Latino, rich, poor—it just depends what block you stumble upon. Head above 96th Street for some of the best Mexican food on the planet, or head west to Central Park, where you'll find kids and adults playing soccer, softball, and football. Get some culture at the neighborhoods museums, get some knowledge at a lecture at the 92nd Street Y, but most importantly, get ready to be somewhere where people can actually live, work, and shop. Nothing hip or cool here, this is just a good old-fashioned New York neighborhood.

Much of this part of the Upper East Side is known as Carnegie Hill, named for the Carneqie Mansion on 91st and Fifth Avenue (it's now the **Cooper-Hewitt Design Museum**). Though he doesn't actually live there, you may still catch a glimpse of Mayor Bloomberg at **Gracie Mansion**, which serves as the official residence of New York City mayors. **Henderson Place**, built in 1881 for families of "moderate means" was designed by the architectures of Lamb and Rich and with 24 units still remaining, serves as an example of original middle-class living in the Big Apple.

Ever think a Soviet battle could take place on American soil? The **Russian Orthodox Cathedral of St. Nicholas** was the site of a power struggle between czarist and Soviet Russians after its founding in 1902. Now, it's undergoing renovations and finally conflict-free, but still an amazing sight to see. The **Old Municipal Asphalt Plant** now houses sports fields but was the source of much controversy: some called it the ugliest thing they'd ever seen, but the MOMA hailed it as a masterpiece of functional design. Head over to 91st Street and decide for yourself. **The Museum of the City of New York** can not only help visitors understand the history of Gotham but natives as well, with 1.5 million objects and images connected to the city's past.

The Jewish Museum features works by Chagall, a video and film archive and traveling exhibits that are always worth a peek. Head up to 104th Street and down to the Caribbean at **Museo del Barrio**, where you can find an excellent collection of Latin American art. Another name you've perhaps heard of? **The Guggenheim**, which not only houses Picasso, Chagall, Mondrian and Kandinsky but is also a piece of art itself, with Frank Lloyd Wright's influence seen on the swirling staircase that guides visitors through. One of the best ways to see the Guggenheim is on the first Friday of every month at Art After Dark, where visitors can tour the museum and have some cocktails and music along the way. Before you leave, check the schedule at the **92nd Street Y**, which frequently hosts boldface-name speakers. And the **Graffiti Wall of Fame** at 106th and Park (yes, that 106 & Park for those BET fans out there), is an awesome collection of street art at its best.

Landmarks

Landmarks

- **92nd Street Y** •
  1395 Lexington Ave [E 92nd St]
  212-415-5500
  Community hub for film, theater, and interesting lectures.
- **Asphalt Green** • E 90th St & East End Ave
  212-369-8890
  Industrial architecture turned sports facility.
- **Cooper-Hewitt National Design Museum** •
  2 E 91st St [5th Ave]
  212-849-8400
  Great design shows; run by the Smithsonian.
- **El Museo del Barrio** •
  1230 5th Ave [E 104th St]
  212-831-7272
  NYC's only Latino museum.
- **Glaser's Bake Shop** • 1670 1st Ave [E 87th St]
  212-289-2562
  Best black-and-white cookies for more than a century.
- **Gracie Mansion** • E End Ave & 88th St
  212-570-4751
  Our own Buckingham Palace, right above the FDR drive.
- **Graffiti Wall of Fame** • E 106th St & Park Ave
  This street art will blow you away.
- **Guggenheim Museum** •
  1071 5th Ave [E 88th St]
  212-423-3500
  Wright's only building in NYC, but it's one of the best.
- **Henderson Place** • E End Ave & E 86th St
  Charming Queen Anne-style apartment houses circa 1881-82.
- **Islamic Cultural Center** •
  1711 3rd Ave [E 96th St]
  212-722-5234
  Enormous and extraordinary mosque. Bustling on Fridays.
- **The Jewish Museum** •
  1109 5th Ave [E 92nd St]
  212-423-3200
  Over 28,000 artifacts of Jewish culture and history.
- **Julia de Burgos Latino Cultural Center** •
  1680 Lexington Ave [E 105th St]
  212-831-4333
  Artistic and community hub of East Harlem.
- **Museum of the City of New York** •
  1220 5th Ave [E 103rd St]
  212-534-1672
  Fascinating exhibitions on life in the big city.
- **Papaya King** • 179 E 86th St [3rd Ave]
  212-369-0648
  Dishing out damn good dogs since 1932.
- **Schaller & Weber** • 1654 2nd Ave [E 86th St]
  212-879-3047
  A relic of old Yorkville with great German meats.
- **St. Nicholas Russian Orthodox Cathedral** •
  15 E 97th St [5th Ave]
  This UES cathedral, built in 1902, remains the center of Russian Orthodoxy in the US.

Wanna watch the game or play a few games of beer pong? You've come to the right place. Check out the cheap specials at **Rathbones**, watch the big game at **Kinsale**, or "dive" right into things at **Reif's**. Then, escape the beer-filled Upper East Side bars with a stop for a cozy drink at **Auction House**, or **ABV** and its smartly curated beer and wine lists, or even the mixology of **The Guthrie Inn**.

Bars

- **ABV** • 1504 Lexington Ave [E 97th St]
  212-722-8959
  Nicely curated wine and beer lists in a classy setting.
- **Auction House** • 300 E 89th St [2nd Ave]
  212-427-4458
  Stylish lounge…or at least stylish for the Upper East Side.
- **The District** • 1679 3rd Ave [94th St]
  212-289-2005
  Upscale pub for the grown up frat boys.
- **Earl's Beer & Cheese** •
  1259 Park Ave [E 97th St]
  212-289-1581
  Best beer selection for miles. And awesome food.
- **East End Bar and Grill** •
  1664 1st Ave [E 87th St]
  212-348-3783
  Mellow Irish hang out.
- **The Guthrie Inn** • 1259 Park Ave [E 97th St]
  212-423-9900
  Amazing cocktails from a well-known mixologist
- **Kinsale Tavern** • 1672 3rd Ave [E 94th St]
  212-348-4370
  Right-off-the-boat Irish staff. Good beers.
- **The Lexington Social** •
  1634 Lexington Ave [E 104th St]
  646-820-7013
  Good happy hour and tapas.
- **Marty O'Brien's** • 1696 2nd Ave [E 88th St]
  212-722-3889
  Where kilted firefighters go to enjoy pints on St. Paddy's.
- **Phil Hughes** • 1682 1st Ave [E 88th St]
  212-722-9415
  An honest-to-god dive bar on the UES.
- **Rathbones Pub** • 1702 2nd Ave [E 88th St]
  212-369-7361
  Your basic Manhattan pub.
- **Reif's Tavern** • 302 E 92nd St [2nd Ave]
  212-426-0519
  Dive-o-rama since 1942.

Movie Theaters

- **AMC Loews Orpheum 7** •
  1538 3rd Ave [E 87th St]
  212-876-2111
  The Upper East Side's premiere multiplex.
- **City Cinemas East 86th Street** •
  210 E 86th St [Third Ave]
  212-744-1999
  It wouldn't be our first choice.

Theaters/Performing Arts

- **92nd Street Y** •
  1395 Lexington Ave [E 92nd St]
  212-415-5500
  Check out the terrific Lyrics and Lyricists series.

Restaurants

For brunch, the Upper East Side's signature meal, there's no place like **Sarabeth's**. If you want to spend the money on a good steak, head to the **Parlor Steakhouse**. Other gems: Bar food finds new meaning at **Earl's Beer & Cheese**, cemitas sandwiches at **Cafe Ollin**, and Alsatian at **Cafe D'Alsace**. When you tire of shelling out UES prices for food, head over to **Papaya King** on 86th Street: "Tastier than a filet mignon." Perhaps, but while we're on the topic, one of the nicest branches of **Shake Shack** also happens to be on 86th Street. Go figure.

Restaurants

- **Café D'Alsace** • 1695 2nd Ave [E 88th St] 212-722-5133 • $$$$ Chic Alsatian bistro with an actual beer sommelier.
- **Cafe Ollin** • 339 E 108th St [1st Ave] 212-828-3644 • $ Tiny Mexican hole cranking out awesome cemitas and more.
- **Cafe Sabarsky** • 1048 5th Ave [E 86th St] 212-288-0665 • $$$ Beautiful wood-paneled surroundings for sipping Viennese coffee.
- **Cavatappo Grill** • 1712 1st Ave [E 89th St] 212-987-9260 • $$$$$ Northern Italian standout with loyal neighborhood following.
- **Chef Ho's** • 1720 2nd Ave [E 89th St] 212-348-9444 • $$$ Creative gourmet-ish Chinese cuisine. Try the Banana Chicken—delicious!
- **El Paso** • 1643 Lexington Ave [E 104th St] 212-831-9831 • $ Fantastic Mexican. Try the chilaquiles and spicy guacamole.
- **Ithaka** • 308 E 86th St [2nd Ave] 212-628-9100 • $$$ Fish grilled to perfection. Live music too.
- **Joy Burger Bar** • 1567 Lexington Ave [E 100th St] 212-289-6222 • $ Burgers that, yes, bring joy to your mouth.
- **Moustache** • 1621 Lexington Ave [E 102nd St] 212-828-0030 • $$ Middle Eastern surrounded by Mexican.
- **Naruto Ramen** • 1596 3rd Ave [E 90th St] 212-289-7803 • $$ Sip Japanese soup at the cramped counter.
- **Papaya King** • 179 E 86th St [3rd Ave] 212-369-0648 • $ Dishing out damn good dogs since 1932.
- **Parlor Steakhouse** • 1600 3rd Ave [90th St] 212-423-5888 • $$$$ Sink your teeth into an authentic filet mignon worth the dough.
- **Peri Ela** • 1361 Lexington Ave [E 90th St] 212-410-4300 • $$ Classy Turkish restaurant.
- **Piatto D'Oro** • 349 E 109th St [2nd Ave] 212-828-2929 • $$$ East Harlem Italian.
- **Pinocchio Ristorante** • 1748 1st Ave [E 91st St] 212-828-5810 • $$$$$ Itty bitty sleeper Italian with rave reviews and loyal fans.
- **Pintaile's Pizza** • 1573 York Ave [E 84th St] 212-396-3479 • $$ Tasty thin-crust stuff.
- **Pio Pio** • 1746 1st Ave [E 91st St] 212-426-5800 • $$ The Matador chicken combo will feed the whole family.
- **Sabor A Mexico** • 1744 1st Ave [E 90th St] 212-289-2641 • $$ Small, home-cooked, cheap and delicious.
- **Sarabeth's** • 1295 Madison Ave [E 92nd St] 212-410-7335 • $$$ Good upper class breakfast, if you can get in.
- **Sfoglia** • 1402 Lexington Ave [E 92nd St] 212-831-1402 • $$$$ Exquisite and experimental Italian by 92nd Street Y.
- **Shake Shack** • 154 E 86th St [Lexington Ave] 646-237-5035 • $ Finally, something good on 86th Street.
- **Table d'Hote** • 44 E 92nd St [Madison Ave] 212-348-8125 • $$$$ Cozy French vibe. Good Prix Fixe.
- **Tokubei 86** • 314 E 86th St [2nd Ave] 212-628-5334 • Long time UES friendly Japanese pub with sushi.
- **Yo In Yo Out** • 1569 Lexington Ave [E 100th St] 212-987-5350 • $$ French trifecta: crepes, croissants, and coffee.
- **Zebu Grill** • 305 E 92nd St [2nd Ave] 212-426-7500 • $$$$$ Candlelit Brazilian bistro with exposed brick and earthy wooden tables.

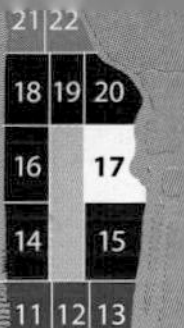

op to feed your mind at **The Corner Bookstore** before heading over to **Eli's** negar Shop for an overpriced but delicious bag of groceries. For German treats id meats, **Schaller & Weber** is the place. **Mister Wright** knows his wine and ooze. **Wankel's** is the best for hardware. Got kids? Make them happy at **The** ildren's General Store. But all that aside, we know what you're really here for: e black & white cookies at **Glaser's**, of course.

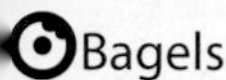

Bagels

- **Tal Bagels** • 333 E 86th St [Second Ave]
  212-427-6811
  Pretty good. Lots of cream cheese options.

Coffee

- **East Harlem Cafe** •
  1651 Lexington Ave [E 104th St]
  212-996-2080
  Best coffee in the 'hood.

Shopping

- **Blacker & Kooby Stationers** •
  1204 Madison Ave [E 88th St]
  212-369-8308
  Good selection of stationery, pens, and art supplies.
- **The Children's General Store** •
  168 E 91st St [Lexington Ave]
  212-426-4479
  Toys, games, crafts, and all things kids love.
- **Corner Bookstore** •
  1313 Madison Ave [E 93rd St]
  212-831-3554
  Tiny, old-school shop. Great selection.
- **Fresh From the Farm** •
  141 E 96th St [Lexington]
  212-534-6444
  Excellent produce and unique Turkish products.
- **Glaser's Bake Shop** • 1670 1st Ave [E 87th St]
  212-289-2562
  Best black-and-white cookies for more than a century.
- **Goliath** • 175 E 105th St [3rd Ave]
  212-360-7683
  Super cool urban sneaker emporium.
- **Gourmet Garage** • 1245 Park Ave [E 96th St]
  212-348-5850
  Not really gourmet, but better than the average market.
- **Housing Works Thrift Shop** •
  1730 2nd Ave [E 90th St]
  212-722-8306
  Uptown outpost of our favorite thrift shop.
- **Kitchen Arts & Letters** •
  1435 Lexington Ave [E 93rd St]
  212-876-5550
  Fine selection of food and wine books.
- **La Casa Azul Bookstore** •
  143 E 103rd St [Lexington Ave]
  212-426-2626
  Spanish and English books, art gallery and a lovely backyard.
- **La Tropezienne Bakery** • 2131 1st Ave [E 110th St]
  212-860-5324
  Excellent French bakery in El Barrio.
- **London Candy Company** •
  1442 Lexington Ave [E 94th St]
  212-427-2129
  English sweets, Stumptown coffee and candy galore.
- **Milano Market** • 1582 3rd Ave [E 88th St]
  212-996-6681
  Gem of an Italian market.
- **Mister Wright Fine Wines & Spirits** •
  1593 3rd Ave [E 90th St]
  212-722-4564
  Good liquor store with huge selection and tastings.
- **Orva Shoes** • 155 E 86th St [Lexington Ave]
  212-369-3448
  Ladies' discount department store.
- **Pickles, Olives Etc** • 1647 1st Ave [E 86th St]
  212-717-8966
  Pickle barrel-sized shop worth a visit.
- **Schaller & Weber** • 1654 2nd Ave [E 86th St]
  212-879-3047
  A relic of old Yorkville with countless German meats.
- **Shatzi** • 243 E 86th St [3rd Ave]
  212-289-1830
  The saving grace of strip mall-ish, chain-hogged 86th Street.
- **Super Runners Shop** •
  1337 Lexington Ave [E 89th St]
  212-369-6010
  Think before you buy running shorts that are too tight.
- **Vinyl Wine** • 1491 Lexington Ave [E 96th St]
  646-370-4100
  Excellent hand-picked selection. And a record player.
- **Wankel's Hardware** • 1573 3rd Ave [E 88th St]
  212-369-1200
  The best hardware store around.

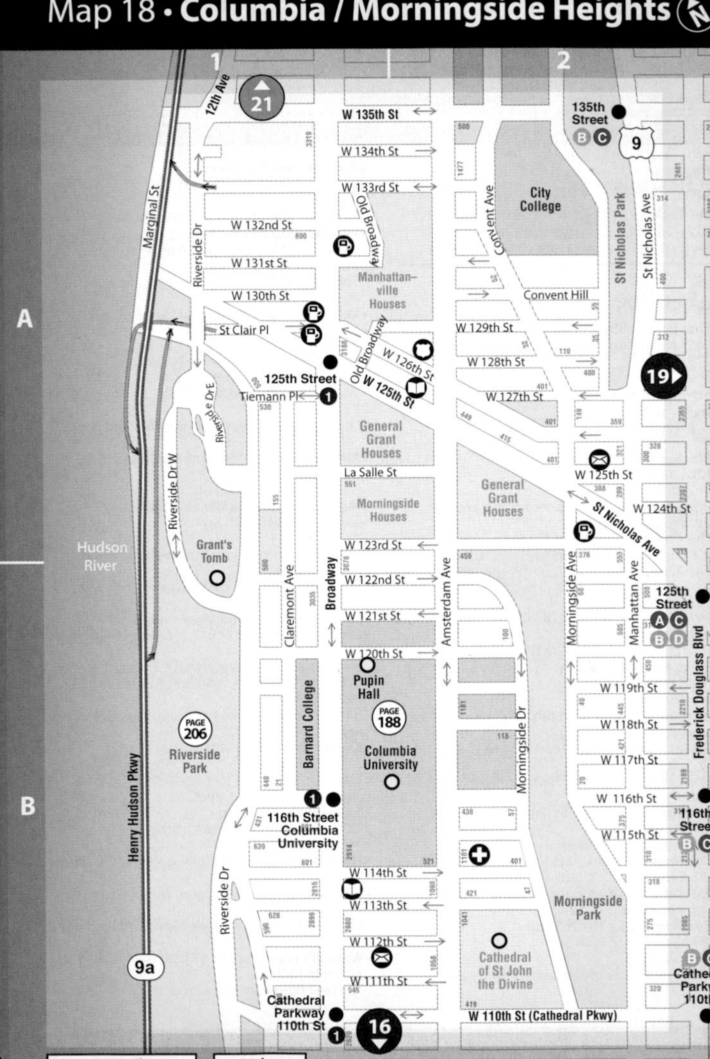

W 135th St
135th Street
City College
Manhattanville Houses
Convent Hill
125th Street
General Grant Houses
Morningside Houses
St Nicholas Ave
St Nicholas Park
Hudson River
Grant's Tomb
Riverside Park
PAGE 206
Barnard College
Pupin Hall
PAGE 188
Columbia University
116th Street Columbia University
116th Street
Morningside Park
Cathedral of St John the Divine
Cathedral Parkway 110th St
W 110th St (Cathedral Pkwy)
Henry Hudson Pkwy
Broadway
Amsterdam Ave
Claremont Ave
Morningside Ave
Manhattan Ave
Frederick Douglass Blvd
Riverside Dr
Marginal St
12th Ave
Tiemann Pl
St Clair Pl
La Salle St
Old Broadway
1/4 mile
.25 km

Neighborhood Overview

\ Until the late 19th century, Morningside Heights was mostly undeveloped farmland. Then in 1895, **Columbia University** moved from midtown Manhattan to 116th and Broadway, the site of a former insane asylum. The rest is history. Columbia and Morningside Heights, which occupies the area of New York squeezed in between the Upper West Side and Harlem, are now forever linked for better or worse. Smack dab in the center of Morningside Heights at 116th Street between Broadway and Amsterdam is the gorgeous main campus of Columbia. A stroll through here quickly replenishes the soul and provides a nice escape from the chaotic city. Just watch out for the freshmen rushing to and from class.

Like many neighborhoods in other cities dominated by an elite university, Morningside Heights had been historically mischaracterized as being a Gibraltar of culture within a barren, dangerous part of town. But the stereotypes from the '70s and '80s couldn't be further from the truth. The Morningside Heights area is one of the safer areas of New York City. Morningside Park still provides a clear line dividing line between the Columbia and residential side of town, but because of the skyrocketing rents that also came with the '90s, the lines between the two have increasingly blurred. Over the years, the relationship between the community and the nearby affluent campus has ebbed and flowed with the university's plans for expansion, land disputes, and greater gentrfi cation.

Not all development has had mixed consequences. In 2008, the **Cathedral of St. John the Divine** reopened after prolonged renovations following a fire in 2001. The wait was worth it; the world's largest Anglican church and fourth largest church in the world in an awe-inspiring display of architecture, scholarship, and local, national, and world history. Built around the same time as the University (in the same lot once belonging to an asylum), St. John the Divine provides a link between the neighborhood and the millennia of history that seemingly preceded it.

If American history and nature is more your style, the neighborhood features grounds arguably just as hallowed. While corny jokes from grade school should tell you who's buried in Grant's Tomb, the mausoleum of the head of the Union Army, the 18th President of the United States and the 19th First Lady is a national landmark under the supervision of the National Park Service. Following an extensive renovation in the early '90s, **Grant's Tomb** is now one of the best places in the neighborhood to get in touch with nature due to its size, proximity to Riverside Park, and supervision by U.S. Park Services.

Right across the street from Grant's Tomb is **Riverside Church**, a nexus point of American social history, where Martin Luther King, Jr., Nelson Mandela, and Kofi Annan have all given notable speeches. Dr. King most famously denounced the Vietnam war here. An interdenominational church with longstanding ties to the city's black residents, Riverside Church is one of the bully pulpits of African-American and civil rights discussion.

Landmarks

O Landmarks

- **Cathedral Church of St. John the Divine •** 1047 Amsterdam Ave [W 112th St]
  212-316-7540
  Our favorite cathedral. Completely unfinished and usually in disarray, just the way we like it.
- **Columbia University •** 2960 Broadway [W 116th St]
  212-854-1754
  A nice little sanctuary amid the roiling masses.
- **Grant's Tomb •** W 122nd St & Riverside Dr
  212-666-1640
  A totally underrated experience, interesting, great grounds.
- **Pupin Hall •** 550 W 120th St [Broadway]
  Original site of the Manhattan Project.

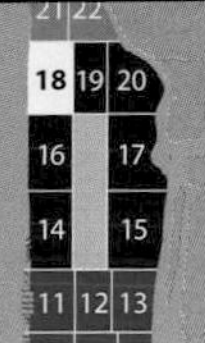

Since outsiders rarely head uptown, neighborhood nightlife mostly consists of grad students avoiding dissertations in beer bars (**1020 Bar**), undergrads avoiding papers with heavier drinking (**The Heights Bar & Grill**), and residents avoiding that all in dives (**Patrick Ryan's**). Columbia will regularly bring in word-class operas at the **Miller Theater**.

Bars

- **1020 Bar** • 1020 Amsterdam Ave [W 110th St]
  212-531-3468
  Columbia dive with super cheap beer.
- **Cafe Amrita** • 301 W 110th St [Central Park W]
  212-222-0683
  Caffeinated Columbia students, snacks, wine, beer.
- **Cotton Club** • 656 W 125th St [St Clair Pl]
  212-663-7980
  Good, fun swingin' uptown joint.
- **The Heights Bar & Grill** •
  2867 Broadway [W 111th St]
  212-866-7035
  Hang out on the rooftop with Columbia students.
- **Lerner Hall** • 2920 Broadway [W 114th St]
  212-854-9067
  Columbia student union features coffee, conventions, and wacky parties.
- **Max Caffe** •
  1262 Amsterdam Ave [W 122nd St]
  212-531-1210
  Low-key date place. Wine, good food, and sweet patio.
- **Patrick Ryan's** • 3155 Broadway [Tiemann Pl]
  212-537-7660
  New ownership provides ridiculously cheap drink specials.
- **Showman's** •
  375 W 125th St [Morningside Ave]
  212-864-8941
  Live jazz. In Harlem. That's all you need to know.

Theaters/Performing Arts

- **Manhattan School of Music** •
  120 Claremont Ave [W 122nd St]
  212-749-2802
  Classics played by students and guest artists.
- **Miller Theater—Columbia University** •
  2960 Broadway [W 116th St]
  212-854-7799
  Making chamber music hip for the college kiddies.

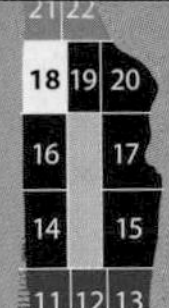

Restaurants

The Columbia kids have many long-standing quick favorites such as the giant slices of **Koronet Pizza** or the quick Middle Eastern food of **Amir's**. For something more relaxed, try Ethiopian at **Massawa**, brunch time at **Kitchenette**, or the dangerously delicious meat emporium of **Dinosaur BBQ**. Italian lovers get their fix at cozy **Max SoHa** and the wonderful **Pisticci**.

Restaurants

- **Ajanta** • 1237 Amsterdam Ave [W 121st St]
  212-316-6776 • $$
  Morningside Heights' prime Indian lunch/dinner place.
- **Amir's Falafel** • 2911 Broadway [W 113th St]
  212-749-7500 • $
  A for price. B- for quality.
- **Bettolona** • 3143 Broadway [La Salle St]
  212-749-1125 • $$$
  Pizza from a wood burning oven in a sleek dining room.
- **Bistro Ten 18** •
  1018 Amsterdam Ave [W 110th St]
  212-662-7600 • $$$
  Excellent uptown American bistro.
- **Community Food and Juice** •
  2893 Broadway [W 113th St]
  212-665-2800 • $$$
  Columbia foodies dig this place. And so should you.
- **Covo** • 701 W 135th St [12th Ave]
  212-234-9573 • $$$
  Uptown gets wood-fired pizzas in an industrial chic setting.
- **Deluxe** • 2896 Broadway [W 113th St]
  212-662-7900 • $$
  Hip diner with good brunch and happy hour.
- **Dinosaur Bar-B-Que** •
  700 W 125th St [Broadway]
  212-694-1777 • $$$
  Not just for Syracuse fans. Head WAY uptown.
- **Havana Central** • 2911 Broadway [W 113th St]
  212-662-8830 • $$$
  The old West End gone Cuban. Bring earplugs.
- **The Heights Bar & Grill** •
  2867 Broadway [W 111th St]
  212-866-7035 • $$
  Columbia students can't drink all the time so they eat here.
- **Hungarian Pastry Shop** •
  1030 Amsterdam Ave [W 111th St]
  212-866-4230 • $
  Exactly what it is—and excellent.
- **Jin Ramen** • 3183 Broadway [Tiemann Pl]
  646-559-2862 • $$
  Kickin' ramen for Columbia crowd to slurp on.
- **Kitchenette** •
  1272 Amsterdam Ave [W 123rd St]
  212-531-7600 • $$
  Cozy and good for everything.
- **Koronet Pizza** • 2848 Broadway [W 111th St]
  212-222-1566 • $
  Just one slice. Really. That's all you'll need.
- **Le Monde** • 2885 Broadway [W 112th St]
  212-531-3939 • $$
  French bistro pub with a nice bar.
- **Maison Harlem** •
  341 Saint Nicholas Ave [W 127th St]
  212-222-9224 • $$
  Brasserie atmosphere and food comes Uptown.
- **Massawa** • 1239 Amsterdam Ave [W 121st St]
  212-663-0505 • $$
  Neighborhood Ethiopian joint.
- **Max Soha** • 1274 Amsterdam Ave [W 123rd St]
  212-531-2221 • $$
  The Italian genius of Max, uptown.
- **Mill Korean** • 2895 Broadway [W 113th St]
  212-666-7653 • $$
  Good Korean for Columbia kids.
- **Miss Mamie's Spoonbread Too** •
  366 W 110th St [Manhattan Ave]
  212-865-6744 • $$
  Soul food spectacular.
- **Panino Sportivo** •
  1231 Amsterdam Ave [W 121st St]
  212-662-2066 • $$
  Gooooaaaal on the TV. And pricey Italian sandwiches.
- **Pisticci** • 125 La Salle St [Broadway]
  212-932-3500 • $$
  Wonderful, friendly Italian. A true gem.
- **Presidential Pizza** •
  357 W 125th St [St Nicholas Ave]
  212-222-7744 • $
  Grab a handful of napkins for 125th street's best slice.
- **Sezz Medi'** •
  1260 Amsterdam Ave [W 122nd St]
  212-932-2901 • $$
  Popular brick oven pizza.
- **Symposium** •
  544 W 113th St [Amsterdam Ave]
  212-865-1011 • $$
  Traditional underground (literally) Greek fare.
- **Tom's Restaurant** •
  2880 Broadway [W 112th St]
  212-864-6137 • $
  Yes. This is the Seinfeld diner. Can we go now?
- **V&T Pizzeria** •
  1024 Amsterdam Ave [W 110th St]
  212-666-8051 • $
  Columbia pizza and pasta. Family friendly if you're into that.

Bagels, Coffee, & Shopping

he newly-expanded **Book Culture** is a world-class academic bookstore and **icky's** provides a resource for style needs. Coffee on the go at **Oren's** or sit nd talk Nietzsche at **Hungarian Pastry Shop**. Groceries and free samples at e 24-hour **Westside Market**. Or everything at the massive **Fairway**. And en you have a world-class neighborhood wine store in **Vino Fino**.

Bagels

- **Nussbaum & Wu** • 2897 Broadway [W 113th St] 212-280-5344 Fine but it's worth the walk to Absolute.

Coffee

- **Cafe Amrita** • 301 W 110th St [Central Park W] 212-222-0683 Study (or update your blog) while you caffeinate.
- **Hungarian Pastry Shop** • 1030 Amsterdam Ave [W 111th St] 212-866-4230 Professors and grad students love to read here.
- **Max Caffe** • 1262 Amsterdam Ave [W 122nd St] 212-531-1210 Great spot to hang out. Open at 8 am.
- **Oren's Daily Roast** • 2882 Broadway [W 112th St] 212-749-8779 Hip staff pours superior java at local mini-chain.

Shopping

- **Amsterdam Liquor & Wine** • 1356 Amsterdam Ave [W 126th St] 212-222-1334 Stock up on your way to that beer pong party.
- **Appletree Market** • 1225 Amsterdam Ave [W 120th St] 212-865-8840 One of the better grocery options for Columbia kids.
- **Book Culture** • 536 W 112th St [Amsterdam Ave] 212-865-1588 Excellent bookstore servicing Columbia/ Barnard students.
- **Book Culture** • 2915 Broadway [W 114th St] 646-403-3000 Offshoot of the original location that Columbia students love.
- **C-Town** • 560 W 125th St [Old Broadway] 212-662-2388 No-frills market way cheaper than your local bodega.
- **Clinton Supply Co.** • 1256 Amsterdam Ave [W 122nd St] 212-222-8245 Random hardware stuff for your new dorm or apartment.
- **Fairway Market** • 2328 12th Ave [W 133rd St] 212-234-3883 So big. So good. So New York.
- **Franklin & Lennon Paint Co.** • 537 W 125th St [Broadway] 212-864-2460 Long-standing outlet with biggest selection of paint and supplies.
- **Hartley Pharmacy** • 1219 Amsterdam Ave [W 120th St] 212-749-8481 Mom & Pop pharmacy with staff that knows you personally.
- **M2M Asian Market** • 2935 Broadway [W 115th St] 212-280-4600 Sushi, soba, Asian groceries. Perfect for a quick stop.
- **Mondel Chocolates** • 2913 Broadway [W 114th St] 212-864-2111 Mom-and-pop candy shop with great chocolates.
- **Ricky's** • 2906 Broadway [W 112th St] 212-280-2861 If a drug store can be hip…
- **Samad's Gourmet** • 2867 Broadway [W 111th St] 212-749-7555 Hard to find Middle Eastern and world delicacies.
- **Sea & Sea Fish Market** • 310 St Nicholas Ave [W 125th St] 212-222-7427 Fish and more fish. They'll fry it up for you!
- **University Hardware** • 2905 Broadway [W 113th St] 212-662-2150 Where the smart kids get their hammers.
- **Vino Fino** • 1252 Amsterdam Ave [W 122nd St] 212-222-0388 Lots of tastings and friendly owners.
- **Westside Market** • 2840 Broadway [W 110th St] 212-222-3367 Bordering on gourmet shopping for Columbia U.

Map 19 • Harlem (Lower)

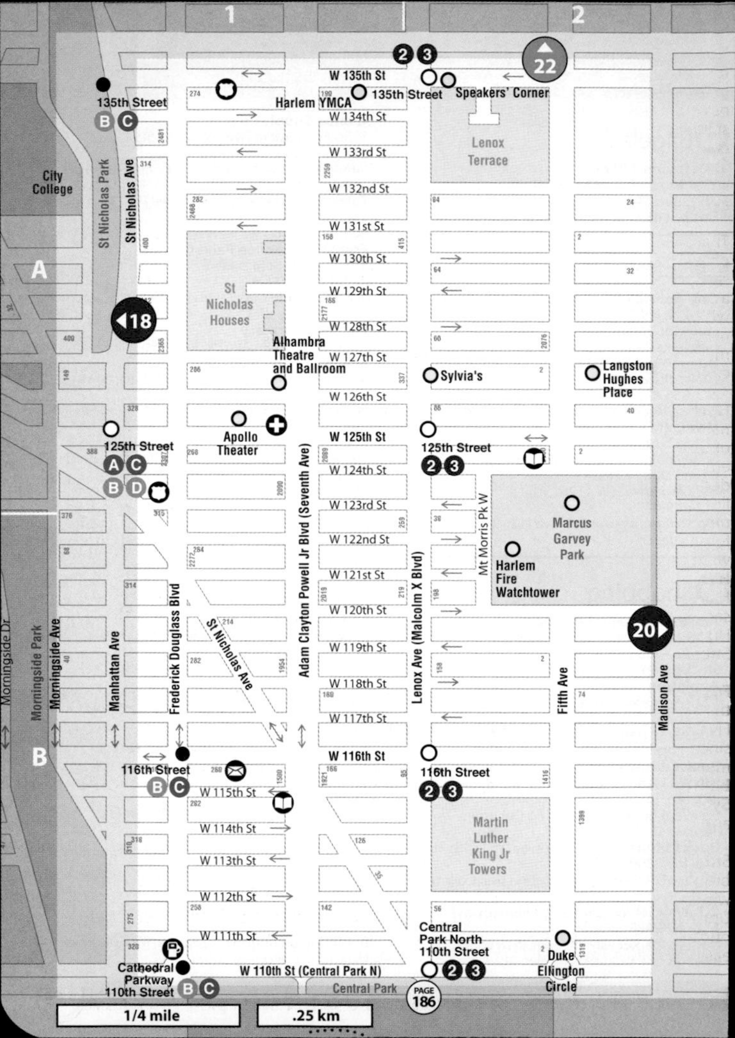

135th Street
B C
St Nicholas Park
St Nicholas Ave
City College
Harlem YMCA
W 135th St
135th Street
2 3
Speakers' Corner
22
W 134th St
W 133rd St
Lenox Terrace
W 132nd St
W 131st St
W 130th St
St Nicholas Houses
W 129th St
18
W 128th St
Alhambra Theatre and Ballroom
W 127th St
Sylvia's
Langston Hughes Place
W 126th St
Apollo Theater
W 125th St
125th Street
A C
B D
125th Street
2 3
W 124th St
W 123rd St
Marcus Garvey Park
Mt Morris Pk W
W 122nd St
Harlem Fire Watchtower
W 121st St
W 120th St
20
W 119th St
Adam Clayton Powell Jr Blvd (Seventh Ave)
Lenox Ave (Malcolm X Blvd)
Fifth Ave
Madison Ave
W 118th St
St Nicholas Ave
Frederick Douglass Blvd
Manhattan Ave
Morningside Ave
Morningside Park
Morningside Dr
W 117th St
W 116th St
116th Street
B C
116th Street
2 3
W 115th St
Martin Luther King Jr Towers
W 114th St
W 113th St
W 112th St
W 111th St
Central Park North 110th Street
2 3
Duke Ellington Circle
Cathedral Parkway 110th Street
B C
W 110th St (Central Park N)
Central Park

PAGE 186

1/4 mile
.25 km

Neighborhood Overview

New Yorkers below 96th Street rarely venture above the park for more than a chicken-and-waffles feast or an amateur night ticket. Well, the joke's on them. Harlem is a thriving neighborhood in every sense of the word—great community spirit, great street life, great architecture, great arts and culture...pretty much great everything. The lifeline of this neighborhood is 125th Street, a thoroughfare known for the Apollo Theater, a zillion stores, and players strutting their stuff. With some of the tastiest grub in town, bargains lining the streets, and locals who keep it real, Harlem is a nabe for New Yorkers who like a little gruff.

That said, Harlem has been evolving for some time now. Bill Clinton maintains an office on 125th Street. Chi-chi cupcake cafes push uptown. And chic French bistros hold shop next to grubby bodegas. But even as American Apparel wrangles itself a spot across from the Apollo, the nabe retains a sense of gritty pride. 125th Street is packed with vendors selling everything from fur vests to coco helado. A random TV in the wall next door to the Apollo plays Soul Train on repeat. Storefront churches fill Sunday mornings with Gospel ballads. Just journey uptown to check it out, and leave the credit card at home—125th can still be a cash-only kind of street.

Historically, a mind-boggling number of writers, artists, and civil rights leaders made names for themselves in Harlem, and the community is proud of its past. At the tip-top of Central Park, **Duke Ellington** sits at an oversized grand piano; the statue was erected in 1997. Shockingly, this relatively recent memorial was the first to be dedicated to an African-American in New York City. Within the Morris Historical District lies **Marcus Garvey Park**, renamed for the famous civil rights leader in 1973. On a more literary note, visit Langston Hughes Place, the street where the poet lived. Look for the ivy-covered building halfway down the block, but just snap a photo—the home went on the market in 2009. Then, check out his first residence at the still-operating **Harlem YMCA**. The facilities became an oasis for black visitors and artists during the Harlem Renaissance, when many of New York's hotels, theaters and restaurants were segregated. The list of short-term residents reads like an artsy walk of fame, with Hughes, Ralph Ellison, Claude McKay, and James Baldwin all once calling the 135th Street location home.

Food, music, and entertainment happily collide in Harlem. **The Apollo Theater** is easily the area's most notable landmark, with everyone from Ella Fitzgerald to the Jackson Five kicking off their careers on that stage. The Amateur Night show has been running since 1934 and still happens on Wednesdays—just prepare for a line. Even more musical greats—Billie Holiday, Bessie Smith—haunted the **Alhambra Theatre and Ballroom**. If it had been around, we like to think they all would have chowed at **Sylvia's**, a soul food institution that has dished out piping hot fried chicken, waffles and mashed potatoes since 1962.

Stroll the residential blocks for a complete view of changing Harlem. Sure, brownstones sell for upwards of a million dollars, but row-houses with shattered windows and planked doors remain. Harlem is a neighborhood in flux, but it's not the Upper West Side. That means old-school New York tactics still apply. Walk fast, with purpose and with a sense of direction (even if you managed to get lost in the very easy-to-understand grid).

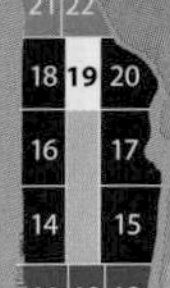

Landmarks

Landmarks

- **Alhambra Ballroom •**
  2116 Adam Clayton Powell Blvd [W 121st St]
  212-222-6940
  Last Harlem dance hall.
- **Apollo Theater •**
  253 W 125th St [Frederick Douglass Blvd]
  212-531-5300
  The one and the only.
- **Duke Ellington Circle •**
  5th Ave & Central Park N
  Nice monument to a jazz great.
- **Harlem Fire Watchtower •**
  Marcus Garvey Park
  It's tall.
- **Harlem YMCA •** 180 W 135th St [7th Ave]
  212-912-2100
  Sidney Poitier, James Earl Jones and Eartha Kitt have performed in this Y's "Little Theatre."
- **Langston Hughes Place •**
  20 E 127th St [5th Ave]
  212-534-5992
  Where the prolific poet lived and worked 1947-1967.
- **Marcus Garvey Park •**
  E 120th St & Madison Ave
  Appeallingly mountainous park.
- **Speaker's Corner •** Lenox Ave & W 135th St
  Famous soapbox for civil rights leaders, including Marcus Garvey.
- **Sylvia's •** 328 Lenox Ave [W 126th St]
  212-996-0660
  This restaurant is worth the trip.

Nightlife

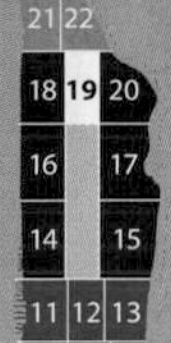

Dive bars, underground jazz, and live music spectacles mesh for a diverse scene. Catch a show at the landmark Apollo Theater (Harlem residents, bring proof of address for a discount); sip fancy cocktails at **67 Orange Street;** or slip into the **Lenox Lounge** for classic jazz. Watch indie movies (many about Harlem) at **Maysles Cinema**.

Bars

- **67 Orange Street •**
  2082 Frederick Douglass Blvd [W 113th St]
  212-662-2030
  Classy cocktail bar with speakeasy style.
- **Bier International •**
  2099 Frederick Douglass Blvd [W 113th St]
  212-280-0944
  Tons of top foreign brews on tap, so bring freunds.
- **Ginny's Supper Club •**
  310 Lenox Ave [W 126th St]
  212-421-3821
  Hopping jazz club under Red Rooster.
- **Harlem Tavern •**
  2153 Frederick Douglass Blvd [W 116th St]
  212-866-4500
  Hybrid duties: Beer garden, sport bar, and pub food.
- **Lenox Lounge •** 288 Lenox Ave [W 124th St]
  212-427-0253
  Old-time Harlem hangout; bar in the front, jazz in the back room.
- **Moca Bar & Lounge •**
  2210 Frederick Douglass Blvd [W 119th St]
  212-665-8081
  Serving up hip hop, classics, and R&B.
- **Paris Blues •**
  2021 Adam Clayton Powell Jr Blvd [W 121st St]
  212-222-9878
  Nothing fancy, just a solid bar.
- **Shrine •**
  2271 Adam Clayton Powell Jr Blvd [W 134th St]
  212-690-7807
  Drink for cheap while Harlem and Columbia bands play.
- **W XYZ Bar •**
  2296 Frederick Douglass Blvd [W 124th St]
  212-749-4000
  Drinkin' and mixin' inside the Harlem Aloft Hotel.

Movie Theaters

- **AMC Magic Johnson Harlem 9 •**
  2309 Frederick Douglass Blvd [W 124th St]
  212-665-6923
  Owned by Magic. Best choice for Upper Manhattan.
- **Maysles Cinema •**
  343 Malcolm X Blvd [127th St]
  212-582-6050
  Amazing indies and documentaries from local film-makers.

Theaters/Performing Arts

- **Apollo Theater •**
  253 W 125th St [Frederick Douglass Blvd]
  212-531-5300
  Where booing is not only allowed, it's encouraged!
- **National Black Theatre •**
  2031 5th Ave [E 126th St]
  212-722-3800
  No, they don't do Neil Simon here.

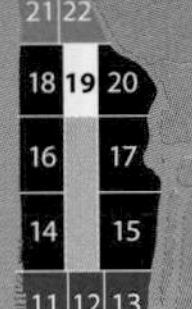

Restaurants

Harlem dining is increasingly global and Marcus Samuelsson's **Red Rooster** has brought a lot of foot traffic to 125th Street, but don't stop there. Kick off the morning at **Il Caffe Latte** with steaming lattes and breakfast wraps. Settle in at **Patisserie des Ambassades** for French-Senegalese entrees. For straight up Senegalese, try **Africa Kine.** And head to **Amy Ruth's** or **Sylvia's** when home-style cooking beckons.

Restaurants

- **The 5 & Diamond •** 2072 Frederick Douglass Blvd [W 112th St] 917-860-4444 • $$$ Cozy, comfy comfort food.
- **Africa Kine Restaurant •** 256 W 116th St [Frederick Douglass Blvd] 212-666-9400 • $ Senegalese with nice little dining room.
- **Amy Ruth's •** 113 W 116th St [Lenox Ave] 212-280-8779 • $$ Soul food, incredible fried chicken.
- **Bad Horse Pizza •** 2224 Frederick Douglass Blvd [W 120th St] 212-749-1258 • $$ Thin crust pizza, pasta and booze.
- **Billie's Black •** 271 W 119th St [St Nicholas Ave] 212-280-2248 • $$ Good food + live entertainment.
- **Chez Lucienne •** 308 Malcolm X Blvd [W 125th St] 212-289-5555 • $$ Cozy little French bistro. Authentic and affordable!
- **Corner Social •** 321 Lenox Ave [W 126th St] 212-510-8552 • $$$ A solid backup when the Rooster is packed across the street.
- **Fishers of Men •** 121 W 125th St [Malcolm X Blvd] 212-678-4268 • $ Sequel to the East side store: fried fish, plus franks.
- **Harlem BBQ •** 2367 Frederick Douglass Blvd [W 127th St] 212-222-1922 • $$ Football-sized frozen cocktails and entire $6 chickens to-go.
- **Il Caffe Latte •** 189 Lenox Ave [W 119th St] 212-222-2241 • $ Fresh sandwiches, massive $3 lattes and a stellar Latin wrap.
- **Island Salad •** 22 E 125th St [5th Ave] 212-860-3000 • $ A healthy food oasis.
- **Jacob Restaurant •** 373 Malcolm X Blvd [W 129th St] 212-866-3663 • $ Soul food and salad by the pound for cheap.
- **Le Baobab •** 120 W 116th St [Lenox Ave] 212-864-4700 • $ Satisfying Senegalese complete with TV in French.
- **Lido •** 2168 Frederick Douglass Blvd [W 117th St] 646-490-8575 • $$$ Sophisticated Northern Italian with requisite exposed brick atmosphere.
- **Lolita's Cafe •** 57 Lenox Ave [W 113th St] 212-222-6969 • $$ Cheap and cozy neighborhood Mexican joint.
- **Manna's •** 2331 Frederick Douglass Blvd [W 125th St] 212-749-9084 • $$ Pile a buffet plate with everything from oxtail to collard greens.
- **Melba's •** 300 W 114th St [Frederick Douglass Blvd] 212-864-7777 • $$$ Upscale soul food.
- **Mobay Uptown Restaurant •** 17 W 125th St [5th Ave] 212-876-7300 • $$$ Throwdown Caribbean soul food at this Food Network fave.
- **Native •** 161 Lenox Ave [W 118th St] 212-665-2525 • $ Excellent soul food.
- **Ottomanelli Brothers •** 1325 5th Ave [W 111th St] 212-828-8900 • $$ Solid Italian food comes to Harlem.
- **Patisserie Des Ambassades •** 2200 Frederick Douglass Blvd [W 119th St] 212-666-0078 • $ Great breakfast pastries. Senegalese food too.
- **Red Rooster •** 310 Lenox Ave [W 125th St] 212-792-9001 • $$$ The latest uptown craze from chef star Marcus Samuelsson.
- **Sylvia's •** 328 Lenox Ave [W 126th St] 212-996-0660 • $$$ An institution. Not overrated.
- **Tonnie's Minis •** 264 Lenox Ave [W 123rd St] 212-831-5292 • $ New York's cupcake obsession pushes uptown.
- **Zoma •** 2084 Frederick Douglass Blvd [W 113th St] 212-662-0620 • $$ Tasty Ethiopian in a tasteful setting.

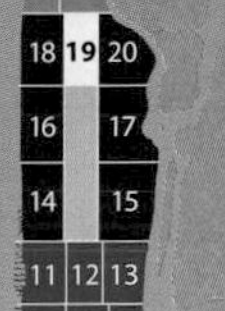

With everything from **Champ's** to **M.A.C. Makeup**, 125th Street anchors Harlem shopping. **H&M** stocks the same trendy threads as everywhere else, without the long lines. Street vendors fill any other gaps. Everything you want is here, guaranteed. And when you want to take the plunge and indulge any and all dashiki-wearing fantasies, check out the open-air **Malcolm Shabazz Harlem Market**.

Coffee

- **Lenox Coffee** • 60 W 129th St [Lenox]
646-833-7839
Classy café with lots of lattes and laptops.
- **Starbucks** • 77 W 125th St [Lenox Ave]
917-492-2454
Use the bathroom. Then head to the closest indie shop.

Shopping

- **467 Lenox Liquors** •
467 Lenox Ave [W 133rd St]
212-234-7722
Standard liquor store, sans bullet-proof glass.
- **Adja Khady Food** •
243 West 116th St [Frederick Douglass]
646-645-7505
Friendly West African culinary supplies and community hang out.
- **Atmos** •
203 W 125th St [Adam Clayton Powell Jr Blvd]
212-666-2242
Palace of popular urban streetwear.
- **B.O.R.N. Boutique** •
52 W 125th St [Malcolm X Blvd]
917-865-9194
Upscale vintage for stylish Harlemites.
- **The Brownstone** •
24 E 125th St [Madison Ave]
212-996-7980
Clothing boutique featuring local designers.
- **Carol's Daughter** • 24 W 125th St [5th Ave]
212-828-6757
Nature-inspired skin care presented with love.
- **Champs** • 208 W 125th St [7th Ave]
212-280-0296
Sports, street shoes, and wear. For losers too.
- **Dr. Jay's** •
256 W 125th St [Frederick Douglass Blvd]
212-665-7795
Urban fashions is just what the doctor ordered.
- **Grandma's Place** • 84 W 120th St [Lenox Ave]
212-360-6776
Harlem toy store. Your grandkid will probably love it.
- **H&M** • 125 W 125th St [Lenox Ave]
855-466-7467
Sort-of-hip, disposable fashion.
- **Harlem Underground** •
20 E 125th St [5th Ave]
212-987-9385
Embroidered Harlem t-shirts.
- **Hats by Bunn** • 2283 7th Ave [W 134th St]
212-694-3590
Cool caps.
- **Jimmy Jazz** • 132 W 125th St [Lenox Ave]
212-665-4198
Urban designers with a range of sizes.
- **MAC** • 202 W 125th St [7th Ave]
212-665-0676
Beauty products in many colors and shades.
- **Make My Cake** •
121 St Nicholas Ave [W 116th St]
212-932-0833
Red. Velvet. Cheesecake. Bonus: In-store WiFi.
- **Malcolm Shabazz Harlem Market** •
58 W 116th St [Lenox Ave]
212-987-8131
An open-air market for all your daishiki needs.
- **Paragon Department Store** •
488 Lenox Ave [135th St]
212-926-9470
It's like a compulsive hoarder decided to sell everything.
- **Settepani** • 196 Lenox Ave [W 120th St]
917-492-4806
Lovely baked goods.
- **Trunk Show Consignment** •
275 W 113th St [8th Ave]
212-662-0009
Cool designer fashions recycled, but just bring a fat wad of cash.
- **United Hardware** •
2160 Frederick Douglass Blvd [W 117th St]
212-666-7778
Good for basic tools; that's about all.

Map 20 • El Barrio / East Harlem

Major Deegan Expwy
E 134th St
E 135th St
RR Bridge
Lincoln Ave
Alexander Ave
Bruckner Blvd
E 132nd St
THE BRONX
PAGE 176
Abraham Lincoln Housing
Abraham Lincoln Housing
E 132nd St
Third Ave Bridge
E 131st St
Willis Ave
Harlem River
E 130th St
Harlem River Dr
E 129th St
Willis Ave Bridge
E 128th St
Keith Haring "Crack is Wack" Mural
E 127th St
Metro North Harlem 125th St
E 126th St
125th Street
Robert F Kennedy Bridge
E 125th St (Dr Martin Luther King Jr Blvd)
E 124th St
Harlem Fire Watchtower
E 123rd St
Marcus Garvey Park
Taino Towers
Paladino Ave
Ronald McNair Pl
E 122nd St
Sen R Wagner Sr Houses
Sen R Wagner Sr Houses
Harlem Courthouse
Sylvan Pl
E 121st St
E 120th St
19
E 119th St
E 118th St
Fifth Ave
Madison Ave
Park Ave
Lexington Ave
Third Ave
E 117th St
Second Ave
First Ave
Pleasant Ave
Bobby Wagner Walk
E 116th St
Pete Pascale Pl
Church of Our Lady of Mt Carmel
116th Street
E 115th St
Danny's Club & Fashion
E 114th St
FDR Dr
Sen R Taft Houses
Sen R Taft Houses
JW Johnson Housing
JW Johnson Housing
Jefferson Houses
Jefferson Houses
Jefferson Park
E 112th St
La Marqueta
E 111th St
110th Street
E 110th St
17
Duke Ellington Circle
1/4 mile
.25 km

Neighborhood Overview

El Barrio, also known as Spanish Harlem or East Harlem (just don't call it "SpaHa"), is a neighborhood that is alive with history and culture—Puerto Rican, African-American, Mexican, Italian, Dominican and increasingly Asian…it's really one of the most diverse neighborhoods in the city. It's not uncommon to find people playing congas on the street or riding tricked-out bicycles with Puerto Rican tunes blasting from their radios. You can feel a real sense of community in the bodegas and on the streets as residents chat up their neighbors and warmly greet one another with "Papi" or "Mami." In the summer locals crowd into **Thomas Jefferson Park** and the abundant community gardens provide locals with the perfect chill out spots. Exploring this neighborhood is highly recommended.

But it's not all pretty. East Harlem has been through some tough times in the past few decades to say the least. And unfortunately, to a lot of New Yorkers, it is still a place to avoid. **Keith Haring's "Crack is Wack" Mural** is a symbol of the urban decay in the 1970s and '80s when drugs, poverty, and violence ravaged the neighborhood. Burnt-out buildings were the norm and social problems skyrocketed. Today concrete housing projects dominate the landscape (some very unique like **Taino Towers**) with a few vacant lots here and there, but crime is way down and rents are creeping up.

In recent years the neighborhood has rapidly changed with new condos sprouting up everywhere (some even with doormen), a growing Mexican population moving in (check out 116th Street between Second and Third for amazing food and groceries), and even a touch of suburbia with the gigantic **Costco** that opened in 2009.

Before the Puerto Rican migration, Italians used to call East Harlem home. In the 1930s there were tens of thousands of immigrants from Southern Italy living here. The Italian legacy has almost entirely disappeared with the last of the great bakeries closing a few years ago. Today there are only a few remnants left including the gorgeous **Church of Our Lady of Mount Carmel** (the first Italian church in New York), the **Virgen del Carmen Shrine**, and restaurants like **Rao's** and **Patsy's Pizza**.

Underneath the Metro-North viaduct is another remnant of the old neighborhood, the historic public market **La Marqueta**. Established by Mayor LaGuardia in 1936, this place was the hub of shopping activity for decades with over 500 vendors. Now it only has a few businesses left selling Puerto Rican delicacies like bacalao. But it is slowly being revived by the city with new vendors selling everything from baked goods to garden supplies. In the meantime, locals pack the public plaza (that looks more like a cage) between 115th & 116th Street on Saturdays in the summer for live music and dancing.

To see the neighborhood in full party mode, head here for the second weekend in June when the Puerto Rican Day Parade is in full swing. On Sunday the parade strolls down Fifth Avenue, but on Saturday Third Avenue and 116th Street come alive for a full-on Puerto Rican party—live music, barbecues on the sidewalk, and lots of Nuyorican pride.

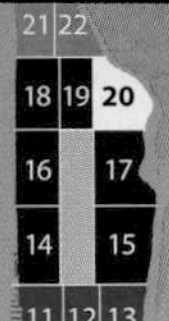

Landmarks

Landmarks

- **Church of Our Lady of Mt Carmel** • 448 E 116th St [Pleasant Ave]
212-534-0681
The first Italian parish in NYC.
- **Danny's Club & Fashion** • 1st Ave & E 114th St
Funky neighborhood fashion shop going strong for 30+ years.
- **Harlem Courthouse** • 170 E 121st St [Lexington Ave]
One of the most impressive buildings in Manhattan.
- **Keith Haring "Crack is Wack" Mural** • 2nd Ave & E 127th St
Keith was right.
- **La Marqueta** • 1590 Park Ave [E 115th St]
212-312-3603
This public market used to be bustling; not so much anymore.
- **Taino Towers** • 3rd Ave & E 123rd St
Unique low-income housing development opened in 1979.
- **Thomas Jefferson Park** • 2180 1st Ave [E 112th St]
212-860-1383
Green space with a giant pool and bbqs in the summer.

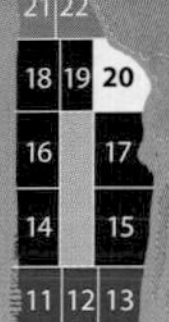

Camaradas is your one-stop hot spot for drinks and live entertainment from old-school DJs to Latin grooves. **Mojitos** has a friendly bar to knock back a few drinks. **Cafe Creole** gets the juices flowing with live Latin jazz while **The Duck** plays country music and women dance on the bar.

Bars

- **Amor Cubano** • 2018 3rd Ave [E 111th St]
  212-996-1220
  The house band always has this place grooving.
- **Café Creole** • 2167 3rd Ave [E 118th St]
  212-876-8838
  Live entertainment: Jazz, etc.
- **Camaradas El Barrio** •
  2241 1st Ave [E 115th St]
  212-348-2703
  Ececltic live music and tasty bar food. Great vibe.
- **The Duck** • 2171 2nd Ave [E 112th St]
  212-831-0000
  Uptown country dive. Weird as it sounds.
- **Mojitos** • 227 E 116th St [3rd Ave]
  212-828-8635
  Good Mexican happy hour destination.

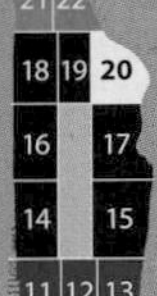

Restaurants

Patsy's pizza really is the "original" New York thin-crust pizza. The slices from the take-out window are the best in NYC. Unless you know the Mayor, **Rao's** is another New York restaurant you'll never see the inside of. 116th Street is a budget culinary wonderland. Try **Taco Mix**, **Sandy**, or **El Nuevo Caridad**.

Restaurants

- **A Taste of Seafood** • 59 E 125th St [Madison Ave] 212-831-5584 • $ Fried fish sandwiches on white bread. Lord, have mercy!
- **Agua Fresca** • 207 E 117th St [3rd Ave] 212-996-2500 • $$$ Nuevo Latino galore from ceviches to tacos.
- **Amor Cubano** • 2018 3rd Ave [E 111th St] 212-996-1220 • $$ Good Cuban food. Great live music.
- **Café Creole** • 2167 3rd Ave [E 118th St] 212-876-8838 • $$ Okra gumbo, jambalaya, and good veggie options.
- **Camaradas El Barrio** • 2241 1st Ave [E 115th St] 212-348-2703 • $$ Spanish/Puerto Rican/tapas/music. Nice!
- **Charlie's Place** • 1960 Madison Ave [E 125th St] 212-410-0277 • $$ Harlem's first sushi bar.
- **Cuchifritos** • 168 E 116th St [Lexington Ave] 212-876-4846 • $ Puerto Rican fried treats.
- **El Aguila** • 137 E 116th St [Lexington Ave] 212-410-2450 • $ Porktastic bustling taco joint. Open 24-7!
- **El Nuevo Caridad** • 2257 2nd Ave [E 116th St] 212-860-8187 • $ Dominican baseball stars approve of this chicken.
- **El Paso Taqueria** • 237 E 116th St [3rd Ave] 212-860-4875 • $$ Great Mexican with fantastic daily specials.
- **El Tapatio Mexican Restaurant** • 209 E 116th St [3rd Ave] 212-876-3055 • $$ Tiny but good.
- **Fishers of Men** • 32 E 130th St [Madison Ave] 212-828-4447 • $ Anything deep fried tastes good. Especially this seafood.
- **Golden Krust** • 2085 Lexington Ave [E 126th St] 212-722-5253 • $ It's all about the patties.
- **Harley's Smokeshack** • 355 E 116th St [1st Ave] 212-828-6723 • $$$ They smoke it, so you can eat it—turkey wings to meatballs.
- **IHOP** • 2082 Lexington Ave [E 125th St] 212-860-0844 • $$ Pancakes and carafes of coffee, plus a 24-hour window.
- **Kahlua's Café** • 2117 3rd Ave [E 116th St] 212-348-0311 • $$ Awesome Mexi-grub. Tiny, loud, and fun.
- **La Corsa** • 123 E 110th St [Park Ave] 212-860-1133 • $ Pizza. Good grandma slices.
- **Makana** • 2245 1st Ave [E 115th St] 212-996-3534 • $$ A great little Hawaiian-Japanese BBQ takes Manhattan.
- **Mojitos** • 227 E 116th St [3rd Ave] 212-828-8635 • $$ Live music Thursday, Friday and Saturday.
- **Patsy's Pizzeria** • 2287 1st Ave [E 118th St] 212-534-9783 • $$ The original thin-crust pizza. Best take-out slices in NY.
- **Pee Dee Steakhouse** • 2006 3rd Ave [E 110th St] 212-996-3300 • $ Grilled meats for cheap.
- **Polash** • 2179 3rd Ave [E 119th St] 212-410-0276 • $$ Surprisingly solid uptown Indian Restaurant.
- **Rao's** • 455 E 114th St [1st Ave] 212-722-6709 • $$$$$ An Italian institution, but you'll never get in.
- **Ricardo Steakhouse** • 2145 2nd Ave [E 110th St] 212-289-5895 • $$ Steak, bar, outside patio with upscale vibe and valet parking.
- **Sandy Restaurant** • 2261 2nd Ave [E 116th St] 212-348-8654 • $ Neighborhood Dominican joint. Try the lechon asado.
- **Taco Mix** • 234 E 116 St [Third Ave] 347-664-3002 • $ The best tacos in El Barrio. Go for the al pastor.

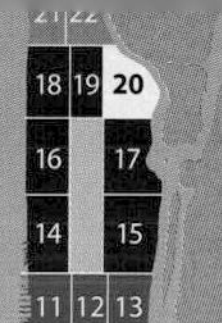

asablanca Meat Market** is always packed, and for good reason with :cellent homemade sausages. For do-it-yourself projects **The emolition Depot** is a gold mine. Latin music fans swear by **Casa Latina usic Store**. There's even a touch of suburbia in East Harlem with the :cent opening of **Costco**.

Coffee

- **Love Cafe** • 283 Pleasant Ave [115th]
  212-369-6916
  Super friendly indie shop almost too good to be true.

Shopping

- **115 R & P Beer Distributors** •
  77 E 115th St [Park Ave]
  212-828-5511
  Beer at a good price if you buy in bulk.
- **Capri Bakery** • 186 E 116th St [3rd Ave]
  212-410-1876
  Spanish El Barrio bakery.
- **Casa Latina Music Shop** •
  151 E 116th St [Lexington Ave]
  212-427-6062
  El Barrio's oldest record store.
- **Casablanca Meat Market** •
  125 E 110th St [Park Ave]
  212-534-7350
  The line out the door every Saturday says it all.
- **Costco** • 517 E 117 St [Pleasant Ave]
  212-896-5873
  Giving Long Islanders another reason to drive into the city.
- **The Demolition Depot** •
  216 E 125th St [3rd Ave]
  212-860-1138
  Amazing selection of architectural salvage.
- **Don Paco Lopez Panaderia** •
  2129 3rd Ave [E 116th St]
  212-876-0700
  Mexican bakery famous for Three Kings Day cake.
- **Eagle Home Centers** •
  2254 2nd Ave [E 115th St]
  212-423-0333
  Jpdate the tile in your kitchen or bathroom
- **Goodwill Thrift Store** •
  2231 3rd Ave [E 122nd St]
  212-410-0973
  A few floors of used stuff (some of it pretty good).
- **Heavy Metal Bike Shop** •
  2016 3rd Ave [E 110th St]
  212-410-1144
  Pedal to the metal for repairs and parts.
- **La Marqueta** • 1590 Park Ave [E 115th St]
  212-312-3603
  A couple Puerto Rican food stalls. Still waiting to be revived.
- **Lore Decorators** • 2201 3rd Ave [E 120th St]
  212-534-1025
  Well Known by Madison Avenue clientele, Reupholster your sidewalk/dumpster chair.
- **Mi Mexico Lindo Bakery** •
  2267 2nd Ave [E 116th St]
  212-996-5223
  Grab a tray at this old-school bakery.
- **Motherhood Maternity** •
  163 E 125th St [Lexington Ave]
  212-987-8808
  Casual wear for soon-to-be mommies.
- **Pathmark** • 160 E 125th St [Lexington Ave]
  212-722-9155
  Huge supermarket. One of the only to sell fresh foods.
- **Raices Dominican Cigars** •
  2250 1st Ave [E 116th St]
  212-410-6824
  Hand-rolled cigars. With a smoking room!
- **Raskin Carpets** • 2246 3rd Ave [E 122nd St]
  212-369-1100
  Long time East Harlem store has Santa at Xmas.
- **Savoy Bakery** • 170 E 110th St [3rd Ave]
  212-828-8896
  Lots of tasty sponge cakes.
- **SpaHa Cafe** • 1872 Lexington Ave [E 116th St]
  212-427-1767
  Pretty decent coffee and baked goods.
- **V&M American Outlet** •
  2226 3rd Ave [E 121st St]
  212-987-6459
  Everything for your apartment
- **V.I.M.** • 2239 3rd Ave [E 122nd St]
  212-369-5033
  Street wear—jeans, sneakers, tops—for all.
- **Young Fish Market** • 2004 3rd Ave [E 110th St]
  212-876-3427
  Get it fresh or fried.

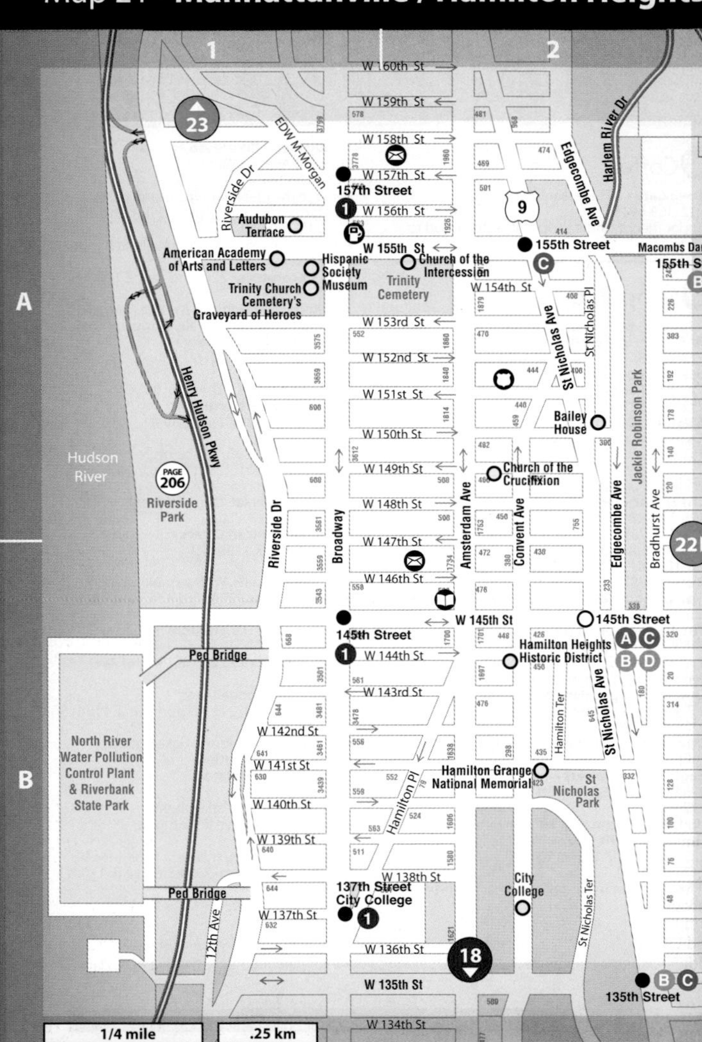

W 160th St
W 159th St
W 158th St
W 157th St
157th Street
W 156th St
W 155th St
155th Street
Macombs Dam
155th Str
W 154th St
W 153rd St
W 152nd St
W 151st St
W 150th St
W 149th St
W 148th St
W 147th St
W 146th St
W 145th St
145th Street
145th Street
W 144th St
W 143rd St
W 142nd St
W 141st St
W 140th St
W 139th St
W 138th St
137th Street City College
W 137th St
W 136th St
W 135th St
135th Street
W 134th St
EDW M-Morgan
Riverside Dr
Audubon Terrace
American Academy of Arts and Letters
Hispanic Society Museum
Trinity Church Cemetery's Graveyard of Heroes
Church of the Intercession
Trinity Cemetery
Edgecombe Ave
Harlem River Dr
St Nicholas Ave
St Nicholas Pl
Jackie Robinson Park
Bailey House
Henry Hudson Pkwy
Hudson River
Riverside Park
PAGE 206
Broadway
Amsterdam Ave
Convent Ave
Church of the Crucifixion
Bradhurst Ave
Hamilton Heights Historic District
Hamilton Ter
Ped Bridge
North River Water Pollution Control Plant & Riverbank State Park
Hamilton Grange National Memorial
St Nicholas Park
Hamilton Pl
City College
St Nicholas Ter
12th Ave
1/4 mile
.25 km

Neighborhood Overview

Hamilton Heights doesn't quite feel like Manhattan. A stew of college students, Neo-Gothic architecture and vibrant Dominican culture brings a foreign flavor to the upper, upper west side of the island. Like everywhere above the park, Columbia University's expansion threatens to throw gentrification into double-time. Even in the face of rising rent, however, Alexander Hamilton's former country estate still seems vaguely bucolic. Gently sloping parks, free museums and striking brownstones anchor the neighborhood. Street vendors dish out spicy tacos and wrap juicy tamales. Winding streets lined with row-houses tempt anyone to stroll for hours. Sandwiched between the Hudson and St. Nicholas Park, this section of the country's most chaotic city offers much needed respite from the concrete and steel.

Counting landmark status buildings in Hamilton Heights is like keeping track of nuns in Rome. The number is staggering, but none are as striking as **City College's** white and brick Neo-Gothic buildings. Turrets, towers and gargoyles practically litter the historic college's campus. For classic New York, mosey up to the **Hamilton Heights Historic District**, just north of City College. Trademark row-houses line the streets where Alexander Hamilton's original home sat. **Hamilton Grange National Memorial** is now hanging out in St. Nicholas Park. The Bailey House is one of the coolest houses in Manhattan, and probably the only one built on a circus fortune. It was the home of P.T. Barnum's partner James Bailey. For crazy concrete church design, nothing beats the whacked out **Church of the Crucifixion**.

Central Park gets all of the fanfare, but uptown green space is hillier and virtually tourist-free. Sure, the authorities built Riverbank State Park to appease residents after the city dumped a sewage plant along the river. But the State rolled out the red carpet. The facilities, set inside the more expansive Riverside Park, boast a roller skating rink, running track and soccer field. Skip the gym fees, and swim laps at the indoor pool, which costs a paltry $2 to enter. The **Trinity Cemetery Graveyard of Heroes** feels almost otherworldly, with enough rolling paths for a rural European plot. Several Astors, Charles Dickens' son and John James Audubon are all buried here, as is three-term mayor Ed Koch. St. Nicholas Park is worth a daytime visit just for its spacious lawns, but don't miss Hamilton Grange. The National Park Service restored the building after moving it to the park in 2009.

In a city where museums charge $20 just to elbow strangers for a glimpse of a Botticelli, the **Hispanic Society of America** Museum and Library seems nearly miraculous. Admission is free to the museum and reference library, which showcases the arts and cultures of Spain, Portugal, and Latin America. Browse the society's prints, paintings and artifacts, but linger in **Audubon Terrace**. The square-city block plot was named for the famous naturalist, John James Audubon, who once farmed in Washington Heights. The land became a cultural center in 1904 and also houses the **American Academy of Arts and Letters**. Years of neglect left the terrace looking drab, but a a recent glass structure addition linking the Academy of Arts and Letters and the Hispanic Society signals a welcome rejuvenation.

Landmarks

- **American Academy of Arts & Letters** • 633 W 155th St [Riverside Dr] 212-368-5900
New glass structure links it to the Hispanic Society.
- **Audubon Terrace** • Broadway & W 155th St
Pleasant, if lonely, Beaux Arts complex. What's it doing here?
- **Bailey House** • 10 St Nicholas Pl [W 150th St]
Romanesque revival mansion from PT Barnum's partner James Bailey.
- **City College** • 160 Convent Ave [W 130th St] 212-650-7000
Peaceful gothic campus.
- **The Episcopal Church Of The Crucifixion** • 459 W 149th St [Convent Ave] 212-281-0900
Whacked-out concrete church by Costas Machlouzarides, circa 1967.
- **Hamilton Grange National Memorial** • 414 W 141st St [St Nicholas Ave]
Alexander Hamilton's house, twice relocated and now facing the wrong way. Damn those Jeffersonians!
- **Hamilton Heights Historic District** • W 140th & W 145th St b/n Amsterdam & St Nicholas Ave
192 houses, apartments and churches on the National Registry of Historic Places. Who knew?
- **Hispanic Society Museum** • 613 W 155th St [Broadway] 212-926-2234
Free museum (Tues-Sat) with Spanish masterpieces.
- **Trinity Church Cemetery Graveyard of Heroes** • 3699 Broadway [W 153rd St]
Hilly, almost countryish cemetery.

RIP to one of our favorite night spots: **St. Nick's Pub** what was probably the best jazz bar anywhere in the world. The African nights on Saturdays were the stuff of legends. Let's hope it makes a miraculous comeback! In lieu of that, **Harlem Public** serves up good food and great drinks and is a welcome addition to a somewhat sparse nightlife scene.

Bars

• **Harlem Public** • 3612 Broadway [149th St]
212-939-9404
Good food, good drinks, exciting addition to neighborhood.

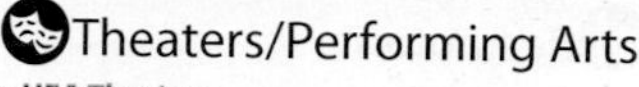
Theaters/Performing Arts

• **HSA Theater** •
645 St Nicholas Ave [W 141st St]
212-868-4444
The Harlem School of the Arts.

Restaurants

Authenticity reigns in Hamilton Heights. Meander up Broadway for your pick of taquerias and Dominican eats. Picante boasts some of the nabe's best sit-down Mexican. Cheap Middle Eastern can be found at **Queen Sheeba**. **Trufa** and its sister restaurant **Tonalli Cafe Bar** provide some bistro options to the sparse Hamilton Heights food scene.

Restaurants

- **Devin's Fish & Chips** • 747 St Nicholas Ave [W 147th St] 212-491-5518 • $ Greasy goodness just steps from St. Nick's Pub. Recommended.
- **Ecuatoriana Restaurant** • 1685 Amsterdam Ave [W 143rd St] 212-491-4626 • $$ Legit Ecuadorian fare, sans guinea pig.
- **Famous Fish Market** • 684 St Nicholas Ave [W 145th St] 212-491-8323 • $ Deep fried and from the sea.
- **Food Hut** • 1709 Amsterdam Ave [W 144th St] 212-491-4492 • $ Jerk chicken with a smile.
- **Jesus' Taco** • 501 W 145th St [Amsterdam Ave] 212-234-3330 • $ Tacos and burgers.
- **Jimbo's Hamburger Palace** • 528 W 145th St [Amsterdam Ave] 212-926-0338 • $ Cheap, fast, easy burgers.
- **La Oaxaquena Restaurant** • 1969 Amsterdam Ave [W 157th St] 212-283-7752 • $ One of the best in a parade of taquerias.
- **Olga's Pizza** • 3409 Broadway [W 138th St] 212-234-7878 • $ Bare-bones pies, whole or by the slice.
- **Picante** • 3424 Broadway [W 139th St] 212-234-6479 • $$ Arguably Manhattanville's best Mexican, plus affordable margs.
- **Queen Sheeba** • 317 W 141st St [Frederick Douglass Blvd] 212-862-6149 • $ Cafeteria style Middle Eastern that's friendly on the wallet.
- **Sunshine Kitchen** • 695 St Nicholas Ave [W 145th St] 212-368-4972 • $ Delicious curried goat.
- **Tonalli Cafe Bar** • 3628 Broadway [W 149th St] 212-926-0399 • $$ Rare Italian bistro cuisine in Hamilton Heights.
- **Trufa** • 3431 Broadway [140th St] 212-281-6165 • $$ Bistro featuring pastas and New American entrees.

Bagels, Coffee, & Shopping

'ou can browse Broadway for mom-and-pop storefronts, and there is not a goshdarn hing you can do about it. You might as well dance with the one you walked to, so check ut **B-Jays USA** for every sneaker under the sun, **Felix Supply Hardware** for stocking up n basics on the way to Trinity Cemetery (we don't question what you might do), and njoy (without smirking) **V.I.M.**; when someone says they're the best jeans and sneaker tore in America, you should probably pay attention.

Coffee

- **Café One** • 1619 Amsterdam Ave [W 139th St]
  212-690-0060
  Free wifi, quality pastries and reliable java.

Shopping

- **B-Jays USA** • 540 W 143rd St [Hamilton Pl]
  212-694-3160
  Every sneaker under the sun.
- **Bronx Spirits Liquors** •
  3375 Broadway [W 137th St]
  212-926-2888
  For wine, sometimes reliable is all you need.
- **Felix Supply Hardware** •
  3650 Broadway [W 150th St]
  212-283-1988
  Stock up on basics near Trinity Cemetery.
- **Foot Locker** • 3549 Broadway [W 146th St]
  212-491-0927
  Get your sneakers from a fake referee.
- **Unity Liquors** •
  708 St Nicholas Ave [W 146th St]
  212-491-7821
  Right by the subway, where all liquor stores should be.
- **V.I.M.** • 508 W 145th St [Amsterdam Ave]
  212-491-1143
  Street wear—jeans, sneakers, tops—for all.

Map 22 • Harlem (Upper)

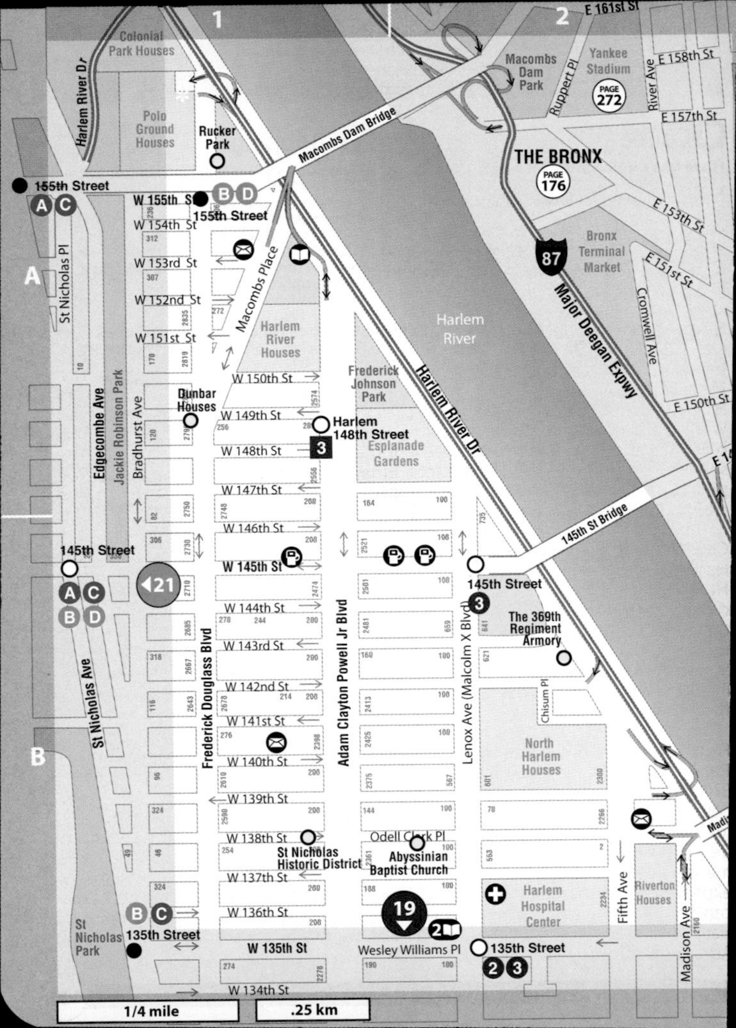

1
2
E 161st St
E 158th St
E 157th St
Colonial Park Houses
Harlem River Dr
Polo Ground Houses
Rucker Park
Macombs Dam Bridge
Macombs Dam Park
Ruppert Pl
Yankee Stadium
PAGE 272
River Ave
THE BRONX
PAGE 176
155th Street
W 155th St
155th Street
W 154th St
W 153rd St
W 152nd St
W 151st St
W 150th St
W 149th St
W 148th St
W 147th St
W 146th St
W 145th St
W 144th St
W 143rd St
W 142nd St
W 141st St
W 140th St
W 139th St
W 138th St
W 137th St
W 136th St
W 135th St
W 134th St
E 153rd St
E 151st St
E 150th St
Bronx Terminal Market
87
Major Deegan Expwy
Cromwell Ave
Harlem River
Macombs Place
Harlem River Houses
Frederick Johnson Park
Harlem River Dr
St Nicholas Pl
Edgecombe Ave
Jackie Robinson Park
Bradhurst Ave
Dunbar Houses
Harlem 148th Street
Esplanade Gardens
145th St Bridge
145th Street
145th Street
21
The 369th Regiment Armory
St Nicholas Ave
Frederick Douglass Blvd
Adam Clayton Powell Jr Blvd
Lenox Ave (Malcolm X Blvd)
Chisum Pl
North Harlem Houses
Odell Clark Pl
St Nicholas Historic District
Abyssinian Baptist Church
19
Harlem Hospital Center
Fifth Ave
Riverton Houses
Madison Ave
St Nicholas Park
135th Street
Wesley Williams Pl
135th Street
1/4 mile
.25 km

Neighborhood Overview

At first glance, upper Harlem lacks character. Generic buffets and 99-cent stores line Lenox, one of the nabe's anchor streets. 145th Street sprawls with suburban gas stations and an entrance to the 145th Street Bridge. High-rises dot the uptown skyline. But this 20-block triangle sandwiched between St. Nicholas and the Harlem River is the lifeline of black culture in New York. Everyone from starving artists to self-made millionaires have called upper Harlem home, and a visit to the **Schomburg Center for Research** reveals the neighborhood's significant impact. Not surprisingly, gentrification is a sensitive point of controversy. But for now, the culture remains intact. Old churches maintain a sense of community. Heavenly soul food attracts locals and tourists. Historic districts recreate a sense of time. Upper Harlem has it all—you just have to dig a little.

History buffs, perk up. A stroll through upper Harlem is one of Manhattan's densest walks. Start at 135th Street and Lenox, or "Speaker's Corner," an intersection where back in the day anyone shouted their concerns and critiques of current events. Most famously, Marcus Garvey presented his views on race at this corner. The Harlem Hellfighters, an all-black military unit that fought in World War I and World War II, housed their headquarters at the imposing **369th Regiment Armory**. The building still operates as a sustainment brigade, but an obelisk outside honors the soldiers. Long before the Hellfighters, Ethiopian traders protested segregation policies by founding the **Abyssinian Baptist Church** in 1808. After 203 years, the congregation only moved once, in 1923, to its striking Neo-Gothic building.

Classic row-houses, historic churches, and apartment complexes define upper Harlem's architecture scene. Most notably, the Rockefeller family built the **Dunbar Houses** in 1926 to provide affordable housing in Harlem. Instead of families, the complex attracted writers, artists, musicians and poets, including W.E.B. DuBois, the first African-American to graduate from Harvard. Similarly ambitious residents moved in to the **St. Nicholas Historic District**. Sometimes called "Strivers' Row," Stanford White designed the houses, where many upwardly mobile residents lived. Note the original "Walk your Horses" signs (there aren't any carriage rides in the neighborhood).

From libraries to basketball courts, Harlem's cultural options are distinct. **Rucker Park** is home to famously intense pickup games. Kareem Abdul-Jabbar, Kobe Bryant, and hundreds of exceedingly talented locals have dribbled on those courts. Swing by to try your hand or just enjoy the show. The Schomburg Center for Research in Black Culture focuses on preserving the history of people of African descent worldwide. The center's dizzying array of artifacts, prints, images and manuscripts includes more than 100,000 items. For a more low-key library experience, visit the **Countee Cullen Regional Branch Library**. At the turn of the century, Madame C.J. Walker lived at this same address. The "richest woman in Harlem" earned her fortune by selling hair care products specifically for African-American women.

Landmarks

O Landmarks

- **The 369th Regiment Armory •**
  2366 5th Ave [W 142nd St]
  Home of the Harlem Hellfighters.
- **Abyssinian Baptist Church •**
  132 Odell Clark Pl [Lenox Ave]
  212-862-7474
  NY's oldest black congregation.
- **The Dunbar Houses •**
  W 149th St & Frederick Douglass Blvd
  Historic multi-family houses.
- **Holcombe Rucker Park •**
  Frederick Douglass Blvd & W 155th St
  Kareem Abdul-Jabar's, and a ton of talented locals', Harlem court.
- **St. Nicholas Historic District •**
  202 W 138th St [7th Ave]
  Beautiful neo-Georgian townhouses.

There isn't a lot of nightlife above 135th Street but stalwart **Londel's Supper Club** has classic jazz on Fridays and Saturdays with no cover.

Bars

- **Londel's Supper Club** • 2620 Frederick Douglass Blvd [W 140th St]
  212-234-6114
  Great live music on Friday & Saturdays.

Restaurants

The parade of routine delis on Lenox hides some of Manhattan's tastiest eats. **Miss Maude's Spoonbread** dishes out calorically foolish comfort food. Do not miss **Charles' Country Pan Fried Chicken** to chow down on mindblowing hot birds. If you want a taste of the sea, hit up the window service at **O'Fishole Seafood** for fried fishy take-out goodness.

Restaurants

- **Charles' Country Pan Fried Kitchen •** 2839 Frederick Douglass Blvd [W 151st St] 212-281-1800 • $ The fried chicken they serve in heaven.
- **Grini's Grill •** 100 W 143rd St [Lenox Ave] 212-694-6274 • $ This "tapas bar" actually serves heaping plates of meat and rice.
- **Londel's •** 2620 Frederick Douglass Blvd [W 140th St] 212-234-6114 • $$$ Good Southern with live music on the weekend.
- **Mama Tina's Pizza •** 2649 Frederick Douglass Blvd [W 141st St] 212-368-2820 • $ Decent pizza for late-night pangs.
- **Miss Maude's Spoonbread Too •** 547 Lenox Ave [W 138th St] 212-690-3100 • $$ Harlem food for the soul.
- **O'Fishole Seafood •** 274 W 145th St [8th Ave] 212-234-2601 • $$ Jimbo's, the burger place, does fish; equally greasy and delicious.
- **People's Choice •** 2733 Frederick Douglass Blvd [W 145th St] 212-281-3830 • $$ Jerk chicken and oxtail stews worth a taste.

Bagels, Coffee, & Shopping

Wandering Lenox and 145th Streets will unearth everything from cheap, expansive supermarkets like **Pathmark** to niche sneaker shops like **Sneaker Q. Make My Cake** has sugary cupcakes, cheesecakes and regular cakes.

Coffee

- **Dunkin' Donuts** • 110 W 145th St [Lenox Ave]
  212-234-3440
  Decent coffee served in gigantic Styrofoam cups.
- **Dunkin' Donuts** •
  2730 Frederick Douglass Blvd [W 145th St]
  212-862-0635
  Decent coffee served in gigantic Styrofoam cups.
- **Starbucks** •
  301 W 145th St [Frederick Douglass Blvd]
  212-690-7835
  One of the few coffee spots around here.
- **T & J Bakery** •
  2541 Adam Clayton Powell Jr Blvd [W 148th St]
  212-234-5662
  Amazing baked goods. And coffee too.

Shopping

- **B. Oyama** • 2330 7th Ave [W 137th St]
  212-234-5128
  Fashion for men.
- **Baskin-Robbins** •
  2730 Frederick Douglass Blvd [W 145th St]
  212-862-0635
  Do they still have 31 flavors?
- **Harlem Liquors** •
  2302 Adam Clayton Powell Jr Blvd [W 135th St]
  212-234-5958
  Do you need to know more than "discount" and "liquor"?
- **Luis Liquor** • 108 W 145th St [Lenox Ave]
  212-694-6619
  Perfect grab-and-go shop near the subway.
- **Make My Cake** •
  2380 Adam Clayton Powell Jr Blvd [W 139th St]
  212-234-2344
  Freshly baked cakes from a Southern family recipe.
- **Pathmark** •
  300 W 145th St [Frederick Douglass Blvd]
  212-281-3158
  No-frills market that gets the job done.
- **The Schomburg Shop** •
  515 Malcolm X Blvd [W 135th St]
  212-491-2206
  Shop specializing in Black history and culture.
- **Sneaker Q** • 693 Lenox Ave [142nd St]
  212-491-9179
  Get your kicks at this Lenox storefront.

Map 23 • Washington Heights

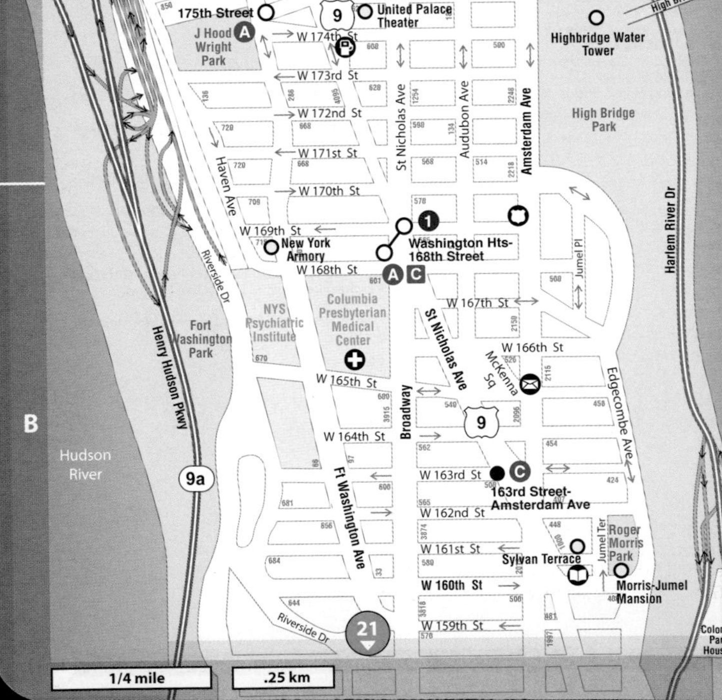

Neighborhood Overview

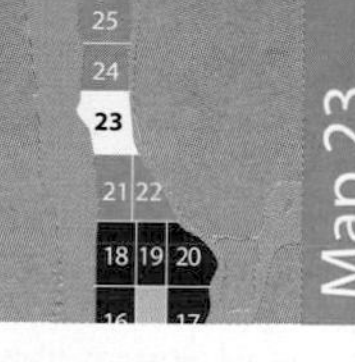

Washington Heights is a veritable United Nations of immigrant stories. Irish settlers moved up north in the 1900s. After World War I, European Jews called this hilly stretch of Manhattan home. Now, the 'hood swings to an undeniable merengue beat. The largely Dominican sliver of northern Manhattan probably claims more authenticity than any Punta Cana all-inclusive. Street vendors whip up delectable chimichurris, a sort of Dominican hamburger. Broadway houses a seemingly limitless number of chicken-and-rice eateries. English almost feels like a second language. As with all of Manhattan, this swath of delis and pollerias sees change in the future. Hipsters searching for cheap rent keep hiking uptown, and higher end Dominican fusion eateries are breaking into the restaurant scene. It looks like everyone knows that all you have to do is take the A train even farther than Harlem.

Some of Manhattan's most storied buildings live far uptown, and The Heights are no exception. Most notable is the **Morris-Jumel Mansion**, a hilltop home that looks like it belongs in Gone With the Wind, not Gotham. British Colonel Roger Morris built the abode in 1765, but George Washington famously stationed his headquarters here in the fall of 1776. After the Revolutionary War, Morris left the estate, which stretched up from Harlem. If that's not impressive enough, note that Washington also took John Adams, Thomas Jefferson, and John Quincy Adams to dine there in 1790. The museum is open for visits, but beware: There have been rumors of hauntings. For a less ghostly architecture tour, check out the two-block historic district of **Sylvan Terrace**. This stretch of wooden row-houses line the skinny street leading up to the mansion. Although the turn of the century homes underwent a few incarnations—from wooden to faux brick to stucco—they are now largely restored to their original facades. Another turn of the century creation, the **New York Armory**, had a similar rebirth. The armory first served as a training center for the National Guard in 1909. It rose to fame as a center for track and field competitions until the 1980s, when it became a homeless shelter. Now, the armory has been restored and functions as a track and field center.

This skinny expanse of Manhattan boasts some of the country's top transportation accomplishments. Construction began in 1948 for the **Cross-Bronx Expressway**, one of the country's first highways to forge through such a densely populated urban area. Heading west into Fort Lee, NJ, the **George Washington Bridge** is the only 14-lane suspension crossing in the country. Hikers, bikers and skaters can skip the pricey tolls and enjoy views of Palisades Interstate Park in New Jersey. The best part about the bridge: **The Little Red Lighthouse** that rests underneath. The charmingly out-of-place tower only operated between 1921 and 1948, but it earned fame from the 1942 children's book *The Little Red Lighthouse and the Great Gray Bridge*, by Hildegarde Swift and Lynd Ward.

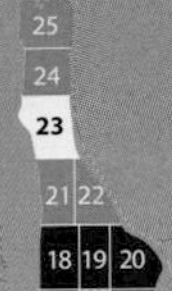

Landmarks

Landmarks

- **The Armory •**
216 Fort Washington Ave [W 169th St]
212-923-1803
World class running facility houses Track & Field Hall of Fame.
- **Cross Bronx Expressway •**
Cross Bronx Expressway [Ittner Pl]
Worst. Highway. Ever.
- **George Washington Bridge •**
W 178th St [Henry Hudson Pkwy]
Try to see it when it's lit up. Drive down from Riverdale on the Henry Hudson at night and you'll understand.
- **High Bridge Water Tower •** Highbridge Park
Defunct but cool water tower; tours inside are worth the hassle.
- **The Little Red Lighthouse •**
Fort Washington Park [W 178th St]
Enter from 181st Street. It's there, really!
- **Morris-Jumel Mansion •**
65 Jumel Terrace [W 162nd St]
212-923-8008
The oldest building in New York, at least until someone changes it again.
- **Sylvan Terrace •**
b/n Jumel Ter & St Nicholas Ave
The most un-Manhattanlike place in all the world.
- **United Palace Theater •**
4140 Broadway [W 175th St]
Movie theater, then church, now rock venue. Gorgeous inside.

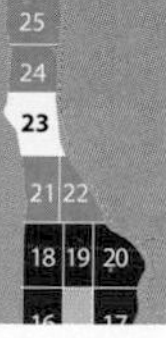

From hopping gay bars to suave wine lounges, The Heights nightlife scene won't leave you wanting. Groove to salsa and Reggaeton at **No Parking** or duck into **Coogan's** or **Le Chéile** for a pint. When the live music itch strikes, the shabby but grand **United Palace** hosts a bevy of artists.

Bars

- **Coogan's** • 4015 Broadway [W 169th St]
  212-928-1234
  Join doctors, professors and off-duty cops for a cold one.
- **Le Chéile** • 839 W 181st St [Cabrini Blvd]
  212-740-3111
  Nice-looking Irish bar with good beer & food.
- **No Parking** • 4168 Broadway [W 177th St]
  212-923-8700
  The Heights gets a gay bar.
- **The Red Room Lounge** • 1 Bennett Ave [W 181st St]
  917-975-2690
  Dionysus would be proud.

Restaurants

Dominican eats dominate the food scene up here; **Restaurant Margot** is easily one of the best. Hit up **Malecon** for unsurpassed roast chicken. When variety beckons **Sushi Yu** dishes up a tasty alternative and **Saggio** is a pleasant Italian trattoria. And good luck choosing from the massive **Hudson View** menu (though we're sorry to report that there is not much of a view).

Restaurants

- **181 Cabrini** • 854 W 181st St [Cabrini Blvd]
  212-923-2233 • $$
  Seasonal American bistro.
- **Aqua Marina** • 4060 Broadway [W 171st St]
  212-928-0070 • $
  OK Uptown Italian.
- **Carrot Top Pastries** •
  3931 Broadway [W 165th St]
  212-927-4800 • $
  Baked goods and coffee too!
- **Coogan's** • 4015 Broadway [W 169th St]
  212-928-1234 • $$
  Where med students and cops go.
- **Dallas BBQ** • 3956 Broadway [W 166th St]
  212-568-3700 • $$
  When you can't get to Virgil's.
- **El Conde** • 4139 Broadway [W 175th St]
  212-781-3231 • $$$
  Big slabs of MEAT.
- **Empire Szechuan Noodle House** •
  4041 Broadway [W 170th St]
  212-568-1600 • $$
  Take a guess at what they serve.
- **Flaco's Pizza** • 3876 Broadway [W 162nd St]
  212-923-3733 • $
  Chowing on this cheap, delish pizza won't keep you flaco.
- **Hudson View Restaurant** •
  770 W 181st St [Fort Washington Ave]
  212-781-0303 • $$
  Ch ch ch choices.
- **Jimmy Oro Restaurant** •
  711 W 181st St [Broadway]
  212-795-1414 • $
  Chinese/Spanish. Huge variety.
- **Malecon** • 4141 Broadway [W 175th St]
  212-927-3812 • $
  Fabulous roast chicken.
- **Margot Restaurant** •
  3822 Broadway [W 159th St]
  212-781-8494 • $$
  Arguably, The Heights' very best Dominican.
- **Parrilla Steakhouse** •
  3920 Broadway [W 164th St]
  212-543-9500 • $$
  Argentinean with cool-ass grill.
- **Reme Restaurant** •
  4021 Broadway [W 169th St]
  212-923-5452 • $
  New York comfort food at this typical diner.
- **Saggio Restaurant** •
  829 W 181st St [Cabrini Blvd]
  212-795-3080 • $$$
  Every good neighborhood needs a solid Italian trattoria.
- **Silver Palace Chinese Restaurant** •
  3846 Broadway [W 160th St]
  212-927-8300 • $$
  Standard storefront Chinese fare.
- **Sushi Yu II** • 827 W 181st St [Pinehurst Ave]
  212-781-8833 • $
  Raw fish for when you need to take a plantain break.
- **Tipico Dominicano** •
  4172 Broadway [W 177th St]
  212-781-3900 • $
  Family place to watch the game. Gooooooal!
- **University Deli** • 603 W 168th St [Broadway]
  212-568-3838 • $
  Standard deli fare, with a large doctor clientele.

Bagels, Coffee, & Shopping

Broadway's chaos anchors this nabe's shopping options. Stroll the street for a mind-boggling number of hardware stores, check out oodles of vendors at **La Plaza de las Americas**, and score free delivery on groceries at **Liberato**. For a taste of Russia, check out **Moscow on the Hudson**. It's all here.

Bagels

- **Mike's Bagels** • 4003 Broadway [W 168th St]
  212-928-2300
  More like Bob's than Murray's.

Coffee

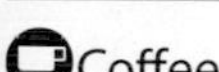

- **Dunkin' Donuts** •
  1416 St Nicholas Ave [W 181st St]
  212-928-1900
  Decent coffee served in gigantic Styrofoam cups.
- **Jou Jou** • 603 W 168th St [Broadway]
  212-781-2222
  Open 24 hours!
- **Jou Jou Café** • 3959 Broadway [W 166th St]
  212-740-8081
  Serving your soup, sandwich and espresso needs all day and night.
- **X Caffe** • 3952 Broadway [W 165th St]
  212-543-1999
  Hip and comfortable.

Shopping

- **3841 Hardware** • 3841 Broadway [W 160th St]
  212-927-9320
  No name required at this classic, Broadway tool supply shop.
- **Bravo Supermarket** •
  1331 St Nicholas Ave [W 177th St]
  212-927-1331
  Clean and well-supplied.
- **Carrot Top Pastries** •
  3931 Broadway [W 165th St]
  212-927-4800
  Top carrot cake, muffins, chocolate cake, rugalach, and more.
- **The Children's Place** •
  600 W 181st St [St Nicholas Ave]
  212-923-7244
  Cute clothes for little ones.
- **Columbia Wine** • 4038 Broadway [169th St]
  212-543-2633
  Well-appointed, non-plexiglass wine & liquor store.
- **Fort Washington Bakery & Deli** •
  808 W 181st St [Fort Washington Ave]
  212-795-1891
  Damn good looking cookies.
- **Goodwill Thrift Store** •
  512 W 181st St [Amsterdam Ave]
  212-923-7910
  Everything and anything for cheaper.
- **Jumel Terrace Books** •
  426 W 160th St [Jumel Terrace]
  212-928-9525
  African-American and Mostly out of print books.
- **La Bella Nails & Spa** •
  4033 Broadway [W 169th St]
  212-927-2023
  Time for that bi-weekly pedicure.
- **La Plaza de Las Americas** •
  Broadway & W 175th St
  Outdoor street vendor market.
- **Liberato Grocery** •
  3900 Broadway [W 163rd St]
  212-927-8250
  Get your fruits and veggies delivered—free!
- **Modell's** • 606 W 181st St [St Nicholas Ave]
  212-568-3000
  Lots and lots of sporting goods.
- **Moscow on the Hudson** •
  801 W 181st St [Fort Washington Ave]
  212-740-7397
  Comrades, this place is Russian culinary heaven.
- **Nunez Hardware** •
  4147 Broadway [W 175th St]
  212-927-8518
  Scavenge for tools at this old-school, stocked-to-bursting shop.
- **Santana Banana** •
  661 W 181st St [Wadsworth Ave]
  212-568-4096
  Leather shoes for men and women who are into leather.
- **Total Beauty Supplies** •
  650 W 181st St [Wadsworth Ave]
  212-923-6139
  Bad hair days are over.
- **Vargas Liquor Store** •
  114 Audubon Ave [W 171st St]
  212-781-5195
  Convenient for paper-bag-drinking in Highbridge Park, if that's your thing.

Map 24 • Fort George / Fort Tryon

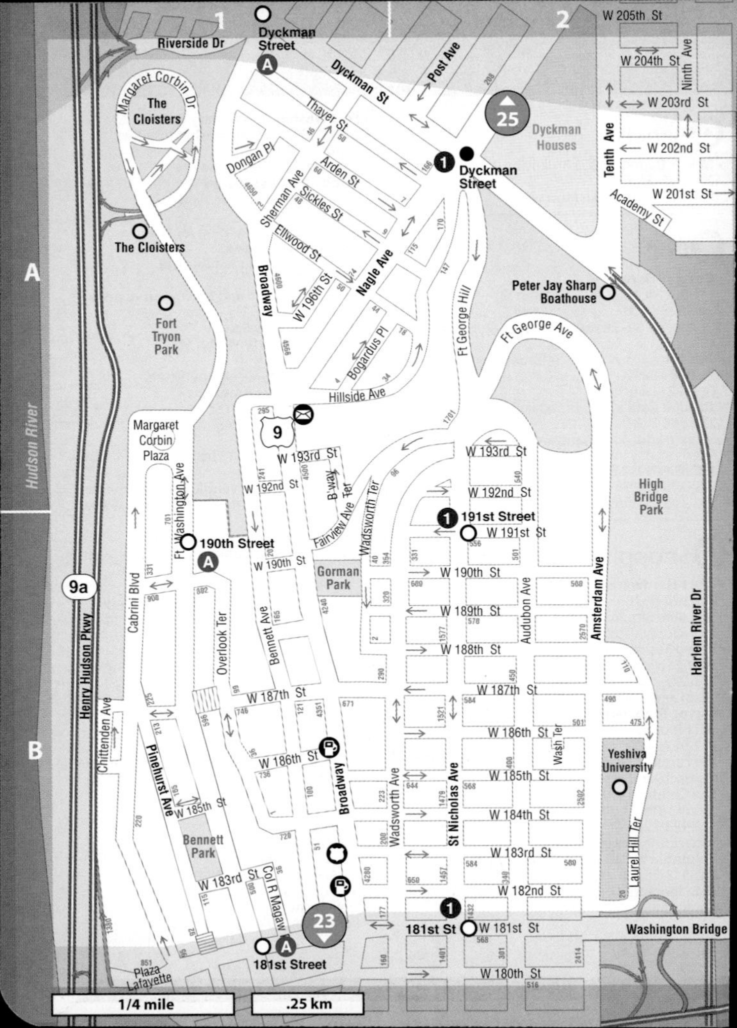

1
2
A
B
W 205th St
W 204th St
Ninth Ave
W 203rd St
W 202nd St
W 201st St
Tenth Ave
Academy St
Dyckman Street
Riverside Dr
Margaret Corbin Dr
The Cloisters
Dyckman St
Post Ave
Thayer St
Dongan Pl
Arden St
Sherman Ave
Sickles St
Ellwood St
Nagle Ave
W 196th St
Broadway
25
Dyckman Houses
Dyckman Street
Peter Jay Sharp Boathouse
Fort Tryon Park
Ft George Hill
Ft George Ave
Bogardus Pl
Hillside Ave
9
Margaret Corbin Plaza
W 193rd St
W 192nd St
B'way Ter
Fairview Ave
Wadsworth Ter
191st Street
W 191st St
Ft Washington Ave
190th Street
W 190th St
Gorman Park
Hudson River
9a
Henry Hudson Pkwy
Cabrini Blvd
Overlook Ter
Bennett Ave
W 189th St
W 188th St
W 187th St
Audubon Ave
Amsterdam Ave
High Bridge Park
Harlem River Dr
Chittenden Ave
Pinehurst Ave
W 186th St
Wash Ter
W 185th St
Yeshiva University
Wadsworth Ave
St Nicholas Ave
W 184th St
W 183rd St
Bennett Park
Col R Magaw
Laurel Hill Ter
W 182nd St
23
181st St
W 181st St
Washington Bridge
181st Street
W 180th St
Plaza Lafayette
1/4 mile
.25 km

Neighborhood Overview

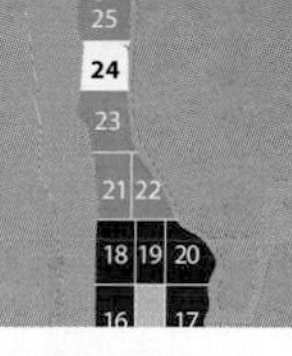

The Fort George/Fort Tryon area is also known locally as Hudson Heights, mostly for the benefit of realtors showing off this area's huge upside (literally!). Fort George is the name of the last fort of its kind, built in 1776 at the intersection of Audubon Avenue and 192nd Street. The area is diverse: The neighborhoods surrounding Fort Tryon Park and Yeshiva University are predominantly Jewish, while east of Broadway tends to be more Latin and Caribbean. The streets are some of the steepest on the island, and provide pleasant views (and a lower-body workout). Residents appreciate the quiet streets and better values and best of all, the commute to Lower Manhattan is just a half-hour.

Built in 1935 by Frederick Law Olmsted, Jr. (the son of one of the master architects behind both Central and Prospect Parks) on land donated to the city by John D. Rockefeller, **Fort Tryon Park** is the 67-acre chunk of green high up on the bluff above the Hudson River. From here, the Hudson is stunning; the pristine Palisades on the New Jersey side of the river were also made possible by Rockefeller philanthropy, in an effort to protect the view for future generations. In 1995 Bette Midler's New York Restoration Project assisted on a much-needed renovation of the park. If you are feeling cultural, pay a visit to **The Cloisters**. The complex, an extension of the Metropolitan Museum of Art, is a fully formed Medieval wonderland, with elements from four French cloisters, stained glass windows, tapestries and gardens. Don't miss the Medieval Festival that takes place every year in Fort Tryon Park when reenactors reimagine life in the Middle Ages. Wardererel

Down at the edge of the Harlem River stands the **Peter Jay Sharp Boathouse**. The first new community boathouse in New York City in years, it opened in 2004 and offers rowing lessons to members of the community. To reach the boathouse go to Tenth Avenue and Dyckman and walk south on the Lillian Goldman Walkway. Just before you get there, you'll pass by the restored Swindler Cove Park, a nice spot to stare at ducks or contemplate the river. If you decide to continue south on the walkway, the only way out is through the bridge that connects to 155th Street in Harlem.

On the campus of Yeshiva University, the unusual **Zysman Hall** was designed by Charles B. Meyers and blends Art-Deco and Moorish styles. Today, the building is home to Yeshiva's High School for Boys. If you feel the need to stock up on kosher goodies, now is the time. Cross the street for a full selection of delis, restaurants and bodegas that carry them.

Landmarks

Landmarks

- **The Cloisters** •
99 Margaret Corbin Dr [Ft Tryon Pl]
212-923-3700
The Met's storehouse of medieval art. Great herb garden, nice views.
- **Fort Tryon Park** •
W 181st St & Hudson River Greenway
A totally beautiful and scenic park on New York's north edge.
- **Peter Jay Sharp Boathouse** •
Swindler Cove Park
See the West Bronx by boat.
- **Yeshiva University Zysman Hall** •
2540 Amsterdam Ave [W 186th St]
Interesting Byzantine-style building.

There isn't a ginormous selection of bars but don't leave the neighborhood just yet. Get some drinks and placate late-afternoon hunger at **Bleu Evolution**. **The Monkey Room** is ideal for game nights or late-night drinks. Quaff craft beer to your heart's content at **Buddha Beer Bar**. For a good neighborhood spot, try **Locksmith Wine Bar**.

Bars

- **Arka Lounge** • 4488 Broadway [W 192nd St]
  212-567-9425
  Caribbean club scene.
- **Bleu Evolution** •
  808 W 187th St [Fort Washington Ave]
  212-928-6006
  Have a drink in the lounge.
- **Buddha Beer Bar** •
  4476 Broadway [W 191st St]
  646-861-2595
  Nice set of taps and Korean/Mexi fusion worth the trip.
- **Locksmith Wine & Burger Bar** •
  4463 Broadway [W 192nd St]
  212-304-9463
  Friendly spot to grab a glass of wine or beer.
- **Monkey Room** •
  589 Fort Washington Ave [W 187th St]
  212-543-9888
  Tiny like a capuchin.
- **Next Door by 107 West** •
  813 W 187th St [Fort Washington Ave]
  212-543-2111
  Half-price bottles of organic wine on Thursdays. Awesome!
- **Umbrella Bar & Lounge** •
  440 W 202nd St [9th Ave]
  212-942-5921
  Hispanic dance club.

Restaurants

In case of empty picnic baskets, visitors to Fort Tryon can go to **New Leaf Restaurant**, an upscale restaurant in a historic building within the park. Find great Indian cuisine at **Kismat**. Enjoy a real Caribbean meal at **La Casa Del Mofongo** or go Venezuelan at **Cachapas Y Mas**. The Mexican food can't be beat at **Tacos El Paisa**. For perfect falafel make your way to **Golan Heights**.

Restaurants

- **107 West** • 811 W 187th St [Fort Washington Ave] 212-923-3311 • $$ Salads, burgers, chicken...you get the idea.
- **809 Bar & Grill** • 112 Dyckman St [Nagle Ave] 212-304-3800 • $$$ Dominican grilled meat-a-thon.
- **Bleu Evolution** • 808 W 187th St [Fort Washington Ave] 212-928-6006 • $$ Uptown bohemian. Calm.
- **Cachapas Y Mas** • 107 Dyckman St [Post Ave] 212-304-2224 • $ Fried Latin tastiness in corn and meat form.
- **Golan Heights** • 2553 Amsterdam Ave [W 187th St] 212-795-7842 • $ Tasty Israeli falafel and shawarma. Popular for lunch.
- **Kismat** • 603 Fort Washington Ave [W 187th St] 212-795-8633 • $$ Throw your taste buds a surprise party.
- **La Casa Del Mofongo** • 1447 St Nicholas Ave [W 182nd St] 212-740-1200 • $$ The obvious: have the mofongo.
- **New Leaf Restaurant & Bar** • 1 Margaret Corbin Dr [Henry Hudson Pkwy] 212-568-5323 • $$$$ Uptown haven for a fancier dinner or brunch.
- **Next Door by 107 West** • 813 W 187th St [Fort Washington Ave] 212-543-2111 • $$ Organic specialties served in a warm atmosphere.
- **Tacos El Paisa** • 1548 St Nicholas Ave [W 188th St] 917-521-0972 • $ Fantastic hole-the-wall Mexican.

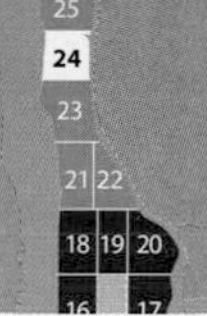

This area is home to one-of-a-kind shops like **Gideons Bakery**, for kosher sweets, and **Food Palace**, for caviar and other Russian goodies. Buy your furry friend a treat and a makeover at **Critter Outfitter**. Get gourmet edibles at **Frank's Market** or enjoy a rhyme by buying wine from **Vines on Pine**.

Bagels

- **Gideon's Bakery** •
  810 W 187th St [Fort Washington Ave]
  212-927-9262
  Get there early. These bagels go fast.

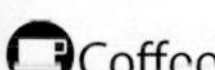

Coffee

- **Dunkin' Donuts** •
  1599 St Nicholas Ave [W 190th St]
  212-568-1039
  Decent coffee served in gigantic Styrofoam cups.
- **La Sala 78** • 111 Dyckman St [Nagle Ave]
  212-304-0667
  Enjoy some art with your latte.

Shopping

- **Apex Supply Co.** •
  4580 Broadway [W 196th St]
  212-304-0808
  Where eggshell is considered a color.
- **Associated Supermarkets** •
  592 Fort Washington Ave [W 187th St]
  212-543-0721
  No-frills market way cheaper than your local bodega.
- **Century Hardware** •
  4309 Broadway [W 184th St]
  212-927-9000
  Experts in nuts and bolts.
- **The Cloisters Museum Store** •
  99 Margaret Corbin Dr [Fort Tyron Park]
  212-650-2277
  Dark Age trinkets.
- **Critter Outfitter** •
  210 Pinehurst Ave [W 187th St]
  212-928-0342
  Pet stuff galore!
- **Fine Fare Supermarkets** •
  1617 St Nicholas Ave [W 191st St]
  212-543-3008
  Decent supermarket. "Fine" may be stretching it.
- **Food Palace** • 4407 Broadway [189th St]
  212-928-3038
  Your local Russian supermarket.
- **Foot Locker** • 146 Dyckman St [Sherman Ave]
  212-544-8613
  No lockers. But lots of sneakers.
- **Frank's Gourmet Market** •
  807 W 187th St [Fort Washington Ave]
  212-795-2929
  Best food shopping around. 15 types of olives.
- **Gideon's Bakery** •
  810 W 187th St [Fort Washington Ave]
  212-927-9262
  Kosher sugar coma.
- **JP Discount Liquors** •
  377 Audubon Ave [W 184th St]
  212-740-4027
  Who doesn't like cheaper liquor?
- **Metropolitan Museum of Art Bookshop Cloisters Branch** •
  799 Fort Washington Ave [Margaret Corbin Dr]
  212-650-2277
  Specialty - Art books.
- **NHS Hardware** •
  1539 St Nicholas Ave [W 187th St]
  212-927-3549
  Get into the DIY spirit.
- **Radio Shack** •
  180 Dyckman St [Vermilyea Ave]
  212-304-0364
  Official post-nuclear-war survivor, w/ Keith Richards and cockroaches.
- **Vines on Pine** •
  814 West 187th Street [Pinehurst Ave]
  212-923-0584
  One-of-a-kind selections.

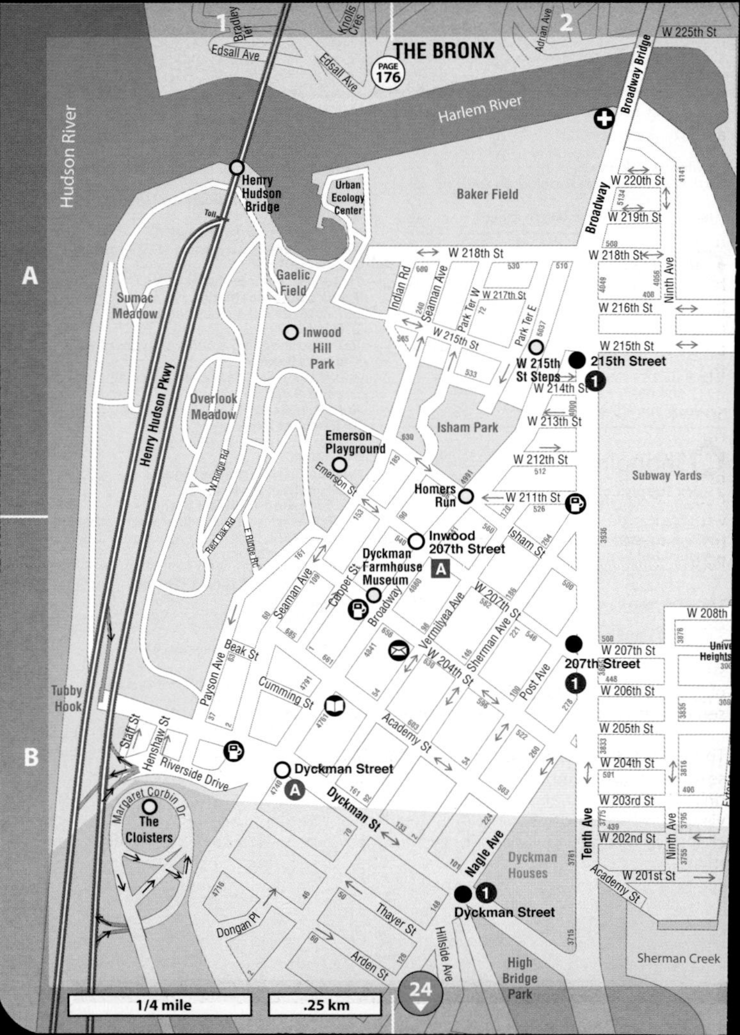

Map 25 • Inwood

PAGE 176

24

Neighborhood Overview

Located on the northernmost tip of the island, the hilly neighborhood of Inwood has something for everyone. And at a moment when there are so few places left in Manhattan where you can get affordable housing and fit all your belongings in something bigger than a shoebox, the 'hood is a solid alternative for those considering abandoning the island for one of the outer boroughs.

West of Broadway offers views, pathways, quiet streets, and artsy cafes. Parking is tricky, but possible—worst-case scenario is parking in one of the many lots around the area, which are still an affordable option. Rents west of Broadway can be higher because of the aforementioned perks and because it's right next to Inwood Hill Park, which is arguably the best neighborhood resource. The grass might be greener on this side of Broadway, but the predominantly Dominican area east of Broadway has even cheaper housing alternatives. That, and you'll find the air is filled with free bachata, especially during the summer.

Speaking of **Inwood Hill Park**, its 160 acres of greenspace stretch along the Hudson from Dyckman Street to the northern tip of the island. The park is home to last remaining natural forest in Manhattan, affording one the opportunity to brag about hiking through real woods without leaving the city. Take your kids (or nephews or nieces) to **Emerson Playground** on a sunny day, let your dog play with its kinfolk at **Homer's Run** or use one of several outdoor tennis courts. The **Inwood Greenmarket** happens rain or shine Saturdays at the foot of Inwood Hill Park.

That little house on the hill at 204th Street that looks out of place among the low-slung apartment buildings along Broadway is the **Dyckman Farmhouse** (c. 1784). Originally part of several hundred acres of farmland owned by a family with roots stretching back to New York's Dutch beginnings, today it's a stark visual reminder of just how much the city has evolved. On weekends say hello (or hola) to the seniors sitting on the benches by the farmhouse's garden.

The **Henry Hudson Bridge** connects Manhattan and The Bronx via a two-level, seven-lane structure. With thousands of vehicles crossing back and forth each day, drivers and passengers can take a minute to admire the lavish engineering efforts, views of the Hudson River and the Harlem Ship Canal below. And speaking of channels, channel your inner Rocky by climbing the **West 215th Steps**. All 111 of them (yep, we counted). On the way up note Park Terrace East to see a few rare species: Actual houses with driveways.

Landmarks

- **Dyckman Farmhouse Museum •**
  4881 Broadway [W 204th St]
  212-304-9422
  Oldest farmhouse in Manhattan, now restored as a museum.
- **Emerson Playground •**
  Seaman Ave & Isham St
  Kids (and adults) love playing around on the iron wolf.
- **Henry Hudson Bridge •** Henry Hudson Pkwy
  Affords a nice view from the Inwood Hill Park side.
- **Homer's Run •** Isham St [W 211th St]
  Where dogs par-tay.
- **Inwood Hill Park •** Dyckman St & Payson Ave
  The last natural forest and salt marsh in Manhattan!
- **West 215th Street Steps •**
  W 215th St & Park Terrace E
  Elevation of sidewalk requires steps.

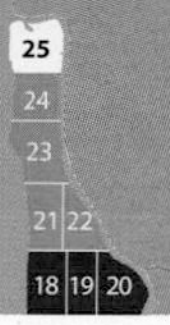

Well, if you refuse to take the 1 or A trains south for more exciting options, then dive into **Piper's Kilt of Inwood** for a perfect pint of Guinness and a burger. **Inwood Local** has many brews on tap and a fun neighborhood feel. For some vino, hit up **Corcho** for a glass and some tapas.

Bars

- **Corcho** • 231 Dyckman St [Seaman Ave]
  212-203-3371
  Cozy spot to sip and nibble; happy hour and wine classes a bonus.
- **Inwood Local** • 4957 Broadway [W 207th St]
  212-544-8900
  Beer garden, wine bar, and sports pub with a side of tasty grub.
- **Irish Eyes** • 5008 Broadway [W 213th St]
  212-567-9072
  Knock on the window if the light is on.
- **Piper's Kilt** • 4946 Broadway [W 207th St]
  212-569-7071
  A bit more spiffed up than it used to be.

Billiards

- **Post Billiards Café** • 154 Post Ave [W 207th St]
  212-569-1840
  When you need to play way way uptown.

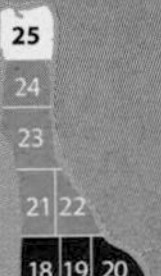

Restaurants

Get brunch at **Garden Cafe**. Go calorie crazy at **Elsa La Reina del Chicharron** with the best pork rinds in town. Sushi lovers go to **Mama Sushi** and Italian aficionados go to **Il Sole** or **La Estufa**. Practice your Spanish at **Mamajuana Cafe** and be artsy at **Indian Road Cafe**.

Restaurants

- **Capitol Restaurant** • 4933 Broadway [W 207th St] 212-942-5090 • $$ Nice neighborhood diner.
- **Daniel's Fruit-opia** • 510 W 207th St [10th Ave] 212-304-0029 • $ Who knew fruit shakes could be addictive?
- **Elsa La Reina Del Chicharron** • 4840 Broadway [W 204th St] 212-304-1070 • $ It's worth the coronary bypass.
- **Garden Café** • 4961 Broadway [Isham St] 212-544-9480 • $$ Homestyle brunch for less than 10 bucks.
- **Grandpa's Brick Oven Pizza** • 4973 Broadway [Isham St] 212-304-1185 • $$ Personal brick oven pies and catering.
- **Guadalupe** • 597 W 207th St [Broadway] 212-304-1083 • $$ High class Mexican.
- **Hashi** • 5009 Broadway [W 213th St] 646-837-6891 • $$$ Sushi, stir frys, and slick atmosphere.
- **Il Sole** • 233 Dyckman St [Seaman Ave] 212-544-0406 • $$ Neighborhood Italian.
- **La Estufa** • 5035 Broadway [W 215th St] 212-567-6640 • $$ This Italian can't be beat north of 14th street.
- **Mama Sushi** • 237 Dyckman St [Broadway] 212-567-2450 • $ As good as uptown sushi gets.
- **Mamajuana Cafe** • 247 Dyckman St [Seaman Ave] 212-304-1217 • $$$ Tasty Nuevo Latino cuisine.
- **Pizza Haven** • 4942 Broadway [W 207th St] 212-569-3720 • $ They bring-a the pizza.

Bagels, Coffee, & Shopping

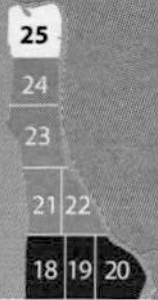

Shopping isn't exactly Inwood's forte but **El Nuevo Azteca** does have a huge selection of typical/junk Mexican foods. Order a fresh-rolled cigar to go at **Q Cigars**, take that old couch for an upholstery makeover to **The Victorian House** or relieve your sweet tooth fix at **Carrot Top Pastries**.

Coffee

- **Beans & Vines** • 4842 Broadway [Academy]
  212-544-2326
  Cozy coffee shop and wine bar serving food.
- **Dunkin' Donuts** •
  4942 Broadway [W 207th St]
  212-544-0453
  Decent coffee served in gigantic Styrofoam cups.
- **Indian Road Cafe** • 600 W 218th St [Indian Rd]
  212-942-7451
  Friendly neighborhood cafe.

Shopping

- **Carrot Top Pastries** •
  5025 Broadway [W 214th St]
  212-569-1532
  Top carrot cake, muffins, chocolate cake, rugalach, and more.
- **El Nuevo Azteca** • 3861 10th Ave [206th St]
  212-567-6028
  For the Mexican junkfood junky.
- **Gopher Broke** • 4926 Broadway [W 204th St]
  917-692-7749
  All I want for Xmas is a piece of forest.
- **Inwood Paint & Hardware** •
  165 Sherman Ave [W 204th St]
  212-569-6002
  High security locks and more.
- **Q Cigars** • 5009 Broadway [W 214th St]
  212-544-9623
  Fresh out of the hand cigars.
- **Richie's Cleaners and Tailors** •
  4915 Broadway [W 204th St]
  212-304-0289
  Trust the R. man.
- **Scavengers** • 600 W 218th St [Indian Rd]
  212-569-8343
  Funky little shop with lots of cool vintage stuff.
- **V.I.M.** • 565 W 207th St [Vermilyea Ave]
  212-942-7478
  Street wear—jeans, sneakers, tops—for all.
- **The Victorian House** •
  4961 Broadway [W 207th St]
  212-304-0202
  Upholstery sanctuary.

Map 26 • Astoria

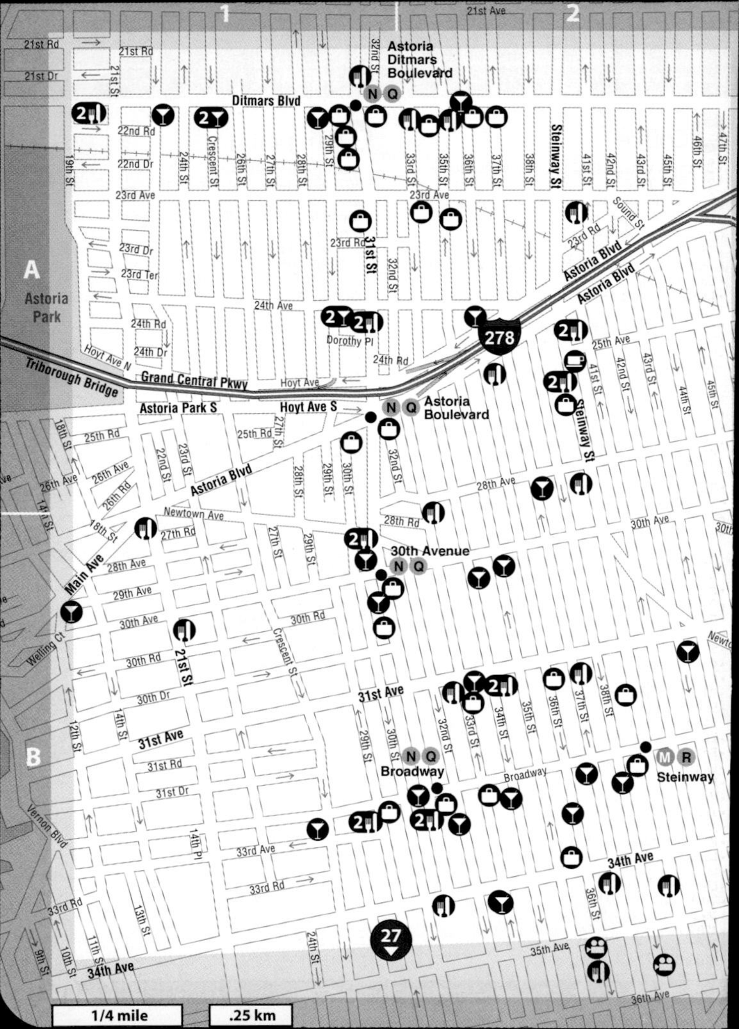

Astoria Ditmars Boulevard

N Q

Astoria Park

Astoria Boulevard

N Q

30th Avenue

N Q

Broadway

N Q

Steinway

M R

278

Triborough Bridge

Grand Central Pkwy

Ditmars Blvd

Astoria Blvd

Steinway St

31st Ave

34th Ave

21st Ave

21st Rd

21st Dr

22nd Rd

22nd Dr

23rd Ave

23rd Rd

23rd Dr

23rd Ter

24th Ave

24th Rd

24th Dr

Hoyt Ave N

Hoyt Ave

Hoyt Ave S

Astoria Park S

Dorothy Pl

25th Ave

25th Rd

26th Ave

26th Rd

Newtown Ave

27th Rd

28th Ave

28th Rd

29th Ave

30th Ave

30th Rd

30th Dr

31st Rd

31st Dr

33rd Ave

33rd Rd

35th Ave

36th Ave

Broadway

Main Ave

Welling Ct

Vernon Blvd

Sound St

Crescent St

1/4 mile

.25 km

27

Entertainment

The Irish have their wonderful way at the Rover **Sissy McGinty's**, the cool kids congregate at **The Sparrow** and **Queens Kickshaw**, but a summer night in the Beer Garden is an experience all its own. There's always something worth seeing at the **Museum of the Moving Image**. For food, go Greek at **Taverna Kyclades**, hit up **Vesta** for Italian or try the Mexican barbecue at **MexiBBQ**.

Nightlife

- **Albatross Bar** • 36-19 24th Ave
- **Avenue Café** • 35-27 30th Ave
- **Astor Room** • 34-12 36th St
- **Bohemian Hall & Beer Garden** • 29-19 24th Ave
- **Brick Café** • 30-95 33rd St
- **Café Bar** • 32-90 36th St
- **Crescent & Vine** • 25-03 Ditmars Blvd
- **Crescent Lounge** • 32-05 Crescent St
- **Cronin & Phelan** • 38-14 Broadway
- **Daly's Pub** • 31-86 31st St
- **DiWine** • 41-15 31st Ave
- **Fatty's Café** • 25-01 Ditmars Blvd
- **Gilbey's of Astoria** • 32-01 Broadway
- **Hell Gate Social** • 12-21 Astoria Blvd
- **Indigo** • 28-50 31st St
- **Irish Rover** • 37-18 28th Ave
- **Locale** • 33-02 34th Ave
- **McCann's Pub & Grill** • 36-15 Ditmars Blvd
- **The Sparrow** • 24-01 29th St
- **Sunswick Limited** • 35-02 35th St
- **Sweet Afton** • 30-09 34th St
- **Winegasm** • 31-86 37th St

Restaurants

- **Agnanti Meze**• 19-06 Ditmars Blvd
- **Aliada** • 29-19 Broadway
- **Astor Bake Shop** • 12-23 Astoria Blvd
- **Bareburger** • 33-21 31st Ave
- **Bear** • 12-14 31st Ave
- **Bistro 33** • 19-33 Ditmas Blvd
- **Cevabdzinica Sarajevo** • 37-18 34th Ave
- **Christos Steak House** • 41-08 23rd Ave
- **Crave** • 28-55 36th St
- **Djerdan** • 34-04 31st Ave
- **El Boqueron Tapas Restaurant** • 31-01 34th Ave
- **Elias Corner** • 24-02 31st St
- **Favela** • 33-18 28th Ave
- **Himalaya Teahouse** • 33-17 31st Ave
- **HinoMaru Ramen** • 33-18 Ditmars Blvd
- **Il Bambino** • 34-08 31st Ave
- **JJ's Restaurant** • 37-05 31st Ave
- **Jour et Nuit** • 28-04 Steinway St
- **Kabab Café** • 25-12 Steinway St
- **Latin Cabana Restaurant** • 34-44 Steinway St
- **Lil Bistro 33** • 19-33 Ditmars Blvd
- **Linn** • 29-13 Broadway
- **Little Morocco** • 24-39 Steinway St
- **MexiBBQ** • 37-11 30th Ave
- **MP Taverna** • 31-29 Ditmars Blvd
- **Mombar** • 25-22 Steinway St
- **Mundo Cafe** • 31-18 Broadway
- **Ornella Trattoria Italiana** • 29-17 23rd Ave
- **Pachanga Patterson** • 33-17 31st Ave
- **Pasha** • 31-01 Newtown Ave
- **Queens Comfort** • 40-09 30th Ave
- **The Queens Kickshaw** • 40-17 Broadway
- **Roti Boti Restaurant** • 27-09 21st St
- **Sabry's** • 24-25 Steinway St
- **Sal, Chris, and Charlie Deli** • 33-12 23rd Ave
- **San Antonio II** • 36-20 Astoria Blvd
- **Sugar Freak** • 36-18 30th Ave
- **Taverna Kyclades** • 33-07 Ditmars Blvd
- **The Thirsty Koala** • 35-12 Ditmars Blvd
- **Trattoria L'Incontro** • 21-76 31st St
- **Tufino Pizzeria** • 36-08 Ditmars Blvd
- **Vesta** • 21-02 30th Ave
- **Watawa** • 33-10 Ditmars Blvd
- **William Hallett** • 36-10 30th Ave
- **Zenon** • 34-10 31st Ave
- **Zlata Praha** • 28-48 31st St

Shopping

- **Artopolis Bakery** • 23-18 31st St
- **Astoria Bier and Cheese** • 34-14 Broadway
- **Astoria Park Wine and Spirits** • 28-07 24th Ave
- **Astoria Wine & Spirits** • 34-12 Broadway
- **babyNOIR**• 26-16 23rd Ave
- **Belief** • 29-20 23rd Ave
- **Bike Stop** • 37-19 28th Ave
- **Butcher Bar**• 37-08 30th Ave
- **Cassinelli Food Products, Inc.** • 31-12 23rd Ave
- **Euro Market** • 30-42 31st St
- **Family Market** • 2915 Broadway
- **Fresh Start**• 29-13 23rd Ave
- **Grand Wine & Liquor** • 30-05 31st St
- **Inside Astoria** • 28-07 Ditmars Blvd
- **International Meat Market**• 36-12 30th Ave
- **K&T Quality Meats** • 33-14 Ditmars Blvd
- **La Guli Pastry Shop** • 29-15 Ditmars Blvd
- **Loveday 31** • 33-06 31st Ave
- **Martha's Country Bakery** • 36-21 Ditmars Blvd
- **Mediterranean Foods** • 23-18 31st St
- **New York City Bagel & Coffee House** • 29-08 23rd Ave
- **Nook 'n Crannie** • 29-18 Ditmars Blvd
- **Parrot Coffee** • 31-12 Ditmars Blvd
- **Raising Astoria** • 26-11 23rd Ave
- **Rosario's Deli**• 22-55 31st St
- **Rose & Joe's Italian Bakery** • 22-40 31st St
- **Second Best Thrift Shop** • 30-07 Astoria Blvd
- **SingleCut Beersmiths** • 19-33 37th St
- **SITE** • 35-11 34th Ave
- **Titan Foods** • 25-56 31st St
- **Tony's Bicycles** • 35-01 23rd Ave
- **Triboro Beverage** • 41-08 Astoria Blvd S

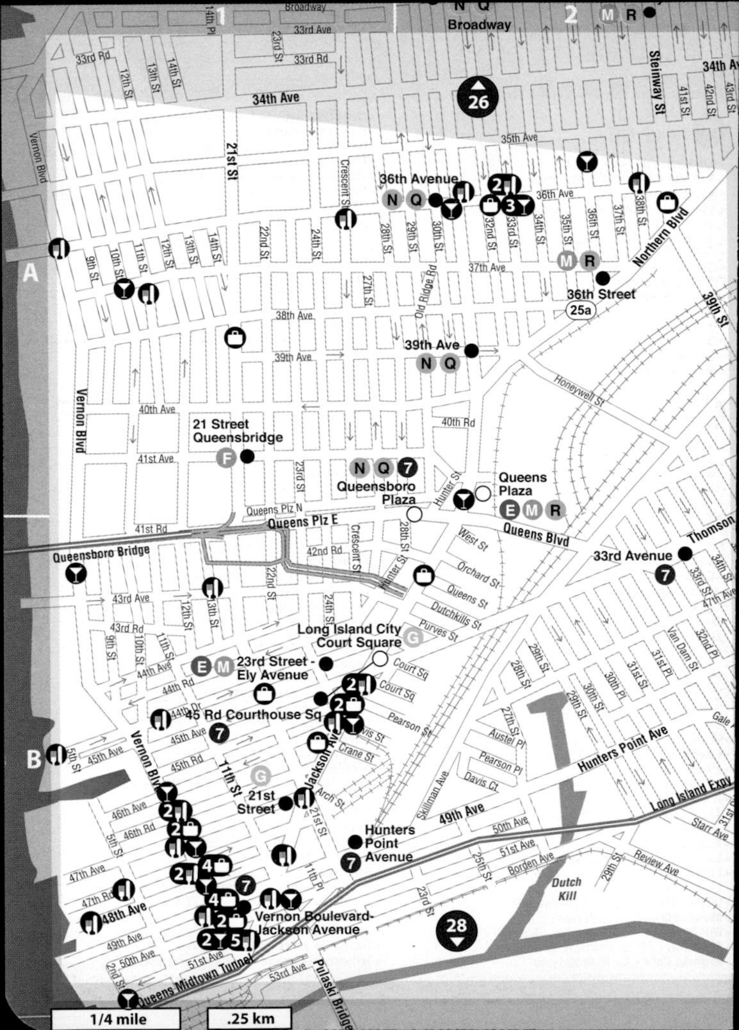
Broadway
36th Avenue
36th Street
39th Ave
21 Street Queensbridge
Queensboro Plaza
Queens Plaza
33rd Avenue
Long Island City Court Square
23rd Street - Ely Avenue
45 Rd Courthouse Sq
21st Street
Hunters Point Avenue
Vernon Boulevard-Jackson Avenue
Queensboro Bridge
Queens Midtown Tunnel
Pulaski Bridge
Dutch Kill
Vernon Blvd
21st St
34th Ave
Northern Blvd
Queens Blvd
Thomson
Hunters Point Ave
Long Island Expy
Jackson Ave
11th St
49th Ave
Steinway St
1/4 mile
.25 km

Queens' version of Battery Park City has brought new amenities to this once sleepy outpost. Try some mixology at **Dutch Kills** or join the locals at **LIC Bar**. For food, rely on standbys like **Manducatis**, **Bella Via** and **Tournesol** or seek comfort at **El Ay Si**. Boutiques come and go and then there's **Just Things**, a quirky amalgamation of thrift, junk and antique store that we hope never ever leaves.

Nightlife

- **Alewife** • 5-14 51st Ave
- **The Cave** • 10-93 Jackson Ave
- **Domaine Bar a Vins** • 50-04 Vernon Blvd
- **Dominie's Hoek** • 48-17 Vernon Blvd
- **Dutch Kills** • 27-24 Jackson Ave
- **The Laughing Devil** • 47-38 Vernon Blvd
- **LIC Bar** • 45-58 Vernon Blvd
- **Penthouse 808 at the Ravel Hotel** • 8-08 Queens Plaza S
- **PJ Leahy's** • 50-02 Vernon Blvd
- **The Rooftop at Ravel** • 8-08 Queens Plaza S
- **Shannon Pot** • 45-06 Davis St
- **Studio Square** • 35-33 36th St
- **Veronica's Bar** • 34-01 36th Ave

Restaurants

- **5 Star Punjabi Diner** • 13-05 43rd Ave
- **Alobar** • 46-42 Vernon Blvd
- **Arepas Cafe** • 33-07 36th Ave
- **Bella Via** • 47-46 Vernon Blvd
- **Blend** • 47-04 Vernon Blvd
- **Breadbox Cafe** • 47-11 11th St
- **Brooks 1890 Restaurant** • 24-28 Jackson Ave
- **Cafe Henri** • 10-10 50th Ave
- **Cafe Ole** • 38-09 36th Ave
- **Cafe Triskell** • 33-04 36th Ave
- **Casa Enrique** • 5-48 49th Ave
- **Corner Bistro** • 47-18 Vernon Blvd
- **Court Square Diner** • 45-30 23rd St
- **Cyclo** • 5-51 47th Ave
- **Dorian Café** • 10-01 50th Ave
- **El Ay Si** • 47-38 Vernon Blvd
- **El Sitio** • 35-55 31st St
- **Gaw Gai Thai Express** • 23-06 Jackson Ave
- **Ihawan 2** • 10-07 50th Ave
- **John Brown Smokehouse** • 10-43 44th Dr
- **Junior's Café** • 46-18 Vernon Blvd
- **LIC Market** • 21-52 44th Dr
- **M. Wells Dinette** • 22-25 Jackson Ave
- **Malagueta** • 25-35 36th Ave
- **Manducatis** • 13-27 Jackson Ave
- **Manducatis Rustica** • 46-35 Vernon Blvd
- **Manetta's** • 10-76 Jackson Ave
- **Sage General Store** • 24-20 Jackson Ave
- **Shi** • 4720 Center Blvd
- **Skinny's Cantina** • 47-05 Center Blvd
- **Tournesol** • 50-12 Vernon Blvd
- **Tuk Tuk** • 49-06 Vernon Blvd
- **Water's Edge** • 44th Dr & East River
- **Waterfront Crab House** • 203 Borden Ave

Shopping

- **Artbook @ MoMa PS1** • 22-25 Jackson Ave
- **Blue Streak Wine & Spirits** • 4720 Center Blvd
- **Camp Bow Wow** • 47-16 Austell Pl
- **Coffeed** • 37-18 Northern Blvd
- **Key Food** • 44-65 21st St
- **Court Square Wine & Spirits** • 24-20 Jackson Ave
- **Food Cellar** • 4-85 47th Rd
- **Greenmarket** • 48th Ave & Vernon Blvd
- **Hunter's Point Wines & Spirits** • 47-07 Vernon Blvd
- **Just Things** • 47-28 Vernon Blvd
- **Mario's** • 47-23 Vernon Blvd
- **Nook 'n Crannie** • 47-42 Vernon Blvd
- **PS 1 Bookstore** • 22-25 Jackson Ave
- **Rio Bonito Market** • 32-15 36th Ave
- **Rio Bonito Market** • 32-15 36th Ave
- **Sage General Store** • 24-20 Jackson Ave
- **Sadowsky Guitars** • 21-07 41st Ave
- **Vernon Blvd Pharmacy** • 48-15 Vernon Blvd
- **Vernon Wine & Liquor** • 50-06 Vernon Blvd
- **Western Beef** • 36-20 Steinway St
- **WMD Lilien Hardware** • 27-43 Jackson Ave

Map 28 • Greenpoint

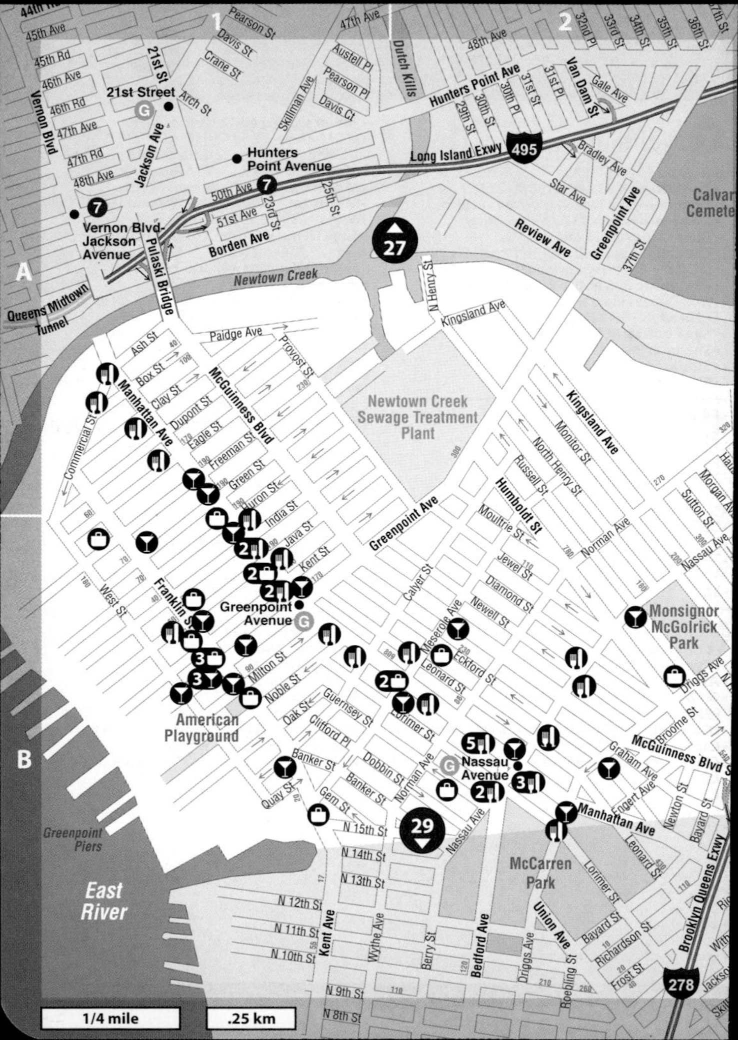

Vernon Blvd
45th Ave
45th Rd
46th Ave
46th Rd
47th Ave
47th Rd
48th Ave
21st St
21st Street
Jackson Ave
Arch St
Pearson St
Davis St
Crane St
47th Ave
Austell Pl
Pearson Pl
Davis Ct
Skillman Ave
Dutch Kills
48th Ave
Hunters Point Ave
29th St
30th St
30th Pl
31st St
31st Pl
Van Dam St
Gale Ave
32nd Pl
33rd St
34th St
35th St
36th St
37th St
Long Island Exwy
495
Bradley Ave
Star Ave
Hunters Point Avenue
50th Ave
51st Ave
23rd St
25th St
Vernon Blvd-Jackson Avenue
Pulaski Bridge
Borden Ave
27
Review Ave
Greenpoint Ave
37th St
Calvary Cemetery
Newtown Creek
Queens Midtown Tunnel
N Henry St
Kingsland Ave
Paidge Ave
Ash St
Box St
Clay St
Dupont St
Eagle St
Freeman St
Green St
Huron St
India St
Java St
Kent St
Provost St
McGuinness Blvd
Manhattan Ave
Commercial St
Newtown Creek Sewage Treatment Plant
Kingsland Ave
Monitor St
North Henry St
Russell St
Humboldt St
Moultrie St
Jewel St
Diamond St
Newell St
Norman Ave
Morgan Ave
Sutton St
Nassau Ave
Greenpoint Ave
Calyer St
Meserole Ave
Eckford St
Leonard St
Lorimer St
West St
Franklin St
Greenpoint Avenue
Milton St
Noble St
Oak St
Guernsey St
Clifford Pl
Banker St
Dobbin St
Quay St
Gem St
American Playground
Monsignor McGolrick Park
Driggs Ave
Broome St
McGuinness Blvd S
Graham Ave
Engert Ave
Newton St
Bayard St
Nassau Avenue
Manhattan Ave
Leonard St
29
N 15th St
N 14th St
N 13th St
N 12th St
N 11th St
N 10th St
N 9th St
N 8th St
Kent Ave
Wythe Ave
Berry St
Bedford Ave
Driggs Ave
Roebling St
Union Ave
McCarren Park
Lorimer St
Bayard St
Richardson St
Frost St
Brooklyn Queens Exwy
278
Greenpoint Piers
East River

1/4 mile
.25 km

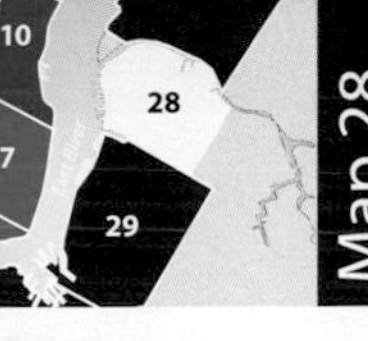

The **Pencil Factory** remains the nightlife favorite of a certain demographic; Polish dance clubs cater to another. Where **Wedel's** churns out fancy Polish chocolates, legions of Manhattan Avenue meat markets slash out infinite slabs of bloody flesh. **The Thing's** got everything you never thought would merit a thrift store. Best Polish food? Answer: **Lomzynianka**.

Nightlife

- **Alligator Lounge II** • 113 Franklin St [Greenpoint Ave]
- **Black Rabbit** • 91 Greenpoint Ave [Franklin St]
- **Blackout** • 916 Manhattan Ave [Kent St]
- **Coco 66** • 66 Greenpoint Ave [Franklin St]
- **The Diamond** • 43 Franklin St [Calyer St]
- **Enid's** • 560 Manhattan Ave [Driggs Ave]
- **Europa** • 98 Meserole Ave [Manhattan Ave]
- **The Habitat** • 988 Manhattan Ave [Huron St]
- **Lulu's** • 113 Franklin St [Greenpoint Ave]
- **The Manhattan Inn** • 632 Manhattan Ave [Nassau Ave]
- **The Mark Bar** • 1025 Manhattan Ave [Green St]
- **Matchless** • 557 Manhattan Ave [Driggs Ave]
- **Palace Café** • 206 Nassau Ave [Russell St]
- **Pencil Factory** • 142 Franklin St [Greenpoint Ave]
- **Pit Stop Bar** • 152 Meserole Ave [McGuinness Blvd]
- **Red Star** • 37 Greenpoint Ave [West St]
- **Shayz Lounge** • 130 Franklin St [Milton St]
- **Spritzenhaus** • 33 Nassau Ave [Dobbin St]
- **TBD Bar** • 224 Franklin St [Green St]
- **Tommy's Tavern** • 1041 Manhattan Ave [Freeman St]
- **Warsaw** • 261 Driggs Ave [Eckford St]

Restaurants

- **Acapulco** • 1116 Manhattan Ave [Clay St]
- **Ashbox** • 1154 Manhattan Ave [Ash St]
- **Brooklyn Ice Cream Factory** • 97 Commercial St [Box St]
- **Brooklyn Label** • 180 Franklin St [Java St]
- **Cafecito Bogota** • 1015 Manhattan Ave
- **Christina's** • 853 Manhattan Ave [Noble St]
- **Eat** • 124 Meserole Ave [Leonard St]
- **Enid's** • 560 Manhattan Ave [Driggs Ave]
- **Erb** • 681 Manhattan Ave [Norman Ave]
- **Five Leaves** • 18 Bedford Ave [Nassau Ave]
- **Fresca Tortilla** • 620 Manhattan Ave [Nassau]
- **God Bless Deli** • 818 Manhattan Ave [Calyer]
- **Kestane Kebab** • 110 Nassau Ave [Eckford St]
- **Kyoto Sushi** • 161 Nassau Ave [Diamond St]
- **La Brique** • 645 Manhattan Ave [Bedford Ave]
- **La Taverna** • 946 Manhattan Ave [Java St]
- **Lokal** • 905 Lorimer St [Nassau Ave]
- **Lomzynianka** • 646 Manhattan Ave [Nassau]
- **Manhattan 3 Decker** • 695 Manhattan Ave [Norman Ave]
- **Ott** • 970 Manhattan Ave [India St]
- **Peter Pan Doughnuts** • 727 Manhattan Ave [Norman Ave]
- **Pio Pio Riko** • 996 Manhattan Ave [Huron St]
- **Relax** • 68 Newell St [Nassau Ave]
- **Sapporo Haru** • 622 Manhattan Ave [Nassau]
- **Thai Café** • 925 Manhattan Ave [Kent St]
- **Valdiano** • 659 Manhattan Ave [Bedford Ave]

Shopping

- **Alter** • 109 Franklin St [Greenpoint Ave]
- **Bellocq Tea Atelier** • 104 West St [Kent St]
- **Brouwerij Lane** • 78 Greenpoint Ave [Franklin]
- **Charlotte Parisserie** • 596 Manhattan Ave [Driggs Ave]
- **Cracovia Liquors** • 130 Nassau Ave [Newell St]
- **Dalaga** • 150 Franklin St [Greenpoint Ave]
- **Dandelion Wine** • 153 Franklin St [Java St]
- **Eastern District** • 1053 Manhattan Ave [Freeman St]
- **Fox & Fawn Vinatge** • 570 Manhattan Ave [Driggs Ave]
- **Fred Flare** • 131 Messerole Ave [Leonard]
- **The Garden** • 921 Manhattan Ave [Kent St]
- **Hayden-Harnett** • 211 Franklin St [Freeman]
- **Jaslowiczanka Bakery** • 163 Nassau Ave [Diamond St]
- **Kill Devil Hill** • 170 Franklin St [Java St]
- **Luddite** • 201 Franklin St [Freeman St]
- **Maria's Deli** • 136 Meserole Ave [Eckford St]
- **New Warsaw Bakery** • 866 Lorimer St [Driggs Ave]
- **Old Hollywood** • 110 Meserole Ave [Manhattan Ave]
- **The One Well** • 165 Greenpoint Ave [Leonard St]
- **Open Air Modern** • 606 Manhattan Ave [Nassau Ave]
- **Permanent Records** • 181 Franklin St [Huron]
- **Photoplay** • 928 Manhattan Ave [Kent St]
- **Pop's Popular Clothing** • 7 Franklin St [Meserole Ave]
- **Steve's Meat Market** • 104 Nassau Ave [Leonard]
- **The Thing** • 1001 Manhattan Ave [Huron St]
- **Wedel** • 772 Manhattan Ave [Meserole Ave]
- **Word** • 126 Franklin St [Milton St]

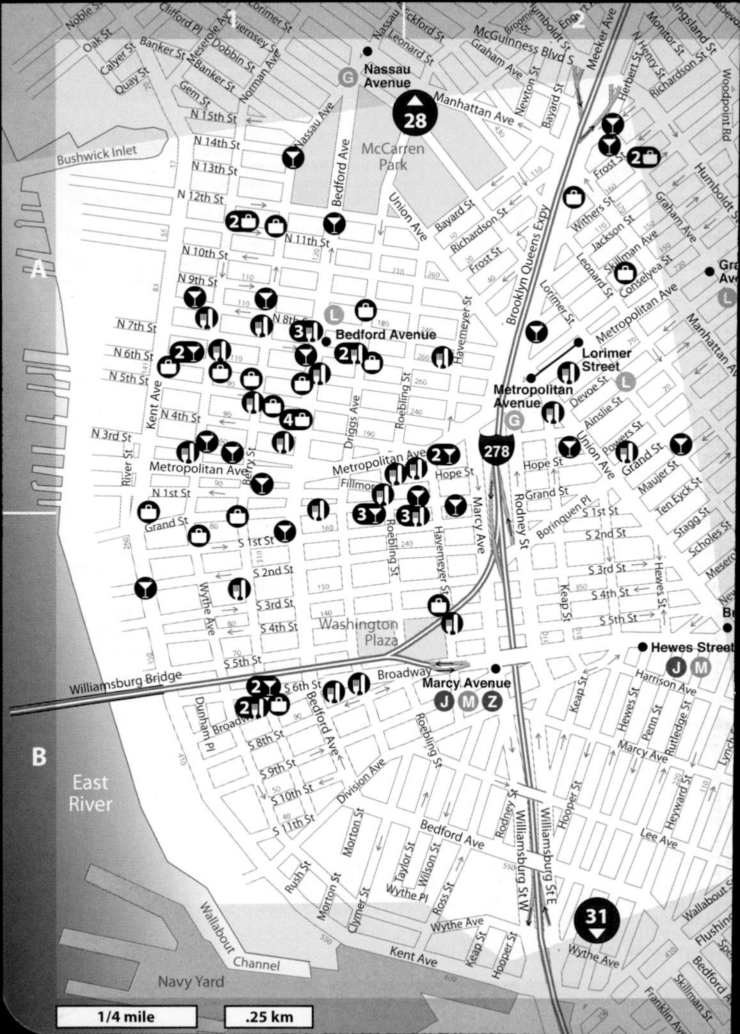

Map 29 • Williamsburg

Nassau Avenue

28

McCarren Park

Bushwick Inlet

Bedford Avenue

Lorimer Street

Metropolitan Avenue

278

Washington Plaza

Williamsburg Bridge

Marcy Avenue

Hewes Street

East River

Wallabout Channel

Navy Yard

31

Noble St
Oak St
Calyer St
Quay St
Banker St
Clifford Pl
Meserole Ave
Guernsey St
Dobbin St
Lorimer St
Norman Ave
Gem St
N 15th St
N 14th St
N 13th St
N 12th St
N 11th St
N 10th St
N 9th St
N 8th St
N 7th St
N 6th St
N 5th St
N 4th St
N 3rd St
N 1st St
Kent Ave
River St
Metropolitan Ave
Berry St
Grand St
S 1st St
S 2nd St
S 3rd St
S 4th St
S 5th St
S 6th St
S 8th St
S 9th St
S 10th St
S 11th St
Wythe Ave
Dunham Pl
Broadway
Bedford Ave
Driggs Ave
Roebling St
Havemeyer St
Marcy Ave
Fillmore Pl
Hope St
Nassau Ave
Eckford St
Leonard St
McGuinness Blvd S
Graham Ave
Broome St
Humboldt St
Engert Ave
Meeker Ave
Manhattan Ave
Newton St
Bayard St
Union Ave
Richardson St
Frost St
Brooklyn Queens Expy
Withers St
Jackson St
Skillman Ave
Conselyea St
Monitor St
Kingsland St
N Henry St
Herbert St
Richardson St
Woodpoint Rd
Humboldt St
Devoe St
Ainslie St
Powers St
Grand St
Maujer St
Ten Eyck St
Stagg St
Scholes St
Rodney St
Borinquen Pl
S 1st St
S 2nd St
S 3rd St
S 4th St
S 5th St
Hewes St
Keap St
Harrison Ave
Penn St
Rutledge St
Marcy Ave
Heyward St
Lee Ave
Division Ave
Morton St
Rush St
Taylor St
Wilson St
Wythe Pl
Ross St
Clymer St
Wythe Ave
Kent Ave
Keap St
Hooper St
Williamsburg St W
Williamsburg St E
Wallabout St
Flushing Ave
Bedford Ave
Skillman St
Franklin Ave

A

B

1

2

1/4 mile

.25 km

Entertainment

You want it, it's here. Carnivores flock to **Peter Luger** and **Fette Sau**, beer-lovers throw 'em back at **Spuyten Duyvil** and **Radegast**, while **Barcade** gives joystick junkies their fix. Live music? **Glasslands**, **Pete's Candy Store**, or **Music Hall** should do it for ya. And if you want to listen at home, stop by **Earwax**, **Academy Annex**, or **Soundfix**.

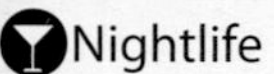

Nightlife

- **Barcade** • 388 Union Ave [Ainslie St]
- **Ba'sik** • 323 Graham Ave [Devoe St]
- **Bembe** • 81 S 6th St [Berry St]
- **Berry Park** • 4 Berry St [N 14th St]
- **Brooklyn Bowl** • 61 Wythe Ave [N12th St]
- **Clem's** • 264 Grand St [Roebling St]
- **Daddy's** • 437 Graham Ave [Frost St]
- **Dram** • 177 S 4th St [Driggs Ave]
- **East River Bar** • 97 S 6th St [Berry St]
- **Glasslands Gallery** • 289 Kent Ave [S 2nd St]
- **Greenpoint Tavern** • 188 Bedford Ave [N 7th]
- **The Gutter** • 200 N 14th St [Wyth Ave]
- **Hotel Delmano** • 82 Berry St [N 9th St]
- **Huckleberry Bar** • 588 Grand St [Lorimer St]
- **Iona** • 180 Grand St [Bedford Ave]
- **Knitting Factory Brooklyn** • 361 Metropolitan Ave [Havemeyer St]
- **Larry Lawrence** • 295 Grand St [Havemeyer]
- **The Levee** • 212 Berry St [Metropolitan Ave]
- **Maison Premiere** • 298 Bedford Ave [Grand St]
- **Music Hall of Williamsburg** • 66 N 6th St [Kent]
- **Nita Nita** • 146 Wythe Ave [N 8th St]
- **Nitehawk Cinema** • 136 Metropolitan Ave [Berry St]
- **Pete's Candy Store** • 709 Lorimer St [Richardson]
- **Public Assembly** • 70 N 6th St [Wythe Ave]
- **Radegast Hall** • 113 N 3rd St [Berry St]
- **Rose** • 345 Grand St [Havemeyer St]
- **Spuyten Duyvil** • 359 Metropolitan Ave [Havemeyer St]
- **Trash** • 256 Grand St [Roebling St]
- **Turkey's Nest** • 94 Bedford Ave [N 12th St]
- **Union Pool** • 484 Union Ave [Rodney St]

Restaurants

- **Acqua Santa** • 556 Driggs Ave [N 7th St]
- **Baci & Abbracci** • 204 Grand St [Driggs Ave]
- **Bakeri** • 150 Wythe Ave [N 8th St]
- **Bozu** • 296 Grand St [Havemeyer St]
- **Cadaques**• 188 Grand St [Bedford Ave]
- **The Brooklyn Star** • 33 Havemeyer St [N 8th]
- **Diner** • 85 Broadway [Berry St]
- **Dressler** • 149 Broadway [Bedford Ave]
- **DuMont** • 432 Union Ave [Devoe St]
- **Egg** • 135 N 5th St [Bedford Ave]
- **Fatty 'Cue** • 91 S 6th St [Berry St]
- **Fette Sau** • 354 Metropolitan Ave [Roebling St]
- **Fiore** • 284 Grand St [Roebling St]
- **Juliette** • 135 N 5th St [Bedford Ave]
- **La Superior** • 295 Berry St [S 2nd St]
- **Le Barricou** • 533 Grand St [Union Ave]
- **Mable's Smokehouse & Banquet Hall**• 44 Berry St [N 12th St]
- **Marlow & Sons** • 81 Broadway [Berry St]
- **Moto** • 394 Broadway [Hooper St]
- **Northside Bakery** • 149 N 8th St [Bedford Ave]
- **Oasis** • 161 N 7th St [Bedford Ave]
- **Pates et Traditions** • 52 Havemeyer St [N 6th St]
- **Peter Luger Steak House** • 178 Broadway [Driggs Ave]
- **Roebling Tea Room** • 143 Roebling St [Metropolitan Ave]
- **Rye** • 247 S 1st St [Roebling St]
- **Teddy's Bar and Grill** • 96 Berry St [N 8th St]
- **Vinnie's** • 148 Bedford Ave [N 9th St]
- **Walter Foods** • 253 Grand St [Roebling St]
- **Yola's Café** • 524 Metropolitan Ave [Union Ave]
- **Zenkichi** • 77 N 6th St [Wythe Ave]

Shopping

- **Academy Annex** • 96 N 6th St [Wythe Ave]
- **Amarcord** • 223 Bedford Ave [N 4th St]
- **Beacon's Closet** • 88 N 11th St [Wythe Ave]
- **Bedford Cheese Shop** • 229 Bedford Ave [N 5th]
- **The Brooklyn Kitchen** • 100 Frost St [Meeker]
- **Buffalo Exchange** • 504 Driggs Ave [N 9th St]
- **Earwax Records** • 218 Bedford Ave [N 5th St]
- **Emily's Pork Store** • 426 Graham Ave [Withers]
- **Fuego 718** • 249 Grand St [Roebling St]
- **Future Perfect** • 115 N 6th St [Berry St]
- **KCDC Skateshop** • 90 N 11th St [Wythe Ave]
- **Marlow & Daughters** • 95 Broadway [Berry St]
- **The Mini-Market** • 218 Bedford Ave [N 5th St]
- **Savino's Quality Pasta** • 111 Conselyea St [Manhattan Ave]
- **Sound Fix Records** • 44 Berry St [N 11th St]
- **Spoonbill & Sugartown** • 218 Bedford Ave [N 5th St]
- **Sprout** • 44 Grand St [Kent Ave]
- **Treehouse** • 430 Graham Ave [Frost St]
- **Two Jakes** • 320 Wythe Ave [Grand St]
- **Ugly Luggage** • 214 Bedford Ave [N 5th St]
- **Uva Wines** • 199 Bedford Ave [N 5th St]
- **Whisk** • 231 Bedford Ave [N 3rd St]

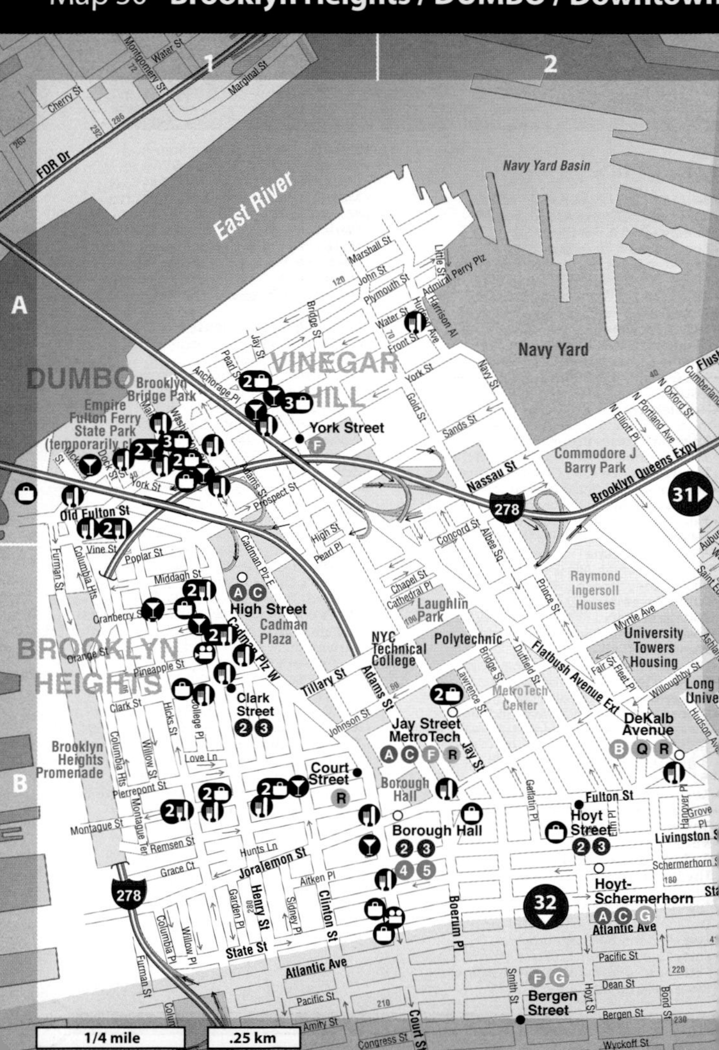

East River
Navy Yard Basin
Navy Yard
DUMBO
VINEGAR HILL
Brooklyn Bridge Park
Empire Fulton Ferry State Park
York Street
Commodore J Barry Park
Brooklyn Queens Expy
Nassau St
278
31
High Street
Cadman Plaza
Raymond Ingersoll Houses
University Towers Housing
BROOKLYN HEIGHTS
NYC Technical College
Polytechnic
MetroTech Center
Clark Street
Jay Street MetroTech
DeKalb Avenue
Brooklyn Heights Promenade
Court Street
Borough Hall
Fulton St
Hoyt Street
Hoyt-Schermerhorn
Atlantic Ave
32
Bergen Street
1/4 mile
.25 km

Entertainment

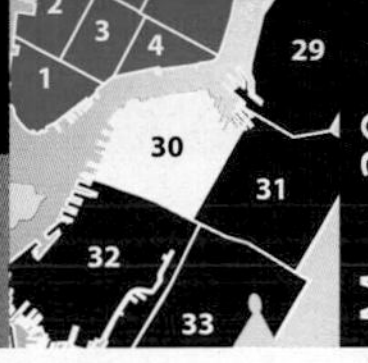

Old-world **Henry's End** is at the top of our list for food, but also check out ultrahip **Superfine**, good slices at **Fascati**, and posh gastropub **Jack the Horse**. For culture, **St. Ann's** is the place. For chocolate, two words: **Jacques Torres**. When Tim and Jason move in together, they accessorize at **West Elm**. The Brooklyn Heights Cinema, is one our our favorite small movie theaters.

Nightlife

- **68 Jay Street Bar** • 68 Jay St [Front St]
- **Eamonn's** • 174 Montague St [Clinton St]
- **Galapagos Art Space** • 16 Main St [Water St]
- **Henry Street Ale House** • 62 Henry St [Cranberry St]
- **Jack the Horse Tavern** • 66 Hicks St [Cranberry St]
- **O'Keefe's** • 62 Court St [Livingston St]
- **reBar** • 147 Front St [Pearl St]
- **St Ann's Warehouse** • 38 Water St [Dock St]
- **Water Street Bar** • 66 Water St [Main St]

Restaurants

- **Bubby's** • 1 Main St [Plymouth St]
- **Fascati Pizzeria** • 80 Henry St [Orange St]
- **Five Guys** • 138 Montague St [Henry St]
- **Grimaldi's** • 1 Front St [Old Fulton St]
- **Hale & Hearty Soup** • 32 Court St [Remsen St]
- **Heights Café** • 84 Montague St [Hicks St]
- **Henry's End** • 44 Henry St [Middagh St]
- **Iron Chef House** • 92 Clark St [Monroe Pl]
- **Jack the Horse Tavern** • 66 Hicks St [Cranberry St]
- **Junior's Restaurant** • 386 Flatbush Avenue Ext [St Johns Pl]
- **Lantern Thai** • 101 Montague St [Hicks St]
- **Miso** • 40 Main St [Front St]
- **Noodle Pudding** • 38 Henry St [Middagh St]
- **Park Plaza Restaurant** • 220 Cadman Plaza W [Clark St]
- **Queen Ristorante** • 84 Court St [Livingston St]
- **Rice** • 81 Washington St [York St]
- **River Café** • 1 Water St [Old Fulton St]
- **Siggy's Good Food** • 76 Henry St [Orange St]
- **Superfine** • 126 Front St [Pearl St]
- **Sushi Gallery** • 71 Clark St [Henry St]
- **Teresa's** • 80 Montague St [Hicks St]
- **The River Cafe** • 1 Water St [Old Fulton St]
- **Vinegar Hill House** • 72 Hudson Ave [Water St]

Shopping

- **Almondine Bakery** • 85 Water St [Main St]
- **Barnes & Noble** • 106 Court St [State St]
- **Bridge Fresh Market** • 68 Jay St [Water St]
- **Brooklyn Ice Cream Factory** • 1 Water St [Old Fulton St]
- **Cranberry's** • 48 Henry St [Cranberry St]
- **Design Within Reach** • 76 Montague St [Hicks St]
- **Egg Baby** • 72 Jay St [Water St]
- **Halcyon** • 57 Pearl St [Water St]
- **Half Pint** • 55 Washington St [Front St]
- **Heights Prime Meats** • 59 Clark St [Henry St]
- **Housing Works-Brooklyn Thrift Shop** • 122 Montague St [Henry St]
- **Jacques Torres Chocolate** • 66 Water St [Main]
- **Lassen & Hennigs** • 114 Montague St [Henry]
- **Macy's** • 422 Fulton St [Hoyt St]
- **Modell's** • 360 Fulton St [Red Hook Ln]
- **Peas & Pickles** • 55 Washington St [Front St]
- **Pomme** • 81 Washington St [York St]
- **powerHouse Arena** • 37 Main St [Water St]
- **Recycle-A-Bicycle** • 35 Pearl St [Plymouth St]
- **Sid's Hardware & Homecenter** • 345 Jay St [Myrtle Prom]
- **Stewart/Stand** • 165 Front St [Jay St]
- **Super Runners Shop** • 123 Court St [State St]
- **Tango** • 145 Montague St [Henry St]
- **TKTS Booth** • 1 Metrotech Center [Johnson St]
- **West Elm** • 75 Front St [Main St]

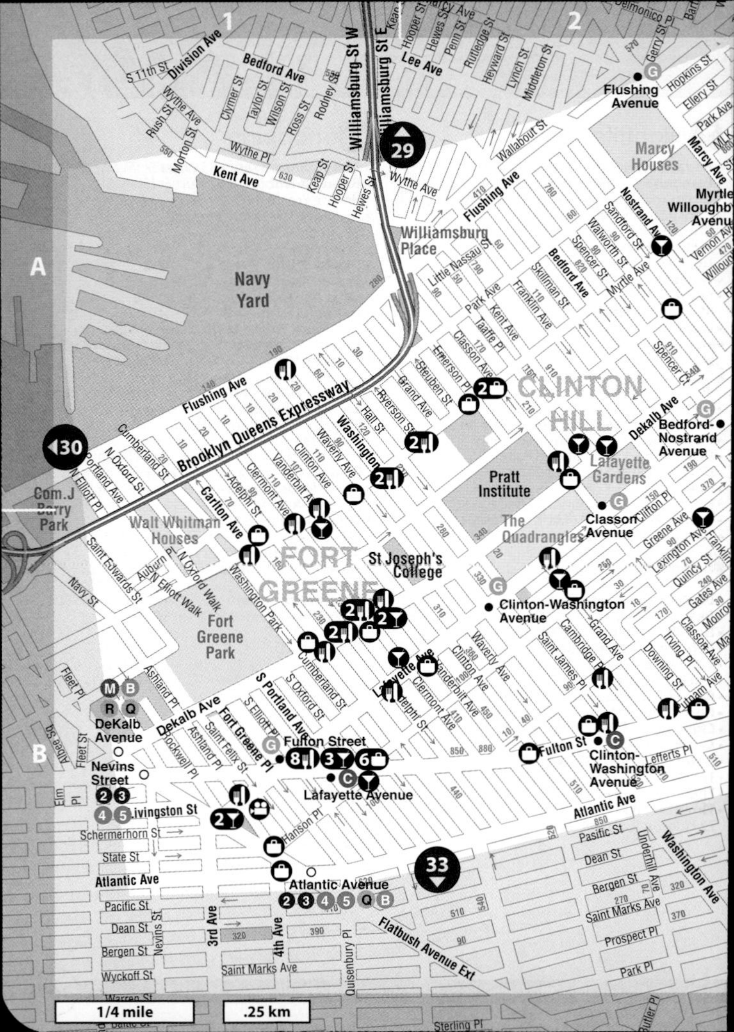

1
2
A
B
Navy Yard
Williamsburg Place
Marcy Houses
CLINTON HILL
FORT GREENE
Pratt Institute
The Quadrangles
Lafayette Gardens
St Joseph's College
Walt Whitman Houses
Fort Greene Park
Com.J Barry Park
Brooklyn Queens Expressway
Flushing Ave
Kent Ave
Wythe Ave
Wythe Pl
Division Ave
Bedford Ave
Lee Ave
Williamsburg St W
Williamsburg St E
Wallabout St
Myrtle Ave
Dekalb Ave
Lafayette Ave
Fulton St
Atlantic Ave
Pacific St
Dean St
Bergen St
Saint Marks Ave
Prospect Pl
Park Pl
Sterling Pl
Flatbush Avenue Ext
Washington Ave
Classon Ave
Grand Ave
Vanderbilt Ave
Clinton Ave
Waverly Ave
Clermont Ave
Adelphi St
Carlton Ave
Cumberland St
Washington Park
S Portland Ave
S Oxford St
Fort Greene Pl
Ashland Pl
Saint Felix St
Hanson Pl
3rd Ave
4th Ave
Nevins St
Livingston St
Schermerhorn St
State St
Wyckoff St
Warren St
Quisenbury Pl
Underhill Ave
Nostrand Ave
Flushing Avenue
Myrtle Willoughby Avenue
Bedford-Nostrand Avenue
Classon Avenue
Clinton-Washington Avenue
Fulton Street
Lafayette Avenue
Atlantic Avenue
DeKalb Avenue
Nevins Street
29
30
33
1/4 mile
.25 km

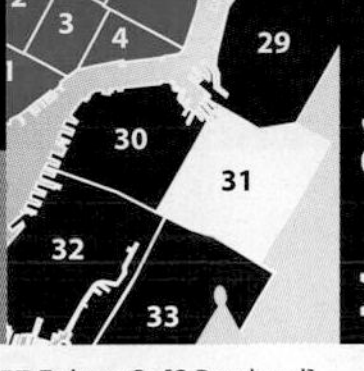

Choice Greene & **Greene Grape's** great gourmet food selections have just raised rents here. Otherwise, head for hipsterish eats **The General Greene**, friendly French at **Chez Oskar**, pre-BAM hipness at **No. 7**, killer cheap Mexican at **Castro's**, posh Italian at **Locanda**, and short rib heaven at **Smoke Joint**. **Frank's**, and **The Alibi** are both good local watering holes.

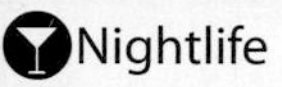

Nightlife

- **The Alibi** • 242 Dekalb Ave [Vanderbilt Ave]
- **BAMcafé** • 30 Lafayette Ave [Ashland Pl]
- **Brooklyn Masonic Temple** • 317 Clermont Ave [Lafayette Ave]
- **Brooklyn Public House** • 247 Dekalb Ave [Vanderbilt Ave]
- **Der Schwarze Kolner** • 710 Fulton St [S Oxford St]
- **Frank's Cocktail Lounge** • 660 Fulton St [S Elliott Pl]
- **Grand Dakar** • 285 Grand Ave [Clifton Pl]
- **Navy Yard Cocktail Lounge** • 200 Flushing Ave [Waverly Ave]
- **One Last Shag** • 348 Franklin Ave [Lexington Ave]
- **Project Parlor** • 742 Myrtle Ave [Sanford St]
- **Rope** • 415 Myrtle Ave [Clinton Ave]
- **Rustik** • 471 Dekalb Ave [Franklin Ave]
- **Stonehome Wine Bar** • 87 Lafayette Ave [S Portland Ave]
- **Sweet Revenge** • 348 Franklin Ave [Lexington Ave]
- **Thomas Boid** • 25 Lafayette Ave [Ashland Pl]

Restaurants

- **67 Burger** • 67 Lafayette Ave [S Elliott Pl]
- **Bati** • 747 Fulton St [S Portland Ave]
- **Black Iris** • 228 Dekalb Ave [Clermont Ave]
- **Cafe Lafayette** • 99 S Portland Ave [Fulton St]
- **Caribbean Soul** • 920 Fulton St [Washington Ave]
- **Castro's Restaurant** • 511 Myrtle Ave [Grand]
- **Chez Lola** • 387 Myrtle Ave [Clermont Ave]
- **Chez Oskar** • 211 Dekalb Ave [Adelphi St]
- **Choice Market** • 318 Lafayette Ave [Grand]
- **Dolores Deli Grocery** • 173 Park Ave [Adelphi St]
- **Five Spot** • 495 Myrtle Ave [Ryerson St]
- **The General Greene** • 229 Dekalb Ave [Clerrmont Ave]
- **Habana Outpost** • 757 Fulton St [S Portland]
- **Ici** • 246 Dekalb Ave [Vanderbilt Ave]
- **Il Porto** • 37 Washington Ave [Flushing Ave]
- **Kif** • 219 Dekalb Ave [Adelphi St]
- **Locanda Vini & Olii** • 129 Gates Ave [Cambridge Pl]
- **Luz** • 177 Vanderbilt Ave [Myrtle Ave]
- **Madiba** • 195 Dekalb Ave [Carlton Ave]
- **Night of the Cookers** • 767 Fulton St [S Oxford]
- **No. 7** • 7 Greene Ave [Fulton St]
- **Olea** • 171 Lafayette Ave [Adelphi St]
- **Scopello** • 63 Lafayette Ave [S Elliott Pl]
- **The Smoke Joint** • 87 S Elliot Pl [Lafayette Ave]
- **Soule** • 920 Fulton St [Washington Ave]
- **Umi Nom** • 433 Dekalb Ave [Classon Ave]
- **Walter's** • 166 Dekalb Ave Cumberland
- **Yamashiro** • 466 Myrtle Ave [Washington Ave]

Shopping

- **Bespoke Bicycles** • 64 Lafayette Ave [S Elliott]
- **Brooklyn Flea** • 176 Lafayette Ave [Clermont]
- **Cake Man Raven Confectionary** • 708 Fulton St [Hanson Pl]
- **Choice Greene** • 214 Greene Ave [Grand Ave]
- **Dope Jams** • 580 Myrtle Ave [Classon Ave]
- **Gnarly Vines** • 350 Myrtle Ave [Carlton Ave]
- **Green in BKLYN** • 432 Myrtle Ave [Clinton]
- **The Greene Grape** • 765 Fulton St [S Oxford]
- **Greene Grape Provisions** • 753 Fulton St [S Portland Ave]
- **Greenlight Bookstore** • 686 Fulton St [S Portland Ave]
- **Malchijah Hats** • 225 Dekalb Ave [Clermont]
- **The Midtown Greenhouse Garden Center** • 115 Flatbush Ave [Hanson Pl]
- **Olivino** • 905 Fulton St [Clinton Ave]
- **Pratt Institute Bookstore** • 550 Myrtle Ave [Emerson Pl]
- **Sister's Community Hardware** • 900 Fulton St [Washington Ave]
- **Target** • 139 Flatbush Ave [Atlantic Ave]
- **Thirst Wine Merchants** • 187 Dekalb Ave [Carlton Ave]
- **Yu Interiors** • 15 Greene Ave [Cumberland St]

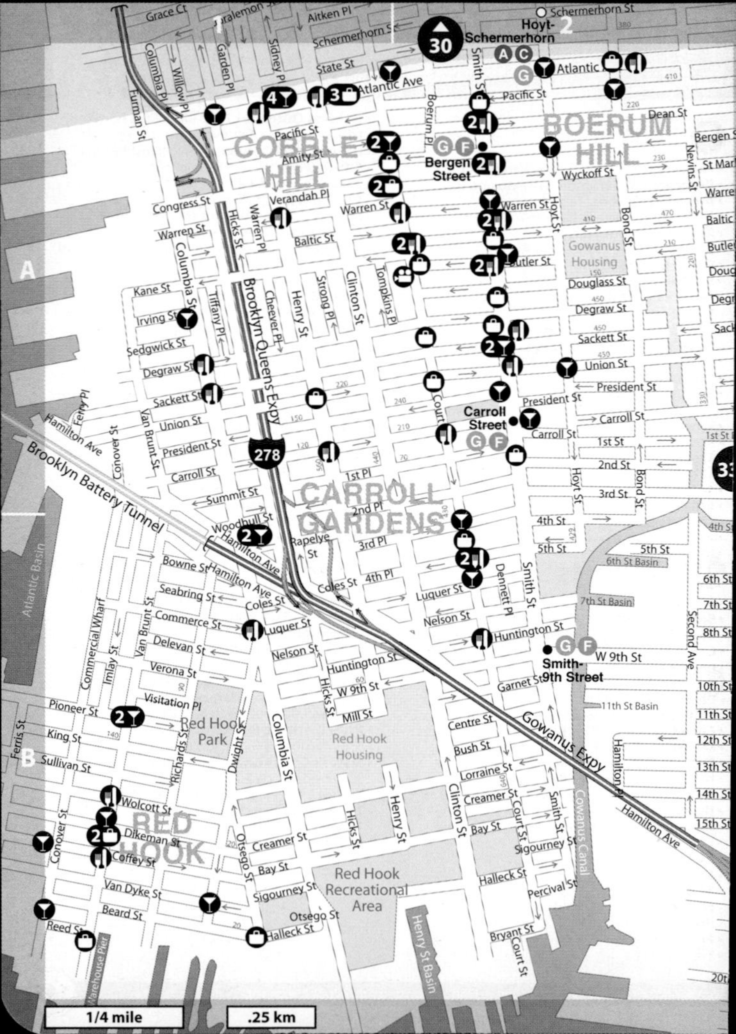

Map 32 • BoCoCa / Red Hook

1/4 mile

.25 km

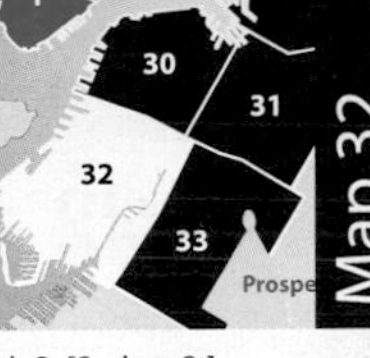

Nightlife? Head for **Boat** (jukebox), **Brooklyn Inn** (classic), **Brooklyn Social** (cool), or **Sunny's** (dive). Restaurants? Hit **Alma** (Mexican), **Char No. 4** (hip), **Ferdinando's** (Sicilian), and **Frankie's** (brunch). Shopping? **D'Amico's** (coffee), **Stinky** (cheese), **Staubitz** (meat), **Swallow** (beautiful stuff), and **Sahadi's** (imports). Full yet?

Nightlife

- **Abilene** • 442 Court St [3rd Pl]
- **Bar Great Harry** • 280 Smith St [Sackett St]
- **Black Mountain** • 415 Union St [Hoyt St]
- **Boat** • 175 Smith St [Wyckoff St]
- **Botanica** • 220 Conover St [Coffey St]
- **Brazen Head** • 228 Atlantic Ave [Court St]
- **Brooklyn Inn** • 148 Hoyt St [Bergen St]
- **Brooklyn Social** • 335 Smith St [Carroll St]
- **Building on Bond** • 112 Bond St [Pacific St]
- **Clover Club** • 210 Smith St [Baltic St]
- **Cody's** • 154 Court St [Dean St]
- **Downtown Bar & Grill** • 160 Court St [Amity]
- **Floyd** • 131 Atlantic Ave [Henry St]
- **Fort Defiance** • 365 Van Brunt St [Dikeman St]
- **Gowanus Yacht Club** • 323 Smith St [President]
- **Henry Public** • 329 Henry St [Atlantic Ave]
- **home/made** • 293 Van Brunt St [Pioneer St]
- **The Jakewalk** • 282 Smith St [Sackett St]
- **Jalopy** • 315 Columbia St [Hamilton Ave]
- **Last Exit** • 136 Atlantic Ave [Henry St]
- **Montero's Bar and Grill** • 73 Atlantic Ave [Hicks]
- **PJ Hanley's** • 449 Court St [4th Pl]
- **Red Hook Bait & Tackle** • 320 Van Brunt St [Pioneer St]
- **Rocky Sullivan's** • 34 Van Dyke St [Dwight St]
- **Sunny's** • 253 Conover St [Reed St]
- **Waterfront Ale House** • 155 Atlantic Ave [Clinton]

Restaurants

- **Alma** • 187 Columbia St [Degraw St]
- **Atlantic Chip Shop** • 129 Atlantic Ave [Henry]
- **Bar Tabac** • 128 Smith St [Dean St]
- **Bedouin Tent** • 405 Atlantic Ave [Bond St]
- **Black Gold** • 461 Court St Luquer St
- **Bocca Lupo** • 391 Henry St [Warren St]
- **Buttermilk Channel** • 524 Court [Huntington]
- **Caserta Vecchia** • 221 Smith St [Butler St]
- **Chance** • 223 Smith St [Butler St]
- **Char No. 4** • 196 Smith St [Baltic St]
- **DeFonte's Sandwich Shop** • 379 Columbia St [Luquer St]
- **Ferdinando's Focacceria** • 151 Union St [Hicks]
- **Fragole** • 394 Court St [Carroll St]
- **Frankie's 457** • 457 Court St [Luquer St]
- **The Good Fork** • 391 Van Brunt St [Coffey St]
- **The Grocery** • 288 Smith St [Sackett St]
- **Hadramout** • 172 Atlantic Ave [Clinton St]
- **Hanco's** • 85 Bergen St [Smith St]
- **Hope & Anchor** • 347 Van Brunt St [Wolcott]
- **Joya** • 215 Court St [Warren St]
- **Karloff** • 254 Court St [Kane St]
- **Ki Sushi** • 122 Smith St [Dean St]
- **Lucali** • 575 Henry St [Carroll St]
- **Prime Meats**• 465 Court Street [Luquer St]
- **Quercy** • 242 Court St [Baltic St]
- **Saul** • 140 Smith St [Bergen St]
- **Seersucker** • 329 Smith Street [President St]
- **South Brooklyn Pizza** • 451 Court St [4th Pl]
- **Watty & Meg** • 248 Court St [Kane St]

Shopping

- **A Cook's Companion** • 197 Atlantic Ave [Court]
- **American Beer Distributors** • 256 Court St [Kane St]
- **Caputo's Fine Foods** • 460 Columbia St [Degraw St]
- **Claywoks on Columbia** • 195 Columbia St [Degraw St]
- **Blue Marble** • 196 Court St [Wyckoff St]
- **Butter** • 389 Atlantic Ave [Bond St]
- **By Brooklyn**• 261 Smith St [Degraw St]
- **Caputo's Fine Foods** • 460 Court St [3rd Pl]
- **D'Amico Foods** • 309 Court St [Degraw St]
- **Dear Fieldbinder** • 198 Smith St [Baltic St]
- **Enamoo** • 109 Smith St [Pacific St]
- **Erie Basin** • 388 Van Brunt St [Dikeman St]
- **Eva Gentry Consignment** • 371 Atlantic Ave [Hoyt St]
- **Exit 9** • 127 Smith St [Dean St]
- **Fairway** • 480 Van Brunt St [Reed St]
- **Fish Tales** • 191 Court St [Wyckoff St]
- **Flight 001** • 132 Smith St [Dean St]
- **G Esposito & Sons** • 357 Court St [President]
- **Ikea** • 1 Beard St [Otsego St]
- **Malko Karkanni Bros.** • 174 Atlantic [Clinton]
- **Mazzola Bakery** • 192 Union St [Henry St]
- **Metal and Thread** • 398 Van Brunt St [Coffey]
- **Sahadi Importing Company** • 187 Atlantic Ave [Court St]
- **Smith & Vine** • 268 Smith St [Douglass St]
- **Staubitz Meat Market** • 222 Court St [Baltic]
- **Stinky** • 215 Smith St [Baltic St]
- **Swallow** • 361 Smith St [2nd St]

Flatbush Ave
State St
Atlantic Avenue
Atlantic Ave
Pacific Street
Pacific St
Dean St
Bergen St
Bergen Street
St Mark's Pl
St Mark's Ave
Carlton Ave
7th Avenue
Park Pl
Prospect Pl
Warren St
Baltic St
Butler St
Douglass St
Degraw St
Sackett St
Union Street
Union St
President St
Carroll St
Garfield Pl
1st St
2nd St
3rd St
4th St
5th St
6th St
7th St
8th St
9th St
10th St
11th St
12th St
13th St
14th St
15th St
16th St
17th St
18th St
Third Ave
Fourth Ave
Fifth Ave
Sixth Ave
Seventh Ave
Eighth Ave
Quisenbury Pl
Sterling Pl
St Johns Pl
Lincoln Pl
Berkeley Pl
Vanderbilt Ave
Washington Ave
Grand Ave
Underhill Ave
Butler Pl
Plaza St E
Grand Army Plaza
Grand Army Plz
PROSPECT HEIGHTS
Brooklyn Botanic Garden
Flatbush Ave
West Dr
East Dr
Montgomery Pl
Polhemus Pl
Fiske Pl
PARK SLOPE
Prospect Park
Prospect Park W
Nevins St
1st St Basin
4th St Basin
Whitwell Pl
Denton Pl
4th Avenue-9th Street
7th Avenue
15th Street-Prospect Park
W Lake Dr
Prospect Park SW
WINDSOR TERRACE
Tenth Ave
Eleventh Ave
Sherman St
Howard Pl
Fuller Pl
Prospect Avenue
Prospect Expy
Prospect Ave
Windsor Pl
Webster Pl
Jackson Pl
Calder Pl
Hamilton Ave
278
27
31
32
1/4 mile
.25 km

Entertainment

As if 7th and 5th Avenues didn't have enough already, now 4th (**Sheep Station**, **Cherry Tree**, etc.) gets into the act. Top food abounds—**Applewood**, **Franny's**, **Blue Ribbon**, **Stone Park**—as does great nabe hangouts **Beast**, **The Gate**, and **Flatbush Farm**. For live acts, head to **Barbes**, and **Union Hall**.

Nightlife

- **Bar Toto** • 411 11th St [6th Ave]
- **Barbes** • 376 9th St [6th Ave]
- **Beast** • 638 Bergen St [Vanderbilt Ave]
- **Beer Table** • 427 7th Ave [14th St]
- **The Bell House** • 149 7th St [3rd Ave]
- **Black Horse Pub** • 568 5th Ave [16th St]
- **Buttermilk Bar** • 577 5th Ave [16th St]
- **Canal Bar** • 270 3rd Ave [President St]
- **Cherry Tree** • 65 4th Ave [Bergen St]
- **Commonwealth** • 497 5th Ave [12th St]
- **Cornelius** • 565 Vanderbilt Ave [Pacific St]
- **Draft Barn** • 530 3rd Ave [13th St]
- **Flatbush Farm** • 76 St Marks Ave [6th Ave]
- **Freddy's Bar and Backroom** • 485 Dean St [6th Ave]
- **The Gate** • 321 5th Ave [3rd St]
- **Hank's Saloon** • 46 3rd Ave [Atlantic Ave]
- **Issue Project Room** • 232 3rd St [3rd Ave]
- **littlefield** • 622 Degraw St [4th Ave]
- **Loki Lounge** • 304 5th Ave [2nd St]
- **O'Connor's** • 39 5th Ave [Bergen St]
- **Pacific Standard** • 82 4th Ave [St Marks Pl]
- **Park Slope Ale House** • 356 6th Ave [5th St]
- **Soda** • 629 Vanderbilt Ave [Prospect Pl]
- **Southpaw** • 125 5th Ave [Sterling Pl]
- **Starlite Lounge** • 1084 Bergen St [Flatbush]
- **Tavern on Dean** • 755 Dean St [Underhill Ave]
- **Union Hall** • 702 Union St [5th Ave]
- **Washington Commons** • 748 Washington Ave [Park Pl]

Restaurants

- **12th Street Bar and Grill** • 1123 8th Ave [11th St]
- **Al Di La Trattoria** • 248 5th Ave [Carroll St]
- **Applewood** • 501 11th St [7th Ave]
- **Beast** • 638 Bergen St [Vanderbilt Ave]
- **Belleville** • 332 5th Ave [3rd St]
- **Blue Ribbon Brooklyn** • 280 5th Ave [1st St]
- **Brooklyn Fish Camp** • 162 5th Ave [Douglass St]
- **Cheryl's Global Soul** • 236 Underhill Ave [Lincoln Pl]
- **The Cocolate Room** • 86 5th Ave [Warren St]
- **ChipShop** • 383 5th Ave [6th St]
- **Convivium Osteria** • 68 5th Ave [St Marks Pl]
- **Flatbush Farm** • 76 St Marks Ave [6th Ave]
- **Franny's** • 295 Flatbush Ave [Prospect Pl]
- **Gen Restaurant** • 659 Washington Ave [St Marks Ave]
- **Ghenet** • 348 Douglass St [4th Ave]
- **Hanco's** • 350 7th Ave [10th St]
- **Jpan Sushi** • 287 5th Ave [1st St]
- **La Taqueria** • 72 7th Ave [Berkeley Pl]
- **Moim** • 206 Garfield Pl [7th Ave]
- **Nana** • 155 5th Ave [Lincoln Pl]
- **Rawstar Vegan Live Cuisine** • 687 Washington Ave [Prospect Pl]
- **Rose Water** • 787 Union St [6th Ave]
- **Scalino** • 347 7th Ave [10th St]
- **Sheep Station** • 149 4th Ave [Douglass St]
- **Smiling Pizzeria** • 323 7th Ave [9th St]
- **Stone Park Cafe** • 324 5th Ave [3rd St]
- **Taro Sushi** • 446 Dean St [5th Ave]
- **Tom's** • 782 Washington Ave [Sterling Pl]
- **The Usual** • 637 Vanderbilt Ave [Prospect Pl]
- **The V-Spot** • 156 5th Ave [Degraw St]
- **Watana** • 420 7th Ave [14th St]

Shopping

- **Beacon's Closet** • 92 5th Ave [Warren St]
- **Bierkraft** • 191 5th Ave [Union St]
- **Bklyn Larder** • 228 Flatbush Ave [Bergen St]
- **Blue Apron Foods** • 814 Union St [7th Ave]
- **Blue Marble Ice Cream** • 186 Underhill Ave [St Johns Pl]
- **Brooklyn Superhero Supply** • 372 5th Ave [5th St]
- **Clay Pot** • 162 7th Ave [Garfield Pl]
- **Cog and Pearl** • 190 5th Ave [Berkeley Pl]
- **Dixon's Bicycle Shop** • 792 Union St [7th Ave]
- **Grab** • 438 7th Ave [15th St]
- **Gureje** • 886 Pacific St [Underhill Ave]
- **JackRabbit Sports** • 151 7th Ave [Garfield Pl]
- **Loom** • 115 7th Ave [President St]
- **Midtown Florist & Greenhouse** • 565 Atlantic Ave [Hanson Pl]
- **Pie Shop** • 211 Prospect Park West [16th St]
- **Rare Device** • 453 7th Ave [16th St]
- **Razor** • 329 5th Ave [4th St]
- **Russo's Fresh Mozzarella** • 363 7th Ave [11th]
- **Stitch Therapy** • 335 5th Ave [4th St]
- **United Meat Market** • 219 Prospect Park West [16th St]

Map 34 • Hoboken

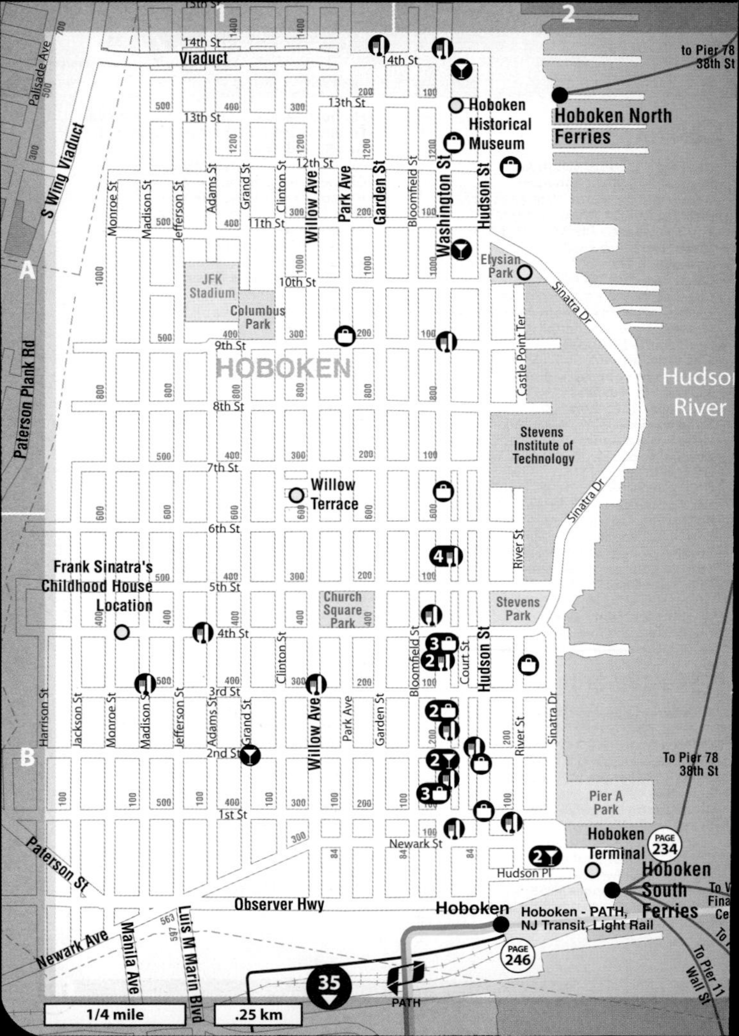

HOBOKEN
Hudson River
Hoboken North Ferries
to Pier 78 38th St
Hoboken Historical Museum
Elysian Park
Sinatra Dr
Stevens Institute of Technology
Stevens Park
Willow Terrace
Church Square Park
JFK Stadium
Columbus Park
Frank Sinatra's Childhood House Location
Pier A Park
To Pier 78 38th St
Hoboken Terminal
PAGE 234
Hoboken South Ferries
To Pier 11 Wall St
Hoboken
Hoboken - PATH, NJ Transit, Light Rail
PAGE 246
35
PATH
Viaduct
14th St
13th St
12th St
11th St
10th St
9th St
8th St
7th St
6th St
5th St
4th St
3rd St
2nd St
1st St
Newark St
Hudson Pl
Observer Hwy
Newark Ave
Paterson St
Manila Ave
Luis M Marin Blvd
Paterson Plank Rd
S Wing Viaduct
Palisade Ave
Harrison St
Jackson St
Monroe St
Madison St
Jefferson St
Adams St
Grand St
Clinton St
Willow Ave
Park Ave
Garden St
Bloomfield St
Washington St
Court St
Hudson St
Castle Point Ter
River St
Sinatra Dr
1/4 mile
.25 km

Entertainment

It's only a short trip from the Village by PATH or ferry, but Hoboken feels more like an upscale college town. The salty longshoremen have moved on to that great pier in the sky, or at least to a members-only social club in town, leaving the waterfront to parkland, luxury condos, and many, many yuppies. Best bets for explorers are the raw clams at **Biggies**, and beer and brats at **Helmer's**.

Landmarks

- **Elysian Park** • Hudson St & Sinatra Dr
- **Frank Sinatra's Childhood House Location** • 415 Monroe St [4th St]
- **Hoboken Historical Museum** • 1301 Hudson St [13th St]
- **Hoboken Terminal** • 1 Hudson Pl [River St]
- **Willow Terrace** • 6th & 7th St b/w Willow Ave & Clinton St

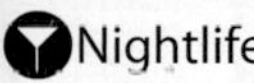

Nightlife

- **City Bistro** • 56 14th St [Washington St]
- **Leo's Grandezvous** • 200 Grand St [2nd St]
- **Maxwell's** • 1039 Washington St [10th St]
- **Oddfellows** • 80 River St [Warren St]

Restaurants

- **Amanda's** • 908 Washington St [9th St]
- **Arthur's Tavern** • 237 Washington St [2nd St]
- **Baja** • 104 14th St [Washington St]
- **Bangkok City** • 335 Washington St [3rd St]
- **Biggie's Clam Bar** • 318 Madison St [3rd St]
- **Brass Rail** • 135 Washington St [1st St]
- **Far Side Bar & Grill** • 531 Washington St [5th St]
- **Gaslight** • 400 Adams St [4th St]
- **Helmer's** • 1036 Washington St [10th St]
- **Hoboken Gourmet Company** • 423 Washington St [4th St]
- **Karma Kafe** • 505 Washington St [5th St]
- **La Isla** • 104 Washington St [1st St]
- **Oddfellows Restaurant** • 80 River St [Warren St]
- **Robongi** • 520 Washington St [5th St]
- **Sushi Lounge** • 200 Hudson St [2nd St]
- **Trattoria Saporito** • 328 Washington St [3rd St]
- **Zafra** • 301 Willow Ave [3rd St]

Shopping

- **Big Fun Toys** • 602 Washington St [6th St]
- **City Paint & Hardware** • 130 Washington St [1st St]
- **Galatea** • 1224 Washington St [12th St]
- **Kings Fresh Ideas** • 325 River St [3rd St]
- **Lisa's Italian Deli** • 901 Park Ave [9th St]
- **Peper** • 1028 Washington St [10th St]
- **Sparrow Wine and Liquor** • 1224 Shipyard Ln [12th St]
- **Sparrow Wine and Liquor** • 126 Washington St [1st St]
- **Tunes New & Used CDs** • 225 Washington St [2nd St]
- **Yes I Do** • 312 Washington St [3rd St]

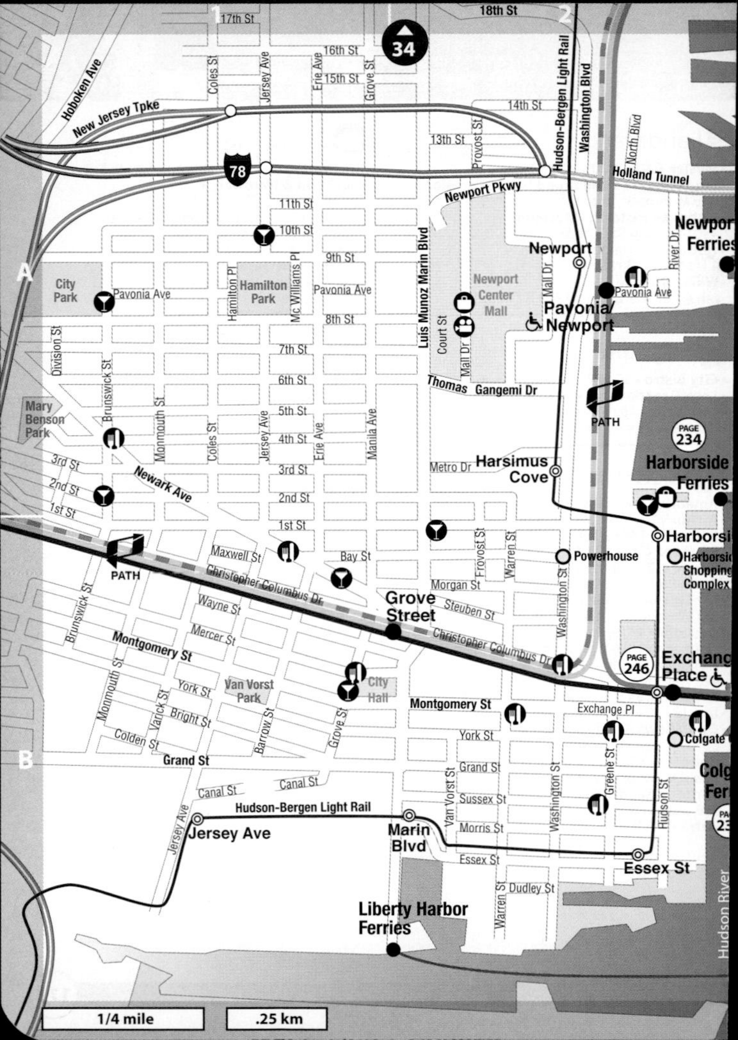

Map 35 • Jersey City

17th St
18th St
16th St
15th St
14th St
13th St
11th St
10th St
9th St
8th St
7th St
6th St
5th St
4th St
3rd St
2nd St
1st St
Hoboken Ave
New Jersey Tpke
Coles St
Jersey Ave
Erie Ave
Grove St
Provost St
Hudson-Bergen Light Rail
Washington Blvd
North Blvd
Holland Tunnel
78
34
Newport Pkwy
Newport
Newport Ferries
River Dr
Pavonia Ave
City Park
Hamilton Pl
Hamilton Park
Mc Williams Pl
Luis Munoz Marin Blvd
Court St
Mall Dr
Newport Center Mall
Pavonia/Newport
Division St
Brunswick St
Monmouth St
Mary Benson Park
Manila Ave
Thomas Gangemi Dr
PATH
PAGE 234
Harborside Ferries
Metro Dr
Harsimus Cove
Newark Ave
Harborside
Powerhouse
Harborside Shopping Complex
Maxwell St
Bay St
Christopher Columbus Dr
Wayne St
Mercer St
Montgomery St
Grove Street
Steuben St
Morgan St
Warren St
Washington St
PAGE 246
Exchange Place
York St
Van Vorst Park
City Hall
Bright St
Varick St
Colden St
Barrow St
Exchange Pl
Colgate
Grand St
Canal St
Van Vorst St
Greene St
Sussex St
Morris St
Hudson St
Marin Blvd
Jersey Ave
Essex St
Dudley St
Liberty Harbor Ferries
Hudson River
1/4 mile
.25 km

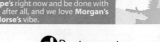

Entertainment

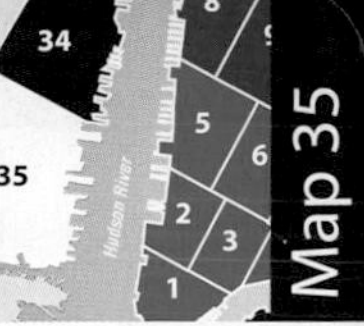

Jersey City has a siren song that lures dissatisfied New Yorkers to its mall-studded shores. First it came for the artists, then for our young families and yuppies. Next it came for our offices and suburbanites. Maybe you should start hanging out at **Marco and Pepe's** right now and be done with it. **White Mana's** is a bona fide landmark, after all, and we love **Morgan's** octopus platter, **Ibby's** falafel, and **Light Horse's** vibe.

Landmarks

- **Colgate Clock** • 30 Hudson St [Essex St]
- **Harborside Shopping Complex** • n/a
- **Powerhouse** • 344 Washington St [Bay St]
- **White Mana** • 470 Tonnele Ave [Bleecker St]

Nightlife

- **Hamilton Park Ale House** • 708 Jersey Ave [10th St]
- **Lamp Post Bar and Grille** • 382 2nd St [Brunswick St]
- **LITM** • 140 Newark Ave [Grove St]
- **The Merchant** • 279 Grove St [Montgomery St]
- **PJ Ryan's** • 172 1st St [Luiz Munoz Marin Blvd]
- **White Star** • 230 Brunswick St [Pavonia Ave]

Restaurants

- **Amelia's Bistro** • 187 Warren St [Essex St]
- **Exchange Market Place** • 10 Exchange Pl [Hudson St]
- **Beechwood Cafe** • 290 Grove St [Mercer St]
- **Ibby's** • 303 Grove St [Wayne St]
- **Iron Monkey** • 97 Greene St [York St]
- **It's Greek to Me** • 194 Newark Ave [Jersey Ave]
- **Komegashi** • 103 Montgomery St [Warren St]
- **Komegashi Too** • 99 Pavonia Ave [River Dr S]
- **Light Horse Tavern** • 199 Washington St [Morris St]
- **Madame Claude** • 364 4th St [Brunswick St]
- **Marco and Pepe** • 289 Grove St [Mercer St]
- **Medina Restaurant** • 287 Grove St [Mercer St]
- **Morgan Seafood** • 2801 John F Kennedy Blvd [Sip Ave]
- **Presto's Restaurant** • 199 Warren St [Morris St]
- **Rumi Turkish Grill** • 60 Sussex St [Greene St]
- **Saigon Café** • 188 Newark Ave [Jersey Ave]
- **Sri Ganesh** • 809 Newark Ave [Liberty Ave]
- **White Mana** • 470 Tonnele Ave [Bleecker St]

Shopping

- **Harborside Shopping Complex** • Exchange Pl
- **Newport Center Mall** • 30 Mall Dr W [Thomas Gangemi Dr]
- **Patel Snacks** • 785 Newark Ave [Herpert Pl]

N

Westchester
Woodlawn
Van Cortlandt Golf Course
Woodlawn Cemetery
Jerome Ave
Wakefield
Baychester Ave
E 233rd St.
Seton Falls Park
New England Thwy
Hutchinson River Pkwy
Shore Rd
Pelham Bay Park
Orchard Beach
Hunters Island
Eastchester
Co-Op City
Haften Park
Rodman Neck
Williamsbridge
Webster Ave
Bronx River Pkwy
White Plain
Gun Hill Rd
Boston Rd
Baychester
BRONX
Pelham Bay Park
Eastchester Bay
Riverdale Park
Wave Hill
Van Cortlandt Park
Mosholu Golf Course
Norwood
Mosholu Pkwy
Bedford Park
Harris Park
Kings-Bridge Heights
Riverdale
Marble Hill
Major Deegan Expy
Bronx and Pelham Expwy
Morris Park
Williams Bridge Rd
Bruckner Expy
Pelham Bay
New York Botanical Garden
Fordham University
Bronx Park
Henry Hudson Bridge
Belmont
Bronx Zoo
East Tremont
E Tremont Ave
Parkchester
Westchester
Cross Bronx Expy
St Raymond's Cemetery
University Heights Bridge
University Heights
Tremont
West Farms
Bronx River
Ferry Point Park
Henry Hudson Pkwy
Morris Heights
Cross Bronx Expy
Crotona Park
Sheridan Expwy
Bruckner Expy
Castle Hill
Castle Hill Ave
Washington Bridge
Claremont Park
Boston Rd.
Locombe Ave
Hamilton Bridge
Grand Concourse
Third Ave
Claremont Village
Soundview
Clason Point
Bronx River
Sound View Park
Whitestone Bridge
Harlem River
Broa
Morrisania
Westchester Ave
E 161 St
Yankee Stadium
Hunts Point
Flushing Bay
Hudson River
Macombs Dam Bridge
E 149th St
Longwood
St Mary's Park
Bruckner Blvd
Bruckner Expy
145 St Bridge
Third Ave
Mott Haven
Riker's Island
Madison Ave Bridge
Port Morris
3rd Ave Bridge
Willis Ave Bridge
Triborough Bridge
Park Ave
QUEENS
MANHATTAN

Don't be afraid of the Boogie Down Bronx. Decades of entrenched poverty and poor urban planning once frayed many neighborhoods, but the borough today is no longer the burning wreck your parents warned you about years ago.

Communities

Belmont's Arthur Avenue (3) is still an authentic Little Italy even though many businesses now belong to Albanians. Woodlawn (9) is home to many Irish Immigrants and it's got the pubs to prove it. With 15,372 units, towering Co-op City (13) is rightly called a city within the city; it even has its own mall! The Mott Haven (14) and Longwood (15) historic districts boast beautiful homes, but "The Hub" (16) features the grand architecture of the past conveniently filled with the discount shopping of today. For antiques, visit the cobblestone corridor of Bruckner Boulevard (17) at Alexander Avenue. Some of the city's grandest homes sit in the wooded environs of Riverdale (4), while City Island (12) resembles nothing so much as a New England fishing village crossed with a New Jersey suburb.

Culture

The New York Botanical Garden (8) and the Bronx Zoo (10) are justly famous, well worth whatever effort it may take to get there. For a beautiful view of the Hudson and the Palisades beyond, choose the botanical garden and historic estate Wave Hill (5) or the quirky Hall of Fame for Great Americans (2) featuring 98 bronze busts of notable citizens in a grand outdoor colonnade. Explore your inner Goth at historic Woodlawn Cemetery (7) or Poe Cottage (18), the American poet's final home. Bronx Museum focuses on 20th- and 21st-century art by African, Asian, and Latin American artists, and it's completely free (and open late on Fridays).

Sports

New Yankee Stadium (1) is not so new anymore, and Old Yankee Stadium is a distant memory, except for its field, which has been preserved across the street. Get the cheapest ticket you can find and just spend the game walking around the concourses, which have the best views of the field. Van Cortlandt Park (6) offers playgrounds, ball fields, tennis and basketball courts, hiking trails, stables for horseback riding, and one of golf's classic courses, "Vanny."

Nature

The restoration of the Bronx River (19) coincides with the improvement of green spaces throughout the borough. Pelham Bay Park (11) is the city's largest at 2,764 acres, offering many recreational opportunities in addition to the Thomas Pell Wildlife Sanctuary, two nature centers, and immensely popular Orchard Beach.

Food

Belmont:
- Dominick's, 2335 Arthur Ave, 718-733-2807—Famous, old-school Italian-American where there are no menus and no set prices.
- Full Moon, 602 East 187th St, 718-584-3451—Wonderful pizza and calzones.
- Roberto Restaurant, 603 Crescent Ave, 718-733-9503—Classic fare, rumored to be the best around.
- Trattoria Zero Otto Nove, 2357 Arthur Ave, 718-220-1027 Best high-end pizza in the borough at Roberto sister restaurant.
- Arthur Avenue Retail Market, 2344 Arthur Ave—Get all the right ingredients for home-cooked Italian meals.

City Island:
- Johnny's Reef, 2 City Island Ave, 718-885-2086—Local favorite for fresh, inexpensive seafood.

Riverdale:
- Riverdale Garden, 4576 Manhattan College Pkwy, 347-346-8497—Upscale American and Continental food in a beautiful setting.
- An Beal Bocht, 445 West 238th St, 718-884-7127—Café/bar/coffee shop hangout for the hip, young, and Irish.
- S&S Cheesecake, 222 West 238th St, 718-549-3888—Forget Junior's, this is the city's best.

University Heights:
- Ebe Ye Yie, 2364 Jerome Ave, 718-563-6064—Hearty Ghanaian meals.

Concourse Village:
- The Feeding Tree, 892 Gerard Ave, 718-293-5025—Delicious Jamaican food close to Yankee Stadium.

Kingsbridge:
- El Economico, 5589 Broadway, 718-796-4851—Home-style Puerto Rican meals.
- Com Tam Ninh Kieu, 2641 Jerome Ave, 718-365-2680—best Vietnamese in the Bronx; great pho.

Pelham Bay:
- Louie & Ernie's, 1300 Crosby Ave, 718-829-6230—Their thin-crust pizza is the best in the borough.

Parkchester:
- Taqueria Tlaxcalli, 2103 Starling Ave, 347-851-3085—destination Mexican.

Landmarks

1 Yankee Stadium
2 Hall of Fame for Great Americans
3 Arthur Avenue
4 Riverdale
5 Wave Hill
6 Van Cortlandt Park
7 Woodlawn Cemetery
8 New York Botanical Garden
9 Woodlawn
10 Bronx Zoo
11 Pelham Bay Park
12 City Island
13 Co-op City
14 Mott Haven
15 Longwood
16 The Hub
17 Bruckner Boulevard
18 Poe Cottage
19 Bronx River
20 Bronx Museum of the Arts

N
Holland Tunnel
West Side Expy
MANHATTAN
Hudson River
9A
SOHO
TRIBECA
BATTERY PARK CITY
FINANCIAL DISTRICT
WEST VILLAGE
STUYVESANT TOWN
EAST VILLAGE
CHINATOWN
LOWER EAST SIDE
E 14th St
E Houston St
First Ave
FDR Dr
East River
Williamsburg Bridge
Manhattan Bridge
Brooklyn Bridge
Brooklyn Battery Tunnel
Governors Island
Manhattan Ave
Greenpoint Ave
Greenpoint
Northside
Sunnyside
278
495
Long Island Expy
Maspeth
Metropolitan Ave
Grand Ave
Williamsburg
QUEENS
Bushwick
Vinegar Hill
Flushing Ave
Brooklyn-Queens Expy
Myrtle Ave
Fort Greene
Brooklyn Heights
Jackie Robinson Pkwy
Broadway
Bedford-Stuyvesant
BQE
Clinton St
Atlantic Ave
Cobble Hill
Boerum Hill
Carroll Gardens
Red Hook
Barclays Center
Crown Heights
Kings Hwy
Pitkin Ave
Brownsville
Pennsylvania Ave
East New Y
Park Slope
Eastern Pkwy
Empire Blvd
Prospect Park
Prospect Expy
Wingate
Rockaway Pkwy
Linden Blvd
27
Gowanus Expy
4th Ave
Green-Wood Cemetery
39th St
Sunset Park
Ocean Ave
Nostrand Ave
Holy Cross Cemetery
Utica Ave
Remsen Ave
Starrett City
Canarsie
Ave D
Flatbush
Farragut
Flatlands Ave
Seaview Ave
Fort Hamilton Pkwy
Borough Park
Bay Ridge
Fourth Ave
Dyker Heights
47th St
18th Ave
Ave J
Flatlands
Flatbush Ave
Canarsie Park
Midwood
Ocean Pkwy
Coney Island Ave
Bay Ridge Pkwy
65th St
Washington Cemetery
Bensonhurst
Marine Park
Jamaica Bay
86th St
Dyker Beach Park
Fort Hamilton
Ave P
Ave U
Mill Basin
Bergen Beach
Verrazano-Narrows Bridge
Kings Hwy
Ocean Parkway
Cropsey Ave
Bath Beach
Bay Pkwy
Stillwell Ave
Gerritsen Ave
Belt
Floyd Bennett Field
Lower Bay
Bensonhurst Park
Ave X
Gravesend
Sheepshead Bay
Shore/Belt Pkwy
Drier-Offerman Park
Manhattan Beach
Sea Gate
Neptune Ave
Brighton Beach
Manhattan Beach Park
Surf Ave
Coney Island
Rockaway Inlet
Rockaway

The Great Mistake of 1898, Brooklyn is no longer its own city, but that little technicality hasn't kept the Borough of Kings down. As Manhattan becomes prohibitively expensive and middle-Americanized, Brooklyn's popularity is at an all-time high. Scores of recent college grads, immigrants, ex-Manhattanites, and even celebrities are calling Brooklyn home, whether in a row of brownstones, a pre-war house, or a brand-new loft. Along with the residential boom, Brooklyn has firmly arrived as a cultural and entertainment mecca, and it boasts some of the hottest bars, astounding cultural diversity, and stellar parks. Atlantic Yards is now a reality after much protest, but Brooklyn won't let go of its unique character that easily.

Communities

As the largest borough by population (over 2.5 million!), Brooklyn holds a special place as one of the nation's most remarkable urban areas. As many as one in four people can trace their roots here! In Brooklyn, you can find pretty much any type of community—for better or worse. As gentrification marches deeper into Brooklyn, the borough is changing fast. Neighborhoods most likely to see their first baby boutiques open soon include Red Hook, East Williamsburg, Prospect-Lefferts Gardens, and Crown Heights.

The first thing you notice when looking at Brooklyn on a map is the sheer size of it. Yet much of Brooklyn is largely unknown to most New Yorkers. Yes, Brooklyn Heights, Williamsburg, and Park Slope are nice communities that are fun to explore. However, if you've never ventured further out into Brooklyn than the obligatory trip to Coney Island, you're missing some fantastic neighborhoods. For instance, Bay Ridge (4) has beautiful single-family homes along its western edge, a killer view of the Verrazano Bridge, and a host of excellent shops and restaurants. Dyker Heights (6) is composed of almost all single-family homes, many of which go all-out with Christmas light displays during the holiday season. Brighton Beach (8) continues to be a haven for many Russian expatriates. The quiet, tree-lined streets of both Ocean Parkway (10) and Midwood (11) can make one forget all about the hustle and bustle of downtown Brooklyn, or downtown anywhere else for that matter. Finally, Bedford-Stuyvesant (12) has a host of cool public buildings, fun eateries, and beautiful brownstones.

Sports

No, the Dodgers are never coming back. This is still hard for many older Brooklynites to accept and accounts for much of the nostalgia that is still associated with the borough. If you can get beyond the fact that Ebbets Field is now a giant concrete housing complex, then you will enjoy spending a fine summer evening watching the Cyclones at Coney Island (7). But really, Brooklynites need to get over it. The Barclays Center (15) already captured one major professional sports team (the Nets) and soon another will begin playing there (the Islanders). Elsewhere, Kensington Stables in Prospect Park (1) provides lessons for wannabe equestrians.

Attractions

Coney Island's (7) redevelopment is well underway but has left untouched the Cyclone, the Wonder Wheel, Nathan's, Totonno's pizza, movies at the Coney Island Museum, the beach, the freaks, and The Warriors. Close by is the Aquarium (13). Nature trails, parked blimps, views of the water, scenic marinas, live events and overnight camping all make historical Floyd Bennett Field (9) a worthwhile trip. For more beautiful views, you can check out Owl's Point Park (3) in Bay Ridge, or the parking lot underneath the Verrazano-Narrows Bridge (5) (located right off the Shore Parkway). The Verrazano might not be New York's most beautiful bridge, but it's hands-down the most awe-inspiring. Both Green-Wood Cemetery (2) and Prospect Park (1) provide enough greenery to keep you happy until you get to Yosemite. Finally, Brooklyn Heights (14) is the most beautiful residential neighborhood in all of New York. Don't believe us? Go stand on the corner of Willow and Orange Streets and find out for yourself.

Food

Here are some restaurants in some of the outlying areas of Brooklyn: See pages 160 to 171 for other Brooklyn eateries.

Bay Ridge: Casablanca Restaurant, 484 77th St, 718-748-2077—highly recommended Moroccan.

Midwood: DiFara's Pizzeria, E 15th St & Ave J, 718-258-1367— Dirty, cheap, and fresh as hell.

Sunset Park: Nyonya, 5223 Eighth Ave, 718-633-0808—Good quality Malaysian.

Sheepshead Bay: The restaurant at Russian Bath of NY, 1200 Gravesend Neck Rd, 718-332-1676, delicious Russian food after a schvitz.

Landmarks

1 Prospect Park
2 Green-Wood Cemetery
3 Owl's Point Park
4 Bay Ridge
5 Verrazano-Narrows Bridge
6 Dyker Heights
7 Coney Island
8 Brighton Beach
9 Floyd Bennett Field
10 Ocean Parkway
11 Midwood
12 Bedford-Stuyvesant
13 New York Aquarium
14 Brooklyn Heights
15 Barclays Center

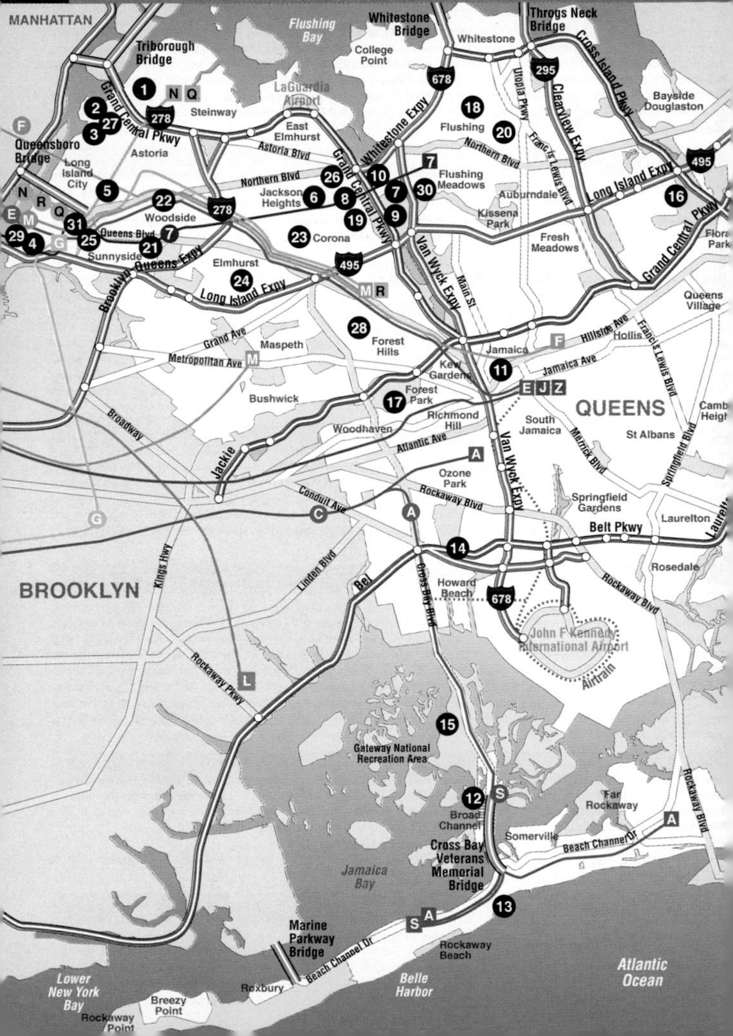

N
MANHATTAN
Flushing Bay
Whitestone Bridge
Throgs Neck Bridge
Triborough Bridge
College Point
Whitestone
Cross Island Pkwy
LaGuardia Airport
Steinway
Grand Central Pkwy
East Elmhurst
Whitestone Expy
Flushing
Utopia Pkwy
Clearview Expy
Bayside Douglaston
Queensboro Bridge
Astoria
Astoria Blvd
Northern Blvd
Francis Lewis Blvd
Long Island City
Jackson Heights
Flushing Meadows
Auburndale
Long Island Expy
Woodside
Queens Blvd
Kissena Park
Fresh Meadows
Corona
Sunnyside
Brooklyn-Queens Expy
Elmhurst
Van Wyck Expy
Main St
Floral Park
Queens Village
Grand Ave
Maspeth
Forest Hills
Hillside Ave
Hollis
Jamaica
Metropolitan Ave
Kew Gardens
Jamaica Ave
Bushwick
Forest Park
Richmond Hill
QUEENS
Cambria Heights
Broadway
Woodhaven
South Jamaica
St Albans
Merrick Blvd
Springfield Blvd
Atlantic Ave
Jackie
Ozone Park
Conduit Ave
Rockaway Blvd
Springfield Gardens
Laurelton
Belt Pkwy
Rosedale
Linden Blvd
Kings Hwy
BROOKLYN
Cross Bay Blvd
Howard Beach
John F Kennedy International Airport
Airtrain
Rockaway Pkwy
Gateway National Recreation Area
Rockaway Blvd
Broad Channel
Far Rockaway
Somerville
Beach Channel Dr
Cross Bay Veterans Memorial Bridge
Jamaica Bay
Marine Parkway Bridge
Rockaway Beach
Atlantic Ocean
Lower New York Bay
Belle Harbor
Roxbury
Breezy Point
Rockaway Point

The most diverse borough in the city, people from all over have been "discovering" Queens for years, making it home to some of the city's best ethnic restaurants and neighborhoods; Flushing's Chinatown is rivaling Manhattan's as the center of New York's Chinese community. Queens also has some of the city's best open spaces with everything from forestland to surfing beaches. And at a time when Brooklyn real estate prices push higher and higher toward Manhattan extremes, Queens is looking like a better and better option to those who are willing to explore a little.

Communities

From the stately Tudor homes of Forest Hills Gardens (28) to the hip-hop beat of Jamaica Avenue (11), Queens has it all. Eastern Queens tends toward suburbia, while the communities along the borough's southern border often include active industrial districts. All things Asian can be found in Flushing (20), the city's largest Chinatown. Sunnyside (21) and Woodside (22) are home to Irish and Mexican immigrants alike, making it easy to find a proper pint and a fabulous taco on the same block. Jackson Heights' (6) 74th Street is Little India, while 82nd Street is packed with South and Central American businesses. Corona (23) blends old-school Italian-American delis with Latino dance clubs. Elmhurst (24) has attracted Asian, Southeast Asian, and South American immigrants to set up shop on its crowded streets. Island Broad Channel (12) feels like a sleepy village, while the Rockaways (13) offer the only surfing beaches in the city.

Culture

Fans of contemporary art have long known P.S.1 (4) is the place to be, especially during its summer weekend WarmUp parties. Then head over to the Sculpture Center (31), to see what new exhibit they've cooked up for us. The Noguchi Museum (3), dedicated to the work of the Japanese-American sculptor, and neighboring Socrates Sculpture Park (2), a waterfront space with changing exhibitions, attract visitors from far beyond the five boroughs. The Fisher Landau Center for Art (25) features a world-class collection of modern art (and is free, to boot). Movie buffs should look for repertory screenings at the American Museum of the Moving Image (5). The delightfully kitschy Louis Armstrong House (26) is a must-see for jazz lovers. In Flushing Meadows-Corona Park, the New York Hall of Science (8) beckons the geeky kid in all of us with its hands-on exhibits while the Queens Museum of Art's (9) scale model of the entire city will wow even the most jaded New Yorkers.

Sports

In 2009, the Mets inaugurated a brand new place to make memories of exquisite disappointment, Jackie Robinson...err, sorry, kids...Citi Field. Enjoy the ersatz Ebbets Field façade. Feel free to root for the visiting team if you like—Mets supporters are far more subdued than their Yankee rivals. The U.S. Open takes place right across the street at the Billie Jean King National Tennis Center (7). See girls gone wild when our local ladies, The Queens of Pain, compete in the Gotham Girls Roller Derby league. See the ponies and fritter away your hard-earned cash at the Aqueduct Racetrack (14). Hitch a ride to Rockaway Beach (13) for swimming and surfing or paddle out in a kayak on loan from the Long Island City Community Boathouse (27). Astoria Pool (1) is the city's largest with room for 3,000 swimmers. For bowling, all-night Whitestone Lanes (18) is the place to be.

Nature

Gantry Plaza State Park's (29) spacious piers attract strollers and urban fishermen alike with panoramic views of the Manhattan skyline, and a major park expansion will eventually connect the waterfront from Anable Basin to the north all the way down to Newtown Creek. The Jamaica Bay Wildlife Refuge (15) in Gateway National Recreation Area is internationally known for bird-watching. Queens Botanical Garden is a peaceful refuge with its own bee hives out in Flushing. Fort Tilden is becoming more popular, but it's still one of New York's prettiest, natural, non-commercial beaches. Flushing Meadows-Corona Park (30) is designed for active recreation, but Alley Pond Park (16) and Forest Park (17) have wooded trails perfect for wandering.

Food

Entire books have been written on where to eat in Queens (none as good as NFT, natch!), so these are just a handful of suggestions:
Corona: Leo's Latticini (a.k.a. Mama's), 46-02 104th St, 718-898-6069—Insanely good Italian sandwiches that pair well with dessert from the Lemon Ice King, 52-02 108th Street, 718-699-5133, just a few blocks away.
Rego Park: Cheburechnaya, 92-09 63rd Dr, 718-897-9080—grilled meats are the speciality at this Kosher Uzbek gem.
Sunnyside: De Mole, 45-02 48th Ave, 718-392-2161— Fresh, simply prepared Mexican food in bistro setting.
Bayside: Uncle Jack's, 39-40 Bell Blvd, 718-229-1100—Mayor Bloomberg's favorite steakhouse serves up fine flesh.
Flushing: Spicy and Tasty, 39-07 Prince Street, 718-359-1601—The name of this Sichuan place is entirely accurate.
Woodside:

- Sripraphai, 64-13 39th Ave, 718-899-9599—Easily the best Thai food in the city.
- La Flor, 53-02 Roosevelt Ave, 718-426-8023—Fantastic neighborhood café with Mexican-inflected dishes.

Landmarks

Astoria Pool
Socrates Sculpture Park
Noguchi Museum
P.S.1 Art Museum
American Museum of the Moving Image
Jackson Heights
US Open/National Tennis Center
Hall of Science
9 Queens Museum of Art
10 Citi Field
11 Jamaica
12 Broad Channel
13 The Rockaways
14 Aqueduct Racetrack
15 Jamaica Bay Wildlife Refuge
16 Alley Pond Park
17 Forest Park
18 Whitestone Lanes
19 Queens Zoo
20 Flushing
21 Sunnyside
22 Woodside
23 Corona
24 Elmhurst
25 Fisher Landau Center for Art
26 Louis Armstrong House
27 Long Island City Community Boathouse
28 Forest Hills
29 Gantry Plaza State Park
30 Flushing Meadows-Corona Park

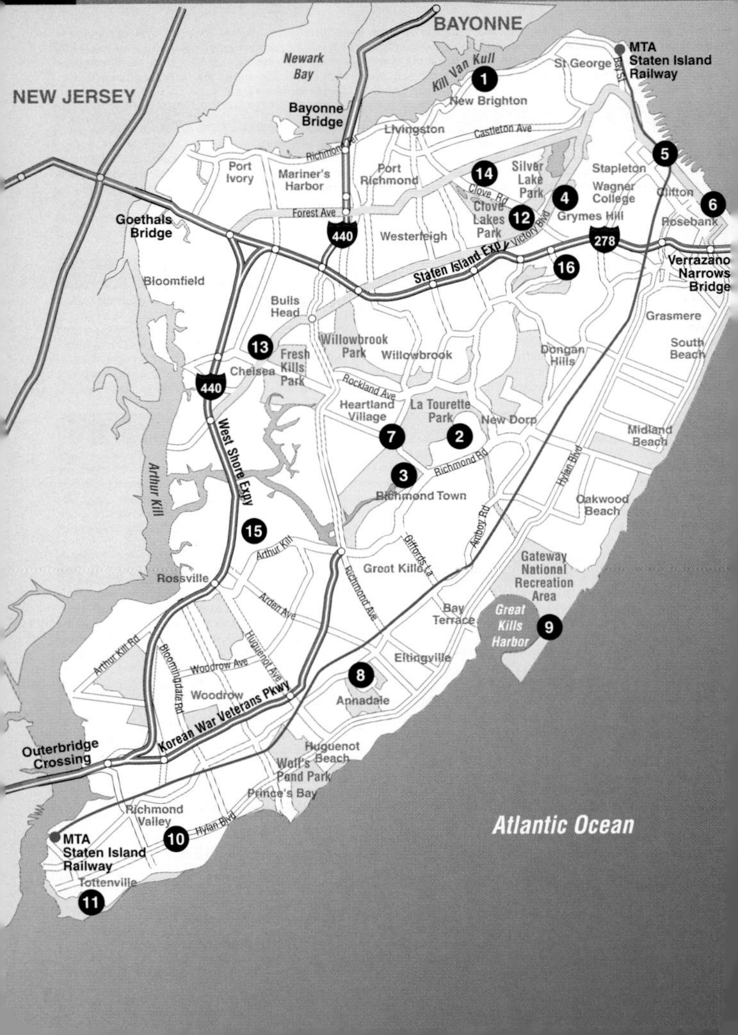

Outer Boroughs • **Staten Island**

BAYONNE
Newark Bay
Kill Van Kull
1
St George
Bay St
MTA Staten Island Railway
NEW JERSEY
New Brighton
Bayonne Bridge
Livingston
Castleton Ave
Richmond Ter
Port Ivory
Mariner's Harbor
Port Richmond
14
Silver Lake Park
Stapleton
5
Wagner College
4
Clifton
6
Clove Rd
Clove Lakes Park
12
Grymes Hill
Rosebank
Forest Ave
Goethals Bridge
440
Westerleigh
Victory Blvd
278
Staten Island Exp
16
Verrazano Narrows Bridge
Bloomfield
Bulls Head
Grasmere
13
Willowbrook Park
Willowbrook
Fresh Kills Park
Chelsea
Dongan Hills
South Beach
440
Rockland Ave
Heartland Village
La Tourette Park
New Dorp
7
2
Midland Beach
West Shore Expy
Arthur Kill
Richmond Rd
3
Richmond Town
Hylan Blvd
Oakwood Beach
15
Arthur Kill
Giffords La
Amboy Rd
Great Kills
Gateway National Recreation Area
Rossville
Richmond Ave
Arden Ave
Bay Terrace
Great Kills Harbor
9
Arthur Kill Rd
Huguenot Ave
Bloomingdale Rd
Woodrow Ave
Eltingville
8
Woodrow
Korean War Veterans Pkwy
Annadale
Outerbridge Crossing
Huguenot Beach
Wolf's Pond Park
Prince's Bay
Richmond Valley
Atlantic Ocean
10
Hylan Blvd
MTA Staten Island Railway
Tottenville
11

Staten Island, of thee we sing! Don't let the sight of jabronis with fake tans and gelled hair hold you back from exploring, lest you miss out on heaps of excellent pizza, the wildflower meadows at Mount Loretto, the windows on the past at Historic Richmond Town, the small-town charm of minor league baseball at St. George, and the striking design of the Chinese Scholars' Garden at Snug Harbor. It's high time you pulled your head out of your borough and hitched a ride on the ferry, if only to eat at one of SI's "holy trinity" of pizzerias.

Culture

1 Snug Harbor Cultural Center, 1000 Richmond Ter, 718-448-2500. A former sailors' home transformed to a waterfront arts complex, Snug Harbor's 83 acres include classrooms, studio spaces, performance venues, galleries, three museums, and a truly noteworthy botanical garden. Call to learn about cultural events and exhibits on site.

2 Jacques Marchais Museum of Tibetan Art, 338 Lighthouse Ave, 718-987-3500. A world-class collection of Tibetan art, courtesy of former New York art collector Edna Coblentz, who had the surprising French pseudonym Jacques Marchais.

3 Historic Richmond Town, 441 Clarke Ave, 718-351-1611. Get back to old-timey times visiting restored homes from the 17th to the 19th centuries, most populated by costumed guides. Great for kids and adults who want to learn how to churn butter/forge metal.

4 Wagner College, 1 Campus Rd, 718-390-3100. Wagner's tranquil hilltop location rewards visitors with beautiful views of the serene surroundings, but its best feature is the planetarium.

5 Staten Island Village Hall, 111 Canal St. Last remaining village hall building in Staten Island, a reminder of the borough's rural past.

6 Alice Austen House, 2 Hylan Blvd, 718-816-4506. Alice Austen was an early twentieth-century amateur photographer, and now she's got a museum and a ferry boat named after her. Go figure. Some of her 8,000 images are on view at her house, which has a great view of lower New York Harbor.

Nature

7 Staten Island Greenbelt, 200 Nevada Ave, 718-667-2165. This 2,800-acre swath of land (comprising several different parks) in the center of the island contains a golf course, a hospital, a scout camp, several graveyards, and plenty of wooded areas that remain relatively undeveloped and can be accessed only by walking trails. A good starting point is High Rock Park. Panoramic views abound.

8 Blue Heron Park, 222 Poillon Ave, 718-967-3542. This quiet, 236-acre park has a fantastic Nature Center and plenty of ponds, wetlands, and streams to explore. Noted for bird-watching, hence the name.

9 Great Kills Park, 718-987-6790. Part of the Gateway National Recreation Area, Great Kills boasts clean beaches, a marina, and a nature preserve.

10 Mount Loretto Unique Area, 6450 Hylan Blvd, 718-482-7287. Flourishing wetlands, grasslands, and beaches all rolled into one serenely beautiful waterfront park. Mysterious sculptures dot the beach.

11 Conference House Park, 7455 Hylan Blvd, 718-984-6046.The historic house is worth a look, but watching the sunset from the restored waterfront pavilion is a must. You'll also find NYC's very own "South Pole" on the beach here.

12 Clove Lakes Park, Clove Rd and Victory Blvd, 311. Who needs Central Park? Check out these romantic rowboats on the lake in season.

13 Freshkills Park, off Route 440. Former landfill, now a park. Sorta. They're working on it over the next 30 years. Free tours by appointment.

Other

14 110/120 Longfellow Road. Celebrate one of the greatest American films without having to schlep to Sicily. This address is where the Corleone family held court in The Godfather.

15 Ship Graveyard, at Arthur Kill Rd and Rossville Ave. These ships of the damned make a perfect backdrop for Goth photo shoots.

16 Staten Island Zoo, 614 Broadway, 718-442-3100. Kids will go wild here, near the stunning Clove Lakes Park. Be sure to bring them to the vampire bat feedings.

Food

Tompkinsville:
New Asha, 322 Victory Blvd, 718-420-0649. Great Sri Lankan food on the cheap. Spicy!
Port Richmond:
Denino's, 524 Port Richmond Ave, 718-442-9401. Some of the best pizza in town.
Dongan Hills:
Lee's Tavern, 60 Hancock St, 718-667-9749. Great bar with great pizza—get the fresh mozzarella.
Grant City:
Nunzio's, 2155 Hylan Blvd, 718-667-9647. More great pizza. Notice a theme here?
Tottenville:
Egger's Ice Cream Parlor, 7437 Amboy Rd, 718-605-9335. Old time ice cream and sweets. Kids love it.
Killmeyer's Old Bavaria Inn, 4254 Arthur Kill Rd, 718-984-1202. Historic German beer garden and eats. Jå!
Castleton Corners
Joe & Pats, 1758 Victory Blvd, 718-981-0887. Completing SI's "Holy Trinity" of pizza.
West Brighton:
Nurnberger Bierhaus, 817 Castleton Ave, 718-816-7461—German beer and food.

Driving In / Through Staten Island

To visit Staten Island, one must either drive/take a bus/take a cab over the Verrazano Bridge ($15 toll) from Bay Ridge, Brooklyn, or catch the ferry from Lower Manhattan. If you elect to do the latter, you'll find myriad buses departing from the St. George side of the ferry as well as the terminal of the Staten Island Railway, ready to whisk you all the way down to Tottenville and back with one swipe of the Metrocard. To reach New Jersey via Staten Island, take the Verrazano to the Staten Island Expressway (Route 278) to Route 440 to the Outerbridge Crossing, and you're almost halfway to Princeton or the Jersey shore. However…the Staten Island Expressway often gets jammed. Two scenic, though not really quicker, alternatives: one, take Hylan Boulevard all the way south to almost the southwest tip of Staten Island, and then cut up to the Outerbridge Crossing; two, take Richmond Terrace around the north shore and cross to New Jersey at the Goethals Bridge. Remember, neither is really faster, but at least you'll be moving.

General Information

Battery Park Parks Conservancy: 212-267-9700
Websites: www.lowermanhattan.info
www.bpcparks.org
www.bpcdogs.org

Overview

Welcome to Battery Park City—a master-planned community reminiscent of *Pleasantville*. Originally the brainchild of Nelson Rockefeller, this urban experiment transformed a WTC construction landfill into a 92-acre planned enclave on the southwestern tip of Manhattan. As space in Manhattan continues to disappear into the stratosphere (literally, the only way to build is up), the idea of BPC requires a double-take. It's about making public spaces (about 30% of those 92 acres) work within private entities. Imagine taking Central Park, cutting it up, and saying, "Here, your neighborhood can have a chunk of it, and that street down there, and that street over there, too." Admit it: walking among private, commercial spaces day in and day out is enough to make anyone claustrophobic (thank you, Financial District). In BPC you walk through spacious parks with weird statues and brick pavers all on your way to work, the grocery store, the gym, or the movie theater. BPC will have you asking: "What's outside Battery Park City?"

Those looking for all-night eateries and party spots should pass it up, but if you've got kids this is the place for you. Many NY families—roughly 25,000 people—occupy the 40% of BPC that's dedicated residential space, including a future-forward "green" building, the Solaire. Robert F. Wagner Jr. and Rector are good choices for a picnic; The Esplanade or South Cove to walk along the Hudson; Nelson A. Rockefeller to play frisbee; North Cove to park your yacht; and Teardrop Park for the kids. People of all ages have welcomed the ever-popular Shake Shack (the cheapest meal in the neighborhood), live music at the World Financial Center, and the new eco-friendly Public Library, Manhattan's first green LEED-certified branch.

Seeing: Amazing sculptures by Bourgeois, Otterness, Puryear, Dine, and Cragg. Inspired architecture: Stuyvesant High School, Siah Armajani's Tribeca Bridge, Kevin Roche's Museum of Jewish Heritage, Caesar Pelli's Winter Garden, and the World Financial Center. If you like things nice, neat, and compartmentalized, this 'hood is for you.

Bagels

• **Pick A Bagel** • Embassy Suites • 102 North End Ave [Vesey St]

Banks

BA • **Bank of America (ATM)** • 3 World Financial Center [Vesey St]
BA • **Bank of America (ATM)** • 4 World Financial Ctr [Vesey St]
CH • **Chase** • 325 North End Ave [Vesey St]
CH • **Chase** • 331 South End Ave [Albany St]
HS • **HSBC (ATM)** • NY Mercantile Exchange • 1 N End Ave [Vesey St]

Car Rental

• **Avis Gateway Plaza** • 345 South End Ave [Albany St]

Coffee

• **Au Bon Pain** • WFC • 200 Liberty St [West St]
• **Cosi** • 200 Vesey St [West St]
• **Financier Patisserie** • 3 World Financial Center [W Side Hwy]
• **Starbucks** • 250 Vesey St [W Side Hwy]

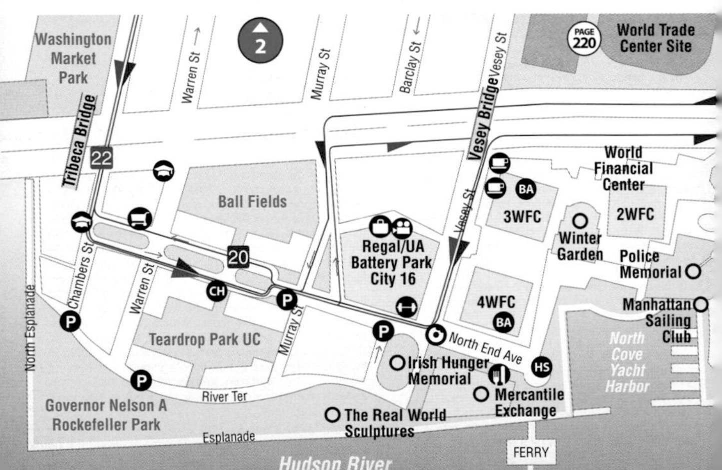

Community Gardens

Gyms

- **Battery Park Swim & Fitness Center** • 375 South End Ave [Liberty St]
- **Liberty Club MCB** •200 Rector Pl [South End Ave]
- **NYSC** • 102 North End Ave [Vesey St]

Landmarks

- **The Irish Hunger Memorial** • Vesey St & North End Ave
- **Manhattan Sailing Club** • North Cove (Liberty St & North End Ave)
- **Mercantile Exchange** • 1 North End Ave [Vesey St]
- **Museum of Jewish Heritage** • 36 Battery Pl [Little West St]
- **Police Memorial** • Liberty St & South End Ave
- **The Real World Sculptures** • Rockefeller Park
- **Skyscraper Museum** • 39 Battery Pl [Little West St]
- **Winter Garden** • 37 Vesey St [Church St]

Liquor Stores

- **Bulls & Bears Winery** • 309 South End Ave [Albany St]

Movie Theaters

- **Regal Battery Park Stadium 11** • Conrad New York • 102 North End Ave [Vesey St]

Nightlife

- **Rise Bar** • Ritz Carlton • 2 West St [Little West St]

Parking

Pet Shops

- **Le Pet Spa** • 300 Rector Pl [South End Ave]

Restaurants

- **Gigino at Wagner Park** • 20 Battery Pl [Washington St]
- **Grill Room** • WFC • 225 Liberty St [W Side Hwy]
- **Picasso Pizza** • 303 South End Ave [Albany St]
- **PJ Clarke's** • 4 World Financial Ctr [Vesey St]
- **Samantha's Fine Foods** • 235 South End Ave [Rector Pl]
- **Steamer's Landing** • 375 South End Ave [Liberty St]

Schools

- **PS 89** • 201 Warren St [Clinton St]
- **Stuyvesant High** • 345 Chambers St [North End Ave]

Shopping

- **DSW Shoe Warehouse** • 102 North End Ave [Vesey]

Supermarkets

- **Gourmet Heaven** • 450 North End Ave [Chambers St]
- **Gristedes** • 315 South End Ave [Albany St] ㉔
- **Gristedes** • 71 South End Ave [W Thames St]

Video Rental

- **Video Room** • 300 Rector Pl [South End Ave]

General Information

Website:	www.centralparknyc.org
Central Park Conservancy:	212-310-6600
Shakespeare in the Park:	212-539-8750

Overview

Taking a stroll through Central Park is something that tourists and residents can always agree on. This world-class sanctuary is a huge, peaceful, lush oasis in the concrete jungle, and who hasn't skipped therapy once or twice in favor of clearing your mind the old-fashioned way, by taking a long walk in the park? On any given day, you'll see people disco roller-skating, playing jazz, juggling, walking their dogs, running, making out, meditating, playing softball, whining through soccer practice, getting married, picnicking, and playing chess.

Designed by Frederick Law Olmsted and Calvert Vaux in the 1850s, Central Park has a diverse mix of attractions. The Central Park Conservancy (www.centralparknyc.org) leads walking tours, and you can always hail a horse-drawn carriage or bike taxi for a ride through the park if you want to look like a true tourist.

Practicalities

Central Park is easily accessible by subway, since the A C B D N R Q 1 2 3 trains all circle the park. Parking along CPW is harder, so try side streets. Unless you're heading to the park for a big concert, a softball game, or Shakespeare in the Park, walking or hanging out (especially alone!) in the park at night is not recommended.

Nature

Central Park is the place to see and be seen, for birds, actually; 230 species can be spotted and The Ramble **27** is a good place to stake out. There are an amazing number of both plant and animal species that inhabit the park, including the creatures housed in its two zoos **4** & **8**. Some people forage for edible plants throughout the park, perhaps out of curiosity, perhaps as a response to the stagnant economy and rising price of groceries, though parks officials are trying to stop this practice. A good source of information on all of the park's flora and fauna is NYC schoolteacher Leslie Day's book, *Field Guide to the Natural World of New York City*.

Architecture & Sculpture

Central Park was designed to thrill visitors at every turn. The Bethesda Fountain **11,** designed by Emma Stebbins, is one of the main attractions of the park. Don't miss the view of Turtle Pond from Belvedere Castle **16** (home of the Central Park Learning Center). The Arsenal **5** is a wonderful ivy-clad building that houses the Parks Department headquarters. The original Greensward plan for Central Park is located in the Arsenal's third-floor conference room—if there isn't a meeting going on, you might be able to sneak a peek. Two of the most notable sculptures in the park are Alice in Wonderland **15** and the Obelisk **19**. Oh, and one other tiny point of interest…the Metropolitan Museum of Art **24** also happens to be in the park.

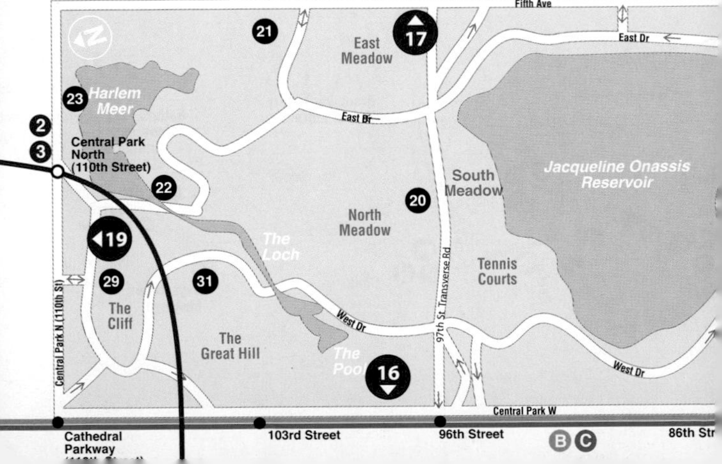

Open Spaces

New Yorkers covet space. Since they rarely get it in their apartments, they rely on large open areas such as Strawberry Fields **10**, the Great Lawn **26**, and Sheep Meadow **28.** The Ramble **27** and the Cliff **29** are still heavily forested and are good for hiking around, but don't go near them after dark. When it snows, you can find great sledding on Cedar Hill **30**, which is otherwise perfect for picnicking and sunbathing.

Performance

In warmer weather, Central Park is a microcosm of the great cultural attractions New York has to offer. The Delacorte Theater **18** is the home of Shakespeare in the Park, a New York tradition begun by famous director Joseph Papp. SummerStage **9** is now an extremely popular concert venue for all types of music, including the occasional killer rock concert. Opera companies and classical philharmonics also show up in the park frequently, as does the odd mega-star (Beastie Boys, Diana Ross, etc.). If you crave something truly outlandish, try the loinclothed Thoth, a self-proclaimed emotional hermaphrodite who plays the violin and sings in his own language, under the Angel Tunnel by the Bethesda Fountain **11**.

Sports

Rollerblading and roller skating are very popular (not just at the Roller Skating Rink **7**—see www.centralparkskate.com, www.cpdsa.org, www.skatecity.com), as is jogging, especially around the reservoir (1.57 mi). The Great Lawn **26** boasts beautiful softball fields. Central Park has 30 tennis courts (if you make a reservation, you can walk right on to the clay court with tennis shoes only—212-280-0205), fishing at Harlem Meer, gondola rides and boat rentals at the Loeb Boathouse **13**, model boat rentals at the Conservatory Water **14**, chess and checkers at the Chess & Checkers House **25**, two ice-skating rinks **1** & **22**, croquet and lawn bowling just north of Sheep Meadow **28**, and rock-climbing lessons at the North Meadow Rec Center **20**. You will also see volleyball, basketball, skateboarding, bicycling, and many pick-up soccer, frisbee, football, and kill-the-carrier games to join. During heavy snows, bust out your snowboard, cross-country skis, or homemade sled. Finally, Central Park is where the NYC Marathon ends each year.

Landmarks

1 Wollman Rink
2 Carousel
3 The Dairy
4 Central Park Zoo
5 The Arsenal
6 Tavern on the Green
7 Roller Skating Rink
8 Children's Zoo
9 SummerStage
10 Strawberry Fields
11 Bethesda Fountain
12 Bow Bridge
13 Loeb Boathouse
14 Model Boat Racing
15 Alice in Wonderland
16 Belvedere Castle
17 Shakespeare Gardens
18 Delacorte Theater
19 The Obelisk
20 North Meadow Recreation Center
21 Conservatory Garden
22 Lasker Rink
23 Dana Discovery Center
24 Metropolitan Museum of Art
25 Chess & Checkers House
26 The Great Lawn
27 The Ramble
28 Sheep Meadow
29 The Cliff
30 Cedar Hill
31 The Great Hill

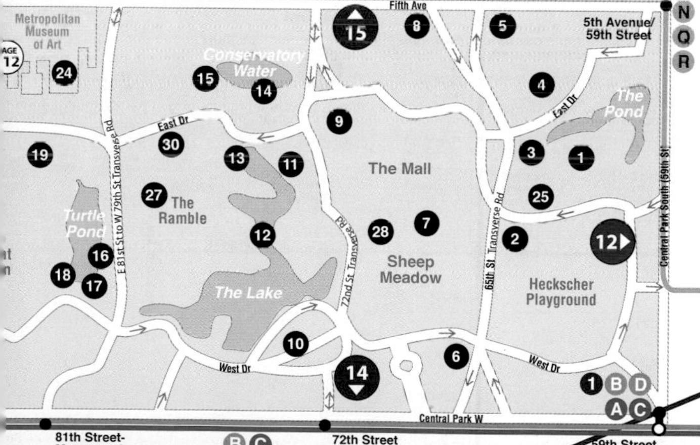

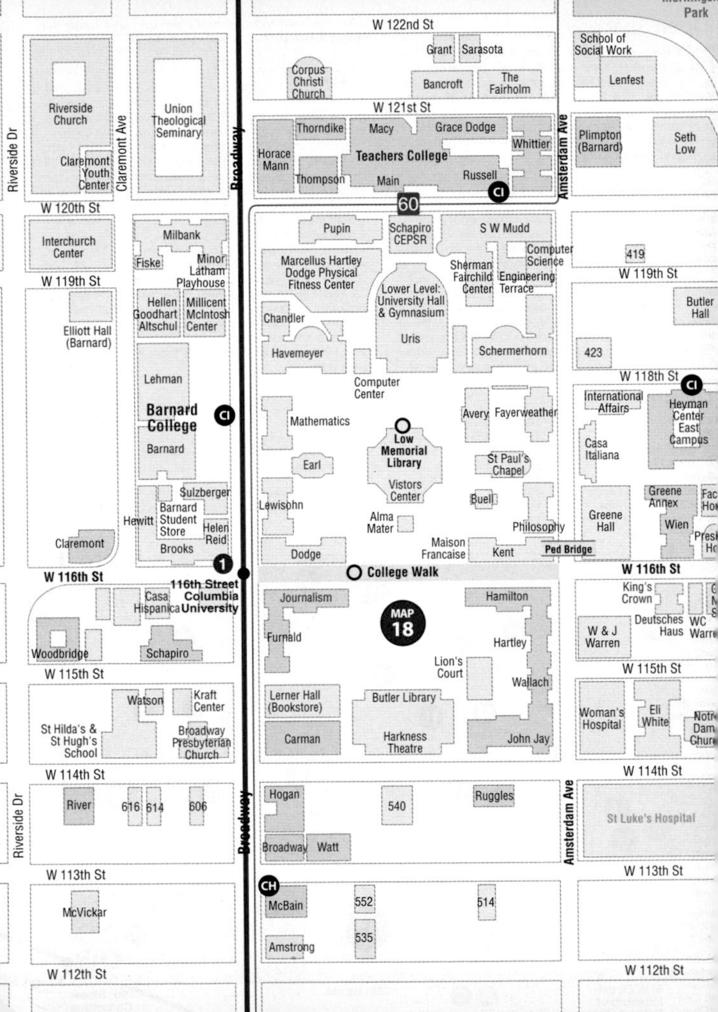
Morningside Park
W 122nd St
Grant
Sarasota
School of Social Work
Lenfest
Corpus Christi Church
Bancroft
The Fairholm
W 121st St
Riverside Church
Union Theological Seminary
Claremont Youth Center
Thorndike
Macy
Grace Dodge
Horace Mann
Teachers College
Whittier
Thompson
Main
Russell
Plimpton (Barnard)
Seth Low
Riverside Dr
Claremont Ave
Broadway
Amsterdam Ave
W 120th St
60
Interchurch Center
Milbank
Fiske
Minor Latham Playhouse
Pupin
Schapiro CEPSR
S W Mudd
Computer Science
419
Marcellus Hartley Dodge Physical Fitness Center
Sherman Fairchild Center
Engineering Terrace
W 119th St
Hellen Goodhart Altschul
Millicent McIntosh Center
Elliott Hall (Barnard)
Lower Level: University Hall & Gymnasium
Uris
Chandler
Havemeyer
Schermerhorn
Butler Hall
423
Lehman
Computer Center
W 118th St
International Affairs
Heyman Center East Campus
Barnard College
Mathematics
Avery
Fayerweather
Barnard
Low Memorial Library
Vistors Center
Earl
St Paul's Chapel
Casa Italiana
Sulzberger
Barnard Student Store
Hewitt
Helen Reid
Brooks
Lewisohn
Buell
Alma Mater
Greene Annex
Greene Hall
Wien
Philosophy
Claremont
Dodge
Maison Francaise
Kent
Ped Bridge
W 116th St
116th Street Columbia University
College Walk
Casa Hispanica
Journalism
Hamilton
King's Crown
Deutsches Haus
W & J Warren
Woodbridge
Schapiro
Furnald
MAP 18
Hartley
Lion's Court
Wallach
W 115th St
Watson
Kraft Center
Lerner Hall (Bookstore)
Butler Library
Woman's Hospital
Eli White
St Hilda's & St Hugh's School
Broadway Presbyterian Church
Carman
Harkness Theatre
John Jay
W 114th St
River
616
614
606
Hogan
540
Ruggles
St Luke's Hospital
Broadway
Watt
W 113th St
CH
McBain
552
514
McVickar
535
Amstrong
W 112th St

General Information

NFT Map:	18
Morningside Heights:	2960 Broadway & 116th St
Medical Center:	601 W 168th St
Phone:	212-854-1754
Website:	www.columbia.edu
Students Enrolled:	27,606
Endowment:	Market value as of 2012 was $7.6 billion

Overview

Yearning for those carefree days spent debating nihilism in the quad and wearing pajamas in public? Look no further than a quick trip to the Ivy League haven of Columbia University. Unlike the other collegiate institutions that pepper Manhattan's real estate, Columbia actually *has* a campus. The main campus, located in Morningside Heights, spans six blocks between Broadway and Amsterdam Avenues. Most of the undergraduate classes are held here, along with several of the graduate schools. Other graduate schools, including the Law School and School of International and Public Affairs, are close by on Amsterdam Avenue. The main libraries, Miller Theater, and St. Paul's Chapel are also located on the Morningside Heights campus. You can even get your intramural fix on a few fields for frisbee-throwing and pick-up soccer games.

Founded in 1754 as King's College, Columbia University is one of the country's most prestigious academic institutions. The university is well known for its core curriculum, a program of requirements that gives students an introduction to the most influential works in literature, philosophy, science, and other disciplines. It also prepares them for the rigors of those pesky dinner parties.

After residing in two different downtown locations, Columbia moved to its present campus (designed by McKim, Mead, and White) in 1897. Low Library remains the focal point of the campus as does the Alma Mater statue in front—a landmark that continues to inspire student superstitions (find the hidden owl and you might be the next valedictorian) thanks to a thwarted plot to blow it up by the radical Weather Underground in the 60s. Students line the stairs in front of the library on sunny days, eating lunch and chatting with classmates. Columbia even has its own spooky network of underground tunnels (third largest in the world) that date back to the old Morningside mental asylum and were utilized by students and police during the 1968 strike.

Town/gown relations in Morningside Heights are quite controversial. While Columbia students show local businesses the money, the university continues to relentlessly buy up property and expand into the community, to the chagrin of many New Yorkers city-wide. The most famous of these struggles came in response to Columbia's plans to build a gymnasium in Morningside Park. Contentious proposals, approved in 2009, for a 17-acre expansion into Manhattanville (the area north of 125th Street) by 2030 still cause tension and fear of evictions, and the debate between the university and old-time residents continues.

Columbia's medical school is the second oldest in the nation, and the world's first academic medical center. The school is affiliated with the Columbia-Presbyterian Medical Center in Washington Heights and encompasses the graduate schools of medicine, dentistry, nursing, and public health. Columbia is the only Ivy League university with a journalism school, which was founded at the bequest of Joseph Pulitzer in 1912. (The prize is still administered there.) The school is also affiliated with Barnard College, Jewish Theological Seminary, Teachers College, and Union Theological Seminary.

Numerous movies have been filmed on or around the campus including *Ghostbusters*, *Hannah and Her Sisters*, and *Spiderman* and *II*.

Notable alums and faculty include artists James Cagney, Art Garfunkel, Georgia O'Keeffe, Rodgers and Hammerstein, Paul Robeson, and Twyla Tharp; critic Lionel Trilling; baseball player Lou Gehrig; and writers Isaac Asimov, Joseph Heller, Carson McCullers, Eudora Welty, Zora Neale Hurston, and Herman Wouk. Business alumni include Warren Buffet, Alfred Knopf, Joseph Pulitzer, and Milton Friedman, while government officials Madeline Albright, Dwight Eisenhower, Alexander Hamilton, Robert Moses, Franklin Delano Roosevelt, and Teddy Roosevelt all graced the university's classrooms. In the field of law, Benjamin Cardozo, Ruth Bader Ginsburg, Charles Evans Hughes, and John Jay called Columbia home, and Stephen Jay Gould, Margaret Mead, and Benjamin Spock make the list of notable science alumni.

Tuition

Undergraduate tuition can exceed $47,000 per year plus room, board, books, illegal substances, therapy for your inferiority/superiority complex, etc. We suggest: Shacking up with your Aunt Agatha on the Upper West Side for the duration.

Sports

The Columbia Marching Band plays "Roar, Lion, Roar" after every touchdown, but their instruments remain tragically roarless most of the time. The Lions almost set the record for straight losses by a major college football team when they dropped 44 consecutive games between 1983 and 1988. Not much has changed—their 1-9 record in 2011 was par for the course. The Lions play their mostly Ivy League opponents at Lawrence A. Wien Stadium (Baker Field), located way up at the top of Manhattan.

Columbia excels in other sports including crew, fencing, golf, tennis, and sailing (silver spoon not included). The university is represented by 29 men's and women's teams in the NCAA Division I. It also has the oldest wrestling team in the country.

Culture on Campus

The ire evoked by its controversial immigration speech, when students stormed the stage, pales when compared to Columbia's 2007 invitation to Iranian president Mahmoud Ahmadinejad to participate in a debate. Good or bad, it created much hype and put the campus in the spotlight for a day or two. Columbia does, however, feature plenty of other less volatile dance, film, music, theater, lectures, readings, and talks. Venues include: the Macy Gallery at the Teacher's College, which exhibits works by a variety of artists, including faculty and children's artwork; the fabulous Miller Theatre at 2960 Broadway, which primarily features musical performances and lectures; the student-run Postcrypt Art Gallery in the basement of St. Paul's Chapel; the Theatre of the Riverside Church for theatrical performances from their top-rated graduate program; and the Wallach Art Gallery on the 8th floor of Schermerhorn Hall, featuring art and architecture exhibits. Check the website for a calendar of events. And bring your rubber bullets, just in case.

Phone Numbers

Morningside Campus	212-854-1754
Medical Center	212-305-2500
Visitors Center	212-854-4900
Public Affairs	212-854-2037
University Development and Alumni Relations	877-854-ALUM(2586)
Library Information	212-854-3533
Graduate School of Architecture, Planning, and Preservation	212-854-3414
School of the Arts	212-854-2875
Graduate School of Arts and Sciences	212-854-4737
School of Dental and Oral Surgery	212-305-6726
School of Engineering	212-854-2993
School of General Studies	212-854-2772
School of International and Public Affairs	212-854-5406
Graduate School of Journalism	212-854-8608
School of Law	212-854-2640
School of Nursing	212-305-5756
School of Public Health	212-305-4797
School of Social Work	212-851-2300

Overview

East River Park is now a wonderfully-renovated, long, thin slice of land, sandwiched between the FDR Drive and the East River, and running from Montgomery Street up to 12th Street. Built in the late 1930s as part of the FDR Drive, the park's recent refurbishments have made its sporting facilities some of the best Manhattan has to offer. The East River Esplanade is now in gorgeous shape, welcoming runners, rollerbladers, dog-walkers, and those who just want to enjoy up-close views of the Williamsburg Bridge. Look, wave to your North Brooklyn counterparts sunbathing across the river! The overall plan is to someday create one continuous green stretch from Maine to Florida, part of the highly ambitious East Coast Greenway project (www.greenway.org). But first we'll see if we can get East River Park to stretch as far as the UN. (Initial city plans are aiming to grow the park from Battery Park to Harlem.)

Attractions

The park comes alive in the summer and on weekends, when hundreds of families barbecue in the areas between the athletic fi elds, blaring music and eating to their hearts' content. Others take leisurely strolls or jogs along the East River Esplanade, which offers dramatic views of the river and Brooklyn. Many have turned the park's unused areas into unofficial dog runs, places for pick-up games of ultimate frisbee or soccer, and sunbathing areas. And aside from bathing beauties, you'll even find fishermen waiting patiently for striped bass (not that we have to tell you, but nothing caught in the East River should be eaten—while the water quality has improved dramatically, it's still full of pollutants).

Sports

The sports facilities at East River Park have undergone heavy reconstruction. The park now includes facilities for football, softball, basketball, soccer, tennis, and even cricket. Thankfully, many of the fi elds have been resurfaced with a resilient synthetic turf—a smart move given the amount of use the park gets by all the different sports leagues.

Facilities

There are three bathroom facilities located in the park—one at the tennis courts, one at the soccer/track fi eld, and one up in the northern part of the park by the playground. The reconstruction has provided East River Park with new benches, gvame tables, seal sprinklers for the kids, and new wate

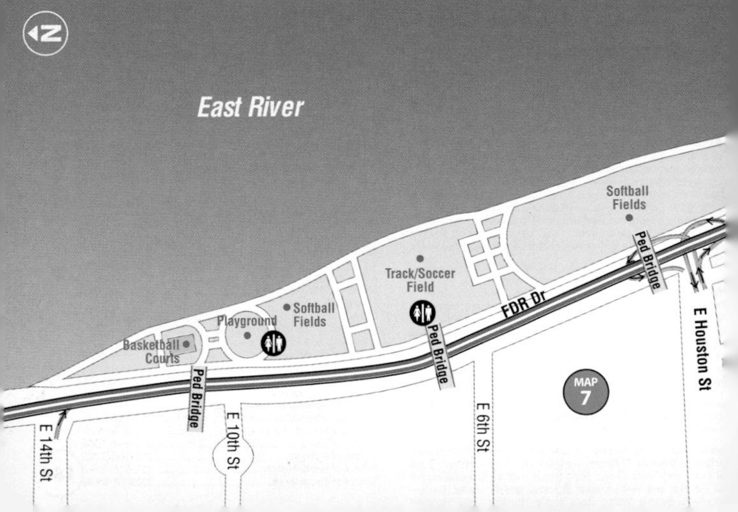

fountains. Aside from the occasional guy with a cart full of cold drinks, there are no food or drink options close by. Your best bet is to arrive at the park with any supplies you might need—if that's too difficult, try a bodega on Avenue D.

Safety

East River Park is relatively safe, especially during the daytime, but we would not recommend hanging out there—or in any other city park, for that matter—after dark, even if you're just passing through.

Esoterica

Built in 1941, the Corlears Hook Pavilion was the original home of Joseph Papp's Shakespeare in the Park. However, it closed in 1973, and has never quite returned to its glory days. Plans for the fancy $3.5 million amphitheater/restaurant that was to replace the sad-looking, abandoned, graffiti-covered Corlears Hook Pavilion band shell have been canned. A less ambitious reconstruction took place in 2001, however, and with new seating, a renovated band shell, and a good scrubbing, the facility is currently open for use.

How to Get There

Two FDR Drive exits will get you very close to East River Park—the Houston Street exit and the Grand Street exit. Technically, cars are not allowed in the park. There is some parking available at the extreme south end of the park by Jackson Street off the access road, but it's hard to get to and poorly marked. Plan to find street parking just west of the FDR and cross over on a footbridge.

If you are taking the subway, you'd better have your hiking boots on—the fact that the closest subways (the J M Z F at Delancey/Essex St and the L at First Ave) are so far away (at least four avenue blocks) is one of the reasons East River Park has stayed mainly a neighborhood park. Fortunately, if you're into buses, the 21, 14, and 8 get you pretty close. Regardless of the bus or subway lines, you will have to cross one of the five pedestrian bridges that traverse the FDR Drive, unless you approach via the East River Esplanade.

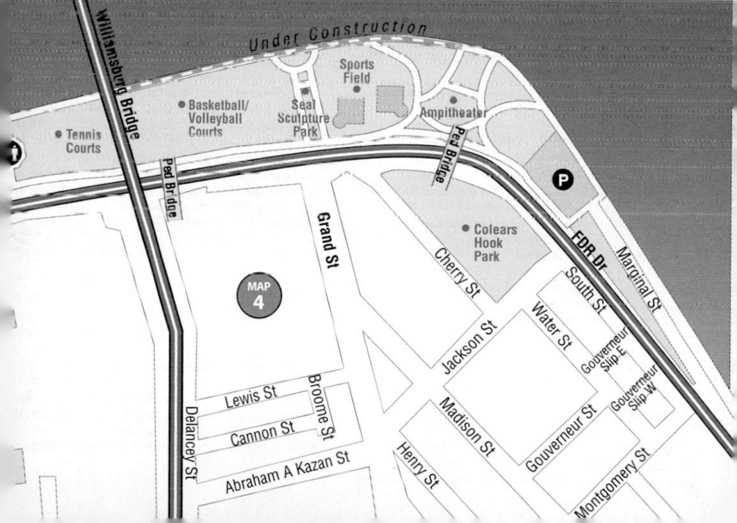

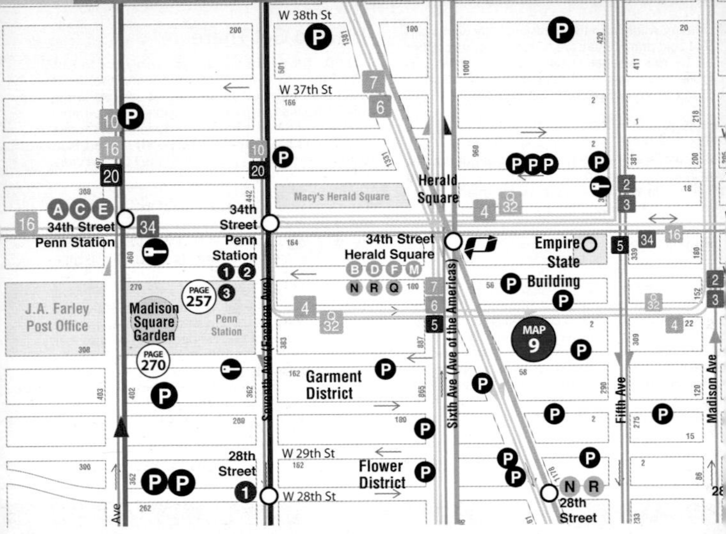

General Information

NFT Map: 9
Address: 350 Fifth Ave (& 34th St)
Phone: 212-736-3100
Website: www.esbnyc.com
Observatory Hours: Open daily 365 days a year 8 am–2 am. Last elevators go up at 1:15 am
Observatory Admission: $25 for adults, $19 for kids, $22 for seniors, $47.50 if you want to be a show off and cut in front of everyone to the front of the line (we're not lying with this one, folks…our society is indeed morally bankrupt).

Overview

There may not be a gorilla climbing it, but if you don't already know the Empire State Building, the jig is up, Mac. Put down the NFT and back away slooowly. You're not a true Manhattanite; you're not even a well-researched tourist. So, folks, how did the giant end up perching on our block? In 1930, at the hands of raw men compounding raw material day after day, four-and-a-half stories were erected per week. Those ravaged from the Depression and eager to put their minds to work built the 1,500-foot structure in just 14 months, way ahead of schedule. A year later, it served as an ambassador to visitin dignitaries like Queen Elizabeth and, years late your Aunt Elizabeth. These days it is one of New Yor City's (and the world's) most famous landmark Movies have been shot there. Big shots work there Wherever you are in Manhattan (and sometime Brooklyn or Queens), it's there to orient you. An you can take plenty of snapshots from the reason you-go-there-observation-deck on the 86th floo No trick questions asked. Some New Yorkers thir it's hip to have never been to the Empire Sta Building. These people are idiots. Whether yo choose to go during the day or at night, it's a total different but amazing experience either way.

The Lights

As far away as downtown and all the way uptow the lights of the Empire State Building soar abo the clouds, signifying an international holiday an or an interminable disease. On the 86th floor, a ma with binoculars and a direct line to the lightir engineers waits. His raison d'être? Close-flying floc of birds. One phone call, and the lights go out, le the poor suckers smash their beaks and plunge their death from the mesmerizing lights. True stor

Lighting Schedule (for updates/changes, check www.esbnyc.com)

- January • Martin Luther King, Jr. Day
- January • March of Dimes
- January–February • Lunar New Year
- February 14 • Valentine's Day
- February • President's Day
- February • Westminster Kennel Club
- February • Swisspeaks Festival for Switzerland
- February • World Cup Archery Championship
- March 17 • St. Patrick's Day
- March • Greek Independence Day
- March • Equal Parents Day/ Children's Rights
- March • Wales/St. David's Day
- March • Oscar Week in NYC
- March • Colon Cancer Awareness
- March • Red Cross Month
- March -April • Spring/Easter Week
- April • Earth Day
- April • Child Abuse Prevention
- April • National Osteoporosis Society
- April • Rain Forest Day
- April • Israel Independence Day
- April • Dutch Queen's Day
- April • Tartan Day
- May • Muscular Dystrophy
- May • Armed Forces Day
- May • Memorial Day
- May • Police Memorial Day
- May • Fire Department Memorial Day
- May • Haitian Culture Awareness
- June 14 • Flag Day
- June • Portugal Day
- June • NYC Triathlon
- June • Stonewall Anniversary/ Gay Pride
- July 4 • Independence Day
- July • Bahamas Independence Day
- July • Bastille Day
- July • Peru Independence
- July • Columbia Heritage & Independence
- August • US Open
- August • Jamaica Independence Day
- August • India Independence Day
- August • Pakistan Independence Day
- September • Mexico Independence Day
- September • Labor Day
- September • Brazil Independence Day
- September • Pulaski Day
- September • Race for the Cure
- September • Switzerland admitted to the UN
- September • Qatar Independence
- September • Fleet Week/Support our Servicemen and Servicewomen/ Memorial for 9/11
- September • Feast of San Gennaro
- October • Breast Cancer Awareness
- October • German Reunification Day
- October • Columbus Day
- October 24 • United Nations Day
- October • Big Apple Circus
- October • Pennant/World Series win for the Yankees
- October • Pennant/World Series win for the Mets [Ha!]
- October • NY Knicks Opening Day
- October–November • Autumn
- October • Walk to End Domestic Violence
- November • NYC Marathon
- November • Veterans' Day
- November • Alzheimer's Awareness
- December • First night of Hanukkah
- December • "Day Without Art/Night Without Lights"/AIDS Awareness
- December–January 7 (with interruptions) • Holiday Season

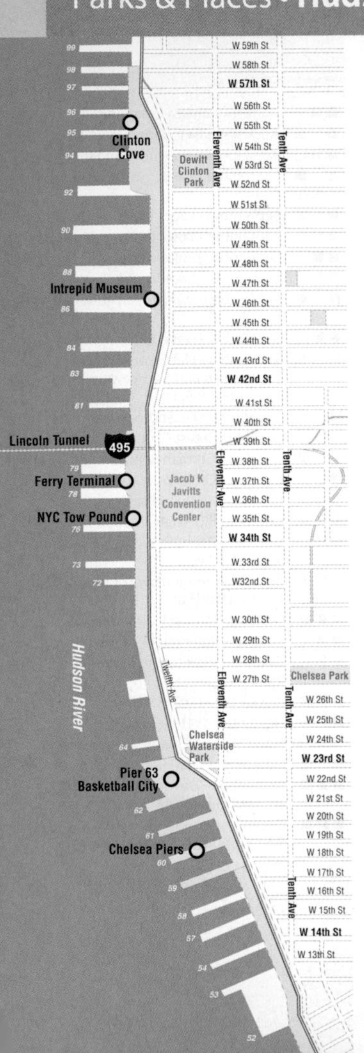

General Information

Hudson River Park Trust:	212-627-2020
Websites:	www.hudsonriverpark.org www.friendsofhudsonriverpark.org

Overview

It's up for debate whether Hudson River Park is a beacon for downtown joggers or a Bermuda triangle that pilots should fly away from. In a matter of months, this western stretch of green torpedoed into infamy when two planes and a helicopter crash-landed off the banks of the park. Most famously, the U.S. Airways "Miracle on the Hudson" skidded to a safe water landing in early 2009. Seven months later, a helicopter and a small plane collided in nearly the same spot and killed nine people.

Of course, we'd rather talk about the park's safer aerial acrobatics, like the trapezes and half-pipes that define this 550-acre, $330 million park development along the south and southwest coastline of Manhattan, stretching from Battery Place to West 59th Street.

As part of the New York State Significant Coastal Fish and Wildlife Habitat, 400 acres of the total 550 thrive as estuarine sanctuary. This means the seventy fish species (there are fish in the Hudson?) and thirty bird species on the waterfront won't go belly up or beak down with all the marine preservation. Thanks to this effort, you'll be able to enjoy the winter flounder, white perch, owls, hawks, and songbirds for generations to come. (That's fantastic! Bob, tell them what else they've won…) What downtown, nature-loving, organic-eating savers of the planet have won is in what they've lost. As a mandate, office buildings, hotels, casino gambling boats, and manufacturing plants are prohibited from the HRP, as are residences (sorry, no water-front property next to your yacht) and jet skis (better to leave them in the Caymans). Check out the Intrepid aircraft carrier/sea-air-space museum, especially during Fleet Week each year (usually the week of Memorial Day, in May). You'll get to see teeming Navy personnel and much more modern vessels, some of which absolutely dwarf the Intrepid itself. A sight not to be missed.

Art

HRP takes its culture cue from the surrounding downtown art scene of TriBeCa, SoHo, and Chelsea. Perhaps you saw one of Merce Cunningham Dance Company's final performances before they shut down. Or maybe you were waiting in line to see *Ashes and Snow*, Gregory Colbert's rendition of the interactions between animals and humans took form in the temporary Nomadic Museum on Pier 54. Or maybe you checked out Malcolm Cochran's *Private Passage* on Clinton Cove (55th–57th St). Similar to your late night antics, you peered into a gigantic wine bottle. There, from portholes carved on the sides, you coul see the interior of the stateroom of the Queen Mary. Or, hearkening back to an early time, the *Shadow of the Lusitania*. Justen Ladda recreated the shadow of the famous ship on the south side of Pier 54 (also home to reconstructed historic ships, not just their shadows), its original docking place, with glass and planters. Jutting out where Pier 49 used to sit is one of the park's more somber exhibits, the New York City AIDS memorial. Dedicated on World AIDS Day in 2008 after 14 years of fundraising and planning, the 42-foot-long memorial is both a striking accomplishment and a sober nod to those whose lives have been lost to the disease. A more permanent piece in HRP: *Salinity Gradient* in TriBeCa. Paver stones spanning 2000 feet take the shape of Hudson marine creatures. Striped bass included. Not impressed? HRP Trust hired different designers for each segment of the five-mile park, with only the esplanade and waterfront railing as universal pieces. Check out the landscape design of each segment.

Attractions

Season-specific events are held year-round at HRP. During the summer, experience fi ght-night basics on Pier 84 for Rumble on the River with live blood splattering with each KO. Sundays in the summer host Moon Dances on Pier 84 with free dance lessons before live New York bands play. Wednesday and Fridays in the summer boast River Flicks on Pier 54 and Pier 84 with throwback films like *The Goonies*. Pier of Fear is mainly a Halloween party for the kiddies, but if you're still down with dressing up as the *Scream* guy, hey, no one will stop you. An estuarium (dedicated to the science of the river) and a TriBeCa dog run, among other projects, are next on the list of improvements for HRP.

Sports

Think of sports in terms of piers. You already know about ritzy Chelsea Piers, but soon enough "Pier 40" or "Pier 63" will also become vernacular to sports freaks. And there are far less expensive piers beyond CP. Most crucial to athletic-minded souls, a five-mile running/biking/blading path that threads through the piers. It's a miniature divided highway—smooth, simple, and super crowded during peak times (early evening and weekends). You'll fi nd sunbathing lawns throughout (the most sport some will ever do). Pier 40: three and a half ball fi elds. Area south of Houston: three tennis courts. Mini-golf. Batting cages. Skateboard park. Beach volleyball. Trapeze lessons. Pier 40, CP, Pier 63, Pier 96: free kayaking. Those are the highlights; for more that's up your particular sports alley, check out the website.

How to Get There

Hmmm. How to most efficiently make your way through all the concrete to the shoreline? The 1 and A C E between Chambers and 59th Streets will get you the closest. Go west 'til you hit water. You're there.

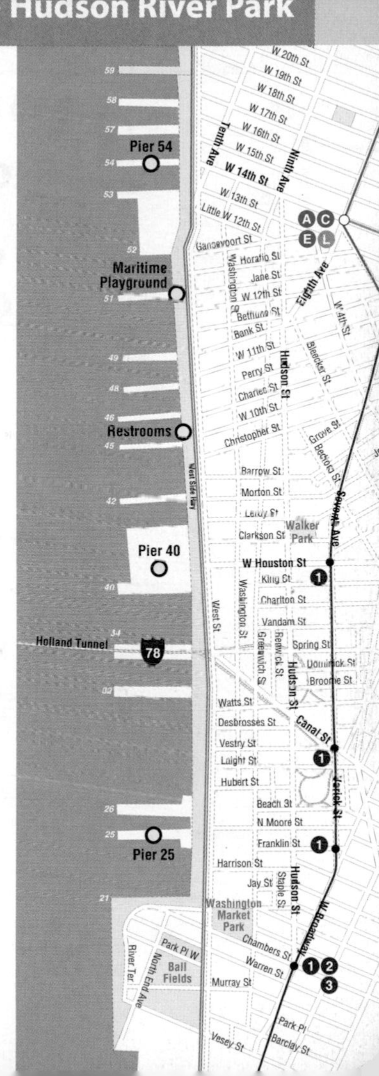

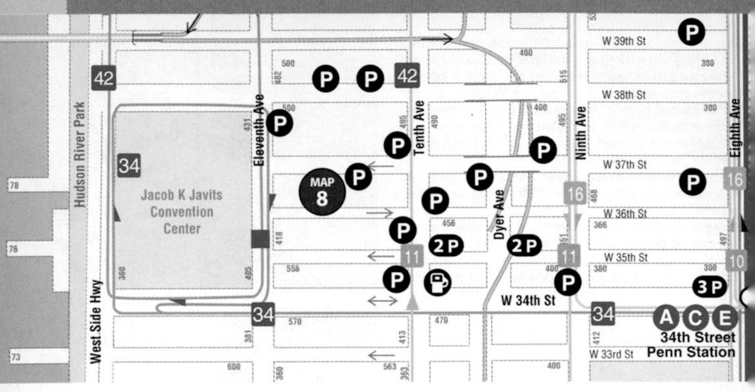

LEVEL ONE

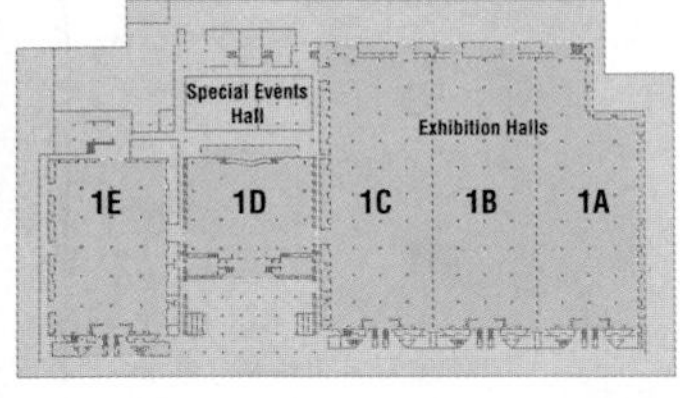

LEVEL THREE

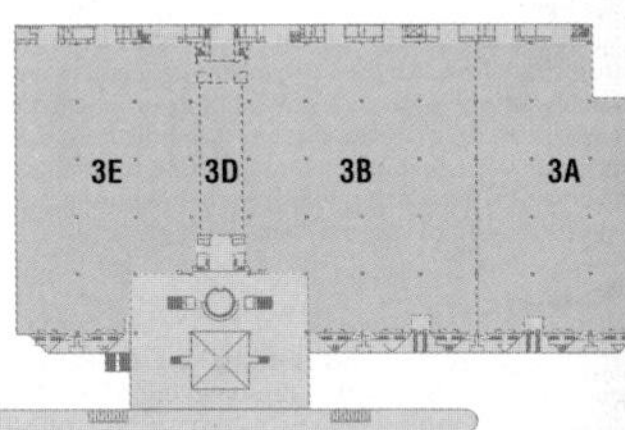

LEVEL TWO

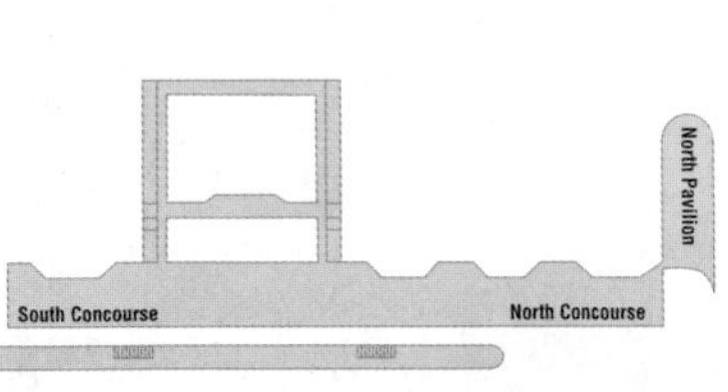

LEVEL FOUR

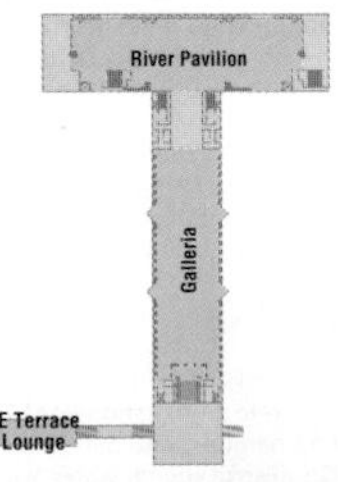

General Information

NFT Map: 8
Address: 655 W 34th St
Website: www.javitscenter.com
Phone Number: 212-216-2000
Fax Number: 212-216-2588

Overview

This massive glass-and-steel behemoth of a convention hall next to the Hudson River was officially built to house big trade shows, conventions and expositions, but clearly its true purpose is to annoy anyone who has to go there. Located between 34th and 38th streets, the James Ingo Freed design has been sitting in the middle of nowhere sans subway link for an appalling 25 years. Dissatisfaction with the convention center has brewed for a number of years, with complaints ranging from the aesthetic (big ugly box) to the practical (lack of space). Various plans have been proposed over the years to expand the center up or over the adjoining west side rail yards, and overhaul the building's facade. The Javits even got dragged into the Jets stadium fiasco, but seems to have emerged with some concrete progress towards a revamping: in late-2006, ground was broken on an expansion that would more than double the size of the Center. Shockingly, the election of a new governor (Spitzer), and resignation of a governor due to prostitution allegations (Spitzer again) has resulted in a re-evaluation of the plans. When discovered that most of the $1.6 billion budget would go towards fixing—not expanding—the project was essentially nixed.

The latest news is the possibility that Javits will be demolished completely, to be replaced by a larger version out at the Aqueduct racetrack in Jamaica, Queens. Until that happens, if it ever does, the new High Line park is being expanded up to West 34th Street, ending at Javits' southern edge—perhaps the nearby existence of something beautiful will rub off on the old eyesore.

What is most important to know about the Javits, and most other convention centers in the world, is that they are essentially soulless, dehumanizing spaces with crappy bathrooms, horrific food, nowhere to sit, and filled (generally) with absolutely slimy, soulless, moronic sales and marketing people; it just depends on which industry is in town that moment as to what exact breed you're getting. Even the presence of cool sports cars (i.e. the Auto Show each Easter week) can't overcome a feeling, after spending even two hours in this convention center, of an absolute black nihilism. Surely someone's come up with something better? Perhaps all trade shows should simply be outdoors in Southern California in the spring—at least, that's our vote.

ATMs

H • Chase • Level One
H • Chase • Level Three

Services

Coat/Luggage Check
Concierge Services
FedEx Kinko's Office and Print Center
First Aid
Hudson News
Information
Lost and Found
Mailboxes Etc
Shoeshine
Wi-Fi (hourly, daily, and show plans available)

Food

The food at the Javits Center is, of course, rapaciously expensive, and, if you're exhibiting, usually sold out by 2:30 in the afternoon. Our suggestion is to look for people handing out Chinese food menus and have them deliver to your booth. (And yes, they take credit cards. And yes, it's bad Chinese food.)

Level 1
Boar's Head Deli
Caliente Cab Company
Carvel Ice Cream Bakery
Feast of the Dragon
Gourmet Coffee Bar
Market Fair/Korean Deli Buffet
Nathan's
Villa Cucina Italiana
Villa Pizza

Level 3
The Bakery
Boar's Head Deli
Carvels
Caliente Cab Company
Dai Kichi Sushi
The Dining Car
Feast of the Dragon
Go Gourmet
The Grille
Villa Pizza

North Concourse
New York Pretzel
Panini

How to Get There—Mass Transit

Until they extend that 7 train, there's no direct subway access to the center. The closest subway stop is at 34th Street/Penn Station, but even that's a good 4- to 5-block hike away. You can also take the buses from the 42nd Street 42 and 34th Street 34 subway stops, which will both drop you off right outside the center.

There are also numerous shuttle buses that run to various participating hotels and other locales free of charge for convention goers. Schedules and routes vary for each convention, so ask at the information desk on the first floor.

From New Jersey, the NY Waterway operates ferries from Weehawken, Hoboken, and Jersey City that ship you across the Hudson River to 39th Street and Twelfth Avenue in 15 minutes or less, dropping you just one block from the Javits Center. The ferries leave every 15–30 minutes during peak hours. Call 1-800-53-FERRY or go to www.nywaterway.com for a schedule and more information.

Lincoln Center / Columbus Circle

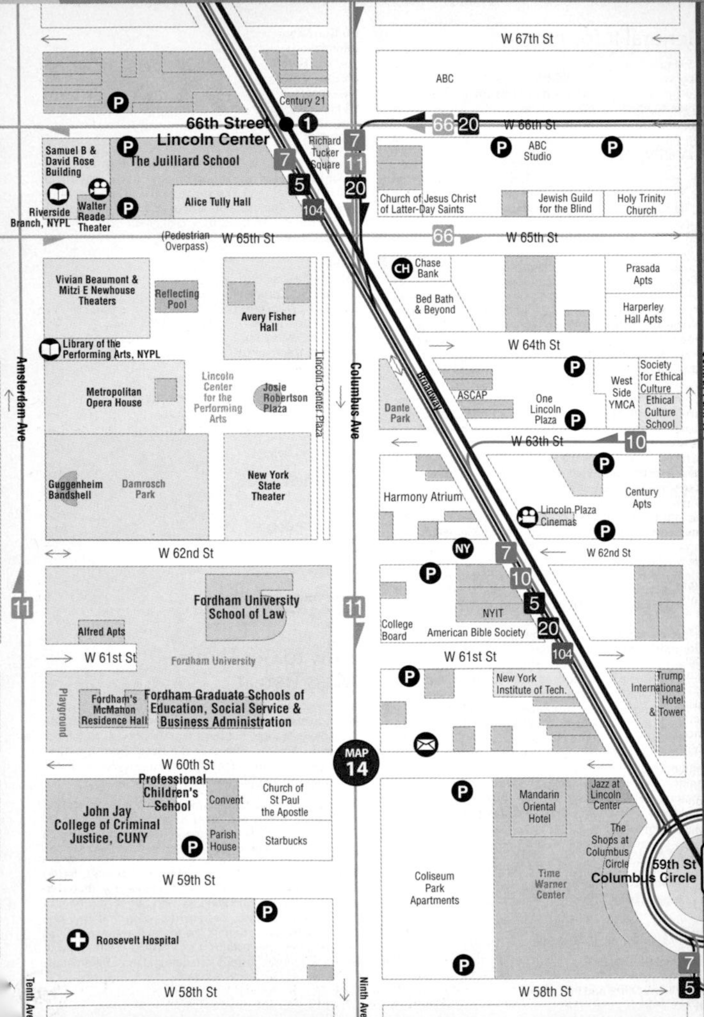

W 67th St
ABC
Century 21
66th Street Lincoln Center
Richard Tucker Square
W 66th St
ABC Studio
Samuel B & David Rose Building
The Juilliard School
Riverside Branch, NYPL
Walter Reade Theater
Alice Tully Hall
Church of Jesus Christ of Latter-Day Saints
Jewish Guild for the Blind
Holy Trinity Church
(Pedestrian Overpass)
W 65th St
Vivian Beaumont & Mitzi E Newhouse Theaters
Reflecting Pool
Avery Fisher Hall
Chase Bank
Bed Bath & Beyond
Prasada Apts
Harperley Hall Apts
Library of the Performing Arts, NYPL
W 64th St
Metropolitan Opera House
Lincoln Center for the Performing Arts
Josie Robertson Plaza
Lincoln Center Plaza
Columbus Ave
Amsterdam Ave
Dante Park
Broadway
ASCAP
One Lincoln Plaza
West Side YMCA
Society for Ethical Culture
Ethical Culture School
Central Park W
W 63rd St
Guggenheim Bandshell
Damrosch Park
New York State Theater
Harmony Atrium
Lincoln Plaza Cinemas
Century Apts
W 62nd St
Fordham University School of Law
Alfred Apts
College Board
NYIT
American Bible Society
W 61st St
Fordham University
Playground
Fordham's McMahon Residence Hall
Fordham Graduate Schools of Education, Social Service & Business Administration
New York Institute of Tech.
Trump International Hotel & Tower
MAP 14
W 60th St
Professional Children's School
John Jay College of Criminal Justice, CUNY
Convent
Church of St Paul the Apostle
Parish House
Starbucks
Mandarin Oriental Hotel
Jazz at Lincoln Center
The Shops at Columbus Circle
59th St Columbus Circle
Time Warner Center
Coliseum Park Apartments
W 59th St
Roosevelt Hospital
W 58th St
Tenth Ave
Ninth Ave

Lincoln Center / Columbus Circle

General Information

NFT Map: 14
Website: www.lincolncenter.org
General Information: 212-546-2656 (212-LINCOLN)
Customer Service: 212-875-5456
Alice Tully Hall: 212-875-5050
Avery Fisher Hall: 212-875-5030
The Chamber Music Society: 212-875-5775
Film Society of Lincoln Center: 212-875-5610
Guided Tours: 212-875-5350
Jazz at Lincoln Center: 212-258-9800
The Julliard School: 212-799-5000
Lincoln Center Theater: 212-362-7600
The Metropolitan Opera House: 212-362-6000
New York City Ballet: 212 870-5500
New York Philharmonic: 212-875-5656
New York State Theater: 212-870-5570
Parking Garage: 212-874-9021
Walter Reade Theater: 212-875-5600

Ticket Purchase Phone Numbers

Alice Tully Hall: 212-721-5050
Avery Fisher Hall: 212-721-5030
CenterCharge: 212-721-6500
Film Society of Lincoln Center: 212-496-3809
MovieFone, Walter Reade Theater: 212-777-FILM
TeleCharge, Lincoln Center Theater: 212-239-6200
Ticketmaster, New York State Theater: 212-307 4100
Ticketmaster, Met & Ballet: 212-362-6000

Overview

Lincoln Center is the largest performing arts center in the world, which means it's a beloved icon, but it's also guilty of some cultural Disneyfication. It sets the gold standard, but it also needs to make money, which it does by presenting the same venerable artists performing the same standard works, geared toward an aging, wealthy, elitist audience. However, that shouldn't stop you from seeing the Met Opera, hearing the New York Philharmonic, and taking a photo by the fountain at least once in your life. Go ahead, wear jeans to the ballet, in the name of the people!

LC recently underwent a massive $1.2 billion renovation, which included a much-needed facelift (inside and out) for Alice Tully Hall and the addition of a lawn-covered café, among other worthy attractions. Don't miss out on discount tickets at the new Atrium, one small step toward lowering LC's snob factor. But not for long, as LC now hosts Mercedes Benz Fashion Week.

The latest news is the contentious departure of New York City Opera, spurred by financial difficulties, after many decades as LC's "people's opera." Jazz at Lincoln Center is quite a newbie by comparison, having opened only in 2004. Its artistic director, trumpet player Wynton Marsalis, has done wonders for promoting jazz education, but JALC embodies the same disparity as the rest of LC: it's an esteemed heavyweight in the jazz world, but it caters to the 1%, despite jazz having been conceived as accessible music for regular folks like you and me.

Who Lives Where

A mecca of tulle, tin, and strings, Lincoln Center houses companies upon troupes upon societies. Matching the performing group to the building means you won't end up watching *Swan Lake* when you should be listening to Mozart. The most confusing part about Lincoln Center is that "Lincoln Center Theater" is two theaters—the Vivian Beaumont and the Mitzi E. Newhouse theaters. Jazz at Lincoln Center moved into the Frederick P. Rose Hall in the AOL/Time Warner Center.

American Ballet Theater — Metropolitan Opera House
Chamber Music Society — Alice Tully Hall
Film Society of Lincoln Center — Walter Reade Theater
Jazz at Lincoln Center — Frederick P. Rose Hall
Julliard Orchestra & Symphony — Alice Tully Hall
Metropolitan Opera Company — Metropolitan Opera House
Lincoln Center Theater — Vivian Beaumont Theater and Mitzi E. Newhouse Theater
Mostly Mozart Festival — Avery Fisher Hall
New York City Ballet — New York State Theater
New York Philharmonic — Avery Fisher Hall
School of American Ballet — Samuel B. and David Rose Building

Columbus Circle

Hooray! Something that isn't completely soulless in Columbus Circle! Cue: the Museum of Arts and Design, which opened up on the south side of the circle in 2008. Definitely check out its sublime permanent collection, its excellent temporary exhibits, and its cool design shop. Other than that, head for the Whole Foods or Lincoln Center. This mothership, inside one of the closest things to a shopping mall in NYC, anchors the Time Warner Center and the Mandarin Oriental Hotel, which, by the way, has pillows on which your out-of-town guests will not sleep, unless they own a small kingdom. Ditto for eating at Per Se ($250 per person, plus drinks). Other highlights for us common folk include Thomas Keller's Bouchon Bakery, the uptown outpost of TriBeCa's cool Landmarc restaurant. The Trump International Hotel and Tower soars nearby. Nougatine, of Jean-Georges fame, features as its premier lunch spot…ahh…the other reason you go to Columbus Circle.

How to Get There

Lincoln Center is right off Broadway and only a few blocks north of Columbus Circle, which makes getting there easy. The closest subway is the 66th Street 1 stop, which has an exit right on the edge of the center. It's also an easy walk from the trains that roll into Columbus Circle. If you prefer above-ground transportation, the 5 7 10 11 66 104 bus lines all stop within one block of Lincoln Center. There is also a parking lot underneath the complex.

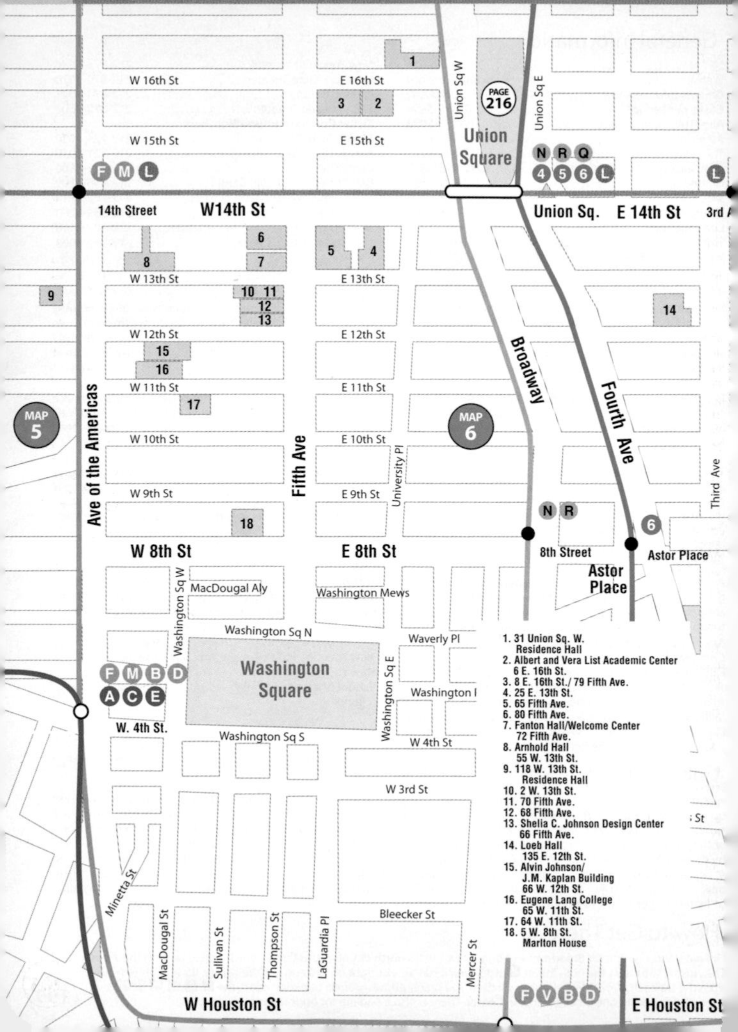

W 16th St
E 16th St
W 15th St
E 15th St
Union Sq W
Union Sq E
PAGE 216
Union Square
N R Q
4 5 6 L
F M L
L
14th Street
W14th St
Union Sq.
E 14th St
3rd A
W 13th St
E 13th St
W 12th St
E 12th St
W 11th St
E 11th St
W 10th St
E 10th St
W 9th St
E 9th St
MAP 5
MAP 6
Ave of the Americas
Fifth Ave
University Pl
Broadway
Fourth Ave
Third Ave
N R
6
W 8th St
E 8th St
8th Street
Astor Place
Astor Place
Washington Sq W
MacDougal Aly
Washington Mews
Washington Sq N
Waverly Pl
Washington Square
Washington Sq E
Washington Pl
F M B D
A C E
W. 4th St.
Washington Sq S
W 4th St
W 3rd St
Minetta St
MacDougal St
Sullivan St
Thompson St
LaGuardia Pl
Bleecker St
Mercer St
F V B D
W Houston St
E Houston St
1. 31 Union Sq. W. Residence Hall
2. Albert and Vera List Academic Center 6 E. 16th St.
3. 8 E. 16th St./ 79 Fifth Ave.
4. 25 E. 13th St.
5. 65 Fifth Ave.
6. 80 Fifth Ave.
7. Fanton Hall/Welcome Center 72 Fifth Ave.
8. Arnhold Hall 55 W. 13th St.
9. 118 W. 13th St. Residence Hall
10. 2 W. 13th St.
11. 70 Fifth Ave.
12. 68 Fifth Ave.
13. Shelia C. Johnson Design Center 66 Fifth Ave.
14. Loeb Hall 135 E. 12th St.
15. Alvin Johnson/ J.M. Kaplan Building 66 W. 12th St.
16. Eugene Lang College 65 W. 11th St.
17. 64 W. 11th St.
18. 5 W. 8th St. Marlton House

General Information

NFT Maps: 5 & 6
Phone: 212-229-5600
Website: www.newschool.edu
Enrollment: 10,547

Overview

The graffiti logoed New School, formerly The New School for Social Research, is a legendary progressive university located around Greenwich Village, housing seven major divisions, a world-renowned think tank and the backdrop for Project Runway. Founded in 1919 as a refuge for intellectual nonconformists (including historian Charles Beard, philosopher John Dewey, and several former Columbia professors), The New School credits its philosophy to the fusing of American intellectual rigor and European critical thought.

The university annually enrolls 9,300 students within seven undergraduate and graduate divisions, including Parsons The New School for Design, The New School for Public Engagement, Eugene Lang College The New School for Liberal Arts, Mannes College The New School for Music, The New School for Drama, The New School for Social Research, and The New School for Jazz and Contemporary Music.

The current New School for Social Research, formerly the Graduate Faculty of Political and Social Science, formerly the University in Exile was a division founded as a haven for dismissed teachers from totalitarian regimes in Europe. Original members included psychologist Erich Fromm and political philosopher Leo Strauss. Quite a lineage with which more recent graduates as Sufjan Stevens and Marc Jacobs have to contend.

Tuition

Tuition for undergraduates can exceed $39,000 per year plus nearly $14,000 to share an apartment with two or three other students. Yes, that's over $1,650 per month to share a living space for the school year (not the full calendar year). See website for details.

Culture on Campus

Parsons is always showcasing something or other, from student shows to MoMa-presented conferences to fine arts lectures. The John L. Tischman Auditorium is the egg-shaped art deco venue for the masses. The quad courtyard, between buildings on 12th and 13th Streets, is the closest thing to a college campus. Otherwise, there's the city.

Transportation

All the subways that Union Square has to offer! N, Q, R, W, 4, 5, 6 and the L.

General Phone Numbers

Student Financial Services (Mannes) 212-580-0210
Career Development 212-229-1324
Counseling Services 212-229-1671
Financial Aid 212-229-8930
Food Services 212-229-5161
Health Education 212-229-5687
Health Services 212-598-4796
HEOP 212-229-8996
Student Housing 212-229-5459
Intercultural Support 212-229-8996
International Student Services 212-229-5592
International Student Services (Mannes) ... 212-580-0210
Student Ombuds 212-229-8996
Registrar 212-229-5620
Registration (Mannes) 212-580-0210
Student Development 212-229-5687
Student Financial Services 212-229-8930
Student Rights & Responsibilites 212-229-5349
Fogelman Library 212-229-5307
Gimbel Library 212-229-8914
Scherman Library 212-580-0210

Residence Hall Phone Numbers

Loeb Hall 212-229-1167
Marlton House 212-473-7014
Union Square 212-229-5343
William Street 646-414-0216
13th Street 646-414-2671
Security (24 Hours) 212-229-7001

Academic Phone Numbers

The New School for General Studies 212-998-8040
Milano The New School for Management and Urban Policy 212-998-3011
Parsons The New School for Design 212-998-6060
Eugene Lang College The New School for Liberal Arts 212-263-7300
The New School for Social Research 212-998-7200
Mannes College The New School for Music 212-998-7200
The New School for Drama 212-998-0100
The New School for Jazz and Contemporary Music 212 998-1800

1. Carlyle Court
2. Coral Towers
3. Thirteenth St Residence Hall
4. 145 Fourth Avenue
5. University Hall
6. Palladium Hall
7. 113 University Place
8. 838 Broadway
9. 7 E 12th Street
10. Casa Italiana Zerilli-Marimò
11. Founder's Hall
12. Third Avenue North Residence Hall
13. Rubin Residence Hall
14. Bronfman Center
15. Brittany Residence Hall
16. Lillian Vernon Creative Writers House
17. Alumni Hall
18. Barney Building
19. 13 University Place
20. Cantor Film Center
21. 10 Astor Place
22. Deutches Haus
23. Glucksman Ireland House
24. Institute of French Studies/ La Maison Française
25. Weinstein Residence Hall
26. Straus Institute
27. 19 Washington Sq. North
28. One-Half Fifth Avenue
29. 1-6 Washington Square North
- School of Social Work
- Graduate School of Arts and Science
30. Rufus D Smith Hall
31. Seventh Street Residence
32. 111, 113A Second Avenue
33. Silver Center Block
- Silver Center for Arts and Science
- Waverly Building
- Brown Building
- Grey Art Gallery
34. Kimball Block
- Kimball Hall
- Torch Club
- Copy Central
- 285 Mercer Street
35. Broadway Block
- 715 Broadway
- 719 Broadway
- 721 Broadway
- 1 Washington Pla
- 3 Washington Pla
- 5 Washington Pla
36. NYU Health Cente
College of Nursing
37. 411 Lafayette Stre
PAGE 216
Union Square
MAP 6
14th Street-Union Square
3rd Avenue
8th Street
Astor Place
Cooper Square
Washington Square
W 4th Street
Washington Square Village
Bleecker Street
2nd Avenue
Broadway-Lafayette Street
Prince Street
38. 48 Cooper Square
39. Hayden Residence Hall
40. Education Block
- Pless Hall
- Pless Annex
- NYU Bookstore
- East Building
- Faye's @ the Square
- Goddard Hall
41. Student Services Block
- 25 West Fourth Street
- Public Safety
- 242 Greene Street
- 14A Washington Place
- 19 West Fourth Street
- 8 Washington Place
- 10 Washington Place
42. Meyer Block
- Meyer Hall
- Psychology Building
43. Provincetown Playhouse
- Wilf Hall
44. Vanderbilt Hall
45. Judson Block
- Kevorkian Center
- Skirball Department
- King Juan Carlos I Center
- Furman Hall
46. 58 Washington Square South
47. Kimmel Center for University Life
- Skirball Center for the Performing Arts
48. Bobst Library
49. Schwartz Plaza
50. Shimkin Hall
- Gould Welcome Center
51. Kaufman Management Center
52. Tisch Hall
53. Courant Institute
54. Silk Building
55. Housing
56. D'Agostino Hall
57. 561 La Guardia Place
58. Mercer Street Residence
59. 530 La Guardia Place
60. Mail Services
61. Off Campus Housing
62. 665 Broadway
63. Second Street Residence Hall
64. University Plaza
65. Silver Towers
66. Coles Sports and Recreation Center
67. 194, 196 Mercer Street
68. Puck Building
- Wagner Graduate School of Public Service

General Information

NFT Map: 6
Phone: 212-998-1212
Website: www.nyu.edu
Enrollment: 50,917

Overview

Founded in 1831, one of the nation's largest private universities sprawls throughout Manhattan, though its most recognizable buildings border Washington Square. Total enrollment is just over 50,000, about half of whom are undergrads, many of whom will flood the city with their artistic product upon graduation, as if there wasn't enough competition for young artists here.

The expansion of NYU during recent years has not been welcomed by local residents. Some Village folks blame NYU's sprawl for higher rents and diminished neighborhood character. On the other hand, the students are a financial boom for businesses in the area, and many historical buildings (such as the row houses on Washington Square) are owned and kept in good condition by the university.

NYU comprises fourteen colleges, schools, and faculties, including the well-regarded Stern School of Business, the School of Law, and the Tisch School of Arts. It also has a school of Continuing and Professional Studies, with offerings in publishing, real estate, and just about every other city-centric industry you could imagine. 42,242 people applied to NYU for undergrad last year, 30% were accepted, and the gender ration still holds at about 60:40 ladies:gents.

Unfortunately, the Chick-fil-A within the Weinstein Hall dining facility closed a few years ago. We're still in mourning.

Tuition

Tuition for undergraduates can cost over $45,000, plus $15,000 for room and board. Just something to think about.

Sports

NYU isn't big on athletics. They don't have a football team. (Where would they play anyway?) It does have a number of other sports teams, though. The school competes in Division III and its mascot is the Bobcat, although all of their teams are nicknamed the Violets. Go figure.

Culture on Campus

The Grey Art Gallery usually has something cool (www.nyu.edu/greyart), and the Skirball Center for the Performing Arts hosts live performances (www.skirballcenter.nyu.edu). NYU doesn't host nearly as many events as decent liberal arts schools in the middle of nowhere. Why bother? It's in Greenwich Village, surrounded by some of the world's best rock and jazz clubs, and on the same island as 700+ art galleries, thousands of restaurants, and tons of revival and new cinema. This is both the blessing and the curse of NYU—no true "campus," but situated in the middle of the greatest cultural square mileage in the world.

Transportation

NYU runs its own campus transportation service for students, faculty, staff, and alumni with school ID cards. They run 7 am to 2 am weekdays and 10 am to 2 am weekends.

Route A: 200 Water St (South Street Seaport) to 715 Broadway (near 4th St), stopping at the Lafayette and Broome Street dorms on the way.
Route B: Woolworth Building to 715 Broadway, passing through the same areas as Route A.
Route C: 715 Broadway loop, passing through SoHo, NoHo, and the East Village.
Route D: 715 Broadway loop through the West Village via the Greenwich Street dorm.
Route E: Midtown Center (SCPS near 42nd St and Fifth Ave) to 715 Broadway, stopping at the NYU Medical Center on the east side and passing through the Gramercy Park area.

General Phone Numbers

Gould Welcome Center: 212-998-INFO (4636)
NYU Protection and Transportation Services 212-998-2222
Undergraduate Admissions: 212-998-4500
Financial Aid: 212-998-4444
University Registrar: 212-998-4800
University Employment Office: 212-998-1250
Student Health Services: 212-443-1000
Kimmel Center for University Life: 212-998-4900
Bobst Library: 212-998-2500
Coles Sports Center: 212-998-2020
NYU Card: 212-443-CARD (2273)

Academic Phone Numbers

All undergraduate programs: 212-998-4500
Summer Session: 212-998-2292
Dental School: 212-998-9800
Steinhardt School of Education: 212-998-5000
Ehrenkranz School of Social Work: 212-998-5910
Gallatin School of Individualized Study: 212-998-7370
Graduate School of Arts & Science: 212-998-8040
Graduate Computer Science: 212-998-3011
Law School: 212-998-6060
School of Medicine: 212-263-7300
School of Continuing and Professional Studies Degree Program: 212-998-7200
School of Continuing and Professional Studies Real Estate Institute: 212-998-7200
School of Continuing and Professional Studies Non-Credit Program: 212-998-7171
Stern School of Business: 212-998-0100
Tisch School of the Arts: 212-998-1800
Wagner School of Public Service: 212-998-7414

PAGE 176
Bronx
Bronx Kill
Bronx Shore Fields
RFK Bridge
10
Parks 5 Boro Complex
9
Triborough Bridge
Golf Center
1
Discus Thrower
Picnic Area
Sunken Meadows Fields
Randall's Island
Tennis Center
8
Paladino Ave
E 120th St
E 119th St
E 118th St
MAP 20
Manhattan
2
Harlem River Event Area
Icahn Stadium
FDNY Fire Academy
7
E 116th St
Pleasant Ave
278
Island Rd
Nature Center
FDR Dr
E 114th St
East River
Harlem River
Manhattan Psychiatric Center
6
Wards Island Treatment Plant
Roosevelt Dr
Central Fields
Wards Island
Kantor Fields
5
Children's Playground
Hell Gate Bridge
3
Sunken Garden Fields
Picnic Area
Hell Gate Fields
Wards Meadow Fields
E 103 St Footbridge
4
East River Fields
RFK Bridge
Hell Gate
Que

General Information

Randall's Island Park Alliance: 212-830-7722; www.risf.org

Overview

If landfills, minimal food options, and a treacherous mix of the Harlem and East Rivers called "Hell Gate" don't entice you over the Triborough Bridge, you probably have good instincts.

But put Randall's & Wards Islands' sullied past aside, and its 440 acres of public park space just across the bridge will surprise you. Conceived by Robert Moses, the two landfill-connected islands have undergone a major overhaul since 1999 and boast some of the city's top athletic fields and parks. Look to the Randall's Island Park Alliance, which operates the greenspace, to keep progress humming. The foundation kicked off the park's renovation by replacing Downing Stadium with the state-of-the-art Icahn Track & Field Stadium in 2005. Since then, the RISF restored 66 fields, marshes, and wetlands, and built new waterfront bike and pedestrian paths. In 2007, local activists put the kibosh on an eight-year-old plan to build a fancy suburban-style water park. Maybe the island has some bad ju-ju: Hell Gate, where the Harlem and East Rivers meet, has caused hundreds of ships to sink.

No mater what, we hope future plans bring in more food facilities. Currently, the only culinary options are a smattering of food trucks near the Icahn Stadium and the golf center's snack bar One suggestion: Make a Whole Foods pit stop before enjoying a chill, weekend afternoon in the park.

How to Get There

By Car: Take the Triborough Bridge, exit left to Randall's Island. There's a $7.50 toll to get on the island with your car. It's free to leave!

By Subway/Bus: From Manhattan: take the 4 5 6 train to 125th Street, then transfer on the corner of 125th Street and Lexington Avenue for the 35 bus to Randall's Island. There's a bus about every 40 minutes during the day. From Queens: take the Q53 from 61st Street-Woodside.

By Foot: A pedestrian footbridge at 103rd Street was built by Robert Moses in the '50s to provide Harlem residents access to the recreational facilities of the parks after then-City Council President Newbold Morris criticized the lack of facilities in Harlem. The bridge is open to pedestrians and cyclists 24/7.

1 **Randall's Island Golf Center** • 212-427-5689 • The golf center on Randall's Island has a driving range open year-round with 80 heated stalls, along with two 18-hole mini-golf courses, nine batting cages, a snack bar, and a beer garden. A weekend shuttle service is available every hour on the hour, 10 am–5 pm from Manhattan (86th Street and Third Avenue) and costs $10 round-trip. Summer hours are 6 am–11 pm Tuesday–Sunday and 11 am–11 pm on Mondays, with off-season hours from 8 am–8 pm Tuesday–Sunday and 1 pm–8 pm on Mondays.

2 **Icahn Track & Field Stadium** • 212- 860-1899 x101 • Named for financier Carl Icahn, the 10,000-seat stadium is the only state-of-the-art outdoor track and field venue in New York City with a 400-meter running track and a regulation-size soccer field.

3 **Supportive Employment Center** • 212-534-3866

4 **Charles H. Gay Shelter Care Center for Men** • Volunteers of America - Greater New York • 212-369-8900 • www.voa-gny.org

5 **Odyssey House Drug Rehab Center** • Mabon Building • 212-426-6677

6 **DEP Water Pollution Control Plant** • 718-595-6600 • www.ci.nyc.ny.us/html/dep/html/drainage.html

7 **Fire Department Training Center** • The NYC Fire Academy is located on 27 acres of landfill on the east side of Randall's Island. In an effort to keep the city's "bravest" in shape, the academy utilizes the easily accessible 68 acres of parkland for physical fitness programs. The ultra-cool training facility includes 11 Universal Studios–like buildings for simulations training, a 200,000 gallon water supply tank, gasoline and diesel fuel pumps, and a 300-car parking lot. In addition, the New York Transit Authority installed tracks and subway cars for learning and developing techniques to battle subway fires and other emergencies. It's really too bad they don't sell tickets and offer tours!

8 **Tennis Center** • 212- 427-6150 • 11 outdoor courts. Indoor courts heated for winter use.

9 **Robert Moses Building** • We're sure many an urban planning student has made a pilgrimage here.

10 **NYPD** • They launch cool-looking police boats from here.

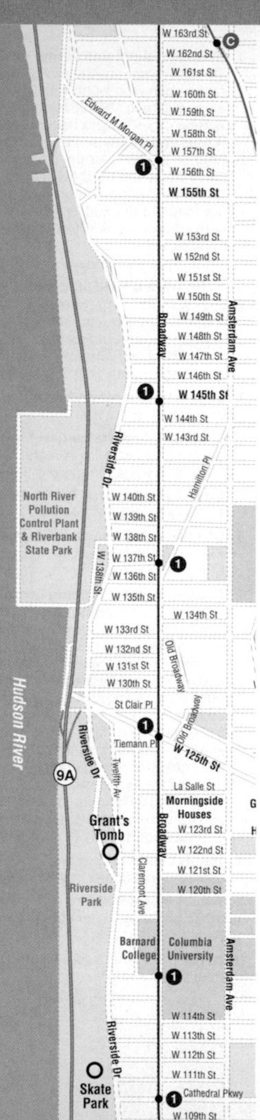

General Information

Website:
www.nycparks.org or www.riversideparkfund.org
Riverside Park Administrator:
212-408-0264
79th Street Boat Basin - Public Marina:
212-496-2105

Overview

If Sally Struthers taught you anything about saving the world, your ticket to heaven awaits at Riverside Park. Pick a program and you're saved: Sponsor a Bench or Sponsor a Tree. Yes, apparently crabapple (or "crab apple" otherwise risking the tongue twister, "crap-abble") and London plane trees need your desperate help. For years, they've been subject to the cruelty of noxious gases from passing cars and dogs' territorial marks, but you, even you, cannot justify lovesick children carving hearts and initials in their bark. You may even remember those poor, diseased-looking trees, like cobras shedding their skins, bark peeling to reveal a lighter inner bark. Light bulb on yet? Those are London plane trees (no diseases involved). And don't forget those benches suffering the wrath of a million deadweights, as they stop to rest their walking feet.

After you've sponsored your new friend, revel in the four miles of pure, parkalicious plain. Spanning from 72nd to 158th Street, Riverside Park was designed in 1875 by Frederick Law Olmsted. It was expanded and adapted for active recreational use during the early 20th Century without losing too much of its charm. In 1980, the New York City Landmarks Preservation Commission crowned Riverside Park between 72nd and 125th a "scenic landmark."

Things to do along 300 acres of green goodness: Walk. Run. Cycle. Skate. Kayak. Play ball, any ball. (Especially tennis on those gorgeous red clay courts). Throw in a couple of dog walkers, and sure as sugar, you've got yourself a bona fide park (see Hudson River Park, Battery Park City, Central Park for reference).

Sights & Sounds

North waterfront between 147th and 152nd streets: It's a looker. To excite the secret Oscar slave in you, head to the Crabapple Grove at 91st for a self-guided tour of *You've Got Mail*, where Tom Hanks finally met Meg Ryan (as if they didn't know each other the whole time). While you're there, check out the Garden for All Seasons. You can take a guess at what kind of garden that is. Whistle not wet? Take a gander at the American elms that surreptitiously line Riverside Drive. Remember what it's like to have trees—real trees—where you live. Or, if you're so over the tree thing, the Soldiers' and Sailors' Monument at 89th gives homage to Civil War heroes from New York and gives you +1 in preparing for that all-important tavern trivia game. Same goes for Grant's Tomb at 122nd, an intriguing monument, especially with Jazzmobile strumming serious beats on a lazy summer day. Who knew the key to heaven's gates was in your backyard?

Swing a Ring

Located at Riverside Park's Hudson Beach (W 105th St), Swing a Ring is a unique fitness apparatus that exists only in New York City (lucky us); Santa Monica, CA; and Providence, RI. There's a set for adults and a set for ankle-biters. It's free, permanent, open year-round, and virtually indestructible (read: won't be destroyed by wayward youth with too much spare time on their hands). Each May there's a "Swing a Ring Day" celebration featuring expert instruction for adults and youngsters. For more information about the rings and special events, visit www.swingaring.com. Once you try it, you'll never stop swinging! (Well, not until the big guy with the lycra bicycle shorts wants a turn.) For those whose swinging only extends to an ice cold Corona with a passable burger to wash it down, the tables at the Hudson Beach Café, overlooking the swing set, offer a scenic (and more sedentary) view of the action.

Practicalities

Take the 1 2 3 train to any stop between 72nd and 157th and it's just a short walk west to Riverside Park. Or just drive along Riverside Drive and park (no pun intended). And hey, be safe. Don't hang out there alone after dark.

Think Your Apartment is Cool?

Guess again, you Village Vamps and NoHo Stars. Ain't nothin' beats living on a houseboat at the 79th Street Boat Basin. But will Zabar's deliver?

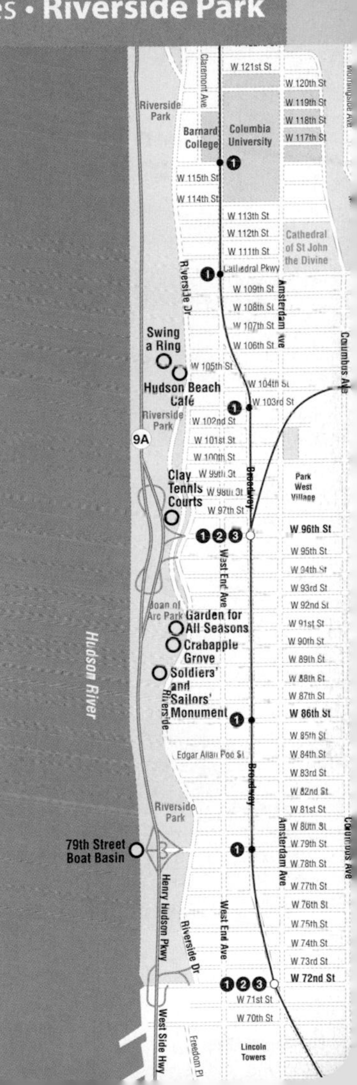

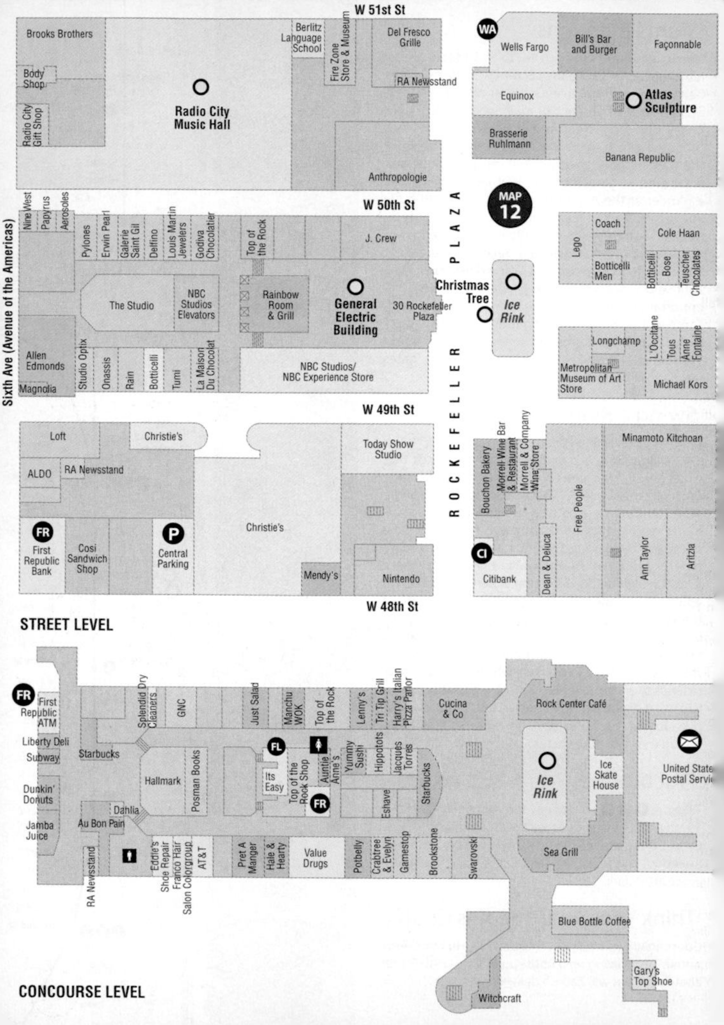

W 51st St
Brooks Brothers
Body Shop
Radio City Gift Shop
Radio City Music Hall
Berlitz Language School
Fire Zone Store & Museum
Del Fresco Grille
RA Newsstand
Anthropologie
WA
Wells Fargo
Bill's Bar and Burger
Façonnable
Equinox
Atlas Sculpture
Brasserie Ruhlmann
Banana Republic
W 50th St
MAP 12
Nine West
Papyrus
Aerosoles
Pylones
Erwin Pearl
Galerie Saint Gil
Delfino
Louis Martin Jewelers
Godiva Chocolatier
Top of the Rock
J. Crew
Lego
Coach
Cole Haan
Botticelli Men
Botticelli
Bose
Teuscher Chocolates
The Studio
NBC Studios Elevators
Rainbow Room & Grill
General Electric Building
30 Rockefeller Plaza
Christmas Tree
Ice Rink
Allen Edmonds
Magnolia
Studio Optix
Onassis
Rain
Botticelli
Tumi
La Maison Du Chocolat
NBC Studios/ NBC Experience Store
Longchamp
L'Occitane
Tous
Anne Fontaine
Metropolitan Museum of Art Store
Michael Kors
Sixth Ave (Avenue of the Americas)
ROCKEFELLER PLAZA
W 49th St
Loft
Christie's
Today Show Studio
ALDO
RA Newsstand
Bouchon Bakery
Morrell Wine Bar & Restaurant
Morrell & Company Wine Store
Free People
Minamoto Kitchoan
FR
First Republic Bank
Cosi Sandwich Shop
P
Central Parking
Christie's
Mendy's
Nintendo
CI
Citibank
Dean & Deluca
Ann Taylor
Aritzia
W 48th St
STREET LEVEL
FR
First Republic ATM
Liberty Deli
Subway
Dunkin' Donuts
Jamba Juice
Starbucks
Splendid Dry Cleaners
GNC
Just Salad
Manchu WOK
Top of the Rock
Lenny's
Tri Tip Grill
Harry's Italian Pizza Parlor
Cucina & Co
Rock Center Café
Hallmark
Posman Books
FL
Its Easy
Top of the Rock Shop
Auntie Anne's
FR
Yummy Sushi
Hippototos
Jacques Torres
Eshave
Starbucks
Ice Rink
Ice Skate House
United States Postal Service
Dahlia
Au Bon Pain
RA Newsstand
Eddie's Shoe Repair
Franco Hair Salon Colorgroup
AT&T
Pret A Manger
Hale & Hearty
Value Drugs
Potbelly
Crabtree & Evelyn
Gamestop
Brookstone
Swarovski
Sea Grill
Blue Bottle Coffee
Gary's Top Shoe
Witchcraft
CONCOURSE LEVEL

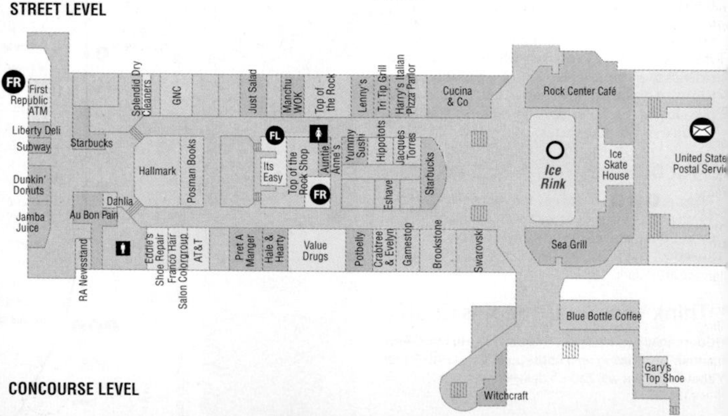

General Information

NFT Map:	12
Phone:	212-632-3975
Website:	www.rockefellercenter.com
Rink Phone:	212-332-7654
Rink Website:	www.therinkatrockcenter.com
NBC Tour Phone:	212-664-3700
Top of the Rock:	www.topoftherocknyc.com

Overview

Perhaps you've been blinded five streets away by 25,000 Swarovski crystals. Or maybe you've glimpsed a gargantuan King Kong of a tree shooting seventy feet in the air and wondered how on earth such vegetation could grow in concrete. Regardless, you fall for antics, arrive in bewilderment at Rockefeller Center, and stay for the ice-skating rink, services at St. Patrick's, and the Rockettes at Radio City Music Hall.

When there's not a huge pine tree to distract you, you'll note that Rockefeller Center occupies three square blocks with a slew of retail, dining, and office facilities. Midtown corporate just ain't the same without its magic. Embodying the Art Deco architecture of the era, the center's legacy began during the Great Depression.

The Top of the Rock Observation Deck, first opened more than 70 years ago by John D. Rockefeller, has nally reopened to the masses. Enjoy jaw dropping, 60-degree views of the skyline.

oday, the Associated Press, General Electric, and IBC call Rock their 9–5. (You've seen Dean & Deluca n TV during the *Today Show*'s outdoor broadcasts.) nd "30 Rock" has *Saturday Night Live* and *Late Night* ith *Jimmy Fallon*. Not bad for a tree-hugger, huh?

Where to Eat

ow hungry are you? Rock Center isn't a prime dining estination, but you won't starve if you find yourself the area. For cheaper fare, try places down in the oncourse such as Pret A Manger, Hale & Hearty, or ichcraft. For fancier (read: overpriced) food, try the ea Grill (overlooking the skating rink). The food isn't raight out of *Gourmet*—you're paying for the view. sate your sweet tooth, Magnolia Bakery operates midtown location here. (Although, if you're paying mage to a certain Bradshaw, we think you deserve battle the crazed Sex and the City fans in the West lage.) Many restaurants in Rockefeller Center e open on Saturdays, but aside from the "nice" staurants, only a few open their doors on Sundays. far your best option is to walk north to 54th St and th Ave and chow down at the Hallo Berlin food nd. Wurst and sausage here will be far better than ything you get in the center itself, and will cost you lf as much. Just sayin'.

Where to Shop

For all the mall-lovers out there, Rockefeller Center has its own underground version—heck, there's even a Sharper Image and a Brookstone! For original, non-commercialized goods, check out these stores in Rockefeller Center and the surrounding area:

FireZone Store and Museum • 50 Rockefeller Plaza • Official seller of FDNY merchandise.
Kinokuniya Bookstore • 10 W 49th St • Japanese-language and Asian-themed, English language books.
Minamoto Kitchoan • 608 Fifth Ave • Authentic Japanese pastries and cakes.
La Maison Du Chocolat • 30 Rockefeller Plaza • French chocolates.
Posman Books• 30 Rockefeller Plaza • family-owned independent bookstore.
Teuscher Chocolates • 620 Fifth Ave • Swiss chocolates.

And for the practical parts of your life: Dahlia (flowers), Eddie's Shoe Repair, Kodak/Alpha Photo, and Splendid Dry Cleaners. They're all located near the entrance to the Sixth Avenue subway (B D F M). A US Post Office is on the Eastern end of Concourse near the rink and UPS is in the area perpendicular to the Sea Grill. But they, like many of the stores in the Concourse, are closed on weekends. Unless you work in Rockefeller Center, it's not likely that you'll need to use them anyway.

The Rink

To practice your double loop: The rink opens Columbus Day weekend and closes in April to make way for the Rink Bar. Skating hours are 9 am–10:30 pm Monday–Thursday, 8:30 am–midnight Friday/ Saturday, and 8:30 am–10 pm on Sundays. Skating prices range from $24.50 to $26.50 for adults, depending on the day you visit. (Weekends and holidays are the most expensive times to skate.) The skating rate for children ranges from $19.50 to $21.50 per session. Skate rentals are included in the cost. Lessons are available for $30 during the week and $35 during the weekend—call 212-332-7655 for more information. With hefty skating rates and a crowded rink, better to shoot for an early weekday morning or afternoon, or very early on the weekend. (Or maybe go to Bryant Park and glide for free.)

Overview

Once upon a time, Roosevelt Island was much like the rest of New York—populated by criminals, the sick, and the mentally ill. The difference was that they were the residents of the island's various mental institutions, hospitals, and jails, but these days this slender tract of land between Manhattan and Queens has become prime real estate for families and UN officials.

The 147-acre island, formerly known as "Welfare Island" because of its population of outcasts and the poor, was renamed for Franklin D. Roosevelt in 1973, when the island began changing its image. The first residential housing complex opened in 1975. Some of the old "monuments" remain, including the Smallpox Hospital and the Blackwell House (one of the oldest farmhouses in the city), while the Octagon Building, formerly a 19th-century mental hospital known for its deplorable conditions, has been turned into luxury condos (so yes, you're still in New York). The island also boasts a renovated riverside promenade and a farmers market on Saturdays. Four Freedoms Park, designed by Louis I. Kahn, is the latest addition.

The island's northern tip is a popular destination for fi shermen with iron gullets. It's also the home of a lighthouse designed by James Renwick, Jr., of St. Patrick's Cathedral fame. The two rehab/convalescent hospitals on the island don't offer emergency services, so if you're in need of medical attention right away, you're out of luck. The island's main drag, Main Street (where did they come up with the name?), resembles a cement-block college campus circa 1968. Just south, closer to the tram, is a newly developed stretch of condos that are fetching top dollar. Two of these buildings are residences for Memorial Sloan-Kettering Cancer Center and Rockefeller and Cornell University employees.

Perhaps the best way to experience the island is to spend a little while on the local shuttle bus that runs the length of the island. You'll see a wonderful mix of folks, some crazy characters, and have a chance to grill the friendly bus drivers about all things Roosevelt Island. Trust us.

How to Get There

Roosevelt Island can be reached by the F train, but it's much more fun to take the tram. Plus, your-out-of town friends will love that this is the tram Tobey Maguire saved as Spiderman in the first movie. You can board it with a Metrocard (including an unlimited!) at 60th Street and Second Avenue in Manhattan—look for the big hulking mass drifting through the sky. It takes 4 minutes to cross and runs every 15 minutes (every 7 minutes during rush hour) 6 am–2 am, Sunday through Thursday, and 'til 3:30 am on Fridays and Saturdays. To get there by car take the Queensboro Bridge and follow signs for the 21st Street-North exit. Go north on 21st Street and make a left on 36th Avenue. Go west on 36th Avenue and cross over the red Roosevelt Island Bridge. The only legal parking is at Motorgate Plaza at the end of the bridge at Main Street.

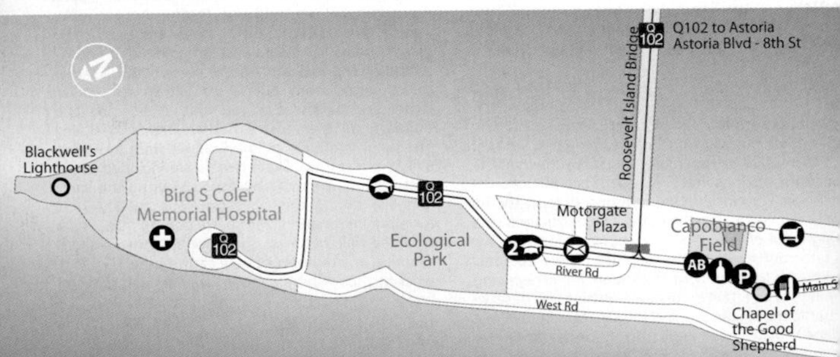

Banks
AB • **Amalgamated Bank** • 619 Main St

Coffee
• **Starbucks** • 455 Main St

Hospitals
• **Coler Goldwater–Coler Campus (No ER)** • 900 Main St [West Rd]
• **Coler Goldwater–Goldwater Campus (No ER)** • 1 Main St [River Rd]

Landmarks
• **Blackwell House** • 591 Main St
• **Blackwell's Lighthouse** • North tip of Roosevelt Island
• **Chapel of the Good Shepherd** • 543 Main St
• **Smallpox Hospital** • Near south tip of Roosevelt Island
• **Tramway** • 346 Main St [2nd Av]

Libraries
• **Roosevelt Island** • 524 Main St [East Rd]

Liquor Stores
• **Grog Shop** • 605 Main St

Post Offices
• **Roosevelt Island** • 694 Main St [River Rd]

Restaurants
• **Trellis** • 549 Main St

Schools
• **Lillie's International Christian** • 851 Main St
• **MS 271 Building (M271)** • 645 Main St
• **PS 217 Roosevelt Island** • 645 Main St

Supermarkets
• **Gristedes** • 686 Main St [River Rd]

Video Rental
• **Liberty Roosevelt Island** • 544 Main St [East Rd]
• **Roosevelt Island Video** • 544 Main St

Subways
F .... Roosevelt Island

Bus Lines
Q102 .... Main St / East and West Rds

Parking

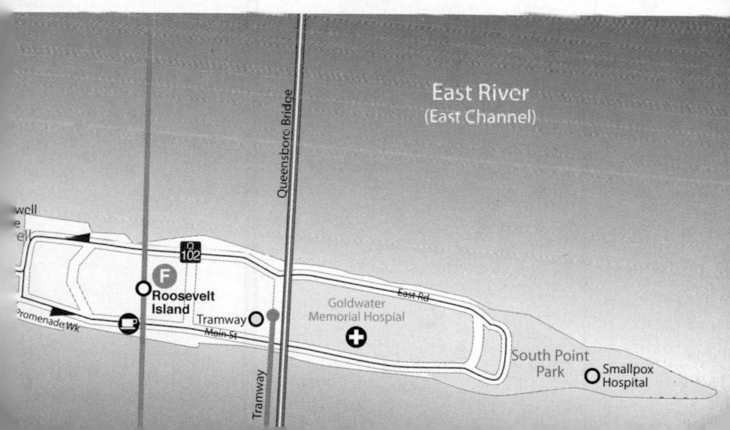

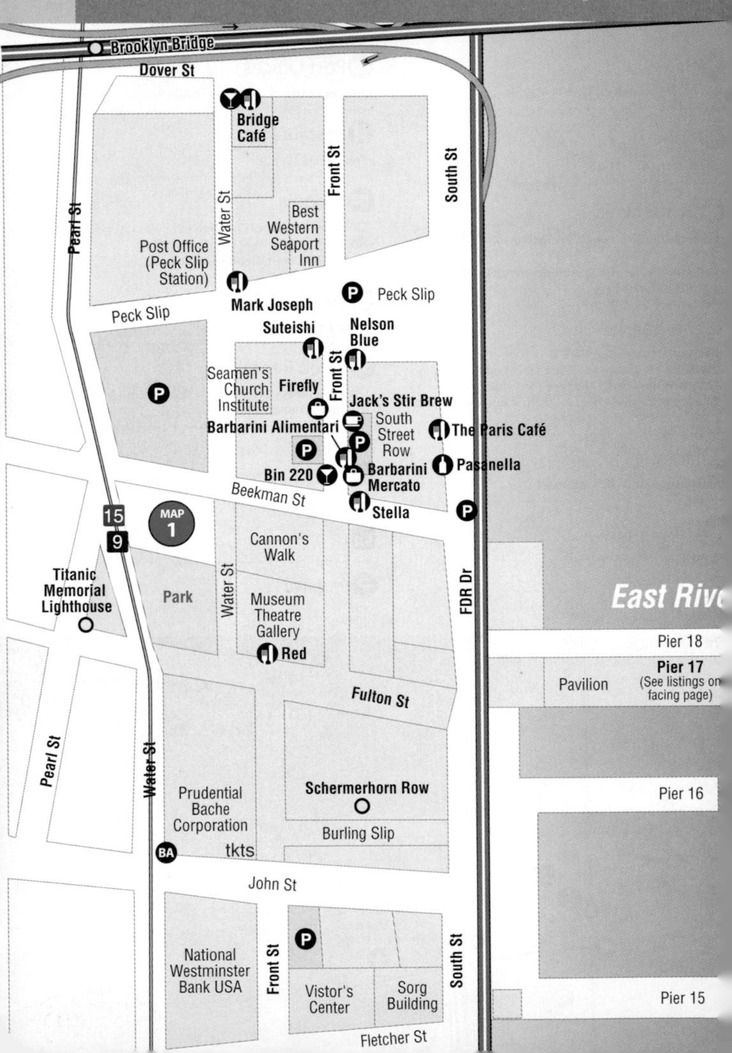
Brooklyn Bridge
Dover St
Bridge Café
Front St
South St
Water St
Pearl St
Best Western Seaport Inn
Post Office (Peck Slip Station)
Mark Joseph
Peck Slip
Peck Slip
Suteishi
Nelson Blue
Seamen's Church Institute
Firefly
Front St
Jack's Stir Brew
South Street Row
The Paris Café
Barbarini Alimentari
Pasanella
Bin 220
Barbarini Mercato
Beekman St
Stella
15
9
MAP 1
Cannon's Walk
Titanic Memorial Lighthouse
Park
Water St
Museum Theatre Gallery
FDR Dr
East Riv
Red
Pier 18
Pier 17
(See listings on facing page)
Pavilion
Fulton St
Pearl St
Water St
Schermerhorn Row
Pier 16
Prudential Bache Corporation
Burling Slip
BA
tkts
John St
National Westminster Bank USA
Front St
Vistor's Center
Sorg Building
South St
Pier 15
Fletcher St

General Information

NFT Maps:	1 & 3
Phone:	212-SEAPORT
Phone (museum):	212-748-8600
Museum:	12 Fulton St www.southstseaport.org Hours vary by season. Visit the website or call for information.
Retail:	www.southstreet seaport.com
Hours:	Mon–Sat: 10 am–9 pm Sun: 11 am–8 pm

Overview

Time was, you could be forgiven if you assumed South Street Seaport was just a mall and a bunch of chain stores. After Superstorm Sandy, however, the area has undergone quite a physical and spiritual change. Today the Seaport has been rebranded as a spot for container ship pop-ups, artisanal vendors from Brooklyn and a space for live events. Even the bad old mall is scheduled for a major renovation.

Where to start? By far our favorite stop is friendly and crowded **Nelson Blue**, with its crisp, clean New Zealand cuisine. It can get crowded early evenings with Wall Streeters, but off times and weekends it's a perfect respite from walking the pavement. **Suteishi**, right across the street, does excellent sushi rolls, while **Barbarini Alimentari** gives great Italian take-out (**Barbarini Mercato** next door is a great little greens/cheese/charcuterie market, one of a whole slew that have opened up in every up-and coming 'nabe in NYC).

Fun kid stuff (including clothes) can be found at **firefly**, and a gourmet cuppa joe can be sipped at **Jack's Stir Brew**. Have a glass of wine at **Bin 220** and then snag some seafood at posh **Stella**. You really can't go wrong down here now—this is a MAJOR change from five, and especially ten years ago.

Of course, there are some longer-standing places that should still be explored—including brunch at 19th-century spot **Bridge Café**, drinks at former fishmonger hangout **Paris Café**, succulent steaks at **Mark Joseph**, and satisfyingly above-average Mexican at mainstay **Red**.

The next wave for the Seaport was shaping up to be all the empty fish market stalls on **South Street**. Cool liquor store **Pasanella** is riding the wave down here, but unfortunately, a few other businesses have opened and closed already. It remains to be seen if the South Street can support another wave of hipness now that Front Street is saturated, or if it will get converted to even more tourist crapola à la Pier 17 mall, or—most likely given the state of the economy—nothing much of anything will happen for the next 12 months or so. But the infrastructure exists—wouldn't it be nice if the city just said "Hey, let's have a big permanent market with cool stalls like Reading Terminal Mall in Philadelphia or the Ferry Building in San Francisco."

Well, we all have dreams.

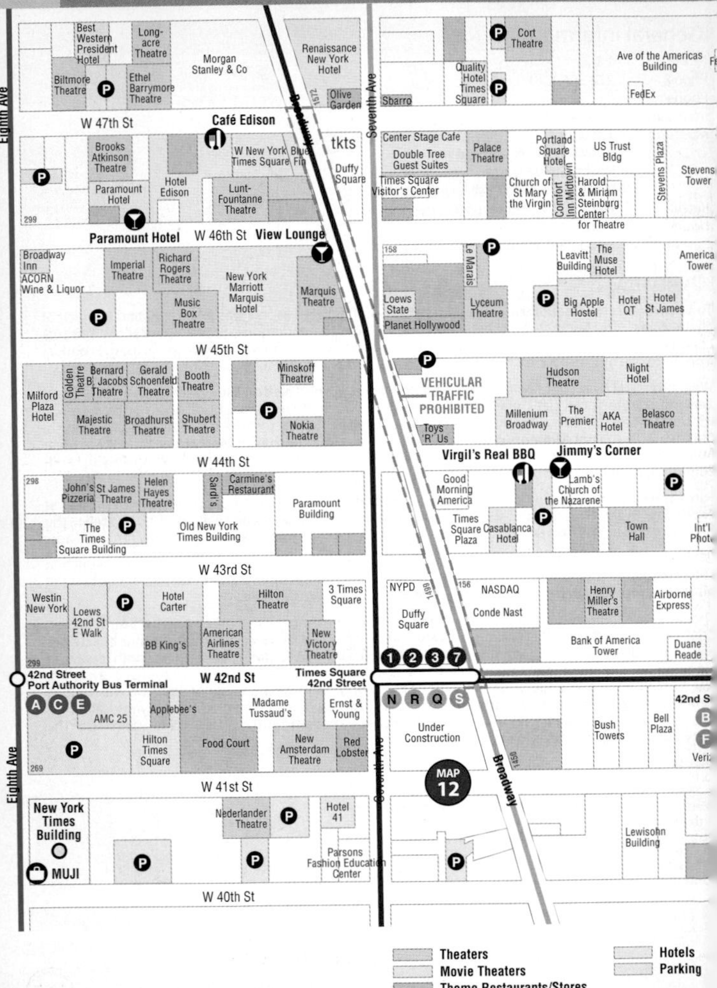
Eighth Ave
Best Western President Hotel
Long-acre Theatre
Morgan Stanley & Co
Renaissance New York Hotel
Cort Theatre
Ave of the Americas Building
Biltmore Theatre
Ethel Barrymore Theatre
Olive Garden
Seventh Ave
Sbarro
Quality Hotel Times Square
FedEx
W 47th St
Café Edison
Broadway
tkts
Center Stage Cafe
Palace Theatre
Portland Square Hotel
US Trust Bldg
Stevens Plaza
Stevens Tower
Brooks Atkinson Theatre
W New York Times Square
Duffy Square
Double Tree Guest Suites
Times Square Visitor's Center
Church of St Mary the Virgin
Comfort Inn Midtown
Harold & Miriam Steinburg Center for Theatre
Paramount Hotel
Hotel Edison
Lunt-Fountanne Theatre
Paramount Hotel
W 46th St
View Lounge
Le Marais
Leavitt Building
The Muse Hotel
America Tower
Broadway Inn
ACORN Wine & Liquor
Imperial Theatre
Richard Rogers Theatre
New York Marriott Marquis Hotel
Marquis Theatre
Music Box Theatre
Loews State
Planet Hollywood
Lyceum Theatre
Big Apple Hostel
Hotel QT
Hotel St James
W 45th St
VEHICULAR TRAFFIC PROHIBITED
Hudson Theatre
Night Hotel
Milford Plaza Hotel
Golden Theatre
Bernard B. Jacobs Theatre
Gerald Schoenfeld Theatre
Booth Theatre
Minskoff Theatre
Majestic Theatre
Broadhurst Theatre
Shubert Theatre
Nokia Theatre
Toys 'R' Us
Millenium Broadway
The Premier
AKA Hotel
Belasco Theatre
W 44th St
Virgil's Real BBQ
Jimmy's Corner
John's Pizzeria
St James Theatre
Helen Hayes Theatre
Sardi's
Carmine's Restaurant
Paramount Building
Good Morning America
Lamb's Church of the Nazarene
The Times Square Building
Old New York Times Building
Times Square Plaza
Casablanca Hotel
Town Hall
Int'l Photo
W 43rd St
Westin New York
Loews 42nd St E Walk
Hotel Carter
Hilton Theatre
3 Times Square
NYPD
Duffy Square
NASDAQ
Conde Nast
Henry Miller's Theatre
Airborne Express
BB King's
American Airlines Theatre
New Victory Theatre
Bank of America Tower
Duane Reade
42nd Street Port Authority Bus Terminal
W 42nd St
Times Square 42nd Street
A C E
1 2 3 7
N R Q S
AMC 25
Applebee's
Madame Tussaud's
Ernst & Young
Under Construction
42nd St
B F
Bush Towers
Bell Plaza
Hilton Times Square
Food Court
New Amsterdam Theatre
Red Lobster
MAP 12
W 41st St
New York Times Building
Nederlander Theatre
Hotel 41
Lewisohn Building
MUJI
Parsons Fashion Education Center
W 40th St
Theaters
Movie Theaters
Theme Restaurants/Stores
Hotels
Parking

General Information

NFT Map: 12
Website: www.timessquare.com
www.timessquarenyc.org
Transit: Take the 1 2 3 7 N Q R W and S trains to get to the center of everything at the 42nd Street/Times Square stop.

Overview

Is Times Square cool? Well, if you're not sure what our answer is, then close the book and read the title again. ***NOT*** for tourists, remember? Between the sheer mass of humanity and idiotic "attractions" such as the Bubba Gump Shrimp Company and, of course, the Hard Rock Café, spending any significant amount of time here will definitely turn your brain into strawberry Jell-o.

But all is not lost, faithful travelers. There are a few places, mostly on the edges of the madness (really, it's always the edge of things anyway, isn't it?), that are worth checking out, while your family is waiting on line for the Toys-R-Us ferris wheel or attempting to convince themselves that Chevy's serves good Mexican food.

In 2009 the city added lots of pedestrian plazas and bike lanes to make this part of the city much more friendly for hanging out. Between 42nd and 47th Streets, the area is closed to cars and you'll find tourists waiting for discounted day of Broadway tickets at the renovated TKTS booth, or taking a load off before heading down to Macy's or up to Central Park. They even added beach chairs for summertime lounging in the middle of all that concrete!

Sights

Our favorite sight in the area is the new **New York Times Building**, on the corner of 43rd Street and Eighth Avenue, across from the heinous Port Authority Bus Terminal (can we please just drop a bomb on that and be done with it?). Designed by Renzo Piano, it's a brilliant architectural addition to the area, has several "green" building components, and also houses a hip **MUJI** (620 Eighth Ave) store.

Aside from standing in the middle of Times Square one warm summer night after dropping something mind-expanding, the only other suggestion we have is to have a drink once (once is enough) at the Marriott's **View Lounge** (1535 Broadway), which is a 360-degree rotating bar at the top of the Marriott. Overpriced drinks, nice view, you've done it, now it's time to leave.

Restaurants

About every fifth restaurant in NYC serves good food; the percentage goes way down in Times Square. There re still a few gems, though—including **Virgil's Real Barbeque** (152 W 44th St) (quite good food, although they ush you out like you're in Chinatown), the 24-hour French haven **Maison** (1700 Broadway, off the map) (an xcellent beer selection as well), another French destination in **Marseille** (630 Ninth Ave, off the map), and the ow-Michelin-starred Italian **Insieme** (777 Seventh Ave, off the map). For cheap and honest deli fare, you can't o better than the old-school **Café Edison** (228 W 47th St).

Nightlife

ortunately, there is something decent to do here now—the **Iridium Jazz Club** (off the map) moved down o 1650 Broadway from Lincoln Center a few years ago. Les Paul jammed here every Monday before dying of neumonia in 2009 at 94, but major acts like Pharoah Sanders still blow in occasionally. For a drink, the bar t the **Paramount Hotel** (235 W 46th St) is cool (merci, Monsieur Starck), though (of course) not cheap. Our ecommendation: head a few blocks north to the **Russian Vodka Room** (265 W 52nd St, off the map) for a ngular experience. You won't remember it, but you'll have fun doing it. And finally, for people who say the old mes Square is gone forever, stop in for a shot, a beer, and some lively conservation with the locals at **Jimmy's orner** (140 W 44th St)—every neighborhood should have a bar like this.

Everything Else

ere isn't. Go to the Village. Doesn't matter which one. Just get the hell out of here.

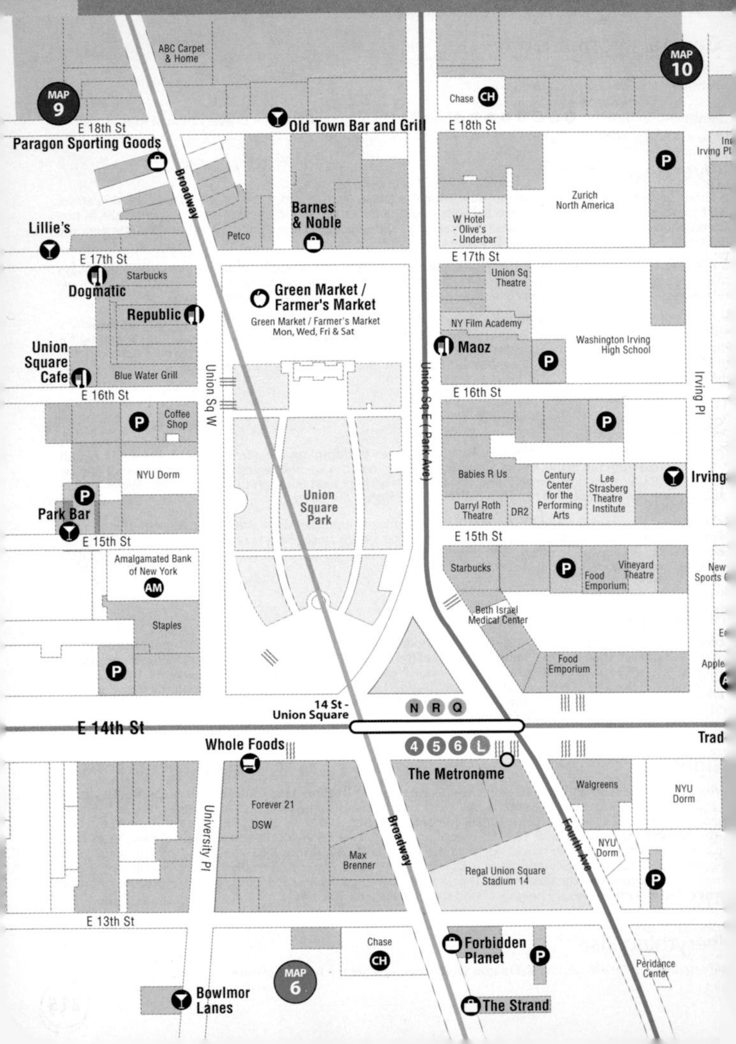
ABC Carpet & Home
MAP 9
MAP 10
Chase
E 18th St
Old Town Bar and Grill
Paragon Sporting Goods
Broadway
Barnes & Noble
Zurich North America
Irving Pl
W Hotel - Olive's - Underbar
Lillie's
Petco
E 17th St
Starbucks
Dogmatic
Green Market / Farmer's Market
Green Market / Farmer's Market Mon, Wed, Fri & Sat
Union Sq Theatre
NY Film Academy
Republic
Maoz
Washington Irving High School
Union Square Cafe
Blue Water Grill
Union Sq W
Union Sq E (Park Ave)
E 16th St
Coffee Shop
NYU Dorm
Babies R Us
Century Center for the Performing Arts
Lee Strasberg Theatre Institute
Irving
Union Square Park
Darryl Roth Theatre
DR2
Park Bar
E 15th St
Amalgamated Bank of New York
Starbucks
Food Emporium
Vineyard Theatre
Beth Israel Medical Center
Staples
Food Emporium
14 St - Union Square
E 14th St
Whole Foods
The Metronome
Walgreens
NYU Dorm
Forever 21
DSW
University Pl
Max Brenner
Broadway
Fourth Ave
NYU Dorm
Regal Union Square Stadium 14
E 13th St
Chase
Forbidden Planet
Peridance Center
MAP 6
Bowlmor Lanes
The Strand

General Information

NFT Maps: 6, 9, & 10

Overview

Want to find the real pulse of Manhattan? Head straight to Union Square where thousands of people surge through here everyday to hang out on the steps, shop at the excellent farmers market, protest whatever's wrong with our country this week, occasionally shoot up, and watch the city roll on by. Part of the charm is that there's no real attraction here. There's a park with some benches, a statue, a dog run, the aforementioned market, and that's about it. After 9-11 New Yorkers congregated here to console each other and remember the perished. Since that fateful day, Union Square has become the de facto living room of Downtown. Between New School and NYU kids rushing to class, crazy street entertainers, lost tourists, and locals just trying to get to work, this place is always jumping. Historical note: The first ever Labor Day celebration took place here, so next time you're sitting in the park enjoying your lunch from the **Whole Foods** salad bar, give thanks that the legal days of working 14-hour shifts are long over. At least for some of us.

Shopping

Unfortunately like the rest of Manhattan, the area around Union Square has slowly been transformed into a giant outdoor mall. You've got chain stores galore flanking the park, but if you look very carefully, you'll find a couple of good shopping options in these parts. High on the list is **The Strand** (828 Broadway), the iconic bookstore that keeps on truckin' (thank goodness) with discounted books and literary readings, and don't forget **Alabaster Bookshop** (122 4th Ave) just around the corner. There's also **Forbidden Planet** (840 Broadway), a comic book nerd's heaven. For the sports nuts **Paragon Sporting Goods** (867 Broadway) is the place to get any kind of racquet, ball, or bat you can think of. And if your feet need some new duds, hike over to **Shoemania** (853 Broadway) where the selection will overwhelm you as much as the in-your-face staff. If you must choose a big name, the **Barnes & Noble** (33 E 17th) at the north end of the park has an amazing magazine selection and of course an incredible selection of NFTs. But the main draw is the **Union Square Farmers Market**—going strong for over thirty years this is the best place in the city to stock up on produce, cheese, baked goods, and meat. Fantastic.

Restaurants

For a true splurge make reservations at **Union Square Café** (21 E 16th St). Despite the 1980s décor, the food is truly wonderful (or so we hear…we're still trying to get a table). For a quick bite that won't break the bank, **Republic** (37 Union Sq W) serves up noisy noodles. To eat really cheap you can't beat **Maoz** (38 Union Sq E) for fast food vegetarian or **Dogmatic** (26 E 17th St) for a tasty sausage sandwich. Or do what the locals do and make a trip to the **Whole Food's** (4 Union Sq E) salad bar section. In the warmer months you can sit in the park, but on colder days walk up to the second floor cafeteria and enjoy an amazing view of the city. For dessert, Union Square happens to have two superior places for hot chocolate: **Max Brenner** (841 Broadway) and **Michel Cluizel** in the back of **ABC Carpet & Home** (888 Broadway).

Nightlife

Ready for a stiff drink? **Old Town Bar and Restaurant** (45 E 18th St) is the prime choice. It has character, cheap cocktails, and the crowd isn't totally lame (yeah, it's that tough of a neighborhood to find a decent bar). Just west of the square is **Park Bar** (15 E 15th St), a perfect place to meet up for an after work blind date—it's small enough to force conversation with your new friend. Or try **Lillie's** (13 E 17th St) just up the block if you have a Irish-Victorian bar décor fetish. You'll know what we're talking about the second you walk in. If you like your bowling alleys with fancy cocktails and a doorman, then **Bowlmor** (110 University Pl) will do you just fine. And for live music, the **Irving Plaza** (17 Irving Pl) is a staple on the New York rock scene.

Just Plain Weird

See that giant smoking magic wand clocky thingy on the south side of the square? It's actually got a name—*The Metronome*. Installed in 1999, artists Andrew Ginzel and Kristen Jones created something that's supposed to inspire reflection on the pace of time in the city…or something like that. Unfortunately, every time we glance up at it, we feel even more on edge than we already are. The clock just keeps moving faster and faster and faster and faster and faster… So much for finding any peace and quiet in this part of town.

Just Off The Map

Unlike Guantanamo, NFT does not condone torture in any way. But we will submit to it on occasion by braving the ridiculous mobs at **Trader Joe's** (142 E 14th St) . It's worth a few bruises and scratches to save a few bucks on Wasabi-Ginger Almonds and Organic Fair Trade Italian Coffee. Ditto for the "Two Buck Chuck" (that actually costs $2.99) at their wine shop (138 E 14th St). We'll drink to that, over at **Beauty Bar** (231 E 14th St), hip drinks and dancing in a former hair salon.

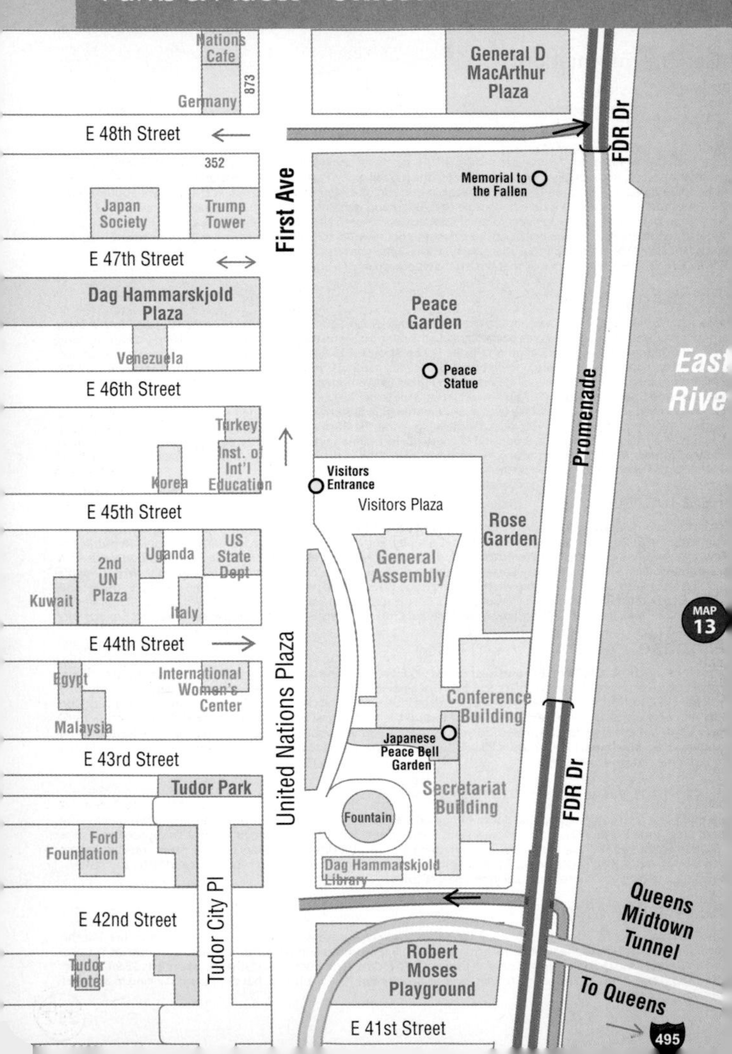
Nations Cafe
873
Germany
E 48th Street
General D MacArthur Plaza
FDR Dr
352
Japan Society
Trump Tower
First Ave
Memorial to the Fallen
E 47th Street
Dag Hammarskjold Plaza
Peace Garden
Venezuela
E 46th Street
Peace Statue
East River
Promenade
Turkey
Inst. of Int'l Education
Korea
Visitors Entrance
Visitors Plaza
E 45th Street
Rose Garden
US State Dept
Uganda
2nd UN Plaza
General Assembly
Kuwait
Italy
MAP 13
E 44th Street
United Nations Plaza
Egypt
International Women's Center
Conference Building
Malaysia
Japanese Peace Bell Garden
E 43rd Street
Tudor Park
Secretariat Building
FDR Dr
Fountain
Ford Foundation
Dag Hammarskjold Library
Tudor City Pl
Queens Midtown Tunnel
E 42nd Street
Robert Moses Playground
Tudor Hotel
To Queens
E 41st Street
495

General Information

NFT Map: 13
Address: First Ave b/w 42nd & 48th Sts
Phone: 212-963-TOUR(8687)
Website: www.un.org
Guided Tour Hours: 9:45 am-4:45 pm (audio tours available weekends 10 am-4:15 pm) except national holidays and weekends in January and February.
Guided Tour Admission: $16 for adults, $11 for seniors, $11 for students, and $9 for children ages 5–12.

Overview

The United Nations Headquarters building, that giant domino teetering on the bank of the East River, opened its doors in 1951. It's here that the 193 member countries of the United Nations meet to fulfill the UN's mandate of maintaining international peace, developing friendly relations among nations, promoting development and human rights, and getting all the free f*#%ing parking they want. The UN is divided into bodies: the General Assembly, the Security Council, the Economic and Social Council, the Trusteeship Council, the Secretariat, and the International Court of Justice (located in the Hague). Specialized agencies like the World Health Organization (located in Geneva) and the UN Children's Fund (UNICEF) (located in New York) are part of the UN family.

The United Nations was founded at the end of World War II by world powers intending to create a body that would prevent war by fostering an ideal of collective security. New York was chosen to be home base when John D. Rockefeller Jr. donated $8.5 million to purchase the 18 acres the complex occupies. The UN is responsible for a lot of good—its staff and agencies have been awarded nine Nobel Peace Prizes over the years. However, the difficult truth is that the United Nations hasn't completely lived up to the ideals of its 1945 charter. Scandals involving abuses by UN troops in Haiti and other countries have certainly not boosted the UN's reputation recently.

However, this place is definitely worth a tour. After all, the people in this building do change the world, for better or worse. The UN Headquarters complex is an international zone complete with its own security force, fire department, and post office (which issues UN stamps). It consists of four buildings: the Secretariat building (the 39-story tower), the General Assembly building, the Conference building, and the Dag Hammarskjöld Library. Once you clear what feels like airport security, you'll find yourself in the visitors' lobby where there are shops, a coffee shop, and a scattering of topical small exhibits that come and go. The guided tour is your ticket out of the lobby and into important rooms like the Security Council Chambers and the impressive and inspiring General Assembly Hall. Sometimes tour groups are allowed to briefly sit in on meetings, but don't expect to spy Ban Ki-moon roaming the halls. Take a stroll through the Peace Bell Garden (off limits to the public, but it can be seen from the inside during the guided tour). The bell, a gift from Japan in 1954, was cast from coins collected by children from 60 different countries. A bronze statue by Henry Moore, *Reclining Figure: Hand*, is located north of the Secretariat Building. The UN grounds are especially impressive when the 500 prize-winning rose bushes and 140 flowering cherry trees are in bloom.

UN Headquarters is undergoing a massive $2 billion renovation. The project is estimated to be completed in 2013 or around the same time the UN finally ends world poverty. We can still dream, right?

N
Barclay St
Washington St
7 WTC
Greenwich St
Vesey Park
West Broadway
Vesey St
Tower 1: Freedom Tower 1 Retail Floors 70 Office Floors
Performing Arts Complex
Tower 2: 2 Retail Floors 65 Office Floors
Fulton St
Fulton St
Wedge of Light Plaza
PATH Terminal
PATH Plaza
WTC Memorial North Pool
Visitors Center
West St
Tower 3: 3 Retail Floors 62 Office Floors
Church St
Memorial Museum
Greenwich St
Museum Entrance
9A
World Financial Center
WTC Memorial South Pool
MAP 1
Tower 4: 3 Retail Floors 58 Office Floors
Liberty St
St Nicholas Church
Liberty Park
Cedar St
Cedar St
Washington St
Tower 5: 57 Office Floors
Albany St

Overview

It's been 12 years since 9/11, and though many New Yorkers are experiencing 9/11-fatigue, there is still a literal and figurative void in the Financial District.

Much is on the docket for the neighborhood's continuing rehabilitation. At the top of the list s 1 World Trade Center, the epic 1,776-foot skyscraper (formerly called the Freedom Tower), and the number of feet high is no accident. It will nclude an observation deck, restaurants, offices, and broadcasting facilities. Whenever it's actually inished, it'll be environmentally sound and ultra-safe.

'he National September 11th Memorial is now open o the public, designed by Michael Arad and Peter Valker, featuring a pair of recessed reflecting pools n the footprints of the twin towers. The pools are ed by waterfalls and surrounded by 225 newly lanted trees and the nearly 3,000 names of those vho tragically passed away. The accompanying nuseum is stlll in progress.

he World Trade Center MTA-PATH station Is being edesigned by architect Santiago Calatrava for a nere $3.8 billion, Chambers, Fulton, Hudson, and ther downtown streets are being structurally nproved, and downtown parks are also being evitalized.

/hat will it look like? The spire-like Freedom Tower vill climb roughly 1,800 feet in the sky. Its footprint ill match the footprints of the Twin Towers at 00 by 200 feet. Boasting 2.6 million square feet of ffice space, restaurants, an observation deck, and roadcasting facilities for the Metropolitan Television lliance, it will be environmentally sound and ultra-fe. If it ever gets built, that is.

nd the memorial? Michael Arad designed *Reflecting bsence* as waterfalls flowing into the sunken ootprints" of the twin towers, cascading onto the ames etched in stone of those who died there. e plans also include a visitor's center designed by orwegian firm Snohetta.

ebate still rages regarding many aspects of the oject, from the height and look of the other towers how many streets will be allowed to run through e site (many were de-mapped when the WTC was ginally built). Also raging are class-action lawsuits eging inadequate protection against toxins for orkers. And with the economy still in the dumps, nstruction projects across the city have been put hold. Stay tuned.

Transit has been restored to pre–September 11th order, with all subway lines resuming service to the area, along with PATH service to the newly constructed PATH station.

Useful Websites

- Lower Manhattan Info provides current details about construction and future plans for the WTC site and the surrounding area: www.lowermanhattan.info
- The World Trade Center Health Registry will track the health survey of thousands of people directly exposed to the events of 9/11: www.nyc.gov/html/doh/html/wtc/index.html
- The findings of the National Commission on Terrorist Attacks Upon the United States (the 9/11 Commission): www.9-11commission.gov
- "New York New Visions" is a coalition of several groups looking at different options for rebuilding the area: www.nynv.aiga.org
- The New York Skyscraper Museum continues to add Information about the WTC and downtown NYC in general; they also contributed to the historical panels placed on the viewing wall around the site: www.skyscraper.org
- Official National September 11th Memorial & Museum site: www.911memorial.org

W 34th St
34th Street
Penn Station
W 33rd St
J A Farley
Post Office
W 31st St
W 30th St
West Side
Rail Yards
Hudson
River
Park
W 29th St
W 28th St
Chelsea Park
Penn
Station
South
Houses
W 27th St
West Side Hwy
Eleventh Ave
Tenth Ave
Ninth Ave
Eighth Ave
W 26th St
W 25th St
9a
MAP
8
W 24th St
Chelsea
Waterside
Park
W 23rd St
23rd Street
W 22nd St
Gallery
District
CHELSEA
Hudson
River
Chelsea Piers
W 21st St
W 20th St
W 19th St
Chelsea Grasslands
W 18th St
W 17th St
10th Avenue Square
W 16th St
Chelsea
Market
Chelsea Market Public Art
W 15th St
Diller - Von Furstenberg
Sundeck & Water Feature
MEATPACKING
DISTRICT
W 14th St
14th Street
W 13th St
Washington Grasslands
Gansevoort Woodland
Little W 12th St
Gansevoort St
Hudson St
Gansevoort Plaza
MAP
5
Horatio St
Washington
Jane St
Greenwich St
Eighth Ave
WEST
VILLAGE
Stairs
Elevator
Sections 1 & 2
Section 3
Pending development

Overview

Welcome to New York's newest, and instantly one of its coolest, parks. Open from 7 am to 10 pm daily and built on top of a disused portion of freight rail elevated train tracks, The High Line is at once both an escape from the sturm und drang of the city's streets and a celebration of Manhattan's west side, especially its architecture. Section 2, which opened in June 2011, doubles the length of the park up to 30th Street , and the entire thing is wheelchair accessible.

The flora planted along the High Line is well suited to the region's native ecology. 50% of the plants are native to North America and 30% are native to the Northeast. This naturally becomes a home for birds and butterflies living in the area, and the park absorbs (and uses!) lots of rainwater that would otherwise be flooding our disgusting gutters. Given that the old high line was doing nothing but rusting, this park is essentially one big recycling center.

What's more, it's obvious that the presence of the High Line itself, stretching from the uber-hip Meatpacking District north into the heart of Chelsea's glut of art galleries, is going to have a huge impact on further architectural and cultural development in the area. More and more folks are simply going to take the extra two-block schlep from the nearest subway stop (8th Avenue's A/C/E/L) to check out the park, its surrounding buildings, and the ever-increasing number of cultural, gastronomic, and nightlife options directly underneath (and above!) it.

One major example of new architectural work can simply be seen by looking UP when you're on the High Line; namely Polshek Partnerships' brilliant **Standard Hotel**, which straddles the High Line just south of 14th Street. The hotel sports a posh restaurant as well as a beer garden, both directly underneath the High Line. Two other stunning architectural gems visible from the High Line (looking west) are Frank Gehry's first commercial office building in New York, Barry Diller's **IAC Headquarters**, and Jean Nouvel's new **condo building** right across the street. The IAC is one of the most wonderfully luminescent buildings in all of New York, and Nouvel's façade of hundreds of differently-sized panes of glass will become an instant classic. Of course, the work on the High Line itself, by architects Diller Scofidio + Renfro and landscape architects James Corner Field Operations, is simply amazing. The 10th Avenue Square area, with amphitheater-style seating and a living-room-window view of the northbound traffic of Tenth Avenue, is a favorite as well as a perfect place for a picnic (a picnic that can be perfectly constructed using wonderful **Chelsea Market** food vendors).

While weekend days during summer on the High Line is already a madhouse, we recommend an early-morning or evening stroll during spring and fall. The cityscape views at night are stunning; early morning is quiet and generally cool, until the sun moves above the skyscrapers to the east of the park.

Essentially, however, there is no bad time to visit the High Line. The views will be great no matter what time of day it is, and fantastic food options are always waiting for you, including hip **Cookshop (Map 8)**, French haven **La Lunchonette (Map 8)**, neighborhood standby **Red Cat (Map 8)**, Jean-Georges Vongerichten's **Spice Market (Map 5)**, and warm **Italian Bottino (Map 8)**. Want cheaper fare? Hit greasy spoon **Hector's (Map 5)** or wait for one of the gourmet trucks to pull up around the corner from the Gansevoort stairs, or go DIY by buying food at **Chelsea Market (Map 8)**. On the High Line itself, look out for stands selling delicious popsicles (People's Pops and La Newyorkina), ice cream sandwiches from Melt Bakery, and Blue Bottle Coffee.

At night, you can hang around to rock out at **The High Line Ballroom (Map 8)**, or drink at pubs **The Half King (Map 8)**, **Brass Monkey (Map 5)**, or the Standard's **Biergarten (Map 5)**, or, better yet, walk the streets of the West 20s in search of gallery openings (read: free wine and cheese). No matter how you slice it, a visit to the High Line will only make you happier. We promise.

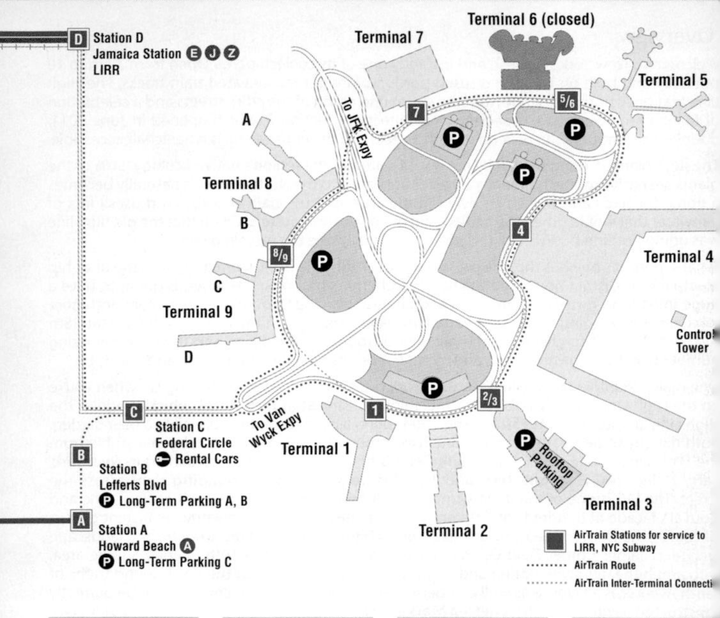

Airline	Terminal
Aer Lingus	4
Aeroflot	1
Aerolineas Argentinas	4
Aero Gal	4
Aero Mexico	1
Aerosvit Ukrainian	4
Air Berlin	8
Air Canada	7
Air China	1
Air Europa	4
Air France	1
Air India	4
Air Jamaica	4
AirPlus Comet	1
Air Tahiti Nui	4
Alitalia	1
Allegro (seasonal)	4
American	8
American Eagle	8
ANA	7
Asiana	4
Austrian Airlines	1
Avianca	4
Azteca	4
Biman Bangladesh	4
British Airways	7
Caribbean	4
Cathay Pacific	7
Cayman Airways	1
China Airlines	1
China Eastern	1
Comair	3
Copa Airlines	4
Czech Airlines	4
Delta	3
Egypt Air	4
El Al	4
Emirates	4
Etihad	4
Eurofly	4
Finnair	8
Flyglobespan	4
Iberia	7
Icelandair	7
Japan Airlines	1
Jet Airways	8
Jetblue(San Juan)	4
JetBlue Airways	5
KLM	4
Korean Air	1
Kuwait Airways	4
Lacsa	4
Lan Chile	4
Lan Ecuador	4
Lan Peru	4
LOT	4
Lufthansa	1
Malev Hungarian	8
Mexicana	8
Miami Air (charter)	4
North American	4
Northwest	4
Olympic	1
Pakistan	4
Qantas	7
Qatar	4
Royal Air Maroc	1
Royal Jordanian	4
Saudi Arabian Airlines	1
Singapore	4
South African	4
SN Brussels Airlines	8
Sun Country	4
Swiss International	4
TACA International	[illegible]
TAM	[illegible]
Travel Span	4
Turkish	
United Airlines	
US Airways/ America West	
US Helicopter	
Uzbekistan	
Virgin American	
Virgin Atlantic	
XL Airways	

General Information

Address: JFK Expy
Jamaica, NY 11430
Phone: 718-244 4444
Lost & Found: 718-244-4225
Website: www.kennedyairport.com
AirTrain: www.airtrainjfk.com
AirTrain Phone: 718-570-1048
Long Island Rail Road: www.mta.info/lirr

Overview

Ah, JFK. It's long been a nemesis to Manhattanites due to the fact that it's the farthest of the three airports from the city. Nonetheless, more than 49 million people go through JFK every year. A $9.5 billion expansion and modernization program will transform the airport, with JetBlue taking about $900 million of that for its gigantic, 26-gate, new HQ to address the ten million of you who, in spite of JFK's distance, wake up an hour earlier to save a buck.

JetBlue's Terminal 5 rises just behind the landmark TWA building, which you should check out if you have time to kill after getting up an hour earlier. Its bubbilicious curves make this 1960s gem a glam spaceship aptly prepared to handle any swanky NY soiree. Top that, Newark.

Rental Cars (On-Airport)

The rental car offices are all located along the Van Wyck Expressway near the entrance to the airport. Just follow the signs.

1 • **Avis** • 718-244-5406 or 800-230-4898
2 • **Budget** • 718-656-6010 or 800-527-0700
3 • **Dollar** • 718-656-2400 or 800-800-4000
5 • **Enterprise** • 718-659-1200 or 800-RENT-A-CAR
4 • **Hertz** • 718-656-7600 or 800-654-3131
5 • **National** • 718-632-8300 or 800-CAR-RENTAL

Hotels

Crown Plaza JFK • 151-20 Baisley Blvd • 718-489-1000
Comfort Inn JFK • 144-36 153rd Ln • 718-977-0001
Double Tree Club Hotel • 135-40 140th St • 718-276-2188
Holiday Inn JFK Airport • 144-02 135th Ave • 718-659-0200
Ramada Plaza Hotel • Van Wyck Expy • 718-995-9000
Ramada Plaza Hotel • Van Wyck Expy • 718-995-9000
Best Western JFK Airport • 144-25 153rd Lane • 718-977-2100
Courtyard by Marriott JFK Airport • 145-11 North Conduit Ave. • 718-848-2121
Days Inn • 144-26 153rd Court • 718-527-9025
Fairfield Inn by Marriott • 156-08 Rockaway Blvd. • 718-977-3300
Hampton Inn • 144-10 135th Avenue • 718-322-7500
Hilton Garden Inn • 148-18 134th Street • 718-322-4448
Holiday Inn Express Kennedy Airport • 153-70 South Conduit Ave • 718-977-3100
Howard Johnson Express Inn at JFK Airport • 153-95 Rockaway Blvd • 718-723-6700
JFK Inn • 154-10 South Conduit Ave • 718-723-5100
Sheraton JFK Airport Hotel • 132-26 South Conduit Ave • 718-322-7190

G Washington Bridge
Cross Bronx Expy
BRONX
NEW JERSEY
Throgs Neck Expy
Bruckner Expy
Hudson River
Henry Hudson Pkwy
MANHATTAN
RFK Bridge
Flushing Bay
Whitestone Bridge
Throgs Neck Bridge
Whitestone Expy
LaGuardia Airport
Central Park
Grand Central Pkwy
FDR Dr
East River
Lincoln Tunnel
57th St
34th St
Astoria Blvd
Northern Blvd
Queensboro Bridge
Midtown Tunnel
Queens Blvd
West St
Long Island Expy
Brooklyn-Queens Expy
Holland Tunnel
QUEENS
Woodhaven Blvd
Grand Central Pkwy
Williamsburg Bridge
Metropolitan Ave
Manhattan Bridge
Brooklyn Bridge
Brooklyn-Battery Tunnel
Broadway
Van Wyck Expy
Atlantic Ave
Jamaica Ave
Flatbush Ave
Atlantic Ave
N Conduit Ave
Prospect Park
Prospect Expy
Green-Wood Cemetery
BROOKLYN
Cross Bay Blvd
Ocean Pkwy
Ocean Ave
Belt Pkwy
Floyd Bennett Field
Jamaica Bay
Lower Bay
ROCKAWAY BEACH
Rockaway Inlet

Car Services & Taxis

All County Express • 914-381-4223 or 800-914-4223
Classic Limousine • 631-567-5100 or 800-666-4949
Dial 7 Car & Limo Service • 212-777-7777 or 800-777-8888
Super Saver by Carmel • 800-922-7635 or 212-666-6666
Tel Aviv Limo Service • 800-222-9888 or 212-777-7777

Taxis from the airport to anywhere in Manhattan cost a flat $52 + tolls and tip, while fares to the airport are metered + tolls and tip. The SuperShuttle (800-258-3826) will drop you anywhere between Battery Park and 227th, including all hotels, for $13–$22, but be warned it could end up taking a while, depending on where your fellow passengers are going. Nevertheless, it's a good option if you want door-to-door service and have a lot of time to kill, but not a lot of cash.

How to Get There—Driving

You can take the lovely and scenic Belt Parkway straight to JFK, as long as it's not rush hour. The Belt Parkway route is about 30 miles long, even though JFK is only 15 or so miles from Manhattan. You can access the Belt by taking the Brooklyn-Battery Tunnel to the Gowanus (the best route) or by taking the Brooklyn, Manhattan, or Williamsburg Bridges to the Brooklyn-Queens Expressway to the Gowanus. If you're sick of stop-and-go highway traffic and prefer using local roads, take Atlantic Avenue in Brooklyn and drive east until you hit Conduit Avenue. Follow this straight to JFK—it's direct and fairly simple. You can get to Atlantic Avenue from any of the three downtown bridges (look at one of our maps first!). From midtown, you can take the Queens Midtown Tunnel to the Long Island Expressway to the Van Wyck Expressway South (there's never much traffic on the LIE, of course…). From uptown, you can take the Robery F. Kennedy Bridge to the Grand Central Parkway to the Van Wyck Expressway S. JFK also has two new AM frequencies solely devoted to keeping you abreast of all of the airport's endeavors that may affect traffic. Tune into 1630AM for general airport information and 1700AM for construction updates en route to your next flight. It might save you a sizeable headache.

How to Get There—Mass Transit

This is your chance to finish *War and Peace*. Replacing the free shuttle from the subway is the AirTrain, which will make your journey marginally smoother, but also make your wallet a little lighter. Running 24/7, you can board the AirTrain from the subway on the A line at either the Howard Beach stop or the E, J, and Z lines at the Sutphin/Archer Ave-Jamaica Station stop. The ride takes around 15-25 minutes, depending on which airport terminal you need.

A one-way ride on the AirTrain sets you back $5, so a ride on the subway and then hopping the AirTrain will be a total of $7.50. If you're anywhere near Penn Station and your time is valuable, the LIRR to Jamaica will cost you $7 off-peak, $9.50 during peak times and $4 on weekends using a MTA CityTicket. The AirTrain portion of the trip will still cost you an additional $5 and round out your travel time to less than an hour.

If you want to give your MetroCard a workout, you can take the E or the F to the Turnpike/Kew Gardens stop and transfer to the Q10. Another possibility is the 3 or 4 to New Lots Avenue, where you transfer to the B15 to JFK. The easiest and most direct option is to take a New York Airport Service Express bus (718-875-8200) from either Grand Central Station, Penn Station, or the Port Authority for $15. Since the buses travel on service roads, Friday afternoon is not an advisable time to try them out.

Parking

Daily rates for the Central Terminal Area lots cost $3 for the first half-hour, $6 for up to one hour, $3 for every hour after that, up to $33 per day. Long-term parking costs $18 for the first 24-hours, then $6 in each 8-hour increment thereafter. Be warned, though—many of the ongoing construction projects at JFK affect both their short-term and long-term lots, so be sure to allow extra time for any unpleasant surprises. For updated parking availability, call 718-244-4080.

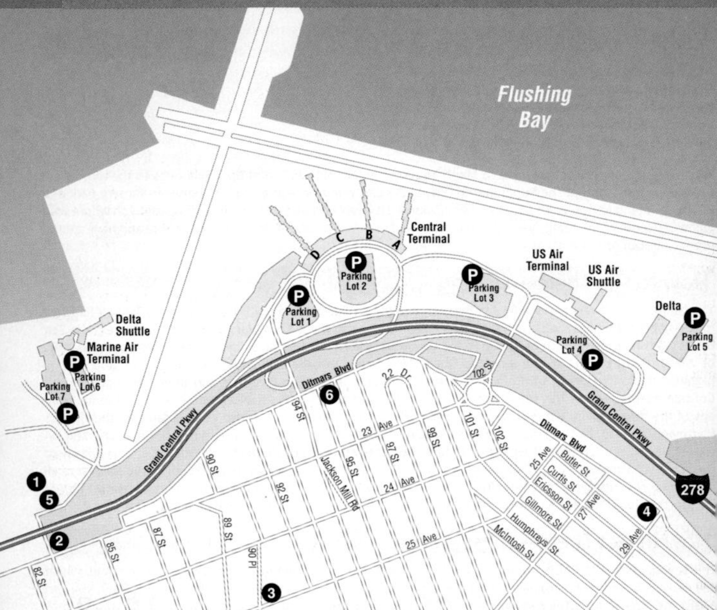

Airline	*Terminal*
Air Canada	B
Air Tran Airways	B
American Airlines	B
American Eagle	B
Delta	C
Delta Connection	D
Delta Shuttle	A
Frontier Airlines	B
JetBlue Airways	B
Southwest Airlines	B
Spirit	B
United	B
United Express	B
US Airways	C
US Airways Express	C
US Airways Shuttle	C
WestJet	C

General Information

Address:	LaGuardia Airport Flushing, NY 11371
Recorded Information:	718-533-3400
Lost & Found:	718-533-3988
Police:	718-533-3900
Website:	www.laguardiaairport.com

Overview

The reason to fly from LaGuardia (affectionately known as LGA on your baggage tags) is that it is geographically the closest airport to Manhattan and thus a cheap(er) cab ride when your delayed flight touches down at 1 in the morning. The reason not to fly to and from here is that there is no subway line (HELLO, city officials!) and the check-in areas are just too darn small to accommodate the many passengers and their many bags that crowd the terminals at just about every hour of the day. Food is not a great option, so eat before you leave home. If you must dine, there are 5 Au Bon Pains throughout the terminals—find them as they are the most palatable choice available.

How to Get There—Driving (or directing your cabbie)

LaGuardia is mere inches away from Grand Central Parkway, which can be reached from both the Brooklyn-Queens Expressway (BQE) or from the Robert F. Kennedy Bridge. From Lower Manhattan, take the Brooklyn, Manhattan, or Williamsburg Bridges to the BQE to Grand Central Parkway E. From Midtown Manhattan, take FDR Drive to the Robert F. Kennedy Bridge to Grand Central. A potential alternate route (and money-saver) would be to take the 59th Street Bridge to 21st Street in Queens. Once you're heading north on 21st Street, you can make a right on Astoria Boulevard and follow it all the way to 94th Street, where you can make a left and drive straight into LaGuardia. This alternate route is good if the FDR and/or the BQE is jammed, although that probably means that the 59th Street Bridge won't be much better.

How to Get There—Mass Transit

Alas, no subway line goes to LaGuardia (although there SHOULD be one running across 96th Street in Manhattan, through Astoria, and ending at LaGuardia—but that's another story). The closest the subway comes is the 7 E F G R Jackson Heights/Roosevelt Avenue/74th Street stop in Queens, where you can transfer to the Q33 or Q47 bus bus to LaGuardia. Sound exciting? Well, it's not. A better bus to take is the M60, which runs across 125th Street to the airport. An even better bet would be to pay the extra few bucks and take the New York Airport Service Express Bus ($12 one-way, 718-875-8200) from Grand Central Station. It departs every 20–30 minutes and takes approximately 45 minutes; also catch it on Park Avenue between 41st and 42nd Streets, Penn Station, and the Port Authority Bus Terminal. The improbably named SuperShuttle Manhattan is a shared mini-bus that picks you up anywhere within the city limits ($13–$22 one-way, 212-258-3826). If you want a taxi, search for the "hidden" cab line tucked around Terminal D as the line is almost always shorter than the others.

How to Get There—Really

Plan ahead and call a car service to guarantee that you won't spend the morning of your flight fighting for a taxi. Nothing beats door to door service. Allstate Car and Limousine: 212-333-3333 ($32 in the am & $40 in the pm + tolls from Union Square); LimoRes: 888-546-6794 ($38 + tolls from Union Square; best to call in the morning); Dial 7: 212-777-7777 ($30 in the am & $40 in the pm + tolls from Union Square), Carmel: 212-666-6666 ($33 + tolls to LGA, $28–$35 + tolls from LGA).

Parking

Daily parking rates at LaGuardia cost $3 for the first half-hour, $6 for up to one hour, $3 for every hour thereafter, and up to $33 per day. Long-term parking is $33 per day for the first two 24 hour periods, and $6 for each subsequent 8 hour period. (though only in Lot 3). You can use cash, credit card, or E-Z Pass to pay. Another option is independent parking lots, such as The Crowne Plaza (104-04 Ditmars Blvd, 718-457-6300 x295), Clarion Airport Parking (Ditmars Blvd & 94th St, 718-335-6713) and AviStar (23rd Ave & 90th St, 800-621-PARK). They run their own shuttle buses from their lots, and they usually charge $14–$17 per day. If all the parking garages onsite are full, follow the "P" signs to the airport exit and park in one of the off-airport locations.

Rental Cars

1 Avis • LGA	800-230-4898
2 Budget • 83-34 23rd Ave	800-527-0700
3 Dollar • 90-05 25th Ave	800-800-4000
4 Enterprise • 104-04 Ditmars Blvd	718-457-2900
5 Hertz • LGA	800-654-3131
6 National • Ditmars Blvd & 95th St	800-227-7368

Hotels

Airway Inn • 82-20 Astoria Boulevard • 718-565-5100

Clarion • 94-00 Ditmars Blvd • 718-335-1200

Courtyard • 90-10 Grand Central Pkwy • 718-446-4800

Crowne Plaza • 104-04 Ditmars Blvd • 718-457-6300

Eden Park Hotel • 113-10 Corona Ave • 718-699-4500

Holiday Inn • 37-10 114th Street • 718-651-2100

Howard Johnson • 135-33 38th Avenue • 718-461-3888

LaGuardia Airport Hotel • 100-15 Ditmars Boulevard • 888-307-7555

LaGuardia Marriott • 102-05 Ditmars Blvd • 718-565-8900

Lexington Marco LaGuardia Hotel • 137-07 Northern Boulevard • 718-445-3300

Paris Suites • 109-17 Horace Harding Expy • 718-760-2820

Sheraton • 135-20 39th Ave • 718-460-6666

Skyway Motel at LaGuardia • 102-10 Ditmars Boulevard • 718-899-6900

Wyndham Garden • 100-15 Ditmars Blvd • 718-426-1500

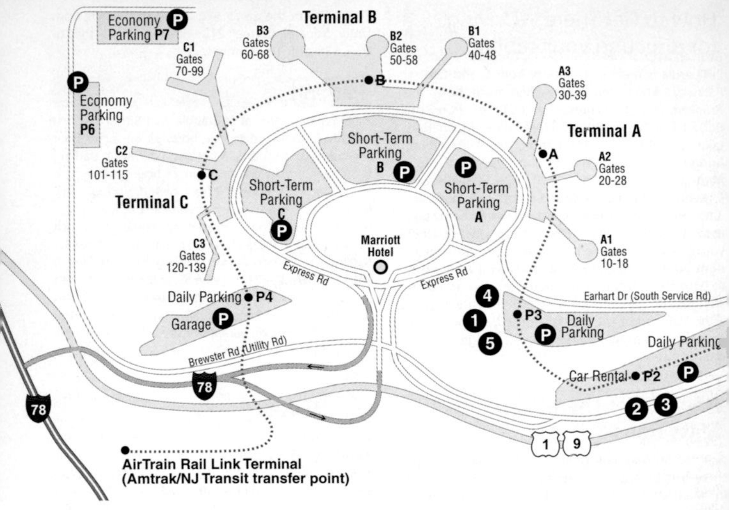

Airline	Terminal
Air Canada	A
Air India	B
Alaska Airlines	B
American	A
American Eagle	A
British Airways	B
Delta	B
El Al	B
Jet Airways	B
JetBlue	A
Lufthansa	B
OpenSkies	B
Porter Airlines	B
SAS	B
Singapore Airlines	B
Southwest	A
Swiss	B
TAP Portugal	B
United	C
United Express	A/C
US Airways	A
US Airways Express	A
Virgin America	A
Virgin Atlantic	B
WestJet	A

General Information

Address:	10 Toler Pl, Newark, NJ 07114
Phone:	888-EWR-INFO
Police/Lost & Found:	973-961-6230
Airport Information:	973-961-6000
Transportation Info:	800-AIR-RIDE (247-7533)
Radio Station:	530 AM
Website:	www.newarkairport.com

Overview

Newark Airport is easily the nicest of the three majo metropolitan airports. The monorail that connect the terminals and the parking lots, the AirTrair link from Penn Station, and the diverse food cour (in Terminal C), make it the city's preferred poin of departure and arrival. There are also plenty o international departures, making it a great seconc option to the miserable experience of doing JFK.

If your flight gets delayed or you find yourself wit time on your hands, check out the d-parture Sp in Terminals B or C to unwind, or, if you're feelin carnivorous after your screaming match with airlin personnel, Gallagher's Steakhouse (Terminal C).

How to Get There–Driving

The route to Newark Airport is easy—just take the Holland Tunnel or the Lincoln Tunnel to the New Jersey Turnpike South. You can use either Exit 14 or Exit 13A. If you want a cheaper and slightly more scenic (from an industrial standpoint) drive, follow signs for the Pulaski Skyway once you exit the Holland Tunnel. It's free, it's one of the coolest bridges in America, and it leads you to the airport just fine. If possible, check a traffic report before leaving Manhattan—sometimes there are viciously long tie-ups, especially at the Holland Tunnel. It's always worth it to see which outbound tunnel has the shortest wait.

How to Get There–Mass Transit

If you're allergic to traffic, try taking the AirTrain service from Penn Station. It's run by Amtrak ($25–$48 one-way) and NJ Transit Airtrain ($12.50 one-way). If you use NJ Transit, choose a train that runs on the Northeast Corridor or North Jersey Coast Line with a scheduled stop for Newark Airport. If you use Amtrak, choose a train that runs on the Northeast Corridor Line with a scheduled stop for Newark Airport. The cheapest option is to take the PATH train ($2.00) to Newark Penn Station then switch to NJ Transit bus #62 ($1.50), which hits all the terminals. Just be alert at night since the area around Newark Penn Station can be a bit shady. You can also catch direct buses departing from Port Authority Bus Terminal (with the advantage of a bus-only lane running right out of the station and into the Lincoln Tunnel), Grand Central Terminal, and Penn Station (the New York version) on Olympia for $14. The SuperShuttle will set you back $13–$22, and a taxi from Manhattan will cost you around $50.

How to Get There–Car Services

Car services are always the simplest option, although they're a bit more expensive for Newark Airport than they are for LaGuardia. Allstate Car and Limousine: 212-333-3333 ($46 in the am & $52 in the pm + tolls from Union Square); Tri-State: 212-777-7171 ($43 + tolls from Union Square; best to call in the morning); Dial 7: 212-777-7777 ($48 in the am & $49 in the pm + tolls from Union Square).

Parking

Short term parking is $3 for every half-hour, up to $33 per day." Long-term parking rates are $3 for the first half-hour, $6 for up to one hour, $3 for every hour after that, $24 per day for the P1 and P3 lots, and $27 per day for the P4 lot. The P6 parking lot is much farther away and only serviced by a shuttle bus. Lot P6 costs $18 for first 24 hours, $6 for each 8-hour period or part thereof. There are some off-airport lots that you can sometimes score for $18 per day, especially if you have a business card. Most of them are on the local southbound lanes of Route 1 & 9. Valet parking costs $40 per day, $20 for each additional 12 hours.

Rental Cars

1 • **Avis**	800-230-4898
2 • **Budget**	800-527-0700
3 • **Dollar**	866-434-2226
4 • **Hertz**	800-654-3131
5 • **National**	800-227-7368
6 • **Enterprise** (Off-Airport)	800-325-8007

Hotels

Marriott (On-Airport) • 973-623-0006
Courtyard Marriott • 600 Rte 1 & 9 S • 973-643-8500
Hilton • 1170 Spring St • 908-351-3900
Howard Johnson • 20 Frontage Rd • 973-344-1500
Sheraton • 128 Frontage Rd • 973-690-5500
Hampton Inn • 1128-38 Spring St • 908-355-0500
Best Western • 101 International Wy • 973-621-6200
Holiday Inn North • 160 Frontage Rd • 973-589-1000
Days Inn • 450 Rte 1 South • 973-242-0900
Ramada Inn • 1 Haynes Ave • 973-824-4000
Wyndham Garden Hotel •
550 US Route 9 • 973-824-4000

Free Harlem River Crossing
A Broadway Bridge
B University Heights Bridge
C Washington Bridge
D A Hamilton Bridge
E Macombs Dam Bridge
F 145th St Bridge
G Madison Ave Bridge
H 3rd Ave Bridge
I Willis Ave Bridge
1 George Washington Bridge
2 Lincoln Tunnel
3 Holland Tunnel
4 Verrazano-Narrows Bridge
5 Brooklyn-Battery Tunnel
6 Brooklyn Bridge
7 Manhattan Bridge
8 Williamsburg Bridge
9 Queens Midtown Tunnel
10 Queensboro Bridge
11 Triborough Bridge
12 Henry Hudson Bridge
13 Bronx-Whitestone Bridge
14 Throgs Neck Bridge
16 Marine Parkway Gil Hodges Memorial Bridge
17 Bayonne Bridge
18 Goethals Bridge
Outerbridge Crossing
The Bronx
Manhattan
Queens
Brooklyn
New Jersey
Staten Island
Hudson River
Flushing Bay
La Guardia Airport
Upper New York Bay
Lower New York Bay
Jamaica Bay

General Information

Port Authority of NY and NJ: www.panynj.gov
DOT: www.ci.nyc.ny.us/html/dot/home.html • 212-NEW-YORK
MTA: www.mta.info
EZPass: www.e-zpassny.com • 800-333-TOLL
Transportation Alternatives: www.transalt.org
Best overall site: www.nycroads.com

Overview

Since NYC is an archipelago, it's no wonder there are so many bridges and four major tunnels. Most of the bridges listed in the chart below are considered landmarks, either for their sheer beauty or because they were the first of their kind at one time. The traffic-jammed Holland Tunnel, finished in 1927, was the first vehicular tunnel connecting New Jersey and New York. King's Bridge, built between Manhattan and the Bronx in 1693, was sadly demolished in 1917. Highbridge, the oldest existing bridge in NYC (completed 1848), is scheduled to reopen to pedestrians in 2013. Brooklyn Bridge, built in 1883, is the city's oldest functioning bridge, still open to vehicles and pedestrians alike, and is considered one of the most beautiful bridges ever built.

The '70s was a decade of neglect for city bridges. Inspections in the '80s and maintenance and refurbishment plans in the '90s/'00s have made the bridges stronger and safer than ever before. On certain holidays when the weather permits, the world's largest free-flying American flag flies from the upper arch of the New Jersey tower on the George Washington Bridge. The Williamsburg Bridge has been completely rebuilt and is almost unrecognizable from its pre-renovation form, especially the pedestrian pathways. The Triborough has been renamed the "RFK" Bridge, and the Queensboro is now officially called Ed Koch Queensboro, just to confuse everyone immensely.

		Toll/E-Z Pass Peak/E-Z Pass off-peak	# of lanes	Pedestrians/bicyclists?	# of vehicles/day (in thousands)	Original cost (in millions)	Engineer	Main span	Operated by	Opened to traffic
1	Geo. Washington Bridge	13.00/10.25/8.25 (inbound only)	14	yes	300	59	Othmar H. Ammann	4,760'	PANYNJ	10/25/31
2	Lincoln Tunnel	13.00/10.25/8.25 (inbound only)	6	no	120	75	Othmar H. Ammann Ole Singstad	8,216'	PANYNJ	12/22/37
3	Holland Tunnel	13.00/10.25/8.25 (inbound only)	4	no	100	54	Clifford Holland/ Ole Singstad	8,558'	PANYNJ	11/13/27
4	Verrazano-Narrows Bridge	*15.00/10.66	12	no	190	320	Othmar H. Ammann	4,260'	MTA	11/21/64
5	Brooklyn-Battery Tunnel	7.50/5.33	4	no	60	90	Ole Singstad	9,117'	MTA	5/25/50
6	Brooklyn Bridge	free	6	yes	140	15	John Roebling/ Washington Roebling	1,595.5'	DOT	5/24/1883
7	Manhattan Bridge	free	4	yes	150	31	Leon Moisseiff	1,470'	DOT	12/31/09
8	Williamsburg Bridge	free	8	yes	140	24.2	Leffert L. Buck	1,600'	DOT	12/19/03
9	Queens-Midtown Tunnel	7.50/5.33	4	no	80	52	Ole Singstad	6,414'	MTA	11/15/40
10	Ed Koch Queensboro	free	10	yes	200	20	Gustav Lindenthal	1,182'	DOT	3/30/09
11	Robert F. Kennedy Bridge	7.50/5.33	8/6/8	yes	200	60.3	Othmar H. Ammann	1,380'	MTA	7/11/36
12	Henry Hudson Bridge	5.00/2.44	7	no	75	5	David Steinman	840'	MTA	12/12/36
13	Bronx-Whitestone Bridge	7.50/5.33	6	no	110	20	Othmar H. Ammann	2,300'	MTA	4/29/39
14	Throgs Neck Bridge	7.50/5.33	6	no	100	92	Othmar H. Ammann	1,800'	MTA	1/11/61
15	Cross Bay Veterans Memorial Bridge	3.75/2.00	6	yes	20	29	n/a	3,000'	MTA	5/28/70
16	Marine Parkway Gil Hodges Memorial Bridge	3.75/2.00	4	yes	25	12	Madigan and Hyland	540'	MTA	7/3/37
17	Bayonne Bridge	13.00/10.25/8.25	4	yes	20	13	Othmar H. Ammann	5,780'	PANY/NJ	11/13/31
18	Goethals Bridge	13.00/10.25/8.25	4	no	75	7.2	Othmar H. Ammann	8,600'	PANY/NJ	6/29/28
19	Outerbridge Crossing	13.00/10.25/8.25	4	no	80	9.6	Othmar H. Ammann	750'	PANY/NJ	6/29/28

* $7.72 with EZPass to Staten Island ($5.76 for registered Staten Island residents with EZPass), $2.25 with three or more occupants—cash only. Free to Brooklyn.

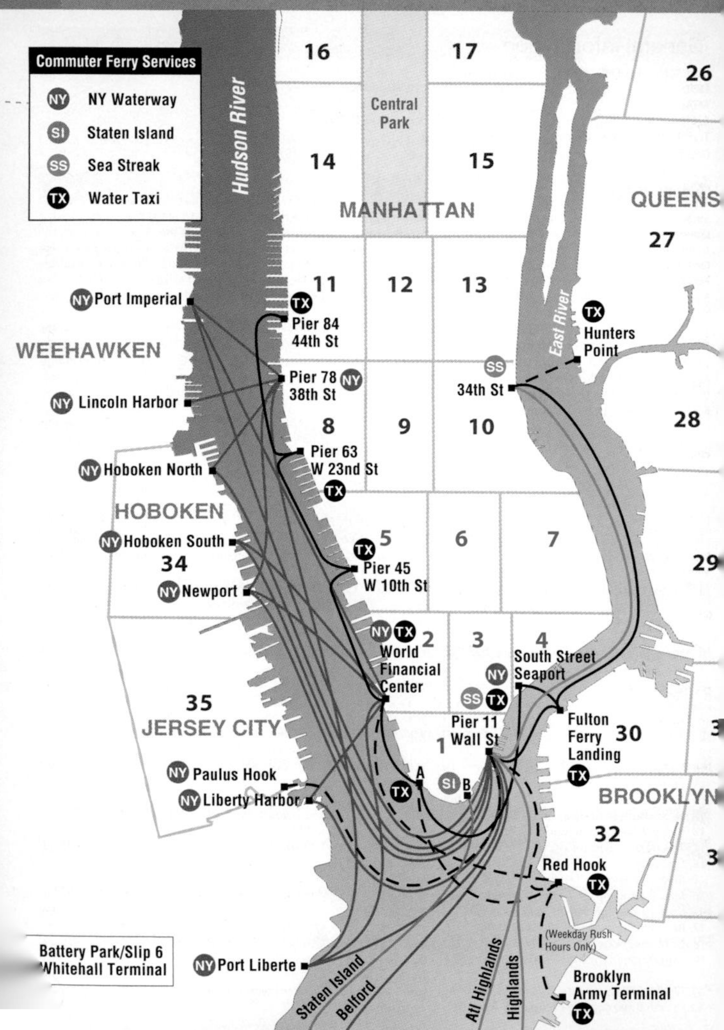
Commuter Ferry Services
NY NY Waterway
SI Staten Island
SS Sea Streak
TX Water Taxi
Hudson River
East River
MANHATTAN
Central Park
QUEENS
WEEHAWKEN
HOBOKEN
JERSEY CITY
BROOKLYN
16
17
26
14
15
27
11
12
13
28
8
9
10
5
6
7
29
2
3
4
1
30
32
34
35
Port Imperial
Lincoln Harbor
Hoboken North
Hoboken South
Newport
Paulus Hook
Liberty Harbor
Port Liberte
Pier 84 44th St
Pier 78 38th St
Pier 63 W 23nd St
Pier 45 W 10th St
World Financial Center
South Street Seaport
Pier 11 Wall St
Fulton Ferry Landing
34th St
Hunters Point
Red Hook
(Weekday Rush Hours Only)
Brooklyn Army Terminal
A
B
Battery Park/Slip 6
Whitehall Terminal
Staten Island
Belford
Atl Highlands
Highlands

Ferries/Boat Tours, Rentals & Charters

Name	*Contact Info*
Staten Island Ferry	311 • www.siferry.com This free ferry travels between Battery Park and Staten Island. On weekdays it leaves every 15–30 minutes 12 am–11:30 pm. On weekends, it leaves every hour 1:30 am–11:30 am and every half-hour at all other times.
NY Waterway	800-53-FERRY • www.nywaterway.com The largest ferry service in NY, NYWaterway offers many commuter routes (mostly from New Jersey), sightseeing tours. They also started a popular East River Ferry service to shuttle folks from 34th Street in Manhattan to Long Island City, Greenpoint, and Williamsburg.
NY Water Taxi	212 742-1969 • www.nywatertaxi.com Available for commuting, sightseeing, charter, and shuttles to Yankees and Mets games. Commuter tickets range between $4.50 and $6 and tours cost $20 to $25. For chartered trips or tours, call for a quote.
Sea Streak	800-BOAT-RIDE • www.seastreakusa.com Catamarans that go pretty fast from the Highlands in NJ to Wall Street and E 34th Street.
Circle Line Sightseeing Cruises	212-269-5755 • www.circleline42.com Circle Line offers many sightseeing tours, including a visit to Ellis Island (departs from Pier 16 at South Street Seaport—$11 for adults, $4.50 for kids)
Circle Line Downtown	www.circlelinedowntown.com Take a tour, ride a speed boat, or use their hop on/off service for many downtown attractions.
Spirit of New York	212-727-7735 • www.spiritcruises.com Offers lunch and dinner cruises. Prices start at $43. Leaves from Pier 62 at Chelsea Piers. Make a reservation at least one week in advance, but the earlier the better.
Loeb Boathouse	212-517-2233 • www.thecentralparkboathouse.com You can rent rowboats from March through October at the Lake in Central Park, open seven days a week, weather permitting. Boat rentals cost $12 for the first hour and $3 for every additional 15 minutes (rentals also require a $30 cash deposit). The boathouse is open 10 am–5 pm, but the last boat goes out at 4:30 pm. Up to four people per boat. No reservations needed.
World Yacht Cruises	212-630-8100 or 800-498-4271 • www.worldyacht.com These fancy, three-hour dinner cruises start at $70.00 per person. The cruises depart from Pier 81 (41st Street) and require reservations. The cruise boards at 6 pm, sails at 7 pm, and returns at 10 pm. There's also a Sunday brunch cruise April -December that costs $50.00 per person.

Marinas/Passenger Ship Terminal

Name	*Contact Info*	*Map*
MarineMax Manhattan	212-336-7873 • www.marinemax.com Dockage at Chelsea Piers. They offer daily, weekly, and seasonal per-foot rates (there's always a waiting list).	8
NY Skyports Inc	212-686-4546 Located on the East River at E 23rd Street. Transient dockage costs $3 per foot.	10
79th St Marina	212-496-2105 This city-operated dock is filled with long-term houseboat residents. It's located at W 79th Street and the Hudson River. Open from May to October.	14
Dyckman Marina	212-496-2105 Transient dockage on the Hudson River at 348 Dyckman Street	25
Manhattan Cruise Terminal	212-246-5450 • www.nycruise.com If *Love Boat* re-runs aren't enough and you decide to go on a cruise yourself, you'll leave from the Manhattan Cruise Terminal. W 55th Street at 12th Avenue. Take the West Side Highway to Piers 88-92.	11
North Cove Yacht Harbor	212-786-1200 • www.thenorthcove.com A very, very fancy place to park your yacht in Battery Park City.	p 184

Helicopter Services

Name	*Contact Info*	*Map*
Helicopter Flight Services	212-355-0801 • www.heliny.com For a minimum of $149, you can hop on a helicopter at the Downtown Manhattan Heliport at Pier 6 on the East River on weekdays or on weekends and spend 15 minutes gazing down on Manhattan. Reservations are recommended, and there's a minimum of two passengers per flight.	3, 8
Liberty Helicopter Tours	212-967-6464 • www.libertyhelicopters.com Leaves from the Downtown Manhattan Heliport at Pier 6 on the East River (9 am–6:30 pm). Prices start at $150, and reservations are needed only when boarding at the Seaport. Flights depart every 5–10 minutes. Minimum of four passengers per flight.	3, 8

General Information

E-ZPass Information:	800-333-TOLL, www.e-zpassny.com
Radio Station Traffic Updates:	1010 WINS on the 1s for a 5 boroughs focus and 880 on the 8s for a suburbs focus
DOT Website:	www.nyc.gov/dot
Real-Time NYC Traffic Cameras:	www.nyc.gov/html/dot/html/motorist/atis.shtml

Driving in Manhattan

Avoid it. Why drive when you can see the city so well on foot or by bus? (We don't count the subway as seeing the city, but rather as a cultural experience in and of itself.) We know that sometimes you just *have* to drive in the city, so we've made you a list of essentials.

- Great auto insurance that doesn't care if the guy who hit you doesn't have insurance and doesn't speak any English.
- Thick skin on driver, passengers, and car. Needed for the fender benders and screamed profanity from the cabbies that are ticked anyone but cabbies are on the road.
- Meditation CD to counteract cardiac arrest–inducing "almost" accidents.
- NFT. But we know you would never leave home without it.
- E-ZPass. Saves time and lives. Maybe not lives, but definitely time and some money.
- New York State license plates. Even pedestrians will curse you out if you represent anywhere other than the Empire State, especially NJ or CT or Texas.
- A tiny car that can fit into a spot slightly larger than a postage stamp or tons of cash for parking garages.
- Patience with pedestrians—they own the streets of New York. Well, co-own them with the cabbies, sanitation trucks, cops, and fire engines.

The following are some tips that we've picked up over the years:

Hudson River Crossings

In the Bridge or Tunnel battle, the Bridge almost always wins. The George Washington Bridge is by far the best Hudson River crossing. It's got more lanes and better access than either tunnel with a fantastic view to boot. If you're going anywhere in the country that's north of central New Jersey, take it. However, inbound traffic on the George can back up for hours in the morning because they don't have enough toll booth operators to handle all those nuts who don't have E-ZPass. The Lincoln Tunnel is decent inbound, but check 1010 AM (WINS) if you have the chance—even though they can be horribly inaccurate and frustrating. Avoid the Lincoln like the plague during evening rush hour (starts at about 3:30 pm). If you have to take the Holland Tunnel outbound, try the Broome Street approach, but don't even bother between 5 and 7 pm on weekdays.

East River Crossings

Brooklyn

Pearl Street to the Brooklyn Bridge is the least-known approach. Only the Williamsburg Bridge has direct access (i.e. no traffic lights) to the northbound BQE in Brooklyn, and only the Brooklyn Bridge has direct access to the FDR Drive in Manhattan. Again, listen to the radio if you can, but all three bridges can be disastrous as they seem to be constantly under construction (or, in a fabulous new twist, having one lane closed by the NYPD to for some unknown (terrorism?) reason). The Williamsburg is by far the best free route into North Brooklyn, but make sure to take the outer roadway to keep your options open in case the BQE is jammed. Your best option to go anywhere else in Brooklyn is usually the Brooklyn-Battery Tunnel, which can be reached from the FDR as well as the West Side Highway. Fun fact: The water you pass was so dirty in the '50s that it used to catch fire. The tunnel is not free, but if you followed our instructions you've got E-ZPass anyway. The bridges from south to north can be remembered as B-M-W, but they are not as cool as the cars hat share the initials.

Queens

There are three options for crossing into Queens by car. The Queens Midtown Tunnel is usually miserable, since it feeds directly onto the parking lot known as the Long Island Expressway. The 59th Street Bridge (known as the Queensboro to mapmakers) is the only free crossing to Queens. The best approach to it is First Avenue to 57th Street (after that, follow the signs) or to 59th Street if you want to jump on the outer roadway that saves a ton of time and only precludes easy access to Northern Boulevard. If you're in Queens and want to go downtown in Manhattan, you can take the lower level of the 59th Street Bridge since it will feed directly onto Second Avenue, which of course goes downtown. The Triborough Bridge (RFK) is usually the best option (especially if you're going to LaGuardia, Shea, Astoria for Greek food, or Flushing for dim sum). The FDR to the Triborough is good except for rush hour—then try Third Avenue to 124th Street.

Harlem River Crossings

The Triborough (RFK) will get you to the Bronx in pretty good shape, especially if you are heading east on the Bruckner towards 95 or the Hutchinson (which will take you to eastern Westchester and Connecticut). To get to Yankee Stadium, take the Willis or the Macomb's Dam (which are both free). When you feel comfortable maneuvering the tight turns approaching the Willis, use it for all travel to Westchester and Connecticut in order to save toll money. The Henry Hudson Bridge will take you up to western Westchester along the Hudson, and, except for the antiquated and completely unnecessary toll plaza, is pretty good. It wins the fast and pretty prize for its beautiful surroundings. The Cross-Bronx Expressway will take years off your life. Avoid it at all costs.

Manhattan's "Highways"

There are two so-called highways in Manhattan—the Harlem River Drive/FDR Drive/East River Drive (which prohibits commercial vehicles) and the Henry Hudson Parkway/West Side Highway/Joe Dimaggio Highway. The main advantage of the FDR is that it has no traffic lights, while the West Side Highway has lights from Battery Park up through 57th Street. The main disadvantages of the FDR are (1) the potholes and (2) the narrow lanes. If there's been a lot of rain, both highways will flood, so you're out of luck (but the FDR floods first). Although the West Side Highway can fly, we would rather look at Brooklyn and Queens than Jersey, so the FDR wins.

Driving Uptown

The 96th Street transverse across Central Park is usually the best one, although if there's been a lot of rain, it will flood. If you're driving on the west side, Riverside Drive is the best route, followed next by West End Avenue. People drive like morons on Broadway, and Columbus jams up in the mid 60s before Lincoln Center and the mid 40s before the Lincoln Tunnel but it's still the best way to get all the way downtown without changing avenues. Amsterdam is a good uptown route if you can get to it. For the east side, you can take Fifth Avenue downtown to about 65th Street, whereupon you should bail out and cut over to Park Avenue for the rest of the trip. Do NOT drive on Fifth Avenue below 65th Street within a month of Christmas, and check the parade schedules before attempting it on weekends throughout the year. The 96th Street entrance to the FDR screws up First and Third Avenues going north and the 59th Street Bridge screws up Lexington and Second Avenues going downtown. Getting stuck in 59th Street Bridge traffic is one of the most frustrating things in the universe because there is absolutely no way out of it.

Driving in Midtown

Good luck! Sometimes Broadway is best because everyone's trying to get out of Manhattan, jamming up the west side (via the Lincoln Tunnel) and the east side (via the 59th Street Bridge and the Queens Midtown Tunnel). Friday nights at 9:30 pm can be a breeze, but from 10 pm to midnight, you're screwed as shows let out. The "interior" of the city is the last place to get jammed up—it's surprisingly quiet at 8 am. At 10 am, however, it's a parking lot. Those who plan to drive in Midtown on weekends from about March–October should check parade schedules for Fifth AND Sixth avenues.

The demarcation of several "THRU Streets" running east-west in Midtown has been with the city for a couple of years and folks are finally getting the hang of it. Still, it may screw you up. See the next page for more information.

Driving in the Village

People get confused walking in the village, so you can imagine how challenging driving can be in the maze of one ways and short streets. Beware. If you're coming into the Village from the northwest, 14th Street is the safest crosstown route heading east. However, going west, take 13th Street. Houston Street is under construction at a number of points along its length but it has the great benefit of direct access to FDR Drive, both getting onto it and coming off of it. If you want to get to Houston Street from the Holland Tunnel, take Hudson Street to King Street to the Avenue of the Americas to Houston Street (this is the **only** efficient way to get to the Village from the Holland Tunnel). First Avenue is good going north and Fifth Avenue is good going south. Washington Street is the only way to make any headway southbound and Hudson Street is the only way to make any headway northbound in the West Village.

Driving Downtown

Don't do it unless you have to. Western TriBeCa is okay and so is the Lower East Side—try not to "turn in" to SoHo, Chinatown, or the Civic Center. Canal Street is a complete mess during the day (avoid it), since on its western end, everyone is trying to get to the Holland Tunnel, and on its eastern end, everyone is mistakenly driving over the Manhattan Bridge (your only other option when heading east on Canal is to turn **right** on Bowery!). Watch the potholes! Chatham Square (the confluence of Bowery, Catherine, East Broadway, Oliver, St. James, Park Row, Worth, and Mott) is due for another major "reorg" starting summer 2009; that should be fun, no?

DMV Locations in Manhattan

If you're going to the DMV to get your first NY license (including drivers with other states' licenses), you'll need extensive documentation of your identity. The offices have a long list of accepted documents, but your best bet is a US passport and a Social Security card. If you don't have these things, birth certificates from the US, foreign passports, and various INS documents will be okay under certain conditions. Do not be surprised if you are turned away the first time. This trip requires great amounts of patience. Plan on spending three to six hours here. We're not kidding. This is not a lunch-hour errand.

Greenwich Street Office
11 Greenwich St
New York, NY 10004
(Cross Streets Battery Park Pl & Morris St)
M–F 8:30 am–4 pm
212-645-5550 or 718-966-6155

Harlem Office
159 E 125th St, 3rd Fl
New York, NY 10035
(Lexington and Third)
M, T, W & F 8:30 am–4 pm, Thursday 10 am–6 pm
212-645-5550 or 718-966-6155

Herald Square Office
1293-1311 Broadway, 8th Fl
New York, NY 10001
(Between W 33 & W 34th Sts)
* To exchange an out-of-state license for a New York license, you must go to License X-Press.
M–F 8:30 am–4 pm
212-645-5550 or 718-966-6155

Manhattan
License X-Press Office*
300 W 34th St
New York, NY 10001
(Between Eighth & Ninth aves)
*Service limited to license and registration renewals and out-of-state exchange. You can't get your snowmobile or boat license here, but you can surrender your license plate. Oh, and no permit renewals.
M–F 8:30 am–4 pm
212-645-5550 or 718-966-6155

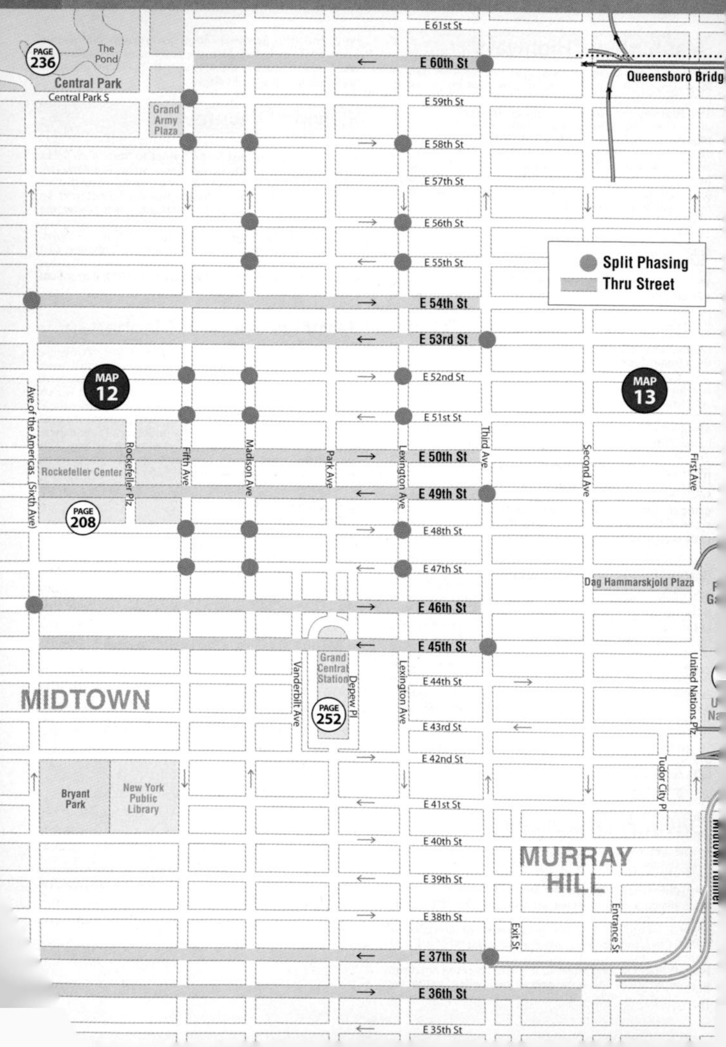

PAGE 236
The Pond
Central Park
Central Park S
Grand Army Plaza
E 61st St
E 60th St
Queensboro Bridg
E 59th St
E 58th St
E 57th St
E 56th St
E 55th St
Split Phasing
Thru Street
E 54th St
E 53rd St
MAP 12
E 52nd St
MAP 13
E 51st St
Ave of the Americas (Sixth Ave)
Rockefeller Plz
Fifth Ave
Madison Ave
Park Ave
Lexington Ave
Third Ave
Second Ave
First Ave
E 50th St
Rockefeller Center
E 49th St
PAGE 208
E 48th St
E 47th St
Dag Hammarskjold Plaza
E 46th St
E 45th St
Grand Central Station
Vanderbilt Ave
Depew Pl
E 44th St
United Nations Plz
MIDTOWN
PAGE 252
E 43rd St
E 42nd St
Tudor City Pl
Bryant Park
New York Public Library
E 41st St
E 40th St
MURRAY HILL
E 39th St
E 38th St
Exit St
Entrance St
E 37th St
E 36th St
E 35th St

General Information

NFT Maps: 12 & 13
DOT Website: www.nyc.gov/html/dot/html/motorist/streetprog.shtml
DOT Phone: 311

Overview

In the tradition of "don't block the box" and other traffic solutions (such as randomly arresting political protesters), the city introduced "THRU Streets," a program initially tested in 2002, as a permanent fixture in Midtown in 2004. The plan was implemented on some crosstown streets in Midtown in order to reduce travel times, relieve congestion, and provide a safer environment for pedestrians and cyclists. They are still working on clearing up the exhaust fume issue, for those concerned about said environment.

On certain streets, cars are not allowed to make turns between Sixth and Third Avenues (with the exception of Park Avenue). The regulations are in effect between 10 am and 6 pm on weekdays. The affected streets are:

36th & 37th Streets
45th & 46th Streets
49th & 50th Streets
53rd & 54th Streets
60th Street (between Third and Fifth Avenues)

The good news is that turns from 59th Street are permitted. Oh joy.

The above streets are easily identifiable by big, purple "THRU Streets" signs. With everything that's going on in midtown Manhattan though, you'd be forgiven for missing a sign (by us, not by the NYPD). If you happen to unwittingly find yourself on a THRU Street and can't escape on Park Avenue, you're going to have to suck it up until you get to Sixth Avenue or Third Avenue, depending on the direction you're heading. If you attempt to turn before the designated avenue, you'll find yourself with an insanely expensive ticket. Of course, if you're trying to drive crosstown, it's in your best interests to take one of these streets.

Both sides of almost every non-THRU Street in this grid have been stuck with "No Standing Except Trucks Loading and Unloading" regulations, supposedly creating up to 150 spaces for truck loading (if you were ever stuck behind a truck in morning rush hour on a THRU Street in 2004, you would rejoice at this news). Additionally, one side of each non-THRU street has been "daylighted" for 80–100 feet in advance of the intersection. We are not exactly sure how they came up with the term "daylighted," but the DOT tells us it allows space for turning vehicles

According to the DOT, THRU Streets are working—since the program began, travel times have fallen by 25% (as people have decided to emigrate to New Zealand) and vehicle speeds have increased by an average of 33% (from 4 mph to 5.3 mph). The THRU Streets combined now carry 4,854 vehicles per hour (up from 4,187), which means that each of the THRU Streets accommodates an average of 74 additional vehicles per hour.

Split Signal Phasing

Another traffic innovation in Midtown is "split signal phasing," which allows pedestrians to cross the street without having to worry about vehicles turning in their path at about 40 non-THRU Street intersections in this same grid. Of course, this system assumes that both pedestrians and drivers follow the rules of the road. In spite of the disregard that most New Yorkers display for crossing signals, the number of pedestrian accidents in the eight-month trial period (compared to the eight months prior to implementation) fell from 81 to 74. The number of cycling accidents fell from 30 to 17. Accidents not related to pedestrians or bikes fell from 168 to 102. We don't know if this accounts for accidents caused by drivers who became confused by the pretty purple signs. We have to admit that something must be working—though there would be no accidents if no one ever left their house…

Now if the DOT and NYPD could get traffic to flow smoothly onto bridges and into tunnels, they might actually be onto something. They can save you 1.5 minutes getting crosstown, just don't try leaving the city. Ever.

Information

Department of Transportation (DOT): 311 (24 hours) or 212-NEW-YORK (Out-of-state)
TTY Hearing-Impaired: 212-504-4115
Website: www.nyc.gov/dot
Parking Violations Help Line: 311
TTY Automated Information for the Hearing Impaired: 718-802-8555
Website: www.nyc.gov/html/dof/html/parking/parking.shtml

Standing, Stopping and Parking Rules

In "No Stopping" areas, you **can't** wait in your car, drop off passengers, or load/unload.

In "No Standing" areas, you **can't** wait in your car or load/unload, but you **can** drop off passengers.

In "No Parking" areas, you **can't** wait in your car or drop off passengers, but you **can** load/unload.

NYC has just enacted a "no idling" law. That means, when you're doing one of the three illegal things mentioned above, shut your car off, so at least you only get one ticket, not two!

Parking Meter Zones

On holidays when street cleaning rules are suspended (see calendar), the "no parking" cleaning regulations for metered parking are also suspended. You can park in these spots but have to pay the meters. Also, metered spots are still subject to rules not suspended on holidays (see below). On MLH (major legal holidays), meter rules are suspended (so no need to feed the meter).

Meters

At a broken meter, parking is allowed only up to one hour. Where a meter is missing, parking is still allowed for the maximum time on the posted sign (an hour for a one-hour meter, two hours for a two-hour meter, etc.).

Instead of old-fashioned individual meters, muni-meters have spread like a virus throughout NYC. The machines let you purchase time-stamped slips which you stick in your windshield to show you paid. These machines accept coins, parking cards, and some (we wish it was all!) accept credit cards (for example, the machines in the theater district). In the case of a non-functional muni-meter, the one-hour time limit applies.

The DOT sells parking cards that come in $20, $50, and $100 denominations and can be used in muni-meters, municipal parking lots, and some single-space meters (look for a yellow decal). The cards can be purchased through the DOT website (www.nyc.gov/html/dot/home.html), by calling 311 (or 212-NEW-YORK if you're calling from outside the city), or by going to the Staten Island Ferry Terminal or one of the two City Stores.

As of spring 2006, you don't have to pay meters on Sunday, even if the signs say you do (unless the law changes again with the political winds).

Signs

New York City Traffic Rules state that one parking sign per block is sufficient notification. Check the entire block and read all signs carefully before you park. Then read them again.

If there is more than one sign posted for the same area, the more restrictive sign takes effect (of course). If a sign is missing on a block, the remaining posted regulations are the ones in effect.

The Blue Zone

The Blue Zone is a "No Parking" (Mon–Fri, 7 am–7 pm) area in Lower Manhattan. Its perimeter has been designated with blue paint; however, there are no individual "Blue Zone" signs posted. Any other signs posted in that area supersede Blue Zone regulations. Confused yet?

General

- All of NYC was designated a Tow Away Zone under the State's Vehicle & Traffic Law and the NYC Traffic Rules. This means that any vehicle parked or operated illegally, or with missing or expired registration or inspection stickers, may, and probably will, be towed.
- On major legal holidays, stopping, standing, and parking are permitted except in areas where stopping, standing, and parking rules are in effect seven days a week (for example, "No Standing Anytime").
- It is illegal to park in a spot where SCR are in effect, even if the street cleaner has already passed. If you sit in your car, the metermaid will usually let you stay
- Double-parking of passenger vehicles is illegal at all times, including street-cleaning days, regardless of location, purpose, or duration. Everyone, of course, does this anyway. If everyone is double parked on a certain block during street cleaning, the NYPD probably is not ticketing. However, leave your phone number in the window in case the person you blocked in feels vindictive and demand that a cop write you a ticket.
- It is illegal to park within 15 feet of either side of a fire hydrant. The painted curbs at hydrant locations do not indicate where you can park. Isn't New York great? Metermaids will tell you that each cement block on the sidewalk is five feet, so make sure you are three cement blocks from the hydrant (2.5 will not do).

If you think you're parked legally in Manhattan, you're probably not, so go and read the signs again. Cops will now just write you parking tickets and mail them to you if you are parked in a bus stop, so you won't even know it's happening unless you're very alert.

There is now clearly an all-out effort to harass everyone who is insane enough to drive and/or park during the day in downtown Manhattan. Beware.

Tow Pounds

Manhattan
Pier 76 at W 38th St & Twelfth Ave
open 24 hours: Monday 7 am–Monday 5 am
212-971-0771 or 212-971-0772

Bronx
745 E 141st St b/w Bruckner Expy & East River
Open Monday-Friday: 8 am-10 pm, Saturday: 8 am-3 pm,
Sunday: Closed
718-585-1385 or 718-585-1391

Brooklyn
Brooklyn Navy Yard; corner of Sands St & Navy St
Open Monday-Friday 8 am-10 pm, Saturday 8 am-3 pm, and on the second Sunday of each month from 11 am-6 pm. 718-694-0696

Queens
Under the Kosciusko Bridge at 56th Rd & Laurel Hill Blvd
Open Monday-Friday from 8 am-10 pm, Saturday from 8 am-3 pm, and closed on Sunday; 718-786-7122, 718-786-7123, or 718-786-7136

Find out if your car was towed (and not stolen or disintegrated): 718-422-7800 or 718-802-3555 (TTY)

http://nycserv.nyc.gov/NYCServWeb/NYCSERVMain

Once you've discovered that your car has indeed been towed, your next challenge is to find out which borough it's been towed to. This depends on who exactly towed your car—the DOT, the Marshal, etc. Don't assume that since your car was parked in Manhattan that they will tow it to Manhattan—always call first.

So you've located your car, now come the particulars: If you own said towed car, you're required to present your license, registration, insurance, and payment of your fine before you can collect the impounded vehicle. If you are not the owner of the car, you can usually get it back with all of the above, if your last name matches the registration (i.e. the car belongs to a relative or spouse); otherwise, you'll need a notarized letter with the owner's signature authorizing you to take the car. The tow fee is $185, plus a $70 execution fee, plus $10–$15 for each day it's in the pound. If they've put a boot on it instead, it's still $185. You can pay with cash or debit card; if you own the car, you can also pay by credit card or certified check. We recommend bringing a wad of cash and a long Russian novel for this experience.

General Information

In New York State	call 511
All inquiries (24/7)	say "Long Island Rail Road"
From Outside New York State:	877-690-5116
International Callers:	212-878-7000
Schedule Information (24/7)	Say "Schedules"
Fare Information (24/7)	Say "Fares"
Mail & Ride (M-F, 7:30 am-5 pm)	Say "Mail and Ride"
Group Travel and Getaways (M-F, 8 am-4 pm)	Say "Group Travel"
Lost & Found (M-F, 6 am-10 pm)	Say "Lost & Found"
Refunds (M-F, 8 am-4 pm)	Say "More Options" then "Ticket Refunds"
Ticket Machine Assistance (M-F, 6:30 am-3:30 pm)	Say "More Options" then "Ticket Machines"
Hamptons Reserve Service (May-Sept)	Say "More Options" then "Hamptons Reserve"
MTA Police:	212-878-1001
Website:	www.mta.info/lirr

Overview

The Long Island Railroad is the busiest railroad in North America. It has eleven lines with 124 stations stretching from Penn Station in midtown Manhattan, to the eastern tip of Long Island, Montauk Point. An estimated 81 million people ride the LIRR every year. If you enjoy traveling on overcrowded trains with intermittent air-conditioning, then the LIRR is for you. If you are going anywhere on Long Island and you don't have a car, the LIRR is your best bet. Don't be surprised if the feeling of being in a seedy bar creeps over you during evening rush—those middle-aged business men like their beer en route. Despite a recent movement to ban the sale of alcohol on LIRR station platforms and trains, for now, it's still legal to get your buzz on.

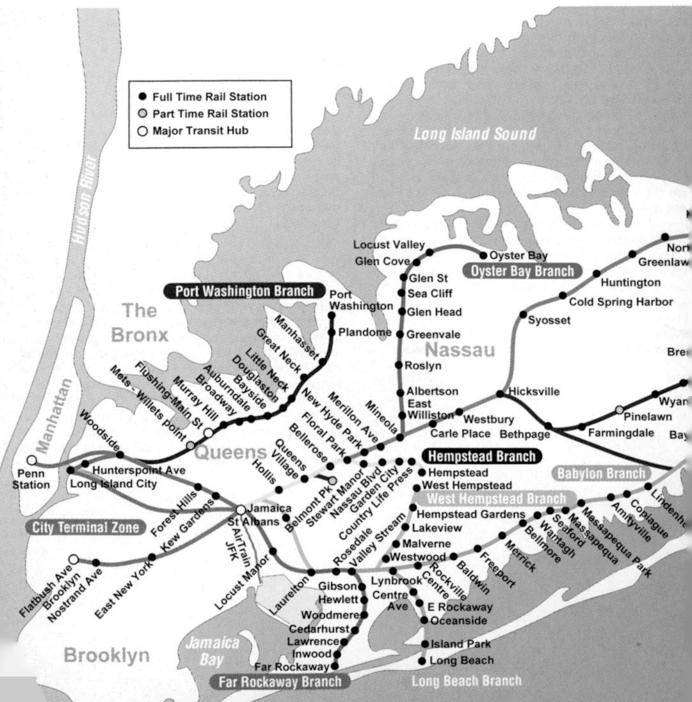

If you're not a regular LIRR user, you might find yourself taking the train to Shea Stadium for a Mets game (Port Washington Branch), Long Beach for some summer surfing (Long Beach Branch), or to Jamaica to transfer to the AirTrain to JFK (tip– the subway is cheaper). For the truly adventurous, take the LIRR all the way out to the Hamptons beach house you are visiting for the weekend (Hamptons Reserve seating is available during the summer for passengers taking 6 or more trips). Bring a book as it is a long ride.

Fares and Schedules

Fares and schedules can be obtained by calling one of the general information lines, depending on your area. They can also be found on the LIRR website. Make sure to buy your ticket before you get on the train at a ticket window or at one of the ticket vending machines in the station. Otherwise it'll cost you an extra $6 to $5.75 to $6.50 depending on your destination. As it is a commuter railroad, the LIRR offers weekly and monthly passes, as well as ten-trip packages for on- or off-peak hours. The LIRR's CityTicket program offers discounted one-way tickets for $3.75

Pets on the LIRR

Trained service animals accompanying passengers with disabilities are permitted on LIRR trains. Other small pets are allowed on trains, but they must be confined to closed, ventilated containers.

Bikes on the LIRR

You need a permit ($5) to take your bicycle onto the Long Island Railroad. Pick one up at a ticket window or online at the LIRR website.

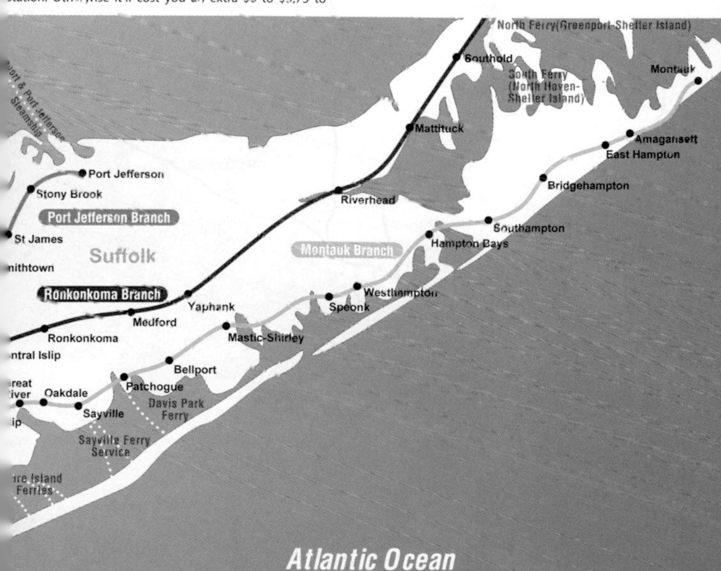

Transit • Metro-North Railroad

General Information

In New York State	call 511
All inquiries	say "Metro-North Railroad"
From Connecticut:	877-690-5114
From Outside New York State:	877-690-5116
International Callers:	212-878-7000
Schedule Information (24/7)	Say "Schedules"
Fare Information (24/7)	Say "Fares"
Mail & Ride (M-F, 6:30 am-5 pm)	Say "More Options" then "Mail and Ride"
Group Sales (M-F, 8:30 am-5 pm)	Say "More Options" then "Group Sales"
Lost & Found (M-F, 6 am-10 pm)	Say "More Options" then "Lost & Found"
Ticket Machine Assistance (24/7)	Say "More Options" then "Ticket Machines"
MTA Police:	212-878-1001
Website:	www.mta.info/mnr

Overview

Metro-North is an extremely accessible and efficient railroad with three of its main lines (Hudson, Harlem, and New Haven) originating in Grand Central Station in Manhattan (42nd St & Park Ave). Those three lines east of the Hudson River, along with two lines west of the Hudson River that operate out of Hoboken, NJ (not shown on map), form the second-largest commuter railroad system in the US. Approximately 250,000 commuters use the tri-state Metro-North service each day for travel between New Jersey, New York, and Connecticut. Metro-North rail lines cover roughly 2,700 square miles of territory. The best thing about Metro-North is that it lands you at Grand Central Station, one of the city's finest pieces of architecture. On weekdays, sneak into the land of platforms via the North Passage, accessible at 47th & 48th Streets. At least for now, it's still legal to have an after work drink on Metro-North. During happy hour (starting somewhere around 3 pm), hit the bar car or buy your booze in advance on the platform at Grand Central. It might make you feel better about being a wage slave. But beware of having too happy of an hour as the bathrooms can be stinky and not all cars have them.

Fares and Schedules

Fare information is available on Metro-North's extraordinarily detailed website (along with in-depth information on each station, full timetables, and excellent maps) or at Grand Central Station. The cost of a ticket to ride varies depending on your destination so you should probably check the website before setting out. Buy advance tickets on MTA's WebTicket site for the cheapest fares. If you wait until you're on the train to pay, it'll cost you an extra $4.75–$5.50. Monthly and weekly rail passes are also available for commuters. Daily commuters save [illegible]% on fares when they purchase a monthly travel pass.

Hours

Train frequency depends on your destination and the time of day that you're traveling. On weekdays, peak-period trains east of the Hudson River run every 20–30 minutes; off-peak trains run every 30–60 minutes; and weekend trains run hourly. Hours of operation are approximately 5 am to 3 am. Don't miss the last train out as they leave on time and wait for no one.

Bikes on Board

If you're planning on taking your two wheeler onboard, you'll need to apply for a bicycle permit first. An application form can be found on the Metro-North website at http://mta.info/mnr/html/mnrbikepermit.htm. The $5 permit fee and application can either be mailed into the MTA, or processed right away at window 27 at Grand Central Terminal.

Common sense rules for taking bikes on board include: no bikes on escalators, no riding on the platform, and board the train after other passengers have boarded. Unfortunately there are restrictions on bicycles during peak travel times. Bicycles are not allowed on trains departing from Grand Central Terminal 7 am–9 am and 3:01 pm–8:15 pm. Bikes are not permitted on trains arriving at Grand Central 5 am–10 am and 4 pm–8 pm. Don't even think about taking your bike with you on New Year's Eve, New Year's Day, St. Patrick's Day, Mother's Day, eve of Rosh Hashanah, eve of Yom Kippur, eve of Thanksgiving, Thanksgiving Day, Christmas Eve, or Christmas Day—they're not allowed. The Friday before any long weekend is also a no-no. There's a limit of two bikes per carriage, and four bikes per train at all times. Unfortunately, the same restrictions are not imposed on passengers with 4 Vera Bradley overnight bags heading off to the country house, but that is another story.

Riders of folding bikes do not require a permit and do not have to comply with the above rules, provided that the bike is folded at all times at stations and on trains.

Pets

Only seeing-eye dogs and small pets, if restrained or confined, are allowed aboard the trains.

One-Day Getaways

Metro-North offers "One-Day Getaway" packages on its website. Packages include reduced rail fare and discounted entry to destinations along MNR lines including Bruce Museum $18.25, Dia:Beacon $33.50, Hudson River Museum/Andrus Planetarium $14.50, Maritime Aquarium at Norwalk $31.25, Mohegan Sun Casino $48.75, New York Botanical Garden ($18.00), and Wave Hill ($17.50). Tickets are available at Metro-North ticket offices or full service ticket vending machines. The website also suggests one-day hiking and biking excursions.

Transit • PATH & Light Rail

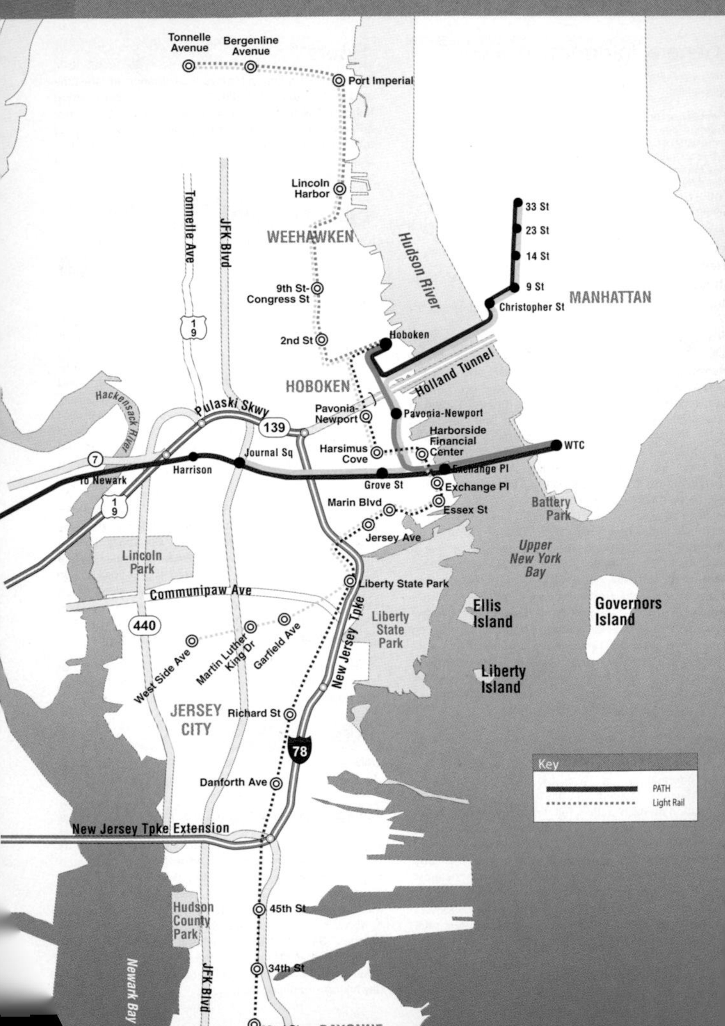

PATH Train

General Information

Website:	www.panynj.gov/path
Phone:	800-234-7284
Police/Lost & Found:	201-216-6078

Overview

The PATH (Port Authority Trans-Hudson Corp.) is an excellent small rail system that services Newark, Jersey City, Hoboken, and Manhattan. There are a few basic lines that run directly between 33rd Street (Herald Square) in Manhattan & Hoboken, 33rd Street & Jersey City, and Newark & the WTC. Transfers between the lines are available at most stations. The PATH can be quite useful for commuters on the west side of Manhattan when the subway isn't running, say, due to a sick passenger or mysterious police investigation. Additionally, you can catch the PATH to Newark and then either jump in a cheap cab or take New Jersey Transit one stop to Newark Airport. It's a more economical option than taking a car all the way in from Manhattan, and you can take it back to the Village late at night when you've finished seeing a show at Maxwell's in Hoboken.

Check the front or the sides of incoming trains to determine their destination. Don't be fooled by the TV screens installed at stations; they occasionally announce the time of the next arrival, but as their main purpose is low-quality advertising, they are often incorrect. Also, don't assume that if a Journal Square train just passed through, the next train is going to Hoboken. Often there will be two Journal Square trains in a row, followed by two Hoboken trains. During the weekend, PATH service can be excruciatingly slow and confusing, and is best only endeavored with a seasoned rider.

Fares

The PATH costs $2.25 one-way. Regular riders can purchase 10-trip, 20-trip, and 40-trip SmartLink cards, which reduce the fare per journey to $1.70. The fare for seniors (65+) is $1 per ride. You can also use pay-per-ride MTA MetroCards for easy transition between the PATH and subway.

Hours

The PATH runs 24/7 (although a modified service operates between 11pm–6am, M–F, and 7:30pm–9am, S, S, & H). Daytime service is pretty consistent, but the night schedule for the PATH is a bit confusing, so make sure to look at the map. You may be waiting underground for up to a half an hour. During off hours the train runs on the same track through the tunnel. This allows for maintenance to be completed on the unused track.

Hudson-Bergen Light Rail

General Information

Website:	http://www.mylightrail.com/
Phone:	800-772-2222

Overview

Even though it's called the Hudson-Bergen Light Rail system (HBLR, operated by NJ Transit), it actually only serves Hudson county. Bergen County residents are still waiting for their long promised connection. The HBLR has brought about some exciting changes (a.k.a. "gentrification") in Jersey City, though Bayonne remains (for the moment) totally, well…Bayonne. Currently there are 24 stops in the system, including service to Jersey City, Hoboken, Weehawken, and Union City

Fares

The Light Rail is $2.10 per trip; reduced fare is $1.05. Ten-trip tickets are $21, monthly passes cost $64. Unless you have a monthly pass, you need to validate your ticket before boarding at a Ticket Validating Machine (TVM). Once validated, tickets are only valid for 90 minutes, so don't buy too far in advance. The trains and stations have random fare inspection and the fine for fare evasion is $100.

Hours

Light rail service operates between 5 am and 1:30 am. Times are approximate, check the website for exact schedules on each line.

Bikes on Board

Bikes are allowed (no permit or fee required) on board during off-peak times—weekdays from 9:30 am to 4 pm and 7 pm to 6 am, and all day Saturday, Sunday, and NJ state holidays. Bicycles have to be accompanied on the low-floor vestibule section of each rail car.

Pets

Small pets are allowed, as long as they're confined to a carry container. Service animals are permitted at all times.

Station
Under Contruction Station
Port Jervis Line
Main Line & Bergen County Line
Pascack Valley Line
Montclair-Boonton Line
Morris and Essex Lines
Raritan Valley Line
Northeast Corridor Line
Princeton Branch
North Jersey Coast Line
PENNSYLVANIA
NEW YORK
NEW JERSEY
Orange
Rockland
Sussex
Passaic
Warren
Morris
Essex
Union
Hudson
HACKENSACK
Staten Island
Hunterdon
Somerset
Middlesex
Monmouth
Bucks
Burlington
Ocean
Atlantic Ocean
Otisville
Middletown
Campbell Hall
Salisbury Mills - Cornwall
Port Jervis
Harriman
Tuxedo
Sloatsburg
Suffern
Spring Valley
Nanuet
Mahwah
Ramsey Route 17
Ramsey
Pearl River
Montvale
Allendale
Park Ridge
Waldwick
Woodcliff Lake
Ho-Ho-Kus
Hillsdale
Ridgewood
Westwood
Glen Rock-Main Line
Glen Rock-Boro Hall
Emerson
Hawthorne
Radburn-Fair Lawn
Oradell
Paterson
River Edge
Broadway-Fair Lawn
Anderson St
Garfield
Essex St
Clifton
Passaic
Delawanna
Lyndhurst
Kingsland
Rutherford
Wood-Ridge
Meadowlands Sports Complex
Secaucus Junction
New York Penn Sta
Hoboken
Hackettstown
Mt Olive
Netcong
Lake Hopatcong
Mount Arlington
Dover
Denville
Boonton
Mountain Lakes
Towaco
Lincoln Park
Mtn View-Wayne
Little Falls
Great Notch
Montclair State Univ
Montclair Heights
Mountain Ave
Upper Montclair
Watchung Ave
Walnut St
Bay St
Glen Ridge
Bloomfield
Watsessing
Mt Tabor
Morris Plains
Morristown
Convent
Madison
Chatham
Highland Ave
Mountain Station
South Orange
Orange
Brick Church
East Orange
Newark Broad St
Gladstone
Peapack
Bernardsville
Far Hills
Basking Ridge
Lyons
New Providence
Murray Hill
Summit
Short Hills
Millburn
Maplewood
Millington
Stirling
Gillette
Berkeley Heights
Newark Penn Station
Newark Liberty International Airport
Union
North Elizabeth
Elizabeth
Roselle Park
Cranford
Garwood
Westfield
Fanwood
Netherwood
Plainfield
Dunellen
Linden
Rahway
Avenel
Woodbridge
Metropark
Metuchen
Edison
Perth Amboy
South Amboy
High Bridge
Annandale
Lebanon
White House
North Branch
Raritan
Somerville
Bridgewater
Bound Brook
New Brunswick
Jersey Ave
Aberdeen-Matawan
Hazlet
Middletown
Red Bank
Little Silver
Monmouth Park (seasonal service)
Long
Belmar
Manasquan
Princeton
Princeton Junction
Hamilton
Trenton

General Information

Address:	1 Penn Plz E Newark, NJ 07105
Phone:	973-275-5555 or 800-772-2222
Website:	www.njtransit.com
Quik-Tik (monthly passes):	866-QUIK-TIK
Emergency Hotline:	973-378-6565
Newark Lost and Found:	973-491-8792
Hoboken Lost and Found:	201-714-2739
New York Lost and Found:	212-630-7389
AirTrain:	973-961-6230
Atlantic City Terminal:	609-343-7174

Overview

The trains are usually clean (and immune to the weirdness that plagues the LIRR), but some lines (*like* the Pascack Valley Line) seem to just creep along, which can be problematic when you're trying to make a transfer before reaching the Big Apple. But with many new stations, including the renovated transfer station at Secaucus, and an expanded Light Rail system (see PATH page), NJ Transit is staying competitive with all other modes of transportation into and out of the city. NJ Transit also runs an AirTrain to Newark Airport. As the rails have been prone to power loss and broken switches lately, NJ Transit won't be competing with Japanese rail systems any time soon, but riding their rails generally beats waiting in traffic at the three measly Hudson River automobile crossings. NJ Transit also offers bus lines to Hoboken and Newark for areas not served by train lines. The newest station is the Meadowlands stop on the Pascack Valley line. You'll be able to get off right at the stadium for the big game or to check out American Dream Meadowlands (formerly known as Xanadu, no joke!), a giant entertainment complex.

Secaucus Junction Station

The three-level train hub at Secaucus is celebrating its fifth birthday! The station cost around $450 million and took 14 years to complete. The building is dedicated to Democratic New Jersey Senator Frank R. Lautenberg, who was responsible for securing the federal funds necessary for construction. The former Secaucus Junction Station is now officially known as the Frank R. Lautenberg Station at Secaucus Junction (which, if you want to get technical, is not actually a junction). We're certain that most commuters will adopt this name whenever referring to the station, or maybe they'll just call it "Secaucus."

For riders, the biggest advantage of the new station is that they no longer have to travel out to Hoboken to get to Penn Station. (Secaucus is just an 8-minute ride from Penn Station.) The Secaucus hub connects ten of NJ Transit's 11 rail lines, and also offers service to Newark Airport, downtown Newark, Trenton, and the Jersey Shore.

Fares and Schedules

Fares and schedules can be obtained at Hoboken, Newark, Penn Station, on NJ Transit's website, or by calling NJ Transit. If you wait to pay until you're on the train, you'll pay an extra five bucks for the privilege. NJ Transit also offers discounted monthly, weekly, weekend, and ten-trip tickets for regular commuters.

Pets

Only seeing-eye dogs and small pets in carry-on containers are allowed aboard the trains and buses.

Bikes

You can take your bicycle onboard a NJ Transit train only during off-peak hours (weekdays from 9:30 am–4 pm, and from 7 pm–5 am) and during all hours on the weekends. Bikes are not allowed on board most holidays, or the Fridays prior to any holiday weekend; however, a folding frame bicycle can be taken onboard at any time. Most NJ Transit buses participate in the "Rack 'n' Roll" program, which allows you to load your bike right on to the front of the bus.

Overview

Phone: 800-USA-RAIL
Website: www.amtrak.com

General Information

Amtrak is our national train system, and while it's not particularly punctual or affordable, it *will* take you to many major northeastern cities in half a day or less. Spending a few hours on Amtrak also makes you want to move to Europe where France is now running trains at 357 mph (as opposed to 35 mph in the US). But if you plan a trip at the last minute and miss the requisite advance on buying airline tickets or want to bring liquids with you with checking baggage, you might want to shop Amtrak's fares. Bonus: Amtrak allows you to talk on cell phones in most cars and has plugs for laptop computers at your seat.

Amtrak was created by the federal government in 1971. Today, Amtrak services 500+ stations in 46 states (Alaska, Hawaii, South Dakota, and Wyoming sadly do not have the pleasure of being serviced by Amtrak). While not being as advanced as the Eurail system, Amtrak serves over 24 million passengers a year, employs 19,000 people, still has the same décor it did in the early 1970s, and provides "contract-commuter services" for several state and regional rail lines.

Red Caps (station agents) are very helpful, especially for passengers traveling with children and strollers. The only problem is finding an available one!

Amtrak in New York

In New York City, Amtrak runs out of Pennsylvania Station, an eyesore currently located underneath Madison Square Garden. We treat the station like our annoying little brother, calling it Penn for short and avoiding it when we can. But don't despair—chances are the city you'll wind up in will have a very nice station, and, if all goes well, so will we, once the front half of the Farley Post Office is converted to a "new" Penn Station. Warning: If you hop in a cab to get to Amtrak, specify that you want to be dropped off at Eighth Avenue and 33rd Street in order to avoid LIRR and Madison Square Garden foot traffic. Don't let the cabbie argue with you, especially if you have luggage. He is just trying to make his life easier.

Popular Destinations

Many New Yorkers use Amtrak to get to Boston, Philadelphia, or Washington DC. Of course, these are the New Yorkers who are traveling on an expense account or fear the Chinatown bus service. Amtrak also runs a line up to Montreal and through western New York state (making stops in Buffalo, Rochester, Albany, etc.) Check Amtrak's website for a complete listing of all Amtrak stations.

Going to Boston

Amtrak usually runs 18 trains daily to Boston. One-way fares cost $59–$101, and the trip, which ends at South Station in downtown Boston, takes about four-and-a-half hours door-to-door. For $117 one-way, you can ride the high speed Acela ("acceleration" and "excellence" combined into one word, though perhaps "expensive" would have been more appropriate) and complete the journey in three to three-and-a-half hours—if there are not track problems.

Going to Philadelphia

About 40 Amtrak trains pass through Philadelphia every day. One-way tickets cost about $45–$60 on a regular Amtrak train; if you're really in a hurry, you can take the special "Metroliner" service for $87, which will get you there in an hour and fifteen minutes, or the Acela for $81, which takes about one hour from station to station. The cheapest rail option to Philly is actually to take NJ Transit to Trenton and then hook up with Eastern Pennsylvania's excellent SEPTA service—this will take longer, but will cost you under $25. Some commuters take this EVERY day. Thank your lucky stars you're probably not one of them.

Going to Washington DC

(Subtitle: *How Much is Your Time Worth?*)
Amtrak runs over 40 trains daily to DC and the prices vary dramatically. The cheapest trains cost $69 one-way and take just under four hours. The Acela service costs more than double at $125-$146 one-way, and delivers you to our nation's capital in less than three hours (sometimes). Worth it? Only you can say. Depending on what time of day you travel, you may be better off taking the cheaper train when the Acela will only save you 30 minutes.

A Note About Fares

While the prices quoted above for Boston, Philly, and DC destinations tend to remain fairly consistent, fare rates to other destinations, such as Cleveland, Chicago, etc can vary depending on how far in advance you book your seat. For "rail sales" and other discounts, check www.amtrak.com. Military IDs will save you a bundle, so use them if you have them. Occasionally (or rarely), Amtrak offers discounts that can be found on their website under "Hot Deals."

Baggage Check (Amtrak Passengers)

A maximum of three items may be checked up to thirty minutes before departure. Up to three additional bags may be checked for a fee of $10 (two carry-on items allowed). No electronic equipment, plastic bags, or paper bags may be checked. See the "Amtrak Policies" section of their website for details.

General Information

NFT Map:	9
Address:	Seventh Ave & 33rd St
General Information (Amtrak):	800-872-7245
MTA Subway Stops:	1 2 3 A C E
MTA Bus Lines:	4 10 16 34
Train Lines:	LIRR, Amtrak, NJ Transit
LaGuardia Airport Bus Service:	NY Airport Service, 212-875-8200, $12
JFK Airport Bus Service:	NY Airport Service, 212-875-8200, $15
Passengers per day:	600,000

Overview

Penn Station, designed by McKim, Mead & White (New York's greatest architects), is a Beaux-Arts treasure, filled with light and… oh wait, that's the one that was torn down. Penn Station is essentially a basement, complete with well-weathered leather chairs, unidentifiable dust particles, and high-cholesterol snack food. Its claim to fame is that it is the busiest Amtrak station in the country. If the government gods are with us, the plan to convert the eastern half of the Farley Post Office (also designed by McKim, Mead & White) next door to an above-ground, light-filled station will come to fruition. With bureaucracy at hand, we aren't holding our collective breath. Until then, Penn Station will go on servicing 600,000 people per day in the rat's maze under Madison Square Garden.

Penn Station services Amtrak, the LIRR, and NJ Transit trains. Amtrak, which is surely the worst national train system of any first-world country, administers the station. How is it that the Europeans have bullet trains and it still takes 3 or more hours to get from NYC to DC? While we're hoping the new station proposal will come through, will it help the crazed LIRR commuters struggling to squish down stairwells to catch the 6:05 to Ronkonkoma? We can only hope.

Dieters traveling through Penn Station should pre-pack snacks. The fast food joints are just too tempting. Donuts and ice cream and KFC, oh my! Leave yourself time to pick up some magazines and a bottle of water for your train trip. It may turn out to be longer than you think.

The plus side to Penn is that it's easy to get to from just about anywhere in the city via subway or bus. If you are just too ritzy to take the MTA (or you have an abundance of baggage), have your cab driver drop you off anywhere surrounding the station except for Seventh Avenue—it is constantly jammed with tour buses and cabs trying to drop off desperately late passengers.

Terminal Shops

On the LIRR Level

Food & Drink

Auntie Anne's Soft Pretzels
Blimpie
Caruso's Pizza
Carvel
Cinnabon
Colombo Frozen Yogurt
Europan Café
Haagen Dazs
Hot & Crusty
Hot Dog Stand
KFC
Knot Just Pretzels
Le Bon Café
McDonald's
Nedick's
Pizza Hut
Primo! Cappuccino
Rose Pizza and Pasta
Salad Chef/Burger Chef
Tim Horton's
Seattle Coffee Roasters
Soup King
Soup Man/Smoothie King (2)
Starbucks
Subway
TGI Friday's
Tracks Raw Bar & Grill

Other

Carlton Cards
Dreyfus Financial Center
Duane Reade
GNC
Hudson News (4)
K-Mart
Petal Pusher
Penn Books
Perfumania
Soleman—Shoe repair, locksmith
Verizon Wireless

On the Amtrak Level

Food & Drink

Auntie Anne's Soft Pretzels (2)
Baskin Robbins
Deli
Don Pepi Pizza
Houlihan's Restaurant & Bar
Nathan's/Carvel
Kabooz's Bar and Grille
Krispy Kreme Doughnuts
Penn Sushi
Pizza Hut
Primo! Cappuccino (3)
Roy Rogers
Soup Man/Smoothie King/
Sodutto Ice Cream
Tim Horton's
Zaro's Bread Basket (2)

Other

Book Corner
Duane Reade
Elegance
Gifts & Electronics
GNC
Hudson News (3)
Joseph Lawrence Jewelers
New York New York
Shoetrician—Shoe repair and shine
Tiecoon
The Petal Pusher
Staples
Tourist Information Center
Verizon Wireless

There is a Wachovia 24-hour ATM and a PNC Bank ATM located on the Amtrak level. There is a Bank of America 24-hour ATM and a 24-hour HSBC ATM located on the LIRR level, in addition to the generic (money-thieving) ATMs located in several stores throughout the station.

Temporary Parcel/Baggage Check

The only facility for storing parcels and baggage in Penn Station is at the Baggage Check on the Amtrak level (to the left of the ticket counter). There are no locker facilities at Penn Station. The Baggage Check is open from 5:15 am until 10 pm and costs $4.50 per item for each 24-hour period.

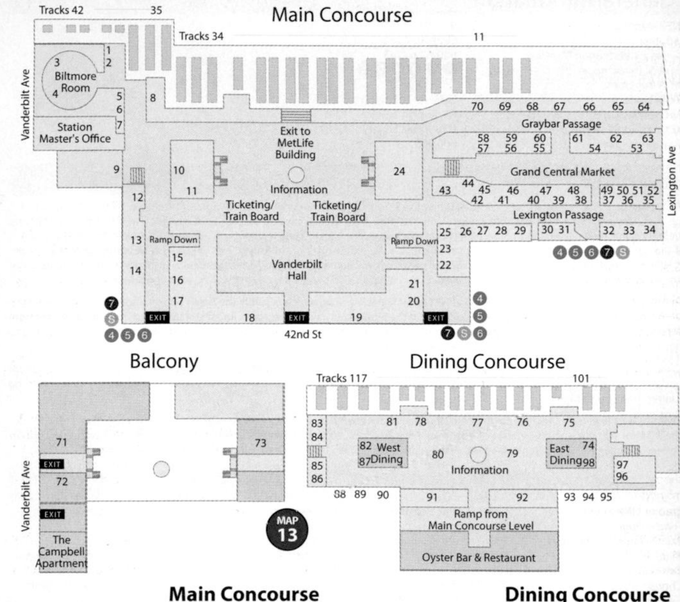

Main Concourse

1. Central Watch Band
2. Grand Central Racquet
3. Eddie's Service Shop
4. Dahlia
5. Eddie's Shoeshine & Repair
6. Papyrus
7. Junior's Brooklyn NYC
8. Starbucks
9. New York Transit Museum
10. Zaro's Bakery
11. Chase Bank
12. Pylones
13. Posman Books
14. Rite Aid
15. The Beverage Bar
16. Francesco's Hair Salon, Barber Shop & Day Spa
17. Hot & Crusty
18. Banana Republic
19. Kenneth Cole
20. Brooklyn Industries
21. Super Runners Shop
22. Financier
23. Papyrus
24. Hudson News
25. Swatch
26. Capital One Bank
27. L'occitane
28. Grand Central Optical
29. The Art Of Shaving
30. Tumi
31. LittleMissMatched
32. Joon Jewelry
33. La Crasia
34. Pink Slip
35. Starbucks
36. Aveda
37. InnaSense
38. Tea & Honey Store
39. Mac
40. Tia's Place
41. Origins
42. Cursive
43. Forever Silver
44. Pescatore
45. Dishes At Home
46. Li-La Chocolates
47. Oren's Daily Roast Coffees & Teas
48. Penzeys Spices
49. Zaro's Bread Basket
50. Wild Edibles
51. Murray's Real Salami
52. Bread Corrado Pastry
53. Greenwich Produce
54. Ceriello
55. Murray's Cheese
56. German Royal Hams - Koglin
57. Greenwich Produce
58. O & Co
59. Grande Harvest Wines
60. Cobbler Shine
61. Toto
62. Joe - Art Of Coffee
63. GNC
64. Rosetta Stone
65. Tibet Kailash
66. D-Line Jewelry
67. Windhorse
68. The Soap Bar
69. Selen Design
70. Zaro's Bakery
71. Michael Jordan's The NYC Steakhouse
72. Dipriani Dolce
73. Apple Store

Dining Concourse

74. Zaro's Bread Basket
75. Eddie's Shoeshine
76. Golden Krust
77. Hudson News
78. New York Pretzel
79. Caffe Pepe Rosso
80. Dishes
81. Dahlia
82. Ciao Bella Gelato
83. Paninoteca Italiana
84. Chirping Chicken
85. Eata Pita
86. Feng Shui Chinese Cuisine
87. Hale & Hearty Soups
88. Mendy's Dairy & Appetizing
89. Mendy's Kosher Delicatessen
90. Masa's
91. Junior's
92. Zocalo
93. Central Market Grill
94. The Manhattan Chili
95. Brother Jimmy's BBQ
96. Two Boots Pizzeria
97. Cafe Spice Express
98. Magnolia Bakery

General Information

NFT Map:	13
Address:	42nd St & Park Ave
General Information:	212-340-2210
Lost and Found:	212-340-2555
Website:	www.grandcentralterminal.com
MTA Subway Stops:	4 5 6 7 S
MTA Bus Lines:	1 2 3 4 42 98 101 102 104
Other Rail Lines:	Metro-North
Newark Airport Bus Service:	Olympia, 877-8-NEWARK, $16
LaGuardia Airport Bus Service:	NY Airport Express, 718-875-8200, $13
JFK Airport Bus Service:	NY Airport Express, 718-875-8200, $16

Overview

Grand Central Terminal, designed in the Beaux-Arts style by Warren & Wetmore, is by far the most beautiful of Manhattan's major terminals, and it is considered one of the most stunning terminals in the world. Its convenient location in the heart of Midtown and its refurbishments only add to its intrinsic appeal. The only downside is that the station will only get you on a train as far north as Dutchess County or as far east as New Haven via Metro-North—in order to head to the Island or Jersey, you'll have to hoof it over to GCT's architecturally ugly stepsister Penn Station.

If you ever find yourself underestimating the importance of the Grand Central renovations (begun in 1996 with continued work and maintenance today), just take a peek at the ceiling toward the Vanderbilt Avenue side—the small patch of black shows how dirty the ceiling was previously. And it was really dirty…

Diners have any number of choices including Michael Jordan's The Steak House N.Y.C. or Cipriani Dolci for nice views overlooking the main concourse or the food court on the lower level (perfect for commuters or those intent on saving a few bucks). After hitting the raw stuff at Oyster Bar, go right outside its entrance to hear a strange audio anomaly: If you and a friend stand in opposite corners and whisper, you'll be able to hear each other clearly. You can even do some grocery shopping in the Grand Central Market on the east side of the main concourse. Alternatively, folks looking to hit the sauce may do so in 1920s grandeur in The Campbell Apartment near the Vanderbilt Avenue entrance, or for a non-edible treat, grab an iPad for your train ride at the shiny Apple Store on the east balcony overlooking the main concourse.

By far the coolest food option, however, is Grand Central Market, located between the east passages of the terminal as you head out towards Lexington Avenue. Instead of paying for overpriced food, build your own bread-meat-cheese extravaganza, or take home fresh fish or perfected butchered meat to cook at home later on. Our favorite vendors: Murray's Cheese, Murray's Real Salami, Wild Edibles, and Dishes at Home.

There are some great tours of Grand Central Terminal including: the Municipal Arts Society Tour (212-935-3960, $20) and the Grand Central Partnership Tour (212-883-2420, free). Grand Central's website also offers a headset audio tour ($7) and an app version of the tour ($4.99) for visitors who want to wander on their own.

ATMs

Chase

Numerous generic (money-thieving) ATMs at stores throughout the station.

East Dining

Brother Jimmy's BBQ
Café Spice
Central Market Grill
Golden Krust Patties
Jacques-Imo's to Geaux
Little Pie Company
Caffé Pepe Rosso
Two Boots
Zaro's Bread Basket
Zócalo Bar and Restaurant

West Dining

Dishes
Ciao Bella Gelateria
Chirping Chicken
Eata Pita
Feng Shui
Hale and Hearty Soups
Junior's
Masa Sushi
Mendy's Kosher Dairy
Mendy's Kosher Delicatessen
New York Pretzel
Paninoteca Italiana

General Information

NFT Map:	11
Address:	41st St & Eighth Ave
General Information:	212-564-8484
Kinney Garage:	212-502-2341
Website:	www.panynj.gov/CommutingTravel/bus/html/pa.html
Subway:	A C E Port Authority 1 2 3 7 N R Q S Times Square
MTA Bus Lines:	10 11 16 20 27 42 104
Newark Airport Bus Service:	Olympia, 212-964-6233, $13
LaGuardia Airport Bus Service:	NY Airport Express, 718-875-8200, $12
JFK Airport Bus Service:	NY Airport Express, 718-875-8200, $15

Overview

Devised as a solution to New York City's horrendous bus congestion, the Port Authority Bus Terminal was completed in 1950. The colossal structure consolidated midtown Manhattan's eight, separate, interstate bus stations into one convenient drop-off and pick-up point. Back in the day the Port Authority held the title of "largest bus terminal in the world," but for now we'll have to be content with merely the biggest depot in the United States. The Port Authority is located on the north and south sides of W 41st Street (b/w Eighth Ave & Ninth Ave) in a neighborhood that real-estate agents haven't yet graced with an official name. How about Greyhound Gardens?

There are plenty of things to do should you find that you've got some time to kill here. Send a postcard from the post office, donate blood at the blood bank on the main floor, use the refurbished bathrooms, roll a few strikes and enjoy a cocktail at "Frames" bowling lounge, or chug a couple of decent brews at mini-chain Heartland Brewery. There are also many souvenir carts, newsstands, and on-the-go restaurants, as well as a statue of beloved bus driver Ralph Kramden located outside of the south wing. The grungiest area of the terminal is the lower bus level, which is dirty and exhaust-filled, best visited just a few minutes before you need to board your bus. The chart on the right shows which bus companies run out of the Port Authority and provides a basic description of their destinations.

If you can, avoid interstate bus rides from the Port Authority on the busiest travel days of the year. The lines are long, the people are cranky, and some of the larger bus companies hire anyone who shows up with a valid bus operator's license and their very own bus (apparently easier to obtain than you might think). The odds of having a disastrous trip skyrocket when the driver is unfamiliar with the usual itinerary.

On Easter Sunday, Christmas Eve, or Thanksgiving, one can see all the angst-ridden sons and daughters of suburban New Jersey parents joyfully waiting in cramped, disgusting corridors for that nauseating bus ride back to Leonia or Morristown or Plainfield or wherever. A fascinating sight.

Terminal Shops

South Wing—Lower Bus Level
Green Trees
Hudson News

South Wing—Subway Mezzanine
Au Bon Pain
Hudson News
Music Explosion

South Wing—Main Concourse
Heartland Brewery
Au Bon Pain
Auntie Anne's
Casa Java
Deli Plus
Duane Reade
GNC
Jamba Juice
Hudson News
Hudson News Book Corner
Marrella Men's Hair Stylist
NY Blood Center
Radio Shack
Ruthie's Hallmark
Stop 'n Go Wireless
Strawberry
US Postal Service
Villa Pizza
World's Fare Restaurant Bar
Zaro's Bakery

South Wing—Second Floor
Café Metro
Drago Shoe Repair
Bank of America
Hudson News Book Corner
Kelly Film Express
Frames
Center McAnn's Pub
Mrs Fields Bakery Café
Munchy's Gourmet
Sak's Florist
Sweet Factory

South Wing—Fourth Floor
First Stop-Last Stop Café
Hudson News

North Wing-Lower Bus Level
Snacks-N-Wheels

North Wing—Subway Mezzanine
Bank of America (ATM)
Green Trees
Hudson News

North Wing—Main Concourse
Continental Airlines
Hudson News
Mrs Fields Cookies

North Wing—on 42nd Street
Big Apple Café

North Wing—Second Floor
Bank of America (ATM)
Hudson News
Jay's Hallmark Bookstore
Tropica Juice Bar
USO

North Wing—Third Floor
Hudson News
Tropica Juice Bar

Bus Company	*Phone*	*Area Served*
Academy Bus Transportation	800-442-7272	Serves New York City, including Staten Island, Wall Street, Port Authority, and New Jersey, including Hoboken www.academybus.com
Adirondak New York & Pine Hill Trailways	800-776-7548	Serves all of New York State with coach connections throughout the US. www.trailwaysny.com
Capitol Trailways	800-333-8444	Service between Pennsylvania, Virginia, New York State, and New York City. www.capitoltrailways.com
Carl Bieber Bus	800-243-2374	Service to and from Port Authority and Wall Street in New York and Reading, Kutztown, Wescosville, Hellertown, and Easton, Pennsylvania. www.biebertourways.com
Coach USA	800-522-4514	Service between New York City and W Orange, Livingston, Morristown, E Hanover, Whippany, and Floram Park, New Jersey. www.coachusa.com
DeCamp Bus	800-631-1281	Service between New York City and New Jersey, including the Meadowlands. www.decamp.com
Greyhound Bus	800-231-2222	Serves most of the US and Canada. www.greyhound.com
Gray Line Bus	800 669-0051	Service offered throughout the US and Canada. www.grayline.com
Lakeland Bus	973-366-0600	Service between New York and New Jersey. www.lakelandbus.com
Martz Group	800-233-8604	Service between New York and Pennsylvania. www.martzgroup.com
New Jersey Transit	973-275-5555	Serves New York, New Jersey, and Philadelphia. www.njtransit.com
NY Airport Service	212-875-8200	Service between Port Authority and Kennedy and LaGuardia airports. www.nyairportservice.com
Olympia Trails	877-894-9155	Provides express bus service between Manhattan and Newark Airport. Makes stops all over New York City, including Penn Station, Grand Central, and many connections with hotel shuttles. www.olympiabus.com
Peter Pan Lines	800-343-9999	Serves the East, including Boston, New Hampshire, Maine, Philly, DC. Also goes to Canada. www.peterpanbus.com
Rockland Coaches (NY)	845-356-0877	Services New York's Port Authority, GW bridge, 44th Street, and 8th Street to and from most of Bergen County and upstate New York. www.coachusa.com/rockland
ShortLine Bus	800-631-8405	Serves the New York City airports, Atlantic City, and the Hudson Valley. www.shortlinebus.com
Suburban	732-249-1100	Offers commuter service from Central New Jersey to and from Port Authority and Wall Street. Also services between the Route 9 Corridor and New York City. www.coachusa.com/suburban
Susquehanna Trailways	800-692-6314	Service to and from New York City and Newark (Greyhound Terminal) and Summerville, New Jersey, and many stops in Central Pennsylvania, ending in Williamsport and Lock Haven. www.susquehannabus.com
Trans-Bridge Lines	610-868-6001 800-962-9135	Offers service between New York, Pennsylvania and New Jersey, including Newark and Kennedy airports. transbridgelines.com
Red & Tan Hudson County (NJ)	908-354-3330	Serves New York City and Hudson County, New Jersey. www.coachusa.com/redandtan

General Information

NFT Map: 23
Address: 4211 Broadway & 178th St
Phone: 800-221-9903 or 212-564-8484
Website: www.panynj.gov/bus-terminals/gwbbs-about-station.htmll
Subway: A (175th St), A 1 (181st St)
Buses: 100 98 5 4 3 Bx7

Overview

Change is coming slowly to the George Washington Bridge Bus Terminal, though we can hope it will never lose its "lived-in" charm. The Port Authority has cleaned the station up a bit, added some needed signage, and improved the lighting, but any place with pigeons routinely wandering through the indoors can never be too chic. Hit some downtime before your bus arrives and your entertainment options are limited to people-watching or opening a new bank account. If you luck out and the weather's nice, though, the view of the bridge upstairs is pretty sweet.

Stores

Lower Level:
Bridge Stop Newsstand
HealthPlus Healthcare
Subway Pedestrian Walkway
NJT T Ticket Vending Machines
Port of Calls/Retail Pushcarts

Concourse:
ATM
Bridge Stop Newsstand
Dentists—Howard Bloom, DDS; Steve Kaufman DDS
E-Z Visions Travel
Food Plus Café
GW Books and Electronics
HealthPlus Healthcare
Neighborhood Trust Federal Credit Union
New York National Bank
Off-Track Betting
Pizza Palace
Terminal Barber Shop
Washington Heights Optical

Street Level:
Blockbuster Video
Rite-Aid Pharmacy
Urban Pathways—Homeless Outreach Office
Port Authority Business Outreach Center
(179th St underpass)

Bus Companies

Air Brook •
800-800-1990 • airbrook.com
To Atlantic City (Tropicana)

Express Bus Service •
973-742-4700 • expressbusservice.com
To Elmwood Park, Englewood, Fort Lee, Hackensack, Paramus, Paterson, River Edge, and Teaneck (all stops on Route 4).

New Jersey Transit •
973-275-5555
To 60th St, Bergenfield, Bogota, Cliffside Park, Coytesville, Dumont, Edgewater (including Edgewater Commons Mall), Englewood, Englewood Cliffs, West Englewood, Fair Lawn (including the Radburn section), Fairview, Fort Lee, Glen Rock, Guttenberg, Hackensack (including NJ Bus Transfer), Hoboken, North Hackensack (Riverside Square), Irvington, Jersey City, Kearney, Leonia, Maywood, Newark, North Bergen, Paramus (including the Bergen Mall and Garden State Plaza), Paterson (including Broadway Terminal), Ridgewood, Rochelle Park, Teaneck (including Glenpointe and Holy Name Hospital), Union City, Weehawken, and West New York.

Red & Tan/Coach USA •
908-354-3330 • coachusa.com/redandtan
To Alpine, Bergenfield, Blauvelt, Bradlees Shopping Center, Closter, Congers, Creskill, Demarest, Dumont Emerson, Englewood, Englewood Cliffs, Grandview Harrington Park, Haverstraw, Haworth, Hillsdale Linwood Park, Montvale, Nanuet, (including Nanue Shopping Mall), Naurashaun, New City, New Milford Northvale (including Northvale Industrial Park) Norwood, Nyack, Oradell, Orangeburg, Palisades, Park Ridge, Pearl River, Piermont, Rivervale, Rockland Lake Rockland Psych Center, Rockleigh (including Rockleigh Industrial Park), South Nyack, Sparkill, Spring Valley Stony Point, Tappan, Tenafly, Upper Nyack, Valle Cottage, West Haverstraw, Westwood, and Woodcli Lake.

Shortline/Coach USA •
800-631-8405 • www.coachusa.com/shortline
To Upstate NY points, Colleges, Orange, Rocklanc Sullivan, Bergen and Pike Counties, day tours t Woodbury Common Premium Outlets.

General Information

NFT Map: 3
Websites: www.chinatown-bus.com
www.chinatown-bus.org

Overview

There are several inexpensive bus lines running from Chinatown in New York City to the respective Chinatowns in Boston, Philadelphia, Washington DC, Richmond, and Atlanta. If you're lucky, you'll catch a kung-fu movie on board, but be prepared for an '00s "classic" like *Turner & Hooch*. Tickets usually cost $13-20 each way, and can be purchased online or in person at pick-up locations.

Cheaper than planes and trains, the Chinatown buses have become extraordinarily popular. They are in such demand that Greyhound and Trailways have lowered their online fares to compete. That said, Chinatown buses are an infinitely more adventurous mode of transportation. The odds are high that you'll experience at least one problem during the course of your trip including, but not limited to, poor customer service, unmarked bus stops, late departures, less than ideal bus conditions, and hocking or spitting from other passengers. More pertinent problems include cancelled or delayed trips without warning, breakdowns, fires, broken bathrooms (or none at all), stolen luggage, and drop-offs on the side of the road near the highway because bus companies don't have permission to deliver passengers to central transportation hubs. Conversely, service has improved greatly in the past few years, and many people have enjoyed dirt-cheap, hassle free experiences on the Chinatown buses. It's probably not the best choice for families, but anyone else should give it a try.

A few tips to make your trip easier: 1) MAKE SURE YOU GET ON THE RIGHT BUS. We cannot emphasize this enough. Do not be embarrassed to ask everyone on the bus which city they're going to. 2) Do not sit anywhere near the bathroom. You will smell the intense, probably illegal, cleaning products for the first half of the ride, and your fellow passengers' business for the second half. 3) If the bus isn't full, it's perfectly fine to take your luggage onboard with you if you're worried about theft. This is an especially good idea when leaving the New York stations. 4) Arrive at least 30 minutes ahead of time. Trust us. This will save you a chaotic sprint under the Manhattan Bridge while you jump on the wrong bus. Yes, it has happened even to NFT experts.

Another newer option that's a step above Chinatown buses (but still really cheap) are Bolt Bus (www.boltbus.com) and Megabus (www.megabus.com). Check the website for more details, but both leave from the vicinity of Penn Station and travel to Boston, DC, Philly, and even Toronto. And they have Wi-Fi connections so you can surf the NFT website on board. Try that on a Chinatown bus.

Bus Companies

Lucky Star Bus Transportation •
617-426-8801 • www.luckystarbus.com.
To Boston every hour 7 am–10 pm. From **69 Chrystie St** to South Station: one-way $15, round trip $30.

Boston Deluxe •
917-662-7552 or 646-773-3816 • www.bostondeluxe.com
- To Boston at 9 am, 12:30 pm, and 6 pm. From **1250 Broadway & 32nd St** or **88 E Broadway** to 175 Huntington Ave: one-way $15, round trip $30.
- To Hartford at 8:30 am, 12:30 pm, and 5:30 pm. From the same pick-up points to 365 Capital Ave: one-way $15, round trip $30.

Washington Deluxe • 866-BUS-NY-DC • www.washny.com
- To Washington several times a day; From **34th St & 8th Ave**. Additional departures from **Delancey & Allen Sts**, and several locations in **Williamsburg** to various locations in DC. Schedule varies by day of the week, so it's recommended that you check the website for info. $40 round-trip and $25 each way on Saturdays.

Dragon Deluxe •
800-475-1160 or 212-966-5130 • www.dragondeluxe.com
- To Washington DC six times a day between 7:30 am and 11:30 pm. From **153 Lafayette St** or **Broadway & W 32nd St-Herald Square** to 14th & L Sts: one-way $20, round trip $35.
- To Baltimore six times a day between 7:30 am and 11:30 pm. From the same pick-up points to 5600 O'Donnell St: one-way $20, round trip $35.
- To Albany at 7:30 am and 5:30 pm. From the same pick-up points to Madison Ave (between the New York State Museum and Empire State Plaza): one-way $25, round trip $45
- To Woodbury Commons at 7:30 am and 5:30 pm. From the same pick-ups points to Woodbury Commons: one-way $15, round trip $30.

Eastern Travel • 212-244-6132 • www.easternshuttle.com
- To Washington DC 6–12 times a day between 7:30 am and 7:30 pm; From **88 E Broadway**, **430 7th Ave at W 34th St**, or **5 Times Square (in front of the Ernst &Young Building)** to 715 H Street in Washington DC; one-way $20, round trip $35.
- To Baltimore 6–12 times a day between 7:30 am and 7:30 pm. From same pickup-point to 5501 O'Donnell St Cut Off: one-way $20, round trip $35.

Today's Bus • 212-343-3281 • www.todaysbus.com
- To Philadelphia every hour between 7:15 am and 11 pm. From **88 E Broadway** to 1041 Race St: one-way $12, round trip $20.
- To DC 14 times a day between 7:15 am and 11 pm. From **88 E Broadway** to 610 I St NW: one-way $20, round trip $35.
- To Norfolk, VA, at 6 pm. From **13 Allen St** to 649 Newton Rd: one-way $25, round trip $40.
- To Richmond, VA, at 5 pm. From **88 E Broadway** to 5215 W Broad St: one-way $40, round trip $60
- To Atlanta, GA, at 8 pm. From **109 E Broadway** to 5150 Buford Hwy NE: one-way $90, round trip $170.

General Information

Bicycle Defense Fund: www.bicycledefensefund.org
Bike Blog NYC : www.bikeblognyc.com
Bike New York, Five Borough Bike Tour: www.bikenewyork.org
Century Road Club Association (CRCA): www.crca.net
Department of City Planning: www.nyc.gov/html/dcp/html/bike/home.shtml
Department of Parks & Recreation: www.nycgovparks.org
Department of Transportation: www.nyc.gov/html/dot/html/bicyclists/bikemain.shtml
Empire Skate Club: www.empireskate.org
Fast & Fabulous Lesbian & Gay Bike Club: www.fastnfab.org
Five Boro Bicycle Club: www.5bbc.org
League of American Bicyclists: www.bikeleague.org
New York Bicycle Coalition: www.nybc.net
NYC Bike Share www.citibikenyc.com
New York Cycle Club: www.nycc.org
NYC Streets Renaissance: www.nycstreets.org
Recycle-A-Bicycle http://www.recycleabicycle.org/
Streetsblog NYC www.streetsblog.org/
Time's Up! Bicycle Advocacy Group: www.times-up.org
Transportation Alternatives: http://www.transalt.org/

Overview

While not for the faint of heart, biking and skating around Manhattan can be one of the most efficient and exhilarating forms of transportation. Transportation Alternatives estimates that ove 130,000 New Yorkers hop on a bike each day—an all-time high for the city. Manhattan is relatively flat, and the fitness and environmental advantages of using people power are incontrovertible However, there are also some downsides, including, but not limited to: psychotic cab drivers buses, traffic, pedestrians, pavement with potholes, glass, debris, and poor air quality. In 2007 Bloomberg chose bike-friendly Janette Sadik-Khan to head the Department of Transportation Since then things have been looking up for bikers all over the city. Many new miles of bike lanes have been added, and there has been an effort to create well protected lanes wheneve possible including in Times Square, 8th and 9th Avenues in Chelsea, and 2nd and 3rd Avenue in the East Village. These tend to be the safest places to ride, though they often get blocked by parked or standing cars. Central Park is a great place to ride, as is the Greenway along the Hudson River from Battery Park all the way up to the GWB (it's actually a 32-mile loop around the island). East River Park is another nice destination for recreational riding and skating—jus be careful after dark! The most exciting cycling news in recent years is the launch of the Ci Bike share program. Annual, 7 day, or 24-hour memberships are available with a valid cred card. The program is designed for quick trips around town -- less than 30 minutes -- and i meant to be used in conjunction with other forms of mass transit.

Bikes are sometimes less convenient than skates. Where skates can be tucked in a bag an carried onto subways, indoors, or on buses, bikes have to be locked up on the street and ar always at risk of being stolen. Unfortunately, bike racks are hard to come by in NYC, so you ma need to get creative on where to park. Always lock them to immovable objects and don't skim on a cheap bike lock. With over 40,000 bikes a year stolen in NYC, the extra cost for a top-of-the line bike lock is worth it. On the upside, bikes provide a much faster, less demanding form c transportation around the city.

Crossing the Bridges by Bike

Brooklyn Bridge

Separate bicycle and pedestrian lanes run down the center of the bridge, with the bicycle lane on the north side and the pedestrian lane on the south. Cyclists should beware of wayfaring tourists taking photographs. We do not recommend rollerblading across the bridge—the wooden planks make for quite a bumpy ride. The bridge is quite level and, aside from the tourists and planks, fairly easy to traverse.

Brooklyn Access: Stairs to Cadman Plz E and Prospect St, ramp to Johnson & Adams Sts
Manhattan Access: Park Row and Centre St, across from City Hall Park

Manhattan Bridge

The last of the Brooklyn crossings to be outfitted with decent pedestrian and bike paths, the Manhattan Bridge bike and pedestrian paths are on separate sides of the bridge. The walking path is on the south side, and the bike path is on the north side of the bridge. The major drawback to walking across the Manhattan Bridge is that you have to climb a steep set of stairs on the Brooklyn side (not the best conditions for lugging around a stroller or suitcase). Fortunately, the bike path on the north side of the bridge is ramped on both approaches. However, be careful on Jay Street when accessing the bridge in Brooklyn due to the dangerous, fast-moving traffic.

Brooklyn Access: Jay St & Sands St
Manhattan Access: Bike Lane–Canal St & Forsyth St
Pedestrian Lane–Bowery, just south of Canal St

Williamsburg Bridge

The Williamsburg Bridge has the widest pedestrian/bike path of the three bridges to Brooklyn. The path on the north side, shared by cyclists and pedestrians, is 12 feet wide. The southern path, at eight feet wide, is also shared by bikers and walkers. Now that both sides of the bridge are always open to pedestrians and bikes, this is one of the best ways to get to and from Brooklyn. As a bonus fitness feature, the steep gradient on both the Manhattan and Brooklyn sides of the bridge gives bikers and pedestrians a good workout.

Brooklyn Access: North Entrance–Driggs Ave, right by the Washington Plz
South Entrance–Bedford Ave b/w S 5th & S 6th Sts
Manhattan Access: Delancey St & Clinton St/Suffolk St

George Washington Bridge

Bikers get marginalized by the pedestrians on this crossway to New Jersey. The north walkway is for pedestrians only, and the south side is shared by pedestrians and bikers. Cyclists had to fight to keep their right to even bike on this one walkway, as city officials wanted to institute a "walk your bike across" rule to avoid bicycle/pedestrian accidents during construction. The bikers won the battle but are warned to "exercise extra caution" when passing pedestrians.

Manhattan Access: W 178th St & Fort Washington Ave
New Jersey Access: Hudson Ter in Fort Lee

Robert F. Kennedy Bridge

Biking is officially prohibited on this two-mile span that connects the Bronx, Queens, and Manhattan. Unofficially, people ride between the boroughs and over to Wards Island all the time. The bike path is quite narrow, compared to the paths on other bridges, and the lighting at night is mediocre at best. The tight path sees less pedestrian/cycling traffic than other bridges, which, paired with the insufficient lighting, gives the span a rather ominous feeling after dark. If you're worried about safety, or keen on obeying the laws, the 103rd Street footbridge provides an alternative way to reach Wards Island sans car. This pedestrian pass is open only during the warmer months, and then only during daylight hours. See page 297 for more information about the footbridge schedule.

Bronx Access: 133rd St & Cypress Ave
Manhattan Access: Ramps--124/126th Sts & First Ave Stairs–Second Ave and 124/126 Sts
Queens Access: 26th St & Hoyt Ave (beware of extremely steep stairs).

Ed Koch Queensboro Bridge

The north outer roadway of the Ed Koch Queensboro Bridge is open exclusively to bikers, 24/7, except for the day of the New York Marathon. More than 2,500 cyclists and pedestrians per day traverse the bridge. Bikers complain about safety issues on the Manhattan side of the bridge: With no direct connection from Manhattan onto the bridge's West Side, bikers are forced into an awkward five-block detour to get to Second Avenue, where they can finally access the bridge.

Manhattan Entrance: 60th St, b/w First Ave & Second Ave
Queens Entrance: Queens Plz & Crescent St

Citi Bike Bike Share

The membership-only Citi Bike bike sharing program began in 2013. Designed for short jaunts around town, annual memberships cost $95 and entitle the user to unlimited trips of up to 45 minutes. One-day and 7-day "Access Passes" for unlimited trips up to 30 minutes are available for $9.95 and $25, respectively. Trips exceeding the time limit incur steep overage charges; much like ZipCar, the program is not intended to function as a bike rental. At the program's outset, stations were limited to Manhattan south of 60th Street and a small swath of Brooklyn between Brooklyn Heights and Bedford-Stuyvesant, with plans to eventually expand to other neighborhoods. The bikes themselves are functional three-speed machines, with easily adjustable seats, bells and LED safety lights, and multiple logos of main sponsor Citibank, which pledged more than $40 million to start the program. For more information visit citibikenyc.com.

Bike Rentals (and Sales)

Cadence Cycling • 174 Hudson St • 212-226-4400 • Map 2
Canal Street Bicycles • 417 Canal St • 212-334-8000 • Map 2
Gotham Bikes • 112 W Broadway • 212-732-2453 • Map 2
Bike Works • 106 Ridge St • 212-388-1077 • Map 4
Chari & Co. • 175 Stanton St • 212-475-0102 • Map 4
Dah Bike Shop • 134 Division St • Map 4
Frank's Bike Shop • 533 Grand St • 212-533-6332 • Map 4
The Hub Station • 73 Morton St • 212-965-9334 • Map 5
West Village Waterfront Bike Shop • 391 West St • 212-414-2453 • Map 5
Bfold 224 • E 13th St • 212-529-7247 • Map 6
Bicycle Habitat • 244 Lafayette St • 212-431-3315 • Map 6
Metro Bicycles • 332 E 14th St • 212-228-4344 • Map 6
NYC Velo • 64 2nd Ave • 212-253-7771 • Map 6
Track Star NYC • 231 Eldridge St • 212-982-2553 • Map 6
Busy Bee Bikes • 437 E 6th St • 212-228-2347 • Map 7
Continuum Cycles • 199 Avenue B • 212-505-8785 • Map 7
Landmark Bicycles • 136 E 3rd St • 212-674-2343 • Map 7
Recycle-A-Bicycle • 75 Avenue C • 212-475-1655 • Map 7
Larry's Bicycles Plus • 1690 2nd Ave • Map 17
Bike and Roll • 557 12th Ave • 212-260-0400 • Map 8
City Bicycles & Hobby • 315 W 38th St • 212-563-3373 • Map 8
Enoch's Bike Shop • 480 10th Ave • 212-582-0620 • Map 8
A Bicycle Shop • 163 W 22nd St • 212-691-6149 • Map 9
Chelsea Bicycles • 130 W 26th St • 212-727-7278 • Map 9
Metro Bicycles • 546 Avenue of the Americas • 212-255-5100 • Map 9
Paragon Sporting Goods • 867 Broadway • 212-255-8036 • Map 9
Sid's Bikes • 151 W 19th St • 212-989-1060 • Map 9
Manhattan Velo • 141 E 17th St • 212-253-6788 • Map 10
Sid's Bikes • 235 E 34th St • 212-213-8360 • Map 10

Spokesman Cycles • 34 Irving Pl • 212-995-0450 • Map 10
Liberty Bicycles • 846 9th Ave • 212-757-2418 • Map 11
Manhattan Bicycle Shop • 791 9th Ave • 212-262-0111 • Map 11
Metro Bicycles • 360 W 47th St • 212-581-4500 • Map 11
Ferrara Cycle Shop • 6304 20th Ave • 718-232-6716 • Map 12
Conrad's Bike Shop • 25 Tudor City Pl • 212-697-6966 • Map 13
Bay Ridge Bicycle World • 8916 3rd Ave • 718-238-1118 • Map 14
Bicycle Renaissance • 430 Columbus Ave • 212-362-3388 • Map 14
Eddie's Bicycles • 480 Amsterdam Ave • 212-580-2011 • Map 14
Toga Bikes • 110 West End Ave • 212-799-9625 • Map 14
Bicycles NYC • 1400 3rd Ave • 212-794-2929 • Map 15
Bike Heaven • 348 E 62nd St • 212-230-1919 • Map 15
NYC Wheels • 1603 York Ave • 212-737-3078 • Map 15
Pedal Pushers • 1306 2nd Ave • 212-288-5592 • Map 15
Champion Bicycles • 896 Amsterdam Ave • 212-662-2690 • Map 16
Innovation Bike Shop • 105 W 106th St • 212-678-7130 • Map16
Metro Bicycles • 231 W 96th St • 212-663-7531 • Map16
Metro Bicycles • 1311 Lexington Ave • 212-427-4450 • Map 17
ModSquad Cycles • 2119 Frederick Douglass Blvd • 212-865-5050 • Map19
Heavy Metal Bike Shop • 2016 3rd Ave • 212-410-1144 • Map 20
Junior Bicycle Shop • 1820 Amsterdam Ave • 212-690-6511 • Map 21
Mani's Bicycle Shop • 8 Bennett Ave • 212-927-8501 • Map 23
Victor's Bike Repair • 4125 Broadway • 212-740-5137 • Map 23
Tread Bike Shop • 250 Dyckman St • 212-544-7055 • Map 25

Bikes and Mass Transit

Surprisingly, you can take your bike on trains and some buses—just make sure it's not during rush hour and you are courteous to other passengers. The subway requires you to carry your bike down staircases, use the service gate instead of the turnstile, and board at the very front or back end of the train. To ride the commuter railroads with your bike, you may need to purchase a bike permit. For appropriate contact information, see transportation pages.

Amtrak: Train with baggage car required.
LIRR: $5 permit required.
Metro-North: $5 permit required.
New Jersey Transit: No permit required.
PATH: No permit required.
New York Water Taxi: No fee or permit required
NY Waterway: $1 fee.
Staten Island Ferry: Enter at lower level.
Bus companies: Call individual companies.

Ice Skating

Recreational skating venues in Manhattan include Wollman and Lasker Rinks in Central Park, Chelsea Piers, Riverbank State Park (679 Riverside Drive at 145th St), and Rivergate Ice Rink (401 E 34th St). If you're looking for a place to get your skates sharpened to your own personal specifications before hitting the ice, contact Westside Skate & Stick (174 Fifth Ave, 212-228-8400), a custom pro shop for hockey and figure skaters that's by appointment only. For more information on skating venues throughout the boroughs, check out www.skatecity.com. For organized events, visit the Empire Skate Club at www.empireskate.org.

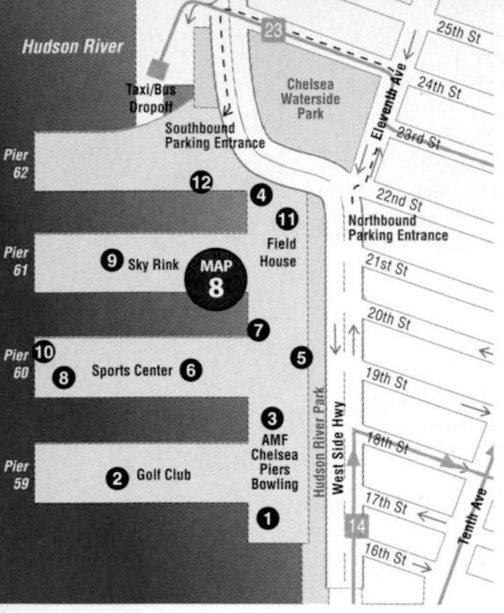

General Information

NFT Map: 8
Website: www.chelseapiers.com

Overview

Opened in 1910 as a popular port for trans-Atlantic ships, Chelsea Piers found itself neglected and deteriorating by the 1960s. In 1992, Roland W. Betts (fraternity brother of George W. Bush) began the plan to renovate and refurbish the piers as a gargantuan 28-acre sports and entertainment center. In 1995, Chelsea Piers re-opened its doors to the public at a final cost of $120 million—all private money. The only help from the state was a very generous 49-year lease. By 1998, Chelsea Piers was the third most popular attraction in New York City, after Times Square.

How to Get There

Unless you live in Chelsea, it's a real pain to get to the Piers. The closest subway is the C E to 23rd Street and Eighth Avenue, and then it's still a three-avenue block hike there. If you're lucky, you can hop a 23 bus on 23rd Street and expedite the last leg of your journey. L train commuters should get off at the Eighth Avenue stop and take the 14 bus across to the West Side Highway where you'll be dropped off at 18th Street.

If you drive, entering from the south can be a little tricky. It's pretty well signed, so keep your eyes peeled. Basically you exit right at Eleventh Avenue and 22nd Street, turn left onto 24th Street, and then make a left onto the West Side Highway. Enter Chelsea Piers the same way you would if you were approaching from the north. Parking costs $15 for the first hour, $20 for two, $24 for three. Street parking in the West 20s is an excellent alternative in the evenings after 6 pm.

Facilities

Chelsea Piers is amazing. There are swimming pools, ice-skating rinks, a bowling alley, spa, restaurants, shops, batting cages—you name it. So, what's the catch? Well, it's gonna cost ya. Like Manhattan rents, only investment bankers can afford this place.

1 **Chelsea Brewing Company** • 212-336-6440. Microbrewery and restaurant. Try the amber ale, wings, nachos, and cheesy fries—all excellent.
2 **The Golf Club at Chelsea Piers** • 212-336-6400. Aside from potentially long wait times, the 250-yard driving range with 52 heated stalls and automated ball-feed (no buckets or bending over!) is pretty awesome. $25 buys you 90 balls (peak) or 147 balls (off-peak). If you don't bring your own, club hire is $4/one club, $5/two, $6/three, or $12/ten. Before 6 pm on weekdays, you can whack all the balls you want for $25 for three hours between 6:30 and 9:30 a.m.
3 **300 New York** • 212-835-BOWL. A very schmancy 40-lane bowling alley equipped with video games and bar. $8/game plus $6 shoe rental.
4 **Wichcraft** • 212-780-0577 Handcrafted sandwiches, soups, salads, and sweets.
5 **New York Presbyterian Sports Medicine Center** • 212-366-5100. Performance physical therapy.
6 **Paul Labrecque Salon & Spa** • 212-988-7186 Hair, skin, nails, and massage services to get you ready for the court, pitch, or pool.
7 **The Sports Center** • 212-336-6000. A very expensive, monster health club with a 10,000-square-foot climbing wall, a quarter-mile track, a swimming pool, and enough fitness equipment for a small army in training. If you have to ask how much the membership is, you can't afford it.
8 **Sky Rink** • 212-336-6100. Two 24/7 ice rinks mainly used for classes, training, and bar mitzvahs.
9 **The Lighthouse** • 212-336-6144. 10,000-square-foot event space for private gatherings catered by Abigail Kirsch.
10 **The Field House** • 212-336-6500. The Field House is an 80,000-square-foot building with a 23-foot climbing wall, a gymnastics training center, four batting cages, two basketball courts, and two indoor soccer fields.
11 **Spirit Cruise** • 866-483-3866; www.spiritofnewyork.com. Ships run out of Chelsea Piers and Weehawken, NJ. Dinner cruises are approximately $80/person, and if you're having a big function, you can rent the entire boat

Unfortunately, but not surprisingly, there are no golf courses on the island of Manhattan. Thankfully, there are two driving ranges where you can at least smack the ball around until you can get to a real course, as well as a golf simulator at Chelsea Piers that lets you play a full round "at" various popular courses (Pebble Beach, St. Andrews, etc.). NYC has a number of private and public courses throughout the outer boroughs and Westchester; however, they don't even come close to satisfying the area's huge demand for courses.

Golf Courses	*Borough*	*Address*	*Phone*	*Par*	*Fee*
Mosholu Golf Course	Bronx	3700 Jerome Ave	718-655-9164	18 holes, par 30	Weekend $27.00 for non-residents $24.25 for residents; weekdays $15.25 for 18 holes before 1 pm, $33.00 for non-residents and $29.00 for residents for 18 holes after 1 pm.
Pelham/Split Rock Golf	Bronx	870 Shore Rd	718-885-1258	18 holes, par 71	Weekend fees $17.75/early, twilight/$39.50 morning and afternoon - weekday fees $16.75 $28, non-residents add $8.
Van Cortlandt Golf Course	Bronx	Van Cortlandt Pk S & Bailey Ave	718-543-4595	18 holes, par 70	9 holes early for $18 M-F, 19.25 weekends; $39-$43 for 18 holes after 12, $21-$25 for Twilight on weekday weekend $38-$42 after 12, $24 twilight
Marine Park Golf Club	Brooklyn	2880 Flatbush Ave	718-338-7149	18 holes, par 72	Weekend fees $19.25/early for 9 holes, afternoon–weekday fees $18–$38, non-residents add $8
Dyker Beach Golf Course	Brooklyn	86th St & Seventh Ave	718-836-9722	18 holes, Par 71	Weekend fees $17/early, twilight/$38 morning and afternoon; weekday fees $16–$27, non-residents add $8
Golf Simulator	New York	Chelsea Piers Golf Club	212-336-6400		$43/hour (see previous Chelsea Piers page)
LaTourette Golf Course	Staten Island	1001 Richmond Hill Rd	718-351-1889	18 holes, par 72	M–F/$16.75–$28; weekend $17.75/early, twilight; $39.50/ morning and afternoon; non-resident add $8.
Silver Lake Golf Course	Staten Island	915 Victory Blvd	718-442-4653	18 holes, par 69	Weekend $22.00/early for 9 holes; 18 holes (before 12:00 pm) $35.00; twilight (adjusted seasonally) $25.00; Weekend (Reservation Fee Included); Early Morning (9 holes) $23.25, 18 holes (before 12:00 pm) $51.00; 18 holes (at or after 12:00 pm) $42.00; Twilight $28.00 plus $8 non resident fee
South Shore Golf Course	Staten Island	200 Huguenot Ave	718-984-0101	18 holes, par 72	Please see Silver Lake Golf Course rates also apply
Clearview Golf Course	Queens	202-12 Willets Point Blvd	718-229-2570	18 holes, par 70	Please see Silver Lake Golf Course rates also apply
Douglaston Golf Course	Queens	63-20 Marathon Pkwy, Douglaston	718-224-6566	18 holes, par 67	Please see Silver Lake Golf Course rates also apply
Forest Park Golf Course	Queens	101 Forest Park Dr, Woodhaven	718-296-0999	18 holes, par 70	Please see Silver Lake Golf Course rates also apply
Kissena Park Golf Course	Queens	164-15 Booth Memorial Ave	718-939-4594	18 holes, Par 64	Weekend fees $17.75/early, twilight/$39.50 morning and afternoon–weekday fees $16.75–$28, non-residents add $8.

Driving Ranges		*Address*	*Phone*	*Fee*
Brooklyn Sports Center	Brooklyn	3200 Flatbush Ave	718-253-6816	$10 for 150 balls, $12 for 285 balls
Chelsea Piers: Pier 59	Manhattan	Pier 59	212-336-6400	$20 for 118 balls, $30 for 186 balls
Randall's Island Golf	Manhattan	1 Randalls Is Rd	212-427-5689	$12 for 119 balls
Center Golden Bear	Queens	232-01 Northern Blvd	718-225-9187	$10 for large bucket, $7.50 for small bucket

For swimming pools in Manhattan, you pretty much have two options: pay exorbitant gym fees or health club fees in order to use the private swimming facilities, or wait until the summer to share the city's free outdoor pools with openly urinating summer camp attendees. OK, so it's not that bad! Some YMCAs and YWCAs have nice indoor pools, and their fees are reasonable. And several of the same New York public recreation centers that have outdoor pools (and some that do not) have indoor pools for year-round swimming. Though plenty of kids use the pools, there are dedicated adult swim hours in the mornings, at lunch time, and in the evenings (pee-free if you get there early). Just don't forget to follow each pool's admittance ritual, strange as it may seem—the locker room attendants generally rule with an iron fist. And if you can wait the obligatory 30 minutes, there's an authentic local food court near the standout public pool in Red Hook (155 Bay St, Brooklyn).

Then there's the Hudson. Yes, we're serious. There are about eight races in the Hudson each year, and the water quality is tested before each race. New York City also has some great beaches for swimming, including Coney Island, Manhattan Beach, and the Rockaways. If you prefer your swimming area enclosed, check out the pool options in Manhattan:

Pools

Pools	*Address*	*Phone*	*Type*	*Fees*	*Map*
Abe Lincoln	E 135 St & 5 Ave	212-491-1714	Outdoor-Summer months		19
Asphalt Green	555 E 90th St	212-369-8890	Indoor	$25/day	17
Asser Levy Recreation Center free,	E 23rd St & Asser Levy Pl 10		212-447-2020	Indoor, OutdoorOutdoor Indoor $75/year	
Athletic and Swim Club at Equitable Center	787 Seventh Ave	212-265-3490	Indoor	Call for fees	12
Bally Toal Fitness	139 W 32nd St	212-465-1750	Indoor	$25/day	9
Bally Toal Fitness	350 W 50th St	212-265-9400	Indoor	$25/day	11
Chelsea Piers Sports Center	19th St & Hudson River Park	212-336-6000	Indoor	Call for fees	8
Chelsea Recreation Center	430 W 25th St	212-255-3705	Indoor	$100/year for adults free for children	8
Dry Dock	Avenue C & E 10th St	212-677-4481	Outdoor - Summer months		7
Frederick Douglass	Amsterdam Ave & W 100 St	212-316-3241	Outdoor - Summer months		16
Gravity Fitness Center at Le Parker 12 Meridien		119 W 56th St	212-708-73400	Indoor	$50/day
Hamilton Fish Recreation Center	128 Pitt St	212-387-7687	Outdoor - Summer months	Free	4
Hansborough Recreation Center	35 W 134th St	212-234-9603	Indoor	$75/year	19
Highbridge	2301 Amsterdam Ave	212-927-2400	Outdoor - Summer months	Free	23
Jackie Robinson Pool	85 Bradhurst Ave	212-234-9606	Outdoor - Summer months	Free	21
John Jay	E 77th St & Cherokee Pl	212-794-6566	Outdoor - Summer months	Free	15
Lasker Pool	110th St & Lenox Ave	212-534-7639	Outdoor - Summer months	Free	19
Lenox Hill Neighborhood House	331 E 70th St	212-744-5022	Indoor	Call for fees	15
Manhattan Plaza Health Club	482 W 43rd St	212-563-7001	Indoor - Summer months	$35/day	11
Marcus Garvey Swimming Pool	13 E 124th St	212-410-2818	Outdoor - Summer months	Free	19
Millennium UN Plaza Hotel Health $30/day or $88/month Club	13	1 United Nations Plaza		212-702-5016	Indoor
New York Health & Racquet Club	110 W 56th St	212-541-7200	Indoor	$50/day or $99/month	12
New York Health & Racquet Club	132 E 45th St	212-986-3100	Indoor	$50/day or $99/month	13
New York Health & Racquet Club	1433 York Ave	212-737-6666	Indoor	$50/day or $99/month	15
New York Health & Racquet Club	20 E 50th St	212-593-1500	Indoor	$50/day or $99/month	12
New York Health & Racquet Club	24 E 13th St	212-924-4600	Indoor	$50/day or $$99/month	6
New York Health & Racquet Club	39 Whitehall St	212-269-9800	Indoor	$50/day or $99/month	1
New York Health & Racquet Club	62 Cooper Sq	212-904-0400	Indoor	$50/day or $99/month	6
New York Sports Club	1601 Broadway	212-977-8880	Indoor	$25/day	12
New York Sports Club	1637 Third Ave	212-987-7200	Indoor	$25/day	17
New York Sports Club	614 Second Ave	212-213-5999	Indoor	$25/day	10
Recreation Center 54	348 E 54th St	212-754-5411	Indoor	$75/year	13
Recreation Center 59	533 W 59th St	212-397-3159	Indoor	$75/year	11
Reebok Sports Club NY	160 Columbus Ave	212-362-6800	Indoor	$188/month	14
Riverbank State Park	679 Riverside Dr	212-694-3600	Indoor - Summer months	$2/day	21
Sheltering Arms	Amsterdam & W 129 St	212-662-6191	Indoor, Outdoor	$75/year	18
Sheraton New York Health Club	811 Seventh Ave	212-621-8591	Indoor - Summer months	$40/day	12
Thomas Jefferson Park	2180 First Ave	212-860-1383	Outdoor - Summer months	Free	20
Tompkins Square Mini Pool	500 E 9th St	212-387-7685	Outdoor - Summer months	Free	7
Tony Dapolito Recreation Center	1 Clarkson St	212-242-5228	Indoor, Outdoor	$75/year	5
West End Sports Club	75 West End Ave	212-265-8200	Indoor	$16/day	14
YMCA	1395 Lexington Ave	212-415-5700	Indoor	$30/day or $88/month	17
YMCA	180 W 135th St	212-281-4100	Indoor	$30/day or $88/month	19
YMCA	224 E 47th St	212-756-9600	Indoor	$30/day or $88/month	13
YMCA	344 E 14th St	212-780-0800	Indoor	$20/day	6

General Information

Manhattan Parks Dept: 212-360-8131 • Website: www.nycgovparks.org
Permit Locations: The Arsenal, 830 Fifth Ave & 64th St; Paragon Sporting Goods Store, 867 Broadway & 18th St

Overview

There are more tennis courts on the island of Manhattan than you might think, although getting to them may be a bit more than you bargained for. Most of the public courts in Manhattan are either smack in the middle of Central Park or are on the edges of the city—such as Hudson River Park (Map 5), East River Park (Map 7) and Riverside Park (Map 16). These courts in particular can make for some pretty windy playing conditions.

Tennis	*Address*	*Phone*	*Type/ # of Cts./Surface*	*Map*
East River Park	East River Park at Broome St	212-533-0656	12 hardcourts, lessons	4
Coles Center, NYU	181 Mercer St	212-998-2045	Schools, 9 courts, Rubber	6
Midtown Tennis Club	341 Eighth Ave	212-989-8572	Private, 8 courts, Har-Tru	8
Manhattan Plz Racquet Club	450 W 43rd St	212-594-0554	Private, 5 courts, Cushioned Hard	11
Millennium UN Plaza Hotel Gym	2nd Ave & 44th St	212-758-1234	Private, 1 court, Supreme	13
Millennium UN Plaza Hotel Health Club	1 United Nations Plaza	212-702-5016	Private, 1 hardcourt	13
River Club	447 E 52nd St	212-751-0100	Private, 2 courts, Clay	13
Town Tennis Club	430 E 56th St	212-752-4059	Private, 2 courts, Clay, Hard	13
Vanderbilt Tennis Club	15 Vanderbilt Ave, 3rd Fl	212-687-3841	Private, 2 courts, Hard	13
Rockefeller University	1230 York Ave	212-327-8000	Schools, 1 court, Hard	15
Sutton East Tennis Club	488 E 60th St	212-751-3452	Private, 8 courts, Clay, Available Oct–April.	15
Central Park Tennis Center	93rd St near West Dr	212-280-0205	Public, Outdoor, 26 Fast-Dry, 4 Hard	16
Riverside Park	Riverside Dr & W 96th St	212-469-2006	Public, Outdoor, 10 courts, Clay	16
PS 146 Ann M Short	421 E 106th St	n/a	Schools, 3 courts, Hard	17
Tower Tennis Courts	1725 York Ave	212-860-2464	Private, 2 courts, Hard	17
PS 125 Ralph Bunche	425 W 123rd St	n/a	Schools, 3 courts, Hard	18
Riverside Park	W 119th St & Riverside Dr	212-978-0277	10 hardcourts, lessons	18
Riverbank State Park	W 145th St & Riverside Dr	212-694-3600	Public, Outdoor, 1 court, Hard	21
F Johnson Playground	W 151st St & Seventh Ave	212-234-9609	Public, Outdoor, 8 courts, Hard	22
Fort Washington Park	Hudson River & 170th St	212-304-2322	Public, Outdoor, 10 courts, Hard	23
The Dick Savitt Tennis Center	575 W 218th St	212-942-7100	Private, 6 courts, Hard	25
Inwood Hill Park	207th St & Seaman Ave	212-304-2381	Public, Outdoor, 9 courts, Hard	25
Roosevelt Island Racquet Club	281 Main St	212-935-0250	Private, 12 courts, Clay	p260
Randall's Island	East & Harlem Rivers	212-860-1827	Public, Outdoor, 11 courts, Hard	p254
Randall's Island Indoor Tennis	Randall's Island Park	212-427-6150	Private, 4 courts, Hard Available Oct–April.	p254

Getting a Permit

The tennis season, according to the NYC Parks Department, lasts from April 7 to November 18. Permits are good for use until the end of the season at all public courts in all boroughs, and are good for one hour of singles or two hours of doubles play. Fees are:

- Juniors (17 yrs and under) $10
- Senior Citizen (62 yrs and over) $20
- Adults (18–61 yrs) $200
- Single-play tickets $15

Billiards Overview

Whether you're looking for a new hobby or need a new atmosphere in which to booze (that isn't your 300 sq. ft. apartment), a good pool-hall is a great way to get the job done. Or perhaps you simply enjoy a hearty game of 8-ball, and it's as simple as that; in any case, an eclectic mix of options dot the island of Manhattan.

	Address	*Phone*	*Map*	*Fee*
Tropical 128	128 Elizabeth St	212-925-8219	3	$8 per hour per person; $12 per hour for 2 people
Fat Cat Billiards	75 Christopher St	212-675-6056	5	$5.50;$6.50 on weekends per hour per player
Amsterdam Billiards and Bar	110 E 11th St	212-995-1314	6	$6 per person per hour
Pressure	110 University Pl	212-352-1161	6	$26 per hour
SoHo Billiards	298 Mulberry St	212-925-3753	6	$7 per hour per table
Slate Restaurant Bar & Billiards	54 W 21st St	212-989-0096	9	$17 per hour for two players
East Side Billiard Club	163 E 86th St	212-831-7665	16	$7.50 per hour per person
Post Billiards Café	154 Post Ave	212-569-1840	25	Weekdays, $8 per hour for 2 people; weekends 10 per hour for 2 people

Bowling Overview

Whether you're looking for a new hobby or need a new atmosphere in which to booze (that isn't your 300 sq. ft. apartment), a good pool-hall is a great way to get the job done. Or perhaps you simply enjoy a hearty game of 8-ball, and it's as simple as that; in any case, an eclectic mix of options dot the island of Manhattan.

If you want to go bowling in Manhattan, you have five options. Keep in mind that there's just about no way to bowl cheaply, so if you're struggling to keep a positive balance in your bank account, you may want to find another activity or head out to New Jersey.

Manhattan	*Address*	*Phone*	*Map*	*Fees*
300	Chelsea Piers, Pier 60	212-835-2695	8	$8.75/game/person. $5 for shoes.
Bowlmor Lanes	110 University Pl	212-255-8188	6	Su–Th: Before 5pm: $9.45/game; After 5pm $9.95/game; Fri-Sat: Before 5pm: $9.95/game; After 5pm: $10.95/ game; Shoes: $6
Bowlmor Lanes	222 W 44th St	212-680-0012	12	
Frames	550 9th Ave	212-268-6909	11	M-F before 5pm, $7/game; All other times, $10.50/game; $6 shoes.
Lucky Strike Lanes	624 W 42nd St	646-829-0170	11	$25 per lane per 1/2 hour, $4 shoes.

Brooklyn	*Address*	*Phone*	*Fees*
Brooklyn Bowl	61 Wythe Ave	718-963-3369	$25 per lane per 1/2 hour, $3.50 shoes.
The Gutter	200 N 14th St, Williamsburg	718-387-3585	$6-$7/game/person, $2 for shoes.
Maple Lanes	1570 60th St, Borough Park	718-331-9000	$4.50–$6.50 per game, $4.25 shoes.
Melody Lanes	461 37th St, Sunset Park	718-832-2695	$5.50–$7.00 per game, $3.50 shoes.
Shell Lanes	1 Bouck Ct, Coney Island	718-336-6700	$3.25–$5.25 per game, $3.50 shoes.
Strike 10 Lanes	6161 Strickland Ave, Marine Park	718-763-3333	$6.00-$8.00, $4.25 for shoes.

Queens	*Address*	*Phone*	*Fees*
AMF 34th Avenue Lanes	69-10 34th Ave, Woodside	718-651-0440	$4–$6 per game, $4.75 for shoes
Astoria Bowl - Maric Lanes	19-45 49th St, Astoria	718-274-1910	$4 per game, $6 on weekends, $4 for shoes
Cozy Bowl	98-18 Rockaway Blvd, Ozone Park	718-843-5553	$3–$6 per game, $3.50 for shoes.
JIB Lanes	67-19 Parsons Blvd, Flushing	718-591-0600	$3.75 per game, $3.50 for shoes.
Whitestone Lanes	30-05 Whitestone Expy, Flushing	718-353-6300	$4.50-$7.50 per game, $4.50 shoes.

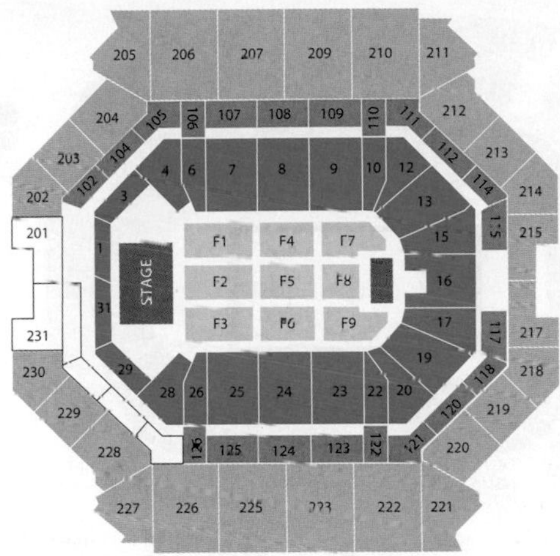

General Information

Address	620 Atlantic Avenue
Website:	barclayscenter.com
Nets:	www.nba.com/nets
Tickets:	877-77-BKTIX

Overview

Barclays Center, the new home for the Brooklyn Nets, opened in 2012 as part of the controversial $4.9 billion Atlantic Yards redevelopment project. Why so controversial? Neighborhood residents were meant to enjoy more jobs and affordable housing as part of the redevelopment, but that hasn't exactly come to pass, and some residents (including a homeless shelter) were forced out by eminent domain. However you may feel about it, it's now a done deal, so let's hope for the best.

The original architectural design was created by Frank Gehry, the king of urban revitalization, but it was horrendously expensive, especially following the 2008 financial collapse, so the fi rm of Ellerbe Becket took over. The Brooklyn Nets began play at the arena for the 2012–13 season after playing in New Jersey since 1977, and for those who don't dig basketball, there are big-name concerts (like Jay-Z, part owner of the Nets) accommodating 19,000 fans.

How To Get There—Driving

Parking is so limited that Barclays Center practically demands that you use public transport, but if you must, you can reserve a spot at the center (should there be any available, being a suiteholder helps), find a nearby garage, or scour for street parking.

How To Get There—Mass Transit

Part of the draw of Barclays Center is its proximity to Brooklyn's largest transportation hub. The 2, 3, 4, 5, B, D, N, Q and R trains all service the arena, and you can also take the C to Lafayette Avenue or the G to Fulton Street. The LIRR stops at Atlantic Terminal, just across the street from the arena. In addition, eleven bus lines stop right outside or nearby.

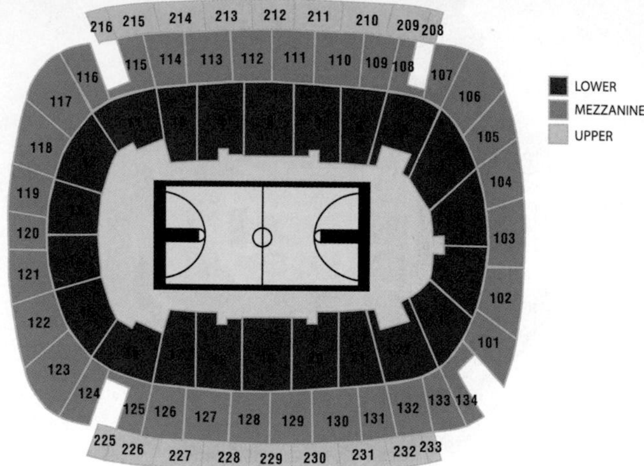

Prudential Center Information

Address: 165 Mulberry St Newark, NJ 07102
Website: www.prucenter.com
Devils: www.devils.nhl.com
Seton Hall: www.shupirates.com
Ticketmaster: 800-745-3000, www.ticketmaster.com

Overview

Opened in October 2007, the Prudential Center (or "The Rock" to the media and fans) is a state of the art arena in downtown Newark. Yes, you heard that right, downtown Newark is now a prime destination for major league sports and top-notch live music. With a capacity of 18,000 and all the bells and whistles of the modern sports going experience, New Jersey Devils fans are loving this place—as are Seton Hall basketball fans. The Rock is hands down a billion times better than the cold and charmless Izod Center which is sitting in the middle of the Meadowlands all alone and empty except for the occasional Doo Wop or Megadeth concert (no joke)—its future is now as murky as a bucketful of Meadowlands swamp water.

How to Get There—Driving

No need to get on a bus anymore at Port Authority, thank goodness, for Devils games. From the NJ Turnpike Southbound take Exit 15W onto I-280 westbound. Turn right on Exit 15 A towards Route 21 southbound. Turn right onto Rector Street. Turn left onto Broad Street southbound. Continue on Broad Street to Lafayette Street and make a left. Prudential Center will be on your left hand side. According to the website The Prudential Center "is one of the most easily accessible arenas in the country." There is lots of parking, but traffic can still be unpredictable. Always allow more time than you think you'll need. Highways surrounding the arena include 280, 78, NJ Turnpike, 1 & 9, 21, 22, Garden State Parkway, 80 and NJ 3.

How to Get There—Mass Transit

No need to get on a bus anymore at Port Authority, thank goodness, for Devils games. Just take NJ Transit to Broad Street Station, then switch to Newark Light Rail to Newark Penn Station, which is only two blocks west of the Prudential Center. Even easier is taking the PATH train to Newark Station. The arena is only a short walk away. Call or check the website for more details.

How to Get Tickets

The box office is open Monday to Friday from 11 am to 6 pm and is closed Saturday and Sunday, unless there is an event. To purchase tickets without going to the box office, call Ticketmaster at 800-745-3000, or visit their website. Or try stubhub.com the day of the game to find some good deals.

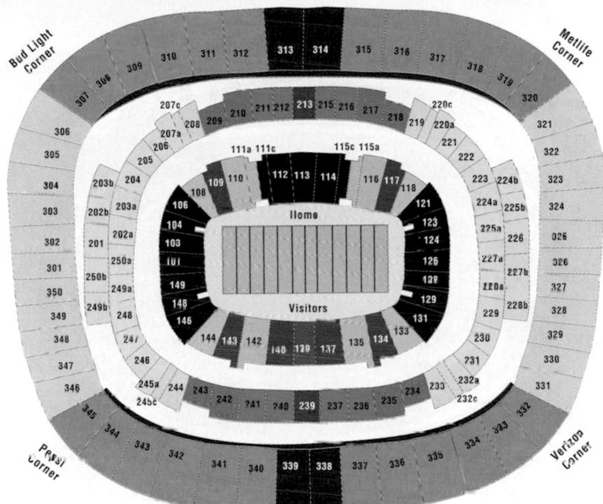

General Information

Address:	East Rutherford, NJ 07073
Phone:	201-935-3900
Giants:	www.giants.com
Jets:	www.newyorkjets.com
Red Bulls:	www.newyorkredbulls.com
Ticketmaster:	800-745-3000, www.ticketmaster.com

Overview

Well, well, how times have changed. Who's the other top team settling into its new shared home field "MetLife Stadium?" That's right—the JETS J-E-T-S JETS! How 'bout dem Jets, fans? Rex Ryan's team continues to play great. Except in the AFC Championship Game. But don't be surprised to see a Super Bowl berth sometime very soon. If not, at least we'll always have memories of the 2014 Super Bowl at the Meadowlands.

Of course, with the Giants having won a Super Bowl as recently as 2011, the claim can be made that there are two very good franchises sharing the new stadium. We'll see how we like it, but the fact remains that they spent a billion dollars to build it and guess what? Still no roof. So we'll be freezing our asses off in December again. But then again, maybe that's the way football is supposed to be…at least if you're a cheese-head.

How to Get There —Driving

MetLife Stadium is only five miles from the Lincoln Tunnel (closer to Midtown than Shea Stadium, even), but leave early if you want to get to the game on time—remember that the Giants and the Jets are a) sold out for every game and b) have tons of fans from both Long Island and the five boroughs. You can take the Lincoln Tunnel to Route 3 W to Route 120 N, or you can try either the Holland Tunnel to the New Jersey Turnpike N to Exit 16W, or the George Washington Bridge to the New Jersey Turnpike S to Exit 16W. Accessing the stadium from Exit 16W allows direct access to parking areas. Parking costs $25 for most events except NFL games where all cars must have pre-paid parking permits only.

How to Get There–Mass Transit

On game days NJ Transit now runs trains directly to the stadium. The new stop is called Meadowland Sports Complex. Train service will begin about 3 ½ hours prior to a major event or football game. After events, trains will depart frequently from the Meadowlands for up to two hours.

How to Get Tickets

For the Jets and the Giants, scalpers and friends are the only options. For the Red Bulls and for concerts, you can call Ticketmaster or visit the website.

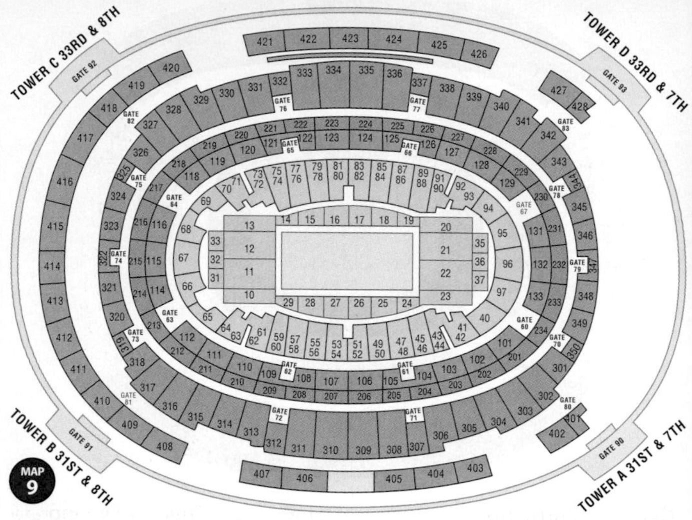

General Information

NFT Map:	9
Address:	4 Pennsylvania Plz New York, NY 10001
Phone:	212-465-6741
Website:	www.thegarden.com
Knicks:	www.nyknicks.com
Liberty:	www.nyliberty.com
Rangers:	www.newyorkrangers.com
Ticketmaster:	800-745-3000, www.ticketmaster.com

Overview

Once resembling the Doge's Palace in Venice (c.1900), the since-relocated Altoid 'tween Seventh and Eighth Avenues atop Penn Station remains one of the legendary venues in sport, becoming so almost solely by way of the sport of boxing. It now, for good and ill, houses the NBA's Knicks (catch Spike Lee and various supermodels courtside), NHL's Rangers, The Liberty of the WNBA, St. John's University's Red Storm, as well as concerts, tennis tournaments, dog shows, political conventions, and, for those of you with 2+ years of graduate school, monster truck rallies and "professional" wrestling. There's also The Theater at Madison Square Garden for more intimate shows. Check out MSG's website for a full calendar of events.

How to Get There–Mass Transit

MSG is right above Penn Station, which makes getting there very easy. You can take the A C E and 1 2 3 lines to 34th Street and Penn Station, or the N R Q B D M and PATH lines to 34th Street and 6th Avenue. The Long Island Rail Road also runs right into Penn Station.

How to Get Tickets

For single seats for the Knicks and the Rangers, you can try Ticketmaster, but a better bet would be to try the "standby" line (show up a half-hour before game time and wait). You can find some decent deals online at Craigslist, Stubhub, and eBay when the Knicks are riding a losing streak (which definitely has been the case in recent years). The ubiquitous ticket scalpers surrounding the Garden are a good last resort for when your rich out-of-town friends breeze in to see a game. Liberty tickets (and tickets for other events) are usually available through Ticketmaster.

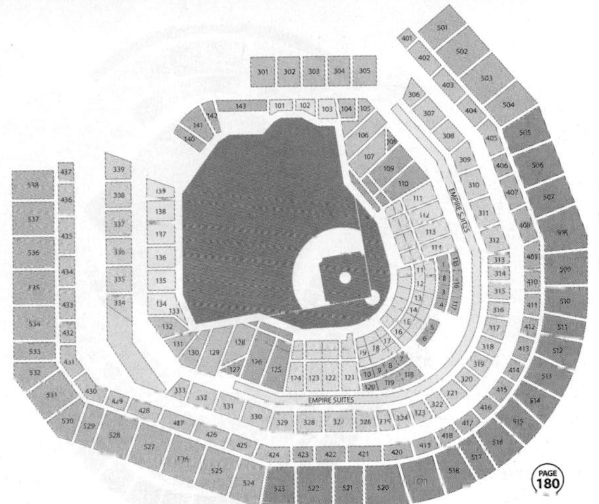

General Information

Address:	123-01 Roosevelt Ave & 126th St Flushing, Queens
Shea Stadium/Citi Field Box Office:	718-507-TIXX
Website:	www.mets.com
Mets Clubhouse Shops:	11 W 42nd St & Roosevelt Field Mall, Garden City, LI
Ferry:	800-BOATRIDE or 732-872-2628

Overview

The t-shirts reading, "I'm Still Calling It Shea," were ready by the new stadium's opening, though given the financial crisis some of us have been referring to it as "Debit's Field" or "Two-Shea," but naming aside it's actually a pretty nice ballpark. Fans enter through The Jackie Robinson Rotunda, guaranteeing that young fans who know nothing of segregated baseball and separate drinking fountains will get a little lesson on civil rights as they read the inspiring quotes etched in the façade and pose for pictures next to Robert Indiana's sculpture of the number 42. Once inside you might get the feeling you're at a food court with a ball game going on in the background, but the selections are pretty good, including Shake Shack, Nathan's, Blue Smoke and El Verano Taquería. There are even some spots where you can get a decent sized beer on tap for $6 (at press time). You can buy nostalgic sports gear at "47" (named for the year Robinson broke into the majors) and women can buy their Mets bikinis and form-fitting jeans with a pair of eye-catching Mets logos on the butt at Touch by Alyssa Milano. There are about 14,000 fewer seats than at Shea, making affordable seating less available, but the Mets tier their ticket prices so that a weeknight game against a lousy team can be a pretty good deal, even if you have no view of the left field corner. Oh yes, and those people protesting nearby are the hard-working small business owners that the city is kicking out in order to improve the surroundings.

How To Get Tickets

You can order Mets tickets by phone through the Mets' box office, on the internet through the Mets' website, or at the Mets Clubhouse Shops (11 West 42nd St, the Manhattan Mall, and Roosevelt Field Mall in Garden City).

How To Get There—Driving

Yeah. Good luck trying to make the first pitch on a weekday night. But if you must, take the Robert F. Kennedy Bridge to the Grand Central Parkway; the Mid-Town Tunnel to the Long Island Expressway to the Grand Central; or the Brooklyn-Queens Expressway to the LIE to the Grand Central. If you want to try and avoid the highways, get yourself over to Astoria Boulevard in Queens, make a right on 108th Street, then a left onto Roosevelt Avenue.

How To Get There—Mass Transit

The 7 train runs straight to Citi Field, and the MTA frequently offers special express trains that make limited stops between Citi Field and Times Square, making it by far the easiest way to get to the stadium. The E F M and R trains connect with the 7 at 74th Street-Roosevelt Avenue. The other option from Midtown is the Port Washington LIRR from Penn Station, which stops at Citi Field on game days.

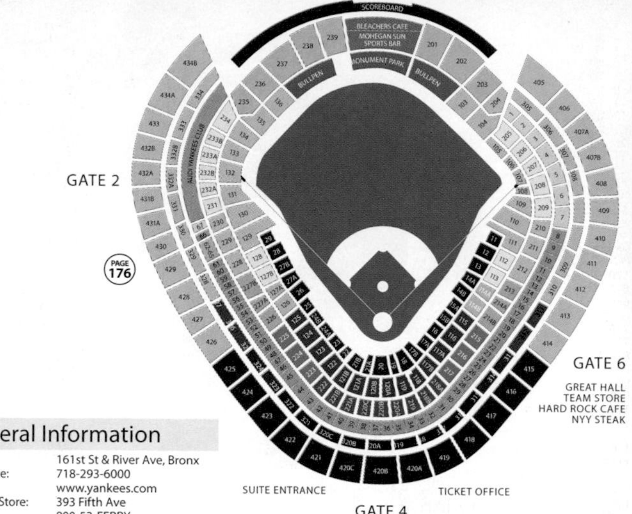

PAGE 176

General Information

Address:	161st St & River Ave, Bronx
Box Office:	718-293-6000
Website:	www.yankees.com
Yankees Store:	393 Fifth Ave
Ferry:	800-53-FERRY
Ticketmaster:	800-745-3000; www.ticketmaster.com

Overview

New Yankee Stadium is here. And it's big. Very, very big. There's a lot of great amenities (the Lobel's Sliced Steak Sandwich Cart is far and away our favorite), but there's also a lot to complain about. In no particular order: seats cost more, most seats are farther away from the field, you can barely hear the crack of the bat, the stadium doesn't get as loud anymore, there is a stupid wire that runs across your field of vision on the first and third base lines on the upper levels, you have to pay extra to get into the outfield bar, you can't get in to one of the restaurants without a fancy seat, half the fancy seats are unsold so there is all this empty space where all the best seats are, the stadium floors are rough plain concrete and the ramps and staircases are so bare as to feel almost prison-like, you still can't bring a bag into the place… we could keep going. While the video screen is amazing, we'd prefer to actually watch the game LIVE by being CLOSE TO THE FIELD. And since the policy of not showing any play that is remotely controversial (i.e. interesting) on replay still seems to be in place, why go at all? Honestly, we're thinking of switching our allegiances; maybe we'll at least wait for Mo to retire. At least the team is good; we say: enjoy watching them on TV.

While the Yanks didn't win it all last year, they were still pretty damned good, making it to the American League Championship Series—but of course, that's rarely good enough for the Bronx Bombers. Biggest question: will the aging team be able to stave off the effects of Father Time? Only (time) will tell…

How to Get There—Driving

Driving to Yankee Stadium from Manhattan isn't as bad as you might think. Your best bet is to take the Willis Avenue Bridge from either First Avenue or FDR Drive and get on the Major Deegan for about one mile until you spot the stadium exit. From the Upper West Side, follow Broadway up to 155th Street and use the Macombs Dam Bridge to cross over the river to the stadium (thus avoiding crosstown traffic). Parking (in contrast to ticket prices) is cheap, especially at lots a few blocks away from the stadium.

How to Get There—Mass Transit

Getting to the stadium by subway is easy. The 4 and D and the B (on weekdays) all run express to the stadium, and you can easily hook up with those lines at several junctions in Manhattan. And now you can take Metro-North, since the city built a dedicated station just for Yankee Stadium.

How to Get Tickets

You can purchase tickets by phone through Ticketmaster, at the box office or the Yankee store, or online through either Ticketmaster or the Yankees website. And of course the illegal scalpers who are all over the damned place.

Television

1	NY1 (24-Hour News)	www.ny1.com
2	WCBS (CBS)	newyork.cbslocal.com
4	WNBC (NBC)	www.nbcnewyork.com
5	WNYW (FOX)	www.myfoxny.com
7	WABC (ABC)	abclocal.go.com/wabc
9	WWOR (My9)	www.my9tv.com
11	11 WPIX (PIX11)	pix11.com
13	WNET (PBS)	www.thirteen.org
21	WLIW (Long Island Public)	www.wliw.org
25	NYC TV (Public)	www.nyc.gov/media
31	WPXN (Ion)	www.ionline.tv
41	WXTV (Univision)	www.univision.com
47	WNJU (Telemundo)	www.telemundo.com
49	CPTV (Conn. Public)	www.cptv.org
50	WNJN (NJ Public)	www.njn.net
63	WMBC (Ethnic/Religious)	www.wmbctv.com

AM Stations

570	WMCA	Religious
620	WSNR	Talk/Ethnic
660	WFAN	Sports/Mets/Giants Nets/Devils
710	WOR	Talk
770	WABC	Talk/Jets
820	WNYC	Talk
880	WCBS	News/Yankees
930	WPAT	Talk/Ethnic (NJ)
970	WNYM	Talk
1010	WINS	News
1050	WEPN	Sports/Jets/Knicks/ Rangers (en Espanol)
1100	WHLI	Easy Listening
1130	WBBR	Talk/Bloomberg/ Islanders
1160	WVNJ	Talk
1190	WLIB	Gospel
1230	WFAS	Adult Standards
1240	WGBB	Mandarin Chinese
1280	WADO	Talk/Sports (en Espanol)Knicks/ Yankees/Jets
1330	WWRV	Religious (en Espanol)
1380	WKDM	Chinese (Mandarin)
1460	WVOX	Talk
1480	WZRC	Cantonese
1520	WTHE	Gospel
1530	WJDM	Religious (en Espanol)
1560	WQEW	Radio Disney
1600	WWRL	Talk/NY Liberty
1660	WWRU	Korean

FM Stations

88.1	WCWP	College (LI)
88.3	WBGO	Jazz (NJ)
88.7	WRHU	College (LI)
88.9	WSIA	College
89.1	WFDU	College (NJ)
89.1	WNYU	College
89.5	WSOU	College/Rock (NJ)
89.9	WKCR	College/Jazz
90.3	WHCR	College
90.3	WHPC	College (LI)
90.7	WFUV	Adult Alternative
91.1	WFMU	Free-form! (NJ)
91.5	WNYE	Radio NY
92.3	WNOW	Top 40
93.1	WPAT	Latin (NJ)
93.5	WVIP	Caribbean
93.9	WNYC	Talk/Classical
94.7	WNSH	Country
95.5	WPLJ (JACK)	Top 40
96.3	WXNY	Latin
96.7	KLV	Contemporary Christian
97.1	WQHT	Hip-Hop/R&B
97.9	WSKQ	Latin
98.3	WKJY	Adult Contemporary
98.7	WEPN	Sports
99.5	WBAI	Talk
100.3	WHTZ (Z-100)	Top 40
100.7	WHUD	Adult Contemporary
101.1	WCBS	Oldies
101.9	WFAN	Sports
102.7	WWFS	Adult Contemporary
103.5	WKTU	Top 40/Dance (LI)
103.9	WFAS	Top 40
104.3	WAXQ	Classic Rock
105.1	WWPR	Hip-Hop/R&B
105.5	WDHA	Rock (NJ)
105.9	WQXR	Classical
106.3	WFME	Religious(NJ)
106.7	WLTW	Adult Contemporary
107.1	WXPK	Adult Alternative
107.5	WBLS	Urban Adult Contemporary

Print Media

AM New York	330 W 34th St, 17th Floor	212-4482970	Free daily; pick it up at the subway.
Daily News	4 New York Plaza	212-210-2100	Daily tabloid; rival of the *Post*. Good sports.
El Diario	1 Metrotech Ctr, 18th Floor	212-807-4600	Daily; America's oldest Spanish-language newspaper.
Magazine	45 Main St, 8th Fl, Brooklyn	718-596-3462	Bi-weekly arts and events focus; free.
Metro NYC	44 Wall St	212-952-1500	Free daily; pick it up at the subway.
Newsday	235 Pinelawn Rd, Melville	631-843-2000	Daily; based in Long Island.
New York Magazine	75 Varick St	212-508-0700	Broad-based upscale weekly.
New York Review of Books	435 Hudson St, 3rd Floor	212-757-8070	Bi-weekly; intellectual lit review. Recommended.
New York Observer	321 W 44th St, 6th Floor	212-755-2400	Weekly.
New York Post	1211 Avenue of the Americas	212-930-8000	Daily tabloid; known for its sensationalist headlines.
New York Times	620 Eighth Ave	212-698-4637	Daily; one of the world's best-known papers.
The New Yorker	4 Times Square	212-286-5400	Weekly; intellectual news, lit, and arts.
Time Out New York	475 Tenth Ave, 12th Fl	646-432-3000	Weekly; the best guide to goings-on in the city.
The Village Voice	36 Cooper Sq	212-475-3300	Free, alternative weekly.
Wall Street Journal	200 Liberty St	212-416-2000	Daily; famous financial paper.

January

Winter Antiques Show	Park Ave at 67th St	Selections from all over the country.
Three Kings Day Parade	El Museo del Barrio	Features a cast of hundreds from all over the city dressed as kings or animals—camels, sheep, and donkeys (early Jan).
Outsider Art Fair	Corner of Lafayette & Houston	Art in many forms of media from an international set. $15 admits one for one day.
National Boat Show	Jacob Javits Convention Center	Don't go expecting a test drive (early Jan).
Chinese New Year	Chinatown	Features dragons, performers, and parades.
NYC Winter Jazzfest	Greenwich Village	A full weekend of jazz at multiple Village venues.

February

Empire State Building Run-Up	Empire State Building	Run until the 86th floor (0.2 miles) or heart seizure.
The Art Show	Park Ave at 67th St	A very large art fair.
Westminster Dog Show	Madison Square Garden	Fancy canines more well groomed than you.
Seventh on Sixth Fall Fashion Show	Bryant Park	Weeklong celeb-studded event.

March

International Cat Show	Madison Square Garden	Fine felines.
St Patrick's Day Parade	Fifth Avenue	Irish pride (March 17). We recommend fleeing.
Orchid Show	Bronx River Parkway	Brought to you by the New York Botanical Garden.
Whitney Biennial	Whitney Museum	Whitney's most important American art, every other year (March–June).
Greek Independence Day Parade	Fifth Avenue	Floats and bands representing area Greek Orthodox churches and Greek federations and organizations (Late March).
The Armory Show	West Side Piers	Brilliant best-of-galleries show—recommended.
New Directors/New Films	MoMA	Film festival featuring new films by emerging directors.

April

Macy's Flower Show	Broadway and 34th St	Flowers and leather-clad vixens. Okay, just flowers really.
Easter Parade	Fifth Avenue	Starts at 11 am, get there early (Easter Sunday).
New York Antiquarian Book Fair	Park Ave at 67th St	170 international booksellers exhibition.
New York International Auto Show	Jacob Javits Convention Center	Traffic jam.
New York City Ballet Spring Season	Lincoln Center	Features new and classical ballet (April–June).

May

Tribeca Film Festival	Various locations including Regal 16 at BPC, BMCC Chambers St, Battery Park	Festival includes film screenings, panels, lectures, discussion groups, and concerts (Early May).
The Great Five Boro Bike Tour	Battery Park to Staten Island	Tour de NYC (first Sunday in May).
Ninth Avenue International Food Festival	Ninth Ave from 37th to 57th Sts	Decent but overrated.
Fleet Week	USS Intrepid	Boats and sailors from many navies (last week in May).
New York AIDS Walk	Central Park	10K walk whose proceeds go toward finding a cure.
Lower East Side Festival of the Arts	Theater for the New City, 155 First Ave	Celebrating Beatniks and Pop Art (last weekend in May).
Spring Flower Exhibition	NY Botanical Garden, Bronx	More flowers.
Cherry Blossom Festival	Brooklyn Botanic Garden	Flowering trees and Japanese cultural events (late April–early May).
Martin Luther King, Jr/369th Regiment Parade	Fifth Avenue	Celebration of equal rights (third Sunday in May).
Thursday Night Concert Series	South Street Seaport	Free varied concerts (May–September).
Affordable Art Fair	Midtown	Prices from $500 to no more than $10,000; worth a look if you're buying.

June

Event	Location	Description
• Puerto Rican Day Parade	Fifth Avenue	Puerto Rican pride.
• Metropolitan Opera Parks Concerts	Various locations	Free performances through June and July.
• Museum Mile Festival	Fifth Avenue	Museum open-house (second Sunday in June).
• Gay and Lesbian Pride Parade	Columbus Circle, Fifth Ave & Christopher St	Commemorates the 1969 Stonewall riots (last Sunday in June).
• Blue Note Jazz Festival	Various locations	All kinds of jazz.
• JVC Jazz Festival	Various locations	Descends from the Newport Jazz Festival.
• Mermaid Parade	Coney Island	Showcase of sea-creatures and freaks—basically, Brooklynites.
• Feast of St Anthony of Padua	Little Italy	Patron saint of expectant mothers, Portugal, seekers of lost articles, shipwrecks, Tigua Indians, and travel hostesses, among other things (Saturday before summer solstice).
• Central Park SummerStage	Central Park	Free concerts, but get there very, VERY early. (June–August).
• Bryant Park Free Summer Season	Sixth Ave at 42nd St	Free music, dance, and film (June–August).
• Midsummer Night Swing	Lincoln Center	Performances with free dance lessons (June–July).
• Big Apple Barbecue Block Party	Madison Sq Park	Outdoor jazz, endless grilled meats. 'Nuff said.
• American Crafts Festival	Lincoln Center	Celebrating quilts and such.
• Village Voice 4Knots Music Festival	South Street Seaport	Free outdoor show featuring renowned and Music Festival emerging artists. For the alternative minded.
• Howl Festival	Tompkins Square Park	Counter culture meets commerce: ah, we love the East Village! Recommended.

July

Event	Location	Description
• Macy's Fireworks Display	East River	Independence Day's literal highlight (July 4).
• Washington Square Music Festival	W 4th St at LaGuardia Pl	Open-air concert (July–August).
• New York Philharmonic Concerts	Various locations	Varied programs (June-July).
• Summergarden	MoMA	Free classical concerts (July–August).
• Celebrate Brooklyn! Performing Arts Festival	Prospect Park Bandshell	Nine weeks of free outdoor events (July–August).
• Mostly Mozart	Lincoln Center	The name says it all (July–August).
• New York Shakespeare Festival	Delacorte Theater in Central Park	Two free plays every summer (June–September)—Zounds!
• Music on the Boardwalk	Coney Island	"Under the Boardwalk" not on the set list, presumably… (July–August).
• PS1 Warm Up	PS1 Contemporary Art Center	An assortment of musical performances every Saturday afternoon (July–August).

August

Event	Location	Description
• Harlem Week	Harlem	Black and Latino culture. The celebration lasts all month.
• Hong Kong Dragon Boat Festival	Flushing-Meadows Park Lake, Queens	Wimpy canoes need not apply.
• The Fringe Festival	Various locations, Lower East Side	Avant-garde theater.
• US Open Tennis Championships	USTA National Tennis Center, Flushing	Final Grand Slam event of the year (August–September).
Lincoln Center Out of Doors	Lincoln Center	Free outdoor performances throughout the month.

September

Event	Location	Description
West Indian Day Carnival	Eastern Parkway from Utica—Grand Army Plaza, Brooklyn	Children's parade on Saturday, adult's parade on Labor Day (Labor Day Weekend).
Richmond County Fair	441 Clarke Ave, Staten Island	Best agricultural competitions (Labor Day).
Feast of San Gennaro	Little Italy	Plenty of greasy street food (third week in September).
Broadway on Broadway	Times Square	Free outdoor concert celebrating musicals

September—*continued*

• Brooklyn BeerFest	N 11th St between Berry and Wythe, Brooklyn	Taste test of over 100 beers. Yum!
• Atlantic Antic	Brooklyn Heights	Multicultural street fair (last Sunday in September).
• New York City Opera Season	Lincoln Center	Popular and classical operas.
• DUMBO Art Festival	DUMBO, Brooklyn	Over 500 artists show you their stuff under a bridge.

October

• Race for the Mayor's Cup	NY Harbor	And the winner gets to find out what he's been drinking (September–November)!
• New York Film Festival	Lincoln Center	Features film premieres (early October).
• Fall Crafts Park Avenue	Seventh Regiment Armory on Park Avenue, b/w 66th and 67th Sts	Display and sale of contemporary American crafts by 175 of the nation's finest craft artists.
• Columbus Day Parade	Fifth Avenue	Celebrating the second person to discover America (Columbus Day).
• Halloween Parade	West Village	Brings a new meaning to costumed event (October 31).
• Halloween Dog Parade	East Village	"Awwww, they're so cuuuute!"
• Blessing of the Animals	St John the Divine, Morningside Heights	Where to take your gecko.
• Big Apple Circus	Lincoln Center	Step right up (October–January)!
• Hispanic Day Parade	Fifth Ave b/w 44th and 86th Sts	A celebration of Latin America's rich heritage (mid October).
• Open House NY	Various locations, all boroughs	Insider access to architecture and design landmarks (early October)—recommended.
• NY Underground Comedy	Various locations	Find undiscovered comedians before Comedy Festival Central does.
• NY Comic Con	Jacob Javits Center	Comic enthusiasts convene at the nerd mecca.

November

• New York City Marathon	Verrazano to Central Park	26 miles of NYC air (first Sunday of November).
• Veteran's Day Parade	Fifth Ave from 42nd St to 79th St	Service at Eternal Light Memorial in Madison Square Park following the parade.
• Macy's Thanksgiving Day Parade	Central Park West at 79th St to Macy's	Santa starts the holiday season.
• The Nutcracker Suite	Lincoln Center	Christmas tradition (November–December).
• Singing Christmas Tree	South Street Seaport	Warning: might scare small children, family pets, and stoners (November–December).
• Christmas Spectacular	Radio City Music Hall	Rockettes star (November–January).
• A Christmas Carol	Madison Square Garden	Dickens by way of New York City (Nov–Jan).
• Origami Christmas Tree	Museum of Natural History	Hopefully not decorated with candles (Nov–Jan).
• The Pier Antiques Show	Pier 94	Look at old things you can't afford..

December

• Christmas Tree Lighting Ceremony	Rockefeller Center	Most enchanting spot in the city, if you don't mind sharing it with about a million others.
• Messiah Sing-In	Call 212-333-5333	Handel would be proud.
• New Year's Eve Fireworks	Central Park	Hot cider and food available (December 31).
• New Year's Eve Ball Drop	Times Square	Welcome the new year with a freezing mob (Dec 31).
• Blessing of the Animals	Central Presbyterian Church	Where to take your other gecko (December 24).
• Menorah Lighting	Fifth Avenue	Yarmulke required.
• New Year's Eve Midnight Run	Central Park	5k for the brave.
• John Lennon Vigil	Strawberry Fields, Central Park	Anniversary of the singer/songwriter's death (December 9).
• Alvin Ailey American Dance Theater	New York City Center	Dance at its best.
• Holiday Window Displays	Saks Fifth Avenue, Macy's, Lord & Taylor	A New York tradition.

"New York is the concentrate of art and commerce and sport and religion and entertainment and finance, bringing to a single compact arena the gladiator, the evangelist, the promoter, the actor, the trader and the merchant." —E. B. White

Useful Phone Numbers

Emergencies:	911
General City Information:	311
MTA Hotline	511
City Board of Elections:	212-VOTE-NYC
Con Edison:	800-752-6633
Time Warner Cable:	212-358-0900 (Manhattan); 718-358-0900 (Queens/ Brooklyn); 718-816-8686 (Staten Island)
Cablevision:	718-617-3500
Verizon:	xxx-890-1550 (add 1 and your local area code plus the seven digit number)
Police Headquarters:	646-610-5905
Public Advocate:	212-669-7200

Bathrooms

When nature calls, New York can make your life excruciatingly difficult. The city-sponsored public bathroom offerings, including dodgy subway restrooms and the sporadic experimentation with self-cleaning super porta-potties, leave a lot to be desired. Your best bet, especially in an emergency, remains bathrooms in stores and other buildings that are open to the public.

The three most popular bathroom choices for needy New Yorkers (and visitors) are Barnes & Noble, Starbucks, and any kind of fast food chain. Barnes & Noble bathrooms are essentially open to everyone (as long as you're willing to walk past countless shelves of books during your navigation to the restrooms). They're usually clean enough, but sometimes you'll find yourself waiting in line during the evening and weekends. Although Starbucks bathrooms are more prevalent, they tend to be more closely guarded (in some places you have to ask for a key) and not as clean as you'd like. Fast food restrooms are similarly unhygienic, but easy to use inconspicuously without needing to purchase anything.

For a comprehensive listing of bathrooms in NYC (including hours and even ratings), try the Bathroom Diaries at www.thebathroomdiaries.com or—if you have a smart phone—try any of a number of apps designed to help you avoid a ticket for peeing in the street.

If you're busting to go and there's no Barnes & Noble, Starbucks, or fast food joint in sight, consider the following options:

- **Public buildings**—including train stations (Grand Central, Penn Station) and malls (South Street Seaport, World Financial Center, Manhattan Mall, The Shops at Columbus Circle).
- **Government buildings**—government offices, courthouses, police stations.
- **Department stores**—Macy's, Bloomingdale's, Saks, etc.
- **Other stores**—Old Navy, Bed Bath & Beyond, FAO Schwartz, NBA store, The Strand, etc.
- **Supermarkets**—Pathmark, Food Emporium, D'Agostino, Gristedes, Key Food, etc. You'll probably have to ask, because the restrooms in supermarkets are usually way in the back amongst the employee lockers.
- **Diners**—they are in every neighborhood, and usually they are busy enough so that if you simply stride in and head towards the back (since that's where the bathroom is most of the time anyway) WITHOUT stopping, they probably won't notice. Works for us, usually.
- **Bars**—a good choice at night when most other places are closed. Try to choose a busy one so as not to arouse suspicion. Most bars have those intimidating signs warning you that the restrooms are for customers only!
- **Museums**—most are closed at night, and most require an entry fee during the day. How desperate are you?
- **Colleges**—better if you're young enough to look like a student.
- **Parks**—great during the day, closed at night.
- **Hotels**—you might have to sneak past the desk though.
- **Times Square visitors centers**—1560 Broadway and 810 Seventh Avenue.
- **Places of worship**—unpredictable hours, and not all have public restrooms.
- **Subways**—how bad do you have to go? Your best bets are express stops on the IND lines, for example, 34th Street and 6th Avenue. Some stations have locked bathrooms, with keys available at the booths.
- **Gyms**—i.e. places where you have a membership.
- **Outdoor public bathrooms**—the city tries these out from time to time—see if you can find one.

Websites

www.bridgeandtunnelclub.com • Musings and explorations of New York.
www.boweryboys.blogspot.com • Riveting podcasts of NYC history
www.chinatownchowdown.com • The ultimate guide to eating in Chinatown.
www.curbed.com • Keeps track of the daily developments in New York real estate.
www.delivery.com • Tell your computer to bring you a sammich.
www.eatingintranslation.com • One guy eats his away through NYC.
www.eater.com • Restaurant gossip galore.
www.famousfatdave.com • The hungry cabbie!
www.fieldtrip.com/ny • Hundreds of suggestions for places to visit in the city.
www.forgotten-ny.com • Fascinating look at the relics of New York's past.
www.gothamist.com • Blog detailing various daily news and goings-on in the city.
www.lowermanhattan.info • An excellent resource for information about what's happening in Lower Manhattan.
www.menupages.com • Menus for almost every restaurant in Manhattan.
www.metropolitanwalks.com • Interesting walking tours.
www.midtownlunch.com • Good eats for the office set.
www.newyork.craigslist.org • Classifieds for every area, including personals, apartments, musicians, jobs, and more.
www.notfortourists.com • The ultimate NYC website.
www.nyc.gov • New York City government resources.
www.nyc-grid.com • Photo blog of NYC, block by block.
www.nycsubway.org • Complete history and overview of the subways.
www.nycgo.com • The official NYC tourism site.
www.overheardinnewyork.com • Say what?
www.porkchop-express.com • Homage du pork by NFT freelancer.
www.scoutingny.com • A film scout chronicles the city.
www.seemless.com • Don't look up from your desk, ever. Order lunch here.
www.theskint.com • Cool events listed daily.
www.vanishingnewyork.blogspot.com • Chronicling the loss of all the good stuff.

New York Timeline — a timeline of significant events in New York history (by no means complete)

1524: Giovanni de Verrazano enters the New York harbor.
1609: Henry Hudson explores what is now called the Hudson River.
1626: The Dutch purchase Manhattan and New Amsterdam is founded.
1647: Peter Stuyvesant becomes Director General of New Amsterdam.
1664: The British capture the colony and rename it "New York."
1754: King's College/Columbia founded.
1776: British drive colonial army from New York and hold it for the duration of the war.
1776: Fire destroys a third of the city.
1789: Washington takes the Oath of Office as the first President of the United States.
1801: Alexander Hamilton founds the *New-York Evening Post*, still published today as the *New York Post*.
1811: The Commissioners Plan dictates a grid plan for the streets of New York.
1812: City Hall completed.
1825: Completion of the Erie Canal connects New York City commerce to the Great Lakes.
1835: *New York Herald* publishes its first edition.
1835: Great Fire destroys 600 buildings and kills 30 New Yorkers.
1854: First Tammany Hall–supported mayor Fernando Woods elected.
1859: Central Park opens.
1863: The Draft Riots terrorize New York for three days.
1868: Prospect Park opens.
1871: Thomas Nast cartoons and *New York Times* exposes lead to the end of the Tweed Ring.
1880: The population of Manhattan reaches over 1 million.
1883: Brooklyn Bridge opens.
1886: The Statue of Liberty is dedicated, inspires first ticker tape parade.
1888: The Blizzard of '88 incapacitates the city for two weeks.
1892: Ellis Island opens; 16 million immigrants will pass through in the next 32 years.
1897: Steeplechase Park opens, first large amusement park in Coney Island.
1898: The City of Greater New York is founded when the five boroughs are merged.
1904: General Slocum disaster kills 1,021.
1904: The subway opens.
1906: First New Year's celebration in Times Square.
1911: Triangle Shirtwaist Fire kills 146, impels work safety movement.
1920: A TNT-packed horse cart explodes on Wall Street, killing 30; the crime goes unsolved.
1923: The Yankees win their first World Championship.
1929: Stock market crashes, signaling the beginning of the Great Depression.
1929: The Chrysler Building is completed.
1930: The Empire State Building is built, then tallest in the world.
1927: The Holland Tunnel opens, making it the world's longest underwater tunnel.
1931: The George Washington Bridge is completed.
1933: Fiorello LaGuardia elected mayor.
1934: Robert Moses becomes Parks Commissioner.
1939: The city's first airport, LaGuardia, opens.
1950: United Nations opens.
1955: Dodgers win the World Series; they move to LA two years later.
1963: Pennsylvania Station is demolished to the dismay of many; preservation efforts gain steam.
1964: The Verrazano-Narrows Bridge is built, at the time the world's longest suspension bridge.
1965: Malcolm X assassinated in the Audubon Ballroom.
1965: Blackout strands hundreds of thousands during rush hour.
1969: The Stonewall Rebellion marks beginning of the gay rights movement.
1969: The Miracle Mets win the World Series.
1970: Knicks win their first championship.
1970: First New York City Marathon takes place.
1971: World Trade Center opens.
1975: Ford to City: Drop Dead.
1977: Thousands arrested for various mischief during a city-wide blackout.
1981: First NYC AIDS death begins a decade of tragedy.
1977: Ed Koch elected mayor to the first of three terms.
1987: Black Monday—stock market plunges.
1993: Giuliani elected mayor.
1993: A bomb explodes in the parking garage of the World Trade Center, killing 5.
1994: Rangers win the Stanley Cup after a 40-year drought.
2000: NFT publishes its first edition.
2001: The World Trade Center is destroyed in a terrorist attack; New Yorkers vow to rebuild.
2003: Blackout becomes best party in NYC history.
2003: Tokens are no longer accepted in subway turnstiles.
2006: Ground is broken on the WTC memorial.
2007: Construction begins (again) on the Second Avenue subway line.
2009: Bloomberg purchases a third term.
2012: 1 WTC is once again tallest in NYC.
2012: Superstorm Sandy ravages Zone A, altering New Yorkers' relationship with the waterfront.

Essential New York Songs

"Sidewalks of New York" — Various, written by James Blake and Charles Lawlor, 1894
"Give My Regards to Broadway" — Various, written by George Cohan, 1904
"I'll Take Manhattan" — Various, written by Rodgers and Hart, 1925
"Puttin' on the Ritz" — Various, written by Irving Berlin, 1929
"42nd Street" — Various, written by Al Dubin and Harry Warren, 1932
"Take the A Train" — Duke Ellington, 1940
"Autumn in New York" — Frank Sinatra, 1947
"Spanish Harlem" — Ben E. King, 1961
"Car 54 Where Are You?" — Nat Hiken and John Strauss, 1961
"On Broadway" — Various, written by Weil/Mann/Leiber/Stoller, 1962
"Talkin' New York" — Bob Dylan, 1962
"Up on the Roof" — The Drifters, 1963
"59th Street Bridge Song" — Simon and Garfunkel, 1966
"I'm Waiting for My Man" — Velvet Underground, 1967
"Brooklyn Roads" — Neil Diamond, 1968
"Crosstown Traffic" — Jimi Hendrix, 1969
"Personality Crisis"— The New York Dolls, 1973
"New York State of Mind" — Billy Joel, 1976
"53rd and 3rd" — The Ramones, 1977
"Shattered" — Rolling Stones, 1978
"New York, New York" — Frank Sinatra, 1979
"Life During Wartime" — Talking Heads, 1979
"New York New York" — Grandmaster Flash and the Furious 5, 1984
"No Sleep Til Brooklyn" — Beastie Boys, 1987
"Christmas in Hollis" — Run-D.M.C., 1987
"New York" — U2, 2000
"I've Got New York" — The 6th's, 2000
"New York, New York" — Ryan Adams, 2001
"The Empty Page" — Sonic Youth, 2002
"New York" — Ja Rule f. Fat Joe, Jadakiss, 2004
"Empire State of Mind" — Jay-Z, 2009

Essential New York Movies

The Crowd (1928)
2nd Street (1933)
King Kong (1933)
Pride of the Yankees (1942)
Arsenic and Old Lace (1944)
Miracle on 34th Street (1947)
On the Town (1949)
On the Waterfront (1954)
The Blackboard Jungle (1955)
n Affair to Remember (1957)
The Apartment (1960)
reakfast at Tiffany's (1961)
Vest Side Story (1961)
arefoot in the Park (1967)
ohn & Mary (1969)
idnight Cowboy (1969)
rench Connection (1970)
he Out of Towners (1970)
haft (1971)
ean Streets (1973)
Serpico (1973)
Godfather II (1974)
The Taking of Pelham One Two Three (1974)
Dog Day Afternoon (1975)
Taxi Driver (1976)
Saturday Night Fever (1977)
Superman (1978)
Manhattan (1979)
The Warriors (1979)
Fame (1980)
Escape From New York (1981)
Nighthawks (1981)
Ghostbusters (1984)
The Muppets Take Manhattan (1984)
After Hours (1985)
Crocodile Dundee (1986)
Wall Street (1987)
Moonstruck (1987)
Big (1988)
Bright Lights, Big City (1988)
Working Girl (1988)
Do the Right Thing (1989)
Last Exit to Brooklyn (1989)
When Harry Met Sally (1989)
A Bronx Tale (1993)
Kids (1995)
Men in Black (1997)
Bringing Out the Dead (1999)
The Royal Tenenbaums (2001)
Gangs of New York (2002)
Spider-Man (2002)
25th Hour (2003)
The Interpreter (2005)
Inside Man (2006)
The Devil Wears Prada (2006)
American Gangster (2007)
Enchanted (2007)
Sex and the City (2008)
New York I Love You (2009)
Whatever Works (2009)

Essential New York Books

Tree Grows in Brooklyn, by Betty Smith
oming of age story set in the slums of Brooklyn.

he Alienist by Caleb Carr
reat portrait of late-19th century New York complete with rial killer, detective, and Teddy Roosevelt.

he Bonfire of the Vanities, by Tom Wolfe
oney, class and politics undo a wealthy bond trader.

ight Lights, Big City, by Jay McInerney
80s yuppie and the temptations of the city.

tcher in the Rye, by J. D. Salinger
fluential portrayal of teenage angst.

e Cricket in Times Square, by George Selden
assic children's book.

e Death and Life of Great American Cities, by Jane Jacobs
luential exposition on what matters in making cities work.

e Encyclopedia of New York City, by Kenneth T. Jackson, ed
ge and definitive reference work.

tham: A History of New York City to 1898, by Edwin G. rrows and Mike Wallace
thoritative history of New York.

The Fuck-Up, by Arthur Nersesian
Scraping by in the East Village of the '80s.

Here is New York, by E. B. White
Reflections on the city.

House of Mirth, by Edith Wharton
Climbing the social ladder in upper crust, late 19th-century NY.

Knickerbocker's History of New York, by Washington Irving
Very early (1809) whimsical "history" of NY.

Manchild in the Promised Land, by Claude Brown
Autobiographical tale of growing up in Harlem.

The Power Broker, by Robert Caro
Biography of Robert Moses, you'll never look at the city the same way after reading it.

The Recognitions, by William Gaddis
Ever thought New Yorkers were phony? They are.

Washington Square, by Henry James
Love and marriage in upper-middle-class 1880s NY.

The Best of the Best

With all the culture the city has to offer, finding activities to amuse children is easy enough. From fencing classes to the funnest parks, our guide will provide you with great ideas for entertaining your little ones.

★ **Neatest Time-Honored Tradition:** The Central Park Carousel (830 Fifth Ave, 212-879-0244) features the largest hand-carved figures ever constructed and has been in residence in the park since 1950. $2.50 will buy you a memory to last forever. Open 10 am to 6 pm on weekdays and 10 am to 7 pm weekends, weather permitting.

★ **Coolest Rainy Day Activity:** The Children's Museum of the Arts (182 Lafayette St, 212-274-0986) offers activities for wee ones as young as 10 months, because its never too early to find out whether your child might be the next Picasso. Budding painters can use the open art studio; dramatic ones stage productions in the performing arts gallery; those who must touch everything delight in the creative play stations. Open Wed–Sun, 12–5 pm; Thurs, 12–6 pm.

★ **Sweetest Place to Get a Cavity:** Jacques Torres (350 Hudson St, 212-414-2462) where kids can watch cocoa beans turn into chocolate bars in the glass-encased factory-emporium. As if you needed another reason: Torres makes chocolate-covered Cheerios, and a host of other fun confections. Open Mon–Sat, 9 am–7 pm, Sun, 10 am–6 pm.

★ **Best Spots for Sledding:** Central Park's Pilgrim Hill and Cedar Hill. Kids pray for a snow day for the chance to try out this slick slope. BYO sled or toboggan.

★ **Funnest Park:** Hudson River Park Playground (Pier 51, Gansevoort St) With a beautiful view of the Hudson River, the park features several sprinklers, a winding "canal," and a boat-themed area complete with prow, mast, and captain's wheel.

★ **No Tears Hair Cuts:** Former Cozy's coiffer Jennifer Bilek (917-548-3643) offers professional in-home services, eliminating the fear of the unknown. She'll cut moms and dads, too…and offers "glamour parties" for girls ages 5–12.

★ **Best Halloween Costume Shopping:** Halloween Adventure (104 Fourth Ave, 212-673-4546) is the city's costume emporium that has every disguise you can possibly imagine, along with wigs, make-up supplies, and magic tricks to complete any child's dress-up fantasy. Open year-round.

★ **Best Place for Sunday Brunch:** There a billion places to take the kids to get pancakes and eggs on Sunday mornings, so why not try something totally different—dim sum in Chinatown! The kids will be entertained as carts of dumplings, pork buns, and unidentified foods constantly roll on by for non-stop eating fun. Try Mandarin Court, 88 Palace, or Dim Sum Go Go which are all located in Map 3 of the book.

Rainy Day Activities

- **American Museum of Natural History** (Central Park West at 79th St, 212- 769-5100) Fantastic for kids of all ages, with something to suit every child's interest. From the larger-than-life dinosaur fossils and the realistic animal dioramas to the out-of-this-world Hayden Planetarium, all attention will be rapt. The hands-on exhibits of the Discovery Room and the IMAX theater are also worth a visit. Open 10 am–5:45 pm daily.
- **Bowlmor Lanes** (110 University Pl, 212-255-8188) Great bowling alley with a retro décor that kids will love. Bumpers are available to cut down on those pesky gutter balls. Children are welcome every day before 5 pm and all day Sunday—a popular birthday spot.
- **Brooklyn Children's Museum** (145 Brooklyn Ave, 718-735-4400) The world's first museum for children (opened in 1899) engages kids in educational hands-on activities and exhibits. Kids can learn about life in New York in the Together in the City exhibit and find out why snakes are so slimy in the Animal Outpost.
- **Staten Island Children's Museum** (1000 Richmond Ter, 718-273-2060) Offers plenty of hands-on opportunities for kids to explore everything from pirate ships to the rainforest. There's also an outdoor play space (weather permitting). Birthday parties. The museum is open Tues–Fri, 12 pm–5 pm; Sat–Sun, 10 pm–5pm.
- **Children's Museum of Manhattan** (212 W 83rd St, 212-721-1234) As soon as you arrive at the museum, sign up for some of the day's activities. While you're waiting, check out the other exhibits in the museum. There's the Word Play area designed for the younger children in your group and the Time/Warner Media Center for the older set, where kids can produce their own television shows. The museum is open Tue–Sun, 10am–5pm.
- **Intrepid Sea Air Space Museum** (Pier 86, 46th St & 12th Ave, 212-245-0072) Tour the *Growler*, a real submarine that was once a top-secret missle command center, or take a virtual trip on one of the simulator rides. After you've taken a look at the authentic aircrafts on deck, visit the museum of the *Intrepid* to see an extensive model airplane collection and a Cockpit Challenge flight video game for those aspiring pilots. The museum is open Mon–Fri, 10 am–5 pm, and Sat–Sun 10 am–6pm .
- **Little Shop of Crafts** (711 Amsterdam Ave, 212-717-6636 Great space to bead/paint. Stay for hours.
- **Lower East Side Tenement Museum** (108 Orchard St, 212-431-0233) The museum offers insight into immigrant life in the late 19th and early 20th centuries by taking groups on tours of an historic tenement building on the Lower East Side. One tour called "Visit the Confino Family" is led by "Victoria Confino," a young girl dressed in authentic costume who teaches children about the lives of immigrants in the early 1900s. A great place to take your kids if they haven't already been there on a school field trip.
- **The Metropolitan Museum of Art** (1000 Fifth Ave, 21 535-7710) A great museum to explore with audio guide designed specifically for children. From the armor exhibit to the Egyptian Wing, the museum offers art exhibits fro all historical periods.
- **Noguchi Museum** (9-01 33rd Rd at Vernon Blvd, Lor Island City, 718-204-7088) This newly renovated museu that features the works of Japanese-American artist Isar Noguchi offers interesting tours and hands-on worksho for toddlers to teens. The fees are nominal, but you mu register beforehand.
- **The Museum of Modern Art** (11 W 53rd St, 212-708-940 Besides the kid-friendly audio guides that help make t renowned museum enjoyable for tykes, MoMA has a of exciting weekend family programs that get kids ta ing about art and film. Lots of fun hands-on programs t Registration is a must—these programs book up fast.

Outdoor *and* Educational

They can't learn *everything* from the Discovery Channel.

• **Central Park Zoo** • 830 Fifth Ave • 212-439-6500 • Houses more than 1,400 animals, including some endangered species. Take a walk through the arctic habitat of the polar bears and penguins to the steamy tropical Rain Forest Pavilion. The Tisch Children's Zoo nearby is more suited for the younger crowd with its smaller, cuddlier animals.

• **Fort Washington Park** • W 155 St to Dyckman, at the Hudson River • 212-304-2365 • Call the Urban Park Rangers to arrange a tour of the little red lighthouse located at the base of the George Washington Bridge. The lighthouse affords some spectacular views—better than anything they'd see from atop Dad's shoulders. The park offers a "Junior Ranger Program" for kids, as well as a playground in Picnic Area "B."

• **Historic Richmond Town** • 441 Clarke Ave, Staten Island • 718-351-1611 • A 100-acre complex with over 40 points of interest and a museum that covers over three centuries of the history of Staten Island. People dressed in authentic period garb lead demonstrations and tours.

New York Botanical Garden • Bronx River Parkway at Fordham Road, Bronx • 718-817-8777 • 250 acres and 50 different indoor and outdoor gardens and plant exhibits to explore. The Children's Adventure Garden changes each season, and kids can get down and dirty in the Family Garden. Keen young botanists can join the Children's Gardening Program and get their own plot to care for.

Classes

With all of their after school classes and camps, the children of New York City are some of the most well-rounded (and programmed) in the country. Help them beef up their college applications with some fancy extracurriculars. It's never too early…

92nd Street Y After-School Programs • 1395 Lexington Ave, 212-415-5500 • The center provides children of all ages with tons of activities, ranging from music lessons and chess to flamenco and yoga. 92nd St is known as "the Y to beat all Ys."

Abrons Arts Center/Henry Street Settlement • 466 Grand St, 212-598-0400 • The Arts Center offers classes and workshops for children of all ages in music, dance, theater, and visual arts.

Archikids • 472 16th St, 718-768-6123 • After-school classes and summer camp for children ages five and up that teach kids about architecture through hands-on building projects.

The Art Farm • 419 E 91st St, 212-410-3117 • "Mommy & Me" art and music classes, baking courses, and small animal care for the very young.

Asphalt Green • 555 E 90th St, 212-369-8890 • Swimming and diving lessons, gymnastics, team sports, and art classes. They've got it all for kids one and up.

Baby Moves • 139 Perry St, 212-255-1685 • A developmental play space that offers classes for infants to six year-olds in movement, music, and play.

Church Street School for Music and Art • 74 Warren St, 212-571-7290 • This community arts center offers a variety of classes in music and art involving several different media, along with private lessons and courses for parents and children.

• **Dieu Donné Papermill** • 315 W 36th St, 212-226-0573 • Workshops in hand papermaking offered for children ages seven and up.

• **FasTracKids.** • 307 E 84th St, 212-737-3344 • The Studio offers hands-on courses in art, science, and yoga, with an emphasis on process and discovery.

• **Greenwich House Music School** • 46 Barrow St, 212-242-4770 • Group classes and private lessons in music and ballet for children of all ages.

• **Greenwich Village Center** • 219 Sullivan St, 212-254-3074 • Run by the Children's Aid Society, the center provides arts and after-school classes ranging from gymnastics to origami, as well as an early childhood program and nursery school.

• **Hamilton Fish Recreation Center** • 128 Pitt St, 212-387-7687 • The center offers free swimming lessons in two outdoor pools along with free after-school programs with classes like astronomy and photography.

• **Hi Art!** • 939 8th Ave, Studio 4A, 917-318-9499• For children ages 2–12, the classes focus on the exploration of art in museums and galleries in the city and giving kids the freedom to develop what they've seen into new concepts in a spacious studio setting.

• **Institute of Culinary Education** • 50 W 23rd St, 800-522-4610 • Hands-on cooking classes.

• **Irish Arts Center** • 553 W 51st St, 212-757-3318 • Introductory Irish step dancing classes for children five and up.

• **Jewish Community Center** • 334 Amsterdam Ave, 646-505-4444 • The center offers swimming lessons, team sports, and courses in arts and cooking. There's even a rooftop playground.

• **Kids at Art** • 431 E 73rd St, 212-410-9780 • Art program that focuses on the basics in a non-competitive environment for kids ages 2–11.

• **Marshall Chess Club** • 23 W 10th St, 212-477-3716 • Membership to the club offers access to weekend chess classes, summer camp, and tournaments for children ages five and up.

Tannen's Magic • 45 W 34th St, Suite 608, 212-929-4500 • Private magic lessons for children eight and up on weekday evenings or group lessons of three to four teens on Monday nights. Their week-long summer sleep-away camp is also very popular.

• **The Techno Team** • 160 Columbus Ave, 212-501-1425 • Computer technology classes for children ages 3–12.

• **Trapeze School** • West St at Houston St, 917-797-1872 • Kids ages six and up can learn how to fly through the air with the greatest of ease.

Babysitting/Nanny Services

Baby Sitter's Guild • 60 E 42nd St, 212-682-0227
Barnard Babysitting Agency • 49 Claremont Ave, 212-854-2035
My Child's Best Friend • 239 E 73rd St, 212-396-4090
New York City Explorers • 244 Fifth Ave, 212-591-2619

Where to go for more info

www.gocitykids.com
www.ny.com/kids

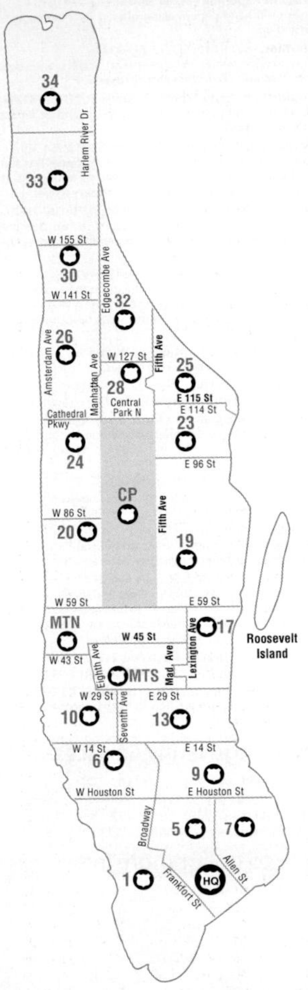

Important Phone Numbers

All Emergencies:	911
Non-Emergencies:	311
Terrorism Hot Line:	888-NYC-SAFE
Crime Stoppers:	800-577-TIPS
Crime Stoppers (Spanish):	888-57-PISTA
Sex Crimes Report Line:	212-267-RAPE
Crime Victims Hotline:	212-577-7777
Cop Shot:	800-COP-SHOT
Missing Persons Case Status:	212-694-7781
Missing Persons Squad:	212-473-2042
Operation Gun Stop:	866-GUNSTOP
Organized Crime Control Bureau Drug Line:	888-374-DRUG
Complaints (Internal Affairs):	212-741-8401
NYPD Switchboard	646-610-6000
Website:	www.nyc.gov/nypd

Statistics

Statistics	*2011*	*2009*	*2008*	*2006*	*2005*
Uniformed Personnel	515	39,787	37,838	37,038	39,110
Murders	1,420	471	523	597	540
Rapes	19,717	1,201	1,298	1,497	1,640
Robberies	18,482	18,533	22,355	23,556	24,417
Felony Assaults	18,720	16,644	16,230	17,124	17,336
Burglaries	38,501	19,318	20,685	22,950	23,997
Grand Larcenies	9,314	39,342	44,166	46,525	47,619
Grand Larcenies (cars)	9,314	10,672	12,481	15,731	17,865

Precinct

Precinct		*Phone*	*Map*
1st Precinct	16 Ericsson Pl	212-334-0611	2
5th Precinct	19 Elizabeth St	212-334-0711	3
7th Precinct	19 1/2 Pitt St	212-477-7311	4
6th Precinct	233 W 10th St	212-741-4811	5
9th Precinct	130 Avenue C	212-477-7811	7
Mid-Town South	357 W 35th St	212-239-9811	8
10th Precinct	230 W 20th St	212-741-8211	9
13th Precinct	230 E 21st St	212-477-7411	10
Mid-Town North	306 W 54th St	212-760-8400	11
17th Precinct	167 E 51st St	212-826-3211	13
20th Precinct	120 W 82nd St	212-580-6411	14
19th Precinct	153 E 67th St	212-452-0600	15
24th Precinct	151 W 100th St	212-678-1811	16
23rd Precinct	162 E 102nd St	212-860-6411	1
26th Precinct	520 W 126th St	212-678-1311	1
28th Precinct	2271 Frederick Douglass Blvd	212-678-1611	1
32nd Precinct	250 W 135th St	212-690-6311	1
25th Precinct	120 E 119th St	212-860-6511	2
30th Precinct	451 W 151st St	212-690-8811	2
33rd Precinct	2207 Amsterdam Ave	212-927-3200	2
34th Precinct	4295 Broadway	212-927-9711	2
Central Park Precinct	86th St & Transverse Rd	212-570-4820	p23

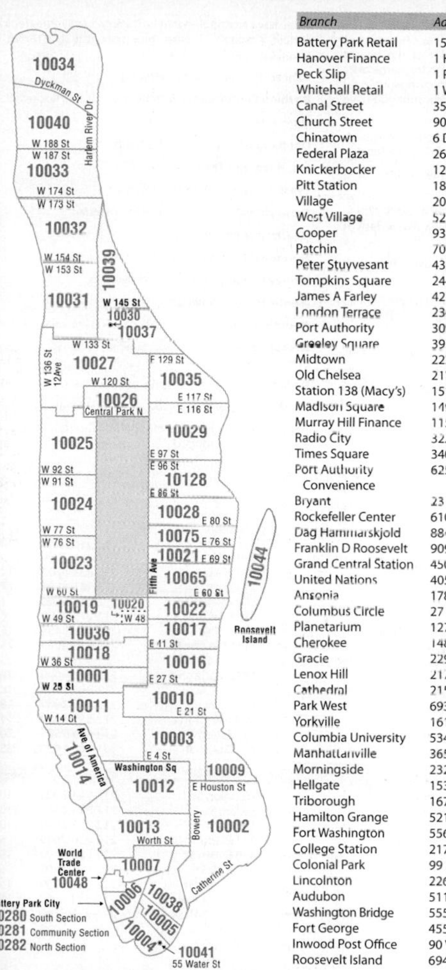

Branch	Address	Phone	Map
Battery Park Retail	15 Rector St	212-330-5151	1
Hanover Finance	1 Hanover St	212-425-5875	1
Peck Slip	1 Peck Slip	212-964-1054	1
Whitehall Retail	1 Whitehall St	212-330-5151	1
Canal Street	350 Canal St	212-925-3378	2
Church Street	90 Church St	212-330-5001	2
Chinatown	6 Doyers St	212-267-3510	3
Federal Plaza	26 Federal Plaza	212-608-2420	3
Knickerbocker	128 East Broadway	212-608-3598	4
Pitt Station	185 Clinton St	212-254-9270	4
Village	201 Varick St	212-645-0327	5
West Village	527 Hudson St	212-989-5084	5
Cooper	93 Fourth Ave	212-254-1390	6
Patchin	70 W 10th St	212-475-2534	6
Peter Stuyvesant	432 E 14th St	212-677-2112	7
Tompkins Square	244 E 3rd St	212-673-6415	7
James A Farley	421 Eighth Ave	212-330-2902	8
London Terrace	234 Tenth Ave	800-275-8777	8
Port Authority	309 W 15th St	212-645-0351	8
Greeley Square	39 W 31st St	212-244-7055	9
Midtown	223 W 38th St	212-819-9604	9
Old Chelsea	217 W 18th St	212-675-0548	9
Station 138 (Macy's)	151 W 34th St	212-494-2688	9
Madison Square	149 E 23rd St	212-673-3771	10
Murray Hill Finance	115 E 34th St	212-689-1124	10
Radio City	322 W 52nd St	212-265-3672	11
Times Square	340 W 42nd St	212-502-0421	11
Port Authority Convenience	625 8th Ave	646-472-0501	11
Bryant	23 W 43rd St	212-279-5960	12
Rockefeller Center	610 Fifth Ave	212-265-3854	12
Dag Hammarskjold	884 Second Ave	800-275-8777	13
Franklin D Roosevelt	909 Third Ave	800-275-8777	13
Grand Central Station	450 Lexington Ave	212-330-5722	13
United Nations	405 E 42nd St	212-963-7353	13
Ansonia	178 Columbus Ave	212-362-1697	14
Columbus Circle	27 W 60th St	212-265-7858	14
Planetarium	127 W 83rd St	212-873-5698	14
Cherokee	1483 York Ave	212-517-8361	15
Gracie	229 E 85th St	212-988-6680	15
Lenox Hill	217 E 70th St	212-330-5561	15
Cathedral	215 W 104th St	212-662-0355	16
Park West	693 Columbus Ave	800-275-8777	16
Yorkville	1617 Third Ave	212-369-2747	17
Columbia University	534 W 112th St	800-275-8777	18
Manhattanville	365 W 125th St	212-662-1540	18
Morningside	232 W 116th St	800-275-8777	19
Hellgate	153 E 110th St	212-860-1896	20
Triborough	167 E 124th St	212-534-0381	20
Hamilton Grange	521 W 146th St	212-281-1538	21
Fort Washington	556 W 158th St	212-923-1763	21
College Station	217 W 140th St	212-283-7096	22
Colonial Park	99 Macombs Pl	212-368-9849	22
Lincolnton	2266 Fifth Ave	212-281-9781	22
Audubon	511 W 165th St	212-568-2387	23
Washington Bridge	555 W 180th St	212-568-2690	23
Fort George	4558 Broadway	212-942-5266	24
Inwood Post Office	90 Vermilyea Ave	212-567-7821	25
Roosevelt Island	694 Main St	800-275-8777	p210

If you have to get to a hospital (especially in an emergency), it's best to go to the closest one. However, as a quick reference, the following is a list of the largest hospitals by neighborhood, complete with the name of its corresponding map. But no matter which hospital you drag yourself into, for heaven's sake make sure you have your insurance card.

Lower Manhattan: NYU Downtown Hospital • William & Beekman Sts, just south of the Brooklyn Bridge • [Map 3]

East Village: Beth Israel Medical Center • 14th St & Broadway/Union Square • [Map 10]

Murray Hill: Bellevue Hospital Center • First Ave & 27th St [Map 10] ; NYU College of Dentistry • First Ave & 24th St [Map 10]

Hell's Kitchen/Upper West Side: St Luke's Roosevelt Hospital • 10th Ave & 58th St [Map 11]

East Side: New York Presbyterian • York Ave & 68th St [Map 15]; Lenox Hill Hospital • Lexington Ave & 77th St [Map 15]; Mt Sinai Medical Center • Madison Ave & 101st St [Map 17]

Columbia/Morningside Heights: St Luke's Hospital Center • Amsterdam Ave & 114th St [Map 18]

Farther Uptown: Columbia Presbyterian Medical Center • 168th St & Broadway [Map 23]

If you have a condition that isn't immediately threatening, certain hospitals in New York specialize and excel in specific areas of medicine:

Cancer: Memorial Sloan-Kettering

Birthing Center/Labor & Delivery: St Luke's Roosevelt

Digestive Disorders: Mt Sinai

Dentistry: NYU College of Dentistry

Ear, Nose, and Throat: Mt Sinai

Eyes: New York Eye and Ear Infirmary

Geriatrics: Mt Sinai, New York Presbyterian

Heart: New York Presbyterian

Hormonal Disorders: New York Presbyterian

Kidney Disease: New York Presbyterian

Mental Health: Bellevue

Neurology: New York Presbyterian, NYU Medical Center

Orthopedics: Hospital for Special Surgery, New York Presbyterian

Pediatrics: Children's Hospital of New York Presbyterian

Psychiatry: New York Presbyterian, NYU Medical Center

Rheumatology: Hospital for Special Surgery, Hospital for Joint Diseases Orthopedic Institute, NYU Medical Center

Emergency Rooms	*Address*	*Phone*	*Map*
Bellevue Hospital Center	462 First Ave	212-562-1000	10
Beth Israel Medical Center	281 First Ave	212-420-2000	10
Harlem Hospital Center	506 Lenox Ave	212-939-1000	22
Hospital for Joint Diseases	301 E 17th St	212-598-6000	10
Lenox Hill Hospital	110 E 77th St	212-434-2000	15
Metropolitan Hospital Center	1901 First Ave	212-423-6262	17
Mount Sinai Medical Center	1190 Fifth Ave	212-241-6500	17
New York Downtown Hospital	170 William St	212-312-5000	1
New York Eye & Ear Infirmary	310 E 14th St	212-979-4000	6
New York Presbyterian–Weill Cornell Medical Center	525 E 68th St	212-746-5454	15
New York-Presbyterian Hospital Allen Pavilion	5141 Broadway	212-932-4000	25
New York-Presbyterian Hospital/Columbia University Medical Center	622 W 168th St	212-305-2500	23
North General Hospital	1879 Madison Ave	212-423-4000	20
NYU Langone Medical Center	550 First Ave	212-263-7300	10
St Luke's Hospital	1111 Amsterdam Ave	212-523-4000	18
St Luke's Roosevelt Hospital Center	1000 Tenth Ave	212-523-4000	11
VA NY Harbor Healthcare System - Manhattan Campus	423 E 23rd St	212-686-7500	10
Wilzig Hospital	355 Grand St	201-309-1090	35

Other Hospitals	*Address*	*Phone*	*Map*
Beth Israel—Phillips Ambulatory Care Center	10 Union Sq E	212-844-8000	10
Coler Goldwater–Coler Campus	1 Main St	212-848-6000	p210
Coler Goldwater–Goldwater Campus	1 Main St	212-318-8000	p210
Gouverneur Healthcare Services	227 Madison St	212-238-7000	4
Gracie Square Hospital	420 E 76th St	212-988-4400	15
Hospital for Special Surgery	535 E 70 St	212-606-1000	15
Manhattan Eye, Ear & Throat	210 E 64th St	212-838-9200	15
Memorial Sloan-Kettering Cancer Center	1275 York Ave	212-639-2000	15
Renaissance Health Care Network Diagnostic and Treatment Center	215 W 125th St	212-932-6500	18

Beginner's mistake: Walk into the "main branch" of the New York Public Library at Bryant Park, and ask how to check out books. Trust us; it's happened. Recognizable for its reclining stone lions, Patience and Fortitude, the famous building is primarily a research library with non-circulating materials that you can peruse only in its iconic reading room. In 2008, the Children's Center, a circulating children's library, moved to this location and now you can check out kids books here too. Otherwise, if you want to read War and Peace or Fifty Shades of Grey, head to your local branch (there are 80 of them spread throughout Manhattan, Staten Island, and the Bronx). Note: Holds can take a very long time to fill, at least a week to a week and a half. If the book you need is only a 20-minute subway ride away, and you need the book now, invest the time and the $5 fare.

If it's reference material you're after, there are four specialized research libraries to help: **The Schomburg Center for Research in Black Culture (Map 22)** is the nation's foremost source on African-American history. The **Science, Industry, and Business Library (Map 9)** is perfect for those wanting to get ahead in business. The **New York Public Library for the Performing Arts (Map 14)**, located at Lincoln Center, houses the Theatre on Film and Tape Archive. If you can give them even a semi-legitimate reason, you can watch taped performances of most Broadway shows from the past 25 years. Located at the Hudson Park Branch is the **Early Childhood Resource & Information Center (Map 12)** which offers parenting workshops and reading programs for kids.

The aforementioned "main branch" of the New York Public Library (Map 12) (one of Manhattan's architectural treasures, designed by Carrère and Hastings and opened to the public in 1911, and renamed for billionaire Stephen A. Schwarzman in 2008) is actually a research library that houses NYPL's preeminent research collections in the humanities and social sciences. The location contains 88 miles of shelves and has more than 10,000 current periodicals from almost 150 countries. Research in the library requires an ACCESS card, which you can apply for at the library and which allows you to request materials in any of the reading rooms. Card sign-up can be slow, so be patient. It never hurts to bring along multiple kinds of ID, or a piece of mail if you're a new NYC resident. The **Andrew Heiskell Braille and Talking Book Library (Map 9)** is also part of NYPL. It contains large collections of special format materials and audio equipment for listening to recorded books and magazines. You can check out the full system online at www.nypl.org.

Library	*Address*	*Phone*	*Map*
115th Street	203 W 115th St	212-666-9393	19
125th St	224 E 125th St	212-534-5050	20
58th St	127 E 58th St	212-759-7358	13
67th St	328 E 67th St	212-734-1717	15
96th Street	112 E 96th St	212-289-0908	17
Aguilar	174 E 110th St	212-534-2930	20
Andrew Heiskell Braille & Talking Book Library	40 W 20th St	212-206-5400	9
Bloomingdale	150 W 100th St	212-222-8030	16
Chatham Square	33 East Broadway	212-964-6598	3
Columbus	742 Tenth Ave	212-586-5098	11
Countee Cullen	104 W 136th St	212-491-2070	22
Early Childhood Resource & Information Center	455 5th Ave	917-275-6975	12
Epiphany	228 E 23rd St	212-679-2645	10
Fort Washington	535 W 179th St	212-927-3533	23
Frick Art Reference Library	10 E 71st St	212-547-0641	15
George Bruce	518 W 125th St	212-662-9727	18
Grand Central Branch	135 E 46th St	212-621-0670	13
Hamilton Fish Park	415 E Houston St	212-673-2290	7
Hamilton Grange	503 W 145th St	212-926-2147	21
Harlem	9 W 124th St	212-348-5620	19
Hudson Park	66 Leroy St	212-243-6876	5
Inwood	4790 Broadway	212-942-2445	25
Jefferson Market	425 Sixth Ave	212-243-4334	5
Kips Bay	446 Third Ave	212-683-2520	10
Macomb's Bridge	2650 Adam Clayton Powell Jr Blvd	212-281-4900	22
Mid-Manhattan Library	455 Fifth Ave	917-275-6975	12
Morningside Heights Library	2900 Broadway	212-864-2530	18
Muhlenberg	209 W 23rd St	212-924-1585	9
Mulberry Street	10 Jersey St	212-966-3424	6
National Archives	201 Varick St	212-401-1620	5
New Amsterdam	9 Murray St	212-732-8186	3
New York Academy of Medicine Library	1216 Fifth Ave	212-822-7200	17
New York Public Library for the Performing Arts	40 Lincoln Center Plz	212-870-1630	14
New York Society Library	53 E 79th St	212-288-6900	15
Ottendorfer	135 Second Ave	212-674-0947	6
Riverside	127 Amsterdam Ave	212-870-1810	14
Roosevelt Island	524 Main St	212-308-6243	p210
Schomburg Center for Research	515 Malcolm X Blvd	212-491-2200	22
Science, Industry, and Business Library	188 Madison Ave	212-592-7000	9
Seward Park	192 East Broadway	212-477-6770	4
St Agnes	444 Amsterdam Ave	212-877-4380	14
Stephen A. Schwarzman Building	42nd St & Fifth Ave	212-340-0849	12
Terence Cardinal Cooke-Cathedral	560 Lexington Ave	212-752-3824	13
Tompkins Square	331 E 10th St	212-228-4747	7
Washington Heights	1000 St Nicholas Ave	212-923-6054	23
Webster	1465 York Ave	212-288-5049	15
Yorkville	222 E 79th St	212-744-5824	15

Very few places, anywhere, rival New York when it comes to quality gay living. Gay men can get almost anything they want, any time of day, with many businesses catering specifically to gay clientele (and let's not even get into the blessing/curse that is Grindr). Bars remain the backbone of the social scene: some, like **Industry**, focus on a chic atmosphere, while places like **Phoenix** and **Ninth Avenue Saloon** are friendly dive bars. You can sing your face off on karaoke nights at **Pieces** or **Xes**, get into trouble at **The Cock**, and dance with the locals at **The Ritz** or with bridge-and-tunnel types at **XL** or **Splash**.

There are more lesbian bars and parties than ever in New York City, so all you have to do is decide what night, which neighborhood and how you'll snag a girl! Although you'll find quality drinks, music, and women at **Henrietta Hudson's**, the notorious and intolerable bathroom line might discourage those lesbians who actually have a bladder. **LovergirlNYC@ Club Cache** on Saturday nights boasts 500+ beautiful women, while **Cubby Hole** promises a homey atmosphere and friendly crowd. Check out **Snapshot at Delancey** on Tuesday nights for steamy Sapphic scenesters and musicians; and **Nowhere** on any night. And if you're not afraid of venturing out of Manhattan, check out **Chueca** in Queens—it's a lesbian bar 7 days a week! In Brooklyn, chill on the patio at **Ginger's**.

Websites

The Lesbian, Gay, Bisexual & Transgender Community Center: www.gaycenter.org — Information about center programs, meetings, publications, and events.

Out & About: www.outandabout.com — Travel website for gays and lesbians including destination information, a gay travel calendar, health information, and listings of gay tour operators.

Gay Cities NYC: www.newyork.gaycities.com — Comprehensive list of all things gay.

Gayellow Pages: www.gayellowpages.com — Yellow pages of gay/lesbian-owned and gay/lesbian-friendly businesses in the US and Canada.

Shescape: www.shescape.com — Hosts lesbian events at various venues in town year round.

Publications

Free at gay and lesbian venues and shops, and some street corners.

Gay City News (formerly LGNY) — Newspaper for lesbian and gay New Yorkers including current local and national news items. www.gaycitynews.com

Next Magazine—Weekly magazine that includes frisky nightlife listings, film reviews, feature articles, and more. www.nextmagazine.net.

Bookshops

Bluestockings, 172 Allen St, 212-777-6028 — Lesbian/radical bookstore and activist center with regular readings and a fair-trade café. www.bluestockings.com

Health Centers and Support Organizations

Callen-Lorde Community Health Center, 356 W 18th St, 212-271-7200 — Primary Care Center for GLBT New Yorkers. www.callen-lorde.org

Gay Men's Health Crisis, 119 W 24th St, 212-367-1000; Hotline: 212-807-6655 — Non-profit organization dedicated to AIDS awareness and support for those living with HIV. www.gmhc.org

The Lesbian, Gay, Bisexual & Transgender Community Center, 208 W 13th, 212-620-7310 — The largest LGBT multi-service organization on the East Coast. www.gaycenter.org

Gay and Lesbian National Hotline, 212-989-0999 — Switchboard for referrals, advice, and counseling. www.glnh.org

Identity House, 208 W 13th St, 212-243-8181 — Offers LGBTQ counseling services, short-term therapy and/or referrals, groups, and workshops. www.identityhouse.org

Lambda Legal Defense and Education Fund, 120 Wall, St Ste 1500, 212 809-8585 — These are the people who fight the good fight in order to secure civil rights for the entire LGBT population. www.lambdalegal.org

National Gay & Lesbian Task Force, 80 Maiden, Ln Ste 1504, 212-604-9830 — This national organization creates change by building LGBT political power and de-marginalizing LGBT issues. www.ngltf.org

New York City Gay & Lesbian Anti-Violence Project, 212-714-1141 — 24-hour crisis support line for violence against LGTBH communities. www.avp.org

PFLAG, 119 W 24th St, 2nd Floor, 212-463-0629 — Parents, Families, and Friends of Lesbians and Gays meet on the second Sunday of every month 3 pm–5 pm for mutual support. www.pflagnyc.org

Lesbian and Gay Immigration Rights Task Force (LGIRTF), 350 W 31st St to 40 Exchange Pl, 17th Floor, 212-714-2904 — Advocates for changing US policy on immigration of permanent partners. www.lgirtf.org

GLAAD (Gay and Lesbian Alliance Against Defamation), W 29th St, 4th Floor, 212-629-3322 — These are the folks who go to bat for you in the media. www.glaad.org

OUTdancing @ Stepping Out Studios, 37 W 26th St, 646-742-9400 — The first LGBT partner dance program in the US. www.steppingoutstudios.com

LGBT Night at Leo Bar, Asia Society, 725 Park Ave, 212-327-9352 — Each third Friday of the month, Asia Society partners with a different LGBT professional organization, mixing people, cocktails, and culture. Free exhibition tours included. www.asiasociety.org

Positive Alliance, 369 W 46th St, 2nd Floor, 212-333-4177 — Weekly social mixer and party for HIV+ gay men, their friends and supporters, also providing email newsletter with links to resources and news updates. www.poznyc.com

Annual Events

Pride Week — Usually the last full week in June; www.hopinc.org (212-807-7433)

New York Gay and Lesbian Film Festival — Showcase o[f] international gay and lesbian films, May/June; www.newfestival.org (212-571-2170)

Mass Red Ribbon Ride — Replacing the old NYC to Boston AIDS ride, this version is a two-day ride across Massachusetts. The 2006 ride begins in Pittsfield and finishes in Weston, mid-August; www.massredribbonride.org (617-450-1100 or 888-MASSRIDE)

Useful websites: www.doglaw.com, www.nycparks.org

It's good to be a dog in New York. NYC's pooches are among the world's most pampered: they celebrate birthdays, don expensive sweaters, and prance down Fifth Avenue in weather-appropriate gear. Even for those of us who can't afford to dress our pups in Burberry raincoats, there are ways to spoil our canine companions. NYC is full of dog runs—both formal and informal—scattered throughout the city's parks and neighborhood community spaces. Good thing too, as the fine for having a dog off-leash can run upward of $100, and park officials are vigilant. While the city takes no active role in the management of the dog runs, it provides space to the community groups who do. These community groups are always eager for help (volunteer time or financial contributions) and many post volunteer information on park bulletin boards. It can take many years and several thousand dollars to build a dog run in New York. NYC boasts dozens of dog runs, but that doesn't seem like very many when you consider that there are more than a million pooches in the five boroughs. Each dog run is different. It's good to know, for example, that Riverside Park at 87th Street has a fountain and hose to keep dogs cool in the summer. Formal runs are probably the safest bet for pets, as most are enclosed and maintained. For safety reasons, choke or pronged collars are forbidden, and identification and rabies tags should remain on the flat collar. Most runs prohibit dogs in heat, aggressive dogs, and dogs without up-to-date shots.

There are no dog runs in Central Park, but before 9 am the park is full of people walking their dogs off-leash. While this is a strict no-no the rest of the day (and punishable by hefty fines), park officials unofficially tolerate the practice as long as dogs maintain a low profile, and are leashed immediately at 9 am. There are also 23 particularly dog-friendly areas throughout the park. Check out www.centralparknyc.org for more info.

Map Name • Address • Comments

While there are too many dog runs to create a complete list, these are some of the best-established ones - and check out the websites mentioned in this section to find more.

2 **P.S. 234** • 300 Greenwich St at Chambers St • Private run. $50/year membership. www.doglaw.com

3 **Fish Bridge Park** • Dover and Pearl Sts • Concrete-surfaced run. Features water hose, wading pool, and lock box with newspapers. www.nycgovparks.org

4 **Coleman Oval Park** • Pike & Monroe Sts • Under the Manhattan Bridge. www.nycgovparks.org

5 **West Village D.O.G. Run** • Little W 12th St • Features benches, water hose, and drink bowl. Membership costs $40 annually, but there's a waiting list. www.wvdog.org

6 **Washington Square Park** • MacDougal St at W 4th St • Located in the southwest corner of the park, this is a large, gravel-surfaced run with many spectators. This popular run gets very crowded, but is well-maintained nonetheless. www.nycgovparks.org

6 **LaGuardia Place** • Mercer St at Houston St • Private run with a membership (and a waiting list). The benefits include running water and a plastic wading pool for your dog to splash in.

6 **Union Square** • Broadway at 15th St • Crushed stone surface. www.nycgovparks.org

7 **Tompkins Square Park** • Avenue B at 10th St • NYC's first dog run opened in 1990 and was renovated in 2007. This community-centered run offers lots of shade, benches, and running water - but be aware: toys, frisbees, balls, and dogs in heat are prohibited. www.firstrunfriends.org

8 **Thomas Smith Triangle** • Eleventh Ave at 23rd St • Concrete-surfaced run. www.nycgovparks.org

8 **Chelsea Waterside Park** • 11th Ave at 22nd St

10 **Madison Square Park** • Madison Ave at 25th St • Medium-sized run with gravel surface and plenty of trees. www.nycgovparks.org

11 **DeWitt Clinton Park** • Eleventh Ave at 52nd & 54th Sts • Two small concrete-surfaced runs. www.nycgovparks.org

11 **Astro's Community Dog Run** • W 39th St at Tenth Ave • A private dog run (membership costs $15 a year) featuring chairs, umbrellas, fenced garden, and woodchip surface. www.astrosdogrun.org

13 **East River Esplanade at 63rd St**• Concrete dog run by the river. www.doglaw.com

13 **Peter Detmold Park** • Beekman Pl at 51st St • Large well-maintained run with cement and dirt surfaces and many trees. www.nycgovparks.org

13 **Robert Moses Park** • First Ave and 42nd St • Concrete surface. www.nycgovparks.org

14 **Theodore Roosevelt Park** • Central Park W at W 81st St • Gravel surface. www.nycgovparks.org

14 **Riverside Park** • Riverside Dr at 72nd St www.nycgovparks.org

14 **Margaret Mead Park** • Columbus Ave at 81st St www.leashline.com

15 **Balto Dog Monument** • Fifth Ave at E 67th St (Central Park)

15,17 **Carl Schurz Park** • East End Ave at 85/86th Sts • Medium-sized enclosed run with pebbled surface and separate space for small dogs. This run has benches and shady trees, and running water is available in the bathrooms. www.nycgovparks.org

16 **Riverside Park** • Riverside Dr at 87th St • Medium-sized run with gravel surface. www.nycgovparks.org

16 **Riverside Park** • Riverside Dr at 105/106th Sts • Medium-sized run with gravel surface. www.nycgovparks.org

18 **Morningside Park** • Morningside Ave b/w 114th & 119th Sts www.nycgovparks.org

20 **Thomas Jefferson Park** • E 112th St at First Ave • Wood chip surface.

23 **J. Hood Wright Park** • Haven Ave at W 173rd St • An enclosed dirt-surfaced run. www.nycgovparks.org

24 **Fort Tryon Park/Sir William's Dog Run** • Margaret Corbin Dr, Washington Heights www.ftdog.org

25 **Inwood Hill Dog Run** • Dyckman St and Payson Ave • Gravel surface. www.nycgovparks.org

184 Kowsky Plaza Dog Run (**Battery Park City**) • Gateway Plaza • Located near the marina, this area has small hills for your dog to run on, as well as a small fountain and bathing pool. www.bpcdogs.org

184 **Battery Park City** • Along River Ter between Park Pl W and Murray St • Concrete-surfaced run with a view of the river.

If you're reading this you're probably not a tourist, and if you're not a tourist you probably don't need a hotel. However, chances are good that at some point your obnoxious friend or relative from out of state will suddenly come a-knockin', bearing news of their long-awaited arrival to the big city. "So I thought I'd stay at your place," they will suggest casually, displaying their complete ignorance of the number of square feet in an average New York apartment—and simultaneously realizing your greatest fear of playing host to someone you greatly dislike. Or there's the possibility that your place is infested with mice, bed bugs, or pigeons and you need to escape, pronto. Or maybe you're just looking for a romantic (or slightly less than romantic) getaway without leaving the city. Whatever the case, be assured that there is a seemingly endless array of possibilities to suit all your overnight desires and needs.

Obviously, your options run from dirt cheap (well, by New York standards) to disgustingly, offensively expensive. For those with tons of extra cash, either call us or check out some of the elite luxury chains—the **Ritz Carlton** (cheaper to stay at the one in Battery Park **(p 184)** than Central Park **(Map 12)**), **The Four Seasons (Map 12)** at E 57th St, **The W** at Union Square **(Map 10)**, Times Square (Map 12), E 39th St **(Map 10)**, and Lexington Ave at 49th St **(Map 13)**, **Le Parker Meridien (Map 12)**, **The Peninsula (Map 12)**, **The St. Regis (Map 12)**, and **The Mandarin-Oriental (Map 11)**.

Those hotels that are more unique to Manhattan include: **The Lowell (Map 15)**, a fortress of pretentiousness nestled beside Central Park, which successfully captures the feel of a snobby, high-class gentleman's club. For a similar feeling, only with a heavy dose of Renaissance Italy and a design dating back to 1882, check into **The New York Palace (Map 12)**. If you prefer more modern surroundings, the swank-tastic **Bryant Park Hotel (Map 12)** (once the landmark Radiator building before it was transformed) is a favorite amongst entertainment and fashion industry folks. Similarly, The **Regency (Map 15)**, nicknamed "Hollywood East" in the 1960s, is a must for all celeb-stalkers and hangers-on alike. Meanwhile, **The Algonquin (Map 12)** offers complimentary delivery of The New Yorker, as if to suggest that they cater to a more literary crowd (maybe in the 1920s, but whether or not that's the case today is up for debate). If you're feeling fabulous, there's **The Muse Hotel (Map 12)**, located in the heart of Times Square, mere steps away from the bright lights of Broadway (*Book of Mormon*, anyone?). If you're more comfortable with the old-money folks (or if you're a nostalgic member of the nouveau-riche), check out the apartment-size rooms at **The Carlyle (Map 15)**. Be a bit easier on your wallet and get a room at **The Excelsior Hotel (Map 14)**—it may be a tad less indulgent, but get over it, you're still right on Central Park. Yet more affordable and not an ounce less attractive is **The Hudson (Map 11)**, a chic boutique hotel from Ian Schrager. Then there's **The Shoreham (Map 12)**, which offers complimentary champagne at the front desk (so it's definitely worth a shot to pose as a guest) in addition to a fantastically retro bar, that looks like it's straight out of *A Clockwork Orange*. If you are gay or have a gay relative or friend coming to visit, consider The Out NYC (Map 11), which is a sleek, new resort hotel billing itself as New York's first straight-friendly hotel. ast but certainly not least, one can always stay at the world-famous **Waldorf-Astoria (Map 13)**, where unrivaled service and a lavish renovation more than justify the cost of staying (at least for the 1% and those who edging close to that elite coterie).

There are additional high-end options downtown, perfect for nights of drunken bar-hopping or cool European friends with deep but chic pockets. The sexier of these hotels include: **The Hotel Gansevoort (Map 5)**, a sleek tower of luxury, located steps away from the Meatpacking District—New York's very own version of Miami Beach! Nearby, you'll find **The Maritime Hotel (Map 10)**, which does a great impression of a cruise ship, replete with porthole-shaped windows and La Bottega, an Italian restaurant with a massive outdoor patio that feels like the deck of a Carnival liner. In trendy SoHo, you'l find **The Mercer Hotel**, **60 Thompson (Map 6)** and **The SoHo Grand (Map 2)** (there's also its sister, **The Tribeca Grand (Map 2)**, farther south)—which vary ever-so-slightly in degrees of coolness, depending on your demands. A little bit north of there, next to Gramercy Park, i **The Inn at Irving Place (Map 10)**. Things are a tad less modern at this upscale bed and breakfast, created from two adjacent townhouses, but the Cibar Lounge, the rock and fashion royalty, and the lack of any visible signage outside are sure to make you feel lik your dreams of achieving super-awesome-hip forever status have come true. On the newest stretch of NYC hipness, The Bowery, there are a few new boutique hotels to make all your rock star dreams come true. **The Bowery Hotel (Map 6)** was the first to make its mark on this former stretch of skid row. The Lobby Bar is worth checking out even if you can't afford a room. Up the street the semi-sleek **Cooper Square Hotel (Map 6)** is competing for models and I-Bankers expense accounts. Check out how they squeezed the fancy hotel in between two existing tenement buildings. Not too far away is the **Crosby Street Hotel (Map 6)**, another of those cool hotels we'll never be able to afford. One thing we can afford is a stroll down the High Line to crane our necks at the exhibitionists who often can be spotted cavorting in the floor-to-ceiling windows of the **Standard Hotel (Map 5)**, which—ahem—straddles the airborne park. Guests are reminded by staff that their rooms will be highly visible and they should be careful, which of course prompts many to be careful to show off as much as they can for onlookers.

But speaking of money and thrills we can't afford, let's get real—most of us can't begin to afford such luxuries as those outlined above. We live in a city where pay is kinda flat (or at least flatter than expenses), there's a rent affordability crisis unlike anything in NYC history, and the only reason you really need a hotel is because as much as you might love Aunt Edna from Des Moines and want to spend time with her during her fortnight in the city, you don't want to step on her as she sleeps on the floor of your studio apartment when you stumble home after last call. For these real-world occasions, rest assured—there are a few hotels in the city where real people can actually afford to stay. Some of these include **The Gershwin Hotel (Map 9)**, **Herald Square Hotel (Map 9)**, **Super 8 Times Square (Map 12)**, **Red Roof Inn (Map 9)**, **Second Home on Second Avenue (Map 6)**, and **The Chelsea Savoy (Map 9)**. These are all solid, safe choices.

More mid-range options include: **Hotel Thirty Thirty (Map 9)**, **The Abington Guest House (Map 5)**, **The Roger Williams Hotel (Map 9)**, **Portland Square Hotel (Map 12)**, **Comfort Inn (Map 9)**, **Clarion Hotel (Map 10)**, and **The New Yorker Hotel (Map 8)**.

Whatever you do, never book your family, friends, or self into a hotel that you don't know or haven't scouted, no matter how appealing the cost—if it seems too good to be true, it may well be. Some of the lowest-priced "hotels" in town appear on some leading hotel booking sites, and they can be really scary. Some are in unsavory neighborhoods, or are in old buildings and barely qualify as hotels. You may arrive and find that someone's suitcases are already in your room, or that there's no heat or hot water, or that the room feels more like a homeless shelter than a hotel. (Yup, this actually happens. Even to seasoned New Yorkers like us, when we get too enamored of a would-be bargain.) And let's not mention the bedbug threat. Suffice it to say, always always always go with a brand you trust, or check it out beforehand in person or online. That's the only way to be sure you or your out-of-town visitors won't end up with the most unwelcome kind of New York story.

No matter what range of hotel you are looking to book, and for whatever reason, note that rates are generally highest during the holiday season and the summer, and lowest during the off season. Other specific events, like Fashion Week or the UN General Assembly, can cause the price of hotel rooms to increase markedly. Regardless of time of year, sometimes you'll get a better deal if you book well in advance, and sometimes you can score an awesome find by booking at the very last minute on a site like Hotwire.com. And sometimes you're just out of luck—rates are ballpark and they are subject to change up until you have the reservation. If you find yourself in a bind and you need to get a room for yourself or someone else, additional websites that may be helpful are Hotels.com, Priceline, Travelocity, Expedia, and Kayak, or individual company websites like Hilton.com, spg.com, holiday-inn.com, and so on. You can also call a hotel directly to ask if they have any specials. Be aware that not all hotels have a star rating and sometimes those that do aren't accurate. The quoted rates will give you an idea of the quality being offered. The bottom line is, like most things in New York, while you have plenty of options, few of them are cheap—but with serendipity and creativity, you may be the lucky one who gets the bargain.

Sure, eating out in New York can be a competitive sport (try getting a reservation at WD50), sometimes a contact sport (try squeezing in the door at Caracas). However, once you're equipped with enough information about New York's 25,000 restaurant choices, the rewards are limitless, and we can confirm that this is one of the best damn towns on Earth to eat in. Certainly you could take advantage of the city's gourmet grocery stores and make fabulous meals at home, but compare your Citarella grocery bill to the check at Westville and you'll be eating out more often. But not to worry, we can always help you find the perfect place. Whether you're looking for a restaurant with a rare 28 from Zagat, or you refuse to let that D health rating get between you and good food (re: Kosher delis and Chinatown basements), you'll never have to settle.

Eating Old

Since New York City is a perpetual culinary hotspot featuring tons of celebrity chefs (and Top Chef contestants who packed their knives and went), it's easy to get wrapped up in trendy food that looks more like a Rorschach test than dinner. Some experimental restaurants are remarkably on the cutting edge, but when you're not in the mood for aerated olive-chocolate foie gras (Wylie Dufresne, we're looking at you), you can rely on the Big Apple's longstanding heavyweights. They've relaxed the tie and jacket rule, but you can still rub elbows with the who's who at the posh **21 Club (circa 1929, Map 12)**; dine on New American cuisine at the 219-year-old **Bridge Café**, the oldest business in the city, older than Chase Manhattan **(circa 1794, Map 1)**; slurp fresh-shucked oysters and enjoy amazing desserts under the vaulted, tiled ceiling at Grand Central Station's **Oyster Bar (circa 1913, Map 13)**; sample more oysters and one of the best burgers in existence at the venerable Midtown watering hole **P.J. Clarke's (circa 1884, Map 13)**; order the sturgeon scrambled with eggs, onions, and a bialy on the side at **Barney Greengrass (circa 1908, Map 16)**; feast like old-world royalty at **The Russian Tea Room (circa 1927, Map 12)**; or expand your culinary horizons with calf's spleen and cheese on a roll at **Ferdinando's Focacceria (circa 1904, Map 32)**.

Eating Cheap

New York has always had options for us broke folks, and the economic collapse (still hanging on, isn't it?) didn't hurt those options either. At **Shake Shack (Maps 2, 9, 14, 17)**, you can still grab a Shack Burger for under $5 or a Shack Stack (twice the goods) for under $10. Ethnic food has always been a great friend to eaters on a budget. For the city's most succulent soup dumplings, head to **Shanghai Café (Map 3)**. For brilliant Middle Eastern go to **Hummus Place (Map 7)**, **Gazala Place (Map 11)**, or **Taïm (Map 5)** for some of the best falafel on the planet. For Mexican check out the taquería at The Corner a.k.a. **La Esquina (Map 6)** or head out to Bushwick's factory-restaurant **Tortillería Los Hermanos**. The Indian lunch buffet at **Tiffin Wallah (Map 10)** is less than ten bucks and veggie friendly to boot. **Papaya King (Map 17)** has kept hot dog lovers grinning since 1932. For a gigantic plate of Puerto Rican food under ten dollars, sit at the counter of **La Taza De Oro (Map 8)**. For a cheap breakfast that even celebs appreciate, **La Bonbonniere (Map 5)** can't be beat. And many of us can't survive a day without the staples of NYC Jewish eats: bagels and knishes. For bagels, go with perennial winner **Ess-a-Bagel (Maps 10, 13)** or try our favorites: **David's Bagels (Map 10)**, **Kossar's Bialys (Map 4)**, **Absolute Bagels (Map 16)**, or the original **Tal Bagels (Maps 13, 15, 16, 17)**. For knishes, nothing beats the **Yonah Schimmel Knish Bakery (Map 6)**. Since the NFT office began in Chinatown and we're always broke (free advice: don't go into publishing), we are certified experts on eating cheap in this part of town. At **Nice Green Bo (Map 3)** get the scallion pancakes, at **Food Shing/Food Sing 88 (Map 3)** get the beef noodle soup, at **Fuleen (Map 3)** get the shrimp with chili sauce, and for Malaysian order the stingray (!) at **Sanur (Map 3)**.

Eating Hip

Eating hip usually involves the food of the moment (kale chips and artisanal popsicles), beautiful people (who couldn't possibly eat another bite of that amuse-bouche), and some kind of exclusivity (unpublished phone numbers and hidden entrances). Although, with this little hiccup in our economic stability, even the hippest places have had to let the dirty, burger-eating plebeians through their doors. That being said, the ultimate in cool dining is, of course, **Rao's (Map 20)**—or so we hear. But unless you're the Mayor, the Governor, or Woody Allen, you probably won't be getting a reservation anytime soon. If you can find the unmarked basement door of **Bobo (Map 5)**, you'll really impress your date. Head east to try the always crowded, no-reservations eatery **Freemans (Map 6)**, which hides itself at the end of an alleyway; do not miss the pork chops. For fans of Japanese izakayas, nothing is quite as fun as an evening at **En Brasserie (Map 5)**. Its gourmet menu brilliantly fuses homemade miso with duck, cod, tofu, and anything else you can think of. And the low lighting will make anyone look good. **Zenkichi (Map 29)** also has killer Japanese, and yes, it's behind a camouflaged front door, but both the food an ambiance are stellar, and it's a great date spot. David Chang's restaurant mini-empire is still on people's radars, so try **Momofuku Ko (Map 6)**. If the lines are too long at the Momofukus or you don't have friends that can afford to score a table at **The Spotted Pig (Map 5)**, try **Kuma Inn (Map 4)** on the Lower East Side. The small plates like Chinese sausage with Thai chili-lime sauce and pork wasabi dumplings are brilliant, it's BYO sake, and there's no secret phone number. If you don't mind waiting and your date isn't a vegetarian, grab a cocktail in the lobby of the slick Ace Hotel and get ready for a dinner you won't soon forget at **The Breslin (Map 9)**.

Eating Late

Some say New York never sleeps, and some (ahem, Madrid) insist that it does, but like any big city it depends on the neighborhood, so let us help you locate some options. **Kang Suh's (Map 9)** Korean barbecue runs all night, as well as the Turkish kebab spot **Bereket (Map 7)**, the bar/burger joint **7A (Map 7)**, and a host of classic diners like **Odessa (Map 7)** and **Waverly Restaurant (Map 5)**. **Veselka (Map 6)** is the place for late-night Ukrainian soul food. You'll find cabbies chowing down past 3 am at **Lahore Deli (Map 6)**, **Big Arc Chicken (Map 7)**, or **99 Cents Fresh Pizza (Map 11)**. **French Roast (Map 5, 14)** serves good croque-monsieurs 24 hours, and that dessert you declined earlier in the evening. If you're near Chinatown at 3 a.m, let the wonton soup and barbecue duck at **Great NY Noodletown (Map 3)** soak up all that beer. And, of course, **Blue Ribbon (Map 6)** is still one of the best places to eat after midnight.

Eating Pizza

We don't care what Chicago says; we do pizza best! The coal oven spots top most lists: **Grimaldi's (Map 30)**, **Lombardi's (Map 6)**, **Luzzo's (Map 7)**, **John's Pizzeria (Map 5)**, and the original **Patsy's (Map 20)** in East Harlem. The coal oven enjoys extra cachet because it's illegal now, except in the aforementioned eateries where they were already in operation. However, the regular brick oven joints, such as **Franny's (Map 33)**, **Keste (Map 5)**, **Co (Map 8)** and **Lucali (Map 32)** are no slouches. For an upscale pie, try the exquisite creations at Mario Batali's **Otto (Map 6)**. Trying to find something edible near Wall Street? Check out **Adrienne's (Map 1)** delicious rectangle pies on Stone Street, or walk up to TriBeCa for a luscious Brussels-sprout-bacon-caramelized-onion pie at **Saluggi's (Map 2)**. For a classic Village scene complete with live jazz, check out **Arturo's (Map 6)** on Houston Street. The outer boroughs seriously represent here: **Louie & Ernie**'s in The Bronx (p 177), **Tufino** in Queens **(Map 26)**, **Denino's** on Staten Island (p 183), and, of course, **Di Fara** in Brooklyn (p 179). Pizza by the slice practically deserves its own category, but the highlights include **Patsy's (Map 20**, definitely the best slice in the city), **Artichoke Basille's Pizza (Map 6**, get the grandma slice), **Farinella (Map 3**, very unique), and **Joe's (Map 5**, classic NY Style).

Eating Ethnic

Spin a globe, blindly stick your finger onto a spot, and chances are you can find that cuisine on offer in New York. And an outstanding offering it will be.

Argentine: **Buenos Aires (Map 7)**

Austrian: **Edi & The Wolf (Map 7)**

Australian: **Tuck Shop (Map 6)** and **The Thirsty Koala (Map 26)**

Chinese: **Joe's Shanghai (Map 3)**, **Old Sichuan (Map 3)** and **Szechuan Gourmet (Map 9)**

Cuban: **Café Habana (Map 6)**

Dominican: **El Malecon (Map 23)** and **El Castillo de Jagua (Map 4)**

Egyptian: **Kabab Café (Map 26)**

Ethiopian: **Ghenet (Map 33)** and **Zoma (Map 19)**

German: **Heidelberg (Map 15)**, **Zum Schneider (Map 7)** and **Hallo Berlin (Map 11)**

Greek: **Kefi (Map 14)**, **Periyali (Map 9)** and **Pylos (Map 7)**

Indian: **Dawat (Map 13)**, **Banjara (Map 7)** and **Indian Tandoor Oven (Map 15)**

Italian: **Babbo (Map 6)**, **Felidia (Map 13)**, **Il Giglio (Map 2)**, **Sfoglia (Map 17)**, **Al Di La (Map 33)**, **I Trulli (Map 10)** and countless others

Japanese: **Nobu (Map 2)**, **Takahachi (Map 7)**, **Ki Sushi (Map 32)** and **about 40 others**

Jewish: **Sammy's Roumanian (Map 6)** and **B&H Dairy (Map 6)**

Korean: **Kang Suh (Map 9)**, **Seoul Garden (Map 9)** and **Dok Suni's (Map 7)**

Malaysian: **New Malaysia (Map 3)**

Mexican: **Alma (Map 32)** and **Mexico 2000 (Map 29)**

New Zealand: **Nelson Blue (Map 1)**

Pakistani: **Pakistan Tea House (Map 2)** and **Haandi (Map 10)**

Polish: **Christina's (Map 28)** and **Lomzynianka (Map 28)**

Russian: **The Russian Vodka Room (Map 12)** and **Russian Samovar (Map 12)**

Scandinavian: **Aquavit (Map 13)** and **Smörgås Chef (Map 1)**

South African: **Madiba (Map 31)**

Southern American: **Sylvia's (Map 19)** and **Cheryl's Global Soul (Map 33)**

Spanish: **Socarrat (Map 9)** and **Tia Pol (Map 8)**

Sri Lankan: **Sigiri (Map 7)**

Thai: **Pongsri Thai (Map 3)** and

Sripraphai (p 181)

Turkish: **Turkish Kitchen (Map 10)**

Eating Meat

New York is home to arguably the world's best steakhouse, **Peter Luger (Map 29)**, but it's competitive at the top, and clawing at Luger's heels are: **Mark Joseph Steakhouse (Map 1)** and classics like **Sparks (Map 13)**, **Palm (Map 13)**, **Smith & Wollensky (Map 13)** and the **Strip House (Map 6)**. For the Brazilian-style "all you can eat meat fest," **Churrascaria Plataforma (Map 11)** does the trick. As for hamburgers, the rankings provide material for eternal debate: **Corner Bistro (Maps 5, 26)**, **Burger Joint** at Le Parker Meridien **(Map 12)**, **J.G. Melon (Map 15)** and **Bonnie's Grill (Map 33)**, to name a few. **Royale (Map 7)** compliments the perfect patty with stellar fixins for a song, and **Korzo Haus (Map 7)** serves a succulent ground beef patty wrapped in Hungarian fried bread, topped with Central European goodies. Texans and Missourians alike can agree that New York has some damn good BBQ, even if we sometimes recruit our BBQ talent from down South: **Daisy May's (Map 11)**, **Hill Country (Map 9)**, **Dinosaur Bar-B-Que (Map 18)** and **Blue Smoke (Map 10)** in Manhattan, and **The Smoke Joint (Map 31)** in Brooklyn.

Eating Veggie

You could live your whole life here, never eat a shred of meat, and feast like a king every day (and probably live longer). Try the quality Indian fare at **Pongal (Map 10)** and **Chennai Garden (Map 10)**, and, for high-end eats, **Franchia (Map 10)**, **Candle 79 (Map 15)**, **Dirt Candy (Map 7)**, and **GoBo (Map 5)**. For those on a budget, try **Atlas Café (Map 7)** for a quick bite and **Angelica Kitchen (Map 6)** for something a step up. For a delicious macrobiotic meal including dessert, **Souen (Maps 5, 6)** has yet to disappoint. For adventurous veggie heads, nothing beats **HanGawi (Map 9)**, consistently voted one of the best vegetarian and Korean restaurants in the city.

Eating Your Wallet

While we technically use the same currency as the rest of the country, it's actually worth about half as much here as elsewhere. Even the most frugal among us have spent 100 New York dollars on a night out and thought we got off easy—the damage can easily exceed $200 per person at a Michelin-starred restaurant. No doubt you're dying to try Eric Ripert's this and Daniel Boulud's that, but treat this like open bar at your holiday office party: Know your limit (financially, emotionally, morally), and try not to do anything you'll regret in the morning. If you can keep your food down after witnessing triple digits on your share of the tab, start on the slippery slope to gastronomically induced bankruptcy at the following restaurants, which rarely disappoint: **Babbo (Map 6)**, **Per Se (Map 11)**, **Gramercy Tavern (Map 9)**, **Le Bernardin (Map 12)**, **Bouley (Map 2)**, **Union Square Cafe (Map 9)**, **Mesa Grill (Map 9)**, **Craft (Map 9)**, **Aquavit (Map 13)** and **Spice Market (Map 5)**. And remember to manage your expectations: unless you fall in love with your server, the experience will probably not change your life. Although **Per Se (Map 11)** comes pretty damn close.

Our Favorite Restaurants

Consensus on this subject is always difficult, but with a group of New Yorkers opinionated enough to produce the NFT, we have to at least try and duke it out. We've historically granted the accolade to **Blue Ribbon (Map 6)**: it's open 'til 4 a.m., it's where the chefs of other restaurants go, it's got fondue, beef marrow, fried chicken, great liquor, a great vibe and great service. And it will always have that special place in our hearts and stomachs, but we also have to give a shout out to a few others: **Alma (Map 32)**, an out-of-the-way rooftop Mexican restaurant with stunning views and equally good tamales, mole, margaritas, and ambiance, **Sigiri (Map 7)**, a spicy Sri Lankan gem that's BYOB to boot; **Babbo (Map 6)**, because it's Babbo (call at least one month ahead); **Arturo's (Map 6)**, a classic, old-school pizza joint with live jazz, Greenwich Village locals and amazing coal-fired pizza and **Kuma Inn (Map 4)**, a hard-to-find Asian tapas restaurant that's cool and hip but also affordable, laid-back and mind-blowingly delicious.

Overview

If you ever get bored in New York City, you have only yourself to blame. When it comes to nightlife in particular, the only difficulty you'll have is in choosing amongst the seemingly infinite options for entertainment. New York's top weeklies—The Village Voice and Time Out New York—offer their round-ups of goings on about town, as do websites such as **Flavorpill** (www.flavorpill.com), **Brooklyn Vegan** (www.brooklynvegan.com), and **Oh My Rockness** (www.ohmyrockness.com). A current favorite for usually cheap and off-beat picks is **The Skint** (www.theskint.com) For those of you who require more than your typical night out, **NonsenseNYC** (www.nonsensenyc.com) is an e-mail newsletter with a ton of dance parties, interactive art shows, guerrilla theater and other unusual events. A word of caution: don't forget to pace yourselves.

Dive Bars

There is no shortage of dumps in this city, so we've done our best to single out the darkest and the dirtiest. The oldest on our list is, of course, **McSorely's Old Ale House (Map 6)**, which has been in operation 1854, and looks it's straight out of Gangs of New York. Best experienced during the day and avoided like the plague on evenings and weekends, it's worth checking out the place where Abe Lincoln drank and soaking in all that old-school barroom atmosphere. A popular choice among our staff is the oh-so-derelict **Milano's (Map 6)**. Tucked away on swiftly gentrifying Houston St., it's been a boozy refuge since 1880. In the East Village Lucy has been a fixture behind the bar at **Lucy's (Map 7)** for 33 years, and **Blarney Cove (Map 7)** is open and ready to serve the thirsty masses at 8am. Other downtown favorites include **Puffy's Tavern (Map 2)**, **Blue & Gold (Map 6)** and **Mona's (Map 7)**. In Midtown, **Jimmy's Corner (Map 12)** is the ultimate escape from Times Square tourist swarms and the classic **Subway Inn (Map 15)** remains a lone holdout amid office towers and Bloomingdale's shoppers. Uptown, we like **Reif's Tavern (Map 17)**, **Dublin House (Map 14)** and **1020 Bar (Map 18)**. On the other side of the East River, check out **Turkey's Nest (Map 29)** in Williamsburg and Red Hook classic **Sunny's (Map 32)**.

Best Beer Selection

It's a marvelous time to be a beer connoisseur in New York City. The number of watering holes with mind-boggling craft beer lists grows every year, so we'll do your liver a favor and suggest a few of the best. If your braving a bar crawl in Greenwich Village, heavily trodden **Peculier Pub (Map 6)** and **Blind Tiger Ale House (Map 5)** offer large and diverse selections, and **Vol de Nuit (Map 5)** has a huge list of Belgian beers. Going several steps further with the Trappist schtick, the East Village's **Burp Castle (Map 6)** has a fine array of Belgians, but use your inside voice or you'll be soundly shushed. **Nearby Jimmy's 43 (Map 6)** and **d.b.a. (Map 7)** are our neighborhood favorites where beer is concerned, and over in Alphabet City, **Zum Schneider (Map 7)** offers a slew of unique choice to wash down its German fare. In the Lower East Side, **Spitzer's Corner (Map 4)** is worth checking out early on a week night (good luck on a weekend). Beer shop **Good Beer (Map 7)** is a great place to order a flight of four beers or a growler to go, and **Top Hops (Map 4)** offers a great selection of bottles and drafts, as well as a standing bar area. In Midtown your best bets are **Rattle n' Hum (Map 9)** or **Ginger Man (Map 9)**, which has an absolutely amazing selection with over 120 bottles and 66 taps. Our Uptown favorite is **Earl's Beer & Cheese (Map 17)**, which has a small but excellent beer list.

If you're seeking good beer in Brooklyn, make Wiliamsburg your first stop. In fact, just head to cozy, Belgian-focused **Spuyten Duyvil (Map 29)**, which has over 100 bottles and a rotating cask ale. From there, **Barcade (Map 29)** achieves an awesome synergy between its classic 80s arcade games and stellar beer list—our only complaint is that we can't drink and play Tetris at the same time. **The d.b.a. (Map 29)** on this side of the river is just as well-stocked as its East Village cousin, with the added bonus of being less crowded. Tricky spellings aside, **Brouwerij Lane (Map 28)** and **Breukelen Bier Merchants (Map 29)** are perfect places to nurse a pint while you shop for bottles. In Gowanus, check out **Draft Barn (Map 33)** to drink ale like a king or queen in a medieval fortress minus the moat. If you're in Park Slope, head straight to **Beer Table (Map 33)**, whose proprietors know more about beer than they probably should (or maybe we're just jealous of their supreme beer nerdery).

Outdoor Spaces

Outdoor space is a precious commodity in NYC, so couple it with booze and you've got the perfect destination for cooped-up city dwellers when the weather turns warm. Actually, you can find New Yorkers stubbornly holding court at outdoor venues in all sorts of weather short of electrical storms and sub-freezing temperatures, and they'll only retreat from those conditions when chased indoors by the staff. Although entry to many of the finest outdoor drinking dens requires supermodel looks or celebrity status, or at the very least a staggering tolerance for douchebags, there are plenty of options for the mere mortals among us. For example, the **Vu Bar (Map 9)** at the top of La Quinta Inn in Koreatown is a low-key establishment that'll let you in no matter what you wear or who you hang out with. For a little fancier but still accessible night out in the open air, try **Bookmarks (Map 12)**, the rooftop bar in the Library Hotel. For drinks with a view, check out **Berry Park (Map 29)** in Williamsburg, which looks out onto Manhattan, or head to South Street Seaport's **Beekman Beer Garden Beach Club (Map 1)**, which makes up for what it lacks in beachiness with stunning views of the Brooklyn Bridge.

Our favorite places to enjoy a drink outside are in the many back patios that turn the darkest, funkiest watering holes into bona fide oases, no matter how small and concrete-laden they may be. Beer lovers congregate in the backyards at **d.b.a. (Map 7)** in the East Village and **Spuyten Duyvil (Map 29)** in Williamsburg, and the aptly named **Gowanus Yacht Club (Map 32)** remains our Carroll Gardens favorite. More outdoor drinking can be had at **Sweet & Vicious (Map 6)** in the Lower East Side, **The Park (Map 8)** in Chelsea, **The Heights Bar & Grill (Map 18)** in Morningside Heights, **The Gate (Map 33)** in Park Slope, and **Union Pool (Map 29)** in Williamsburg. In Long Island City, there's an excellent beer garden called **Studio Square (Map 27)**. Speaking of beer gardens, there's a seeming resurgence of these all-but-disappeared drinking venues, once popular with the central European immigrant set. Predictably packed results can be found at **La Birreria (Map 9)** or **Spritzenhaus (Map 29)**. But if you can only visit one, make it the 100-year-old Bohemian **Hall & Beer Garden (Map 26)** in Astoria. Snag a picnic table in the massive outdoor area with a gang of friends, and knock back frosty pitchers of pilsner just like they did in the old days (polka dancing optional).

Best Jukebox

Personal taste factors heavily in this category of course, but here is a condensed list of NFT picks. For Manhattan: **Ace Bar (Map 7)** (indie rock/punk), **Hi-Fi (Map 7)** (a huge and diverse selection), **7B (Horseshoe Bar)** (Map 7) (rock all the way), **WCOU Radio (Tile Bar) (Map 7)** (eclectic), **Rudy's Bar & Grill (Map 11)** (blues), **Welcome to the Johnsons (Map 4)** (indie rock/punk). For Brooklyn: **Boat Bar (Map 32)** (Carroll Gardens—indie rock), the **Brooklyn Social Club (Map 32)** (Carroll Gardens—country/soul) and **The Levee (Map 29)** (Williamsburg—good all around).

DJs and Dancing

New York's old cabaret laws make it tough to find free dance spots, but they do exist (albeit often with the velvet rope scenario that may deter the impatient). On the weekends, entry into the swankier clubs doesn't come without paying your dues in long lines and pricey cover charges. That's not our style. You'll find us dancing and hanging out at **Santos Party House (Map 3)** as well as **Happy Ending (Map 3)** and **Le Poisson Rouge (Map 6)**. In and around Williamsburg, we suggest checking out the lively dance scenes at **Bembe (Map 29)** or **Glasslands (Map 29)**.

Cocktails

In recent years mixology has practically become a religion in New York, and its temples of worship are clustered in the East Village. For starters, head to **Death & Company (Map 7)**, tell the knowledgeable servers what you like in a drink, and prepare to be converted.

If wait lists aren't your thing (and there often is one) **The Summit Bar (Map 7)**, **Elsa (Map 7)**, **Louis 649 (Map 7)**, **The Beagle (Map 7)**, and bitters-focus **Amor y Amargo (Map 7)** are all solid options nearby. **Mayahuel (Map 6)**, located among Sixth Street's Indian restaurants is practically a crash course in all things tequila and mezcal. If hardly-secret speakeasies are your thing, **PDT (Map 7)** is accessible through a telephone booth in deep-fried-dog haven **Crif Dogs** (reservations recommended), and in the West Village, **Employees Only (Map 5)** is located behind psychic's shop. If you're in the West Village, be sure to check out **Little Branch (Map 5)** for live jazz and some of the strongest mixed drinks we've ever had the pleasure of meeting. A little further uptown, **Rye House (Map 9)** is our preferred after-work headquarters. In Midtown, the classy **The Campbell Apartment (Map 13)**, tucked inside Grand Central Terminal, is a must. And for the blazer/cocktail dress set, there are your opulent hotel bars, such as **Rose Bar (Map 10)** inside the Gramercy Park Hotel, **King Cole Bar (Map 12)** inside the St. Regis Hotel, or **Bemelmans Bar (Map 15)** inside the Caryle Hotel. We're banking on our beverages to ease the pain of that tab.

Considering all the options in Manhattan, it's probably no surprise that Brooklyn has many bars offering just-as-high caliber cocktails, minus some of the crowdedness. Don't believe us? Head to **Dram (Map 29)**, **Hotel Delmano (Map 29)**, **Maison Premiere (Map 29)** or **Huckleberry Bar (Map 29)** in Williamsburg, or venture a little further east to **Ba'sik (Map 29)** or **The Richardson (Map 29)**. **Clover Club (Map 32)** is our favorite for mixed drinks in Cobble Hill. If you're in Long Island City be sure to check out **Dutch Kills (Map 27)** and marvel at that custom-crafted ice that won't water down your drink no matter how slowly you savor it.

Music—Overview

New York caters to a wide array of tastes in everything, and music is no exception. From the indie rock venues of Brooklyn to the history-steeped jazz clubs in Greenwich Village to amateur night at the Apollo, your musical thirst can be quenched in every possible way.

Jazz, Folk and Country

There are plenty of places to see jazz in the city, starting off with classic joints such as the **Village Vanguard (Map 5)** and **Birdland (Map 11)**. There's also the "Jazz at Lincoln Center" complex in the Time Warner Center on Columbus Circle which has three rooms: the 1,000-plus-seat, designed-for-jazz Rose Theater, the Allen Room, an amphitheater with a great view of the park, and the nightclub-esque Dizzy's Club Coca Cola. For a smaller (and cheaper) jazz experience, try **Lenox Lounge (Map 19)**, **Jazz Gallery (Map 9)** and **Arthur's Tavern (Map 5)**. **The Nuyorican Poets Café (Map 7)** has frequent jazz performances. In Brooklyn, one of your best bets is the small back room at Park Slope's **Barbes (Map 33)**. Easily one of the best weekly jazz experiences is the Mingus Big Band's residency at **The Jazz Standard (Map 10)**. If you've never done it, do it—it's a truly great and unpredictable band that even surly Mr. Mingus (might) have been proud of. For folk & country, try **Rodeo Bar (Map 10)**, **Hank's Saloon (Map 33)**, **Parkside Lounge (Map 7)** or **Jalopy (Map 32)**.

Rock and Pop

In case you've just moved back to NYC from, say, ten years in Mumbai, the rock scene is now firmly entrenched in Brooklyn. However, Manhattan's **Bowery Ballroom (Map 6)** remains the top live venue, with excellent sound and a good layout. Other notable spots this side of the East River include **Santos Party House (Map 3)**, **Webster Hall (Map 6)**, and the **Highline Ballroom (Map 8)**. **Irving Plaza (Map 10)**, **Terminal 5 (Map 11)**, and **Hammerstein Ballroom (Map 8)** aren't our favorites, but are worthwhile for the occasional top-notch acts. **Roseland (Map 12)** is billed as an intimate venue for high-profile acts, but good luck getting tickets for the Stones or anyone else of that ilk. The best remaining small club in Manhattan is **Mercury Lounge (Map 7)**, which gets great bands right before they're ready to move up to Bowery Ballroom. As far as the rest of the Lower East Side, it helps if you like your clubs to be punky basements (**Cake Shop, Map 4**) or former bodegas (**Arlene Grocery, Map 4**). **Fat Baby (Map 4)**, and **Fontana's (Map 3)** all offer plenty of goings-on south of Houston Street as well.

When it comes to new talent, it's really the clubs in Brooklyn that shine. If you know your way around Bowery Ballroom, you'll feel right at home at Brooklyn's premiere venue, **Music Hall of Williamsburg (Map 29)**. Then there's **Glasslands Gallery (Map 29)**, **Trash Bar (Map 29)**, **Cameo Gallery (Map 29)**, **Pete's Candy Store (Map 29)**, **Public Assembly (Map 29)**, **Brooklyn Bowl (Map 29)** ... basically, the rocking never stops in Map 29. Maybe we'll even forgive **The Knitting Factory (Map 29)** for leaving Manhattan to move here. In Greenpoint, check out the **Warsaw (Map 28)** in the Polish National Home. We also love the **The Bell House (Map 33)** in Gowanus, Brooklyn **Masonic Temple (Map 31)** in Fort Greene and **Union Hall (Map 33)** in Park Slope.

Experimental

A number of venues in New York provide a place for experimental music to get exposure. **Experimental Intermedia (Map 3)** is fully dedicated to showcasing the avant-garde. John Zorn's performance space, **The Stone (Map 7)**, takes an experimental approach in the venue's concept as well as its music, with a different artist acting as curator for an entire month and artists taking in 100% of the proceeds. **The Kitchen (Map 8)** features experimental music in addition to film, dance, and other art forms. **Le Poisson Rouge (Map 6)** has brought an exciting mix of different sounds back to the heart of Greenwich Village, and is one of our favorite spots. In Brooklyn, the experimental scene is cranking away, especially at **Issue Project Room's (Map 33)** space at the Old American Can Factory, **Glasslands Gallery (Map 29)** in Williamsburg, and **Jalopy (Map 32)** in Carroll Gardens.

Everything Else

A few places run the gamut of musical genres; folksy artists one night, hot Latin tango the next, and a slew of comedy, spoken word, and other acts. **Joe's Pub (Map 6)** presents an excellent variety of popular styles and often hosts celebrated international musicians. Keep an eye on **BAMcafé (Map 31)** for a variety of great performers. For cabaret or piano bar, try **Don't Tell Mama (Map 11)**, **Duplex (Map 5)**, or **Brandy's (Map 15)**. For a more plush experience, try the **Café Carlyle (Map 15)**. But for top cabaret talent at affordable prices, go directly to **The Metropolitan Room (Map 9)**. If you're seeking some R&B or soul, check out the **Apollo Theater (Map 19)**, though they mostly get "oldies" acts. The Apollo's Amateur Night on Wednesday is your chance to see some up-and-comers. **The Pyramid Club (Map 7)** has open mic MC'ing nights. **Barbes (Map 33)** in Park Slope hosts a wide palette of "world music" (for lack of a better term), including Latin American, European, and traditional US styles, plus more experimental fare. For more sounds of the south, **SOB's (Map 5)** has live South American music and dancing and should definitely be experienced at least once. **Nublu (Map 7)** is always reliable for a fun and sweaty night, especially on Wednesdays when they feature Brazilian bands and DJs. For African music, check out **Barbes (Map 33)** on Wednesday nights with the Mandingo Ambassadors as well as performances at **Le Grand Dakar (Map 31)** in Clinton Hill. And oh yeah—then there's all that classical music stuff, at places like **Carnegie Hall (Map 12)** and **Lincoln Center (Map 14)**—maybe you've heard of them?

We don't need to hear Liza Minelli or Frank Sinatra sing it to remember the famous line about New York City: "If I can make it there, I'll make it anywhere." A corollary of sorts might be, "If they'll make it anywhere, I can buy it there." From tasteful to tacky, classic to classless, delicious to dangerous, we've got it all: life-sized stuffed animals, Ming vases, toys for, shall we say, adventuresome adults, live eels, exotic spices, and even illegal fruits (but you didn't hear it from us). It requires enormous self-restraint to take a walk and not buy something here—or maybe we just tell ourselves that. While some of us occasionally lament the "mall-ification" of our fair city, we'll challenge anyone to find another place that combines convenience and quirkiness as well as this town does. You want Prada knock-offs? Chinatown. You want the real thing? Just walk north a few blocks. A real human skeleton? Cross the street. Homemade ricotta? It's practically next door. You can hunt for bargains or blow a year's salary in the blink of an eye. And even if you decide to leave your wallet at home in the interests of self-preservation, you can find endless entertainment in walking the streets and practicing the art of window-shopping..

Clothing and Accessories

Shopping for haute couture is no longer strictly an uptown affair, with a few high-end shops appearing in SoHo and the Meatpacking District, but the Upper East Side is still the ultimate destination for designer labels. Madison Avenue is the main artery, in the 50s, 60s, and 70s, rounded out by Fifth Avenue in the 50s and a few blocks east along 57th St. There you will find **Chanel (Map 12)**, **Burberry (Map 12)**, **Tiffany & Co (Map 12)** and all other names of that ilk. For department store shopping, start off with the little brown shopping bag originator **Bloomingdale's (Map 15)**, which is a short hop to everything else: **Saks Fifth Avenue (Map 12)** for the classics, **Henri Bendel (Map 12)** and **Barneys (Map 15)** for trendier lines, and **Bergdorf Goodman (Map 12)** if money is no object. A less expensive hobby is simply walking by all of these stores' window displays, particularly around the holidays. They're an impressive art form in and of themselves. If you're on a budget and can deal with the crush of tourists, check out **Macy's (Map 9)**. **Century 21 (Maps 1, 14)** can yield deals on name brand clothing, shoes, makeup, accessories, and home wares—the key word being "can." You'll need to have patience to sift through everything and deal with the crowds.

Even though SoHo suspiciously resembles an outdoor mall, it's still a great place to shop because of the wide range of stores in a concentrated area. The big names are all here too, but a standout store is **Prada (Map 6)**, whose Rem Koolhaas design draws as many visitors as Miuccia's clothes do. In addition to the standards, you'll find many street vendors selling everything from handmade jewelry to floppy-eared children's hats. While Broadway during the day is an agoraphobe's nightmare, the side streets on either side of Broadway have cool boutiques that appeal to the shopper who aims to avoid the chain stores.

The West Village has its own enclave of painfully hip, wallet-emptying shops. Head northwest to the Meatpacking District and you can see the results of an impressive urban magic trick that transformed racks of hanging beef into racks of $800 jeans. You can check out cool designs at **Stella McCartney (Map 5)** punk rock-inspired styles at **Alexander McQueen (Map 5)**, and envelope-pushing department store **Jeffrey (Map 5)**, the subject of a Saturday Night Live skit that's a send-up of the clerks' reputed snobbery. But for up-and-coming designers and independent boutiques, head East, to Noho (the area north of Houston and east of Broadway), Nolita (north of Little Italy), and the East Village.

The Upper East Side (particularly along Madison Avenue in the East 80s) has a notable amount of designer consignment stores. **Bis Designer Resale (Map 15)** and others like it sell gently worn items from top-tier designers like Chanel and Armani at a fraction of their original cost. You can also meander along "Thrift Row," a string of Upper East Side thrift shops on and near Third Avenue in the East 70s and 80s. Many of these shops, such as the **Housing Works Thrift Shop (Maps 10, 15, 17)**, carry a nice selection of designer clothing—not to mention the added bonus that the proceeds from your purchases go toward a good cause, like AIDS-related charities, cancer research and adoption programs.

Vintage Shopping

The abundance of vintage shops—over 60 at last count—will impress any shopper, whether you're someone who's just looking for a unique piece for a special occasion or a professional stylist purchasing wardrobe items for a period film (and if you are, check out **What Comes Around Goes Around, Map 2, in SoHo**). Our favorites, by neighborhood: **Tokio 7 (Map 6)** in the East Village, **Ina (Map 6)** in Noho, **Edith Machinist (Map 4)** in the Lower East Side, **Beacon's Closet (Map 29)** in Williamsburg, and for the especially fashion-forward, **Eva Gentry Consignment (Map 32)** in Boerum Hill. For you die-hards, be sure to attend the twice-yearly Manhattan Vintage Clothing Show at the Metropolitan Pavilion, where over 75 dealers sell their vintage finery. It should go without saying that at all of the abovementioned shops and venues, you must be prepared to pay the usual New York City premium.

Flea Markets, Street Vendors, Street Fairs & Bazaars

New Yorkers who once spent weekends perusing the eclectic finds in the asphalt lot at 26th Street and Sixth Avenue are still mourning the loss of the internationally-known Annex Antique Fair & Flea Market. The good news is that many of the same vendors from **Annex sell their wares at the Annex/ Hell's Kitchen Flea Market (Map 11)** on 39th Street between Ninth and Tenth Avenues. Saturdays in Fort Greene belong to **Brooklyn Flea (Map 31)** which features hundreds of vendors hawking everything from vintage maps, to retro eyewear, to furniture, as well as stellar food options (the market moves to Williamsburg waterfront on Sundays). There are many other smaller flea markets throughout the city, as well as numerous street fairs in various neighborhoods during warmer months. The best way to find them is usually by accidentally stumbling upon them during an exploratory walk. A fantastic indoor market to add to your must see list is The **Market NYC (Map 6)** in Nolita, a refreshingly offbeat collection of young, local designers who aren't afraid to be truly creative. Another fun option is shopping street side from designers who sell their one-of-a-kind designs al fresco. You can't always identify them by name, but you can't miss their stands along Prince and Spring Streets in SoHo. Look for made-while-you-wait purses and belts, scrap metal jewelry pieces, handmade leather-bound journals, and other ingular items.

Sports

'aragon Sporting Goods (Map 9) in Union Square is ard to beat as a one-stop shop for all sports gear and ccessories. They also take care of your recreational eeds, with services like all-inclusive ski packages ır Hunter Mountain and permitting for the NYC arks Department tennis courts. **Sports Authority Map 13)**, **Foot Locker (Maps 21, 24)**, and **Modell's Map 23)** provide a broad range of affordable sports othing, shoes, and athletic equipment. For the best ld weather and mountain gear, head to **Tents & ails (Map 2)**, **Patagonia (Map 14)** or **REI (Map 6)**.

lousewares and Home Design

u can lose hours in **ABC Carpet & Home (Map** just off of Union Square. Design fanatics can preciate their exotic array of furnishings (much it antique and imported from Asia and Europe) en if they can't afford the steep prices. For the rest us, more affordable housewares can be found at e Upper West Side's **Gracious Home (Map 14)**, elsea's **The Container Store (Map 9)**, and any e of **Muji**'s three Manhattan locations **(Maps 3, 9, 12)**. For paint, window dressings, and other home decorating supplies, try **Janovic (Maps 11, 16)**. Prepare for sensory overload if you take on the over 200,000 square feet of commercial and residential furnishings at the **A&D Building (Map 13)**. Showrooms are open to the public, unlike at some of the smaller design shops nearby, which require business cards upon entry.

Kitchenware/Tableware

Fishs Eddy (Map 9) is a plateware alternative to mega-chains like Pottery Barn and Bed, Bath & Beyond, and is easily one of our favorite shops in all of New York. **Zabar's (Map 14)** often-ignored second floor is a favorite among the city's cooks. In Brooklyn, we love browsing at **Whisk (Map 29)**, **The Brooklyn Kitchen (Map 29)** and the fabulous **A Cook's Companion (Map 32)**. Downtown, small but sublime **Global Table (Map 6)** has excellent reasonably priced housewares, and **Lancelotti's (Map 7)** collection of cool kitchenware and tableware is always fun to check out.

Furniture

No cash at all? Easy. Troll the Upper East Side on Sunday nights to see what people are throwing out. Chances are, you'll find something better than what you'd buy new at Brooklyn's **Ikea (Map 32)**, which is indubitably the next step up in the food chain of furniture. Otherwise, **West Elm (Map 30)**, **Room & Board (Map 6)** and **Design Within Reach** (not really that within reach) **(Map 30)** will gladly take your hard-earned dollars if you're ready to graduate from "Aksuldnje" and "Fjosell." Have even more money to spend? Easily done, at places such as **Scott Jordan Furniture (Map 5)**, **Ligne Rosset (Map 10)**, and the Meatpacking District's brilliant **Vitra (Map 5)**. If vintage is your bag, head straight to Williamsburg's **Two Jakes (Map 29)** or check out some of the smaller shops around town such as Fort Greene's **Yu Interiors (Map 31)**. Any way you slice it, New York makes spending entire paychecks shockingly convenient.

Electronics

J&R (Map 1) provides most things electronic, including computers and accessories, iPods, games, cameras, music equipment, CDs, DVDs, and household appliances. **B&H (Map 8)** is the top destination for professionals and amateurs when it comes to photographic, audio, and video equipment. It's worth a visit just to witness the pure spectacle of this well-coordinated operation, as well as the outstanding selection of gear. Note that the megastore is run by Orthodox Jews who strictly observe the Sabbath and holidays, and thus you should always check the hours and days of operation posted on their website before heading over. Audiophiles are wonderfully served by **Stereo Exchange (Map 6)** and the jaw-dropping, price-busting **Sound by Singer (Map 9)**. Other places to shop for electronics include the **Apple Store (Maps 6, 8, 12, 13)** and **Tekserve (Map 9)**, the (other) Apple specialists.

Food

With residents from every corner of the globe who collectively speak over 170 languages, New York couldn't help but be an exciting destination for food shopping. The offerings are as diverse as the population, whether you're looking for the best of the basics or exotic spices and other imported specialties. Two revered emporia make the Upper West Side a culinary destination—**Fairway (Maps 14, 15, 18, 32)** and **Zabar's (Map 14)**—and the Zabar's offshoot, **Vinegar Factory (Map 17)**, graces the Upper East Side. The national chain **Whole Foods (Maps 2, 6, 9, 12, 14, 16)** is multiplying, and now there's even two **Trader Joe's (Maps 6, 9)**, though only devotees can brave the crowds there. **The Essex Street Market (Map 4)** on the Lower East Side is a beloved neighborhood institution filled to the brim with amazing meat, produce, fish and cheese (like **Saxelby Cheesemongers, Map 4**). Another great public market filled with gourmet goodness can be found in the heart of Grand Central Terminal—the **Grand Central Market (Map 13)**. **Chelsea Market (Map 8)**, housed in a cool, historic National Biscuit Company factory complex has a number of restaurants, bakeries and gourmet food vendors. If you're looking for fresh-from-the-farm meats and produce, though, the city's greenmarkets are important destinations for chefs and amateur cooks alike. The largest is the **Union Square Greenmarket (Map 9)**, which operates year-round on Mondays, Wednesdays, Fridays, and Saturdays. Meanwhile, outdoor markets like **Smorgasburg (Map 29)** and **Hester Street Fair (Map 4)** on Saturdays and **New Amsterdam Market (Map 1)** on Sundays entice foodies to skip brunch in favor of gourmet food cart bliss.

And then there's the city's real gems: the endless number of ethnic food purveyors stocked with imported goods from around the world. When it comes to Italian, Arthur Ave in the Bronx is famed for its bakeries, butcher shops, grocers, and sundry shops. The more centrally located **Di Palo Fine Foods (Map 3)** offers some of the best imported delicacies as well as their own celebrated fresh ricotta. For Middle Eastern specialties, **Sahadi's (Map 32)** provides an impressive range of top quality products (and many of its neighbors on Atlantic Avenue deserve a visit while you're in the area). **Friendly Despana (Map 3)** in SoHo will satisfy all your Spanish desires, including three different types of Spanish sparkling water and $100-a-pound Spanish Serrano ham. **Eataly (Map 9)** is a sprawling Italian food market with everything from hard-to-find cheeses to unique beers to special pastas. Chinatown's options can overwhelm the savviest of shoppers, and there's even a destination for people in the market for British treats, **Myers of Keswick (Map 5)** in the West Village.

If there's one kind of specialty store we can't do without, it's New York's neighborhood cheese shops. Among the best are **Murray's (Map 5)** in the West Village, classic Lamarca **Cheese Shop (Map 10)** on the East Side, small but powerful **Stinky (Map 32)** in Carroll Gardens, **Bedford Cheese Shop (Map 29)** in Williamsburg, and, of course, the cheese counter at **Dean & Deluca (Map 15)**. If you're low on cash **East Village Cheese (Map 6)** is your go-to shop. They don't give out free samples and the line is always long, but it's the cheapest option in Manhattan by far.

You'll need bread to go with your cheese, of course Our favorites are **Sullivan Street Bakery (Map 11)** **Grandaisy Bakery (Maps 2, 14)**, and **Amy's Bread (Maps 8, 11)**. For meats, hit **Faicco's Pork Store (Map 5)**, **Despana (Map 3)**, **G Esposito & Sons (Map 32)**, or **Choice Greene (Map 31)**.

Art Supplies

Running low on Cadmium Red? Use your last stick c charcoal drawing a nude? The best art stores in NY are scattered loosely around the SoHo area, and th best known of these is **Pearl Paint (Map 3)**. Locate at the corner of Mercer and Canal Streets, the stor occupies a six-story building and stocks every type c art supply you can imagine, including a great sepa rate frame shop out back on Lispenard. Closer to NY and Cooper Union, there's **Blick Art Materials (Ma 6)**. You can find the best selection of paper at **Ne York Central Art Supply (Map 6)** on Third Avenu **SoHo Art Materials (Map 2)** on Wooster Street a small, traditional shop that sells super premiu paints and brushes for fine artists. Don't forget check out both **Sam Flax (Map 13)** and **A.I. Frie man (Map 9)** in the Flatiron area for graphic desig supplies, portfolios, and gifts. **Lee's Art Shop (Ma 12)** is a great store on 57th Street; how it has surviv Midtown rents is anyone's guess. Should you fi yourself on the Upper East Side needing art suppli in a pinch, the fairly decent selection at **Blacker Kooby (Map 17)** will do just fine. As for Williamsbu **Artist & Craftsman (Map 29)** on Metropolitan A enue is a good bet for supplies. In Fort Greene, t **Pratt Store (Map 31)** is a combined art supply sto college bookstore.

For photographic equipment, the holy trinity of **B& Photo (Map 8)**, **Adorama (Map 9)**, and **K & M Ca era (Map 3)** will satisfy every possible photograp (digital or darkroom-based) need that you mi have. B & H is of course the mothership, Adorama is great if you're nearby, and K & M is in the trinity because it's the only one of the three that's open on Saturdays. Remember to flash that student ID card if you've got it, as most art stores offer a decent discount.

Music Equipment & Instruments

New York's large and vibrant music scene supports a thriving instrument trade. 48th Street is not what it once was, with music store after music store between Sixth and Seventh Avenues (anchored by Sam Ash), but **Roberto's Woodwind Repair (Map 12)** is still on 46th Street. If the bustle of Times Square isn't for you anyway and are looking for used, vintage, or just plain cool, then shop elsewhere—some favorites include: **First Flight (Map 7)**, **30th Street Guitars (Map 9)**, **Rogue Music (Map 9)** and **Ludlow Guitars (Map 4)**.

For an exquisite purchase where money is no object, find the perfect grand piano at **Steinway & Sons (Map 12)**, where the salespeople pride themselves on matching everyone, even beginners, with the perfect instrument for their skills and character. Also keep an eye (and an ear) out for special musical evenings at the former, and spontaneous performances at the latter.

Music for Listening

Oops! No record stores left in NYC—or at least that's the way it seems, with Tower, Virgin, and Kim's all now faint memories in our minds. So now it's down to the small boutique record shops, and the slightly-larger selection of **J&R Music World (Map 1)** near City Hall. As for the small shops we still do love hip **Other Music (Map 6)** (look out for occasional in-store performances) and avant-garde **Downtown Music (Map 3)**. If you're into trolling through used bins, head to Bleecker Street to check out **Rebel Rebel (Map 5)** and **Bleecker Street Records (Map 5)**. If you're thirsty for more used music and vinyl, just head to one of North Brooklyn's many record shops, like **Earwax (Map 29)**, **Academy Annex (Map 29)**, **Sound Fix Records (Map 29)**, **Permanent Records (Map 28)** and **The Thing (Map 28)**.

Weird, Odd, Bizarre, and/or Just Plain Fun

Every once in a while, you walk into a shop and say, "what is this place?" And while New York doesn't have anything quite as odd as, say, the taxidermy shops that still dot London, for instance, there are a few places that still make us stop, smile and wonder. First on the list is the quirky **Brooklyn Superhero Supply (Map 33)**, which should cover all your needs in said superhero department. The logical next stop is **Forbidden Planet (Map 6)** for comics, t-shirts, and action figures. More odd toys and collectibles for grown-ups can be found at **Kid Robot (Map 6)**—which is just a couple blocks from skull-and-preserved-butterfly-packed science store **Evolution (Map 6)**. For a true cabinet of curiosities check out **Obscura Antiques (Map 7)**, which is filled unusual and macabre finds. For not-as-vintage, but still unique finds, browse the découpage plates, housewares, and curios at **John Derian (Map 6)**.

Then there are those places that meet any highly-specific interest you could dream up. Pen nerds, head to City Hall's **Fountain Pen Hospital (Map 3)**. Antique button collectors, check out Upper East Side's **Tender Buttons (Map 15)**. If you need to own an authentic piece of NYC memorabilia, whether it be subway token cufflinks or taxi cab medallions, go directly to the **New York City Store (Map 3)**.

Shopping "Districts"

If you are fixated on a specific item, like a sausage maker or a few yards of leopard print fabric, you can investigate the specialty districts around Manhattan. Brave the overwhelming selection throughout the Garment District (25th to 40th Sts, Fifth to Ninth Aves) for fabrics, buttons, zippers, ribbons, and anything else you'd need to design your own clothes. If you're in the market for jewelry, you might want to check out the Diamond and Jewelry District (47th St between Fifth and Sixth Aves), the world's largest market for diamonds. For plants, flowers, and greenery, go to the Flower District (26th to 29th Sts, along and off Sixth Ave), which is right near the Perfume District (along and off Broadway in the West 20s and 30s). Music Row (48th St between Sixth & Seventh Aves) leaves you with no excuses if you've been meaning to learn to play an instrument. The Bowery around Houston St is another well-known strip where you'll find the Kitchenware District for all your culinary endeavors, the Lighting District (past Delancey St) for all your illuminating needs, and the Downtown Jewelry District (turn the corner of Bowery to Canal St) for the more unusual baubles that you can't get uptown. High-end home design stores are concentrated on and around Designers Way and Decorators Way (58th and 59th Sts, between Second and Third Aves). The Flatiron District (from 14th to 34th Sts, between Sixth & Park Aves) is another home furnishing mecca. You can take care of your photography needs just like the pros, by heading to the city's highest concentration of stores and labs (between Fifth and Sixth Aves, from 18th to 22nd Sts). Sadly, Book Row (between 9th and 14th Sts) is no more. What was once an assemblage of over 25 bookstores now houses only the famous Strand Bookstore and Alabaster Bookshop, but we could happily spend days browsing and purchasing in either one of them.

Overview

If you want to see cutting-edge art, go to New York City's galleries. There are more than 500 galleries in the city, with artwork created in every conceivable medium (and of varying quality) on display. SoHo, Chelsea, DUMBO, and Williamsburg are the hot spots for gallery goers, but there are also many famous (and often more traditional) galleries and auction houses uptown, including **Christie's (Map 12)** and **Sotheby's (Map 15)**. With so much to choose from, there's almost always something that's at least *provocative*, if not actually *good*.

The scene at the upscale galleries is sometimes intimidating, especially if you look like you are on a budget. If you aren't interested in buying, they aren't interested in you being there. Some bigger galleries require appointments. Cut your teeth at smaller galleries; they aren't as scary. Also, put your name on the mailing lists. You'll get invites to openings so crowded that no one will try to pressure you into buying (and there's free wine). The Armory Show (www.thearmoryshow.com), an annual show of new art, is also a great way to see what the galleries have to offer without intimidation.

SoHo Area

Five years ago, there were still hundreds of art galleries in SoHo. Now it has practically become an outdoor mall. However, there are still some permanent artworks in gallery spaces, such as Walter De Maria's excellent **The Broken Kilometer (Map 6)** (a Dia-sponsored space at 393 West Broadway), and his sublime **New York Earth Room (Map 6)**. A short jaunt down to TriBeCa will land you in LaMonte Young's awesome aural experience Dream House at the **MELA Foundation (Map 2). Artists Space (Map 2)**, one of the first alternative art galleries in New York, is also in TriBeCa. The **HERE Arts Center (Map 5)** showcases a wide range of work and usually offers an exhibit or performance that warrants a visit. On the Lower East Side check out **Canada (Map 3)** for fun openings and **Envoy Gallery (Map 6)** for cutting edge photography and celebrity sightings.

Chelsea

The commercialization of SoHo has helped make Chelsea the center of the city's gallery scene. Our recommendation is to hit at least two streets—W 24th Street between Tenth and Eleventh Avenues, and W 22nd Street between Tenth and Eleventh Avenues. W 24th Street is anchored by the almost-always-brilliant **Gagosian Gallery (Map 8)** and also includes the **Luhring Augustine (Map 8)**, **Mary Boone (Map 12)**, **Barbara Gladstone (Map 8)**, and **Matthew Marks (Map 8)** galleries. W 22nd favorites include **Julie Saul (Map 8)**, **Leslie Tonkonow (Map 8)**, **Marianne Boesky (Map 8)**, and **Yancey Richardson (Map 8)** galleries. Also, check out the famous "artist's" bookstore Printed Matter (Map 8).

Other recommendations are the **Starrett-Lehigh Building (Map 8)**, not only for the art but also for the great pillars, windows, and converted freight elevators, **Pace Wildenstein (Map 8)**, and the **Jonathan LeVine Gallery (Map 8)**, which consistently features exciting artists.

The New York City book scene has taken a sharp decline in terms of diversity in recent years, with many excellent bookshops—including Coliseum Books, A Different Light, Academy, A Photographer's Place, Rizzoli SoHo, Tower Books, Brentano's, Spring Street Books, and Shortwave—all going the way of the dodo. The remaining independent stores are now the last outposts before everything interesting or alternative disappears altogether. And some of NYC's richest cultural neighborhoods—such as the East Village and the Lower East Side—don't have enough bookstores to even come close to properly serving their populations of literate hipsters. So we thought we'd take this opportunity to list some of our favorite remaining shops...

General New/Used

Strand (Map 6) on Broadway, the largest and arguably most popular independent bookstore in town, boasts staggering range and depth in its offerings (and often the best prices around to boot). Whether you're interested in art tomes, rare first editions, foreign language texts, non-fiction works, or the latest bestseller, it's impossible to be disappointed. **St. Mark's Bookshop (Map 6)** anchors the border between the NYU crowd and the East Village hipster contingent, and has an excellent literary journal selections. **Argosy Book Store (Map 13)** on 59th Street is still a top destination for antiquarian books. Uptown, **Book Culture (Map 18)** serves the Columbia area well. With four locations around the city, the punchy **Shakespeare & Company (Maps 6, 10, 15)** is a local chain that somehow manages to maintain an aura of ndependence. In the West Village, **Three Lives and Co. Map 5)** should be your destination. The **Barnes & Noble Map 9)** in Union Square is their signature store and has a great feel. The **Housing Works Used Book Café (Map 6)** has a vintage coffeehouse feel and is one of our favorite bookstores—all of the profits go to help homeless New orkers living with HIV/AIDS.

Small/Used

ortunately there are still a lot of used bookstores tucked way all over the city. **Mercer Street Books (Map 6)** serves YU and **East Village Books (Map 7)** takes care of hipster eaven. On the Upper East Side both **Corner Bookstore Map 17)** and **Crawford Doyle (Map 15)** keep it old-chool. In Brooklyn, swing by **Unnameable Books (Map 3)** in Prospect Heights for hyper-local poetry. Swing by **Unnameable Books (Map 33)** in Prospect Heights for hyper-local poetry.

Travel

e city's travel book selection is possibly its greatest ength. While independents, such as the elegant **mplete Traveller Bookstore (Map 9)**, are scattered roughout the boroughs, the greatest member of the vel bookstore club is the wonderful **Idlewild Books ap 9)**. Idlewild curates its collection by country ere guidebooks, fiction, and travel writing all happily mingle for a unique way of browsing. So if you can't ord to travel, a trip here is the next best thing.

Art

Printed Matter (Map 8) houses one of the best collections of artists' books in the world and is highly recommended. The **New Museum of Contemporary Art Bookstore (Map 6)** also offers a brilliant selection of both artists' and art books. If you aren't on a budget and have a new coffee table to fill, try **Ursus (Map 15)** in Chelsea. For handsome photography collections, check out **Dashwood Books (Map 6)** on super sleek Bond Street.

NYC/Government

The **City Store (Map 3)** in the Municipal Building is small but carries a solid selection (and is still the only store we've seen that sells old taxicab medallions). The **Civil Service Bookstore (Map 3)** has all the study guides you'll need when you want to change careers and start driving a bus. The **United Nations Bookshop (Map 13)** has a great range of international and governmental titles. The **New York Transit Museum (Map 13)** shop at Grand Central also has an excellent range of books on NYC.

Specialty

Books of Wonder (Map 9) in Chelsea has long been a downtown haven for children's books, and kids love that it adjoins a cupcake bakery. For mystery lovers, **The Mysterious Bookshop (Map 2)** slakes the need for whodunits. The **Drama Book Shop (Map 12)** is a great source for books on acting and the theater. **Bluestockings (Map 4)** is an epicenter for radical and feminist literature. Professional and amateur chefs turn to **Bonnie Slotnick (Map 5)** and **Kitchen Arts and Letters (Map 17)**. Newcomer **La Casa Azul Bookstore (Map 17)** adds much needed lit cred to East Harlem, offering adult and kids books in Spanish and English, an art gallery, and a lovely backyard.

Readings

Anyone can read great authors, but lucky for New Yorkers, we have beaucoup chances to meet the literati, too. The four-story **Barnes & Noble (Map 9)** in Union Square regularly hosts major writers (think: Nick Hornby, Malcolm Gladwell, etc.). **Housing Works Used Book Café (Map 6)** draws some big names; Philip Gourevitch and Jonathan Lethem have discussed their tomes there in the last few years. And **McNally Jackson (Map 6)** in Nolita is another spot known for hosting great author events. Nearly all bookstores present readings, even if irregularly. Check a store's Web page for listings. Literary blogs like www.maudnewton.com list weekly events for bookworms. Even bars have taken a literary turn for the better: KGB Bar features fiction, poetry, and nonfiction readings each week (www.kgbbar.com) and One Story magazine hosts an excellent monthly reading series at Pianos (www.one-story.com). In Brooklyn, Pete's Candy Store and its weekly reading series are a good bet for your weekly dose of literature (www.petescandystore.com).

Map 1 • Financial District

Chameleon Comics	3 Maiden Ln	212-587-3411	Comics
Pace University Bookstore	41 Park Row	212-346-1605	Academic - General

Map 2 • TriBeCa

Barnes & Noble	97 Warren St	212-587-5389	Chain
Manhattan Books	150 Chambers St	212-385-7395	New and used textbooks
The Mysterious Book Shop	58 Warren St	212-587-1011	Specialty - Mystery
NY Law School Bookstore	47 Worth St	212-227-7220	Specialty - Law textbooks

Map 3 • City Hall / Chinatown

Civil Service Book Shop	89 Worth St	212-226-9506	Specialty - Civil Services
Clic	189 Lafayette St	212-966-1161	Art books and an art gallery
Ming Fay Book Store	42 Mott St	212-406-1957	Specialty - Chinese
New York City Store	1 Centre St	212-669-8246	Specialty - NYC books and municipal publications
Oriental Books Stationery & Arts	29 East Broadway	212-962-3634	Specialty - Chinese
Oriental Culture Enterprises	13 Elizabeth St	212-226-8461	Specialty - Chinese

Map 4 • Lower East Side

Bluestockings Bookstore Café and Activist Center	172 Allen St	212-777-6028	Specialty - Political/Left Wing
Eastern Books	15 Pike St	212-964-6869	Specialty - Chinese
World Journal Book Store	379 E Broadway	212-226-5131	Chinese books.

Map 5 • West Village

Barnes & Noble	396 Sixth Ave	212-674-8780	Chain
Bonnie Slotnick Cookbooks	163 W 10th St	212-989-8962	Specialty - Out of print cookbooks
bookbook	266 Bleecker St	212-807-8655	Specialty - Biography
Joanne Hendricks Cookbooks	488 Greenwich St	212-226-5731	Specialty - Wine and Cooking
Left Bank Books	304 W 4th St	212-924-5638	Used; Antiquarian
Partners & Crime Mystery Booksellers	44 Greenwich Ave	212-243-0440	Specialty - Mystery
Three Lives and Co	154 W 10th St	212-741-2069	General Interest
Time Machine	207 W 14th St	212-691-0380	Comics
Unoppressive Non-Imperialist Bargain Books	34 Carmine St	212-229-0079	Used, political, Eastern religious, etc.

Map 6 • Washington Square / NYU / NoHo / SoHo

Alabaster Bookshop	122 Fourth Ave	212-982-3550	Used
Benjamin Cardozo School of Law Bookstore	55 Fifth Ave	212-790-0339	Academic - Law
Dashwood Books	33 Bond St	212-387-8520	Photography
Forbidden Planet	840 Broadway	212-473-1576	Specialty - Fantasy/Sci-fi
Happy Bones Publications	7 Bond St		Tiny book shop with an under-the-rada espresso shop.
Housing Works Used Book Café	126 Crosby St	212-334-3324	Used
Lomography Gallery Store	41 W 8th St	212-529-4353	Super-cool Lomographic cameras & accessories!
McNally Jackson	52 Prince St	212-274-1160	General Interest
Mercer Street Books and Records	206 Mercer St	212-505-8615	Used
myplasticheart nyc	210 Forsyth St	646-290-6866	Designer toy store and gallery.
New Museum of Contemporary Art Bookstore	235 Bowery	212-343-0460	Art books. And NFT!
New York University Book Center-Main Branch	18 Washington Pl	212-998-4667	Academic - General
NYU Bookstore - Computer Store	242 Greene St	212-998-4672	Academic - Computers
Pageant Book & Print Shop	69 E 4th St	212-674-5296	Just prints, really. But really great print
Scholastic Store	557 Broadway	212-343-6166	Specialty - Educational
Shakespeare & Co	716 Broadway	212-529-1330	Good local chain w/ lots of postmoder fiction
St Mark's Bookshop	31 Third Ave	212-260-7853	General Interest.

St Mark's Comics	11 St Marks Pl	212-598-9439	Comics
Strand	828 Broadway	212-473-1452	Used mecca; world's messiest and best bookstore
Surma Book & Music	11 E 7th St	212-477-0729	Specialty - Ukrainian
Taschen	107 Greene St	212-226-2212	God (and the Devil's) gift to publishing

Map 7 • East Village

East Village Books and Records	99 St Marks Pl	212-477-8647	Messy pile of used stuff
Mast Books	66 Avenue A	546-370-1114	Small but excellent selection.

Map 8 • Chelsea

192 Books	192 10th Ave	212-255-4022	Reads like a library—with a premium on art books and literature
Aperture Book Center	547 W 27th St	212-505-5555	Specialty - Photography
Posman Books	75 9th Ave	212-627-0304	Nice location in Chelsea Market
Printed Matter	195 Tenth Ave	212-925-0325	Astounding selection of artist's books; highly recommended

Map 9 • Flatiron / Lower Midtown

Barnes & Noble	33 E 17th St	212-253-0810	Chain
Barnes & Noble College Bookstore	105 Fifth Ave	212-675-5500	Textbook mayhem
Books of Wonder	18 W 18th St	212-989-3270	Top NYC children's bookstore, always has signed copies around too
Center for Book Arts	28 W 27th St, 3rd Fl	212-481-0295	Specialty - Artist/Handmade
The Compleat Strategist	11 E 33rd St	212-685-3880	Specialty - Fantasy/ SciFi
Complete Traveller	199 Madison Ave	212-685-9007	Specialty - Vintage travel books
Fashion Design Books	250 W 27th St	212 633 9646	Specialty Fashion design
Hudson News	Penn Station	212-971-6800	Chain
Idlewild Books	12 W 19th ST	212-414-8888	One of the best travel + literature bookstores on the planet
Jim Hanley's Universe	4 W 33rd St	212-268-7088	Specialty - Comics; SciFi
Koryo Books	35 W 32nd St	212-564-1844	Specialty - Korean
Levine J Co Books & Judaica	5 W 30th St	212 695 6888	Judaica
Metropolis Comics and Collectibles	873 Broadway	212-260-4147	Specialty - Comics
New York Open Center Bookstore	22 E 30th St	212-219-2527	Specialty - New Age; Spiritual
Pathfinder Books	306 W 37th St	212-629-6649	Political books of the working class struggle
Penn Books	1 Penn Plz	212-239-0311	General interest
Revolution Books	9 W 19th St	212-691-3345	Specialty - Political
Rudolf Steiner Bookstore	138 W 15th St	212-242-8945	Specialty - Metaphysics
Russian Bookstore 21	174 Fifth Ave	212-924-5477	Specialty - Russian/Russia
St Francis Friars	139 W 31st St	212-736-8500	Religious Books

Map 10 • Murray Hill / Gramercy

Baruch College Bookstore	55 Lexington Ave	646-312-4850	Academic - General
Kutala Emporium	108 E 28th St	212-684-4447	Indian
Shakespeare & Co	137 E 23rd St	212-505-2021	Chain

Map 11 • Hell's Kitchen

Hudson News	Port Authority Bldg, North Wing	212-563-1030	Chain
John Jay College - Barnes & Noble	841 W 55th St	212-265-3619	Textbooks

Map 12 • Midtown

AMA Management Bookstore	1601 Broadway	212-903 8286	Specialty Management
Assouline	768 5th Ave	212-593-7236	Delicious lavishly-produced art, design and fashion books
Barnes & Noble	555 Fifth Ave	212-697-3048	Chain
Bauman Rare Books	535 Madison Ave	212-751-0011	Antiquarian
Chartwell Booksellers	55 E 52nd St	212-308-0643	Specialty - books about Winston Churchill
Chesh Heritage Fine Books	1775 Broadway, Ste 501	212-265-0600	General interest
Drama Book Shop	250 W 40th St	212-944-0595	Alas, poor Yorick…

FAO Schwarz	767 Fifth Ave	212-644-9400	Specialty - Children's
J N Bartfield-Fine Books	30 W 57th St	212-245-8890	Rare and antiquarian
Metropolitan Museum of Art Bookshop at Rockefeller Center	15 W 49th St	212-332-1360	Specialty - Art books
Midtown Comics–Times Square	200 W 40th St	212-302-8192	Specialty - Comics
Rizzoli destination	31 W 57th St	212-759-2424	Specialty - Art/Design

Map 13 • East Midtown

Argosy Book Store	116 E 59th St	212-753-4455	Rare and antiquarian, great selection of prints, too
Barnes & Noble	160 E 54th St	212-750-8033	Chain
Cohen & Taliaferro	59 E 54th St	212-751-8135	Antique maps and rare travel books. Cool!
Hudson News	89 E 42nd St	212-687-0833	Chain
Martayan LAN	70 E 55th St	212-308-0018	Specialty - Rare and antiquarian maps, atlases, and books
Midtown Comics–Grand Central	459 Lexington Ave	212-302-8192	Specialty - Comics
New York Transit Museum	Grand Central, Main Concourse	212-878-0106	Specialty - NYC/Transit
Posman Books	9 Grand Central Terminal	212-983-1111	Nice little bookshop. Lots of NFTs
Potterton Books	979 Third Ave	212-644-2292	Specialty - Decorative Arts/Architecture/ Design
Quest Book Shop	240 E 53rd St	212-758-5521	Specialty - New Age
United Nations Bookshop	First Ave & E 46th St	212-963-7680	Good range of everything

Map 14 • Upper West Side (Lower)

Barnes & Noble	2289 Broadway	212-362-8835	Chain
Fordham University Bookstore	113 W 60th St	212-636-6080	Academic - General
Juillard School Bookstore	W 66th St b/w Amsterdam Ave & Broadway	212-799-5000	Academic - Music
New York Institute of Technology	1849 Broadway	212-261-1551	Specialty - Technical
Westsider	2246 Broadway	212-362-0706	Used; Antiquarian

Map 15 • Upper East Side (Lower)

Asia Society Bookstore	725 Park Ave	212-327-9217	Specialty - Asian
Bookstore Of The NY Psychoanalytic Institution	247 E 82nd St	212-772-8282	Specialty - Psychoanalysis
Choices Bookshop- Recovery	220 E 78th St	212-794-3858	Specialty - Self-help and recovery
Crawford Doyle Booksellers	1082 Madison Ave	212-288-6300	Lovely place to browse and find a classic
Gagosian Shop	988 Madison Ave	212-744-9200	Top quality (and expensive) art & books. Think Damien Hirst and Jeff Koons originals.
Hunter College Bookstore	695 Park Ave	212-650-3970	Academic - General
Imperial Fine Books	790 Madison Ave, Ste 200	212-861-6620	Antiquarian
James Cummins Book Seller	699 Madison Ave, 7th Fl	212-688-6441	Antiquarian
Logos Book Store	1575 York Ave	212-517-7292	Children's books, spiritual lit, and beyond
Metropolitan Museum of Art Bookshop	Fifth Ave & 82nd St	212-570-3894	Specialty - Art books
Shakespeare & Co	939 Lexington Ave	212-570-0201	Chain
Ursus Books	981 Madison Ave	212-772-8787	Specialty - Art
Weill Cornell Medical College Bookstore	424 E 70th St	212-988-0400	Academic - Medical books.
The Whitney Museum Shop	945 Madison Ave	212-570-3614	Specialty - Art/ Artists' books

Map 16 • Upper West Side (Upper)

Westside Judaica	2412 Broadway	212-362-7846	Judaica

Map 17 • Upper East Side / East Harlem

Barnes & Noble	150 E 86th St	212-369-2180	Chain
Corner Bookstore	1313 Madison Ave	212-831-3554	Tiny, old-school shop. Great selection
Islamic Books & Tapes	1711 Third Ave	212-828-4038	Islamic literature
Kitchen Arts & Letters	1435 Lexington Ave	212-876-5550	Fine selection of food and wine books
La Casa Azul Bookstore	143 E 103rd St	212-426-2626	Spanish and English books, art gallery and a lovely backyard.

Map 18 • Columbia / Morningside Heights

Bank Street College Bookstore	610 W 112th St	212-678-1654	Academic - Education/Children
Book Culture	536 W 112th St	212-865-1588	Excellent bookstore servicing Columbia/ Barnard students.
Book Culture on Broadway	2915 Broadway	646-403-3000	Excellent bookstore servicing Columbia/ Barnard students.
Columbia University Bookstore	2922 Broadway	212-854-4132	Academic - General
Teachers College Bookstore (Columbia University Graduate School of Education)	1224 Amsterdam Ave	212-678-3920	Academic - Education

Map 19 • Harlem (Lower)

Zoe Christian Bookstore	45 W 116th St	212-828-2776	Christian books

Map 21 • Manhattanville / Hamilton Heights

City College Book Store	W 138th St & Convent Ave	212-368-4000	General - Academic
Sisters Uptown	1942 Amsterdam Ave	212-862-3680	African-American books

Map 23 • Washington Heights

Columbia Medical Books	3954 Broadway	212-923-2149	Academic - Medical
Jumel Terrace Books	426 W 160th St	212-928-9525	African-American and mostly out of print

Map 24 • Fort George / Fort Tryon

Metropolitan Museum of Art Bookshop-Cloisters Branch	799 Ft Washington Ave	212-650-2277	Specialty - Art books

Map 25 • Inwood

Libreria Continental	628 W 207th St	212-544-9004	Specialty - Spanish

Map 26 • Astoria

Silver Age Comics	22-55 31st St	718-721-9691	Comics

Map 27 • Long Island City

Artbook @ MoMA PS1	22-25 Jackson Ave	718-784-2084	Fabulous selection of art books

Map 28 • Greenpoint

Ex Libris Polish Book Gallery	140 Nassau Ave	718-349-0468	Polish
Polish American Bookstore	648 Manhattan Ave	718-349-3756	Polish
Polish Bookstore & Publishing	161 Java St	718-349-2738	Polish
Polonia Book Store	882 Manhattan Ave	718-389-1684	Polish
Word	126 Franklin St	718-383-0096	Literary fiction, non-fiction, and kids' books

Map 29 • Williamsburg

Spoonbill & Sugartown	218 Bedford Ave	718-387-7322	Art, architecture, design, philosophy, and literature. New and used

Map 30 • Brooklyn Heights / DUMBO / Downtown

Barnes & Noble	106 Court St	718-246-4996	Chain
Long Island University Book Store	1 University Plz	718-858-3888	General
powerHouse Arena	37 Main St	718-666-3049	One of our favorite gallery/bookstores.
azar's Variety Book Store	40 Hoyt St	718-797-2478	African-American books
akka	155 Plymouth St	718-801-8037	Specialty - Graphic design books

Map 31 • Fort Greene / Clinton Hill

Greenlight Bookstore	686 Fulton St	718-246-0200	Ft. Greene's newest and immediately best bookstore.
Greenlight Bookstore at BAM	30 Lafayette Ave	718-636-4136	General, specializing in film, music and dance.
Pratt Bookstore	550 Myrtle Ave	718-789-1105	Art books

Map 32 • BoCoCa / Red Hook

Anwaar Bookstore	428 Atlantic Ave	718-875-3791	Arabic books
Book Court	163 Court St	718-875-3677	General
Community Bookstore	212 Court St	718-834-9494	General interest.
Dar Us Salam	486 Atlantic Ave	718-625-5925	Islamic books
Freebird Books	123 Columbia St	718-643-8484	Used
Idlewild Books	249 Warren St	718-403-9600	Extensive travel book collection, language classes, second location: viva bookstores!

Map 33 • Park Slope / Prospect Heights / Windsor Terrace

Babbo's Books	242 Prospect Park W	718-788-3475	Used & new
Barnes & Noble	267 Seventh Ave	718-832-9066	Chain
Community Book Store	143 Seventh Ave	718-783-3075	General
Unnameable Books	600 Vanderbilt Ave	718-789-1534	General new and used

Multiplexes abound in NYC, though of course you should brace yourself for far steeper ticket and concession prices than in the rest of the country (with the possible exception of LA). Dinner and a movie turns out to be a rather exorbitant affair, but hey, we don't live in the Big Apple because it's cheap. And whether you're looking for the latest box office hit, or a classic from the French New Wave, there's a theater to meet your needs.

If you're after a first-run Hollywood blockbuster, we highly recommend the **AMC Loews Kips Bay (Map 10)** in Murray Hill. It has spacious theaters with large screens, big sound, comfortable seats, plenty of aisle room, and most importantly, fewer people! The **AMC Loews Village (Map 6)** is gargantuan, too, but movies there sell out hours or days in advance on the weekends. An IMAX theater and a cheesy '30s movie palace decorating theme make **AMC Loews Lincoln Square (Map 14)** a great place to catch a huge film, and its ideal location offers loads of after movie options. Another great choice is the **Regal Battery Park 16 (p 234)**, but it's starting to get just as crowded as the Union Square location.

For independent or foreign films, the **Landmark Sunshine (Map 6)** has surpassed the **Angelika (Map 6)** as the superior downtown movie house. Don't get us wrong—the Angelika still presents great movies, but the tiny screens and constant subway rumble can sometimes make you wish you'd waited for the DVD. The **IFC Center (Map 5)** always shows great indie flicks, and with a recent expansion it's better than ever. If you're looking for revivals, check the listings at the **Film Forum (Map 5)**, **BAM Rose Cinemas (Map 31)**, and the **MoMA (Map 12)**. Regular attendance at those three venues can provide an excellent education in cinema history. For the truly adventurous, there's **Anthology Film Archives (Map 6)**, which plays a repertory of forgotten classics, obscure international hits, and experimental American shorts. Finally, up in Harlem the tiny but terrific **Maysles Cinema (Map 19)** shows truly brilliant indie movies focusing on New York City. This may be the most unique moviegoing experience in Manhattan.

The most decadent and enjoyable movie experiences can be found at the theaters that feel the most "New York." Sadly, the Beekman Theatre immortalized in Woody Allen's Annie Hall was demolished in 2005 to make room for a new ward for Sloan-Kettering (it's hard to argue with a cancer hospital, but film buffs can't help but wish they'd found another space for their expansion). Clearview's **Ziegfeld (Map 12)** on 54th Street is a vestige from a time long past when movie theaters were real works of art. This space is so posh with its gilding and red velvet, you'll feel like you're crossing the Atlantic on an expensive ocean liner. The **Paris Theatre (Map 12)** on 50th Street is one of our favorites in the city—it has the best balcony, hands down!

Oh, and don't forget to use Moviefone (777-FILM; www.moviefone.com) or Fandango (www.fandango.com) to purchase tickets in advance for crowded showtimes (opening weekends, holidays, or pretty much any night when you're trying to see a popular film).

Manhattan	Address	Phone	Map	
92nd Street Y	1395 Lexington Ave	212-415-5500	17	Community hub for film, theater, and interesting lectures.
AMC Empire 25	234 W 42nd St	212-398-2597	12	Buy tickets ahead. It's Times Square.
AMC Loews 19th Street	890 Broadway	212-260-8173	9	Standard multiplex.
AMC Loews 34th Street 14	312 W 34th St	212-244-4556	8	The biggest and most comfortable of the Midtown multiplexes.
AMC Loews 84th St 6	2310 Broadway	212-721-6023	14	Take the subway to Lincoln Square instead.
AMC Loews Kips Bay 15	570 2nd Ave	212-447-0638	10	This multiplex is starting to show its age.
AMC Loews Lincoln Square 13	1998 Broadway	212-336-5020	14	Classy Upper West Side multiplex with IMAX.
AMC Loews Orpheum 7	1538 Third Ave	212-876-2111	17	The Upper East Side's premier multiplex.
AMC Loews Village VII	66 Third Ave	212-982-2116	6	Good-sized multiplex that keeps Union Square crowds in check.
AMC Magic Johnson Harlem 9	2309 Frederick Douglass Blvd	212-665-6923	19	Owned by Magic. Best choice for Upper Manhattan.
American Museum of Natural History IMAX	200 Central Park West	212-769-5200	14	Rest your tired legs and learn something.
Angelika	18 W Houston St	212-995-2570	6	Higher profile indies play here first.
Anthology Film Archives	32 Second Ave	212-505-5181	6	Quirky retrospectives, revivals, and other rarities.
The Asia Society	725 Park Ave	212-288-6400	15	Special country-themed programs every month.
Beekman Theatre	1271 Second Ave	212-585-4141	15	Another good choice owned by the folks behind the Paris.
Bryant Park Summer Film Festival (outdoors)	Bryant Park, b/w 40th & 42nd Sts	212-512-5700	12	Groovy classics outdoors in sweltering summer heat.
Cinema 123	1001 Third Ave	212-753-6022	15	Ideal cure for Bloomingdale's hangover.
Cinema Village	22 E 12th St	212-924-3363	6	Charming and tiny with exclusive documentaries and foreign films.
City Cinemas: East 86th Street	210 E 86th St	212-744-1999	17	It wouldn't be our first choice.
Clearview Cinemas Chelsea	260 W 23rd St	212-691-5519	9	Manhattan's big, comfy, and gay multiplex.
Clearview Cinemas First & 62nd St	400 E 62nd St	212-752-0694	15	You're better off taking the bus down to Kips Bay.
Czech Center New York	321 E 73rd St	646-422-3399	15	Czech premieres and special events.
Film Forum	209 W Houston St	212-727-8110	5	Best place to pick up a film geek.
French Institute	22 E 60th St	212-355-6100	15	Frog-centric activities include movies, plays, talks

				and exhibits.
Guggenheim Museum Movie Theater	1071 Fifth Ave	212-423-3500	17	Special screenings in conjunction with current exhibitions.
IFC Center	323 Sixth Ave	212-924-7771	5	Great midnights, special events, and Manhattan exclusives.
Instituto Cervantes	211 E 49th St	212-308-7720	13	Spanish gems, but call to make sure there's subtitles.
Italian Academy	1161 Amsterdam Ave	212-854-2306	18	Fascinating classic film series at Columbia. Feel smart again.
Jewish Community Center in Manhattan	334 Amsterdam Ave	646-505-4444	14	Jewish premieres, previews, and festivals.
Landmark Sunshine Cinema	143 E Houston St	212-260-7289	6	High luxury indie film multiplex.
Leonard Nimoy Thalia at Symphony Space	2537 Broadway	212-864-5400	16	A different classic movie every week. Good variety.
Lincoln Plaza Cinemas	1886 Broadway	212-757-2280	14	Uptown version of the Angelika.
Maysles Cinema	343 Malcolm X Blvd	212-582-6050	19	Amazing indies and documentaries from local film-makers.
MoMA	11 W 53rd St	212-708-9400	12	Arty programming changes every day.
New York Public Library Jefferson Market Branch	425 6th Ave	212-243-4334	5	Children's films on Tuesdays.
NYU Cantor Film Center	36 E 8th St	212-998-4100	6	Dirt cheap second-run blockbusters on Monday nights.
The Paley Center for Media	25 W 52nd St	212-621-6800	12	Formerly the Museum of Television & Radio.
Paris Theatre	4 W 58th St	212-688-3800	12	Art house equivalent of the Ziegfeld.
Quad Cinema	34 W 13th St	212-255-2243	6	Gay-themed world premieres and second run Hollywood releases.
Regal 64th and 2nd	1210 Second Ave	212-832-1671	15	Nice big theater with two ugly cousins.
Regal Battery Park City 11	102 North End Ave	212-945-4370	p184	Beautiful downtown multiplex. Getting too crowded.
Regal E Walk Stadium 13	247 W 42nd St	212-840-7761	12	Across the street from the Empire, but not nearly as nice.
Regal Union Square Stadium 14	850 Broadway	212-253-6266	6	Extremely crowded but fairly comfortable.
The Scandinavia House	58 Park Ave	212-879-9779	10	Scandinavian movies. Bergman and beyond.
Tribeca Cinemas	54 Varick St	212-941-2001	2	Home base of De Niro's Tribeca Film Festival.
Village East Cinema	181 2nd Ave	212-529-6799	6	Half the theaters are gorgeous, half are dank pits.
Walter Reade Theater	144 W 65th St	212-875-5456	14	Amazing festivals and rare screenings.
Whitney Museum Theater	945 Madison Ave	212-570-3600	15	Artist retrospectives and lectures.
Ziegfeld	141 W 54th St	212-307-1862	12	Beloved NY classic with a gigantic screen. Don't miss.

Brooklyn

BAM Rose Cinemas	30 Lafayette Ave	718-636-4100	31	Great seating and mix of first run + revivals.
Brooklyn Heights Cinema	70 Henry St	718-596-5095	30	Intimate, classy, and just about perfect.
Cobble Hill Cinemas	265 Court St	718-596-9113	32	Great indie destination, though theaters are small.
Indie Screen	285 Kent Ave	347-512-6422	29	Dinner and an art house movie under one roof.
Kent Triplex	1170 Coney Island Ave	718-338-3371	n/a	Moron blockbuster destination.
Nitehawk Cinema	136 Metropolitan Ave	718-384-3980	29	Dinner, cocktails and craft beer while you watch indie flicks.
Pavilion Movie Theatres	188 Prospect Park W	718-369-0838	33	Nice mix of stuff right across from Propsect Park.
Regal Court Street Stadium 12	108 Court St	718-246-8170	30	Audience-participation-friendly megaplex.
reRun Gastropub Theater	147 Front St	718-797-2322	30	Small cinema inside reBar serving up booze and indie films.
Rooftop Films	various locations	718-417-7362	n/a	Summer rooftop series—check website for locations!

Queens

Museum of the Moving Image	36-01 35th Ave	718-777-6888	26	Excellent alternative to blockbuster crap.
Regal Kaufman Astoria Stadium 14	35-30 38th St	718-786-1722	26	Standard blockbuster destination.

New Jersey

AMC Loews Newport Center 11	30 Mall Dr W [Thomas Gangemi Dr]	201-626-3258	35	Jersey stereotypes at their loudest and ugliest.

Make a resolution: Go to at least one museum in New York City every month. There are over 100 museums in the five boroughs, from the **Metropolitan Museum of Art (Map 15)** to the **Dyckman Farmhouse Museum (Map 25)**, an 18th-century relic in upper Manhattan. Many of these museums have special programs and lectures that are open to the public, as well as children's events and summer festivals. When you've found your favorite museums, look into membership. Benefits include free admission, guest passes, party invites, and a discount at the gift shop.

The famous Museum Mile comprises nine world-class museums along Fifth Avenue between 82nd Street and 105th Street, including the **Metropolitan Museum of Art (Map 15)**, and Frank Lloyd Wright's architectural masterpiece, the **Guggenheim (Map 17)**. **El Museo del Barrio (Map 17)**, devoted to early Latin American art, **The Museum of the City of New York (Map 17)**, the **Cooper-Hewitt National Design Museum (Map 17)** (housed in Andrew Carnegie's Mansion), and the **Jewish Museum (Map 17)** are also along the mile. A few blocks off the stretch is the **Whitney Museum of American Art (Map 15)**, which showcases contemporary American artists and features the celebrated Biennial in even-numbered years.

See medieval European art at **The Cloisters (Map 25)** (also a famous picnic spot), exhibitions of up and coming African American artists at the **Studio Museum in Harlem (Map 19)**, and **PS1 (Map 27)** for contemporary art. Take the kids to the **Brooklyn Children's Museum** or the **Children's Museum of Manhattan (Map 14)**. The **Lower East Side Tenement Museum (Map 4)** and the **Ellis Island Immigration Museum (Map 1)** stand as reminders of the past, while the **Hayden Planetarium (Map 14)** offers visions of the future. The treasures of the Orient are on display at the **Asia Society (Map 15)**, and coach potatoes can watch the tube all day at **The Paley Center for Media (Map 12)**, formerly known as the Museum of Television and Radio. The **Brooklyn Museum (Map 33)** supplements its wide-ranging permanent collection with edgy exhibitions, performances, and other special events.

Just about every museum in the city is worth a visit. Other favorites include the **New Museum (Map 6)** (in its spiffy building on The Bowery), the **New-York Historical Society (Map 14)** (which focuses its exhibits on the birth of the city), the **New York Transit Museum (Map 30), the Morgan Library (Map 9)** (with copies of Gutenberg's Bible on display), the **Museum of the Moving Image (Map 26)**, **The Museum of Sex (Map 9)**, and the **Queens Museum of Art** (check out the panorama of New York City). Finally, the **Museum of Arts and Design (Map 12)**, on the southern edge of Columbus Circle, is a bold redesign of Edward Durrell Stone's quirky masterpiece for Huntington Hartford; the new renovation leaves the curves but replaces the cladding. An excellent permanent collection and diverting exhibitions, plus working artists-in-residence and a small lovely museum store, make the Museum a must-see.

Manhattan

Manhattan	Address	Phone	Map
American Academy of Arts & Letters	633 W 155th St	212-368-5900	21
American Folk Art Museum	2 Lincoln Square	212-595-9533	12
American Institute of Graphic Arts	164 Fifth Ave	212-807-1990	9
American Irish Historical Society	991 5th Ave	212-288-2263	15
American Museum of Natural History	Central Park W at 79th St	212-769-5100	15
American Numismatic Society	75 Varick St	212-571-4470	2
Anthology Film Archives	32 Second Ave	212-505-5181	6
Arsenal Gallery	E 64th St & 5th Ave	212-360-8163	15
Asia Society & Museum	725 Park Ave	212-288-6400	15
Asian American Arts Centre	111 Norfolk St	212-233-2154	4
Children's Museum of Manhattan	212 W 83rd St	212-721-1223	14
Children's Museum of the Arts	103 Charlton St	212-274-0986	3
China Institute	125 E 65th St	212-744-8181	15
The Cloisters	99 Margaret Corbin Dr	212-923-3700	24
Cooper-Hewitt National Design Museum	2 E 91st St	212-849-8400	17
Czech Center	321 E 73rd St	646-422-3399	15
Discovery Times Square	226 W 44th St	866-987-9692	12
Dyckman Farmhouse Museum	4881 Broadway	212-304-9422	25
El Museo del Barrio	1230 Fifth Ave	212-831-7272	17
Ellis Island Immigration Museum	Ellis Island, via ferry at Battery Park	212-561-4588	1
Fraunces Tavern Museum	54 Pearl St	212-425-1778	1
Frick Collection	1 E 70th St	212-288-0700	15
Gracie Mansion	East End Ave at 88th St	212-570-4751	17
Grant's Tomb	W 122nd St & Riverside Dr	212-666-1640	18
Grey Art Gallery	100 Washington Sq E	212-998-6780	6
Guggenheim Museum	1071 Fifth Ave	212-423-3500	17

Hayden Planetarium	Central Park West & W 79th St	212-769-5100	14
Hispanic Society Museum	613 W 155th St	212-926-2234	21
International Center of Photography (ICP)	1133 Sixth Ave	212-857-0000	12
Intrepid Sea, Air and Space Museum	12th Ave & W 46th St	212-245-0072	11
Japan Society	333 E 47th St	212-832-1155	13
The Jewish Museum	1109 5th Ave	212-423-3200	17
Madame Tussauds NY	234 W 42nd St	866-841-3505	12
Merchant's House Museum	29 E 4th St	212-777-1089	6
Metropolitan Museum of Art	1000 Fifth Ave	212-535-7710	15
Morgan Library	225 Madison Ave	212-685-0008	9
Morris-Jumel Mansion	65 Jumel Ter	212-923-8008	23
Mount Vernon Hotel Museum and Garden	421 E 61st St	212-838-6878	15
Municipal Art Society	111 W 57th St	212-935-3960	12
Museum at Eldridge Street	12 Eldridge St	212-219-0888	3
Museum at the Fashion Institute of Technology	Seventh Ave & 27th St	212-217-4558	9
Museum of American Finance	48 Wall St	212-908-4110	1
Museum of American Illustration	128 E 63rd St	212-838-2560	15
Museum of Arts & Design	2 Columbus Circle	212-299-7777	12
The Museum of Biblical Art	1865 Broadway	212-408-1500	14
Museum of Chinese in America	215 Centre St	212-619-4785	3
Museum of the City of New York	1220 5th Ave	212-534-1672	17
Museum of Jewish Heritage	36 Battery Pl	646-437-4200	p 184
Museum of Modern Art (MoMA)	11 W 53rd St	212-708-9400	12
Museum of Sex	233 Fifth Ave	212-689-6337	9
National Academy Museum	1083 Fifth Ave	212-369-4880	17
National Museum of the American Indian	1 Bowling Green	212-514-3700	1
Neue Galerie	1048 Fifth Ave	212-628-6200	17
New Museum	235 Bowery	212-219-1222	6
New York City Fire Museum	278 Spring St	212-691-1303	5
New York City Police Museum	100 Old Slip	212-480-3100	1
New York Public Library for the Performing Arts	40 Lincoln Center Plaza	212-870-1600	14
The New York Public Library Humanities & Social Sciences Library	Fifth Ave & 42nd St	212-340-0849	12
New York Transit Museum Gallery Annex & Store	Grand Central Terminal, Main Concourse	212-878-0106	13
New-York Historical Society	170 Central Park W	212-873-3400	14
Nicholas Roerich Museum	319 W 107th St	212-864-7752	16
The Paley Center for Media	25 W 52nd St	212-621-6800	12
Rose Museum	154 W 57th St	212-247-7800	12
Rubin Museum of Art	150 W 17th St	212-620-5000	9
Scandinavia House	58 Park Ave	212-879-9779	10
Skyscraper Museum	39 Battery Pl	212-968-1961	p 184
Sony Wonder Technology Lab	550 Madison Ave	212-833-8100	12
South Street Seaport Museum	12 Fulton St	212-748-8600	1
Statue of Liberty Museum	Liberty Island, via ferry at Battery Park	212-363-3180	1
Studio Museum in Harlem	144 W 125th St	212-864-4500	19
Tenement Museum	108 Orchard St	212-431-0233	4
Tibet House	22 W 15th St	212-807-0563	9
Ukrainian Museum	222 E 6th St	212-228-0110	6
US Archives of American Art	300 Park Ave S	212-399-5015	10
Whitney Museum of American Art	945 Madison Ave	212-570-3600	15
Yeshiva University Museum	15 W 16th St	212-294-8330	9

Brooklyn

Brooklyn Children's Museum	145 Brooklyn Ave	718-735-4400	n/a
Brooklyn Historical Society	128 Pierrepont St	718-222-4111	30
Brooklyn Museum	200 Eastern Pkwy	718-638-5000	n/a
City Reliquary	370 Metropolitan Ave	718-782-4842	29
Coney Island Museum	1208 Surf Ave	718-372-5159	n/a
Harbor Defense Museum	230 Sheridan Loop	718-630-4349	n/a
Museum of Contemporary African Diasporan Arts	80 Hanson Pl	718-230-0492	31
New York Aquarium	Surf Ave & W 8th St	718-265-3474	n/a
New York Transit Museum	130 Livingston St	718-694-1600	30
The Old Stone House	336 3rd St	718-768-3195	33
Toy Museum of NY	157 Montague St	718-243-0820	30
Waterfront Museum	290 Conover St	718-624-4719	32
Weeksville Heritage Center	1698 Bergen St	718-756-5250	n/a
Wyckoff Farmhouse Museum	5816 Clarendon Rd	718-629-5400	n/a

Queens

Bowne House	37-01 Bowne St	718-359 0528	n/a
Fisher Landau Center for Art	38-27 30th St	718-937-0727	27
Godwin-Ternbach Museum	65-30 Kissena Blvd	718-997-4747	n/a
King Manor Museum	Jamaica Ave & 153rd St	718-206-0545	n/a
Kingsland Homestead	Weeping Beech Park, 143-35 37th Ave	718-939-0647	n/a
Louis Armstrong House Museum	34-56 107th St	718-478-8274	n/a
MoMa PS1	22-25 Jackson Ave	718-784-2084	27
Museum of the Moving Image	36-01 35th Ave	718-777-6888	26
New York Hall of Science	47-01 111th St	718-699-0005	n/a
The Noguchi Museum	9-01 33rd Rd	718-204-7088	27
Queens County Farm Museum	73-50 Little Neck Pkwy	718-347-3276	n/a
Queens Museum of Art	Flushing Meadows-Corona Park	718-592-9700	n/a
Socrates Sculpture Park	32-01 Vernon Blvd	718-956-1819	26
Voelker Orth Museum	149-19 38th Ave	718-359-6227	n/a

The Bronx

Bronx County Historical Society	3309 Bainbridge Ave	718-881-8900	112

Metropolitan Museum of Art

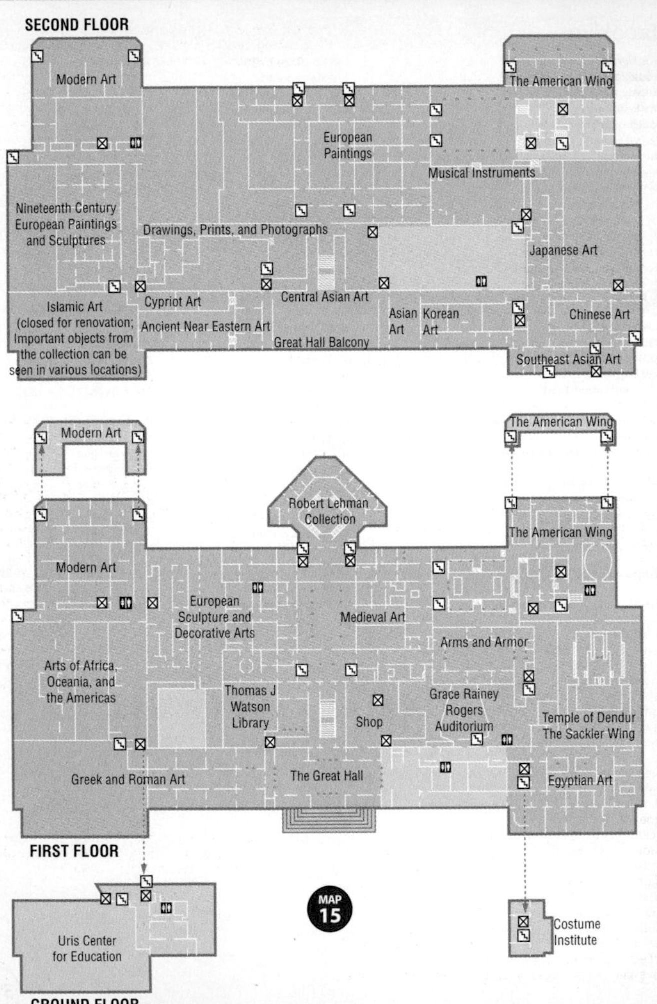
SECOND FLOOR
Modern Art
The American Wing
European Paintings
Musical Instruments
Nineteenth Century European Paintings and Sculptures
Drawings, Prints, and Photographs
Japanese Art
Islamic Art (closed for renovation; Important objects from the collection can be seen in various locations)
Cypriot Art
Central Asian Art
Ancient Near Eastern Art
Great Hall Balcony
Asian Art
Korean Art
Chinese Art
Southeast Asian Art
Modern Art
The American Wing
Robert Lehman Collection
The American Wing
Modern Art
European Sculpture and Decorative Arts
Medieval Art
Arms and Armor
Arts of Africa, Oceania, and the Americas
Thomas J Watson Library
Shop
Grace Rainey Rogers Auditorium
Temple of Dendur The Sackler Wing
Greek and Roman Art
The Great Hall
Egyptian Art
FIRST FLOOR
MAP 15
Uris Center for Education
Costume Institute
GROUND FLOOR

General Information

NFT Map:	15
Address:	1000 Fifth Ave at 82nd St
Phone:	212-535-7710
Website:	www.metmuseum.org
Hours:	Sun-Thurs: 10 am-5:30 pm; Fri & Sat: 10 am-9 pm;; New Year's Day, Christmas & Thanksgiving: closed.
Admission:	A suggested $25 donation for adults, $12 for students, and $17 for senior citizens.

Overview

The Metropolitan Museum of Art is touted as the largest and most comprehensive museum in the Western hemisphere. Established by a group of American businessmen, artists, and thinkers back in 1870, the museum was created to preserve and stimulate appreciation for some of the greatest works of art in history.

In the first few years of its existence, the museum moved from its original location at 681 Fifth Avenue to the Douglas Mansion at 128 W 14th Street, and then finally to its current Central Park location in 1880.

Calvert Vaux and Jacob Wrey Mould designed the museum's Gothic Revival red-brick facade, which was later remodeled in 1926 into the grand, white-columned front entrance that you see today. Part of the original facade was left intact and can still be seen from the Robert Lehman Wing looking toward the European Sculpture and Decorative Arts galleries.

The Met's annual attendance reaches over 4 million visitors who flock to see the more than 2 million works of art housed in the museum's permanent collection. You could visit the museum many times and not see more than a small portion of the permanent collection. The vast paintings anthology had a modest beginning in 1870 with a small donation of 174 European paintings and has now swelled to include works spanning 5,000 years of world culture, from the prehistoric to the present and from every corner of the globe.

The Met is broken down into a series of smaller museums within each building. For instance, the American Wing contains the most complete accumulation of American paintings, sculpture, and decorative arts, including period rooms offering a look at domestic life throughout the nation's history. The Egyptian collection is the finest in the world outside of Cairo, and the Islamic art exhibition remains unparalleled, as does the mass of 2,500 European paintings and Impressionist and Post-Impressionist works. The permanent gallery of Islamic art underwent renovations in 2008, following the 10-15 year renovation of the Greek & Roman collection. The redesigned galleries display works that have been in storage for decades, assuring even the most frequent visitor something fresh to check out including the museum's newly restored, world-famous, non-gas-guzzling **Etruscan chariot**.

Other major collections include the arms and armor, Asian art, costumes, European sculpture and decorative arts, medieval and Renaissance art, musical instruments, drawings, prints, ancient antiquities from around the world, photography, and modern art. Add to this the many special exhibits and performances the Met offers throughout the year, and you have a world-class museum with Central Park as its backyard.

This is a massive museum and seating can be difficult to find during busy weekends. When you need a break from all of the culture, sit down for a snack in the American Wing Café or lunch in the cafeteria. If you pal around with a member (or become one yourself), it is a treat to eat in the Members Dining Room overlooking the park. In the summer climb up to the Roof Garden Café for a glass of wine and the most beautiful view of Central Park that your lack of money can buy.

The Greatest Hits

You can, of course, spend countless hours at the Met. Pick any style of art and chances are you will find a piece here. But if you're rushed for time, check out the sublime space that houses the **Temple of Dendur** in the Sackler Wing, the elegant **Frank Lloyd Wright Room** in the American Wing, the fabulous **Tiffany Glass** and **Tiffany Mosaics**, also in the American Wing, the **choir screen** in the Medieval Sculpture Hall, the **Caravaggios** and **Goyas** in the Renaissance Rooms, the **Picassos** and **Pollocks** in Modern Art, and that huge **canoe** in Arts of Africa and Oceania. For a moment of tranquility, visit the beautiful Chinese Garden Court in the Asian galleries. When it's open, we highly recommend the **Roof Garden**, which has killer views of Central Park as a side dish to cocktails and conversation. When it's not, check out seasonal specials like the **Christmas "Angel" Tree and Neopolitan Baroque Crèche**, an annual favorite set up in front of the medieval choir screen.

How to Get There—Mass Transit

Subway
Take the 4 5 6 to the 86th Street stop and walk three blocks west to Fifth Avenue and four blocks south to 82nd Street.

Bus
Take the 4 bus along Fifth Avenue (from uptown locations) to 82nd Street or along Madison Avenue (from downtown locations) to 83rd Street.

Museum of Natural History

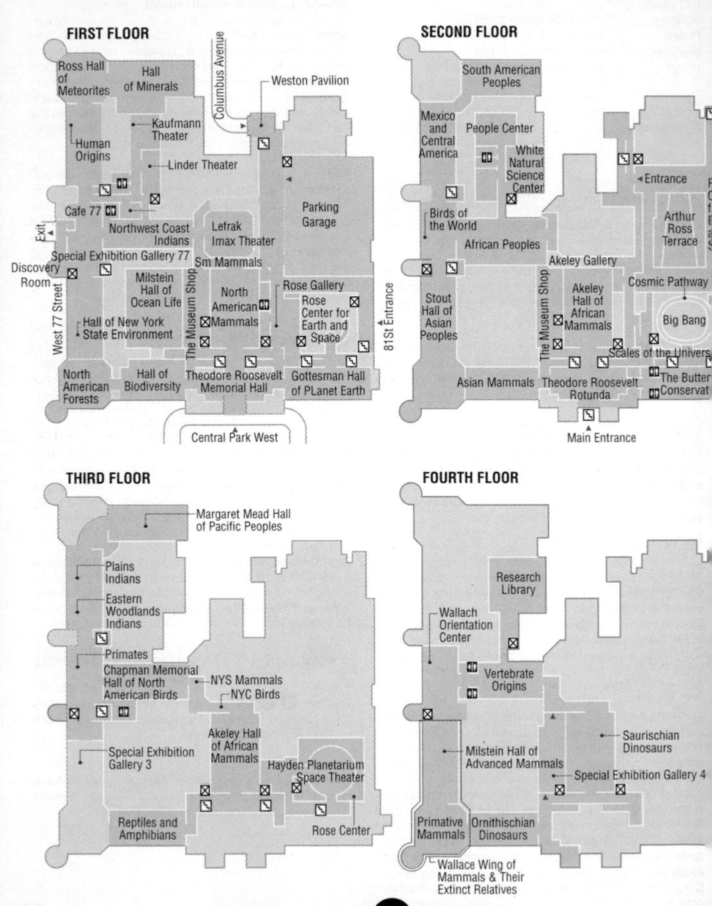
FIRST FLOOR
Ross Hall of Meteorites
Hall of Minerals
Columbus Avenue
Weston Pavilion
Kaufmann Theater
Human Origins
Linder Theater
Cafe 77
Exit
Northwest Coast Indians
Lefrak Imax Theater
Parking Garage
Special Exhibition Gallery 77
Sm Mammals
Discovery Room
Milstein Hall of Ocean Life
The Museum Shop
North American Mammals
Rose Gallery
Rose Center for Earth and Space
81St Entrance
West 77 Street
Hall of New York State Environment
North American Forests
Hall of Biodiversity
Theodore Roosevelt Memorial Hall
Gottesman Hall of PLanet Earth
Central Park West
SECOND FLOOR
South American Peoples
Mexico and Central America
People Center
White Natural Science Center
Entrance
Arthur Ross Terrace
Birds of the World
African Peoples
Akeley Gallery
Cosmic Pathway
Stout Hall of Asian Peoples
The Museum Shop
Akeley Hall of African Mammals
Big Bang
Scales of the Univers
The Butter Conservat
Asian Mammals
Theodore Roosevelt Rotunda
Main Entrance
THIRD FLOOR
Margaret Mead Hall of Pacific Peoples
Plains Indians
Eastern Woodlands Indians
Primates
Chapman Memorial Hall of North American Birds
NYS Mammals
NYC Birds
Akeley Hall of African Mammals
Special Exhibition Gallery 3
Hayden Planetarium Space Theater
Reptiles and Amphibians
Rose Center
FOURTH FLOOR
Research Library
Wallach Orientation Center
Vertebrate Origins
Saurischian Dinosaurs
Milstein Hall of Advanced Mammals
Special Exhibition Gallery 4
Primative Mammals
Ornithischian Dinosaurs
Wallace Wing of Mammals & Their Extinct Relatives

MAP 14

General Information

NFT Map: 14
Address: Central Park West at 79th Street
Phone: 212-769-5100
Website: www.amnh.org
Hours: Daily, 10:00 am–5:45 pm
The Rose Center stays open until 8:45pm the first Friday of every month.
Christmas & Thanksgiving: closed.
Admission: Suggested general admission is $19 for adults, $10.50 for children (2–12), and $14.50 for senior citizens and students. Special exhibitions, IMAX movies, and the space show are extra; packages are available. Free to members.

Overview

Admit it. You secretly TiVo the Discovery Channel and the History Channel. You've even watched one—if not several—episodes of *Star Trek*. Something about African beetles, famous dead guys, and the unknown universe strokes your inner Einstein. Focus your microscope on this one, smarty-pants: the American Museum of Natural History, a paradise for geeks and aspiring geeks alike, not to mention good old nature lovers. And don't worry, your TV-watching secrets are safe with us.

Decades before anyone knew what an atom was, and when relativity was just a twinkle in Einstein's eye, Albert Smith Bickmore established the AMNH. Completed in 1869, the museum held its first exhibition in the Central Park Arsenal a few years later, garnering enough respect to acquire space along classy Central Park West. Architects Calvert Vaux and J. Wrey Mould designed the new, posh building on limited Benjamins and opened it to the public in 1877. Key additions followed: The Hayden Planetarium in 1935, the Theodore Roosevelt Memorial Hall and Rotunda in 1936, and the Rose Center for Earth and Space in 2000.

As Saturday morning museum-going ritual dictates, it's going to be painfully crowded. On those days, you dodge out-of-towners, eyes wide, mouths gaping. It's much the same on weekdays with rowdy school kids on field trips. How to avoid the Excedrin-necessitating atmosphere? Two words: permanent collection. The amazing series of wildlife dioramas even inspired an entire Hollywood movie (albeit not a great one, by adult standards). Don't expect to see any PETA supporters in these halls though.

When you can go at off hours, or if you feel you can brave the crowds, make a point of checking out the fascinating and often provocative special exhibits. Recent highlights have included Darwin and Water: H20=Life.

The Greatest Hits

Five floors of star-lovin', mammal-gazin', bird-watchin', fossil-fuelin' science await. Rain forest fever? Check out the Hall of Biodiversity. Didn't understand why that movie was called *The Squid and The Whale?* Meet the 94-foot long great blue whale and his giant squid companion at the Milstein Hall of Ocean Life. Moby teamed up with MTV2 and the Hayden Planetarium in The Rose Center for Earth and Space to produce SonicVision, an animated alternative music show that poses the question: How do you see your music? Another thought-provoking show with a celebrity element (narration by Whoopi Goldberg) is Journey to the Stars. For more instant thrills, check out the gigantic meteorites at the Arthur Ross Hall of Meteorites, or the five-story tall dinosaur display in the Theodore Roosevelt Rotunda. It's the largest freestanding beast in the world. The AMNH also produces spectacular IMAX features, a great alternative to the museum's amazing but creepy taxidermy. The Hall of Gems houses the Star of India, the largest star sapphire in the world. Finally, for recreation of *The Birds* variety with less evil, visit The Butterfly Conservatory. Tropical butterflies flit all around you from, you guessed it, all over the world. It's enough to put TiVo on pause.

How to Get There—Mass Transit

Subway
Take the B C to the 81st Street stop. Or take the 1 to 79th Street and walk two blocks east.

Bus
The 7 10 and 11 all stop within a block of the museum. Take the 79 across Central Park if you are coming from the East Side.

Museum of Modern Art

General Information

NFT Map: 12
Address: 11 W 53rd St
Phone: 212-708-9400
Website: www.moma.org
Hours: Sun, Mon, Wed, Thurs, Sat: 10:30 am–5:30 pm; Fri 10:30 am–8 pm; closed Tues, Thanksgiving, and Christmas
Admission: $25 for adults, $18 for seniors, $14 for students; free to members and children under 16 accompanied by an adult

Overview

The Museum of Modern Art opened in 1929, back when impressionism and surrealism were truly modern art. Originally in the Heckscher Building at 730 Fifth Avenue, MoMA moved to its current address on West 53rd Street in 1932. What started out as a townhouse eventually expanded into an enormous space, with new buildings and additions in 1939 (by Phillip L. Goodwin and Edward Durell Stone), 1953 (including a sculpture garden by Phillip Johnson), 1964 (another Johnson garden), and 1984 (by Cesar Pelli). During the summer of 2002, the museum closed its Manhattan location and moved temporarily to Long Island City (MoMA's affiliate, PS1 Contemporary Art Center, is still there). After a major expansion and renovation by Yoshio Taniguchi, MoMA reopened in September 2004. Opinion varies as to the success of Taniguchi's new design, but the art is the point, right?

Wrong. Museums are one of the last great bastions of inventive, exciting, fun, not-necessarily-practical architecture. Taniguchi's design uses all available space, which, considering the price of midtown real estate, must have been a selling point for his design. Other than that, you'll have to trek up to the Guggenheim, fly off to Bilbao, or head downtown to the New Museum of Contemporary Art's new Bowery digs to see better marriages of art and design.

The re-Manhattanized museum charges $25. If crowds on a typical Saturday afternoon are any indication, the hefty entry fee is not keeping patrons away. Art lovers take note: The yearly $85 membership ($140 for a dual and $175 for a family) is the way to go. Members get a 10% discount at MoMA stores, free tickets to all film screenings, and you're free to pop in whenever you want to see your favorite Picasso (or use the restroom). For the best deal, visit the museum from 4–8 pm on Fridays, when Target sponsors free admission. The crowds aren't as bad as you might think, and you can usually slide right past the main desk and grab one of the free tickets that they scatter there.

What to See

The fourth and fifth floors are where the big names reside—Johns, Pollock, Warhol (fourth floor), Braque, Cezanne, Dali, Duchamp, Ernst, Hopper, Kandinsky, Klee, Matisse, Miro, Monet, Picasso, Rosseau, Seurat, Van Gogh, and Wyeth (fifth floor). More recent works can be found in the contemporary gallery on the second floor. Special exhibitions are featured on the third and sixth floors. The surrealist collection is outstanding, but we suspect that MoMA has only a tiny fraction of its pop art on display. Well, you can't have everything...

Moving downstairs to the third floor, it's clear that the photography collection is, as always, one of the centerpieces of the museum and is highly recommended (although the Gursky pieces are actually dotted throughout the building). The architecture and design gallery showcases a range of cool consumer items, from chairs to cars to the first Mac computers, and is one of the most popular destinations in the museum.

Recent exhibits, such as Doug Aitken's *Sleepwalkers*—which was the first to project film scenes onto MoMA's exterior walls—provide hope that the museum will only continue to be more innovative in the future.

Breakdown of the Space

Floor One: Lobby, Sculpture Garden, Museum Store, Restaurant
Floor Two: Contemporary Galleries, Media Gallery, Prints and Illustrated Books, Café
Floor Three: Architecture and Design, Drawing, Photography, Special Exhibitions
Floor Four: Painting and Sculpture II
Floor Five: Painting and Sculpture I, Café
Floor Six: Special Exhibitions
There are two theater levels below the first floor.

Amenities

Backpacks and large purses are not allowed in gallery spaces, and the free coat check can become messy when the check-in and check-out lines become intertwined. Leave large items (including laptops) at home.

Bathrooms and water fountains are on all floors. We don't think that there are enough of them, and the bathrooms themselves are way too small to handle the crowds.

There are three places to get food in the museum—you'll pay heavily for the convenience and Danny Meyer experience. Café 2, located on the second floor, offers "seasonal Roman fare," also known as "snooty Italian." They also have an espresso bar. Terrace 5, which overlooks the beautiful sculpture garden, has desserts, chocolates, and sandwiches, along with wine, cocktails, coffee, and tea. Both cafes open half an hour after the museum opens its doors and close half an hour before the museum closes.

For the ultimate museum dining experience, The Modern features the cuisine of Gabriel Kreuther. It has two main rooms—the Dining Room overlooks the sculpture garden, and the Bar Room is more casual and overlooks the bar. An outdoor terrace is also made available when the weather permits. The Modern serves French and New American food and features wild game menu items—sounds great if you've got a platinum card.

The Modern is open beyond museum hours, with the Dining Room closing at 10:30 pm Monday–Thursday, and 11:30 pm on Friday and Saturday. The Bar Room closes at 10:30 pm Monday–Thursday, at 11 pm on Friday and Saturday, and 9:30 pm on Sunday. There's a separate street entrance to allow diners access to The Modern after the museum closes.

On warm summer days, a gelato bar in the sculpture garden offers yummy sorbets.

So long as there are adventurous artists putting on plays in abandoned storefronts and opportunistic real estate developers knocking down beautiful old theaters to put up hotels, the New York theater scene will always be adding a few venues here and deleting a few venues there. What remains constant is that on any given night there are at least dozens, and more often hundreds, of live theater performances to be seen. And the best ones are not always the most expensive.

Broadway (theaters in the Times Square vicinity that hold at least 500 people) still has the reputation of being the place to see American theater at its finest, but the peculiar fact of the matter is that there is much more money to be gained by appealing to the infrequent theatergoer than there is by trying to please the connoisseur. As a result, shows that are looked down on, if not despised, by many lovers of the theater wind up selling out for years (Mamma Mia, anyone?), while more ambitious, artistically admired plays and musicals struggle to find an audience. Check out theater chat boards like BroadwayWorld.com and TalkinBroadway.com to see what the people who see everything have to say.

Nobody gets famous doing live theater anymore, so if you've never heard of the actor whose name is twinkling in lights (Cherry Jones, Brian Stokes Mitchell, Raul Esparza, Christine Ebersole...) chances are that person has the stage experience and acting chops to keep you enthralled for two and a half hours, unlike the big name celebrities (P. Diddy, Melanie Griffith) who make their stage acting debuts in starring roles they're not prepared for. Of course, there are also actors with extensive stage credits who come back to Broadway regularly after becoming famous. That's why we love John Lithgow, Cynthia Nixon, and Phylicia Rashad.

Many great performers work Off-Broadway (Manhattan theaters seating 100–499 people) where the writing and directing are actually more important than spectacle and scores made up of classic pop songs. Off-Off Broadway (fewer than 100 seats) is a terrific grab bag of both beginners and seasoned pros doing material that is often unlikely to draw in masses. And tickets are pretty cheap, too.

TheaterMania.com keeps an extensive list of just about every show in New York, with direct links to the websites that sell tickets. Many shows offer a limited number of inexpensive standing room and/or same-day rush tickets. A detailed directory of such offers can be found at TalkinBroadway.com.

Thousands of same-day tickets for Broadway and Off-Broadway shows are sold for 20%–50% off at the TKTS booths in Times Square (long lines) and at the South Street Seaport (short lines). They take cash, traveler's checks, and credit cards. Check for hours and to see what's been recently available at www.tdf.org. Don't expect to get a bargain for the top-selling hits, but most shows use this booth at some time or another. You can also download discount coupons at Playbill.com that you can use to get seats in advance.

The dirty little secret of New York theatre is that free tickets for high-quality shows (AKA not Wicked, The Lion King, or Jerser Boys etc.) are abundantly available though organizations that specialize in "dressing the house" for productions that depend more on word of mouth than expensive advertising costs. By giving a yearly membership fee of around $100 to AudienceExtras.com or Play-By Play.com, you can check your computer 24-hours a day to find free tickets (there's a small per-ticket service charge) for a dozen or so Off-, Off-Off-, and sometimes Broadway shows available at the last minute. That dinky little play in some church basement that you went to on a whim might wind up being the next great American classic.

Keep an eye out for shows by these lesser-known companies:

The award-winning **Classical Theatre of Harlem (Map 23)** (www.classicaltheatreofharlem.org) has earned a reputation for mounting exciting, edgy revivals of classics from Shakespeare and Brecht, as well as solid productions from more recent greats such as August Wilson and Melvin Van Peebles. A multicultural company that frequently casts against racial type, they draw a youthful audience with imaginative interpretations. As of press time the Classical Theater of Harlem has been left nomadic but we're hoping they find a new permanent home soon.

The **Mint Theatre Company (Map 11)** (www.minttheater.org) specializes in reviving Broadway plays from the past they call "worthy, but neglected." In their tiny space you'll see interesting comedies and dramas from the likes of A. A. Milne, Edith Wharton, and Thomas Wolfe played traditionally with sets and costumes that really make you feel like you're watching a production from over 50 years ago.

Musicals Tonight! does the same kind of thing with forgotten musicals, only presenting them in low budgeted, but highly energized, staged readings. Nowadays most musicals revived on Broadway are revised and updated to the point where they lose their authenticity. But if you're in the mood to see what an Irving Berlin ragtime show from 1915 was really like, or if you want to see a Cole Porter tuner from the '30s with all of the dated topical references that confused audiences even back then, Musicals Tonight! serves up the past as it really was written. And check for their special concerts where Broadway understudies sing songs from the roles they are currently covering. Shows take place at **The Lion Theatre (Map 14)**.

Broadway insiders know that Monday nights, when most shows are dark, is often the hottest night of the week for entertainment. That's when performers use their night off to partake in benefits and special events. Consistently among the best are shows from Scott Siegel's Broadway By The Year series at **Town Hall (Map 12)** (www.the-townhall-nyc.org). Each one-night concert is packed with theater and cabaret stars singing hits and obscurities introduced on Broadway in one selected year. Siegel also produces Broadway Unplugged at Town Hall, a concert of theater performers singing showtunes without amplification. The atmosphere is like a sports event, with the audience wildly cheering each naturally voiced solo.

Located in a former school on First Avenue and 9th Street in the East Village, **P.S. 122 (Map 7)** (www.ps122.org) is a not-for-profit arts center serving New York City's dance and performance community. Shows rotate through on a regular basis, so check the website for the latest schedule. The outdoor **Delacorte Theater (Map 15)** in Central Park hosts performances only during the summer months. Tickets to the ridiculously popular and free Shakespeare in the Park performances are given away at 1pm at the Delacorte on the day of each performance. Hopefully, you enjoy camping because people line up for days in their tents and sleeping bags just to secure a ticket!

Just on the other side of the Manhattan Bridge in Brooklyn is the world famous **Brooklyn Academy of Music (Map 31)**. A thriving urban arts center, BAM brings domestic and international performing arts and film to Brooklyn. The center includes two theaters (**Harvey Lichtenstein Theater (Map 31)** and **Howard Gilman Opera House (Map 31)**, the **BAM Rose Cinemas (Map 31)**, and the **BAMcafé (Map 31)**, a restaurant and live music venue. Our favorite season is the Next Wave Festival, an annual three-month celebration of cutting-edge dance, theater, music, and opera. As an alternative to BAM, **St. Ann's Warehouse (Map 30)** in DUMBO also produces cutting-edge work.

NOT FOR TOURISTS™ Custom Mapping

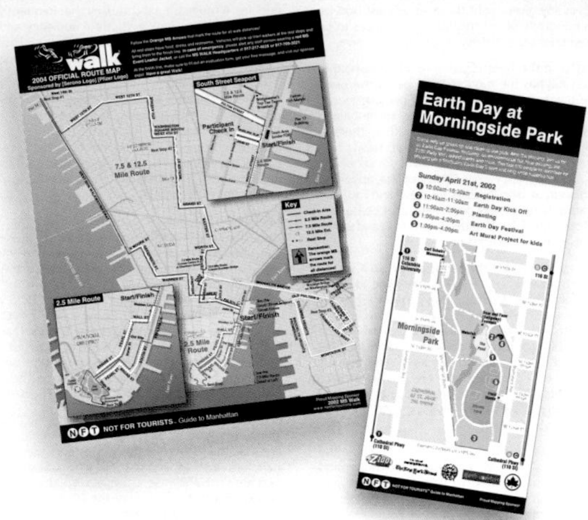

We'll map your world.

Need a custom map?

NFT will work with you to design a custom map that promotes your company or event. NFT's team will come up with something new or put a fresh face on something you already have. We provide custom map-making and information design services to fit your needs—whether simply showing where your organization is located on one of our existing maps, or creating a completely new visual context for the information you wish to convey. NFT will help you—and your audience—make the most of the place you're in, while you're in it.

For more information, call us at 212-965-8650 or visit www.notfortourists.com/custommapping.aspx

Not For Tourists™
www.notfortourists.com
Boston · Brooklyn · Chicago · London · Los Angeles · New York City · San Francisco · Washington DC

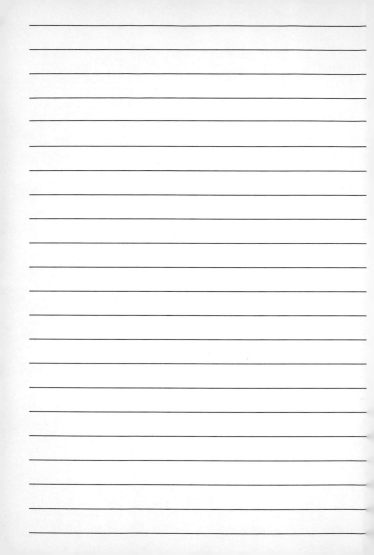

Street Index

Street Index

Street Name	Map No.	Coordinates
Convent Ave (1-155)	18	A2
Convent Ave (156-498)	21	A2/B2
Cooper Sq	6	A2
Cooper St	25	A2/B1
Cornelia St	5	B2
Cortlandt Aly	3	A1
Cortlandt St	1	A1
Crosby St (1-57)	3	A1
Crosby St (58-172)	6	B1
Cumming St	25	B1
Delancey St (1-61)	6	B2
Delancey St (62-336)	4	A1/A2
Depew Pl	13	B1
Desbrosses St	2	A1
Dey St	1	A1
Division St (1-87)	3	A2
Division St (16-136142)	4	A1
Dominick St	5	B2
Dongan Pl	24	A1
Donnellon Sq	21	A2
Dover St	3	B2
Downing St	5	B2
Doyers St	3	A2
Duane St (42-120)	3	B1
Duane St (121-199)	2	B1/B2
Dutch St	1	A2
Dyckman St (25-198)	24	A2
Dyckman St (181-399)	25	B1
Dyer Ave	8	A2
Dyer Ave	11	B2
E 1st St (1-50)	6	B2
E 1st St (51-294)	7	B1
E 2nd St (1-65)	6	B2
E 2nd St (66-398)	7	B1/B2
E 3rd St (1-69)	6	B2
E 3rd St (70-399)	7	B1/B2
E 4th St (1-109)	6	B1/B2
E 4th St (110-399)	7	B1/B2
E 4th Walk	7	B2
E 5th St (200-349)	6	A2
E 5th St (350-799)	7	A1/A2
E 5th Walk	7	A2
E 6th St (200-349)	6	A2
E 6th St (350-998)	7	A1/A2
E 7th St (1-68)	6	A2
E 7th St (69-299)	7	A1/A2
E 8th St (1-199)	6	A1/A2
E 8th St (291-409)	7	A1/A2
E 9th St (1-349)	6	A1/A2
E 9th St (350-753)	7	A1/A2
E 10th St (1-220)	6	A1/A2
E 10th St (221-499)	7	A1/A2
E 11th St (1-349)	6	A1/A2
E 11th St (350-599)	7	A1
E 12th St (1-349)	6	A1/A2
E 12th St (350-751)	7	A1/A2
E 13th St (1-349)	6	A1/A2
E 13th St (350-752)	7	A1/A2
E 14th St (1-399)	6	A1/A2
E 14th St (400-898)	7	A1/A2
E 15th St (1-99)	9	B2
E 15th St (100-821)	10	B1/B2
E 16th St (1-99)	9	B2
E 16th St (100-761)	10	B1/B2
E 17th St (1-64)	9	B2

Street Name	Map No.	Coordinates
E 17th St (65-399)	10	B1
E 18th St (1-63)	9	B2
E 18th St (64-399)	10	B1
E 19th St (1-59)	9	B2
E 19th St (60-399)	10	B1
E 20th St (1-56)	9	B2
E 20th St (57-698)	10	B1/B2
E 21st St (1-56)	9	B2
E 21st St (57-399)	10	B1
E 22nd St (1-52)	9	B2
E 22nd St (53-399)	10	B1
E 23rd St (1-99)	9	B2
E 23rd St (100-599)	10	B1/B2
E 24th St	10	B1
E 25th St	10	B1/B2
E 26th St (1-65)	9	B2
E 26th St (66-399)	10	B1
E 27th St (1-61)	9	B2
E 27th St (62-299)	10	B1
E 28th St (1-61)	9	A2
E 28th St (62-399)	10	A1
E 29th St (1-62)	9	A2
E 29th St (63-399)	10	A1
E 30th St (1-62)	9	A2
E 30th St (63-399)	10	A1
E 31st St (1-64)	9	A2
E 31st St (65-299)	10	A1
E 32nd St (1-63)	9	A2
E 32nd St (64-299)	10	A1
E 33rd St (1-64)	9	A2
E 33rd St (65-399)	10	A1
E 34th St (1-99)	9	A2
E 34th St (72-499)	10	A1/A2
E 35th St (1-59)	9	A2
E 35th St (60-399)	10	A1
E 36th St (1-61)	9	A2
E 36th St (62-399)	10	A1
E 37th St (1-59)	9	A2
E 37th St (60-499)	10	A1/A2
E 38th St (1-60)	9	A2
E 38th St (61-499)	10	A1/A2
E 39th St (1-61)	9	A2
E 39th St (62-399)	10	A1
E 40th St (1-65)	12	B2
E 40th St (66-399)	13	B1/B2
E 41st St (1-64)	12	B2
E 41st St (65-499)	13	B1/B2
E 42nd St (1-52)	12	B2
E 42nd St (33-499)	13	B1/B2
E 43rd St (1-65)	12	B2
E 43rd St (66-399)	13	B1/B2
E 44th St (1-50)	12	B2
E 44th St (50-399)	13	B1/B2
E 45th St (1-59)	12	B2
E 45th St (101-399)	13	B1/B2
E 46th St (1-58)	12	B2
E 46th St (124-399)	13	B1/B2
E 47th St (1-52)	12	B2
E 47th St (50-399)	13	B1/B2
E 48th St (1-64)	12	B2
E 48th St (65-499)	13	B1/B2
E 49th St (1-99)	12	B2
E 49th St (100-499)	13	B1/B2
E 50th St (1-64)	12	A2
E 50th St (65-499)	13	A1/A2
E 51st St (1-61)	12	A2
E 51st St (62-499)	13	A1/A2
E 52nd St (1-99)	12	A2
E 52nd St (100-499)	13	A1/A2

Street Name	Map No.	Coordinates
E 53rd St (1-62)	12	A2
E 53rd St (63-499)	13	A1/A2
E 54th St (1-99)	12	A2
E 54th St (100-499)	13	A1/A2
E 55th St (1-64)	12	A2
E 55th St (65-514)	13	A1/A2
E 56th St (1-74)	12	A2
E 56th St (75-516)	13	A1/A2
E 57th St (1-64)	12	A2
E 57th St (65-503)	13	A1/A2
E 58th St (1-65)	12	A2
E 58th St (66-499)	13	A1/A2
E 59th St (1-65)	12	A2
E 59th St (66-599)	13	A1/A2
E 60th St	15	B1/B2
E 61st St	15	B1/B2
E 62nd St	15	B1/B2
E 63rd St	15	B1/B2
E 64th St	15	B1/B2
E 65th St	15	B1/B2
E 66th St	15	B1/B2
E 67th St	15	B1/B2
E 68th St	15	B1/B2
E 69th St	15	B1/B2
E 70th St	15	B1/B2
E 71st St	15	B1/B2
E 72nd St	15	B1/B2
E 73rd St	15	A1/A2
E 74th St	15	A1/A2
E 75th St	15	A1/A2
E 76th St	15	A1/A2
E 77th St	15	A1/A2
E 78th St	15	A1/A2
E 79th St	15	A1/A2
E 80th St	15	A1/A2
E 81st St	15	A1/A2
E 82nd St	15	A1/A2
E 83rd St	15	A1/A2
E 84th St	15	A1/A2
E 85th St	15	A1/A2
E 86th St	17	B1/B2
E 87th St	17	B1/B2
E 88th St	17	B1/B2
E 89th St	17	B1/B2
E 90th St	17	B1/B2
E 91st St	17	B1/B2
E 92nd St	17	B1/B2
E 93rd St	17	B1/B2
E 94th St	17	B1/B2
E 95th St	17	B1/B2
E 96th St	17	B1/B2
E 97th St	17	B1/B2
E 98th St	17	B1
E 99th St	17	A1/A2
E 100th St	17	A1/A2
E 101st St	17	A1/A2
E 102nd St	17	A1/A2
E 103rd St	17	A1/A2
E 104th St	17	A1/A2
E 105th St	17	A1/A2
E 106th St	17	A1/A2
E 107th St	17	A1/A2
E 108th St	17	A1/A2
E 109th St	17	A1/A2
E 110th St	19	B2
E 110th St (1-499)	20	B1/B2
E 111th St	20	B1/B2

Street Index

Street Name	Map No.	Coordinates
E 112th St	20	B1/B2
E 113th St	20	B1/B2
E 114th St	20	B2
E 115th St	20	B1/B2
E 116th St	20	B1/B2
E 117th St	20	B1/B2
E 118th St	20	B1/B2
E 119th St	20	B1/B2
E 120th St	20	B1/B2
E 121st St	20	B1
E 122nd St	20	B1
E 123rd St	20	A1
E 124th St	20	A1/A2
E 125th St	20	A1/A2
E 126th St	20	A1/A2
E 127th St	20	A1/A2
E 128th St	20	A1
E 129th St	20	A1
E 130th St (1-26)	19	A2
E 130th St (27-198)	20	A1
E 131st St	20	A1
E 132nd St (1-39)	19	A2
E 132nd St (40-99)	20	A1
E 135th St	20	A1
E 138th St	22	B2
E 139th St	22	B2
145th St Brdg	22	B2
E 150th St	17	B2
E Broadway (1-86)	3	A2/B2
E Broadway (86-313)	4	A1/A2
E Houston St (1-170)	6	B1/B2
E Houston St (169-599)	7	B1/B2
East End Ave (1-299)	15	A2
East End Ave (136-298)	17	B2
East River Dr	17	A2/B2
East River Dr	20	B2
Edens Aly	1	A2
Edgar St	1	A1
Edgecombe Ave (2-677)	23	A2/B2
Edgecombe Ave (5-539)	21	A2/B2
Edward M Morgan Pl	21	A1
Eldridge St (1-140)	3	A2
Eldridge St (141-252)	6	B2
Elizabeth St (1-149)	3	A2
Elizabeth St (150-343)	6	B2
Elk St	3	B1
Ellwood St	24	A1/A2
Emerson St	25	A1
Esplanade Gardens Plz	22	B2
Essex St (1-6468)	4	A1
Essex St (95-185)	7	B1
Exchange Aly	1	A1
Exchange Pl	1	A1/A2
Extra Pl	6	B2
Fairview Ave	24	A1/A2/B1
FDR Dr	13	A2/B2
FDR Dr	15	A2/B2
FDR Dr	17	B2
(313-359)	10	A2/B2
(397-566)	4	A2
(567-1399)	7	A2
Fletcher St	1	A2
Foley Sq	3	B1
Footpath	18	A2
Forsyth St (1-131)	3	A2
Forsyth St (124-218)	6	B2
Fort George Ave	24	A2
Fort George Hill	24	A2
Fort Washington Ave		
(1-484)	23	A1/B1
(485-732)	24	B1
Frankfort St	3	B1/B2
Franklin Pl	3	A1
Franklin St (40-83)	3	A1
Franklin St (84-172)	2	A2
Frawley Cir	19	B2
Frederick Douglass Cir	19	B1
Freedom Pl	14	B1
Freeman Aly	6	B2
Front St (77-226)	1	A2
Front St (209-259)	3	B2
Front St (304-395)	4	A2
Fulton St	1	A1/A2
Gansevoort St	5	A1
Gay St	5	A2
Gold St (1-66)	1	A2
Gold St (64-103)	3	B1/B2
Gouverneur Ln	1	A2
Gouverneur Slip E	4	A2
Gouverneur Slip W	4	A2
Gouverneur St	4	A2
Gracie Sq	15	A2
Gracie Ter	15	A2
Gramercy Park E	10	B1
Gramercy Park N	10	B1
Gramercy Park S	10	B1
Gramercy Park W	10	B1
Grand Army Plz	12	A2
Grand St (1-93)	2	A2
Grand St (94-300)	3	A1/A2
Grand St (301-609)	4	A1/A2
Great Jones St	6	B1/B2
Greene St (1-70)	2	A2
Greene St (71-273)	6	A1/B1
Greenwich Ave	5	A2
Greenwich St (1-151)	1	A1/B1
Greenwich St (224-480)	2	A1/B1/B2
Greenwich St (479-846)	5	A1/B1/B2
Grove Ct	5	B2
Grove St	5	A2/B2
Hamill Pl	3	B1
Hamilton Pl	21	B1/B2
Hamilton Ter	21	B2
Hancock Pl	18	A2
Hanover Sq	1	A2
Hanover St	1	A2
Harlem River Dr	20	A1/A2
Harlem River Dr	22	A1/B2
Harlem River Dr	23	A2/B2
Harlem River Dr		
(1-98)	24	A2
(15912-15976)	21	A2
Harlem River Dr Ramp	22	B2
Harrison St	2	B1
Haven Ave	23	A1/B1
Henderson Pl	17	B2
Henry Hudson Pky	11	A1
Henry Hudson Pky	14	A1
Henry Hudson Pky	18	A1/B1
Henry Hudson Pky	25	A1/B1
Henry Hudson Pky		
(1312-1430)	23	A1/B1
(1372-1489)	24	B1
Henry St (1-66)	3	B2
Henry St (63-331)	4	A1/A2
Henshaw St	25	B1
Hester St (38-91)	4	A1
Hester St (84-219)	3	A1/A2
High Brdg	23	A2
Hillside Ave	24	A1/A2
Horatio St	5	A1
Howard St	3	A1
Hubert St	2	A1
Hudson St (1-233)	2	A1/A2/B2
Hudson St (234-685)	5	A1/A2/B2
I-495	10	A1/A2
I-495	11	B1
I-495	13	B2
I-78	5	B2
I-95	23	A1/A2
Indian Rd	25	A1
Irving Pl	10	B1
Isham St	25	A2/B2
Jackson St	4	A2
James St	3	B2
Jane St	5	A1
Jay St	2	B1/B2
Jefferson St	4	A1
Jersey St	6	B2
John St	1	A1/A2
Jones Aly	6	B2
Jones St	5	B2
Joseph P Ward St	1	A1
Jumel Pl	23	B2
Jumel Ter	23	B2
Kenmare St	6	B2
King St	5	B2
LaGuardia Pl	6	B1
La Salle St	18	A1/A2
Lafayette Ct	6	A2
Lafayette St (2-204)	3	A1/B1
Lafayette St (205-456)	6	A2/B2
Laight St	2	A1/A2
Laurel Hill Ter	24	B2
Legion Memorial Sq	1	A2
Lenox Ave (1-509)	19	A2/B2
Lenox Ave (506-548)	22	B2
Lenox Terrace Pl	19	A2
Leonard St (1-64)	2	B2
Leonard St (65-168)	3	A1
Leroy St	5	B1/B2
Lewis St	4	A2
Lexington Ave		
(1-343)	10	A1/B1
(344-753)	13	A1/B1
(754-1270)	15	A1/B1
(1271-1763)	17	A1/B1
(1764-2199)	20	A1/B1
Liberty Pl	1	A1
Liberty St	1	A1/A2
Lispenard St	2	A2
Little W 12th St	5	A1
Ludlow St (1-102)	4	A1
Ludlow St (101-192)	7	B1

Street Index

WHAT IS *THAT?!*
HUH? OH, IT'S WWW.NOTFORTOURISTS.COM
BUT WHY?! WHY WOULD YOU USE ANYTHING OTHER THAN ME?
WELL, THE WEBSITE JUST OFFERS A FEW THINGS THAT YOU DON'T: DAILY CONTENT, FUN PHOTOS, SEARCHABLE DATABASE... COOL STUFF LIKE THAT.
DEVASTATED
OH... I SEE...